Gary Dessler
Florida International University

Nina D. Cole
Ryerson University

Chapter 3 by Julie Bulmash, George Brown College

Human Resources Management in Canada
Canadian Tenth Edition

PEARSON

Prentice
Hall

Toronto

Library and Archives Canada Cataloguing in Publication

Dessler, Gary, 1942–
    Human resources management in Canada / Gary Dessler, Nina D. Cole.—Canadian 10th ed.

Canadian 5th ed. published under title: Human resource management in Canada. Includes index.

ISBN-13: 978-0-13-227087-8
ISBN-10: 0-13-227087-0

1. Personnel management—Textbooks. 2. Personnel management—Canada—Textbooks. I. Cole, Nina D. (Nina Dawn) II. Title.

HF5549.D49 2008   658.3   C2006-905804-0

ISBN-13: 978-0-13-227087-8
ISBN-10: 0-13-227087-0

Editor-in-Chief: Gary Bennett   Production Coordinator: Andrea Falkenberg
Acquisitions Editor: Karen Elliott   Composition: Debbie Kumpf
Executive Marketing Manager: Cas Shields   Photo Research: Dawn du Quesnay
Developmental Editor: Eleanor MacKay   Permissions Research: Beth McAuley
Production Editor: Jen Handel   Art Director: Julia Hall
Copy Editor: Valerie Adams   Interior and Cover Design: Anthony Leung
Proofreader: Dawn Hunter   Cover Image: Getty Images

2 3 4 5   11 10 09 08

Printed and bound in the United States of America.

Dedication

To Claudia

G.D.

To Peggy Martin

N.C.

BRIEF CONTENTS

CONTENTS

PART SIX   Global Issues in Human Resources Management   450

The tenth edition of *Human Resources Management in Canada* is based on the premise that human resources are the most important assets in most Canadian organizations today because they are a source of competitive advantage that is difficult to replicate. The strategic importance of human resources management (HRM) activities is emphasized throughout the book. Knowledge of HRM is thus important for supervisors and managers in every field and employees at every level—not just those working in HR departments or aspiring to do so in the future. This book was designed to provide students specializing in HRM, those in general business or business administration programs, supervisory/managerial staff, and small-business owners with a complete, comprehensive review of HRM concepts and techniques in a highly readable and understandable form.

As in previous editions, the Canadian tenth edition provides extensive coverage of all HRM topics, such as job analysis, HR planning, recruitment, selection, orientation and training, career development, compensation and benefits, performance appraisal, health and safety, and labour relations. Practical applications are discussed in the Tips for the Front Line and Hints for Legal Compliance features. Research Insights are highlighted, and ethical dilemmas are presented for discussion.

NEW TO THE CANADIAN TENTH EDITION

- **Revised Introductory Chapter.** The first chapter has been revised to provide a comprehensive overview of the strategic importance of HR, the advances in measuring HRM's contribution to the bottom line, and HRM's critical role in strategy implementation.

- **New Chapter 3 on HRM and Technology.** This complete chapter on technology and HRM, written by Julie Bulmash of George Brown College, includes information on the evolution of HR technology, different types of human resources information systems, the impact of technology on the role of the HR professional, e-HR, and key trends in technology.

- **Flexible Work Arrangements.** The material on flexible work arrangements has been moved to the human resources planning chapter (Chapter 5), as these arrangements are becoming more and more crucial in attracting and retaining employees for employers who are beginning to experience the approaching labour shortage in Canada.

- **Labour Relations.** The two chapters on labour relations in the ninth edition have been combined into one for more succinct coverage of this material.

- **Boxed Features.** The four boxed features—Strategic HR, Workforce Diversity, Global HRM, and Entrepreneurs and HR—have been updated and revised in all chapters.

- **Required Professional Capabilities (RPCs).** Each chapter indicates where the specific required professional capabilities set out by the Canadian Council of Human Resources Associations for students preparing to write the National Knowledge Exam are discussed.

KEY FEATURES OF THE CANADIAN TENTH EDITION
Highlighted Themes

Workforce Diversity

RBC: A Leader in Diversity

One of the reasons RBC has a strong reputation for leading in diversity is its overall leadership in the Canadian market. RBC executives were on the public stage in 2005 addressing industry issues, as well as receiving awards and recognition for their achievements:

- Three RBC executives were named in the 2005 *Top 100 List of Canada's Most Powerful Women* by the Toronto-based Women's Executive Network: Elisabetta Bigsby, Executive Vice-President, Human Resources; Barbara Stymiest, Chief Operating Officer; and Janice Fukakusa, Chief Financial Officer.
- RBC Capital Markets was rated as one of the most prestigious banking companies in the world in New York–based career information company Vault Inc.'s *2006 Guide to the Top 50 Banking Employers.*

Employers in the banking industry were rated on a number of categories, including how prestigious it would be to work for them, quality of work/life balance, and diversity practices.

- RBC ranked first among banks in Canada's *Gender Intelligent Companies* survey of women consumers (as compiled by the Thomas Yacccato Group 2005).
- RBC is involved in the Aboriginal Stay in School program, aimed at helping high school students find summer employment. In 2005, 45 students participated and 27 were offered casual positions in local branches.
- RBC is sponsoring a multiyear study of visible minorities with Catalyst Canada.
- RBC has partnered with the Institute of Disability Studies at Ryerson University in Toronto on a project to discover how people with disabilities learn inside an organization.

Source: Adapted from Diversity at RBC: 2005 Highlights, May 2006. Used with the permission of RBC Financial Group.

- **Workforce Diversity.** The Workforce Diversity boxes describe some of the issues and challenges involved in managing the diverse workforce found in Canadian organizations. The broad range of types of diversity addressed include generational/age, ethnic, gender, racial, and religious.

Strategic HR

The Most Valuable Car Part? Human Capital

It was only a crack in a die used to stamp out steel body panels, but it was a big headache for Honda. The die might have to be shipped back to Japan to be fixed, costly enough in itself, but a minor issue compared with what could have happened—a horrendously expensive shutdown of the plant in Alliston, Ontario, lasting two weeks or more.

Enter the members of the stamping team at Honda Canada Mfg. They put their heads together and repaired the die themselves in a day and a half, allowing Civics to keep rolling off the assembly line. When Honda executives and other auto industry chiefs point to the Canadian work ethic as a reason that they keep investing here, that's exactly the kind of thing they're talking about.

"It's the dedication of the people to get in there and do those things and make them happen seamlessly," says Jim Miller, senior vice-president of Honda Canada,

which announced that it will build a new engine plant that will create 340 jobs in Alliston.

"They are not happy with us in Michigan these days," says Ontario Premier Dalton McGuinty. "For the second year running, we are the No. 1 auto producer in North America. That's the first time since the invention of the car."

"I think the labour force issue is a really key one," that favours Canada, notes David Cole, chairman of the influential Center for Automotive Research, an industry think tank in Ann Arbor, Michigan. "We have heard of a number of problems with the southern labour force for both suppliers and manufacturers. Education and work ethic are the two major factors."

Ontario assembly plants routinely rank at the top of annual studies on quality and productivity. Ontario is the only jurisdiction in Canada or the United States that is home to assembly plants of each of the top five best-selling automakers.

Source: Adapted from G. Keenan, "The Most Valuable Car Part? People," Globe & Mail, May 22, 2006, p. B1. Reprinted with permission from The Globe and Mail.

- **Strategic HR.** These boxes provide examples that illustrate the ways in which organizations are using effective HRM policies and practices in order to achieve the strategic goals of the organization.

Entrepreneurs and HR

A Practical Approach to Job Analysis and Job Descriptions

Without their own job analysts or even their own HR managers, many small-business owners need a more streamlined approach to job analysis. A resource that includes all of the possible positions that they might encounter, with a detailed listing of the duties normally assigned to these positions, exists in the *National Occupational Classification (NOC)* mentioned earlier. The practical approach to job analysis for small-business owners presented next is built around this invaluable reference tool.

Step 1: Develop an Organization Chart.
Drawing up the organization chart of the present structure comes first. Then, depending on how far in advance planning is being done, a chart can be produced that shows how the organization should look in the immediate future (say, in two months), as well as two or three other charts showing how the organization is likely to evolve over the next two or three years.

Step 2: Use a Job Analysis Questionnaire.
Next, a job analysis questionnaire can be used to determine what each job entails. A shorter version of one of the more comprehensive job analysis questionnaires, such as that in Figure 4.6 (page 91), may be useful for collecting job analysis data. An example of a job summary for a customer service clerk is as follows:

Answers inquiries and gives directions to customers, authorizes cashing of customers' cheques, records and returns lost credit cards, sorts and reviews new credit applications, and works at the customer service desk.

Step 3: Obtain a Copy of the *National Occupational Classification (NOC)* for Reference.
Next, standardized examples of the job descriptions needed should be obtained from the *NOC.* A copy can be found in the reference section of the library in most major centres or purchased through a federal government bookstore or online at http://publications.gc.ca. An online service is also offered at www23.hrdc-drhc. gc.ca/2001/e/generic/welcome.shtml.

Step 4: Choose Appropriate Definitions and Copy Them for Reference.
For each department, the *NOC* job titles and job descriptions that are believed to be appropriate should be chosen. The *NOC* definition will provide a firm foundation for the job description being created. It will provide a standardized list and constant reminder of the specific duties that should be included.

Step 5: Complete the Job Description.
An appropriate job summary for the job under consideration can then be written. The job analysis information, together with the information from the *NOC,* can be used to create a complete listing of the tasks and duties of each of the jobs. The working conditions section can be completed once all of the tasks and duties have been specified.

- **Entrepreneurs and HR.** Suggestions, examples, and practical hints are provided to assist those in smaller businesses who have limited time and resources to implement effective HRM policies and procedures.

Global HRM

Outsourcing HR Functions

Accenture, a global management consulting, technology, and outsourcing company, has recently entered into an agreement with Unilever Corporation. Unilever is a multinational marketing organization with familiar products such as Dove soap, Becel margarine, and Lipton soup, that employs 206 000 people in 100 countries worldwide. To optimize its HR services to its employees, Unilever has decided to outsource its administrative HR functions to Accenture. The agreement will cover three geographic regions—Europe, the Americas, and Asia—and provide services to approximately 200 000 employees

in more than 20 languages. Accenture will manage critical HR software applications. Some of the services it will provide are recruitment, payroll administration, total rewards administration, performance management workforce reporting, and core HR administration.

This arrangement will change the way Unilever manages and delivers its HR services across the company. Once these functions are outsourced, the remaining HR activities will be redesigned to focus more on the customer and establish a targeted service delivery model.

Source: J. Finlaw, "Accenture to Help Unilever Transform Human Resources Operations in 100 Countries with a Seven-Year Outsourcing Agreement," Press Release, June 6, 2006. Used with permission of Accenture.

- **Global HRM.** In recognition of the increasing impact of globalization, topics highlighted in the Global HRM boxes include cultural issues in retirement plans, employment contracts in Europe, and the importance of personal relationships for business success in China.

Additional Features

- **Learning Outcomes.** Specific learning goals are defined on each chapter-opening page.
- **Key Terms.** Key terms appear in boldface within the text, are defined in the margins, and are listed at the end of the chapter.
- **Current Examples.** Numerous real-world examples of HRM policies, procedures, and practices at a wide variety of organizations, ranging from small service providers to huge global corporations, can be found throughout the text.
- **Full-Colour Figures, Tables, and Photographs.** Throughout each chapter, key concepts and applications are illustrated with strong, full-colour visual materials.
- **Weblinks.** Helpful Internet sites are provided throughout the text and are featured in the margins.
- **End-of-Chapter Summaries.** At the end of each chapter, the summary reviews key points related to each of the learning outcomes.
- **End-of-Chapter Review and Discussion Questions.** Each chapter contains a set of review and discussion questions.
- **Critical Thinking Questions.** Each chapter contains end-of-chapter questions designed to provoke critical thinking and stimulate discussion.
- **Running Case.** The running case at the end of each chapter illustrates the types of HRM challenges confronted by small-business owners and front-line supervisors. It is accompanied by critical thinking questions, which provide an opportunity to discuss and apply the text material.
- **Case Incident.** A different case incident can be found at the end of each chapter. These cases present current HRM issues in a real-life setting and are followed by questions designed to encourage discussion and promote the use of problem-solving skills. Almost half the chapters have updated cases.
- **Experiential Exercises.** Each chapter includes a number of individual and group-based experiential exercises, which provide learners with the opportunity to apply the text material and develop some hands-on skills.
- **CBC Videos.** Each of the six parts in the book includes a CBC video case relating to the material in that part, along with several critical thinking questions. For this edition we have placed the cases for each part after the chapters to which they most closely relate. You will find the CBC video cases after Chapters 2, 5, 9, 13, 16, and 17.

Supplements

Human Resources Management in Canada, Canadian Tenth Edition, is accompanied by a complete supplements package:

- **Instructor's Resource CD-ROM (978-0-13-205240-5).** This new supplement for instructors includes the *Instructor's Resource Manual with CBC Video Guide* in PDF and Word format, *Pearson Education Test Generator*, *PowerPoint Lecture Slides*, and access to the CBC Videos. These items are now available in one easy-to-access CD-ROM. A description of each item follows on the next page.

- **Instructor's Manual with CBC Video Guide (978-0-13-205245-0).** This comprehensive guide contains a detailed lecture outline of each chapter, descriptions of the discussion boxes, answers to review and critical thinking questions, answers to the case questions, hints regarding the experiential exercises, and helpful video case notes.

- **Pearson Education Canada TestGen (978-0-13-205244-3).** This powerful computerized testing package contains more than 1500 multiple-choice, true/false, and short essay questions. Each question is rated by level of difficulty and includes a text page reference. This state-of-the-art software package in the Windows platform enables instructors to create tailor-made, error-free tests quickly and easily. The Custom Test allows instructors to create an exam, administer it traditionally or online, and evaluate and track students' results—all with the click of the mouse.

- **PowerPoint® Lecture Slides (978-0-13-205243-6).** This practical set of PowerPoint lecture slides contains more than 350 colour images. The presentation outlines key concepts discussed in the text, and includes selected tables and figures from the text.

- **Image Library (978-0-13-205242-9).** The Image Library is a comprehensive resource to help instructors create vibrant lecture presentations. Almost every figure and table in the text appears in the library organized by chapter. These images can easily be imported into PowerPoint to create new presentations or to add to existing ones.

- **Pearson Education Canada/CBC Video Library (VHS: 978-0-13-205150-7; DVD: 978-0-13-205151-4).** Pearson Education Canada and the CBC have worked together to provide six segments from the CBC series *Venture* and *The National* in VHS and DVD formats. Designed specifically to complement the text, this case collection is an excellent tool for bringing students in contact with the world outside the classroom. These programs have extremely high production quality and have been chosen to relate directly to chapter content.

- **Companion Website (www.pearsoned.ca/dessler).** This site will be of interest to both instructors and students. Instructors can access the password-protected area of the site. It includes additional teaching tools, such as downloadable *PowerPoint Lecture Slides* and the *Instructor's Manual with CBC Video Guide.*

  For a multitude of practice tests, including true/false, multiple-choice, and essay questions, students should take time to explore this site. Also available to students are Weblinks, a glossary, and access to download the CBC Videos featured in the text. Instructors and students can check out the Companion Website by going to **www.pearsoned.ca/dessler** and selecting the book cover for *Human Resources Management in Canada,* Canadian Tenth Edition, by Dessler and Cole.

Other Resources

- **Cawsey/Deszca/Templer,** *Canadian Cases in Human Resources Management,* First Edition. This casebook features 24 Canadian cases in human resource management. (ISBN: 978-0-13-088455-8)

- **Sales/Owen/Lesperance,** *Experiential Exercises in Human Resource Management,* First Edition. Designed to accompany texts in the field of management, this resource meets the demand for more real-life, practical, and experiential material in management courses. In each book, the exercises follow an identical and innovative format to guide both instructors and students and to reinforce the goals of the series: increase students' awareness, apply theory, and build skills. (ISBN: 978-0-13-021805-6)

- **Pearson Practice Tests for Human Resource Certification.** The Pearson Practice Test for Human Resource Certification is comprised of sample Knowledge Assessment and sample National Professional Practice Assessment questions and answers provided by the Canadian Council of Human Resources Associations (CCHRA). This supplement will assist those preparing for their Certified Human Resources Professional (CHRP) designation. (ISBN: 978-0-13-239843-5)

- **HRSim Selection** is available at an additional charge. Please see www.interpretive.com/hrsim/.

- **Pearson Custom Publishing** (**www.prenhall.com/custombusiness**). Pearson Custom Publishing can provide you and your students with texts, cases, and articles to enhance your course. Choose material from Darden, Ivey, Harvard Business School Publishing, NACRA, and Thunderbird to create your own custom casebook. Contact your Pearson sales representative for more details.

- **Online Learning Solutions.** Pearson Education Canada supports instructors interested in using online course management systems. We provide text-related content in WebCT and Blackboard. To find out more about creating your online course using Pearson content in one of these platforms, contact your Pearson sales representative.

- **New! Instructor's ASSET.** Pearson Education is proud to introduce Instructor's ASSET, the Academic Support and Service for Educational Technologies. ASSET is the first integrated Canadian service program committed to meeting the customization, training, and support needs for your course. Ask your Pearson sales representative for details!

- **Your Pearson Sales Representative!** Your Pearson rep is always available to ensure you have everything you need to teach a winning course. Armed with experience, training, and product knowledge, your Pearson rep will support your assessment and adoption of any of the products, services, and technologies outlined here to ensure our offerings are tailored to suit your individual needs and the needs of your students. Whether it's getting instructions for TestGen software or specific content files for your new online course, your Pearson Sales Representative is here to help.

ACKNOWLEDGMENTS

The manuscript was reviewed at various stages of its development by a number of peers across Canada, and we want to thank those who shared their insights and constructive criticism. Among them are

- Gordon Barnard, *Durham College*
- Tony Fang, *York University*
- Wenlu Feng, *Centennial College*
- Beverly Linnell, *Southern Alberta Institute of Technology*
- Barbara Lipton, *Seneca College of Applied Arts and Technology*
- Sean Lyons, *St. Francis Xavier University*
- Carol Ann Samhaber, *Algonquin College*

At Pearson Education Canada, we are very grateful to Karen Elliott, Acquisitions Editor; Cas Shields, Executive Marketing Manager; Eleanor MacKay, Developmental Editor; Jen Handel, Production Editor; Andrea Falkenberg, Production Coordinator; Valerie Adams, Copyeditor; Dawn Hunter, Proofreader; Beth McAuley, Permissions Editor; Dawn du Quesnay, Photo Researcher; and all the other people behind the scenes who have helped make this edition possible.

A special note of thanks is extended to Ashraf (Nia) Khoja, who provided research assistance.

Gary Dessler
Florida International University

Nina D. Cole
Ryerson University

ABOUT THE CANADIAN AUTHOR

Nina Cole

Dr. Nina Cole has 28 years of experience in human resources management as a practitioner, consultant, researcher, and professor. She has 12 years of business experience—8 years as a human resources management consultant with Peat Marwick & Partners, and 4 years as a human resources manager with Federal Industries. The last 16 years have been spent as an academic, teaching and conducting research in human resources management and organizational behaviour. In addition to being an active member of the Human Resources Professionals Association of Ontario for over 20 years, Nina Cole has been associated with other charitable and community groups.

PHOTO CREDITS

A Great Way to Learn and Instruct Online

The Pearson Education Canada Companion Website is easy to navigate and is organized to correspond to the chapters in this textbook. Whether you are a student in the classroom or a distance learner you will discover helpful resources for in-depth study and research that empower you in your quest for greater knowledge and maximize your potential for success in the course.

Companion
Website

[**www.pearsoned.ca/dessler**]

Enter

PEARSON
Prentice
Hall

Jump to... http://www.pearsoned.ca/dessler ⬧ | Home | Search | Help | Profile |

Companion
Website

Home >

Companion Website

Human Resources Management in Canada, Canadian Tenth Edition, by Dessler and Cole

Human Resources
Management in Canada

Student Resources

The modules in this section provide students with tools for learning course material. These modules include:

- Chapter Learning Outcomes
- Required Professional Capabilities
- Chapter Summaries
- Web Destinations
- Quizzes
- Glossary Flashcards

In the quiz modules students can send answers to the grader and receive instant feedback on their progress through the Results Reporter. Coaching comments and references to the textbook may be available to ensure that students take advantage of all available resources to enhance their learning experience.

Instructor Resources

The modules in this section provide instructors with additional teaching tools. Downloadable PowerPoint Presentations, TestGen, and Instructor's Manual are just some of the materials that may be available in this section. Where appropriate, this section will be password protected. To get a password, simply contact your Pearson Education Canada Representative or call Faculty Sales and Services at 1-800-850-5813.

CHAPTER 1

THE STRATEGIC ROLE OF HUMAN RESOURCES MANAGEMENT

LEARNING OUTCOMES

AFTER STUDYING THIS CHAPTER, YOU SHOULD BE ABLE TO

Define human resources management, and **analyze** the strategic significance of human resources management.

Describe the two categories of activities required of HR managers, and **discuss** examples of each.

Discuss the internal and external environmental factors affecting human resources management policies and practices, and **explain** their impact.

Describe the three stages in the evolution of HRM.

Explain how HRM has taken on the four characteristics of a profession.

REQUIRED PROFESSIONAL CAPABILITIES

- Provides services to enable employee success while maintaining the well-being of the organization
- Advises clients on the status of dependent and independent contractors and elements of employee status
- Monitors expenditures and timelines
- Develops requests for proposals (RFPs) and reviews submissions by third parties
- Develops budgeting, monitors expenditures, and evaluates activities of contractors
- Operates within organizational guidelines for procurement of equipment and services

- Develops and maintains a departmental or project budget
- Gathers, analyzes, and reports relevant business and industry information, including global trends
- Stays current in terms of professional development
- Contributes to and promotes the development of the profession
- Understands and adheres to the Canadian Council of Human Resources Association's code of ethics

THE STRATEGIC ROLE OF HUMAN RESOURCES MANAGEMENT

human resources management (HRM)   The management of people in organizations through formulating and implementing human resources management systems that are aligned with organizational strategy in order to produce the workforce competencies and behaviours required to achieve the organization's strategic goals.

Human resources management (HRM) refers to the management of people in organizations. Human resources professionals are responsible for ensuring that the organization attracts, retains, and engages the diverse talent required to meet operational and performance commitments made to customers and shareholders. Their job is to ensure that the organization finds and hires the best individuals available, develops and nurtures their talent, creates a sustaining, productive work environment, and continually builds and monitors these human assets. They have the primary responsibility for managing the workforce that drives organizational performance and success.[1]

More specifically, HRM involves formulating and implementing HRM systems (such as recruitment, performance appraisal, and compensation) that are aligned with the organization's strategy in order to produce a workforce with the competencies and behaviours that are required to achieve the organization's strategic objectives.

human capital   The knowledge, education, training, skills, and expertise of an organization's workforce.

Just as important as the financial capital that is required for an organization to operate, the knowledge, education, training, skills, and expertise of a firm's workers represent the increasingly valuable **human capital**. For example, the reason Ontario is now the number one auto production location in North America (which had been Michigan ever since the invention of the automobile) is the quality of its workforce, as discussed in the Strategic HR box.

Research
Insight   ▷

Research studies have confirmed that effective HR practices are related to better organizational performance. Results show that anywhere between 15 and 30 percent of a company's total value can be substantially correlated with specific HR practices. Early studies found strong correlations between "high-performance

Strategic HR

The Most Valuable Car Part? Human Capital

It was only a crack in a die used to stamp out steel body panels, but it was a big headache for Honda. The die might have to be shipped back to Japan to be fixed, costly enough in itself, but a minor issue compared with what could have happened—a horrendously expensive shutdown of the plant in Alliston, Ontario, lasting two weeks or more.

Enter the members of the stamping team at Honda Canada Mfg. They put their heads together and repaired the die themselves in a day and a half, allowing Civics to keep rolling off the assembly line. When Honda executives and other auto industry chiefs point to the Canadian work ethic as a reason that they keep investing here, that's exactly the kind of thing they're talking about.

"It's the dedication of the people to get in there and do those things and make them happen seamlessly," says Jim Miller, senior vice-president of Honda Canada,

which announced that it will build a new engine plant that will create 340 jobs in Alliston.

"They are not happy with us in Michigan these days," says Ontario Premier Dalton McGuinty. "For the second year running, we are the No. 1 auto producer in North America. That's the first time since the invention of the car."

"I think the labour force issue is a really key one," that favours Canada, notes David Cole, chairman of the influential Center for Automotive Research, an industry think tank in Ann Arbor, Michigan. "We have heard of a number of problems with the southern labour force for both suppliers and manufacturers. Education and work ethic are the two major factors."

Ontario assembly plants routinely rank at the top of annual studies on quality and productivity. Ontario is the only jurisdiction in Canada or the United States that is home to assembly plants of each of the top five best-selling automakers.

Source: Adapted from G. Keenan, "The Most Valuable Car Part? People," *Globe & Mail,* May 22, 2006, p. B1. Reprinted with permission from *The Globe and Mail.*

work systems" (strategically focused HRM) and improved shareholder value, as well as higher return on equity and return on investment. A 2002 study by Anderson Consulting found that human capital practices explained just under half of the difference in market value between companies. A 2004 study by HR consultants Towers Perrin found that mergers became more successful as the amount of HR input increased. The *Watson Wyatt 2005 Human Capital Index* report presented evidence of a strong relationship between recruiting efficiency and organizational performance, and stated, "Companies that fill vacancies faster reduced the disruption and lost productivity associated with turnover." Most recently, a 2006 study by Watson Wyatt and the Human Resource Planning Society found that performance management, rewards, succession planning, recruiting, communication, HR technology, and the overall HR function can significantly contribute to shareholder value if companies design and implement their programs in a formalized way.[2] **Figure 1.1** illustrates the linkage between the market value of the organization and HR practices that support strategy.

For example, one of the most critical strategic HR challenges at the present time is building the leadership pipeline. Canadian organizations have fallen behind in grooming high-potential successors—almost half of incumbents in

FIGURE 1.1   Strategic HRM

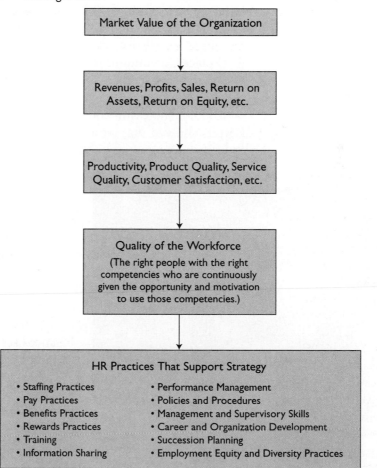

Source: P.A. Mathews, "The HR Image Makeover: From Cost Center to Profit Maker," *workspan*, May 2004, p. 38. Reprinted with permission of WorldatWork, Scottsdale, AZ. www.worldatwork.org.

senior positions achieve top performance ratings, but only 25 percent of second-level executives (the presumed feeder group for future senior executive roles) match that level of performance. For every two current senior executives, there is only one designated job-ready or nearly ready successor. Three out of every ten senior executive positions have no identified potential successors.[3]

Measuring the Impact of HRM

HR professionals now must have hard numbers to take to the executive suite to prove just how much HRM contributes to the bottom line. The HR function must account for the return on resources invested in human capital. HR professionals need to be able to measure the value and impact of their organization's human capital and HRM practices. Traditional operational measures focused on the size and cost of the HR function (such as absenteeism rates, cost per hire), but today's measures need to reflect the quality of people and the effectiveness of HRM initiatives that build workforce capability. These new measures provide critical information that can be linked to organizational outcomes. For example, the percentage of first-choice job candidates accepting first offer to hire indicates the strength of the organization's employment brand in the marketplace and directly affects the quality of the workforce.[4]

Research Insight ▷

Through research linking HR practices and shareholder value at more than 400 companies, Watson Wyatt consultants developed a Human Capital Index (HCI), which outlines 30 key HR practices and indicates their contributions to shareholder value. These 30 practices were summarized into five categories—recruiting excellence, clear rewards and accountability, collegial and flexible workplaces, communications integrity, and prudent use of resources.

Watson Wyatt then conducted a study that went beyond previous correlational findings to investigate whether strong HRM drove financial performance or whether successful companies simply had more resources to put into HRM. Results showed that strong HRM was driving company performance. Looking at 51 large companies in North America and Europe, the study found that those with the best HR practices provided a 64 percent total return to shareholders over a five-year period, more than three times the 21 percent return for companies with weaker HR practices. The bottom line is that effective human capital practices drive business outcomes more than business outcomes lead to good HR practices.[5] **Table 1.1** summarizes these findings on key links between human capital and shareholder value creation.

balanced scorecard A measurement system that translates an organization's strategy into a comprehensive set of performance measures.

Finally, many organizations are using the **balanced scorecard** system that includes measures of the impact of HRM on organizational outcomes. The balanced scorecard approach translates an organization's strategy into a comprehensive set of performance measures. It includes financial measures that tell the results of actions already taken. It complements the financial measures with operational measures of organizational, business unit, or department success that will drive future performance. It balances long-term and short-term actions, and

Many studies have shown that employees are more committed to their jobs when their participation is valued and encouraged.

TABLE 1.1   Key Links between Human Capital and Shareholder Value Creation

Practice	Impact on Market Value
Total rewards and accountability	16.5%
Collegial, flexible workplace	9.0%
Recruiting and retention excellence	7.9%
Communications integrity	7.1%
Focused HR service technologies	6.5%
Prudent use of resources	–33.9%

Expected change in market value associated with a significant one standard deviation (1 SD) improvement in HCI dimension.

Source: Watson Wyatt Human Capital Index®: Human Capital as a Lead Indicator of Shareholder Value. www.watsonwyatt.com/research/resrender.asp?id=W 488&page–1 (August 15, 2006). Reprinted with permission of Watson Wyatt Worldwide.

balances measures of success relating to financial results, customers, internal business processes, and human capital management.[6] For example, one measure relating to HRM is the percentage of senior management positions with fully job-ready successors ready to move up.

Human Resource Management Responsibilities

Human resources management responsibilities and activities fall into two categories. The first is the traditional *operational* (administrative) category, where HR professionals hire and maintain employees, and then manage employee separations. This role requires HR staff to be administrative experts and employee champions. The second is the more recent *strategic* category, where HR is focused on ensuring that the organization is staffed with the most effective human capital to achieve its strategic goals. This role requires HR staff to be strategic partners and change agents.[7] **Table 1.2** illustrates the different focus of operational versus strategic HR activities.

Operational Responsibilities

Every line manager has responsibilities related to employees as they move through the stages of the human-capital life cycle: selection and assimilation into the organization, development of capabilities while working in the organization, and transition out of the organization. HR professionals have traditionally served in a staff role as in-house consultants to line managers, offering advice on HR-related matters, formulating HR policies and procedures, and providing a wide range of HR services.

These services include analyzing jobs, planning future workforce requirements, selecting employees, orienting and training employees, managing compensation and reward plans, and communicating with employees (including counselling and disciplining). These responsibilities also include ensuring fair treatment, appraising performance, ensuring employee health and safety, managing

TABLE 1.2   Operational versus Strategic HR

Operational ⟷	Strategic
Skills	Concepts
Administrative tasks	Planning
Reactive	Proactive
Collecting metrics/measurements	Analyzing metrics/measurements
Working to achieve goals and objectives	Setting the goals and objectives
Following the laws, policies, and procedures	Interpreting, establishing, and revising the laws, policies, and procedures
Employee focus	Organizational focus
Explaining benefits to employees	Designing benefit plans that help the organization achieve its mission and goals
Setting up training sessions for employees	Assessing training needs for the entire organization
Recruiting and selecting employees	Workforce planning and building relationships with external resources
Administering the salary/wage plan	Creating a pay plan that maximizes employees' productivity, morale, and retention
Always doing things the same way	Recognizing that there may be better ways of doing things; recognizing how changes affect the entire organization—not just HR
Works within the organizational culture	Attempts to improve the organizational culture

Source: D.M. Cox & C.H. Cox, "At the Table: Transitioning to Strategic Business Partner," *workspan*, November 2003, p. 22. Reprinted with permission of WorldatWork, Scottsdale, AZ. www.worldatwork.org.

REQUIRED PROFESSIONAL CAPABILITIES

Monitors expenditures and timelines

Develops requests for proposals (RFPs) and reviews submissions by third parties

Develops budgeting, monitors expenditures, and evaluates activities of contractors

Operates within organizational guidelines for procurement of equipment and services

Develops and maintains a departmental or project budget

outsourcing The practice of contracting with outside vendors to handle specified functions on a permanent basis.

CFT Training and Human Resources
www.cfthr.com

HR-Dept.Com
www.hr-dept.com

strategy The company's plan for how it will balance its internal strengths and weaknesses with external opportunities and threats in order to maintain a competitive advantage.

---

labour relations and relationships with unions, handling complaints and grievances, and ensuring compliance with legislation affecting the workplace.

In recent years, there has been a trend to outsourcing much of the operational HR activities, so that HR staff in the organization can focus on strategic HRM. **Outsourcing** involves contracting with outside vendors to handle specified business functions on a permanent basis. Although using outside experts to provide employee counselling and payroll services has been common for many years, the outsourcing of other specific HR functions, including pension and benefits administration, recruitment, management development, and training, has become increasingly common.[8]

For example, Air Canada, CIBC, BMO Financial Group, Hewlett-Packard Canada, IBM Canada, Calgary Health, and Telus have all outsourced part or all of their administrative HR functions, allowing their remaining HR staff to be more strategically focused. Although most have been satisfied with their outsourcing arrangement, some have not realized the full level of cost savings they initially anticipated. RBC Financial Group, for example, brought its recruitment function back in-house after experimenting with outsourcing.[9]

Strategic Responsibilities

More and more HR professionals are now devoting their time to helping their organization achieve its strategic objectives.[10] Traditionally, **strategy**—the company's plan for how it will balance its internal strengths and weaknesses with external opportunities and threats in order to maintain a competitive advantage—was formulated without HR input. Today, HR professionals are increasingly involved in both formulating and implementing organizational strategy.

Role in Formulating Strategy   Organizations are increasingly viewing the HR department as an equal partner in the strategic planning process. HR professionals, together with line managers, play a role in what strategic planners call **environmental scanning**, which involves identifying and analyzing *external* opportunities and threats that may be crucial to the organization's success. These managers can also supply competitive intelligence that may be useful as the company formulates its strategic plans. Details regarding a successful incentive plan being used by a competitor, impending labour shortages, and information about pending legislative changes are examples. HR professionals can also add value to the strategy formulation process by supplying information regarding the company's *internal* strengths and weaknesses, particularly as they relate to the organization's workforce.

environmental scanning
Identifying and analyzing external opportunities and threats that may be crucial to the organization's success.

Role in Executing Strategy   Leading HR researcher Brian Becker says, "It isn't the content of the strategy that differentiates the winners and losers, it is the ability to execute."[11] Strategy execution is typically the area where HR makes the biggest strategic contribution. For example, HR professionals are heavily involved in the execution of downsizing and restructuring strategies through establishing training and retraining programs, arranging for outplacement services, instituting pay-for-performance plans, and helping to redesign jobs.

HR specialists are expected to be *change agents* who lead the organization and its employees through organizational change. Making the enterprise more responsive to product/service innovations and technological change is the objective of many management strategies. Flattening the pyramid, empowering employees, and organizing around teams are ways in which HRM can help an organization to respond quickly to its customers' needs and competitors' challenges.

The competitive strategy may involve differentiating the organization from its competitors by offering superior *customer service* through a highly committed, competent, and customer-oriented workforce. "Getting customer service right means getting HR right," says Lloyd Craig, president and CEO of Surrey Metro Savings Credit Union. His company has developed an extensive list of HR programs designed to help create and support happy, healthy, engaged employees.[12]

employee engagement   The emotional and intellectual involvement of employees in their work.

HR professionals and line managers play a pivotal role in *lowering labour costs*, the single largest operating expense in many organizations, particularly in the service sector. Doing so might involve introducing strategies to reduce turnover, absenteeism, and the rate of incidence of occupational illnesses and injuries. It could also mean adopting more effective recruitment, selection, and training programs. At one international tire manufacturing firm, for example, adopting a behaviour-based interview strategy as the basis for selection of entry-level engineers resulted in savings of $500 000 in three years. These savings were due to lower turnover, lower training costs, and improved capabilities of the engineering staff because of a better fit.[13]

Intense global competition and the need for more responsiveness to environmental changes put a premium on **employee engagement**. Employee engagement is the emotional and intellectual involvement of employees in their work. It is an individual's intensity, focus, and involvement in his or her job and organization. Engaged employees drive desired organizational outcomes—they

Employees in fast-food establishments are taught how to provide courteous, efficient customer service.

go beyond what is required; understand and share the values and goals of the organization; perceive that there are opportunities for growth, development, and advancement; enjoy collegial relationships with managers and co-workers, trust their leaders, and regard the success of the organization as their success.[14] There is a strong positive relationship between engagement and organizational performance (sales growth and total shareholder return), according to an analysis of a Hewitt Associates database of more than 4 million employees from almost 1500 companies.[15]

A 2006 Conference Board of Canada study reported that 57 percent of the workforce is highly engaged, but 14 percent say they are not at all engaged. Employees reported their top reasons for disengagement as lack of recognition (59 percent), lack of opportunities for growth and advancement (46 percent), and ineffectiveness of managers and supervisors (43 percent).[16]

Building employee engagement requires the joint efforts of HR professionals and line managers throughout the firm. Line managers need coaching to learn the skills it takes to build trusting and caring relationships with their employees. Other important strategic HR initiatives to build employee engagement include establishing recognition programs, instituting career-oriented performance-appraisal procedures, and providing management development programs.

ENVIRONMENTAL INFLUENCES ON HRM

There are numerous internal and external environmental influences on HRM. The internal organizational climate, culture, and management practices impact the quality of candidates that a firm can attract, as well as its ability to retain desired workers. There are also a number of external challenges that are driving the strategic focus of HRM.

Internal Environmental Influences

How a firm deals with the following three internal environmental influences has a major impact on its ability to meet its objectives.

organizational culture The core values, beliefs, and assumptions that are widely shared by members of an organization.

First, **organizational culture** consists of the core values, beliefs, and assumptions that are widely shared by members of an organization. Culture is often conveyed through an organization's mission statement, as well as through stories, myths, symbols, and ceremonies. It serves a variety of purposes:

- communicating what the organization "believes in" and "stands for"
- providing employees with a sense of direction and expected behaviour (norms)
- shaping employees' attitudes about themselves, the organization, and their roles
- creating a sense of identity, orderliness, and consistency
- fostering employee loyalty and commitment

All managers with HR responsibilities play an important role in creating and maintaining the type of organizational culture desired. For example, they may organize recognition ceremonies for high-performing employees and be involved in decisions regarding symbols, such as a logo or the design of new company premises. Having a positive culture earns critical acclaim and has a positive impact on recruitment, retention, and productivity.

organizational climate The prevailing atmosphere that exists in an organization and its impact on employees.

Second, **organizational climate** refers to the prevailing atmosphere or "internal weather" that exists in an organization and its impact on employees.[17] It can be friendly or unfriendly, open or secretive, rigid or flexible, innovative or stagnant. The major factors influencing the climate are management's leadership style, HR policies and practices, and amount and style of organizational communication. The type of climate that exists is generally reflected in the level of employee motivation, job satisfaction, performance, and productivity. HR professionals play a key role in helping managers throughout the firm to establish and maintain a positive organizational climate.

Third, *management practices* have changed considerably over the past decade, with many HRM implications. For example, the traditional bureaucratic structure with many levels of management is being replaced by flatter organizational forms using cross-functional teams and improved communication. Since managers have more people reporting to them in flat structures, they cannot supervise their employees as closely, and employee **empowerment** has become more common. **Boundaryless organizations** are also emerging. In this type of structure, relationships (typically joint ventures) are formed with customers, suppliers, and/or competitors, to pool resources for mutual benefit or encourage cooperation in an uncertain environment.

empowerment Providing workers with the skills and authority to make decisions that would traditionally be made by managers.

boundaryless organization structure A structure in which relationships (typically joint ventures) are formed with customers, suppliers, and/or competitors, to pool resources for mutual benefit or encourage cooperation in an uncertain environment.

External Environmental Influences

To be effective, all managers, including those with responsibility for HR, must monitor the environment on an ongoing basis, assess the impact of any changes, and be proactive in responding to such challenges.

Economic Conditions

Economic conditions affect supply and demand for products and services, which, in turn, have a dramatic impact on the number and types of employees required, as well as an employer's ability to pay wages and provide benefits. When the economy is healthy, companies often hire more workers as demand for products and services increases. Consequently, unemployment rates fall, there is more competition for qualified employees, and training and retention strategies increase in importance.[18] Conversely, during a downturn, some firms reduce pay and benefits in order to retain workers. Other employers are forced to downsize, by offering attractive early retirement and early leave programs or by laying off and terminating employees. Unemployment rates rise, and employers are often overwhelmed with applicants when vacancies are advertised.

productivity The ratio of an organization's outputs (goods and services) to its inputs (people, capital, energy, and materials).

Productivity refers to the ratio of an organization's outputs (goods and services) to its inputs (people, capital, energy, and materials).[19] Canada's relatively low productivity growth rate is of concern, because of increasing global competition. To improve productivity, managers must find ways to produce more outputs with current input levels or to use fewer resources to produce current output levels. In most organizations today, productivity improvement is essential for long-term success.

primary sector Agriculture, fishing and trapping, forestry, and mining.

secondary sector Manufacturing and construction.

tertiary or service sector Public administration, personal and business services, finance, trade, public utilities, and transportation/communications.

Employment trends in Canada have been experiencing dramatic change. The **primary sector**, which includes agriculture, fishing and trapping, forestry, and mining, now represents only 4 percent of jobs. Employment in the **secondary sector** (manufacturing and construction) has decreased to 20 percent of jobs. The sector that has grown to represent 76 percent of jobs, dominating the Canadian economy, is the **tertiary or service sector**, which includes public administration, personal and business services, finance, trade, public utilities, and transportation/communications, as shown in **Figure 1.2**.

FIGURE 1.2   Employment by Sector in Canada, 2005

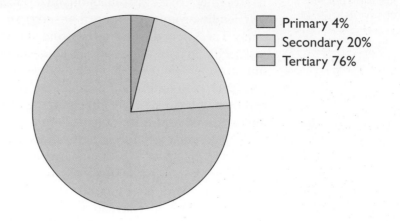

Primary 4%
Secondary 20%
Tertiary 76%

Source: Statistics Canada, CANSIM table 282-0008. Adapted from Statistics Canada website www40. statcan.ca/l01/cst01/labor10b.htm (August 15, 2006).

Since all jobs in the service sector involve the provision of service by employees to individual customers, effectively managing and motivating human resources is critical. Although there are some lesser-skilled jobs (in housekeeping and food services, for example), many service-sector jobs demand highly knowledgeable employees.

Labour Market Issues

Two important labour market issues are labour unions and the increasing numbers of contingent employees doing nonstandard work.

The Labour Union Movement   A labour union is an officially recognized association of employees who have joined together to present a united front and collective voice in dealing with management, with the aim of securing and furthering the social and economic interests and well-being of their membership. Once a union has been certified or recognized to represent a specific group of employees, the company is required by law to recognize the union and bargain with it in good faith.

Labour unions affect organizations in several ways. Management has less discretion and flexibility in implementing and administering HR policies, procedures, and practices when dealing with unionized employees. Labour unions also influence the HR policies and practices in non-unionized organizations wishing to remain union-free. Such organizations monitor bargaining activities in their community and industry, and ensure that their employees are provided with terms and conditions of employment equal to or better than those being negotiated by unions.

contingent employees Workers who do not have regular full-time or regular part-time employment status.

Use of Contingent Employees   The use of **contingent employees** to work in non-standard jobs is increasing. Contingent workers do not have regular full-time or regular part-time employment status. Nonstandard jobs include contract work, self-employment without employees, temporary work and part-year work, or work with multiple jobs with a series of employers. This type of work now accounts for about 41 percent of women's paid jobs and 29 percent of men's jobs. Nonstandard work is often poorly paid, offers little or no job security, and is generally not covered by employment legislation. Some are calling for these laws to be updated so that contingent workers are provided the same legal protection as other workers.[20]

Demographic Trends and Increasing Workforce Diversity   The term **demographics** refers to the characteristics of the workforce, which include age, sex, marital status, and education level. The fact that Canada's labour force is becoming increasingly diverse is one of the major challenges confronting HR managers today. **Diversity** refers to "any attribute that humans are likely to use to tell themselves, 'that person is different from me,'" and thus includes such factors as race, gender, age, values, and cultural norms.[21]

The single most important factor governing the size and composition of the labour force is population growth. Since the population growth has slowed to less than 1 percent per year, the average age of the workforce is increasing. Canada admits more immigrants per capita than any other country, which has created a very diverse labour force.

Age   The **baby boomers**, born between 1946 and 1965, are just beginning to retire. According to Statistics Canada, the proportion of senior citizens will increase rapidly over the next few decades, from 13 percent in 2005 to 25 percent in 2031. The ratio of children and seniors per hundred people in the working population is also expected to increase rapidly, from 44 in 2005 to 61 in 2031.[22]

The aging of the population has had another impact. Growing numbers of middle-aged employees are caught in the **Sandwich Generation**, with responsibilities for rearing young dependants as well as assisting elderly relatives who are no longer capable of functioning totally independently. Most employers provide flexibility in work hours for their "sandwiched" employees, and a few, such as RBC Financial Group, have provided eldercare benefits. The federal government offers a compassionate care benefit to provide job and income protection for up to six weeks to workers who need to take time off work to provide care to a gravely ill or dying family member.[23]

As **Generation X** (individuals born between 1966 and 1980) employees replace aging boomers, flexible work arrangements, continuous skill development, and a balance between work and personal life are becoming increasingly important. This group views command-and-control management styles with disdain and believes that security comes from transferability of skills rather than corporate loyalty.[24] Members of this generation are economically conservative and do not trust institutions. They can provide "out-of-the-box" thinking that can help companies deal with uncertainty.[25]

Generation Y (also known as echo boomers, Nexters, and the Net Generation), born since 1980, are the children of the baby boomers. Members of this sizeable group and are just now beginning to enter the workforce. Although they are masters of technology, comfortable with authority and diversity, and eager to make a contribution, they are also impatient and action-oriented. New approaches to work and career management will be required to keep this group challenged and to manage overall generational diversity in the workplace.[26]

Education   The level of education of the Canadian labour force is increasing at a significant rate. Given the higher expectations of the better-educated labour force, managers are expected to try to ensure that the talents and capabilities of employees are fully utilized and that opportunities are provided for career growth.

Very few working-age Canadians are illiterate in the sense of not being able to read, but a startlingly high proportion (26 percent) have only marginal literacy skills, defined as the ability to understand and use printed and written documents in daily activities to achieve goals and to develop knowledge and potential.

---

demographics   The characteristics of the workforce, which include age, sex, marital status, and education level.

diversity   Any attribute that humans are likely to use to tell themselves, "that person is different from me," and thus includes such factors as race, gender, age, values, and cultural norms.

baby boomers   Individuals born between 1946 and 1965.

Sandwich Generation   Individuals with responsibility for rearing young dependants as well as for assisting elderly relatives who are no longer capable of functioning totally independently.

Generation X   Individuals born between 1966 and 1980.

Generation Y   Individuals born since 1980.

An Ethical Dilemma

The maintenance department supervisor has just come to you, the HR manager, voicing concern about the safety of two of her reporting employees whom she recently discovered are functionally illiterate. What are your responsibilities to these employees, if any?

A frightening reality is that inadequate reading and writing skills have replaced lack of experience as the major reason for rejecting entry-level candidates.[27] About 15 percent of working-age Canadians are *functionally illiterate*—unable to read, write, calculate, or solve problems at a level required for independent functioning or the performance of routine technical tasks.[28] Functional illiteracy is exacting a toll, not only on individual social and economic opportunities but also on organizations' accident rates and productivity levels.

Visible and Ethnic Minorities   The proportion of visible and ethnic minorities entering the Canadian labour market is expected to continue growing at a faster pace than the rest of the population. About two-thirds of visible minorities are immigrants, and approximately 20 percent of the Canadian population could be visible minorities by 2017. Ethnic diversity is also increasing. Currently, more than 200 different ethnic groups are represented among Canadian residents.[29]

Women   The steady convergence of men's and women's employment/population ratios has been one of the most dramatic changes observed in the Canadian labour market over the past 50 years.[30] As shown in **Figure 1.3**, between 1946 and 2003 the employment rate for women steadily increased, while that for men gradually decreased. Many organizations are accommodating working women and shared parenting responsibilities by offering on-site daycare, emergency childcare support, and flexible work arrangements.

Aboriginal Peoples   The Aboriginal population is young and growing at a rate almost twice that of the Canadian population.[31] These young Aboriginal people represent an untapped source of employees who are still facing considerable difficulty in obtaining jobs and advancing in the workplace.

Persons with Disabilities   Canadians with disabilities continue to confront physical barriers to equality every day. Inaccessibility is still the rule, not the exception. Even though studies show that there are no performance differences in terms of productivity, attendance, and average tenure between employees who classify themselves as having a disability and those who do not, persons with disabilities continue, on average, to experience high rates of unemployment and underemployment, and lower pay. Their unemployment rate is 50 percent higher than that for the able-bodied population, and their average income is 17 percent lower.[32]

FIGURE 1.3   Annual Employment Rates for Males and Females: 1946–2003

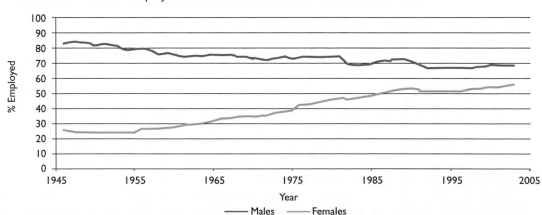

Source: Adapted from Statistics Canada publication *Economic Conference 2004—Emerging Challenges: New Insights on the Economy and Society*, Catalogue 11F0024MIE, release date: November 25, 2004.

Workforce Diversity

BMO Financial Group Values Diversity

At BMO Financial Group, creating and maintaining a diverse workforce and an equitable, supportive workplace is a strategic business priority. Diversity and workplace equity are so integral to the enterprise that they are clearly reflected in the organization's corporate values.

The CEO's Council on the Equitable Workplace, established in 1992, meets at least annually to review the implementation of BMO's diversity strategy. Employee-initiated diversity councils (by line of business) and affinity groups (employees organized by issue; for example, employees with physical disabilities, deaf/deafened/hard of hearing employees) raise awareness, foster dialogue, and model inclusive behaviour.

BMO's commitment to diversity is supported by a comprehensive infrastructure, which includes goal setting, monitoring, and evaluation. The CEO and all BMO executives monitor progress toward these goals on a quarterly basis. Results are further measured and monitored through the Diversity Index (DI) from the Annual Employee Survey. The DI is one of the factors used to assess overall executive performance and compensation.

The demographics of the organization reflect the success of diversity initiatives at BMO. In 2005, the representation of women on BMO's executive team increased to 34 percent—significant progress from 1991, when the representation of women in executive roles was just 9 percent. Representation of visible minorities continued to steadily increase to 22 percent in 2005, and the representation of visible minorities in the middle management ranks has increased to 16 percent.

In 2005, the representation of Aboriginal people at BMO held at just over 1 percent, while the representation of Aboriginal people in middle manager positions increased by 3 percent compared to an increase of only 2 percent in the total population of middle managers. Lastly, while the representation of people with disabilities slipped to just below 3 percent in 2005, the highest level of representation of people with disabilities is in the semi-professional and technician category which increased in 2005 to 4.4 percent.

Source: Adapted from BMO Financial Group, *2005 Employee Equity Narrative Report.* http://www2.bmo.com/bmo/files/images/7/1/BMO_2005_NarrativeRpt.pdf (January 2007). Used with permission.

Robotics is revolutionizing work in many fields. Such technology requires highly trained and committed employees.

Overall, such organizations as BMO Financial Group have led the way in seeking the benefits of workforce diversity, as described in the Workforce Diversity box.

Technology

The overall impact of technological advances in manufacturing and office work is that labour-intensive blue-collar and clerical jobs have been decreasing, while technical, managerial, and professional jobs are on the increase. The training of the Canadian labour force has not kept pace with the rate of technological change and innovation, and there is a scarcity of skills in certain fields. Also, unions have consistently expressed concerns about job displacement and health hazards, such as those related to video display terminals.

Technology is increasingly being used as a delivery mechanism for HR services. Originally, many firms introduced a *Human Resources Information System (HRIS)* to store detailed employee information. More recently, some firms have implemented *enterprise resource software* systems (SAP being the most common) that include a human resources management module.

Questions concerning data control, accuracy, the right to privacy, and ethics are at the core of a growing controversy brought about by the new information technologies. Sophisticated computerized control systems are used to monitor employee speed, accuracy, and efficiency in some firms. More firms are also monitoring employee e-mail, voice mail, telephone conversations, and computer usage, and some now monitor employee behaviour using video surveillance.[33]

An Ethical Dilemma

How much responsibility does a firm have toward employees whose skills will soon become obsolete because of changing technology?

Government

Various laws enacted by governments have had and will continue to have a dramatic impact on the employer–employee relationship in Canada. One of the factors that makes employment law in Canada so challenging is that there are 14 different jurisdictions involved. Each province and territory has its own human rights, employment standards, labour relations, health and safety, and workers' compensation legislation. In addition, about 10 percent of the workforce (including employees of the federal government and Crown corporations, chartered banks, airlines, national railways, and the Canadian armed forces) is covered by federal employment legislation.

Although there is some commonality across jurisdictions, there is also considerable variation. Minimum wage, overtime pay requirements, vacation entitlement, and grounds protected under human rights legislation, for example, vary from one province/territory to another. Furthermore, some jurisdictions have pay and employment equity legislation, while others do not. This means that companies with employees in more than one jurisdiction have different rules applying to different employees. There are, however, certain laws that apply to all employers and employees across Canada, such as Employment Insurance and the Canada/Quebec Pension Plan.

Sometimes changes in a federal law will drive changes in provincial/territorial laws. For example, when the Employment Insurance Act was amended in 2004 to provide income for up to six weeks of paid compassionate leave to care for gravely ill family members, each jurisdiction then had to amend its employment/labour standards legislation to include compassionate leave in order to be consistent with the federal law.[34]

Globalization

The term **globalization** refers to the growing tendency of firms to extend their sales or manufacturing to new markets abroad. As one international business expert put it, "The bottom line is that the growing integration of the world economy into a single, huge marketplace is increasing the intensity of competition in a wide range of manufacturing and service industries."[35]

There are increasing numbers of multinational corporations—firms that conduct a large part of business outside the country in which they are headquartered and that locate a significant percentage of their physical facilities and human resources in other countries. For example, Toyota has a large market share in the United States, Europe, and Africa, and is the market leader in Australia. Toyota has factories all over the world, manufacturing or assembling vehicles, such as the Corolla, for local markets. Notably, Toyota has manufacturing or assembly plants in the United States, Japan, Australia, Canada, Indonesia, Poland, South Africa, Turkey, the United Kingdom, France, and Brazil, and has recently added plants in Pakistan, India, Argentina, the Czech Republic, Mexico, Malaysia, Thailand, China, and Venezuela.[36]

Globalization means that HR professionals may need to become familiar with employment legislation in other countries and manage ethical dilemmas when labour standards are substantially lower than those in Canada. Companies doing business in sub-Saharan Africa, for example, have to deal with a high death rate among employees with AIDS. Some are paying for antiretroviral drugs to keep their employees alive.[37]

Overall, there is a broad range of external environmental influences that can have a substantial impact on HRM and can also affect strategy formulation.

Hints to Ensure Legal Compliance

globalization The tendency of firms to extend their sales or manufacturing to new markets abroad.

REQUIRED PROFESSIONAL CAPABILITIES

Gathers, analyzes, and reports relevant business and industry information, including global trends

A BRIEF HISTORY OF HRM

Frederick Taylor
(1856–1915), the father of
scientific management.

scientific management   The
process of "scientifically" analyzing
manufacturing processes, reducing
production costs, and compensating employees based on their
performance levels.

human relations movement   A
management philosophy based on
the belief that the attitudes and
feelings of workers are important
and deserve more attention.

human resources movement   A
management philosophy focusing
on concern for people and
productivity.

HRM has changed dramatically over time and has assumed an increasingly
strategic role. The demands on HR staff and expectations regarding their role
have evolved as HRM has changed. HR practices have been shaped by society's
prevailing beliefs and attitudes about workers and their rights, which have
evolved in three stages.

Scientific Management: Concern for Production

Frederick Taylor was the driving force behind **scientific management**, the
process of "scientifically" analyzing manufacturing processes, reducing production costs, and compensating employees based on their performance.[38] As a
result, management practices in the late 1800s and early 1900s emphasized task
simplification and performance-based pay. Such incentives were expected to
lead to higher wages for workers, increased profits for the organization, and
workplace harmony. Taylor's views were not accepted by all management theorists. For example, Mary Parker Follett, a writer ahead of her time, advocated
the use of self-management, cross-functional cooperation, empowerment, and
managers as leaders, not dictators.[39]

The Human Relations Movement: Concern for People

The primary aim of the **human relations movement**, which emerged in the 1920s
and 1930s but was not fully embraced until the 1940s, was to consider jobs
from an employee's perspective. Managers who treated workers as machines
were criticized. This management philosophy was based on the results of the
Hawthorne Studies, a series of experiments that examined factors influencing
worker morale and productivity. The conclusions had a significant and far-
reaching impact on management practices.

The researchers discovered that the effect of the social environment was
equal to or greater than that of the physical environment. They learned that
worker morale was greatly influenced by such factors as working conditions,
the supervisor's leadership style, and management's philosophy regarding workers. Treating workers with dignity and respect was found to lead to higher job
satisfaction and productivity levels, with economic incentives being of secondary importance. In the many firms embracing the human relations approach,
working conditions improved substantially. Managers focused on establishing
better channels of communication, allowing employees to exercise more self-
direction, and treating employees with consideration. This movement came
under severe criticism for overcompensating for the dehumanizing effects of scientific management by failing to recognize the importance of structure and
work rules, for oversimplifying the concept of employee motivation, and for
failing to recognize individual differences in beliefs, needs, and abilities.

The Human Resources Movement: Concern for People and Productivity

HRM is currently based on the theoretical assumptions of the **human resources
movement**. Arriving at this joint focus on people and productivity involved four
evolutionary phases.[40]

Phase 1   In the early 1900s, HRM—or personnel administration, as it was then called—played a very subservient or nonexistent role. During this era, personnel administrators assumed responsibility for hiring and firing (a duty formerly looked after by first-line supervisors), ran the payroll department, and administered benefits. Their job consisted largely of ensuring that procedures were followed.

Phase 2   As the scientific management movement gained momentum, operational efficiency increased but wage increases did not keep up, causing workers to distrust management. The resulting increase in unionization led to personnel departments serving as the primary contact for union representatives. Following the depression of the 1930s, various pieces of legislation were enacted, including a minimum wage act, an unemployment insurance program, and protection of workers' right to belong to unions. Legal compliance was subsequently added to the responsibilities of personnel managers. During the 1940s and 1950s, personnel managers were also involved in dealing with the impact of the human relations movement. Orientation, performance appraisal, and employee relations responsibilities were added to their portfolio.

Phase 3   The third major phase in personnel management was a direct result of government legislation passed during the 1960s, 1970s, and 1980s that affected employees' human rights, wages and benefits, working conditions, and health and safety, and established penalties for failure to meet them. The role of personnel departments expanded dramatically. They continued to provide expertise in such areas as recruitment, screening, and training, but in an expanded capacity. During the latter part of this era, the term "human resources management" emerged. This change represented a shift in emphasis—from maintenance and administration to corporate contribution, proactive management, and initiation of change.[41]

Phase 4   The fourth phase of HRM is strategic. Organizations must leverage human capital in order to compete in today's global business world. They require employees who are fully engaged in their jobs, so that the goals and aims of both management and employees can be achieved. In today's organizations, employees are often a firm's best competitive advantage. The role of HR departments has evolved to that of strategic partner.

This transformation has occurred because economic forces, such as deregulation, globalization, and intense competition, are making human capital more important. Many traditional sources of competitive advantage, such as market share, proprietary technology, access to capital, and regulated markets, are becoming less powerful. What remains as a crucial differentiating factor is the organization, its employees, and how they work. Experts believe that the latent creative and innovative capacity among employees of most organizations has the power to eclipse other forms of competitive advantage. They predict that HR managers will be the means through which organizations can realize the untapped potential of their workforces.[42]

According to esteemed HR expert Ed Lawler, "The time is right for HR executives to take on an important new role in organizations. They need to become major players in the development and implementation of business strategy. This is a role that adds a great deal of value and one that HR executives can and should perform."[43]

HR's transformation has been underway for several years, but progress has been slow because of lack of senior management support and the fact that many non-HR managers still view HR as a cost centre. Also, many HR professionals need to acquire more broad-based business knowledge and skill sets. Canadian HR leaders agree that to be considered and respected as equal business partners by other executives in the company, HR professionals must become effective business managers, externally focused, comfortable with saying no and taking risks, and skilled at building relationships with other executives. Although 75 percent of Canadian organizations say they are working toward strategic HR, only one-third of them have a documented HR strategy. In many organizations, HR remains locked in a transactional mode, processing forms and requests, administering compensation and benefits, managing policies and programs, and overseeing hiring and training.[44]

GROWING PROFESSIONALISM IN HRM

certification Recognition for having met certain professional standards.

REQUIRED PROFESSIONAL CAPABILITIES

Stays current in terms of professional development

Contributes to and promotes the development of the profession

Canadian Council of Human Resources Associations (CCHRA)
www.cchra-ccarh.ca

International Personnel Management Association
www.ipma-aigp.ca

REQUIRED PROFESSIONAL CAPABILITIES

Understands and adheres to the Canadian Council of Human Resources Association's code of ethics

Today, HR practitioners must be professionals in terms of both performance and qualifications. Every profession has four major characteristics: (1) a common body of knowledge, (2) **certification** of members, (3) self-regulation, and (4) a code of ethics. Every province has an association of HR practitioners (except Prince Edward Island, which is included in Nova Scotia's) that manages these four areas, ensures information exchange and cooperative problem solving, provides HR training and skills updating, and serves as a voice for HR practitioners regarding proposed legislation. The Canadian Council of Human Resources Associations (CCHRA) is the 30 000-member national body through which all provincial HR associations are affiliated.[45] The International Personnel Management Association (IPMA)—Canada is the national association for public-sector and quasi-public-sector HR professionals.

Other important associations for HR specialists include the Canadian Industrial Relations Association; WorldatWork; health and safety associations, such as the Industrial Accident Prevention Association, the Construction Safety Association, and Safe Communities Canada; and such groups as the Canadian Society for Training and Development for training and development professionals.

The Certified Human Resources Professional (CHRP) designation is a nationally recognized certification for Canadian HR professionals. Managed by the CCHRA and administered through provincial HR associations, the CHRP is similar to other professional designations, such as the Chartered Accountant (CA) and Professional Engineer (P.Eng.), as it recognizes members' qualifications and experience based on established levels of 203 required professional capabilities.[46] The national certification requirements are shown in **Figure 1.4.**

Ethics

The professionalization of HRM has created the need for a uniform code of ethics, as agreement to abide by the code of ethics is one of the requirements of maintaining professional status. The CCHRA Code of Ethics is shown in **Figure 1.5** on page 19. Since what is ethical or unethical is generally open to debate, except in a few very clear-cut cases (such as willful misrepresentation), most codes do not tell employees what they should do. Rather, they provide a guide to help employees discover the best course of action by themselves.[47] Increasingly, HR departments are being given a greater role in providing ethics

FIGURE 1.4   National CHRP Certification Requirements

A. Initial Certification

To fulfill the academic requirement for the CHRP designation, a candidate must:

1. Become a member of a provincial human resources professionals' association; and

2. Complete all nine required courses listed below (Ontario candidates only); and

3. Pass

(1) the national knowledge examination (assesses knowledge of major human resources functions), and

(2) professional practice assessment (measures human resources "experience"); must be written within 5 years of writing the knowledge exam.

Note: Although not currently necessary, by 2011, all CHRP candidates will require a degree.

Required Courses for the National Knowledge Examination (Ontario candidates only)*

Human Resources Management

Organizational Behaviour

Financial and Managerial Accounting

Compensation

Training & Development

Occupational Health & Safety

Labour Relations

Human Resources Planning

Recruitment & Selection

*Challenge exams and executive programs can be substituted.

B. Recertification

Every three years, all CHRPs will be required to recertify based on a set of professional development criteria, including seminars, conferences, volunteer work, or continuing education.

Source: Based on *Become a Certified Human Resources Professional.* Human Resources Professionals Association of Ontario. www.hrpao.org (August 16, 2006). Reproduced with permission.

Human Resources Professionals Association of Ontario
www.hrpao.org

Ethics Resource Center
www.ethics.org

Business for Social Responsibility
www.bsr.org

Canadian Business for Social Responsibility
www.cbsr.ca

An Ethical Dilemma

Can or should an employee reveal information about a troubled co-worker that was disclosed in confidence, and if so, under what circumstances?

training, and monitoring to ensure compliance with the code of ethics. Some organizations have such a commitment to ethics that they have a full-time ethics officer.

The most prevalent ethical issues confronting Canadian organizations today pertain to security of information, employee and client privacy, environmental issues, governance, and conflicts of interest.[48] The major reasons for the failure of ethics programs to achieve the desired results are lack of effective leadership and inadequate training. Positive outcomes associated with properly implemented ethics programs include increased confidence among stakeholders, such as clients, partners, and employees; greater client/customer and employee loyalty; decreased vulnerability to crime; reduced losses because of internal theft; and increased public trust.[49]

FIGURE 1.5   CCHRA National Code of Ethics

1. Preamble

- As HR practitioners in the following categories—
  - Certified Human Resources Professionals,
  - CHRP Candidates, or
  - CHRP Exam Registrants,

  we commit to abide by all requirements of the Code of Ethics of the Canadian Council of Human Resources Associations (CCHRA), as listed in this document. (Where provincial codes are legislated, those will prevail.)

2. Competence

- Maintain competence in carrying out professional responsibilities and provide services in an honest and diligent manner.
- Ensure that activities engaged in are within the limits of one's knowledge, experience and skill.
- When providing services outside one's level of competence, or the profession, the necessary assistance must be sought so as not to compromise professional responsibility.

3. Legal Requirements

- Adhere to any statutory acts, regulation or by-laws which relate to the field of Human Resources Management, as well as all civil and criminal laws, regulations and statutes that apply in one's jurisdiction.
- Not knowingly or otherwise engage in or condone any activity or attempt to circumvent the clear intention of the law.

4. Dignity in the Workplace

- Support, promote and apply the principles of human rights, equity, dignity and respect in the workplace, within the profession and in society as a whole.

5. Balancing Interests

- Strive to balance organizational and employee needs and interests in the practice of the profession.

6. Confidentiality

- Hold in strict confidence all confidential information acquired in the course of the performance of one's duties, and not divulge confidential information unless required by law and/or where serious harm is imminent.

7. Conflict of Interest

- Either avoid or disclose a potential conflict of interest that might influence or might be perceived to influence personal actions or judgments.

8. Professional Growth and Support of Other Professionals

- Maintain personal and professional growth in Human Resources Management by engaging in activities that enhance the credibility and value of the profession.

9. Enforcement

- The Canadian Council of Human Resources Associations works collaboratively with its Member Associations to develop and enforce high standards of ethical practice among all its members.

Source: The CCHRA Code of Ethics. © 2006. www.cchra-ccarh.ca/parc/en/section_2/ss23e.asp (August 16, 2006). Reprinted with the permission of the Canadian Council of Human Resources Associations.

social responsibility   The implied, enforced, or felt obligation of managers, acting in their official capacities, to serve or protect the interests of groups other than themselves.

In recent years, the concept of **social responsibility** has frequently been discussed as a complement to ethics. A company that exercises social responsibility attempts to balance its commitments—not only to its investors but also to its employees and customers, other businesses, and the community or communities in which it operates. The Body Shop, an early and often-cited example of a socially responsible firm, proves that businesses can balance profits and principles. Despite taking a stand on anti-animal testing, human rights protection, and environmental conservation, the Body Shop has been extremely successful.

Chapter Review

Summary

1. Human resources management (HRM) refers to the management of people in organizations. Strategic HRM involves linking HRM with strategic goals and objectives to improve business performance. In more and more firms, HR professionals are becoming strategic partners in strategy formulation and strategy execution.

2. Human resources activities are now being seen as falling into two categories. The first is the traditional operational (administrative) category, where HR hires and maintains employees, and

then manages employee separations. This role requires HR staff to be administrative experts and employee champions. The second is the more recent strategic category, where HR is focused on ensuring that the organization is staffed with the most effective human capital to achieve its strategic goals. This role requires HR staff to be strategic partners and change agents.

3. Internal environmental factors influencing HRM include organizational culture, which consists of the core values, beliefs, and assumptions that are widely shared by members of the organization; organizational climate, which is the prevailing atmosphere; and management practices, such as the shift from traditional bureaucratic structures to flatter organizations where employees are empowered to make more decisions. A number of external factors have an impact on HRM, including economic factors, labour market issues, demographic trends and increasing workforce diversity, technology, government, and globalization.

4. The three stages in the evolution of management thinking about workers are (1) scientific management, which focused on production; (2) the human relations movement, in which the emphasis was on people; and (3) the human resources movement, in which it was recognized that organizational success is linked to both.

5. Every profession has four major characteristics: (1) a common body of knowledge, (2) certification of members, (3) self-regulation, and (4) a code of ethics. The Canadian Council of Human Resources Associations regulates the human resources profession in Canada and has a code of ethics for HR professionals. It has compiled a common body of knowledge based on a list of 203 required professional capabilities that provide the foundation for a certification process leading to the Certified Human Resources Professional designation.

Key Terms

baby boomers   *(p. 11)*
balanced scorecard   *(p. 4)*
boundaryless organization structure   *(p. 9)*
certification   *(p. 17)*
contingent employees   *(p. 10)*
demographics   *(p. 11)*
diversity   *(p. 11)*
employee engagement   *(p. 7)*
empowerment   *(p. 9)*
environmental scanning   *(p. 7)*
Generation X   *(p. 11)*
Generation Y   *(p. 11)*
globalization   *(p. 14)*
human capital   *(p. 2)*
human relations movement   *(p. 15)*
human resources management (HRM)   *(p. 2)*
human resources movement   *(p. 15)*
organizational climate   *(p. 9)*
organizational culture   *(p. 8)*
outsourcing   *(p. 6)*
primary sector   *(p. 9)*
productivity   *(p. 9)*
Sandwich Generation   *(p. 11)*
scientific management   *(p. 15)*
secondary sector   *(p. 9)*
social responsibility   *(p. 19)*
strategy   *(p. 6)*
tertiary or service sector   *(p. 9)*

Review and Discussion Questions

1. Describe the transformation that HRM is currently undergoing.

2. Describe the role of HR in strategy formulation and strategy implementation.

3. Differentiate between organizational culture and organizational climate.

4. Describe the multiple jurisdictions related to employment legislation affecting HRM in Canada.

5. Describe scientific management and explain its impact on organizations.

6. Explain why HRM is a profession.

Critical Thinking Questions

1. If the executive team in your organization was not convinced that the senior HR executive should participate in the strategic planning process, what would you do to try to convince its members?

2. Explain how changing demographics and increasing workforce diversity have had an impact on the organization in which you are working or one in which you have worked.

3. A firm has requested your assistance in ensuring that its multigenerational workforce functions effectively as a team. What strategies and/or programs would you recommend? Why?

4. Identify a company that is known for being both ethical and socially responsible. What types of behaviour and activities typify this organization? How has this behaviour affected the achievement of its corporate strategy?

Application Exercises

Running Case: LearnInMotion.com

Introduction

The main theme of this book is that HRM—activities like recruiting, selecting, training, and rewarding employees—is not just the job of a central HR group, but rather one in which every manager must engage. Perhaps nowhere is this more apparent than in the typical small service business, where the owner-manager usually has no HR staff to rely on. However, the success of such an enterprise often depends largely on the effectiveness with which workers are recruited, hired, trained, evaluated, and rewarded. To help illustrate and emphasize the front-line manager's HR role, throughout this book we will use a continuing ("running") case, based on an actual small business in Ottawa's high-tech region. Each segment will illustrate how the case's main players—owner-managers Jennifer Lau and Pierre LeBlanc—confront and solve HRM problems each day by applying the concepts and techniques presented in that particular chapter. Here's some background information you'll need to answer questions that arise in subsequent chapters.

LearnInMotion.com: A Profile

Jennifer and Pierre graduated from university as business majors in June 2006 and got the idea for LearnInMotion.com as a result of a project they worked on together their last semester in their entrepreurship class. The professor had divided the students into two- or three-person teams and given them the assignment to "create a business plan for a high-tech company." The idea the two came up with was LearnInMotion.com. The basic idea of the Web site was to list a vast array of Web-based, CD-ROM–based, or textbook-based continuing education–type business courses for working people who wanted to take a course from the comfort of their own homes. The idea was that users could come to the Web site to find and then take a course in one of several ways. Some courses could be completed interactively on the Web via the site; others were in a form that was downloadable directly to the user's computer; others (which were either textbook or CD-ROM based) could be ordered and delivered (in several major metropolitan areas) by independent contractor delivery people. Their business mission was "to provide work-related learning when, where, and how you need it."

Based on their research, they knew the market for work-related learning like this was booming. At the same time, professional development activities like these were increasingly Internet-based. Tens of thousands of on- and offline training firms, universities, associations, and other content providers were trying to reach their target customers via the Internet. Jennifer and Pierre understandably thought they were in the right place at the right time. Jennifer's father had some unused loft space in Kanata, Ontario, so with about $45 000 of accumulated savings, Jennifer and Pierre incorporated and were in business. They retained the services of an independent programmer and hired two people—a Web designer to create the graphics for the site (which would then be programmed by the programmer), and a content manager whose job was to enter information onto the site as it came in from content providers. By the end of 2006, they also completed upgrading their business plan into a form they could show to prospective venture capitalists. They sent the first version to three Canadian venture capitalists. Then they waited.

And then they waited some more. They never heard back from the first three venture capitalists, so they sent their plan to five more. They still got no response. But Pierre and Jennifer pressed on. By day they called customers to get people to place ads on their site, to get content providers to list their available courses, and to get someone—anyone—to deliver textbook- and CD-ROM–based courses, as needed, across Canada. By May 2007, they had about 300 content providers offering courses and content through LearnInMotion.com. In the summer, they got their first serious nibble from a venture capital firm. They negotiated with this company through much of the summer, came to terms in the early fall, and closed the deal—getting just over $1 million in venture funding—in November 2007.

After a stunning total of $75 000 in legal fees (they had to pay both their firm's and the venture capital firm's lawyers to navigate the voluminous disclosure documents and agreements), they had just over $900 000 to spend. The funding, according to the business plan, was to go toward accomplishing five main goals: redesigning and expanding the Web site; hiring about seven more employees; moving to a larger office; designing and implementing a personal information manager (PIM)/calendar (users and content providers could use the calendar to interactively keep track of their personal and business schedules); and, last but not least, driving up sales. LearnInMotion was off and running.

Questions

1. Would a company like this with just a few employees and independent contractors have any HR tasks to address? What do you think those might be?

2. What basic HR policies and procedures would you recommend to Jennifer and Pierre?

Case Incident

Jack Nelson's Problem

As a new member of the board of directors for a local bank, Jack Nelson was being introduced to all the employees in the home office. When he was introduced to Ruth Johnson, he was curious about her work and asked her what the machine she was using did. Johnson replied that she really did not know what the machine was called or what it did. She explained that she had only been working there for two months. She did, however, know precisely how to operate the machine. According to her supervisor, she was an excellent employee.

At one of the branch offices, the supervisor in charge spoke to Nelson confidentially, telling him that "something was wrong," but she didn't know what. For one thing, she explained, employee turnover was too high, and no sooner had one employee been put on the job than another one resigned. With customers to see and loans to be made, she continued, she had little time to work with the new employees as they came and went.

All branch supervisors hired their own employees without communication with the home office or other branches. When an opening developed, the supervisor tried to find a suitable employee to replace the worker who had quit.

After touring the 22 branches and finding similar problems in many of them, Nelson wondered what the home office should do or what action he should take. The banking firm was generally regarded as a well-run institution that had grown from 27 to 191 employees during the past eight years. The more he thought about the matter, the more puzzled Nelson became. He couldn't quite put his finger on the problem, and he didn't know whether to report his findings to the president.

Questions

1. What do you think is causing some of the problems in the bank's home office and branches?

2. Do you think setting up an HR unit in the main office would help?

3. What specific functions should an HR unit carry out? What HR functions would then be carried out by supervisors and other line managers? What role should the Internet play in the new HR organization?

Source: From Claude S. George, *Supervision in Action*, 4th ed., 1985. Adapted by permission of Prentice Hall, Inc., Upper Saddle River, NJ.

Experiential Exercises

1. Working alone or with a small group of class-mates, interview an HR manager and prepare a short essay regarding his or her role in strategy formulation and implementation.

2. Prepare a summary of the employment legislation affecting all employers and employees who are not under federal jurisdiction in your province or territory. Explain the impact of each of these laws on HRM policies and practices.

3. Working with a small group of classmates, contact several firms in your community to find out whether or not they have a code of ethics. If so, learn as much as possible about the specific initiatives devised to support and communicate the code. If not, find out if the firm is planning to implement such a code. If so, how does the firm intend to proceed? If not, why not?

CHAPTER 2

THE CHANGING LEGAL EMPHASIS
From Compliance to Valuing Diversity

REQUIRED PROFESSIONAL CAPABILITIES

- Evaluates programs on deliverables

LEARNING OUTCOMES

AFTER STUDYING THIS CHAPTER, YOU SHOULD BE ABLE TO

Explain how employment-related issues are governed in Canada.

Discuss at least five prohibited grounds for discrimination under human rights legislation, and **describe** the requirements for reasonable accommodation.

Describe behaviour that could constitute harassment, and **describe** employers' responsibilities regarding harassment.

Describe the six steps involved in implementing an employment equity program.

Discuss the seven characteristics of successful diversity management initiatives.

THE LEGAL FRAMEWORK FOR EMPLOYMENT LAW IN CANADA

Government of Canada
http://canada.gc.ca

In Canada, the primary responsibility for employment-related laws resides with the provinces and territories. Today, provincial/territorial employment laws govern approximately 90 percent of Canadian workers. The remaining 10 percent of the workforce, employed in the federal civil service, Crown corporations and agencies, and businesses engaged in transportation, banking, and communications, is governed by federal employment legislation. Thus there are 14 jurisdictions—ten provinces, three territories, and Canada as a whole—for employment law.

There is a great deal of commonality to the legislation, both federal and provincial/territorial; however, there are also some differences. For example, vacations, statutory holidays, and minimum wage standards are provided by all jurisdictions, but specific entitlements vary from jurisdiction to jurisdiction.

Therefore, a company with employees in different provinces/territories must monitor the legislation in each of those jurisdictions and remain current as legislation changes. Ensuring legality across multiple jurisdictions can be very complex, since it is possible for a policy, practice, or procedure to be legal in one jurisdiction yet illegal in others.

The legal framework for employment also includes constitutional law, particularly the Charter of Rights and Freedoms; acts of Parliament; **common law**, which is the accumulation of judicial precedents that do not derive from specific pieces of legislation; and **contract law**, which governs collective agreements and individual employment contracts. Such laws impose specific requirements and constraints on management policies, procedures, and practices. One common example of common law is court decisions regarding allegations of wrongful dismissal of an employee by an employer.

To avoid flooding the courts with complaints and the prosecutions of relatively minor infractions, the government in each jurisdiction creates special regulatory bodies to enforce compliance with the law and aid in its interpretation. Such bodies, which include human rights commissions and ministries of labour, develop legally binding rules, called **regulations**, and evaluate complaints.

There are laws that specifically regulate some areas of HRM: occupational health and safety (occupational health and safety acts), union relations (labour relations acts), pensions (pension benefits acts), and compensation (pay equity acts, the Income Tax Act, and others). These will be discussed later in the chapters covering these topics. In this chapter, broader laws affecting the overall practice of HRM will be reviewed. These include employment standards legislation, human rights legislation, and employment equity legislation.

Many organizations have moved beyond legal compliance with human rights and employment equity requirements and have begun to initiate and promote workplace diversity initiatives because the value of having a diverse workforce has proven to make good business sense. The chapter will also provide an overview of diversity management initiatives.

It is illegal in every jurisdiction in Canada to discriminate on the basis of age.

common law   The accumulation of judicial precedents that do not derive from specific pieces of legislation.

contract law   Legislation that governs collective agreements and individual employment contracts.

regulations   Legally binding rules established by the special regulatory bodies created to enforce compliance with the law and aid in its interpretation.

employment (labour) standards legislation   Laws present in every Canadian jurisdiction that establish minimum employee entitlements and set a limit on the maximum number of hours of work permitted per day or week.

EMPLOYMENT/LABOUR STANDARDS LEGISLATION

All employers and employees in Canada, including unionized employees, are covered by **employment (labour) standards legislation**. These laws establish minimum employee entitlements pertaining to such issues as wages; paid holidays

Canadian Association of
Administrators of Labour
Legislation
www.labour-info-travail.org

Workplace Standards
www.workplace.ca/laws/employ_
standard_comp.html

and vacations; leave for some mix of maternity, parenting, and adoption; bereavement leave; compassionate care leave; termination notice; and overtime pay. They also set a limit on the maximum number of hours of work permitted per day or week.

Every jurisdiction in Canada has legislation incorporating the principle of *equal pay for equal work*. In most jurisdictions, this entitlement is found in the employment (labour) standards legislation; otherwise, it is in the human rights legislation. Equal pay for equal work specifies that an employer cannot pay male and female employees differently if they are performing the same or substantially similar work. This principle makes it illegal, for example, for a school board to classify male employees as janitors and female employees doing virtually the same work as housekeepers and provide different wage rates based on these classifications. Pay differences based on a valid merit or seniority system or employee productivity are permitted; it is only sex-based discrimination that is prohibited. Enforcement is complaint-based and violators can be fined.

LEGISLATION PROTECTING HUMAN RIGHTS

Human rights legislation makes it illegal to discriminate, even unintentionally, against various groups. Reactive (complaint-driven) in nature, the focus of such legislation is on the types of acts in which employers should *not* engage. Included in this category are

1. *the Charter of Rights and Freedoms*, federal legislation that is the cornerstone of human rights
2. *human rights legislation*, which is present in every jurisdiction

The Charter of Rights and Freedoms

Charter of Rights and Freedoms
Federal law enacted in 1982 that guarantees fundamental freedoms to all Canadians.

The cornerstone of Canada's legislation pertaining to issues of human rights is the Constitution Act, which contains the **Charter of Rights and Freedoms**. The Charter applies to the actions of all levels of government (federal, provincial/territorial, and municipal) and agencies under their jurisdiction as they go about their work of creating laws. The Charter takes precedence over all other laws, which means that all legislation must meet Charter standards; thus, it is quite far-reaching in scope.

There are two notable exceptions to this generalization. The Charter allows laws to infringe on Charter rights if they can be demonstrably justified as reasonable limits in a "free and democratic society." Since "demonstrably justified" and "reasonable" are open to interpretation, many issues challenged under the Charter eventually end up before the Supreme Court, its ultimate interpreter. The second exception occurs when a legislative body invokes the "notwithstanding" provision, which allows the legislation to be exempted from challenge under the Charter.

Supreme Court of Canada
www.scc-csc.gc.ca

The Charter provides the following fundamental rights and freedoms to every Canadian:

1. freedom of conscience and religion
2. freedom of thought, belief, opinion, and expression, including freedom of the press and other media of communication
3. freedom of peaceful assembly
4. freedom of association

In addition, the Charter provides Canadian multicultural heritage rights, First People's rights, minority language education rights, the right to live and work anywhere in Canada, the right to due process in criminal proceedings, equality rights, and the right to democracy.[1]

Section 15—**equality rights**—provides the basis for human rights legislation, as it guarantees the right to[2]

> equal protection and benefit of the law without discrimination, and, in particular, without discrimination based on race, national or ethnic origin, colour, religion, sex, age, or mental or physical disability.

Section 15 provides the foundation for Canada's human rights legislation.

Human Rights Legislation

Every employer in Canada is affected by human rights legislation, which prohibits intentional and unintentional discrimination in its policies pertaining to all aspects, terms, and conditions of employment. Human rights legislation is extremely broad in scope, affecting almost all aspects of HRM. The ways in which employees should be treated on the job every day and the climate in which they work are also addressed by this legislation. An important feature of the human rights legislation is that it supersedes the terms of any employment contract or collective agreement.[3] For these reasons, supervisors and managers must be thoroughly familiar with the human rights legislation and their legal obligations and responsibilities specified therein.

Human rights legislation prohibits discrimination against all Canadians in a number of areas, including employment. To review individual provincial and territorial human rights laws would be confusing because of the many but generally minor differences among them, often only in terminology (e.g., some provinces use the term "creed," others "religion"). As indicated in **Figure 2.1**, most provincial/territorial laws are similar to the federal statute in terms of scope, interpretation, and application. All jurisdictions prohibit discrimination on the grounds of race, colour, religion/creed, sex, marital status, age, physical and mental disability, and sexual orientation. Some but not all jurisdictions prohibit discrimination on the basis of national or ethnic origin, family status, ancestry or place of origin, and various other grounds.

Discrimination Defined

Central to human rights laws is the concept of **discrimination**. When someone is accused of discrimination, it generally means that he or she is perceived to be acting in an unfair or prejudiced manner. The law prohibits unfair discrimination—making choices on the basis of perceived but inaccurate differences, to the detriment of specific individuals and/or groups. Standards pertaining to unfair discrimination have changed over time.

Both intentional and unintentional discrimination is prohibited.

Intentional Discrimination

Except in specific circumstances that will be described later, intentional discrimination is prohibited. An employer cannot discriminate *directly* by deliberately refusing to hire, train, or promote an individual, for example, on any of the prohibited grounds. It is important to realize that deliberate discrimination

---

equality rights   Section 15 of the Charter of Rights and Freedoms, which guarantees the right to equal protection and equal benefit of the law without discrimination.

The Nunavut Handbook
www.nunavuthandbook.com

Canadian Human Rights Commission
www.chrc-ccdp.ca

Canadian Human Rights Tribunal
www.chrt-tcdp.gc.ca

discrimination   As used in the context of human rights in employment, a distinction, exclusion, or preference, based on one of the prohibited grounds, that has the effect of nullifying or impairing the right of a person to full and equal recognition and exercise of his or her human rights and freedoms.

FIGURE 2.1   Prohibited Grounds of Discrimination in Employment by Jurisdiction

Prohibited Grounds of Discrimination	Federal	Alta.	B.C.	Man.	N.B.	N.L.	N.S.	Ont.	P.E.I.	Que.	Sask.	N.W.T.	Y.T.	Nunavut
Race	♦	♦	♦	♦	♦	♦	♦	♦	♦	♦	♦	♦	♦	♦
Colour	♦	♦	♦	♦	♦	♦	♦	♦	♦	♦	♦	♦	♦	♦
Creed or religion	♦	♦	♦	♦	♦	♦	♦	♦	♦	♦	♦	♦	♦	♦
Sex	♦	♦	♦	♦	♦	♦	♦	♦	♦	♦	♦	♦	♦	♦
Marital status	♦	♦	♦	♦	♦	♦	♦	♦	♦	♦	♦	♦	♦	♦
Age	♦	♦ 18+	♦ 19–65	♦	♦	♦ 19–65	♦	♦ 18+	♦	♦	♦ 18–64	♦	♦	♦
Mental & physical disability	♦	♦	♦	♦	♦	♦	♦	♦	♦	♦	♦	♦	♦	♦
Sexual orientation	♦	♦	♦	♦	♦	♦	♦	♦	♦	♦	♦	♦	♦	♦
National or ethnic origin	♦			♦	♦	♦	♦	♦	♦	♦	♦	♦	♦	♦
Family status	♦	♦	♦	♦				♦	♦	♦	♦	♦	♦	♦
Ancestry or place of origin		♦	♦	♦							♦		♦	
Political belief			♦	♦	♦	♦	♦		♦	♦			♦	
Association			♦	♦			♦		♦	♦		♦	♦	♦
Source of income		♦		♦			♦		♦	♦	♦			
Social condition or origin					♦	♦				♦			♦	
Language								♦		♦			♦	
Pardoned conviction	♦											♦	♦	♦
Record of criminal conviction										♦			♦	
Assignment, attachment, or seizure of pay						♦								

Note: The legislation providing human rights protection and equal pay for equal work in Nunavut is titled the Fair Practices Act.

Source: Canadian Human Rights Commission, *Prohibited Grounds of Discrimination in Canada.* www.chrc-ccdp.ca/pdf/ProhibitedGrounds_en.pdf. Reproduced with the permission of the Ministry of Public Works and Government Services, 2006.

is not necessarily overt. In fact, overt (blatant) discrimination is quite rare today. Subtle direct discrimination can be difficult to prove. For example, if a 60-year-old applicant is not selected for a job and is told that there was a better-qualified candidate, it is often difficult for the rejected job-seeker to determine if someone else truly did more closely match the firm's specifications or if the employer discriminated on the basis of age.

An employer is also prohibited from intentional discrimination in the form of *differential or unequal treatment.* No individuals or groups may be treated differently in any aspects or terms and conditions of employment based on any of the prohibited grounds. For example, it is illegal for an employer to request that only female applicants for a factory job demonstrate their lifting skills, or to insist that any candidates with a physical disability undergo a pre-employment medical, unless all applicants are being asked to do so.

It is also illegal for an employer to engage in intentional discrimination *indirectly,* through another party. This means that an employer may not ask someone else to discriminate on his or her behalf. For example, an employer cannot request that an employment agency refer only male candidates for consideration as management trainees, or instruct supervisors that women of childbearing age are to be excluded from consideration for promotions.

Discrimination because of association is another possible type of intentional discrimination listed specifically as a prohibited ground in eight Canadian jurisdictions. It involves the denial of rights because of friendship or other relationship with a protected group member. An example would be the refusal of a firm to promote a highly qualified male into senior management on the basis of the assumption that his wife, who was recently diagnosed with multiple sclerosis, will require too much of his time and attention, and that her needs may restrict his willingness to travel on company business.

Unintentional Discrimination

Unintentional discrimination (also known as **constructive** or **systemic discrimination**) is the most difficult to detect and combat. Typically, it is embedded in policies and practices that, although appearing neutral on the surface and being implemented impartially, have an adverse impact on specific groups of people for reasons that are not job related or required for the safe and efficient operation of the business. Examples are shown in **Figure 2.2**.

Requirement for Reasonable Accommodation

An important feature of human rights legislation is the requirement for **reasonable accommodation**. Employers are required to adjust employment policies and practices so that no individual is prevented from doing his or her job on the basis of prohibited grounds for discrimination. Accommodation may involve scheduling adjustments to accommodate religious beliefs, or workstation redesign to enable an individual with a physical disability to perform a particular task. Employers are expected to accommodate to the point of **undue hardship**, meaning that the financial cost of the accommodation (even with outside

unintentional/constructive/ systemic discrimination Discrimination that is embedded in policies and practices that appear neutral on the surface, and are implemented impartially, but have an adverse impact on specific groups of people for reasons that are not job related or required for the safe and efficient operation of the business.

reasonable accommodation The adjustment of employment policies and practices that an employer may be expected to make so that no individual is denied benefits, disadvantaged in employment, or prevented from carrying out the essential components of a job because of grounds prohibited in human rights legislation.

undue hardship The point to which employers are expected to accommodate under human rights legislative requirements.

FIGURE 2.2   Examples of Systemic Discrimination

- Minimum height and weight requirements, which screen out disproportionate numbers of women and people from Asia, who tend to be shorter in stature.
- Internal hiring policies or word-of-mouth hiring in workplaces that have not embraced diversity.
- Limited accessibility to company premises, which poses a barrier to persons with mobility limitations.
- Culturally biased or non-job-related employment tests, which discriminate against specific groups.
- Job evaluation systems that are not gender-neutral; that is, they undervalue traditional female-dominated jobs.
- Promotions based exclusively on seniority or experience in firms that have a history of being white-male-dominated.
- Lack of a harassment policy or guidelines, or an organizational climate in which certain groups feel unwelcome and uncomfortable.

Source: Based on material provided by the Ontario Women's Directorate and the Canadian Human Rights Commission.

**bona fide occupational
requirement (BFOR)** A justifiable
reason for discrimination based on
business necessity (that is, required
for the safe and efficient operation
of the organization) or a
requirement that can be clearly
defended as intrinsically required
by the tasks an employee is
expected to perform.

sources of funding) or health and safety risks to the individual concerned or other employees would make accommodation impossible.[4]

Failure to make every reasonable effort to accommodate employees is a violation of human rights legislation in all Canadian jurisdictions. In a Nova Scotia case, a pregnant police officer was denied accommodation. Pregnancy and childbirth are included in the meaning of sex under human rights legislation. The complainant requested lighter duties during her pregnancy. She was told that there were no duties for her at the moment, as other people were currently performing the jobs with the lighter duties that she requested. After completing office duties for about a month, she ceased working. The Nova Scotia Human Rights Commission found that the officer could have been kept in the office for the length of her pregnancy without presenting undue hardship to the police service. The officer was awarded compensation for lost wages, and the police service was ordered to consider the complainant for the next available position and to develop a policy to deal with pregnancy.[5]

Permissible Discrimination

Employers are permitted to discriminate if employment preferences are based on a **bona fide occupational requirement (BFOR)**, defined as a justifiable reason for discrimination based on business necessity, such as the requirement for the safe and efficient operation of the organization (e.g., a person who is blind cannot be employed as a truck driver or bus driver). In some cases, a BFOR exception to human rights protection is fairly obvious. For example, when casting in the theatre, there may be specific roles that justify using age, sex, or national origin as a recruitment and selection criterion.

The issue of BFORs gets more complicated in situations in which the occupational requirement is less obvious; the onus of proof is then placed on the employer. There are a number of instances in which BFORs have been established. For example, adherence to the tenets of the Roman Catholic Church has been deemed a BFOR when selecting faculty to teach in a Roman Catholic school.[6] The Royal Canadian Mounted Police has a requirement that guards be of the same sex as prisoners being guarded, which was also ruled to be a BFOR.[7]

A precedent-setting case involved Tawney Meiorin, who had been employed by the British Columbia government as part of a three-person Initial Attack Fire-Fighting Crew, when the province introduced a new series of four standardized fitness tests for firefighters. Although she successfully completed three of the four tests, she failed the aerobics component in which she was required to run 2.5 kilometres in 11 minutes or less. After four attempts, her fastest time was 49.4 seconds too slow, and she was dismissed. Ms. Meiorin complained that the aerobic standard discriminated against women, as women generally have lower aerobic capacity than their male counterparts. The government argued that this standard was a BFOR for the firefighter position. The Supreme Court determined that this standard was not a BFOR as such a standard was *not* directly related to an individual's performance on the job and, in fact, resulted in systemic discrimination on a prohibited ground.[8]

Human Rights Case Examples

In order to clarify how the human rights legislation is applied, and the types of discrimination prohibited, a few examples follow.

Urban Alliance on Race Relations
www.tgmag.ca/magic/uarr.html

Racial Harassment Guide
www.ohrc.on.ca/english/guides/
racial-harassment.shtml

Race and Colour

Discrimination on the basis of race and colour is illegal in every Canadian jurisdiction. For example, a black man who worked as a federal government records clerk for 13 years endured racial slurs and racist remarks in a poisoned work environment. Some co-workers asked if he sold drugs or stole cars on the side, as well as calling him and other black employees names and accusing them of being liars. The employee's complaint to the Canadian Human Rights Commission alleged that the employer had not done enough to educate employees about harassment and racism. Furthermore, the department had not implemented any of the strategies for resolving discrimination identified by an internal race relations committee. In settling the complaint, the department agreed to pay $18 000 in general damages plus more than $70 000 in early retirement, severance, and pension refund payments to the employee. The department also provided a letter of reference and a letter of apology. The employee agreed to retire from the department and to accept the terms of the settlement as full compensation.[9]

An Ethical Dilemma

Your company president tells you not to hire any gay or lesbian employees to work as part of his office staff because it would make him uncomfortable. What would you do?

Sexual Orientation Harassment Guide
www.ohrc.on.ca/english/guides/
sexual-orientation.shtml

Sexual Orientation

Discrimination on the basis of sexual orientation is prohibited in all jurisdictions. As a result of lawsuits by same-sex couples, the Supreme Court ruled that all laws must define "common-law partners" to include both same-sex and opposite-sex couples.[10]

In a recent federal case, a lesbian employee alleged that she was harassed by a co-worker. She made a complaint to her supervisors but felt the complaint was not investigated properly. She alleged that she was given a poor performance review because of her complaint and that her request for a transfer to another work site was denied. The Canadian Human Rights Commission ordered her employer to provide a letter of apology, financial compensation for pain and suffering, and a transfer to another work site. The Commission also ordered a meeting with the employer's harassment coordinator to talk about the complainant's experiences with the internal complaint process.[11]

Age

Many employers believe that it is justifiable to specify minimum or maximum ages for certain jobs. In actual fact, evidence is rarely available to support the position that age is an accurate indicator of a person's ability to perform a particular type of work.[12]

For example, because of an economic downturn, an Ontario company was forced to lay off staff. The complainant, a foreman, had worked for the company for more than 32 years and was 57 at the time he was selected for termination along with another foreman who was aged 56. Both were offered a generous retirement package. The two foremen who remained were younger than the two released. The vice-president had prepared a note indicating that the two older workers who were terminated were told of the need to reduce people and that they "hoped to keep people with career potential." The Ontario Human Rights Tribunal found age discrimination on the basis of the good employment record of the complainant, the ages of those selected for layoff compared with those retained, and the vice-president's statement, which was found to be a "euphemism; its meaning concerns age."[13]

Religion

Following the 9/11 attacks in 2001, the Canadian Muslim Civil Liberties Association received many calls from Muslims whose employers had previously not had any objections with their praying at work or wearing a *hijaab* (the head-to-ankle covering that leaves only the face, hands, and feet visible in public), but now were expressing discomfort. It is a violation of human rights laws across Canada to deny time to pray or to prohibit the wearing of a *hijaab*. According to a recent survey in Toronto, discriminatory hiring practices and workplace racism toward Muslim women are quite common. Of the 32 women surveyed, 29 said that their employer had commented on their *hijaab*, and 13 said that they were told that they would have to stop wearing their *hijaab* if they wanted the job.[14]

Physical and Mental Disability

In a recent federal complaint, a worker who had Asperger's syndrome alleged that his employer did not renew his term of employment and refused to place his name on the recall list for future employment because of his disability. The settlement resulted in a verbal expression of regret, financial compensation for pain and suffering, a letter of confirmation of employment, and removal of documents from his personnel file.[15]

Harassment

Persons with disabilities are now employed in a wide range of fields and occupations. An example is Nancy Thibeault, the telephone operator and receptionist at PAC Corporation.

Some jurisdictions prohibit harassment on all prescribed grounds, while others only expressly ban sexual harassment. **Harassment** includes unwelcome behaviour that demeans, humiliates, or embarrasses a person, and that a reasonable person should have known would be unwelcome. Examples of harassment are included in **Figure 2.3**.

One type of intentional harassment that is receiving increasing attention is bullying, which involves repeated and deliberate incidents of negative behaviour that cumulatively undermine a person's self-image. In 2004, a Quebec law prohibiting "workplace psychological harassment" came into effect with the intent of ending bullying in the workplace. In the first year, more than 2500 complaints were received, surpassing expectations to such a degree that the number of investigators was increased from 10 to 34.[16]

harassment Unwelcome behaviour that demeans, humiliates, or embarrasses a person, and that a reasonable person should have known would be unwelcome.

Employer Responsibility   The Supreme Court has made it clear that protecting employees from harassment is part of an employer's responsibility to provide a safe and healthy working environment. If harassment is occurring, and employers are aware or ought to have been aware, they can be charged as well as the alleged harasser.[17] Employer responsibility includes employee harassment by clients or customers once it has been reported. In a recent Manitoba decision, a female employee complained to the owner of the company about sexual harassment by her manager. The owner subsequently fired the woman after she filed a human rights complaint. The Human Rights Commission's ruling emphasized that employers are duty bound to take the issue of sexual harassment seriously. They found the owner responsible for the harassment and awarded the woman $3250 for lost wages and $1500 for other damages.[18]

sexual harassment Offensive or humiliating behaviour that is related to a person's sex, as well as behaviour of a sexual nature that creates an intimidating, unwelcome, hostile, or offensive work environment, or that could reasonably be thought to put sexual conditions on a person's job or employment opportunities.

Sexual Harassment   The type of harassment that has attracted the most attention in the workplace is **sexual harassment**. Sexual harassment is offensive or humiliating behaviour that is related to a person's sex, as well as behaviour of a sexual nature that creates an intimidating, unwelcome, hostile, or offensive work environment, or that could reasonably be thought to put sexual conditions on a person's job or employment opportunities. Sixty-four percent of women

FIGURE 2.3   Examples of Harassment

Some examples of harassment include:

- unwelcome remarks, slurs, jokes, taunts, or suggestions about a person's body, clothing, race, national or ethnic origin, colour, religion, age, sex, marital status, family status, physical or mental disability, sexual orientation, pardoned conviction, or other personal characteristics;
- unwelcome sexual remarks, invitations, or requests (including persistent, unwanted contact after the end of a relationship);
- display of sexually explicit, sexist, racist, or other offensive or derogatory material;
- written or verbal abuse or threats;
- practical jokes that embarrass or insult someone;
- leering (suggestive staring) or other offensive gestures;
- unwelcome physical contact, such as patting, touching, pinching, hitting;
- patronizing or condescending behaviour;
- humiliating an employee in front of co-workers;
- abuse of authority that undermines someone's performance or threatens his or her career;
- vandalism of personal property; and
- physical or sexual assault.

Source: Canadian Human Rights Commission, *Anti-Harassment Policies for the Workforce: An Employer's Guide.* www.chrc-ccdp.ca/pdf/AHPoliciesWorkplace_en.pdf. Reproduced with permission of the Ministry of Public Works and Government Services, 2006.

say they have experienced some form of sexual harassment during their careers, and 48 percent of women executives say they left a job because of an inhospitable organizational culture and harassment.[19]

Sexual harassment can be divided into two categories: sexual coercion and sexual annoyance.[20] **Sexual coercion** involves harassment of a sexual nature that results in some direct consequence to the worker's employment status or some gain in or loss of tangible job benefits. Typically, this involves a supervisor using control over employment, pay, performance appraisal results, or promotion to attempt to coerce an employee to grant sexual favours. If the worker agrees to the request, tangible job benefits follow; if the worker refuses, job benefits are denied.

Sexual annoyance is sexually related conduct that is hostile, intimidating, or offensive to the employee but has no direct link to tangible job benefits or loss thereof. Rather, a *"poisoned work environment"* is created for the employee, the tolerance of which effectively becomes a term or condition of employment. The following case provides an illustration of this type of harassment, as well as the consequences of management's failure to take corrective action:

> In 2006, the Supreme Court of British Columbia awarded $950 000 in damages, lost wages and future wages to a former RCMP officer who was harassed by her "old school" detachment commander after she took time off due to complications with her pregnancy. Nancy Sulz was the victim of "humiliating and unfair comments" at her Merritt, British Columbia, detachment relating to her maternity leave and medical absences. The cumulative effect was so severe that Sulz, at the urging of the RCMP, sought and was granted a medical discharge and is likely unable to ever work again.[21]

Harassment Policies   To reduce liability, employers should establish sound harassment policies, communicate such policies to all employees, enforce the policies in a fair and consistent manner, and take an active role in maintaining

sexual coercion   Harassment of a sexual nature that results in some direct consequence to the worker's employment status or some gain in or loss of tangible job benefits.

sexual annoyance   Sexually related conduct that is hostile, intimidating, or offensive to the employee but has no direct link to tangible job benefits or loss thereof.

A poisoned work environment may exist even if no direct threats or promises are made.

a working environment that is free of harassment. Effective harassment policies should include[22]

1. an anti-harassment policy statement, stating the organization's commitment to a safe and respectful work environment, and specifying that harassment is against the law
2. information for victims (e.g., how to identify harassment; what isn't harassment)
3. employees' rights and responsibilities (e.g., respect others, speak up, report harassment)
4. employers' and managers' responsibilities (e.g., put a stop to harassment, be aware, listen to employees)
5. anti-harassment policy procedures (e.g., what to do if you are being harassed, what to do if you are accused of harassment, what to do if you are a third-party employee, investigation guidelines, remedies for the victim and corrective action for harassers, guidelines for handling unsubstantiated complaints and complaints made in bad faith, confidentiality)
6. penalties for retaliation against a complainant
7. guidelines for appeals
8. other options, such as union grievance procedures and human rights complaints
9. how the policy will be monitored and adjusted

Enforcement

Enforcement of human rights acts is the responsibility of the human rights commission in each jurisdiction. It should be noted that all costs are borne by the commission, not by the complainant, which makes the process accessible to all employees, regardless of financial means. The commission itself can initiate a complaint if it has reasonable grounds to assume that a party is engaging in a discriminatory practice.

If discrimination is found, a number of remedies can be imposed. The most common is compensation for lost wages, and other remedies include compensation for general damages, complainant expenses, and pain and humiliation. The violator is generally asked to restore the rights, opportunities, and privileges denied the victim, such as employment or promotion. A written letter of apology may also be required. If a pattern of discrimination is detected, the employer will be ordered to cease such practices and may be required to attend a training session or hold regular human rights workshops.

EMPLOYMENT EQUITY LEGISLATION

The Charter of Rights legalizes employment equity initiatives, which go beyond human rights laws in that they are proactive programs developed by employers to remedy past discrimination and/or prevent future discrimination. Human rights laws focus on prohibiting various kinds of discrimination; however, over time it became obvious that there were certain groups for whom this complaint-based, reactive approach was insufficient. Investigation revealed that four identifiable groups—women, Aboriginal people, persons with disabilities, and visible minorities—had been subjected to pervasive patterns of differential treatment by employers, as evidenced by lower pay on average, occupational segregation, higher rates of unemployment, underemployment, and concentration in low-status jobs with little potential for career growth.

occupational segregation   The existence of certain occupations that have traditionally been male dominated and others that have been female dominated.

R e s e a r c h
I n s i g h t   ▷

glass ceiling   An invisible barrier, caused by attitudinal or organizational bias, which limits the advancement opportunities of qualified designated group members.

Catalyst
www.catalyst.org

For example, historically, the majority of women worked in a very small number of jobs, such as nursing, teaching, sales, and secretarial/clerical work. This is known as **occupational segregation**. Advancement of women and other designated group members into senior management positions has been hindered by the existence of a **glass ceiling,** an "invisible" barrier caused by attitudinal or organizational bias, which limits the advancement opportunities of qualified individuals.

Several studies have confirmed that the glass ceiling is still intact.[23] A study by the Women's Executive Network found that 55 percent of women executives believed that they have faced more barriers to career advancement than similarly qualified males would have encountered in their situation. Fifty-nine percent said they had to work harder and 37 percent said they have had fewer opportunities for advancement, compared with their male counterparts.

A 2005 study involving Canada's Financial Post 500 (FP500)—the 500 largest companies in Canada—conducted by Catalyst is highlighted in **Figure 2.4.** In these firms, there is concrete evidence of underutilization of female employees. Although women make up almost one-half of the Canadian workforce, they are still underrepresented on executive teams, composing 37 percent of management positions, 14 percent of corporate officers, and 12 percent of members on boards of directors. Progress at the highest levels—corporate boards of directors—is shown in **Table 2.1.** According to Catalyst Canada Executive Director Deborah Gillis, "The story of women's advancement in corporate leadership in Canada continues to be one of disturbingly slow growth."

The Plight of the Four Designated Groups

1. Women

Women accounted for 47 percent of the employed workforce in 2004. Two-thirds of all employed women were working in teaching, nursing and related

FIGURE 2.4   The Catalyst Pyramid—Canadian Women in Business, 2005

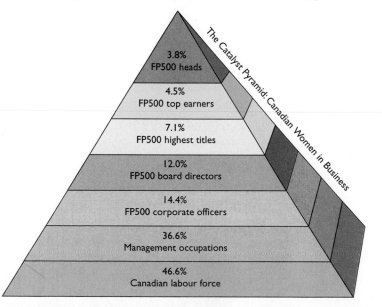

Sources: Statistics Canada Labour Force Survey, 2004; Catalyst, *2005 Catalyst Census of Women Board Directors of the FP500*; and Catalyst, *2004 Catalyst Census of Women Corporate Officers and Top Earners of Canada.* Reproduced by permission of Catalyst, www.catalyst.org.

TABLE 2.1   Representation of Women on Corporate Boards of Canada's FP500

Year	Total Number of Seats	Number of Seats Held by Women	Percentage of Seats Held by Women
2005	4225	508	12.0
2003	4247	476	11.2
2001	4421	431	9.8

Source: Catalyst, *2005 Catalyst Census of Women Board Directors of the FP500*. Reproduced by permission of Catalyst, www.catalyst.org.

health occupations, clerical or other administrative positions, and sales and service occupations. There has been virtually no change in the proportion of women employed in these traditionally female-dominated occupations over the past decade. Women continue to be underrepresented in engineering, natural sciences, and mathematics, a trend unlikely to change in the near future since women are still underrepresented in university programs in these fields.[24]

2. Aboriginals
Almost 60 percent of Aboriginal employees in the workforce are concentrated in three occupational groups, namely clerical, skilled crafts, and trade and semi-skilled manual work.[25] The unemployment rate for Aboriginal people is significantly higher than the rate among non-Aboriginals.[26]

3. People with Disabilities
About 45 percent of people with disabilities are in the labour force, compared with almost 80 percent of the non-disabled population. Although 63 percent of people with a mild disability are in the workforce, only 28 percent of those with a severe or a very severe disability are working. The median employment income of workers with disabilities is 83 percent of that of other Canadian workers.[27]

4. Visible Minorities
Many immigrants are highly educated visible minorities. They are typically unable to obtain employment that takes full advantage of their knowledge, skills, and abilities (**KSAs**), thus facing **underemployment**. It has been estimated that underemployment short-changes skilled immigrants by a total of $2.4 billion a year, and discrimination (whether intentional or unintentional) against immigrants is creating a "brain waste" that costs the Canadian economy up to $15 billion each year.[28]

KSAs Knowledge, skills, and abilities.

underemployment Being employed in a job that does not fully utilize one's knowledge, skills, and abilities (KSAs).

Legislation to Address Employment Barriers
After realizing that simple prohibition of discrimination would not correct these patterns, a number of jurisdictions passed employment equity legislation aimed at identifying and eliminating systemic barriers to employment opportunities that adversely affect these four groups.

Employment equity legislation is focused on bringing the four traditionally disadvantaged groups identified above into the mainstream of Canada's labour force. The use of the term "employment equity" distinguishes Canada's approach from the "affirmative action" used in the United States. Affirmative action has come to be associated with quotas, a divisive political issue.[29]

Employment equity legislation is intended to remove employment barriers and promote equality for the members of the four designated groups. For example, employers under federal jurisdiction must prepare an annual plan with specific goals to achieve better representation of the designated group members at all levels of the organization and timetables for goal implementation. Employers must also submit an annual report on the company's progress in meeting its goals, indicating the representation of designated group members by occupational groups and salary ranges, and information on those hired, promoted, and terminated.

Some companies covered by federal employment equity legislation, such as RBC Financial Group, have made great progress in promoting equality for members of the four designated groups, as outlined in the Workforce Diversity box.

Employment Equity Programs

Mandatory employment equity programs are virtually nonexistent in provincial and territorial jurisdictions. Some provinces have employment equity policies that encourage employment equity plans in provincial departments and ministries. Quebec has a contract compliance program where employers in receipt of more than $100 000 in provincial funding must implement an employment equity plan.[30] In the federal jurisdiction, the Federal Contractors Program requires firms bidding on federal contracts of $200 000 or more to implement an employment equity plan.

employment equity program A detailed plan designed to identify and correct existing discrimination, redress past discrimination, and achieve a balanced representation of designated group members in the organization.

An **employment equity program** is designed to achieve a balanced representation of designated group members in the organization. It is a major management exercise because existing employees must become comfortable working with others from diverse backgrounds, cultures, religions, and so on, and this

Workforce Diversity

RBC: A Leader in Diversity

One of the reasons RBC has a strong reputation for leading in diversity is its overall leadership in the Canadian market. RBC executives were on the public stage in 2005 addressing industry issues, as well as receiving awards and recognition for their achievements:

- Three RBC executives were named in the 2005 *Top 100 List of Canada's Most Powerful Women* by the Toronto-based Women's Executive Network: Elisabetta Bigsby, Executive Vice-President, Human Resources; Barbara Stymiest, Chief Operating Officer; and Janice Fukakusa, Chief Financial Officer.
- RBC Capital Markets was rated as one of the most prestigious banking companies in the world in New York–based career information company Vault Inc.'s *2006 Guide to the Top 50 Banking Employers.*

Employers in the banking industry were rated on a number of categories, including how prestigious it would be to work for them, quality of work/life balance, and diversity practices.

- RBC ranked first among banks in Canada's *Gender Intelligent Companies* survey of women consumers (as compiled by the Thomas Yacccato Group 2005).
- RBC is involved in the Aboriginal Stay in School program, aimed at helping high school students find summer employment. In 2005, 45 students participated and 27 were offered casual positions in local branches.
- RBC is sponsoring a multiyear study of visible minorities with Catalyst Canada.
- RBC has partnered with the Institute of Disability Studies at Ryerson University in Toronto on a project to discover how people with disabilities learn inside an organization.

Source: Adapted from *Diversity at RBC: 2005 Highlights,* May 2006. Used with the permission of RBC Financial Group.

represents a major change in the work environment. A deliberately structured process is involved, which can be tailored to suit the unique needs of the firm. Pelmorex Inc. was featured as an employment equity success story for the 2005 annual report of the Employment Equity Act, as detailed in the Strategic HR box.

The employment equity process includes six main steps, each of which will now be described.

Step 1: Senior-Management Commitment and Support

Senior management's total commitment to employment equity is essential to a program's success. A *written policy*, endorsed by senior management and strategically posted throughout the organization or distributed to every employee, is an essential first step. Manitoba Hydro's employment equity policy, shown in **Figure 2.5**, illustrates how such a policy statement can convey senior management's approval of and commitment to the program's development and successful implementation. The policy statement should be supplemented by various communication initiatives. An organization should *appoint a senior official* (preferably reporting to the CEO) to whom overall responsibility and authority for program design and implementation is assigned.

Step 2: Data Collection and Analysis

The development of an internal workforce profile is necessary in order to compare internal representation with external workforce availability data, set reasonable goals, and measure progress. Such profiles must be based on both

Strategic HR

Diversity at Canada's Weather Network

We see all kinds of weather here in Canada, from the crisp chill of winter, to the pounding rain and wind of a tropical hurricane. Canada's population is just as diverse, and in that variety, we gain strength and experience.

Diversity is a priority at Pelmorex, the parent company of The Weather Network and MétéoMedia, where it has been embraced as an integral component of the corporate philosophy and culture.

Our commitment to equity has improved the organization as a whole. In an annual employee survey, 95 percent of respondents agreed to the statement "Pelmorex is committed to diversity in the workplace." This percentage has increased over the last three years.

We have achieved this by putting equity at the forefront of people management processes, decisions, and hiring practices. Our human resources department conducts a workforce analysis on a quarterly basis, which is one of our most important tools for assessing our internal representation, compared to external availability.

We coordinate several internships every year, actively outreaching to members of designated groups for these opportunities. We award a $1,500 annual scholarship to a female student enrolled in an Atmospheric Science program at a Canadian University. As well, for the 2004/2005 school year, Pelmorex awarded our third annual $2,500 scholarship to a student with a disability enrolled in a Broadcasting Journalism program.

We strive to create and maintain an environment that supports diversity throughout the organization. We provide two special leave days for family matters/emergencies and two days per year for non-statutory religious holiday leave. We have also modified office space to be used as prayer rooms, and our Human Resources managers conduct on-going discussions with employees to discuss job satisfaction, working conditions, and career goals.

Diversity continues to be an on-going focus and our commitment to equity is at all levels within the organization. Pelmorex has a supportive and welcoming environment that is enriched by the diversity of our employees.

Source: Adapted from Human Resources and Social Development Canada, *Annual Report Employment Equity Act 2005*, Chapter 4: "An Employment Equity Success Story." Reproduced with the permission of Her Majesty the Queen in Right of Canada 2006.

FIGURE 2.5   Manitoba Hydro Employment Equity Policy

Our Commitment to Employment Equity

At Manitoba Hydro, we value the background, experience, perspective and talents of each individual. We strive to create a workforce that reflects the diverse populations of the communities in which we serve.

We are committed to the practice of employment equity and we encourage applications from qualified men, women, people of Aboriginal ancestry, persons with disabilities, and members of visible minority groups.

Source: Commitment to Employment Equity, Manitoba Hydro.
www.hydro.mb.ca/careers/overview_equity.shtml. Reproduced with permission.

stock data   Data that provide a snapshot of the organization at a particular point in time, in terms of how many designated group members are employed, in what occupations, and at what salaries.

flow data   Data tracking designated group members by employment transactions and outcomes.

utilization analysis   The comparison of the internal workforce profile with external workforce availability.

stock and flow data. **Stock data** provide a snapshot of the organization at a particular point in time, in terms of how many designated group members are employed, in what occupations, and at what levels and salaries. **Flow data** track designated group members by employment transactions and outcomes. This involves determining how many designated group members apply for jobs with the firm, are interviewed, hired, given opportunities for training, promoted, and terminated.

To obtain data pertaining to the distribution of designated group members, a self-identification process is often used. Under federal employment equity legislation, employers may collect such data, as long as employees voluntarily agree to be identified or identify themselves as designated group members, and the data are only used for employment equity planning and reporting purposes.

Comparison data must also be collected on the number of designated group members available in the labour markets from which the organization recruits. These data may be obtained from Statistics Canada, Human Resources and Social Development Canada (HRSDC), women's directorates, professional associations, and agencies providing specialized assistance to various designated group members. The comparison of the internal workforce profile with external workforce availability is called a **utilization analysis**. This type of comparison is necessary in order to determine the degree of underutilization and concentration of designated group members in specific occupations or at particular organizational levels.

Step 3: Employment Systems Review

employment systems review
A thorough examination of corporate policies and procedures, collective agreements, and informal practices, to determine their impact on designated group members so that existing intentional or systemic barriers can be eliminated.

It is also essential that the organization undertake a comprehensive **employment systems review**. Policies and procedures manuals, collective agreements, and informal practices all have to be examined, to determine their impact on designated group members so that existing intentional or systemic barriers can be eliminated. Typically, employment systems that require review include job classifications and descriptions, recruitment and selection processes, performance appraisal systems, training and development programs, transfer and promotion procedures, compensation policies and practices, and discipline and termination procedures.

To assist in identifying systemic barriers, the following questions should be asked about each policy, procedure, and practice under review:[31]

- Is it job related?
- Is it valid? (Is it directly related to job performance?)
- Is it applied consistently?
- Does it have an adverse impact on designated group members?
- Is it a business necessity? (Is it necessary for the safe and efficient operation of the business?)
- Does it conform to human rights legislation?

Step 4: Plan Development

Once the workforce profile and systems reviews have been completed, the employment equity plan can be prepared. *Goals and timetables* are the core of an employment equity program, since they help to ensure that changes in representation become a reality. Goals, ranging from short- to long-term in duration, should be flexible and tied to reasonable timetables. *Goals are not quotas.*[32] They are estimates of the results that experts in the firm have established based on knowledge of the workplace and its employees, the availability of individuals with the KSAs required by the firm in the external labour force, and the special measures that are planned. Quantitative goals should be set, specifying the number or percentage of qualified designated group members to be hired, trained, or promoted into each occupational group within a specified period of time. Qualitative goals, referred to as special measures, should also be included.

Giving preference to designated group members to the extent that non-members believe they are being discriminated against can result in accusations of **reverse discrimination**. It is possible to avoid the entire issue of reverse discrimination if the approach taken to employment equity is goals. When goals are seen as targets, the end result is that a *better-qualified* candidate who is not a designated group member is never denied an employment-related opportunity. However, when there are two *equally qualified candidates,* based on non-discriminatory job specifications and selection criteria, preference will be given to the designated group member. The term "equally qualified" needs to be explained, since it does not necessarily imply identical educational qualifications or years of work experience, but rather the possession of the qualifications required to perform the job. Thus, if a job requires two years of previous related experience, the candidate with four years of related experience is no more qualified than the individual with two.

Three types of special measures are (1) **positive measures** designed to accelerate the entry, development, and promotion of designated group members, such as targeted recruitment; (2) **accommodation measures** to assist designated group members in carrying out their essential job duties, such as upgrading facilities for an employee with disabilities; and (3) **supportive measures** that enable all employees to achieve a better work/life balance, such as flexible work schedules in northern Canada to allow Aboriginal employees to take part in traditional fishing and hunting activities.

Step 5: Implementation

Implementation is the process that transforms goals, timetables, and special measures into reality. Implementation strategies will be different in every firm, because of each organization's unique culture and climate.

reverse discrimination   Giving preference to designated group members to the extent that nonmembers believe they are being discriminated against.

positive measures   Initiatives designed to accelerate the entry, development, and promotion of designated group members, aimed at overcoming the residual effects of past discrimination.

accommodation measures Strategies to assist designated group members.

supportive measures   Strategies that enable all employees to achieve better balance between work and other responsibilities.

Managers receiving diversity awards

REQUIRED PROFESSIONAL CAPABILITIES

Evaluates programs on
deliverables

Step 6: Monitoring, Evaluating, and Revising

An effective employment equity program requires a control system so that progress and success, or lack thereof, can be evaluated.

Benefits of Employment Equity

A dramatic example of how a more diverse workforce can help a firm to identify differences in customer needs or preferences is provided by DuPont, where a multicultural team increased the company business by $45 million when they changed the way DuPont marketed decorating materials, like its Corian countertops, by recommending a new array of colours that appealed to overseas customers.[33]

Impact of Employment Equity

According to the Canadian Human Rights Commission 2005 annual report, employment equity can make a difference.[34] The representation of women in the federally regulated private sector improved, rising from 40.1 percent in 1987 to 43.4 percent in 2004. Although this was below their estimated availability of 47.3 percent, it still represents a substantial increase. Women represented in the public sector increased to 53.1 percent in 2004, which is a substantial improvement over 1987, when 42 percent of federal public servants were women. The share of executive positions held by women in the federal public sector increased from 25.1 percent in 1997 to 37.2 percent in 2004. Women's representation in executive positions in the federal private sector increased to 20.9 percent in 2004 from 14.8 percent in 1997.

Visible minority group members also made some progress in their representation in the federal private sector, more than doubling from 4.9 percent in 1987 to 13.3 percent in 2004. In 1987, visible minorities held just 2.7 percent of all positions in the federal public sector. By 2004, their representation had increased to 7.8 percent.

In 1987, only 0.6 percent of federal private sector employees were Aboriginal peoples. Although this figure rose to 1.7 percent by 2004, it fell short of the estimated availability of 2.6 percent. Aboriginals fared better in the public sector, where they represented 4.1 percent in 2004, up from 1.8 percent in 1987—higher than their estimated availability.

Of all the designated groups, people with disabilities in the private sector have benefited least from the Employment Equity Act. People with disabilities make up only 2.5 percent of the federal private sector workforce, just a slight increase over the 1.6 percent share reported in 1987 and far below the 5.3 percent labour market availability for this group. The representation of persons with disabilities in the federal public sector increased to 5.7 percent in 2004, up from 2.6 percent in 1987, but still short of their estimated labour market availability.

DIVERSITY MANAGEMENT

Although many people perceive diversity management to be another term for employment equity, the two are very distinct. Managing diversity goes far

diversity management Activities designed to integrate all members of an organization's multicultural workforce and use their diversity to enhance the firm's effectiveness.

Diversity Best Practices
www.diversitybestpractices.com

Diversity Central
www.diversitycentral.com

beyond legal compliance or even implementing an employment equity plan voluntarily. **Diversity management** is broader and more inclusive in scope, and involves a set of activities designed to integrate all members of an organization's multicultural workforce and use their diversity to enhance the firm's effectiveness. Businesses in other countries are also discovering the advantages of a diverse workforce, as outlined in the Global HRM box.

The ethnocultural profile of Canada has been changing since the 1960s, and it will continue to change dramatically over the next 20 years. Canada has seen continued immigration from many lands during the last four decades, and managers are managing an increasingly diverse workforce. Although there are ethical and social responsibility issues involved in embracing diversity, there are other more pragmatic reasons for doing so. Employees with different ethnic backgrounds often possess foreign language skills, knowledge of different cultures and business practices, and may even have established trade links in other nations, which can lead to competitive advantage. Visible minorities can also help to increase an organization's competitiveness and international savvy in the global business arena. Specifically, cultural diversity can help fine-tune product design, marketing, and ultimately customer satisfaction.[35]

Although embracing employee diversity offers opportunities to enhance organizational effectiveness, transforming an organizational culture presents a set of challenges that must be handled properly. Diversity initiatives should be undertaken slowly, since they involve a complex change process. Resistance to change may have to be overcome, along with stereotyped beliefs or prejudices, and employee resentment. Organizations that have been most successful in managing diversity tend to share the following seven characteristics.

1. Top Management Commitment

Tips **for the**
Front Line

As with any major change initiative, unless there is commitment from the top, it is unlikely that other management staff will become champions of diversity. It is no coincidence that organizations that have established themselves as leaders in diversity management, such as BMO Financial Group, Ernst & Young, and IBM Canada, have had senior-level commitment over an extended period of time.

Global HRM

Europe Discovers Diversity Business Case

European firms are reporting positive business results from diversity initiatives. Eighty-three percent of 800 companies that have diversity programs reported seeing business benefits, a European Commission survey found. A stronger pool of quality job applicants, better connections with customers, and an improved ability to innovate were cited as business advantages.

Source: Adapted from "Europe Discovers Diversity Business Case," *Canadian HR Reporter,* December 19, 2005, p. 2.

FedEx Canada president Rajesh Subramaniam says Canada's competitive advantage lies in the array of cultures and peoples inside its borders. In today's global economy, "sameness is suicide," he says.

2. Diversity Training Programs

Diversity training programs are designed to provide awareness of diversity issues and to educate employees about specific types of differences and appropriate ways to handle them. To be successful, diversity training must be ongoing, not a one-day workshop.

3. Inclusive and Representative Communications

Organizations wishing to incorporate the value of diversity into their corporate culture must ensure that all of their internal communications and external publications convey this message. Inclusive language (such as gender-neutral terms) and broad representation in terms of age, gender, race, and so on, in company publications are strategies used.

4. Activities to Celebrate Diversity

Diversity must also be celebrated in organizational activities. The Royal Bank, for instance, recently hosted its first ever in-house diversity fair. There were booths with representatives from each of the designated groups, alongside Pride Employment Network (for gays and lesbians), Toronto's language agency, and other organizations.[36]

5. Support Groups or Mentoring Programs

One goal of diversity programs is to ensure that employees encounter a warm organizational climate, not one that is insensitive to their culture or background. To ensure that no one experiences feelings of alienation, isolation, or tokenism, support groups have been established in some firms to provide a nurturing climate and a means for employees who share the same background to find one another. For example, IBM encourages employees to form special interest clubs, such as the Black Network Group and Aboriginal Peoples Network.[37]

Another option is a mentoring program. The Urban Financial Services Coalition, a trade organization dedicated to promoting minority professionals in financial services, offers mentoring programs for aspiring managers. They believe it is the responsibility of those who have made it to go back and teach others.[38]

6. Diversity Audits

To assess the effectiveness of an organization's diversity initiatives, diversity audits should be conducted. Recommended evaluation criteria include representation of various groups, employee competencies related to diversity KSAs, progress in moving from an initial state of little or no diversity commitment and infrastructure to an ideal state in which diversity is integrated into the fabric of the firm, and results measured by the extent to which diversity management strategies are perceived to have succeeded in promoting diversity.[39]

7. Management Responsibility and Accountability

Diversity management initiatives will not receive high priority unless supervisors and managers are held accountable and results are part of their formal assessment. At FedEx Canada, managers are held accountable for the count of personnel from each of the four designated groups in their departments. A new performance appraisal system for managers considers it a core competency "to ensure the workplace is a diverse workplace."[40]

Chapter Review

Summary

1. The responsibility for employment-related law resides with the provinces/territories, except that employees of the federal civil service, Crown corporations and agencies, and businesses engaged in transportation, banking, and communications are federally regulated. There are 14 jurisdictions for employment law—ten provinces, three territories, and the federal jurisdiction. Ninety percent of Canadians are covered by provincial/territorial employment legislation, and 10 percent are covered by federal employment legislation.

2. All jurisdictions prohibit discrimination on the grounds of race, colour, sexual orientation, religion/creed, physical and mental disability, sex, age, and marital status. Employers are required to make reasonable accommodation for employees by adjusting employment policies and practices so that no one is disadvantaged in employment on any of the prohibited grounds to the point of undue hardship.

3. Harassment includes a wide range of behaviours that a reasonable person *ought to know* are unwelcome. Employers and managers have a responsibility to provide a safe and healthy working environment. If harassment is occurring, and they are aware or ought to have been aware, they can be charged along with the alleged harasser. To reduce liability, employers should establish harassment policies, communicate these to employees, enforce the policies, and play an active role in maintaining a working environment free of harassment.

4. The six steps involved in implementing an employment equity program are (1) senior management commitment and support, (2) data collection and analysis, (3) an employment systems review, (4) plan development, (5) plan implementation, and (6) a follow-up process encompassing monitoring, evaluation, and revision.

5. Seven characteristics of successful diversity management programs are (1) include top management commitment, (2) diversity training, (3) inclusive and representative communication, (4) activities to celebrate diversity, (5) support groups or mentoring programs, (6) diversity audits, and (7) management responsibility and accountability.

Key Terms

accommodation measures   *(p. 40)*
bona fide occupational requirement (BFOR)
    (p. 30)
Charter of Rights and Freedoms   *(p. 26)*
common law   *(p. 25)*
contract law   *(p. 25)*
discrimination   *(p. 27)*
diversity management   *(p. 42)*
employment equity program   *(p. 36)*
employment (labour) standards legislation
    (p. 25)
employment systems review   *(p. 39)*
equality rights   *(p. 27)*
flow data   *(p. 39)*
glass ceiling   *(p. 35)*
harassment   *(p. 32)*
KSAs   *(p. 36)*
occupational segregation   *(p. 35)*
positive measures   *(p. 40)*
reasonable accommodation   *(p. 29)*
regulations   *(p. 25)*
reverse discrimination   *(p. 40)*
sexual annoyance   *(p. 33)*
sexual coercion   *(p. 33)*
sexual harassment   *(p. 32)*
stock data   *(p. 39)*
supportive measures   *(p. 40)*
underemployment   *(p. 36)*
undue hardship   *(p. 29)*
unintentional/constructive/systemic
    discrimination   *(p. 29)*
utilization analysis   *(p. 39)*

Review and Discussion Questions

1. Describe the impact of the Charter of Rights and Freedoms on HRM.

2. Differentiate among the following types of discrimination, and provide one example of each: direct, differential treatment, indirect, because of association, and systemic.

3. Provide five examples of prohibited grounds for discrimination in employment in Canadian jurisdictions.

4. Define "sexual harassment" and describe five types of behaviour that could constitute such harassment.

5. Define the concepts of occupational segregation, underutilization, underemployment, and the glass ceiling.

6. Explain how diversity management differs from employment equity and explain three reasons (other than ethics and social responsibility) for embracing workforce diversity.

Critical Thinking Questions

1. The owner of your company has just informed you, the HR manager, that there are certain moving company jobs, namely the movers, for which he feels minimum strength requirements are BFORs. How would you handle this situation?

2. An employee who has been off for two months with a stress-related ailment has just contacted you, indicating that she would like to return to work next week but won't be able to work full-time for another month or so. How would you handle this?

3. Explain the difference between goals and quotas and discuss the ways in which employers can avoid the issue of reverse discrimination.

4. If your head office in Toronto sent you a diversity poster focusing on GLBT (gay, lesbian, bisexual, and transgendered) employees, and many of your employees are Mormons, what would you do?

Application Exercises

Running Case: LearnInMotion.com

Legal Issues

One of the problems that Jennifer and Pierre faced at LearnInMotion.com concerned the inadequacies of the firm's current human resources management practices and procedures. The previous year had been a swirl of activity—creating and testing the business model, launching the site, writing and rewriting the business plan, and finally getting venture funding. And it would be accurate to say that in all that time, they put absolutely no time into employee manuals, HR policies, or other HR-related matters. Even the 25-page business plan was of no help in this regard. The plan provided considerable detail regarding budgetary projections, competition, market growth, and business strategy. However, it was silent when it came to HR, except for containing short bios of the current employees and projections of the types of positions that would have to be staffed in the first two years.

Almost from the beginning, it was apparent to both Jennifer and Pierre that they were "out of our depth" (as Pierre put it) when it came to the letter and spirit of equal employment opportunity laws. Having both been through business school, they were familiar with the general requirements, such as not asking applicants about their ages. However, those general guidelines weren't always easy to translate into practice during the actual applicant interviews. Two incidents particularly concerned them. One of the applicants for a sales position was in his 50s, which made him about twice as old as any other applicant. Although Pierre didn't mean to be discriminatory, he found himself asking this candidate such questions as "Do you think you'll be able to get up to speed selling an Internet product?" and "You know, we'll be working very long hours here;

are you up to that?"—questions that he did not ask of other, younger candidates. There was also a problem with a candidate for the content manager position. The candidate was a single mother with two children, and Pierre asked her quite pointed questions, such as "What are your children's ages and what daycare arrangements do you have?" And, "This job involves quite a bit of overtime and weekend work, are you sure your kids won't get in the way of that?" Jennifer thought questions like these were probably okay, but she wasn't sure.

There was also a disturbing incident in the office. There were already two content management employees, Maya and Dan, whose job it was to actually place the course and other educational content on the Web site. Dan, along with Alex the Web surfer, occasionally used vulgarity, for instance, when referring to the problems the firm was having getting the computer supplier to come to the office and repair a chronic problem with the firm's server. Pierre's attitude was that "boys will be boys." However, Jennifer and Maya cringed several times when "the boys" were having one of these exchanges, and felt strongly that this behaviour had to stop. However, Jennifer was not sure language like this constituted harassment under the law, although she did feel that at a minimum it was un-civil. The two owners decided it was time to institute and implement some HR policies that would ensure their company and its employees adhered to the letter and the spirit of the various employment laws. Now they want you, their management consultant, to help them actually do it. Here's what they want you to do for them.

Questions

1. The company is located in Ontario and it is small. Given the fact that Pierre and Jennifer now have only five employees and are only planning on hiring three or four more, by what legislation is their company actually covered?

2. Were they within their legal rights to ask the age-related and children-related questions? Why or why not?

3. Did Dan and Alex harass Jennifer and Maya? Why or why not? How should this matter be handled?

4. What have Jennifer and Pierre been doing wrong up to now with respect to the various pieces of employment legislation covering the business, and how do you suggest they rectify the situation in the future?

Case Incident

Harassment

Maria was hired two months ago to supervise the compensation area of the HR department, which you manage. She seems to have been accepted by her peers and reporting employees but you have noticed that, for the past three weeks, she has been the last to arrive at staff meetings and always sits as far as possible from Bob, another supervisor.

Yesterday afternoon, you had a very upsetting conversation with her. She claimed that for more than a month Bob has been repeatedly asking her to go out with him and that her constant refusals seem to be making the situation worse. Bob has accused her of being unfriendly and suggested that she thinks she is too good for him. She said that he has never touched her but that he discusses how "sexy" she looks with the other men in the department, who seem embarrassed by the whole situation. Maria also said that Bob's advances are escalating the more she refuses him and that his behaviour is interfering with her job performance to such an extent that she is thinking of resigning.

With Maria's consent, you have just spoken to Bob, who denied her allegations vehemently and believably.

Questions

1. How would you proceed in dealing with this situation?

2. What are your responsibilities to Maria and Bob?

3. If Maria is telling the truth, are you or Bob legally liable in any way? If so, under what conditions?

4. How would you resolve this matter?

Source: Based on a case in *Equity Works Best: A Manual for Practitioners*, developed by the Ontario Ministry of Labour and published by the Ontario Women's Directorate, 1991. © Queen's Printer for Ontario, 1991. Reproduced with permission.

Experiential Exercises

1. Working in teams of six, role-play an investigation of the harassment claim described in the above case. One member of each team is to be assigned the role of Maria, another the role of Bob, and a third the role of the HR manager. The three remaining team members are to assume the roles of other HR department staff. For the purpose of this role-play, assume that Bob has made comments about how "sexy" Maria is and has asked her out, but claims that he didn't realize his behaviour was bothering Maria.

2. Prepare a report outlining legally acceptable questions that may be asked at a selection interview with a young female engineer applying for the job of engineering project manager at an oil field in rural northern Alberta, with an otherwise all-male group. (Refer to Appendix 7.1 on page 193.)

3. Working with a small group of classmates, search the Web for a company in your community that has an employment equity or diversity management program. Contact the company's HR manager and request more information on the program. Prepare a brief report summarizing its key features.

1 Jeff Rustia

One small Canadian ad agency is enjoying global success by leveraging the multiculturalism of Canada. Jeff Rustia, a young Filipino Canadian, and his diverse team of employees specialize in on-air images for television networks, as well as print and Web marketing. They see themselves as visionary global thinkers who are comfortable with diverse talents, clients, and cultures. They want to export the cultural sensitivity of multicultural Canada.

The basis of Jeff's business strategy and his workforce is diversity. He believes that his staff and his Toronto roots give him an edge in his business. His clients see impressive results from his work. The Aboriginal Peoples Television Network boosted ad revenue by 167 percent after Jeff's company revised the network's on-air image. Now the company is moving on to work with a lifestyle channel for African Americans, a new dance channel, and the Republic of Georgia, who were impressed with the Toronto 1 channel launch that was infused with multiculturalism and diversity.

Questions

1. How does this video illustrate that embracing employee diversity can improve organizational effectiveness?

2. In what ways does having a diverse staff give Jeff an advantage in the advertising business?

Source: Based on "Jeff Rustia Illustrated—Something for Everyone," *CBC Venture 923* (October 17, 2004).

CHAPTER 3

HUMAN RESOURCES MANAGEMENT AND TECHNOLOGY
by Julie Bulmash

LEARNING OUTCOMES
AFTER STUDYING THIS CHAPTER, YOU SHOULD BE ABLE TO

Describe how HR technology has evolved.

Explain what a human resources information system (HRIS) does, and **identify** its main components.

Describe the key functions of an HRIS system and the different types of HRIS systems.

Explain the process organizations use to choose an HRIS system.

Discuss what is meant by e-HR and the benefits of Web-enabled service applications.

Discuss the impact that HR technology has on the role of HR professionals, and **describe** the five core competencies that have emerged.

Identify key trends in technology.

REQUIRED PROFESSIONAL CAPABILITIES

- Ensures that the organization complies with legislated and contractual requirements for information management (e.g., record of hours worked, and records of exposure to hazardous substances)

- Assesses requests for HR information in light of corporate policy, freedom of information legislation, evidentiary privileges, and contractual or other releases

- Contributes to the development of information security measures

HUMAN RESOURCES MANAGEMENT AND TECHNOLOGY

Those of us who have been hired know that it is necessary to complete forms so that we can become an "official" employee. The type of information requested usually includes first name, last name, address, emergency contacts, banking information, beneficiaries for benefit plans, marital status, and of course Social Insurance Number.

These are data and the human resources (HR) department has always been the custodian of employee data. The type of data collected, where the data are

Technology permeates business life today.

stored, how the data are used, and the type of system used for these purposes has changed over time, but the need to collect information relating to hiring, promoting, and firing employees has not changed.

HR technology is increasingly being used by small, medium, and large employers to meet the needs of their stakeholders.[1] What sets high-performing organizations apart from others is how they use technology to deliver HR services.

This chapter is going to explore the relationship of information technology (IT) to HR and how HR leverages technology to manage a firm's human capital. The chapter begins with a discussion of the evolution of HR technology, and then explores HRIS systems, the HR components that make up a system, and the process that organizations engage in to implement an appropriate system. Next we discuss electronic HR (e-HR) and how organizations are using Web-based technologies to enhance their delivery of service. Then we look at the core competencies required to manage in today's technology-driven marketplace in order to meet the expectations of HR stakeholders. To conclude, we discuss some IT-HR trends and how these trends will impact human resources management (HRM).

EVOLUTION OF HUMAN RESOURCES TECHNOLOGY

HR technology Any technology that is used to attract, hire, retain, and maintain human resources, support HR administration, and optimize human resource management.

HR technology can be defined as any technology that is used to attract, hire, retain, and maintain human resources, support HR administration, and optimize HRM.[2] This technology can be used in different types of human resource information systems (HRIS) and by various stakeholders, such as managers, employees, and HR professionals. This technology can be accessed in different ways.

There is no doubt that technology has made it easier and faster to gather, collate, and deliver information and communicate with employees. More importantly, it has the potential to reduce the administrative burden on the HR department so it is better able to focus on more meaningful HR activities, such as providing managers with the expertise they need to make more effective HR-related decisions.[3] Research has indicated that companies that effectively use technology to manage their HR functions will have a significant advantage over those that do not.[4]

However, not all companies have the latest and greatest technology, nor do all companies need the most advanced technology, but all companies do have HR-related information needs. Consider the information needs of a small company as opposed to a large organization of 3000 employees. A small company may use a simple Microsoft Word or Microsoft Excel file to keep basic employee data, whereas a company with 3000 employees manages a greater volume of data. This activity can be daunting without a more sophisticated tool to store and retrieve data!

We can reflect on the various levels of sophistication by examining the evolutionary aspects of HR technology. These aspects can be characterized into four stages of development: (1) paper-based systems, (2) early personal computer (PC) technology, (3) electronic databases, and (4) Web-based technology.[5] **Figure 3.1** illustrates the evolution of HR technology.

Stages in the Evolution of HR Technology

Stage 1: Paper-Based Systems

Initially HR systems were "paper-based." These systems operated independently and did not integrate with any other business-related functions. Features were added as needed. Data were typically stored on mainframe computers, the reporting was very rudimentary, and HR was the sole custodian of the data. It was common for managers during this period to send employees to HR to get all their "personnel" questions answered.

Stage 2: Early Personal Computer (PC) Technology

tombstone data List of basic employee information.

In the next stage, there was a migration of the information resident in these paper-based systems to PCs and local area network (LAN) systems. These HR databases were able to produce reports that simply listed **"tombstone"** data,

FIGURE 3.1   Evolution of HR Technology

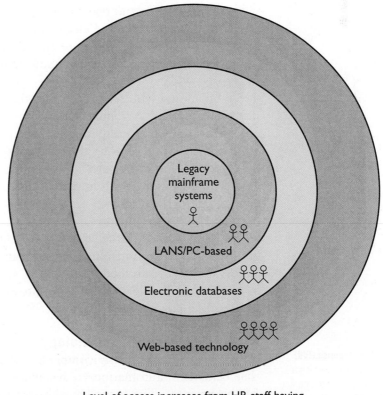

Level of access increases from HR staff having
access through to all managers and employees having access

Source: Julie Bulmash, 2006.

client server A network architecture in which each computer on the network is either a client or a server.

meaning basic employee information. Advances in database technology included payroll and some very basic versions of employee tracking.

The HR data were typically stored on a **client server**—a network architecture in which each computer on the network is either a client or a server. Servers are powerful computers dedicated to managing disk drives (file servers), printers (print servers), or network traffic (network servers). Clients are PCs or other workstations on which users, such as HR professionals, run software applications. Clients rely on servers for resources, such as files; devices, such as printers; and even processing power.[6] For example, when sourcing information from Wikipedia, the user's computer and Web browser would be the *client*, and the computers, databases, and applications that compose Wikipedia would be the *server*. When the user's Web browser requests a particular article from Wikipedia, the Wikipedia server finds all of the information required to display the article in the Wikipedia database, assembles it into a Web page, and sends it back to the Web browser for the user to look at.[7] HR continued to be the only group that had access to the system and continued to be the owner of the data.

Stage 3: Electronic Database Systems

relational database Database in which data can be stored in more than one file, each one containing different types of data. The different files can be linked so that information from the separate files can be used together.

The next stage began with the emergence of relational database technology. A **relational database** means that a piece of data can be stored in more than one file, each one containing different types of data. The different files can be linked so that information from the separate files can be used together. A relational database allows databases to be established in several different locations and the information linked. This technology provided organizations with the ability to develop more complex reports that integrated several data elements.[8] For example a report could be generated from different databases that included name, address, and salary and benefit information.

With this move toward electronic databases, HR systems began to become integrated with other business-related systems. Leading HR organizations began to purchase enterprise-wide systems that included HR-related modules. An enterprise-wide system is defined as a system that supports enterprise-wide or cross-functional requirements, rather than a single department or group within the organization.[9] A popular enterprise-wide system at the time was SAP.

At this time, use of the Internet was increasing, and managers began to consider what it could offer to HR technology. HR continued to own the HR data, but HR began to evolve into a more integral part of the business, as these databases became important in aiding HR with the generation of reports and empowering HR to provide managers with meaningful HR-related information. In addition, other functional areas could share information from these databases. For example, if the company decided it wanted to send out a mass mailing to employees to introduce a new product or organizational change, it would access the data from the HR system.

At this point, HR entered fully into the digital world of electronic HR and the term "e-HR" began to appear.

Stage 4: Web-Based Technology

interactive voice response (IVR) A telephone technology in which a touch-tone phone is used to interact with a database to acquire information from it or enter data into it.

At the present time, many companies have started to embrace HR technology. The benefits of automation are becoming widely known to HR and other areas of the business. The focus has shifted to automating as many transactions as possible to achieve effectiveness and efficiencies. Call centres and interactive voice response systems are widely used by organizations. An **interactive voice** response (IVR) system is a telephone technology in which a touch-tone phone is used to interact with a database to acquire information from it or enter data into it.[10] For example, employees can call in to report their attendance by entering a specific code.

Web-based applications use a Web browser as a user interface (called the "front-end"). Users can access the applications from any computer connected to the Internet via a secure, password-protected login page and from that point forward all the data are encrypted.

For the most part, the HR department continues to be the owner and custodian of HR information but others have begun to recognize the value of this information to the business. The reports that HR is able to produce have become more sophisticated. At this point, the majority of systems are still not Web-based, but some leading-edge organizations have embraced this technology.

Web-based applications
Applications that use a Web browser as a user interface (i.e., the "front-end"). Users can access the applications from any computer connected to the Internet via a secure, password-protected login page and from that point forward all the data are encrypted.

What's Next?

The technology of the future will be about speedy access to accurate current information, and the ability to access this information via multiple systems will give organizations a strategic edge. HR is expected to relinquish its role as sole owner of HR information, so that managers and employees can use this information to solve their own problems using Web-based systems.[11] This new system will not necessarily mean a reduction in HR staff.[12] The new system will enable HR professionals to focus on transforming information into knowledge that can be used by the organization for decision making; it will be about HR and IT working together to leverage this technology.[13] A recent study by the Hackett Group, a business process advisory firm, found that high-performing organizations spend 25 percent less than their peers on HR because they use technology effectively.[14]

Our discussion of HR technology will begin with an examination of HRIS systems, the structural components that make up an HRIS system, the types of data resident in these systems, and how HR uses these data to aid managers in decision making.

HUMAN RESOURCES INFORMATION SYSTEMS

There are more than 140 human resources information systems being offered by more than 100 vendors in Canada and the United States.[15] A recent survey indicated that overall costs of system implementation ranged from US$1000 to US$12 million.[16] Also referred to as human resources management systems (HRMS), **human resources information systems (HRIS)** can be defined as integrated systems used to gather, store, and analyze information regarding an organization's human resources.[17] Using HRIS technology can help HR automate and simplify tasks, reduce administration and record keeping, and provide management with HR-related information when required.

human resources information system (HRIS) Integrated systems used to gather, store, and analyze information regarding an organization's human resources.

These systems provide a repository for information/data to be stored and maintained, and they possess varying degrees of reporting capability. However, for the data to be useful, they need to be transformed into information that is meaningful to managers. This is the challenge facing HR departments today and what will ultimately determine whether HR is able to deliver strategic HR services.

The Relationship of HRM to HRIS

HRIS is the composite of databases, computer applications, and hardware and software necessary to collect, record, store, manage, deliver, manipulate, and present data for human resources.[18] It is important to note that the term "systems" does not just refer to hardware and software. Systems also include the people, policies, procedures, and data required to manage the HR function. In reality, computer technology is not the key to being successful at managing human resource information, but what it does do well is provide a powerful tool for "operationalizing" the information—making it easier to obtain and disseminate and ensuring that it is specific to the organization's HR policies and practices.[19]

A sound HRIS must allow for the assimilation and integration of HR policies and procedures with an organization's computer hardware and its software applications.[20] For example, a simple business rule (e.g., promotions are not to exceed 8 percent of salary) could easily be programmed into the system, and errors could be flagged when they occur.

Let's now look at important HRIS subsystems and the types of data that can be resident in these systems.[21]

HRIS Subsystems

There are several different components, called subsystems, that compose an HRIS. They are employee administration, recruitment, time and attendance, training and development, pension administration, employment equity, performance evaluation, compensation and benefits administration, organizational management, health and safety, labour relations, and payroll interface, as shown in **Figure 3.2**.

FIGURE 3.2   HRIS Subsystems

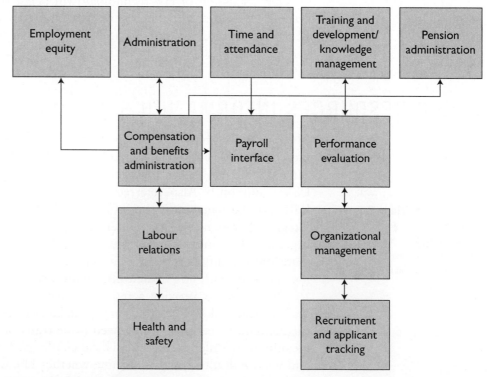

Source: Julie Bulmash, 2006.

Employee Administration

A basic component of an HRIS system is its administrative function. The typical information you would find in an HRIS system for each employee would include hire date, name, address, telephone, e-mail address, birth date, sex, salary, emergency contact information, department code, location, employment status (full-time, part-time, or contract), the start date of each position held, position titles, and benefit information.

Recruitment

This subsystem includes information on the position name and number, the department in which the position resides, whether the position has been approved, and whether the position is full-time or part-time. In some cases, online forms will be available so that applicants can be tracked and résumés can be scanned for key words to identify skills and experience.

Time and Attendance

This subsystem includes the information necessary to calculate vacation time, such as hire date, any leaves of absences (paid or unpaid), termination date if applicable, and any other events that interrupted service. In addition, the company's policy details, such as "use it or lose it," might be programmed into the system. If there are any special rules, then this information is programmed into the system. For example, employees often continue to accumulate vacation on some type of leaves.

Other data in this subsystem often include the number of days an employee was absent, leaves of absence, whether these leaves were sabbatical leave, personal leave, or maternity/paternity/paternal/adoption leaves, and the dates the employee started and ended each leave. Policy details would also be programmed; for example, some companies have a policy that states if absenteeism exceeds a certain number of days, then pay will be decreased by a certain amount. **Figure** 3.3 illustrates a screen from the PeopleSoft Enterprise Time and Labour system.

Training and Development

This subsystem includes data on an employee's skills and competencies, training courses taken, costs of courses, developmental activities, and career planning in terms of which positions might be most appropriate for an employee based on skills and competencies.

FIGURE 3.3   PeopleSoft Enterprise Time and Labour Screen

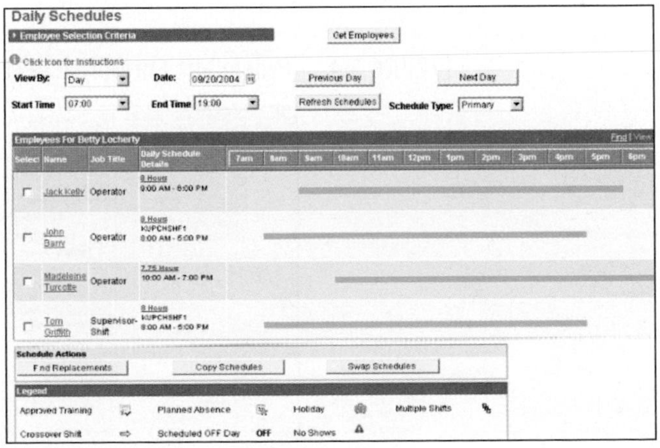

Source: Reproduced with permission of Oracle.

Pension Administration

Information as to the design of the plan is found in this subsystem. In addition, employee contributions and company contributions for each employee would be included.

Employment Equity

Organizations that are subject to employment equity legislation could include information on the number of employees in the four designated groups (women, Aboriginals, visible minorities, and people with disabilities), type of industry, and geographic region in this subsystem in order to provide the information required by the legislation.

Performance Evaluation

This subsystem includes information regarding performance ratings, the date these ratings were received, the type of appraisals that were used, comments about the appraisal, and performance objectives and goals. **Figure 3.4** provides an example of a screen from the PeopleSoft Enterprise ePerformance system.

Compensation and Benefits Administration

Information regarding the company's compensation and benefits plans and the policies relating to these plans are found in this subsystem. For example, policies on the type of increases allowable when an employee receives a promotion, data regarding pay grades and ranges for each position, positions that are entitled to a bonus, and bonus structure could be included. In addition, information regarding the type of benefit plans, whether there is a cost-sharing arrangement, and what that arrangement would be if an employee took an unpaid leave would also be available in this subsystem.

Organizational Management

This subsystem includes the organizational structure and job descriptions. It may have a field to enter the *National Occupational Classification* (*NOC*) *codes* (described in the next chapter). It may also link positions/jobs to specific workers.

Health and Safety

Accidents happen at work and organizations are responsible for reporting these accidents to the Workers' Compensation Board (or equivalent) in their jurisdiction. Data on the number of accidents, types of accidents, health and safety complaints, resolutions, Workers' Compensation claims, and related forms may be included in this subsystem.

FIGURE 3.4   PeopleSoft Enterprise ePerformance Screen

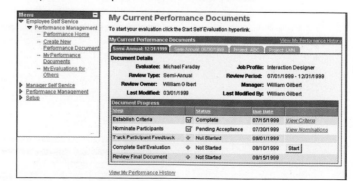

Source: Reproduced with permission of Oracle.

Labour Relations

Such information as seniority lists, union membership, grievances, and resolutions of grievances can be found in this subsystem.

Payroll Interface

This subsystem has information on salary, wages, and benefits to make it easier to interface with accounting (payroll). Most HRIS systems today have a payroll component, and the more sophisticated systems have an ability to directly interface with payroll providers, such as ADP and Ceridian.

Key Functions of an HRIS

<table>
<tr><td>

REQUIRED PROFESSIONAL CAPABILITIES

Ensures that the organization complies with legislated and contractual requirements for information management (e.g., record of hours worked, and records of exposure to hazardous substances)

</td></tr>
</table>

The HRIS is made up of a number of subsystems, and data can be stored, maintained, and generated from the system. These data can be used to create information that will serve different purposes for many different stakeholders.[22] The key functions of an HRIS are shown in **Figure 3.5**.

The HRIS can do the following:

1. create and maintain employee records
2. ensure legal compliance
3. enable managers to forecast and plan future HR requirements
4. provide information to managers and HR so they can manage knowledge and manage talent (career and succession planning)
5. provide information to enable HR plans and activities to align more effectively with the organization's strategic plan
6. assist managers with decision making by providing relevant data so they can make more effective and informed decisions

Create and Maintain Employee Records

The data being entered create an employee record and this record is maintained throughout employment. In most organizations the HRIS administrator is

FIGURE 3.5   Key Functions of an HRIS

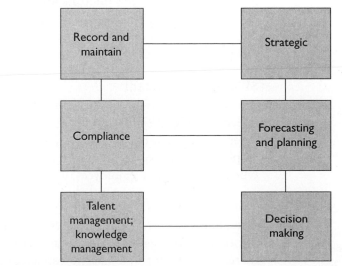

Source: Julie Bulmash, 2006.

responsible for creating (entering the information into the system) and maintaining these records. Accuracy and timeliness are critical. For example, if an employee recently received a promotion and salary increase, this information would need to be entered into the system. Over time, managers, employees, and human resource professionals will all need to access employee records.[23]

> **Hints to Ensure Legal Compliance**

Compliance

Data entered into the HRIS can be used to help the organization comply with government regulations in an accurate and timely fashion. Ensuring data integrity and accuracy is very important and a key responsibility of the HR professional. For example, organizations that are subject to employment equity legislation are required to file an annual report. If the data required to produce the necessary information have been recorded and maintained appropriately, these reports can be generated with ease. Some organizations have software that interfaces directly with the Employment Equity Computerized Reporting System (EECRS) software provided by the federal government,[24] resulting in the information from the HRIS being downloaded directly into the required reporting system. In addition to employment equity, payroll is another example of a function with a multitude of compliance responsibilities, such as the generation of an employee's T4 information.

HR Planning and Forecasting

Information from the recruitment, training and development, and administrative subsystems, such as number of open positions, types of positions, employee skills and competencies, job rates (salaries), retirement eligibility, and employee turnover rates, can be used to help managers develop long-range staffing plans and provide valuable information to HR professionals.

Talent Management/Knowledge Management

The data that are entered into the system, such as skills, competencies, jobs held, training, and employee development interests, can be used to help managers provide development opportunities for their employees, ensure that the appropriate employees are offered positions that will enhance their skills, provide the appropriate training for employees so they can advance in the organization, and highlight an employee's interests and development paths. This information will help HR professionals to provide more targeted advice and counsel to managers and help HR to work more effectively with employees and managers to create a development plan that meets organizational and employee needs.

Strategic Alignment

Information from the system can help organizations align HR activities more effectively with their strategic plan. For example, if the organization's plan was to enter into a new market and it required a certain number of certain types of employees (say, five accountants), the data from the system can tell management whether it has these employees, and if not, when they are expected to be hired.

Enhancing Decision Making

data warehouse Primary data storage repository for all data collected by an organization's business systems.

The ability to extract data from the HRIS and use these data not just to create information but also to improve the quality of management decisions has become increasingly important.[25] HRIS can access a **data warehouse**, or central repository for all the data collected by an organization's business systems.[26]

For example, managers are often asked to recommend an appropriate budget for salary increases. In order to make a "quality" decision, managers might need to confirm the current salaries of their employees, look at the past history of salary increases, review the company policies, and review their employees' performance history. To make a more informed decision, the information needs to be relevant, useful, timely, and accurate.

Some of the most commonly requested reports from the HRIS include

- basic information, such as name, address, phone number
- compensation reports, such as salary history
- performance evaluations
- leaves of absence, paid or unpaid
- number of jobs held and position titles
- number of vacation days taken and number outstanding
- types of training taken and skills acquired

In addition to these reports, managers utilize the system to perform HR calculations. The Saratoga Institute has identified a list of the most common calculations requested by managers: health-care cost per employee, pay and benefits as a percentage of operating expenses, cost per hire, return on training, volunteer turnover rate, turnover cost, time to fill jobs, and return on investment in human capital.[27]

workforce analytics The use of HRIS data to assess the performance of an organization's workforce by using statistics and research design techniques.

Another use of HRIS data is for making decisions regarding the effectiveness of the organization's human resources. **Workforce analytics** refers to the use of HRIS data to assess the performance of an organization's workforce by using statistics and research design techniques.[28] Workforce analytics attempts to analyze factors contributing to effective HR contribution to the achievement of strategic goals.

The ability of HR to use data analytically to aid managers in effective decision making has transformed HR into a "decision science" and enabled it to demonstrate that effective HR management can have a significant and measurable impact on a company's bottom line.[29] **Figure 3.6** summarizes the main user groups for the HRIS and the key information provided to each group.

Types of HRIS

What we have described are some common subsystems that compose an HRIS, who uses these systems, and the major functions of an HRIS. However, it is important to note that there are many different choices in the marketplace, many vendors of software, and different types of systems.

FIGURE 3.6   HRIS Users

	Employee	Manager	HR
Record and maintain		✓	✓
Compliance			✓
Forecasting and planning		✓	✓
Talent management; knowledge management	✓	✓	✓
Strategic		✓	✓
Decision making	✓	✓	✓

Source: Julie Bulmash, 2006.

For example, HRIS can be part of a larger enterprise-wide system. In an enterprise system there are typically "functional modules," one of which can be HR/payroll. An example of an enterprise-wide system is SAP or PeopleSoft (now part of Oracle). In addition to enterprise systems, there are stand-alone systems, meaning they are self-contained and do not rely on other systems to operate. An example would be Halogen Software Inc. or stand-alone HRIS that have several HR-related functions, such as Sage Abra Inc.[30]

These systems can vary with respect to cost, functionality, and level of sophistication. Depending on the organization's requirements, some systems will be more appropriate than others.

Next, we'll examine the process organizations go through to decide what type of system to purchase and the implementation process that they follow.

SELECTING AND IMPLEMENTING AN HRIS

It is clear how beneficial an HRIS can be, but what type of system should a company have? Is it necessary to spend $12 million on a system for a small organization? This section will review how companies decide which system to purchase and the process they follow to implement the system.[31]

The choice of technology can be described in two ways: (1) how much customization does the organization want and (2) what type of system does the organization prefer and need? Organizations can decide if they want to purchase a system that brings "best practice" or, alternatively, they can purchase a system and customize the software to fit their existing processes.

Regarding the type of system, organizations may want a stand-alone system or an **enterprise-wide system** that stores all company data together on a single "platform."[32]

enterprise-wide system   A system that supports enterprise-wide or cross-functional requirements, rather than a single department or group within the organization.

Companies are different in terms of their information needs, their existing technology, and their commitment to technology. They are also different in terms of their ability to afford technology, the value they place on HR information, the size and culture of the organization, and the human resources available to devote to a technology upgrade.[33] A company may need a very simple system that captures time-card and payroll information or it may need a very sophisticated system. But all companies can agree on the key reasons for adoption of HR technology: (1) cost savings, (2) faster processing of information, and (3) a system that will provide relevant information to help the organization achieve its goals.[34]

Typically, organizations follow a process to select an HRIS, as shown in **Figure 3.7**. The process can be divided into three steps: (1) adoption phase, (2) implementation phase, and (3) institutionalization phase.[35] The outcome of the process is that organizations choose a system that is either enterprise-wide (often called ERP systems) or stand-alone. But first they have to be informed consumers!

Tips for the Front Line

Adoption Phase

In this phase, organizations typically engage in a needs analysis to determine what type of system they will purchase. A needs analysis helps the organization decide on what the system should be capable of doing and what the technical specifications will be, and helps the organization develop an information policy about how the information should be managed with respect to storage and access. Additionally, a needs analysis will provide the organization with a framework to use to evaluate vendors of software.

FIGURE 3.7   Three-Step HRIS Implementation Process

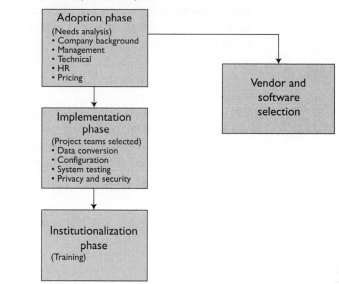

Source: Julie Bulmash, 2006.

There are several main areas to be considered in the needs analysis: company background, management considerations, technical considerations, HR considerations, and pricing.[36]

Company Background

The industry, the size of the company, and the projected growth are important elements to consider. For example, if the company is very small—say, with only four people—and expects to add an additional five people in the next two years, then the type of system that is needed could be something as simple as an Excel spreadsheet. Typically, organizations require HR software after they reach 100 employees.

Management Considerations

Typically, management would have some preconceived views regarding the type of software and what they will require the system to do. They may want a complex system that can assess the value added to the bottom line by HR activities or they may want a very user-friendly system for employees and managers to access regularly.

Technical Considerations

Such elements as hardware, operating systems, networking, databases, and telecommunications all need to be considered. It is very important to understand the kind of technology the company currently has because integrating software into some systems could be costly.

HR Considerations

The requirements of the HR function itself need to be assessed. What type of daily requests and which employee transactions would make the most sense to automate? What types of forms, reports, or listings are maintained? For example, is it necessary to pull together a list manually every time management wants to notify the entire organization about some key event? If so, this activity should be automated. The most critical area that is assessed is the reporting aspect of

HR. As discussed earlier, using reports to help managers make better decisions is an important activity where HR can add value to the organization. The needs assessment should identify the types of data required to produce reports, where these data can be found, and how reliable the data are. HR would look at the manual reports currently being maintained and decide how these can be automated.

Pricing

Organizations want to have the best possible system but might not be able to afford all the "bells and whistles." Factored in to the price are considerations, such as whether additional hardware must be purchased, how much additional staff will be needed during the implementation phase, training costs, and any ongoing support requirements.

request for proposal (RFP)
Request to vendors to schedule demonstrations of the various systems and ultimately choose one that most closely aligns with their needs analysis, budgets, and management requirements.

Once the needs analysis is complete, companies then send out a **request for proposal (RFP)** to vendors, schedule demonstrations of the various systems, and ultimately choose one that most closely aligns with their needs analysis, budgets, and management requirements.

At this point, the adoption phase is complete, and the organization will move on to the implementation phase.

Implementation Phase

In this phase, the company selects a project team. This team typically comprises outside consultants who have the knowledge and expertise on the technical side and also expertise in change management to help the organization with the implementation. In addition to the outside consultants, there is typically a senior project manager who leads the team, subject matter experts from HR and payroll, as well as management from the various functional areas across the organization. After all, these managers will be using the system and it is important for them to ensure that the system is implemented effectively and that their requirements are clearly understood.

The activities involved in this phase focus on getting the system "up and running" within a controlled environment so that the system can be tested to ensure it is functioning as the organization requires. The existing data are "converted" into the new system, requiring the transformation of data from the old system to make them compatible with the new system. The software is tested and users are expected to provide feedback before the system goes "live." Going live means disengaging any other HRIS and only providing users with access to the new system. In this phase, security profiles are established for the users.

Privacy and Security

Major privacy concerns focus on what type of information can be stored on the system. For example, should personal medical histories be stored, who should have access to the computer hardware and software, and who should have access to the databases and be authorized to modify them?[37]

Establishing security profiles is a very important activity when implementing an HRIS system. The staff members who will be working with the HRIS are identified and security profiles are established. These profiles determine who has access to what screen, which data elements or fields each person can have access to, and who will be authorized to change information, enter information, or merely view the information. Security profiles typically are attached to a job description or to an employee number.

Tips for the
Front Line

REQUIRED PROFESSIONAL CAPABILITIES

Assesses requests for HR information in light of corporate policy, freedom of information legislation, evidentiary privileges, and contractual or other releases

Contributes to the development of information security measures

For example, what should the profile look like for an HR administrator whose job it is to enter employee information into the system and who is the point of contact for all changes that employees make to their tombstone data? This individual would be expected to view, enter, and change pertinent data. What about the line manager? What should his or her profile look like? Should the manager have access to an employee's SIN? Is that information necessary? What about the addresses, phone numbers, and performance records for their employees? Typically, managers are able to view information relating to data on their employees, but not confidential data that are irrelevant to the work situation. Additionally, managers can view but not change any records.

A final, critical piece of HRIS security is making sure that system users clearly understand and adhere to the company confidentiality and code of ethics policies. All users need to understand that they must not share passwords, post them in view of others, or compromise them in any way.

Institutionalization Phase

The final step in implementing an HRIS is to train the users on the system. The organization's goal is for the stakeholders to use the system and reap the benefits identified through the needs analysis. However, many difficulties can arise with the implementation of a new system. As with any change, people need to become comfortable. People typically have difficulties in transitioning to an HRIS and the organization can experience inertia.[38] Employees need to be trained but even after training they may not feel fully competent and might not use the system. With any new system, stakeholders typically underestimate the complexity of the system.

HR may have difficulty with the change as well. Very recently, a popular extension of HRIS technology has been self-service for employees and managers in order to automate workflow.[39] With these technological developments, the typical activities that HR used to carry out are no longer required and, as a result, HR staff may feel disenfranchised. A recent survey examined the impact of technology on the number of HR staff and found that the implementation of HR technology does not necessary mean a reduction in HR staff and that, in fact, the number of HR staff increased or remained the same.[40]

One technological development that has impacted HR and the delivery of service has been Web-based self-service applications. The next section will discuss these new self-service options and how organizations have benefited from these innovations.

ELECTRONIC HUMAN RESOURCES

electronic HR (e-HR) A form of technology that enables HR professionals to integrate an organization's HR strategies, processes, and human capital to improve overall HR service delivery.

intranet A network that is interconnected within one organization, using Web technologies for sharing information internally.

Electronic HR (e-HR) is a term that identifies a form of technology that enables HR professionals to integrate an organization's human resources strategies and processes in order to improve overall HR service delivery.[41] Since the mid-1990s organizations have been embracing ways to incorporate electronic and computer functions into their HR strategies.[42] Companies are always looking for better ways to manage costs, provide better service, and effectively manage human capital, and e-HR has become integral to helping organizations achieve these goals. One of the most successful innovations is the migration of HRIS applications onto an intranet.[43] An **intranet** is a network that is interconnected within one organization, using Web technologies for sharing information internally.[44] The Internet has enabled organizations to harness Web-based technology and use Web-based applications to enhance HR services. More than 90 percent of companies are currently using the Web for HR purposes.[45]

In this section we will discuss the more popular Web-based HR service delivery trends, such as manager and employee self-service applications, and briefly discuss how organizations are using the Web to optimize HRM though e-HR systems, such as e-recruiting.

Web-Based Self-Service Trends

The two most popular Web-based HR applications used today are self-service for employees and self-service for managers. These applications have enabled companies to shift responsibility for viewing and updating records onto individual employees and have fundamentally changed the manner in which employees acquire information and relate to their HR departments.

Employee Self-Service

Employee self-service (ESS) systems enable employees to access and manage their personal information directly, without having to go through their HR departments or their managers. ESS systems are set up so that employees can sign onto their company system via the Internet and be immediately authenticated and verified. Recently, HR organizations have utilized portals as a tool to make this access seamless. A **portal** is a single site that can be accessed within an existing Internet site.[46] With this technology, HR departments can set up employee access to HR services. Access can also be provided through IVR or physical kiosks. Employees who have access to these types of ESS systems are able to use this service on a 24/7 basis.

Some common self-service applications these systems feature include allowing employees to update their personal information, such as address, phone number, and emergency contact information; revising banking information; researching benefit options and enrolling in benefit programs; viewing payroll information, such as salary deductions; recording vacation time and sick days; recording travel expenses; accessing HR policies; participating in training delivered via the Web; and accessing company communications and newsletters issued by the HR department. As an example, an employee who recently split with a significant other can change his or her emergency contact name, beneficiary information, and benefit details by logging on to the company intranet site and clicking on the HR portal.

ESS systems have fundamentally changed the way employees relate to their HR departments. Employees are able to access information that is relevant only to them and they no longer need to speak with an HR representative directly for routine updates. These systems have also helped HR departments to reduce their operational costs. From the perspective of the HR professional, the burden of being responsible for basic administrative and transactional activities has been shifted onto the employee. This shift in responsibility allows HR professionals to focus on strategic issues. One study found that the workload of HR generalists was reduced by an average of 15 percent.[47]

Two organizations that have benefited from upgrading their technology and adding employee self-service are the Toronto Police Services and Time Warner.

For the Toronto Police Services, one of the most time-consuming and onerous activities had been the scheduling and payment of both overtime and court time for officers. In 2002, the Police Services spent more than $500 million of their operating budget on salaries, of which $32 million went to paying overtime and court time costs to 7000 officers. With the implementation of an employee self-service system, officers were able to ask for time off online using the ESS system, which in turn reduced administrative costs.[48]

Time Warner's challenge was to find a way to unify its 80 000 employees in geographically diverse regions and give them access to HR services. They created an employee portal, called "Employee Connection," that gives employees varying levels of access to benefits enrollment, compensation planning, merit reviews, stock option information, payroll information, administrative HR forms, expense reimbursement forms, and travel planning information.[49] **Figure 3.8** provides a sample PeopleSoft Enterprise eProfile screen.

Management Self-Service

Management self-service (MSS) systems differ from ESS systems in that they allow managers to access a range of information not only about themselves but also about the employees who report to them. MSS systems also give managers the opportunity to process HR-related paperwork that pertains to their staff. Managers view résumés that are on file, view merit reviews, submit job requisitions, view employee salaries, and keep track of employee performance and training histories. Typically, this type of application system offers a broader range of services than that available to nonmanagerial staff. MSS is broader than just providing HR-related information. Often these systems provide managers with tools to help them with duties such as budget reviews and report writing, and permit them to authorize expense reimbursements.

Research
I n s i g h t ▷

The benefits are that managers have ready access to information that is useful both to them and to their employees, and do not have to go through a third party. In this way, MSS systems reduce overall company workloads. In fact, research has indicated that when used properly, MSS systems reduce the workload of the HR generalists by more than 21 percent because they are not spending the same amount of time on planning annual compensation increases, viewing employee histories, initiating requests for positions, or posting jobs.[50]

Managers are receptive to MSS systems because they contribute to data integrity and accuracy, the number of data validations decreases, and processing time improves.[51] Imagistics International Inc. (formerly Pitney Bowes Office

FIGURE 3.8   PeopleSoft Enterprise eProfile Screen

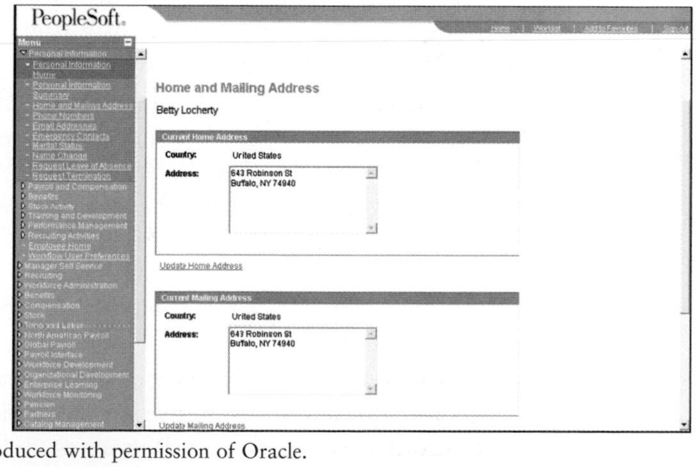

Source: Reproduced with permission of Oracle.

FIGURE 3.9   Web-Based Self-Service Applications and Benefits

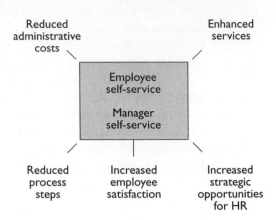

Source: Julie Bulmash, 2006.

Systems) recently implemented an MSS system. Since the system has been in place, the company has reported a significant reduction in administrative costs and process steps, a reduction in entry errors, and an overall streamlining of its reporting process.[52]

MSS can be a very valuable tool, but this technology is currently not as popular as ESS and is slower to gain acceptance. In 2002, 30 to 45 percent of larger organizations (companies with more than 1000 employees) had implemented some form of MSS.[53] **Figure 3.9** summarizes Web-based self-service applications and their benefits.

Web-Based Delivery Trends: Some Cautions

Recent surveys of ESS and MSS system users indicate that 80 percent of respondents agree that Web-based self-service systems can lower HR operation costs, but only 40 percent believe that their company is actually achieving this result. Two-thirds of those surveyed agree that Web-based self-service systems effectively support the transformation of the HR department into a more strategic partner by redirecting some of its responsibilities to employees, but only 37 percent actually feel there was a change.[54]

This discrepancy may be due to employees and managers who view this new technology as the "work of HR" and therefore are resistant to using it, or perhaps the technology is not as user-friendly as it should be. The usefulness of this technology will depend on whether the content is considered beneficial and relevant, on how easy the system is to navigate, and on its cultural fit with the organization. Towers Perrin consultant Minaz Lalani points out that realizing the potential of any application means that processes associated with the technology must be changed. People need to use the system in the right way. Only then will it reap the expected benefits.[55]

E-HR AND HUMAN CAPITAL MANAGEMENT

The management of human capital is critical and the ability to be able to attract, retain, and develop employees will continue to be a major challenge for HR professionals. The use of e-HR systems, including Web-based job sites, portals, and kiosks, to attract job applicants is becoming a necessity. Two technologies have made e-recruiting a reality—Internet job boards, such as Monster.ca, and the Internet applications that allow companies to screen candidates from those boards and facilitate the process.

Research has shown that companies can reduce hiring cycle times by as much as 25 percent when using online recruitment tools. The use of these tools has transitioned HR from hiring faster to hiring "better."[56]

The most common practices used for online recruiting are adding recruitment pages to the Web site of the organization, using specialty recruitment Web sites (job portals and online job boards), developing tools that are interactive so applications can be processed (auto-responding), and adopting online screening tools (e.g., personality assessments and interviews).[57]

Some advantages of online recruiting are reduced time for management of the recruiting process, communication of the company brand, access to a larger number of qualified candidates, reduced recruitment costs from using a standard process, reduced hiring cycle times, and use of the system's reporting functions to analyze the effectiveness of the recruitment strategy. Some disadvantages can be loss of face-to-face contact and discrimination against people who do not have access to the Internet or to information about privacy regarding personal information submitted over the Internet.

Some software vendors who offer e-recruiting tools, such as applicant tracking, are Brass Ring, Deploy, Icarian, Taleo (formally Recruit Soft), and Web Hire.[58] In the next section we will feature some additional software applications that enable organizations to manage HR processes more effectively.

The purchase of a system can reduce operating costs significantly. Hounton and Williams, a major law firm with more than 2000 employees globally, recently purchased an HRIS called UltiPro. According to the HRIS manager, the firm is "saving thousands of dollars each year by relying heavily on electronic transactions using UltiPro rather than paper-based processes."[59]

UltiPro is not particularly well known, but SAP, PeopleSoft, Oracle, and Genesys are more recognizable names of specific software vendors who provide "solutions" to help organizations effectively manage their human capital. This section will provide a brief overview of some specific HRIS software applications and some specialty software vendors. It is not exhaustive nor is it meant to be an endorsement of any particular vendor.

Enterprise-Wide Systems

An enterprise-wide system (called an enterprise resource planning or ERP system) is defined as a system that supports enterprise-wide or cross-functional requirements, rather than a single department or group within the organization. These ERP systems have their origin in software that integrates information from different applications (modules) into one universal database. This means that financial information can be linked to HR information through one database. The most popular high-end enterprise-wide systems are SAP, PeopleSoft, and Oracle.

SAP

SAP was founded as *Systemanalyse und Programmentwicklung* in 1972 by five former IBM employees in Mannheim, Germany. This acronym was changed to *Systeme, Anwendungen und Produkte in der Datenverarbeitung*, which means "systems, applications, and products in data processing," and in 2005, the company name was officially changed to SAP AG.

SAP is the world's third-largest software company and its head office is in Walldorf, Germany. In terms of revenue, SAP is the largest business application and ERP solutions provider. The company's main product is SAP R/3; the "R" stands for real-time data processing and the number "3" relates to a three-tiered system—database, application server, and client.

SAP products are used by more than 12 million people in more than 120 countries, and its market has typically been Fortune 500 companies. Recently SAP has targeted small- to medium-sized organizations with some of its new products.

SAP is made up of individual, integrated software modules that perform various organizational system tasks, such as finance/accounting, controlling, project system, funds management, materials management, and sales distribution. One of its major modules is Human Resource Management Systems (HRMS/HRIS). These systems are very sophisticated and SAP offers a full range of functionality, HR products, and Web-based offerings.[60] Companies using SAP include Allstream, Monsanto, Procter & Gamble, Coca-Cola, and Schlumberger.

PeopleSoft Inc.

PeopleSoft is software that provides HRMS, manufacturing, financial, enterprise performance management, and student administration software solutions to large corporations and governments. The company was founded in 1987 by David Duffied and Ken Morris. Its software is made up of modules, such as HRMS, which includes payroll, all human resources functions and benefits, financials, manufacturing, student administration, and customer relationship management. PeopleSoft is well known for its ability to be easily customized to fit the specific business needs of each client. PeopleSoft was acquired by Oracle in 2005.[61]

One organization using PeopleSoft is the Canadian Imperial Bank of Commerce (CIBC). HR processes at CIBC are streamlined and employees are provided with online access to HR services and information. The system enables employees to add dependants to health insurance, change payroll deductions, enroll in benefits programs, calculate pension benefits, and carry out retirement planning.[62]

Stand-Alone HRIS

HRIS can also be stand-alone. Not all organizations require a sophisticated system and there are many different vendors in the marketplace that offer every size and type of product imaginable. Some considerations for organizations include cost, the number of employees, the degree of efficiency, and the company's existing hardware and software. An effective HRIS requires a balance between what it can do from a technical perspective and how it can meet the needs of that organization. These needs typically increase with the size of the organization.[63]

Smaller firms might use very basic software applications, such as Microsoft Excel and Access. These firms might only require payroll and benefits administration, time and attendance, and employee scheduling functions. Midsize firms typically require compliance tracking and reporting, health claims administration, payroll, compensation, and benefit administration. Managers may require information on performance appraisal, time and attendance, succession planning, skills testing, and employee scheduling, and employees may use the system to aid in career development and self-serve applications. Midsize firms require greater data integration and better backup and recovery capability. In addition, they have many users and require local area network and server-based operations. Typically in these midsize systems, all HRIS functions flow through the single system; therefore, data redundancies can be identified and eliminated.

Some popular HRIS for small to midsize organizations are sold by such vendors as Spectrum Human Resource Management Systems, Genesys Software Systems, Best Software Inc., Ultimate Software (UltiPro workforce management), People Track Inc., and Organization Plus.[64]

Large organizations typically require greater functionality than midsize firms. In addition to those functions mentioned above, large firms will require employee screening, résumé processing and tracking, additional compliance and reporting (such as employment equity), and ESS and MSS for employees and managers. These firms also have a greater need to integrate the HRIS with enterprise-wide software applications. Larger organizations might purchase SAP, PeopleSoft, or Oracle ERP systems.[65]

Specialty Software

With so many vendors in the marketplace, software can be purchased for virtually any HR-related function in any industry, including training and development, performance management, succession planning, and the creation of organization charts. The Entrepreneurs and HR box provides an example of one such company, Cronus Technologies, which is based in Saskatoon, Saskatchewan. Organizations can purchase these applications as stand-alone systems. Specialty software applications are available from Halogen, ExecuTRAK, Org Plus, and Ergowatch.

Entrepreneurs and HR

Cronus Technologies

Cary and Shaun Schuler were awarded the Young Entrepreneur Award by the Business Development Bank of Canada (BDC). Cary, Shaun, and older brother Rodney founded Cronus Technologies Inc., an IT company located in the heart of Saskatoon's high-tech businesses area. Cronus specializes in custom HRIS software development and project management and has won the prestigious HR Technology Excellence Award for its products. Currently Cronus exports to the United States but is also developing partnerships in Western Europe.

"The Schulers epitomize a new generation of young Canadian entrepreneurs who, in creating jobs for themselves and members of their communities, are giving a great deal back to the regions that host their businesses," says BDC President and CEO Michel Vennat. "I salute their drive and determination."

In 2003 Cronus employed approximately 25 employees, and today the company continues to grow as a leading developer of innovative HRIS software. The Schuler brothers are an example of good corporate citizens. They believe in giving back to the community and have sponsored and made donations to various organizations, such as the Arthritis Society, the Hope Cancer Centre, the United Way, and the Dragon Boat Races.

The founders of Cronus Technologies Inc.—Rodney, Cary, and Shaun Schuler.

Source: "Enterprising and Dynamic IT Experts Win BDC's Young Entrepreneur Award for Saskatchewan," 2003 Business Development Bank of Canada. www.bdc.ca/en/about/mediaroom/news_releases/2003/2003102011.htm?iNoC=1 (June 29, 2006).

Halogen Software has a product called e-appraisal. It is a program that uses a Web-based system for employee performance appraisal that can create forms, electronically roll out appraisals, and facilitate 360-degree feedback information. Halogen focuses on the health-care field and is designed to support the accreditation process.[66]

ExecuTRACK Software Group has developed software solutions that create succession-planning matrices, establish career paths, and create candidate placement scenarios, among other functions.[67]

Org Plus is software that has existed since the mid-1970s. It has a sophisticated tool for graphically depicting organizational charts, which can be used as decision-making tools by providing a unified view of critical employee data and enabling the manager and HR to model business scenarios to plan for change.[68]

Ergowatch software was developed at the University of Waterloo, and was originally designed to assess and reduce the risk of back injuries in industrial settings. It is now being transformed into a broader tool that will also be able to evaluate the risk of repetitive stress injuries to workers' hands and arms. The software can assess the load or impact of a task—the combination of weight that is lifted and cumulative time spent in a position or posture, linking that with a worker's physical characteristics (size, age, sex) to predict potential pain and injury. Ergowatch can also conduct a physical demand analysis based on a checklist required by workers' compensation boards to determine what an injured employee can safely do when returning to work.[69]

If this new technology is going to be useful to the organization, HR needs to understand its value. Next we will explore the evolving role of the HR professional in an IT-enabled world.

THE ROLE OF HR IN AN IT-ENABLED ORGANIZATION

The impact of technology has fundamentally changed the HR role. It has enabled HR to (1) decrease its involvement in transactional activities, (2) increase its focus on the customer, and (3) increase its delivery of strategic services. As a result, several core competencies have emerged that are critical to the development of the HR professional, as shown in **Figure 3.10**. Wayne Brockbank and David Ulrich of the University of Michigan Business School have identified five

FIGURE 3.10   Emerging Role of the HR Professional: Five Key Competencies

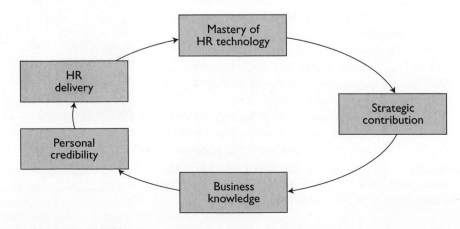

Source: Julie Bulmash, 2006.

key competencies for HR: mastery of HR technology, strategic contribution, personal credibility, HR delivery, and business knowledge.[70] We will briefly examine how these changes have impacted HR, highlighting the influence they have had on the role of the HR professional.

Decreased Transactional Activities

As discussed earlier, technology enables the reduction of the administrative burden, resulting in lowering basic transaction costs. A proactive HR professional needs to think about how best to leverage technology to improve the design and delivery of basic HR services by reacting efficiently to the day-to-day activities, and how best to ensure continuous improvement. To be effective, HR will be required to develop business knowledge with respect to the key drivers of organizational productivity, become cognizant of costs associated with enhancing the efficiency and effectiveness of the workforce, and be capable of selecting the appropriate technology to conduct HR administration.[71] A recent survey published by the Society of Human Resource Management indicated that technical skills, such as software and Internet literacy, and database skills are considered most important for the HR specialist to develop.[72] Proactive approaches using these competencies will result in line managers valuing the strategic contribution of HR.

Increased Client/Customer Focus

In organizations HR deals with internal customers including managers, employees, and all the other departments. These customers expect HR to understand and respond to their requests quickly, reduce "red tape," and provide information that is meaningful, useful, and accurate. It is important for HR to take the time to understand the issues that are keeping managers "up at night." To be effective, HR must understand how technology can best meet these needs regarding key business issues so that the information can be used as a decision support tool to help managers become more competent in their jobs.

When these stakeholders become more comfortable with the fact that HR is listening and cares about their needs, customers will gain respect for HR and trust HR, sharing their concerns and trusting HR with their data needs.

One significant customer that HR works with is the IT department. Next we will discuss how HR can develop a good working relationship with this very critical group of service providers.

HR and IT: Developing Good Working Relationships

One of the key departments that HR works with is the IT department. If HR is going to gain credibility with IT staff and work effectively with them, it must demonstrate its knowledge of and respect for the IT discipline.

What can HR do to build this technological knowledge? There are numerous opportunities that can be viewed as learning opportunities, such as attendance at trade shows, meeting with software vendors, formal courses in IT, and reading about technological trends and issues. Increasing their knowledge of IT will help HR professionals to "talk the language" of IT, and will also help them gain a greater understanding of the IT discipline and the challenges facing IT professionals.[73]

There are a variety of sources for those interested in understanding more about the trends and issues in technology. They include highly respected research

Gartner Inc.
www.gartner.com

Forrester Research
www.forrester.com

International Data Corporation
www.idc.com

Technology Publications
www.bitpipe.com

Software & Information Industry Association
www.siia.com

International Association for Human Resource Information Management
www.IHRIM.org

Society for Human Resource Management
www.SHRM.org

houses, such as Gartner Inc. and Forrester Research; publications, such as *Computing Canada*; and IT/HR associations, such as the International Association for Human Resource Information Management.

Increased Strategic Activities

HR technology is evolving rapidly. HR must use these technologies appropriately in order to help organizations capitalize on their human capital. HR professionals need to focus on the strategic issues identified by executives as critical for organizational sustainability in order to strategically manage human capital within the organization. They need to understand and implement the business strategy using the appropriate technological tools to effectively manage human capital to positively impact the bottom line. HR must be strategically proactive rather than reactive.[74]

To conclude this chapter on HR and technology, some key trends that will have a significant impact on HR in the 21st century will be explored.

TRENDS IN HR AND TECHNOLOGY

Technology is moving at "warp speed" and HR must keep up! Technology will continue to be integral to all business functions, and HR must use technology to continually redefine their services toward driving productivity. Some of the emerging trends that will have a significant impact on HR and on its ability to deliver strategic HR services are emerging technologies, the influence of outsourcing, and the increased focus on determining HR's effectiveness.

Technology Trends

Watson Wyatt consultants have identified several major technology trends that will influence HR management:[75]

1. *The increased use of portals and intranets and a greater focus on the use of virtual tools.* HR will be required to ensure that the organization is aware of the advantages of these tools and provide training and education to ease the transition. These new tools will enable employees to access their own information as opposed to going to HR.[76] So a manager who has a problem first will try and solve it using the tools available on his or her desktop before calling HR.

2. *Greater access to technology.* This increase will require HR to ensure that the appropriate security measures are in place and to be highly diligent in terms of the types of access and who gets access.

3. *Continued optimization of current systems.* This will mean that HR must continue to be "technologically educated."

4. *Enhanced focus on workforce analytics.* This focus will require HR to evolve as a "decision science," providing managers with valued-added decision-making tools.

5. *Increased focus on reducing costs.* This focus will require HR to optimize the functionality of HR technology.

6. *Increased use of standards for data exchange and processes (XML).* HR will need to ensure that the vendors they work with comply with this "standard."

7. *Contingency planning.* HR will be involved in ensuring that plans are in place to deal with disasters, including getting employees back to work and providing them with the appropriate emotional support.

8. *Heightened awareness of HR data privacy.* Government privacy legislation will continue to increase.[77] At present, Canada has two federal privacy acts— the Privacy Information Act and the Personal Information Protection and Electronic Documents Act. Ongoing legal changes will require HR to stay current with respect to legislation and utilize systems to ensure compliance.

Hints to Ensure Legal Compliance

Outsourcing

outsourcing The subcontracting of work that is not considered part of a company's core business.

Outsourcing is the subcontracting of work that is not considered part of a company's core business. The practice has grown exponentially over the past decade. The outsourcing of Unilever's administrative HR functions is highlighted in the Global HRM box. Outsourcing research firm Nelson Hall reported that the overall outsourcing market will grow at 21 percent annually, and that the HR outsourcing market will grow by 11 percent to US$33 billion worldwide by 2008.[78] Another recent report indicates that since 2004, the growth in HR outsourcing has been in areas relating to basic HR transactions and those services that focus on managing the employee life cycle, such as recruiting. Studies have shown that 96 percent of companies with annual earnings of at least US$50 million per year currently outsource some portion of their HR-related activities. The main benefits of HR outsourcing are cost reduction and increased ability for HR professionals to focus on core business objectives.[79]

Determining HR's Effectiveness

With the ability to outsource administrative work and the significant developments in HR technology, HR will now be expected to focus on the strategic management of human capital and those activities that HR undertakes to add value to the organization.

Global HRM

Outsourcing HR Functions

Accenture, a global management consulting, technology, and outsourcing company, has recently entered into an agreement with Unilever Corporation. Unilever is a multi-national marketing organization with familiar products such as Dove soap, Becel margarine, and Lipton soup, that employs 206 000 people in 100 countries worldwide. To optimize its HR services to its employees, Unilever has decided to outsource its administrative HR functions to Accenture. The agreement will cover three geographic regions—Europe, the Americas, and Asia— and provide services to approximately 200 000 employees in more than 20 languages. Accenture will manage critical HR software applications. Some of the services it will provide are recruitment, payroll administration, total rewards administration, performance management workforce reporting, and core HR administration.

This arrangement will change the way Unilever manages and delivers its HR services across the company. Once these functions are outsourced, the remaining HR activities will be redesigned to focus more on the customer and establish a targeted service delivery model.

Source: J. Finlaw, "Accenture to Help Unilever Transform Human Resources Operations in 100 Countries with a Seven-Year Outsourcing Agreement," *Press Release*, June 6, 2006. Used with permission of Accenture.

The HR function, with its newly developed strategic focus, is expected to demonstrate a measurable impact on business results. The expectation is that HR is transforming data into insights and the ability to provide "quality" data that will transcend the need for information and focus key decision makers on relevant information that is meaningful to the business.[80]

Today's HR professionals must be technically savvy and be able to speak the language of business. They must understand the business environment and the major drivers relating to workforce productivity as determined by management. Such techniques as benchmarking and the use of balanced scorecards will be increasingly important for HR. These tools will provide HR with feedback as to whether they are truly listening to the organization and providing customer-focused services.

Finally, how HR utilizes technology to evaluate its own effectiveness and how HR decides to leverage emerging technologies to drive productivity and the management of human capital will make the difference between a mediocre HR department and one that is truly a business partner.

Chapter Review

Summary

1. HR technology has evolved from paper and pencil to PCs to electronic databases to being integrated with company-wide enterprise systems. Web-based technology has been an important development in enabling HR to reduce transactional activities and increase customer and strategic services.

2. The main components of HRIS systems are employee administration, recruitment, time and attendance, training and development, pension administration, employment equity, performance evaluation, compensation and benefits administration, organizational management, health and safety, labour relations, and payroll interface.

3. The main functions of HRIS are creating and maintaining employee records, compliance reporting, HR planning and forecasting, talent management, strategic alignment, and enhancing decision making.

4. The role of the HR professional has changed fundamentally as a result of technology. The core competencies that have developed are mastery of HR technology, strategic contribution, personal credibility, HR delivery, and business knowledge.

5. To choose an HRIS, organizations engage in a three-step process. The first step is the adoption phase, whereby organizations carry out a needs analysis to determine requirements. The second step is the implementation phase, where project teams are created, the software is tested, and privacy and security concerns are addressed. The third step is the institutionalization phase, where training and change management activities are highlighted.

6. The more popular Web-based self-service applications are employee self-service (ESS) and manager self-service (MSS). Some benefits derived from these applications are a reduction in administrative costs, reduction in process steps, enhanced HR service delivery, and increased employee satisfaction.

7. Current technology trends that will impact HR are outsourcing, advances in technology, and a continued focus on measuring the value that HR brings to the organization.

Key Terms

client server   *(p. 52)*
data warehouse   *(p. 58)*
electronic HR (e-HR)   *(p. 63)*
enterprise-wide system   *(p. 60)*
human resources information system (HRIS)
    (p. 53)

human resources (HR) technology   *(p. 50)*
interactive voice response (IVR)   *(p. 52)*
intranet   *(p. 63)*
outsourcing   *(p. 73)*
portal   *(p. 64)*
relational database   *(p. 52)*
request for proposal (RFP)   *(p. 62)*
tombstone data   *(p. 51)*
Web-based applications   *(p. 53)*
workforce analytics   *(p. 59)*

Review and Discussion Questions

1. Explain the four stages in the evolution of HR technology.
2. Describe the stages that organizations engage in to decide on an HRIS.
3. Discuss the five key competencies of an HR professional in an IT-enabled world.
4. Identify two Web-based self-service delivery applications that are popular today.
5. What are some of the trends that HR has to pay attention to?
6. What are the 12 subsystems that reside in an HRIS?
7. Discuss the six key functions of an HRIS.

Critical Thinking Questions

1. Do you think that an HRIS is important for all types of organizations to have? Why or why not?
2. Compare and contrast the cost and benefits of being a member of an HRIS implementation team.

3. Do you think that maintaining security of an HRIS is a major concern for HR technology professionals? Explain what issues you think are most important today.

Application Exercises

Running Case: LearnInMotion.com

Does LearnInMotion Need an HRIS?

Jennifer was getting frustrated. With only a few employees, the company kept a paper-based file for each employee with personal information, benefits forms, and so on. She and Pierre had decided to outsource payroll, but she still had to spend several hours every two weeks gathering payroll information, such as regular hours, overtime hours, vacation time and sick time that had been taken, and so on, to send to the payroll company. The benefits information and calculations were supposed to be carried out by the payroll company, but there had been several instances where mistakes had been made.

Jennifer and Pierre discussed the issue and decided that as a high-tech company, they should investigate the possibility of computerizing their employee files and information. Even with a very small number of employees, they both thought it might be easier for them to use some sort of HRIS. They have asked you, their management consultants, to provide answers to the following questions.

Questions

1. What data should be stored for each employee? How would the company use these data?
2. Conduct an HRIS needs analysis for the company.
3. Would you recommend an HRIS to Jennifer and Pierre? If so, what kind of system?

Case Incident

Integration and Transfer of HR Functions Using HRIS

Jack Newman had recently been appointed regional director of Boomerang Water Corporation, a major service utility in Australia. Jack's previous appointment was with a large manufacturing company in the U.S., where he had made a reputation for himself as a visionary specializing in customer service and performance management. Jack was the youngest person and only non-Australian ever to be appointed as a director of Boomerang Water Corporation. This particular region of the utility employed approximately 2000 workers engaged in the customer service and maintenance provision side of the business. These employees operated in groups of about 30 workers. One supervisor managed each work group. These groups were located in five departments across the region, with each department specializing in a particular customer service or maintenance function. The region serviced about 500 000 customers.

A central division controlled the human resource management functions for the region. This division was located in the region's main town. Elaine Macvain headed the HR division. Elaine had been with the utility for nearly 25 years, and over these years had developed a reputation for running a strong controlled division that provided the customer service and maintenance department with a diversity of HR services. Elaine considered that the main focus of the division was to process day-to-day HR transactions and maintain employee records. Elaine managed a staff of 10 HR professionals. These 10 staff processed employee data that included workers' pay, leave entitlements and requests, and shift work entitlements. The HR department was responsible for recruitment and selection, the performance management system, occupational health and safety records, and career planning. Ron Locat, a member of Elaine's division, had developed a stand-alone HRIS to maintain the HR department's records. Ron had little formal IT training, but had undergone in-house training in the use of Microsoft Access, and had used Access to create the division's database system. Elaine and the other members of the HR division did not have a high level of IT literacy, but they could operate the Access system that Ron had developed. Elaine was indebted to Ron for the work he had put into the

database system, and felt indebted to him for the support that he gave to the HR staff.

A major focus of the utility was training the customer service and maintenance employees. The utility had a promotion system based on the employee's level of technical skills. Employees were promoted to high levels of competency and pay scales on completion of skills training. Peter Noall headed the training division. Peter had been with the utility for about four years. The training division had three staff in addition to Peter. One staff member was an ex–technical college teacher, and two were previously technical supervisors in the organization. Due to the small size of the training division, Peter was forced to outsource much of the organization's training needs. A major responsibility of Peter's was work safety, and he was very proud of the organization's safety record. Peter had contracted the purchase of an expensive dedicated training database system to support the organization's training function. The system provided the training division with a powerful tool with which to profile the total skills base of the organization, identify present and future training needs, track employees' competency levels, and evaluate training outcomes in relation to productivity gains. The training division was proud of its use of high-level technology to support strategic training initiatives.

On commencing his appointment, Jack Newman decided to immediately focus on improving the organization's customer service. He engaged the Fast Track-Immediate Success consultancy group to run a number of focus groups and conduct a strategic analysis related to the delivery of customer service. Eddie Wanton from Fast Track organized focus groups within the HR division, the training division, and ran three focus groups of 20 randomly selected supervisors. Eddie's report to Jack Newman included the following concerns and recommendations aimed to improve customer service.

Report from Fast Track

Concern 1: At present customer complaints are directed to work group supervisors.
Recommendation: Introduce a new division dedicated to customer service quality.

Concern 2: Customer service is not supported by an integration of customer feedback, work group practices, training, and HR strategies.

Recommendation: Link the new customer service quality division to HR, training, and work group supervision.

Concern 3: At present, the HR division has sole responsibility for performance management, not the training division or work group supervisors.

Recommendation: Link performance management responsibilities to work group supervisors via training plans and HR recruitment strategies.

Concern 4: Communications among the HR division, training division, and work group supervisors are low-level and infrequent.

Recommendation: Introduce an organization structure that seamlessly integrates and promotes strategic communication between HR, training, and work group supervision.

Concern 5: The HR division and the training division have created tightly controlled centres of knowledge that do not directly inform work group supervisors.

Recommendation: Introduce the transfer of targeted HR and training responsibilities directly to work group supervisors.

Eddie Wanton's Recommended Strategy

Introduce a database information system that will seamlessly integrate HR functions, training functions, and customer service functions. Use the information system to develop strategic links between these functions. Use the new information system to break down information channel barriers between the HR and training divisions. Use the system to devolve appropriate HR and training operations to work group supervisors. Create a new customer service quality division and use the new IT system to integrate it with the other divisions and work group supervisors. In short, change the organization's communication and information architecture to promote the integration of cross-divisional information sharing, decision making, and control.

Jack Newman's Response

Jack Newman's response to Fast Track's recommendations was to target changes to the organization's structure and design necessary to promote the improvement of customer service. Jack immediately decided to act as champion of the cause, and constituted a taskforce with the responsibility of implementing Fast Tack's recommendations. Jack appointed to the change taskforce Elaine, Peter, Bobby Bea (a work group supervisor who was a union official and had been with the utility for nearly 30 years), and two consultants from IT Now, a company marketing an integrated HRIS. Jack decided to act as chairperson of the taskforce. The objectives of the taskforce were to assist the consultants in identifying the organization's needs, and to inform the consultants as to the type of configuration necessary for the off-the-shelf HRIS to meet those needs. Jack expected the consultants to have the new system up and running within six months.

At the very first meeting of the taskforce it was apparent that, while Peter shared Jack's vision for change, Elaine was very concerned about the implication of these proposed changes for her division. Jack told Elaine that the HR staff would have to significantly upgrade their IT skills, or the organization might have to offer HR division staff redeployment or redundancy packages. Peter quickly pointed out that greater integration between HR and training should place all occupational health and safety responsibilities within the training division. Peter also emphasized that the need to train employees in the new system would entail increasing the number of training division staff. Bobby Bea was concerned that any transfer of HR transactions, such as employees' leave applications, or performance management responsibilities, onto work group supervisors would cut down on their time to oversee service or maintenance operations. Bobby also pointed out that any changes to supervisors' job descriptions would need to be approved by the union and would involve pay raises. The consultant drew the taskforce's attention to the fact that if the organization required the new system to be functional within six months, they would most likely be forced to implement the off-the-shelf version with little specific tailoring to meet organizational needs. Both Elaine and Peter were concerned as to who would head the new customer service quality division, and the implications of the creation of this new division for their divisional budgets.

Questions

1. How can the assignment of a champion facilitate the introduction of the new HRIS? Is Jack Newman the best person to act as champion?

2. Why have the HR and training divisions built quite different database systems? What are the difficulties involved in integrating the functions of these divisions?

3. What are the advantages of integrating the functions of the HR division, training division, and those of the work group supervisors?

4. What are the advantages and disadvantages of the Boomerang Water Corporation buying an off-the-shelf integrated HR database system?

5. In what ways may the transfer of some HR functions to work group supervisors improve the efficiency of the HR division? In what ways may work group supervisors be advantaged or disadvantaged by the transfer of HR functions?

Source: G. Dessler, J. Griffiths, and B. Lloyd-Walker, *Human Resources Management*, 2nd ed. Frenchs Forest, New South Wales: Pearson Education Australia, 2004, pp. 97–99. Reprinted with permission of the publisher.

Experiential Exercises

1. Go to the federal government Web site for the Employment Equity Computerized Reporting System (EECRS; www.hrsdc.gc.ca/asp/gateway. asp?hr=/en/lp/lo/lswe/we/ee_tools/software/eecrs/ index-we.shtml&hs=wzp). Download the software and familiarize yourself with it. What information needs to be in an HRIS in order to provide complete reporting through the EECRS?

2. How could an HRIS be used to help manage a crisis, such as an avian flu epidemic or a terrorist attack?

CHAPTER 4

DESIGNING AND ANALYZING JOBS

LEARNING OUTCOMES

AFTER STUDYING THIS CHAPTER, YOU SHOULD BE ABLE TO

Define job design, and **explain** the difference between a job and a position.

Describe the industrial engineering, behavioural, and human engineering considerations involved in job design.

Explain the six steps in job analysis.

Describe four basic narrative methods of collecting job analysis information and three quantitative methods.

Explain the difference between a job description and a job specification.

Discuss why and how the concept of a job has been changing.

REQUIRED PROFESSIONAL CAPABILITIES

• Contributes to an environment that fosters effective working relationships

ORGANIZING WORK

An organization consists of one or more employees who perform various tasks. The relationships between people and tasks must be structured in such a way that the organization can achieve its goals in an efficient and effective manner.

Organizational structure refers to the formal relationships among jobs in an organization. An **organization chart** is often used to depict the structure. As illustrated in **Figure 4.1**, such a chart indicates the types of departments established and the title of each manager's job. By means of connecting lines, it clarifies the chain of command and shows who is accountable to whom. An organization chart presents a "snapshot" of the firm at a particular point in time, but it does not provide details about actual communication patterns, degree of supervision, amount of power and authority, or specific duties and responsibilities.

Designing an organization involves choosing a structure that is appropriate, given the company's strategic goals. **Figure 4.2** depicts the three basic types of organizational structure: bureaucratic, flat, and boundaryless.

organizational structure   The formal relationships among jobs in an organization.

organization chart   A "snapshot" of the firm, depicting the organization's structure in chart form at a particular point in time.

Example of Online Organization Chart
www.IntranetOrgChart.com

Online Organization Charts
www.nakisa.com

FIGURE 4.1   A Sample Organization Chart

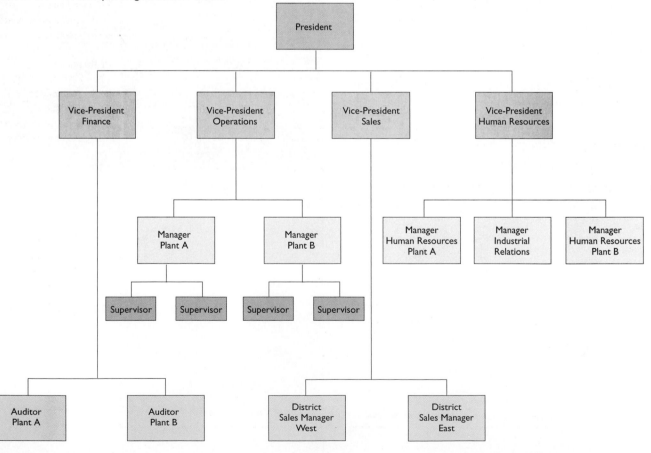

FIGURE 4.2   Bureaucratic, Flat, and Boundaryless Organizational Structures

Structure   **Characteristics**

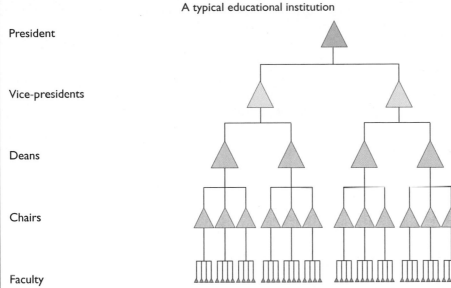
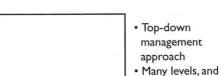
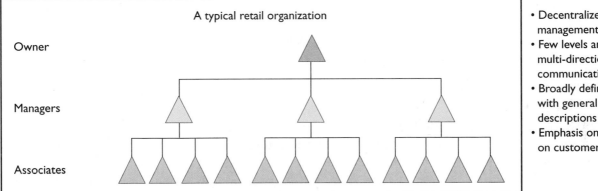
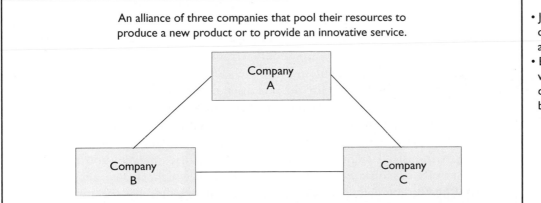

BUREAUCRATIC

A typical educational institution

President

Vice-presidents

Deans

Chairs

Faculty

- Top-down management approach
- Many levels, and hierarchical communication channels and career paths
- Highly specialized jobs with narrowly defined job descriptions
- Focus on independent performance

FLAT

A typical retail organization

Owner

Managers

Associates

- Decentralized management approach
- Few levels and multi-directional communication
- Broadly defined jobs, with general job descriptions
- Emphasis on teams and on customer service

BOUNDARYLESS

An alliance of three companies that pool their resources to produce a new product or to provide an innovative service.

Company A

Company B

Company C

- Joint ventures with customers, suppliers, and/or competitors
- Emphasis on teams whose members may cross organizational boundaries

JOB DESIGN

job design   The process of systematically organizing work into tasks that are required to perform a specific job.

job   A group of related activities and duties, held by a single employee or a number of incumbents.

position   The collection of tasks and responsibilities performed by one person.

REQUIRED PROFESSIONAL CAPABILITIES

Contributes to an environment that fosters effective working relationships

work simplification   An approach to job design that involves assigning most of the administrative aspects of work (such as planning and organizing) to supervisors and managers, while giving lower-level employees narrowly defined tasks to perform according to methods established and specified by management.

industrial engineering   A field of study concerned with analyzing work methods; making work cycles more efficient by modifying, combining, rearranging, or eliminating tasks; and establishing time standards.

In any organization, work has to be divided into manageable units and ultimately into jobs that can be performed by employees. **Job design** is the process of systematically organizing work into tasks that are required to perform a specific job. An organization's strategy and structure influence the ways in which jobs are designed. In bureaucratic organizations, for example, because a hierarchical division of labour exists, jobs are generally highly specialized. In addition, effective job design also takes into consideration human and technological factors.

A **job** consists of a group of related activities and duties. Ideally, the duties of a job should be clear and distinct from those of other jobs, and they should involve natural units of work that are similar and related. This approach helps to minimize conflict and enhance employee performance. A job may be held by a single employee or may have a number of incumbents. The collection of tasks and responsibilities performed by one person is known as a **position**. To clarify, in a department with 1 supervisor, 1 clerk, 40 assemblers, and 3 tow-motor operators, there are 45 positions and 4 jobs.

Specialization and Industrial Engineering Considerations

The term "job" as it is known today is largely an outgrowth of the efficiency demands of the industrial revolution. As the substitution of machine power for people power became more widespread, experts wrote glowingly about the positive correlation between (1) job specialization and (2) productivity and efficiency.[1] The popularity of specialized, short-cycle jobs soared—at least among management experts and managers.

Work simplification evolved from scientific management theory. It is based on the premise that work can be broken down into clearly defined, highly specialized, repetitive tasks to maximize efficiency. This approach to job design involves assigning most of the administrative aspects of work (such as planning and organizing) to supervisors and managers, while giving lower-level employees narrowly defined tasks to perform according to methods established and specified by management.

Although work simplification can increase operating efficiency in a stable environment, and may be very appropriate in settings employing individuals with mental disabilities or those lacking education and training (as in some operations in the developing world), it is not effective in a changing environment in which customers/clients demand custom-designed products and/or high-quality services, or one in which employees want challenging work. Moreover, among educated employees, simplified jobs often lead to lower satisfaction, higher rates of absenteeism and turnover, and sometimes to a demand for premium pay to compensate for the repetitive nature of the work.

Another important contribution of scientific management was the study of work. **Industrial engineering**, which evolved with this movement, is concerned with analyzing work methods and establishing time standards to improve efficiency. Industrial engineers systematically identify, analyze, and time the elements of each job's work cycle and determine which, if any, elements can be modified, combined, rearranged, or eliminated to reduce the time needed to complete the cycle.

Too much emphasis on the concerns of industrial engineering—improving efficiency and simplifying work methods—may result in human considerations being neglected or downplayed. For example, an assembly line, with its simplified and repetitive tasks, embodies the principles of industrial engineering but may lead to repetitive strain injuries, high turnover, and low satisfaction because of the lack of psychological fulfillment. Thus, to be effective, job design must also satisfy human psychological and physiological needs.

Behavioural Considerations

By the mid-1900s, reacting to what they viewed as the "dehumanizing" aspects of highly repetitive and specialized jobs, various management theorists proposed ways of broadening the activities in which employees engaged. **Job enlargement** involves assigning workers additional tasks at the same level of responsibility to increase the number of tasks they have to perform. Thus, if the work was assembling chairs, the worker who previously only bolted the seat to the legs might take on the additional tasks of assembling the legs and attaching the back as well. Also known as **horizontal loading**, job enlargement reduces monotony and fatigue by expanding the job cycle and drawing on a wider range of employee skills. Another technique to relieve monotony and employee boredom is **job rotation**. This involves systematically moving employees from one job to another. Although the jobs themselves don't change, workers experience more task variety, motivation, and productivity. The company gains by having more versatile, multiskilled employees who can cover for one another efficiently.

More recently, psychologist Frederick Herzberg argued that the best way to motivate workers is to build opportunities for challenge and achievement into jobs through **job enrichment**.[2] This is defined as any effort that makes an employee's job more rewarding or satisfying by adding more meaningful tasks and duties. Also known as **vertical loading**, job enrichment involves increasing autonomy and responsibility by allowing employees to assume a greater role in the decision-making process.

Enriching jobs can be accomplished through such activities as

- increasing the level of difficulty and responsibility of the job
- assigning workers more authority and control over outcomes
- providing feedback about individual or unit job performance directly to employees
- adding new tasks requiring training, thereby providing an opportunity for growth
- assigning individuals specific tasks or responsibility for performing a whole job rather than only parts of it

Job design studies explored a new field when behavioural scientists focused on identifying various job dimensions that would simultaneously improve the efficiency of organizations and the satisfaction of employees. One of the best-known theories evolving from such research is the job characteristics model.[3] It proposes that employee motivation and satisfaction are directly linked to five core characteristics:[4]

1. *Skill variety*. The degree to which the job requires a person to do different tasks and involves the use of a number of different talents, skills, and abilities.
2. *Task identity*. The degree to which the job requires completion of a whole and identifiable piece of work—that is, doing a job from beginning to end, with a visible outcome.

job enlargement (horizontal loading) A technique to relieve monotony and boredom that involves assigning workers additional tasks at the same level of responsibility to increase the number of tasks they have to perform.

job rotation Another technique to relieve monotony and employee boredom that involves systematically moving employees from one job to another.

job enrichment (vertical loading) Any effort that makes an employee's job more rewarding or satisfying by adding more meaningful tasks and duties.

Tips for the Front Line

3. *Task significance.* The degree to which the job has a substantial impact on the lives and work of others—both inside and outside the organization.

4. *Autonomy.* The amount of freedom, independence, and discretion the employee has in terms of scheduling work and determining procedures.

5. *Feedback.* The degree to which the job provides the employee with clear and direct information about job outcomes and the effectiveness of his or her performance.

These core job characteristics create the conditions that enable workers to experience three critical psychological states that are related to a number of beneficial work outcomes:[5]

1. *Experienced meaningfulness.* The extent to which the employee experiences the work as important, valuable, and worthwhile.

2. *Experienced responsibility.* The degree to which the employee feels personally responsible or accountable for the outcome of the work.

3. *Knowledge of results.* The degree to which the employee understands, on a regular basis, how effectively he or she is performing.

As illustrated in **Figure 4.3**, skill variety, task identity, and task significance are all linked to experienced meaningfulness; autonomy is related to experienced responsibility; and feedback provides knowledge of results. A job with characteristics that allow an employee to experience all three critical states provides internal rewards that sustain motivation. The benefits to the employer include high-quality performance, higher employee satisfaction, and lower absenteeism and turnover.

Job enrichment and the inclusion of the five core dimensions in jobs is not, however, a panacea. Job enrichment programs are more successful in some jobs and settings than in others. Moreover, not all employees want additional responsibility and challenge. The strength of the linkage among job characteristics, psychological states, and work outcomes is determined by the intensity of an individual employee's need for growth.[6]

FIGURE 4.3   The Job Characteristics Model

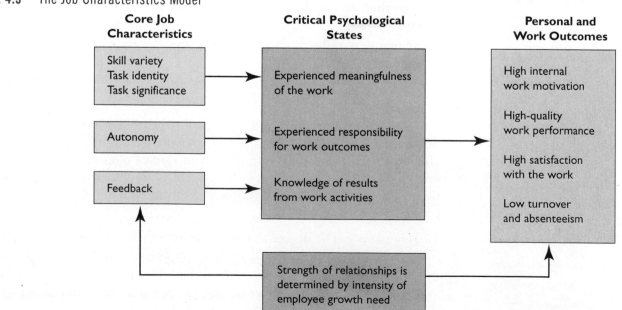

team-based job designs   Job designs that focus on giving a team, rather than an individual, a whole and meaningful piece of work to do and empowering team members to decide among themselves how to accomplish the work.

team   A small group of people, with complementary skills, who work toward common goals for which they hold joint responsibility and accountability.

Some people prefer routine jobs and may resist job redesign efforts. In addition, job redesign efforts almost always fail when employees lack the physical or mental skills, abilities, or education needed to perform the job.

Team-Based Job Designs

A logical outgrowth of job enrichment and the job characteristics model has been the increasing use of **team-based job designs**, which focus on giving a **team**, rather than an individual, a whole and meaningful piece of work to do. Team members are empowered to decide among themselves how to accomplish the work.[7] Often they are cross-trained, and then rotated through performing different tasks. Team-based designs are best suited to flat and boundaryless organization structures.

General Motors' Saturn Division is an extremely high-profile operation that has mastered the use of team-based job design. Initiated as a completely new venture within GM in an attempt to "reinvent the wheel," the Saturn car assembly process involves self-managed teams with 7 to 15 members. Each team operates as a "small business unit," is responsible for statistical process control tasks, has budgeting responsibilities, and is involved in parts and other supply purchasing decisions. The direction in which teamwork at Saturn has evolved could be representative of the future of team production in the auto industry.[8]

Increasingly, organizations are using "virtual teams"—people working together effectively and efficiently across boundaries of time and space, and using software to make team meetings more productive.[9]

Human Engineering Considerations

Over time, it became apparent that in addition to considering psychological needs, effective job design must also take physiological needs and health and safety issues into account. **Human engineering** (or **ergonomics**) seeks to integrate and accommodate the physical needs of workers into the design of jobs. It aims to adapt the entire job system—the work, environment, machines, equipment, and processes—to match human characteristics. Doing so results in eliminating

An Ethical Dilemma

Suppose your organization restructures and adopts a team-based design. One of your top-performing employees before the restructuring then fails to perform to expected standards. Would it be ethical to take disciplinary action against the employee?

human engineering (ergonomics)   An interdisciplinary approach that seeks to integrate and accommodate the physical needs of workers into the design of jobs. It aims to adapt the entire job system—the work, environment, machines, equipment, and processes—to match human characteristics.

An Ethical Dilemma

Some employees clearly require ergonomic aid, while others do not. Should ergonomic issues be addressed only in the redesign of workstations used by employees who have special needs or those used by every employee?

At Saturn's auto factory, team members with complementary skills work toward common goals for which they hold joint responsibility and accountability.

or minimizing product defects, damage to equipment, and worker injuries or illnesses caused by poor work design.

In addition to designing jobs and equipment with the aim of minimizing negative physiological effects for all workers, human engineering can aid in meeting the unique requirements of individuals with special needs, such as older workers, as discussed in the Workforce Diversity box.

Workforce Diversity

Accommodating and Utilizing the Aging Workforce

The aging of the workforce brings new challenges in terms of work performance, employee retention, and disability costs. The employers who will meet these challenges most successfully are those who begin addressing them now. Older workers score high on job skills, loyalty, and reliability. They also have low absenteeism and turnover, and they have the capability to change and adjust. Although older workers face a decrease in their physical strength, they replace this weakness by working smarter and being more safety-conscious at work. Injury rates for older workers are the lowest of any age group, but their injuries are often more severe when they do occur.

Other potential problems that may occur with older workers include the following:

- difficulty maintaining good posture and balance
- problems regulating sleep; how much or how well they sleep can be affected by changing work hours or by light and noise
- trouble maintaining body temperature; they may find heat or cold more difficult to deal with, and hard manual labour may cause overheating more quickly and easily
- deteriorating vision; they might not be able to read small text and may have difficulty when there is poor contrast between text and background
- diminished hearing, which may result in not being able to focus on and listen to a particular voice or sound in a noisy environment
- reduced cognitive ability and memory; they may not think as quickly and clearly, and they may take longer to master new job-related skills
- difficulty multitasking or working in a busy and hectic environment

It is not very difficult or costly to accommodate and use the skills and ability of older workers. With a comprehensive disability management program in place, it can be very easy to accommodate these workers. The following are some suggestions for accommodating older workers:

- Provide brighter lights and well-laid-out documents with large print.
- Have different training techniques for older workers that include learning from previous experience; provide a clear, larger picture, including justification and the logic behind the information, and give sufficient time for training them.
- Do not give them repetitive work that will cause use of the same muscles and, in turn, cause them stress and pain; a job rotation schedule would prevent employees from overworking any part of the body.
- Do not push them to work harder or longer.
- Make adjustments to workstations or work patterns to make them as safe as possible (e.g., design work floors and platforms with smooth and solid decking, while still allowing some cushioning and reducing noise levels).
- Make sure that the person is suited for the particular task and is safely able to do it.
- Provide quality care for and follow-up of injuries.
- Promote comprehensive fitness initiatives, such as participation in a home- or gym-based exercise program (or implement an onsite, supervised fitness program); promote fitness through company-sponsored sports teams and recreational activities, such as company walks.
- Have external health-care providers come in and give informational sessions on nutrition, weight control, smoking cessation, and disease prevention; other topics could focus on coping with age-related conditions, such as arthritis and hearing loss.
- Institutionalize organized stretch and/or walk breaks for older workers.
- Create and maintain a database with the physical demands of each job to properly assign all workers to safe jobs; a database can also help when injured workers come back to work by providing them with lighter tasks to get them started and help them heal.

Source: Adapted from T. McDonald and H.G. Harder, "Older Workers and Disability Management," *International Journal of Disability, Community & Rehabilitation,* 2004, Vol. 3, No. 3. Reprinted with permission from IJDCR.

Research
Insight ▷
It is important to note that the human engineering considerations involved in the design of jobs, workstations, and office space are important to all employees, not just to those with special needs. The Institute for Research in Construction (part of Canada's National Research Council) conducted a field study of the effects of the physical conditions on occupant satisfaction. The results showed that predictable, positive relationships exist among satisfaction with the physical environment, overall environment satisfaction, and job satisfaction. Thus, people who are more satisfied with the physical set-up of their workstations have higher job satisfaction.[10]

THE NATURE OF JOB ANALYSIS

job analysis The procedure for determining the tasks, duties, and responsibilities of each job, and the human attributes (in terms of knowledge, skills, and abilities) required to perform it.

Once jobs have been designed or redesigned, an employer's performance-related expectations need to be defined and communicated. This is best accomplished through job analysis, a process by which information about jobs is systematically gathered and organized. **Job analysis** is the procedure firms use to determine the tasks, duties, and responsibilities of each job, and the human attributes (in terms of knowledge, skills, and abilities) required to perform it. Once this information has been gathered, it is used for developing **job descriptions** (what the job entails) and **job specifications** (what the human requirements are).[11]

job description A list of the duties, responsibilities, reporting relationships, and working conditions of a job—one product of a job analysis.

Uses of Job Analysis Information

Job analysis is sometimes called the cornerstone of HRM. As illustrated in **Figure 4.4,** the information gathered, evaluated, and summarized through job analysis is the basis for a number of interrelated HRM activities.

job specification A list of the "human requirements," that is, the requisite knowledge, skills, and abilities, needed to perform the job—another product of a job analysis.

Human Resources Planning
Knowing the actual requirements of jobs is essential for planning future staffing needs. When this information is combined with knowledge about the skills and qualifications of current employees, it is possible to determine which jobs can be filled internally and which will require external recruitment.

Job Analysis
http://harvey.psyc.vt.edu

FIGURE 4.4 Uses of Job Analysis Information

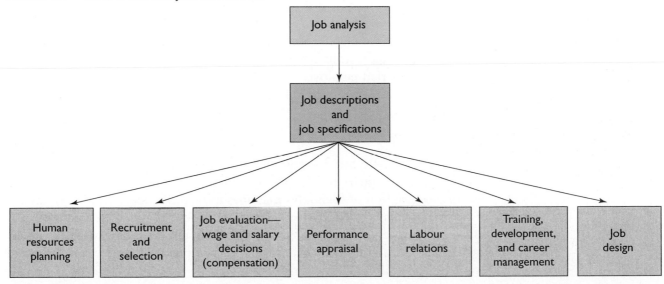

Recruitment and Selection

The job description and job specification information should be used to decide what sort of person to recruit and hire. Identifying bona fide occupational requirements, and ensuring that all activities related to recruitment and selection (such as advertising, screening, and testing) are based on such requirements, is necessary for legal compliance in all Canadian jurisdictions.

Compensation

Job analysis information is also essential for determining the relative value of and appropriate compensation for each job. Job evaluation should be based on the required skills, physical and mental demands, responsibilities, and working conditions—all assessed through job analysis. The relative value of jobs is one of the key factors used to determine appropriate compensation and justify pay differences if challenged under human rights or pay equity legislation. Information about the actual job duties is also necessary to determine whether a job qualifies for overtime pay and maximum hours purposes, as specified in employment standards legislation.

Performance Appraisal

To be legally defensible, the criteria used to assess employee performance must be directly related to the duties and responsibilities identified through job analysis. For many jobs involving routine tasks, especially those of a quantifiable nature, performance standards are determined through job analysis. For more complex jobs, performance standards are often jointly established by employees and their supervisors. To be realistic and achievable, such standards should be based on actual job requirements, as identified through job analysis.

Labour Relations

In unionized environments, the job descriptions developed from the job analysis information are generally subject to union approval before being finalized. Such union-approved job descriptions then become the basis for classifying jobs and bargaining over wages, performance criteria, and working conditions. Once approved, significant changes to job descriptions may have to be negotiated.

Training, Development, and Career Management

By comparing the knowledge, skills, and abilities (KSAs) that employees bring to the job with those that are identified by job analysis, managers can determine the gaps that require training programs. Having accurate information about jobs also means that employees can prepare for future advancement by identifying gaps between their current KSAs and those specified for the jobs to which they aspire.

Job Design

Job analysis is useful for ensuring that all of the duties having to be done have actually been assigned, and for identifying areas of overlap. Also, having an accurate description of each job sometimes leads to the identification of unnecessary requirements, areas of conflict or dissatisfaction, and/or health and safety concerns that can be eliminated through job redesign. Such redesign may increase morale and productivity and ensure compliance with human rights and occupational health and safety regulations.

Steps in Job Analysis

The six steps involved in analyzing jobs are outlined here.

Step 1:   Identify the use to which the information will be put, since this will determine the types of data that should be collected and the techniques used. Some data-collection techniques—such as interviewing the employee and asking what the job entails and what his or her responsibilities are—are good for writing job descriptions and selecting employees for the job. Other job analysis techniques provide numerical ratings for each job, which can be used to compare jobs for compensation purposes.

process chart   A diagram showing the flow of inputs to and outputs from the job under study.

Step 2:   Review relevant background information, such as organization charts, process charts, and existing job descriptions.[12] A **process chart** (like the one in **Figure 4.5**) shows the flow of inputs to and outputs from the job under study. (In Figure 4.5, the inventory control clerk is expected to receive inventory from suppliers, take requests for inventory from the two plant managers, provide requested inventory to these managers, and give information to the plant accountant on the status of in-stock inventories.)

Step 3:   Select the representative positions and jobs to be analyzed. This selection is necessary when there are many incumbents in a single job and when a number of similar jobs are to be analyzed, because it would be too time-consuming to analyze every position and job.

Step 4:   Next, analyze the jobs by collecting data on job activities, required employee behaviours, working conditions, and human traits and abilities needed to perform the job, and using one or more of the job analysis techniques explained later in this chapter.

Step 5:   Review the information with job incumbents. The job analysis information should be verified with any workers performing the job and with the immediate supervisor. This corroboration will help to confirm that the

FIGURE 4.5   Process Chart for Analyzing a Job's Workflow

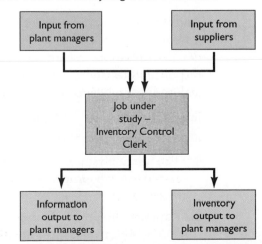

Source: Henderson, Richard I., ed., *Compensation Management in a Knowledge-Based World,* 10th Edition, © 2006, p. 114. Reprinted by permission of Pearson Education, Inc., Upper Saddle River, NJ.

information is factually correct and complete, and it can also help gain the employees' acceptance of the job analysis data.

Step 6:   Develop a job description and job specification, which are the two concrete products of the job analysis.

METHODS OF COLLECTING JOB ANALYSIS INFORMATION

Various qualitative and quantitative techniques are used to collect information about the duties, responsibilities, and requirements of the job; the most important ones will be discussed in this section. In practice, when the information is being used for multiple purposes, ranging from developing recruitment criteria to compensation decisions, several techniques may be used in combination.

Collecting job analysis data usually involves a joint effort by an HR specialist, the incumbent, and the jobholder's supervisor. The HR specialist (an HR manager, job analyst, or consultant) might observe and analyze the work being done and then develop a job description and specification. The supervisor and incumbent generally also get involved, perhaps by filling out questionnaires. The supervisor and incumbent typically review and verify the job analyst's conclusions regarding the job's duties, responsibilities, and requirements.

Qualitative Job Analysis Techniques

The Interview

The interview is probably the most widely used method for determining the duties and responsibilities of a job. Three types of interviews are used to collect job analysis data: individual interviews with each employee; group interviews with employees who have the same job; and supervisory interviews with one or more supervisors who are thoroughly knowledgeable about the job being analyzed. The group interview is used when a large number of employees are performing similar or identical work, and it can be a quick and inexpensive way of learning about the job. As a rule, the immediate supervisor attends the group session; if not, the supervisor should be interviewed separately to get that person's perspective on the duties and responsibilities of the job.

The most fruitful interviews follow a structured or checklist format. A job analysis questionnaire, like the one presented in **Figure 4.6,** may be used to interview job incumbents or may be filled out by them. It includes a series of detailed questions regarding such matters as the general purpose of the job; responsibilities and duties; the education, experience, and skills required; physical and mental demands; and working conditions.

Interview Guidelines   When conducting a job analysis interview, supervisors and job analysts should keep several things in mind:

1. The job analyst and supervisor should work together to identify the employees who know the job best, as well as those who might be expected to be the most objective in describing their duties and responsibilities.

2. Rapport should be established quickly with the interviewee, by using the individual's name, speaking in easily understood language, briefly reviewing the purpose of the interview (job analysis, not performance appraisal), and explaining how the person came to be chosen.

Tips for the Front Line

FIGURE 4.6   Job Analysis Questionnaire

Job title: _____   Job grade: _____
Department: _____   Location: _____
Prepared by: _____   Date: _____

1. Purpose of job
  • What is the purpose of the job? Why does the job exist?
  _____
  _____
  _____

2. Major responsibilities and essential functions (list in order of importance)
  • What are the responsibilities?   • Why is the activity performed?
  • How are they done?   • What is the measure of success?
  • Percentage of time?   • What direction of others is involved?
  _____
  _____
  _____
  _____

3. Knowledge
  • What techniques and/or practices are necessary? Why?
  _____
  _____

  • List specific education requirement(s).
  _____
  _____

  • List experience requirement(s) and number of years required in each.
  _____
  _____

  • List required licences or certificates.
  _____
  _____

4. Problem solving and decision making
  • List how the jobholder solves problems (i.e., planning, scheduling, creativity techniques, complexity of procedures, degree of independent thinking, and resourcefulness or ingenuity required). List examples of required development of new methods. What are the consequences if problems are not solved?
  _____
  _____
  _____
  _____
  _____

5. Resource responsibility
  • List annual pay of personnel who report to jobholder: _____
  • List annual operating budget (include pay): _____

continued

• List any other financial resources (i.e., annual project value/cost, shop order value, total sales, total unit payroll, gross sales booked, purchasing/contracts volume, transportation costs, facilities budget, assets, investment income, program development costs, and gross sales billed):

_____

_____

• What is the jobholder's role in planning, organizing, acquiring, or monitoring these resources?

_____

_____

• What is the jobholder's impact in planning, organizing, acquiring, or monitoring these resources?

_____

_____

6. Skills of persuasion
• Describe the communication skills required in the job (e.g., explaining, convincing, and selling).
• Are contacts inside or outside?
• What are the levels of contacts?
• What type of oral or written communications are involved?
• Who is communicated with and why?

_____

_____

_____

_____

_____

_____

7. Working conditions
Read the list of working conditions below and put a check mark if they impact on your job.

Condition	Amount of Exposure		
	Occasional	Regular	Frequent
Dust, dirt, fumes	_____	_____	_____
Heat, cold	_____	_____	_____
Noise	_____	_____	_____
Vibration	_____	_____	_____
Inclement weather	_____	_____	_____
Lighting	_____	_____	_____

Describe any health or safety hazards related to the job.

_____

_____

_____

Source: T.J. Hackett, E.G. Vogeley, S. Weeks, P. Drouillard, and D.E. Tyson, "Job Analysis and Job Descriptions," in D.E. Tyson, ed., *Carswell's Compensation Guide.* Toronto: Carswell, 2002, pp. 21–23. Reprinted by permission of Thomson Carswell, a division of Thomson Canada Limited.

3. A structured guide or checklist that lists questions and provides spaces for answers should be used. Using a form ensures that crucial questions are identified ahead of time, that complete and accurate information is gathered, and that all interviewers (if there is more than one) glean the same types of data, thereby helping to ensure comparability of results. However, leeway should also be permitted by including some open-ended questions, like "Was there anything that we didn't cover with our questions?"

4. When duties are not performed in a regular manner—for instance, when the incumbent doesn't perform the same tasks or jobs over and over again many times a day—the incumbent should be asked to list his or her duties *in order of importance* and *frequency of occurrence*. This will ensure that crucial activities that occur infrequently—like a nurse's occasional emergency room duties—aren't overlooked.

5. The data should be reviewed and verified by both the interviewee and his or her immediate supervisor.

Questionnaires

Having employees fill out questionnaires to describe their job-related duties and responsibilities is another good method of obtaining job analysis information. The major decision involved is determining how structured the questionnaire should be and what questions to include. Some questionnaires involve structured checklists. Each employee is presented with a long list of specific duties or tasks (such as "change and splice wire") and is asked to indicate whether or not he or she performs each and, if so, how much time is normally spent on it. At the other extreme, the questionnaire can be open-ended and simply ask the employee to describe the major duties of his or her job. In practice, a typical job analysis questionnaire often falls between the two extremes.

Observation

Direct observation is especially useful when jobs consist mainly of observable physical activities. Jobs like those of janitor, assembly-line worker, and accounting clerk are examples. Conversely, observation is usually not appropriate when the job entails a lot of immeasurable mental activity (lawyer, design engineer). Nor is it useful if the employee engages in important activities that might occur only occasionally, such as compiling year-end reports. Direct observation and interviewing are often used together.

Participant Diary/Log

diary/log   Daily listings made by employees of every activity in which they engage, along with the time each activity takes.

Another technique involves asking employees to keep a **diary/log** or list of what they do during the day. Each employee records every activity in which he or she is involved (along with the time spent) in a log. This can produce a very complete picture of the job, especially when supplemented with subsequent interviews with the employee and his or her supervisor. The employee might, of course, try to exaggerate some activities and underplay others. However, the detailed, chronological nature of the log tends to minimize this problem.

Advantages and Disadvantages of Qualitative Methods

Interviews, questionnaires, observation, and participant diaries are all qualitative in nature. They are the most popular methods for gathering job analysis data, and they provide realistic information about what job incumbents actually do and the qualifications and skills required. Associated with each are certain advantages and disadvantages, as summarized in **Table 4.1**. By combining two or more qualitative techniques, some of the disadvantages can be overcome.

TABLE 4.1   A Summary of Conventional Data Collection Methods for Job Analysis and the Advantages/Disadvantages of Each

Method	Variations	Brief Description	Advantages	Disadvantages
Observation	Structured	• Watch people go about their work; record frequency of behaviours or nature of performance on forms prepared in advance	• Third-party observer has more credibility than job incumbents, who may have reasons for distorting information • Focuses more on reality than on perceptions	• Observation can influence behaviour of job incumbents • Meaningless for jobs requiring mental effort (in that case, use information processing method) • Not useful for jobs with a long job cycle
	Unstructured	• Watch people go about their work; describe behaviours/tasks performed		
	Combination	• Part of the form is prepared in advance and is structured; part is unstructured		
Questionnaire	Structured	• Ask job incumbents/supervisors about work performed using fixed responses	• Relatively inexpensive • Structured questionnaires lend themselves easily to computer analyses • Good method when employees are widely scattered or when data must be collected from a large number of employees	• Developing and testing a questionnaire can be time-consuming and costly • Depends on communication skills of respondents • Does not allow for probing • Tends to focus on perceptions of the job
	Unstructured	• Ask job incumbents/supervisors to write essays to describe work performed		
	Combination	• Part of the questionnaire is structured; part is unstructured		
Diary/Log	Structured	• Ask people to record their activities over several days or weeks in a booklet with time increments provided	• Highly detailed information can be collected over the entire job cycle • Quite appropriate for jobs with a long job cycle	• Requires the job incumbent's participation and cooperation • Tends to focus on perceptions of the job
	Unstructured	• Ask people to indicate in a booklet over how long a period they worked on a task or activity		
	Combination	• Part of the diary is structured; part is unstructured		
Individual Interview	Structured	• Read questions and/or fixed response choices to job incumbent and supervisor; must be face to face	• Provides an opportunity to explain the need for and functions of job analysis • Relatively quick and simple way to collect data • More flexible than surveys • Allows for probing to extract information and provides the interviewee with an opportunity to express views and/or vent frustrations that might otherwise go unnoticed • Activities and behaviours may be reported that would be missed during observation	• Depends heavily on rapport between interviewer and respondent • May suffer from validity/reliability problems • Information may be distorted due to outright falsification or honest misunderstanding
	Unstructured	• Ask questions and/or provide general response choices to job incumbent and supervisor; must be face to face		
	Combination	• Part of the interview is structured; part is unstructured		

continued

Group Interview	Structured	• Same as structured individual interviews except that more than one job incumbent/ supervisor is interviewed	• Groups tend to do better than individuals with open-ended problem solving • Reliability/validity are likely to be higher than with individuals because group members cross check each other	• Cost more because more people are taken away from their jobs to participate • Like individual interviews, tends to focus on perceptions of the job
	Unstructured	• Same as unstructured individual interviews except that more than one job incumbent/supervisor is interviewed		
	Combination	• Same as combination individual interview except more than one job incumbent/supervisor is interviewed		

Source: Adapted from William J. Rothwell and H.C. Kazanas, *Planning and Managing Human Resources: Strategic Planning for Personnel Management*, 2nd ed. Amherst, MA: Human Resources Development Press, 2003, pp. 66–68. Reprinted by permission of the publisher.

Quantitative Job Analysis Techniques

Although most employers use interviews, questionnaires, observations, and/or diaries/logs for collecting job analysis data, there are many times when these narrative approaches are not appropriate. For example, when the aim is to assign a quantitative value to each job so that jobs can be compared for pay purposes, a more quantitative job analysis approach may be best. The position analysis questionnaire and functional job analysis are two popular quantitative methods.

Position Analysis Questionnaire

position analysis questionnaire (PAQ) A questionnaire used to collect quantifiable data concerning the duties and responsibilities of various jobs.

PAQ Services Inc.
www.paq.com

The **position analysis questionnaire (PAQ)** is a very structured job analysis questionnaire, a portion of which is shown in **Figure 4.7**.[13] The PAQ itself is filled in by a job analyst, who should already be acquainted with the particular job to be analyzed. The PAQ contains 194 items, each of which represents a basic element that may or may not play an important role in the job. The job analyst decides whether each item plays a role on the job and, if so, to what extent. If, for example, "written materials" received a rating of four, this would indicate that such materials as books, reports, and office notes play a considerable role in this job.

The advantage of the PAQ is that it provides a quantitative score or profile of the job in terms of how that job rates on six basic dimensions: (1) information input, (2) mental processes, (3) work output (physical activities and tools), (4) relationships with others, (5) job context (the physical and social environment, and (6) other job characteristics (such as pace and structure). Because it allows for the assignment of a quantitative score to each job, based on these six dimensions, the PAQ's real strength is in classifying jobs. Results can be used to compare jobs with one another; this information can then be used to determine appropriate pay levels.[14]

Functional Job Analysis

functional job analysis (FJA) A quantitative method for classifying jobs based on types and amounts of responsibility for data, people, and things. Performance standards and training requirements are also identified.

Functional job analysis (FJA) rates the job on responsibilities for data, people, and things from simple to complex. This technique also identifies performance

FIGURE 4.7   Position Analysis Questionnaire (Excerpt)

A1. Visual Sources of Job Information

Using the response scale at the left, rate each of the following items on the basis of the extent to which it is used by the worker as a source of information in performing the job.

1. Written materials
E.g., books, reports, office notes, articles, job instructions, or signs

2 Quantitative materials
Materials that deal with quantities or amounts, e.g., graphs, accounts, specifications, or tables of numbers

3. Pictorial materials
Pictures or picturelike materials used as sources of information, e.g., drawings, blueprints, diagrams, maps, tracings, photographic films, x-ray films, or TV pictures

4. Patterns or related devices
E.g., templates, stencils, or patterns used as sources of information when observed during use (Do not include materials described in item 3.)

5. Visual displays
E.g., dials, gauges, signal lights, radarscopes, speedometers, or clocks

6. Measuring devices
E.g., rules, calipers, tire pressure gauges, scales, thickness gauges, pipettes, thermometers, or protractors used to obtain visual information about physical measurements (Do not include devices described in item 5.)

7. Mechanical devices
E.g., tools, equipment, or machinery that are sources of information when observed during use or operation

8. Materials in process
E.g., parts, materials, or objects which are sources of information when being modified, worked on, or otherwise processed, such as bread dough being mixed, a workpiece being turned in a lathe, fabric being cut, or a shoe being resoled

9. Materials not in process
E.g., parts, materials, or objects not in the process of being changed or modified, which are sources of information when being inspected, handled, packaged, distributed, or selected, such as items or materials in inventory, storage, or distribution channels, or items being inspected

10. Features of nature
E.g., landscapes, fields, geological samples, vegetation, cloud formations, and other natural features that are observed or inspected to provide information

11. Constructed features of environment
E.g., structures, buildings, dams, highways, bridges, docks, railroads, and other "constructed" or altered aspects of the indoor or outdoor environment which are observed or inspected to provide job information (Do not consider equipment, machines, etc., that individuals use in their work, as covered by item 7.)

12. Behaviour
Observing the actions of people or animals, e.g., in teaching, supervising, or sports officiating, where the behaviour is a source of job information

13. Events or circumstances
Events the worker observed and may participate in, such as flow of traffic, movement of materials, or airport control tower operations

14. Art or décor
Artistic or decorative objects or arrangements used as *sources* of job information, e.g., paintings, sculpture, jewellery, window displays, or interior design

Note: The 194 PAQ elements are grouped into six dimensions. This exhibits 14 of the "information input" questions or elements. Other PAQ pages contain questions regarding mental processes, work output, relationships with others, job context, and other job characteristics.

Source: E.J. McCormick, P.R. Jeanneret, and R.D. Mecham, *Position Analysis Questionnaire.* West Lafayette, IN: Purdue Research Foundation, 1989. Copyright © 1989 by Purdue Research Foundation. Reprinted with permission.

standards and training requirements. Thus, FJA allows the analyst to answer the question: "To do this task and meet these standards, what training does the worker require?"[15]

The *National Occupational Classification*

National Occupational Classification (NOC) A reference tool for writing job descriptions and job specifications. Compiled by the federal government, it contains comprehensive, standardized descriptions of about 30 000 occupations and the requirements for each.

occupation A collection of jobs that share some or all of a set of main duties.

The *National Occupational Classification* (**NOC**), the product of systematic, field-based research by Human Resources and Social Development Canada (HRSDC), is an excellent source of standardized job information. It was updated and revised in 2001 and contains comprehensive descriptions of approximately 30 000 occupations and the requirements for each. To illustrate the types of information included, the *NOC* listing for Specialists in Human Resources is shown in **Figure 4.8.**

The *NOC* and its counselling component, the *Career Handbook* (2nd ed.), both focus on occupations rather than jobs. An **occupation** is defined as a collection of jobs that share some or all of a set of main duties. The list of examples of job titles within each of the 520 Unit Groups in the *NOC* provides a frame of reference for the boundaries of that occupational group. The jobs within each group are characterized by similar skills.

To provide a complete representation of work in the Canadian economy, the *NOC* classifies occupations in Major Groups based on two key dimensions—skill level and skill type. The Major Groups, which are identified by two-digit numbers, are then broken down further into Minor Groups, with a third digit added, and Unit Groups, at which level a fourth digit is added. Within these three levels of classification, a Unit Group provides the actual profile of an occupation.[16] For example,

- Major Group 31—Professional Occupations in Health
- Minor Group 311—Physicians, Dentists, and Veterinarians
- Unit Group 3113—Dentists

WRITING JOB DESCRIPTIONS AND JOB SPECIFICATIONS

Job Descriptions

A job description is a written statement of *what* the jobholder actually does, *how* he or she does it, and *under what conditions* the job is performed. The description in **Figure 4.9**—in this case for a Vice-President, Human Resources, Asia-Pacific Region—provides an example. As can be seen, the description is quite comprehensive and includes such essential elements as job identification, summary, and duties and responsibilities, as well as the human qualifications for the job.

No standard format is used in writing job descriptions, but most include the following types of information: job identification, job summary, relationships, duties and responsibilities, authority of incumbent, performance standards, and working conditions. As mentioned previously, job specifications (human qualifications) may also be included, as is the case in Figure 4.9.

Job Identification

As in Figure 4.9, the job identification section generally contains several types of information. The *position title* specifies the title of the job, such as vice-president, marketing manager, recruiter, or inventory control clerk. The *department* and *location* are also indicated, along with the title of the immediate supervisor—in

FIGURE 4.8   *NOC* Job Description for Specialists in Human Resources

Specialists in Human Resources develop, implement, and evaluate human resources and labour relations policies, programs, and procedures and advise managers and employees on personnel matters. Specialists in Human Resources are employed throughout the private and public sectors, or may be self-employed.

Examples of titles classified in this unit group

Business Agent, Labour Organization
Classification Officer
Classification Specialist
Compensation Research Analyst
Conciliator
Consultant, Human Resources
Employee Relations Officer
Employment Equity Officer
Human Resources Research Officer
Job Analyst
Labour Relations Officer
Mediator
Union Representative
Wage Analyst

Main duties

Specialists in Human Resources perform some or all of the following duties:

- Plan, develop, implement, and evaluate personnel and labour relations policies, programs, and procedures to address an organization's human resource requirements
- Advise managers and employees on the interpretation of personnel policies, compensation and benefit programs, and collective agreements
- Negotiate collective agreements on behalf of employers or workers, mediate labour disputes and grievances and provide advice on employee and labour relations
- Research and prepare occupational classifications, job descriptions, salary scales, and competency appraisal measures and systems
- Plan and administer staffing, total compensation, training and career development, employee assistance, employment equity and affirmative action programs
- Manage programs and maintain human resources information and related records systems
- Hire and oversee training of staff
- Coordinate employee performance and appraisal programs
- Research employee benefit and health and safety practices and recommend changes or modifications to existing policies

Employment requirements

- A university degree or college diploma in a field related to personnel management, such as business administration, industrial relations, commerce, or psychology
  or
  Completion of a professional development program in personnel administration is required.
- Some experience in a clerical or administrative position related to personnel administration may be required.

Additional information

- Progression to management positions is possible with experience.

Classified elsewhere

- *Human Resources Managers* (0112)
- *Personnel and Recruitment Officers* (1223)
- *Personnel Clerks* (1442)
- *Professional Occupations in Business Services to Management* (1122)
- Training officers and instructors (in 4131 *College and Other Vocational Instructors*)

Source: Adapted from Human Resources and Social Development Canada, *National Occupational Classification, 2001.* Reproduced with the permission of Her Majesty the Queen in Right of Canada 2006.

FIGURE 4.9 Sample Job Description

Sample Job Description

Position:	Vice-President, Human Resources, Asia-Pacific
Location:	Hong Kong
Division:	Asia-Pacific
Incumbent:	Y. Tanaka
Department:	Human Resources
Job code:	CAP-HRM-001
Reports to:	President Asia-Pacific (administrative), Vice-President, Human Resources—Corporate (functional)
Written by:	Monica Lim, Job Analyst
Date:	2 April 2007
Approved by:	J.A. Wong, President, Asia-Pacific (administrative superior) W.J. Smith, Vice-President, Human Resources—Corporate (functional superior)

Job Summary

Under the administrative direction of the President, Asia-Pacific, and the functional guidance of the Vice-President, Human Resources—Corporate, develop, recommend and implement approved HRM strategies, policies and practices that will facilitate the achievement of the company's stated business and HRM objectives.

Duties and Responsibilities

- Develop and recommend HRM strategies, policies and practices that promote employee commitment, competence, motivation and performance, and that facilitate the achievement of the Asia-Pacific region's business objectives.
- Provide policy guidance to senior management regarding the acquisition, development, reward, maintenance and existence of the division's human resources so as to promote the status of the company as an ethical and preferred employer of choice.
- Identify, analyze and interpret for Asia-Pacific regional senior management and corporate HR management those influences and changes in the division's internal and external environment and their impact on HRM and divisional business objectives, strategies, policies and practices.

Relationships

Internally, relate with senior line and functional managers within the Asia-Pacific region and corporate headquarters in New York. Externally, successfully relate with senior academic, business, government and trade union personnel. Directly supervise the following positions: Manager, Compensation and Benefits, Asia-Pacific and Manager, Training and Development, Asia-Pacific. Functionally supervise the HR managers in 13 geographic locations within the Asia-Pacific region.

Know-How

University degree is required, along with seven to 10 years broad-based HRM experience in a competitive and international (preferably Asian) business environment. A proven track record in managing change is essential. Fluency in English is essential and fluency in Chinese or Japanese is desirable. Excellent human relations and communication skills are essential. Previous experience in marketing, finance or manufacturing is desirable. The ability to positively represent the company at the most senior levels and to actively contribute as a Director of the Asia-Pacific regional Board is essential.

Problem Solving

Diverse cultures and varying stages of economic development within the Asia-Pacific region create a unique and tough business environment. The incumbent will often face complex HR and business problems demanding solutions that need to be creative and, at the same time, sensitive to local and company requirements.

continued

Authority

This position has the authority to:

- approve expenditures on budgeted capital items up to a total value of $100 000 in any one financial year
- hire and fire subordinate personnel in accord with company policies and procedures
- approve expense accounts for subordinate personnel in accord with company policies and procedures
- authorize all non-capital item expenditures within approved budgetary limit
- exercise line authority over all direct reporting positions

Accountability

Employees: 3000. Sales: $4 billion. Direct budget responsibility: $2.7 million. Assets controlled: $780 000. Locations: Australia, China, Hong Kong, India, Indonesia, Japan, South Korea, Malaysia, New Zealand, the Philippines, Singapore, Taiwan, Thailand.

Special Circumstances

Successful performance requires the incumbent to work long hours, to travel extensively (50–60 percent of the time), to quickly adapt to different cultures and business conditions, to successfully handle high-stress situations and to constantly work under pressure in a complex and very competitive business environment.

Performance Indicators

Performance indicators will include both quantitative and qualitative measures as agreed by the President, Asia-Pacific Division, and Vice-President, Human Resources—Corporate and the incumbent. Indicators may be market based (e.g., share price improvement), business based (e.g., division profitability, budget control, days lost through industrial unrest, positive changes in employee commitment, job satisfaction and motivation) and individual based (e.g., performance as a leader and manager as assessed by superiors, peers and subordinates). Performance expectations and performance indicators generally will be defined on an annual basis. A formal performance appraisal will be conducted at least once a year.

Source: R.J. Stone, *Human Resource Management*, 4th ed. Milton, Queensland: John Wiley & Sons, 2002, pp. 131–132. Reprinted with permission of the author.

this case under the heading *reports to*. The *date* refers to the date the job description was actually written, and *written by* identifies the person who wrote it. There is also an indication of whom the description was *approved by*. Many job descriptions also include a *job code,* which permits easy referencing.

Job Summary

The *job summary* should describe the general nature of the job, listing only its major functions or activities. Thus (as in Figure 4.9), the Vice-President, Human Resources, Asia-Pacific will "develop, recommend and implement approved HRM strategies, policies and practices that will facilitate the achievement of the company's stated business and HRM objectives." For the job of materials manager, the summary might state that he or she will "purchase economically, regulate deliveries of, store, and distribute all material necessary on the production line," while that for a mailroom supervisor might indicate that he or she will "receive, sort, and deliver all incoming mail properly, and he or she will handle all outgoing mail, including the accurate and timely posting of such mail."[17]

Relationships

The *relationships* section indicates the jobholder's relationships with others inside and outside the organization, as shown in Figure 4.9. Others directly and indirectly supervised are included, along with peers, superiors, and outsiders relevant to the job.

Duties and Responsibilities

This section presents a detailed list of the job's major duties and responsibilities. As in Figure 4.9, each of the job's major duties should be listed separately and described in a few sentences. In the figure, for instance, the duties of the Vice-President, Human Resources, Asia-Pacific include developing and recommending HRM strategies, policies, and practices; providing policy guidance; and identifying, analyzing, and interpreting internal and external environmental changes. Typical duties of other jobs might include maintaining balanced and controlled inventories, making accurate postings to accounts payable, maintaining favourable purchase price variances, and repairing production line tools and equipment.

Most experts state unequivocally that "one item frequently found that should *never* be included in a job description is a 'cop-out clause' like 'other duties, as assigned.'" This phrase leaves open the nature of the job and the people needed to staff it, and it can be subject to abuse.[18]

Authority

This section of a job description should define the limits of the jobholder's authority, including his or her decision-making authority, direct supervision of other employees, and budgetary limitations. For example, the Vice-President, Human Resources, Asia-Pacific (in Figure 4.9) has the authority to approve all budgeted noncapital expenditures and budgeted capital expenditures up to $100 000; approve expense accounts for subordinates; hire and fire subordinates, and exercise line authority over direct reporting positions.

Performance Standards/Indicators

Some job descriptions also contain a performance standards/indicators section, which indicates the standards the employee is expected to achieve in each of the job description's main duties and responsibilities.

Setting standards is never easy. Most managers soon learn, however, that just telling employees to "do their best" doesn't provide enough guidance to ensure top performance. One straightforward way of setting standards is to finish the statement: "I will be completely satisfied with your work when . . . " This sentence, if completed for each duty listed in the job description, should result in a usable set of performance standards.[19] Some examples would include the following:

Duty: *Accurately Posting Accounts Payable*

- All invoices received are posted within the same working day.
- All invoices are routed to the proper department managers for approval no later than the day following receipt.
- No more than three posting errors per month occur on average.
- The posting ledger is balanced by the end of the third working day of each month.

Duty: *Meeting Daily Production Schedule*

- Work group produces no fewer than 426 units per working day.
- No more than 2 percent of units are rejected at the next workstation, on average.
- Work is completed with no more than 5 percent overtime per week, on average.

Working Conditions and Physical Environment

The job description should also list the general working conditions involved in the job. This section generally includes information about noise level, temperature, lighting, degree of privacy, frequency of interruptions, hours of work, amount of travel, and hazards to which the incumbent may be exposed.

Special guidelines for entrepreneurial and small businesses are provided in the Entrepreneurs and HR box.

Job Descriptions and Human Rights Legislation

Human rights legislation requires employers to ensure that there is no discrimination on any of the prohibited grounds in any aspect of terms and conditions of employment. To ensure that job descriptions comply with this legislation, a few key points should be kept in mind:

Hints to Ensure Legal Compliance

- Job descriptions are not legally required but are highly advisable.
- Essential job duties should be clearly identified in the job description. Indicating the percentage of time spent on each duty and/or listing duties in order of importance are strategies used to differentiate between essential and nonessential tasks and responsibilities.

Entrepreneurs and HR

A Practical Approach to Job Analysis and Job Descriptions

Without their own job analysts or even their own HR managers, many small-business owners need a more streamlined approach to job analysis. A resource that includes all of the possible positions that they might encounter, with a detailed listing of the duties normally assigned to these positions, exists in the *National Occupational Classification* (*NOC*) mentioned earlier. The practical approach to job analysis for small-business owners presented next is built around this invaluable reference tool.

Step 1: Develop an Organization Chart.

Drawing up the organization chart of the present structure comes first. Then, depending on how far in advance planning is being done, a chart can be produced that shows how the organization should look in the immediate future (say, in two months), as well as two or three other charts showing how the organization is likely to evolve over the next two or three years.

Step 2: Use a Job Analysis Questionnaire.

Next, a job analysis questionnaire can be used to determine what each job entails. A shorter version of one of the more comprehensive job analysis questionnaires, such as that in Figure 4.6 (page 91), may be useful for collecting job analysis data. An example of a job summary for a customer service clerk is as follows:

Answers inquiries and gives directions to customers, authorizes cashing of customers' cheques, records and returns lost credit cards, sorts and reviews new credit applications, and works at the customer service desk.

Step 3: Obtain a Copy of the *National Occupational Classification* (*NOC*) for Reference.

Next, standardized examples of the job descriptions needed should be obtained from the *NOC*. A copy can be found in the reference section of the library in most major centres or purchased through a federal government bookstore or online at http://publications.gc.ca. An online service is also offered at www23.hrdc-drhc. gc.ca/2001/e/generic/welcome.shtml.

Step 4: Choose Appropriate Definitions and Copy Them for Reference.

For each department, the *NOC* job titles and job descriptions that are believed to be appropriate should be chosen. The *NOC* definition will provide a firm foundation for the job description being created. It will provide a standardized list and constant reminder of the specific duties that should be included.

Step 5: Complete the Job Description.

An appropriate job summary for the job under consideration can then be written. The job analysis information, together with the information from the *NOC*, can be used to create a complete listing of the tasks and duties of each of the jobs. The working conditions section can be completed once all of the tasks and duties have been specified.

- When assessing suitability for employment, training program enrollment, and transfers or promotions, and when appraising performance, the only criteria examined should be KSAs required for the essential duties of the job.

- When an employee cannot perform one or more of the essential duties because of reasons related to a prohibited ground, such as a physical disability or religion, reasonable accommodation to the point of undue hardship is required.

Job Specifications

Writing the job specification involves examining the duties and responsibilities and answering the question: "What human traits and experience are required to do this job?" Much of this information can be obtained from the job analysis questionnaire. The job specification clarifies what kind of person to recruit and for which qualities that person should be tested. It is sometimes included with the job description.

Complying with human rights legislation means keeping a few pointers in mind:

Hints to Ensure Legal Compliance

physical demands analysis
Identification of the senses used and the type, frequency, and amount of physical effort involved in the job.

- All listed qualifications are bona fide occupational requirements, based on the current job duties and responsibilities.

- Unjustifiably high educational and/or lengthy experience requirements can lead to systemic discrimination.

- The qualifications of the current incumbent should not be confused with the minimum requirements, since he or she might be underqualified or overqualified.

- For entry-level jobs, identifying the actual physical and mental demands is critical. For example, if the job requires detailed manipulation on a circuit-board assembly line, finger dexterity is extremely important and is something for which candidates should be tested. A **physical demands analysis**—which

The job specifications for the call centre operators shown here should clearly indicate which skills, like computer literacy, are job requirements.

identifies the senses used and the type, frequency, and amount of physical effort involved in the job—is often used to supplement the job specification. A sample form is included as **Figure 4.10**. Having such detailed information is particularly beneficial when determining accommodation requirements. The mental and emotional demands of a job are typically missing from job analysis information. They should be specified so that the mental and emotional competencies of job applicants can be assessed and any need for accommodation can be identified.

- Identifying the human requirements for a job can be accomplished through a judgmental approach (based on educated guesses of job incumbents, supervisors, and HR managers) or statistical analysis (based on the relationship between some human trait of skill and some criterion of job effectiveness). Basing job specifications on statistical analysis is more legally defensible.

Personality-Related Job Requirements

The Personality-Related Position Requirements Form (PPRF) is a survey instrument designed to assist managers in identifying potential personality-related traits that may be important in a job. Identifying personality dimensions is difficult when using most job analysis techniques, because they tend to be much better suited to unearthing human aptitudes and skills—like manual dexterity. The PPRF uses questionnaire items to assess the relevance of such basic personality dimensions as agreeableness, conscientiousness, and emotional stability to the job under study. The relevance of these personality traits can then be assessed through statistical analysis.[20]

Completing the Job Specification Form

Once the required human characteristics have been determined, whether using statistical analysis or a judgmental approach, a job specification form should be completed. To illustrate the types of information and amount of detail that should be provided in a well-written job specification, a sample has been included as **Figure 4.11**.

JOB ANALYSIS IN THE 21st CENTURY

The traditional meaning of a "job" as a set of well-defined and clearly delineated responsibilities is changing. Many employees are increasingly expected to adapt to organizational changes, such as reduced hierarchical structure, blurred boundaries, work being done in teams, more focus on organizational goals than on rules, and continual change. In organizations that use self-managed work teams, employees' jobs change daily and the boundaries that typically separate organizational functions (like sales and production) and hierarchical levels are reduced and made more permeable. The focus is on defining the job at hand in terms of the overall best interests of the organization, as is the case at IKEA, described in the Strategic HR box on page 107.

In boundaryless organization structures, relationships are formed with customers, suppliers, and/or competitors to pool resources for mutual benefit in an uncertain environment. Wal-Mart and a major supplier, Procter & Gamble, collaborate by sharing their sales forecasts through a secure Web site. In this way, they are able to best meet consumer needs and to enhance the performance of both companies.[21] Many e-businesses use boundaryless structures because

FIGURE 4.10 Physical Demands Analysis

Division:		Job Title:
Job Code:		Level:
Date:		Date of Last Revision:

Physical Requirements
Review the chart below. Indicate which of the following are essential to perform the functions of this job, with or without accommodation. Check one box in each section.

Section I					Section 2		Section 3			Section 4		
Incumbent Uses:	NA	Right	Left	Both	Repetitive motion		The job requires the use of the first category up to 2 hours per day	The job requires the use of the first category up to 4 hours per day	The job requires the use of the first category up to 8 hours per day	Frequent breaks: Normal breaks plus those caused by performing jobs outside of the area.	Limited breaks: Two short breaks and one lunch break.
					Y	N						
Hands: (requires manual manipulation)												
Feet: (functions requiring foot pedals and the like)												

Lifting capacity: Indicate, by checking the appropriate box, the amount of lifting necessary for this job, with or without accommodation.

	NA	Occasionally (As Needed)	Often (Up to 4 Hours Per Day)	Frequently (Up to 8 Hours Per Day)
5 kg				
5–10 kg				
10–25 kg				
25–50 kg				
50+ kg				

Mobility: Indicate which category the job functions fall under by placing a check next to those that apply.
☐ Sits constantly (6 hours or more with two breaks and one lunch break)
☐ Sits intermittently (6 hours or more with frequent change, due to breaks and getting up to perform jobs outside of the area)
☐ Stands intermittently (6 hours or more with frequent changes, due to breaks and getting up to perform jobs outside of the area)
☐ Bending constantly (4 hours or more with two breaks and one lunch break)
☐ Bending intermittently (4 hours or more with frequent changes, due to breaks and getting up to perform jobs outside of the area)
☐ Walks constantly (6 hours or more with two breaks and one lunch break)
☐ Walks intermittently (6 hours or more with frequent changes, due to breaks and getting up to perform jobs outside of the area)

continued

Visual acuity: Indicate the minimum acceptable level, with or without accommodation, necessary for the job
☐ Excellent visual acuity
☐ Good visual acuity
☐ Not relevant to the job

Auditory acuity: Indicate the minimum acceptable level, with or without accommodation, necessary for the job.
☐ Excellent auditory acuity
☐ Good auditory acuity
☐ Not relevant to the job

Source: M. Rock and D.R. Berger, eds., *The Compensation Handbook: A State-of-the-Art Guide to Compensation Strategy and Design*, 4th ed. Columbus, OH: McGraw-Hill, 2000, pp. 69–70 © 2000 The McGraw-Hill Companies, Inc.

speed, agility, and innovation are the drivers of success, and narrowly defined, rigid, and inflexible jobs are not useful. Employees have complex job roles, with a broad range of responsibilities, and will often work in autonomous teams. This trend is already evident in such jobs as project manager and internal consultant, where roles are broadly defined, encompass a wide array of responsibilities, and are based on empowerment of individuals and teams.[22]

FIGURE 4.11   Job Specification

Job Title: Lifeguard   **Location:** Lethbridge Community Pool
Job Code: LG1   **Supervisor:** Head Lifeguard
Department: Recreation   **Division:** Parks and Recreation
Date: May 1, 2007

Job Summary
The incumbent is required to safeguard the health of pool users by patrolling the pool, rescuing swimmers in difficulty, treating injuries, advising pool users of safety rules, and enforcing safety rules.

Skill
Formal Qualifications: Royal Life Saving Society Bronze Medallion or equivalent
Experience: No prior experience required but would be an asset.
Communication Skills: Good oral communication skills are required. Proficiency in one or more foreign languages would be an asset. The incumbent must be able to communicate courteously and effectively. Strong interpersonal skills are required. All interaction with the public must be handled with tact and diplomacy.

Effort
Physical Effort: The incumbent is required to stand during the majority of working hours. In the event of an emergency where a swimmer is in distress, the incumbent must initiate rescue procedures immediately, which may involve strenuous physical exertion.
Mental Effort: Continuous mental attention to pool users. Must remain vigilant despite many simultaneous demands on his or her attention.
Emotional Effort: Enforcement of safety rules and water rescue can be stressful. Must maintain a professional demeanour when dealing with serious injuries or death.

Working Conditions
Job is performed in humid indoor environment, temperature-controlled. No privacy. Shift work to cover pool hours from 7 A.M. to 11 P.M., seven days a week. Some overtime and split shifts may be required.

Approval Signatures
Incumbent: _____
Supervisor: _____   Date: _____

Strategic HR

IKEA Canada

IKEA Canada doesn't just want to fill jobs; they want to partner with people. They recruit unique individuals who share IKEA's core values of togetherness, cost consciousness, respect, and simplicity. They want to give down-to-earth, straightforward people the possibility to grow, both as individuals and in their professional roles, so that together they are strongly committed to creating a better everyday life for themselves and their customers.

It is important for IKEA coworkers to have a strong desire to learn and the motivation to continually do things better, because the IKEA way of working is less structured than that of many other organizations. IKEA provides a free and open work environment, balanced with expectations that coworkers assume responsibility for their own actions.

IKEA Canada employee Mike, Commercial Activities Manager, says that at his job interview, "they were more interested to know what I wanted to achieve in life rather than what I had already done in life: this really hit home fore me. After having worked in a factory previously . . . I suddenly found myself in a job where people would listen to what I was saying; they valued my judgment no matter what their position within IKEA. I found this very motivating." Mike says that overall "It's the open flow of ideas, the appreciation of individual opinions, and the recognition of those who work hard that I really cherish about IKEA."

Source: Excerpted and adapted from the Ikea Canada websites www.ikea.com/ms/en_CA/jobs/join_us/index.html and www.ikea.com/ms/en_CA/jobs/true_stories/mike/index.html (June 15, 2006). Used with permission of IKEA CANADA.

An Ethical Dilemma

In view of the fact that job descriptions are not required by law and that some organizations have found them no longer relevant, would abolishing job descriptions raise any moral or legal concerns?

All these changes have led work to become more cognitively complex, more team-based and collaborative, more dependent on social skills, more dependent on technological competence, more time pressured, more mobile, and less dependent on geography.[23] This situation has led some organizations to focus on personal competencies and skills in job analysis, hiring, and compensation management, rather than on specific duties and tasks.

The Future of Job Descriptions

Most firms today continue to use job descriptions and to rely on jobs as traditionally defined. However, it is clear that more and more firms are moving toward new organizational structures built around jobs that are broad and that may change every day. As one writer has said, "In such a situation, people no longer take their cues from a job description or a supervisor's instructions. Signals come from the changing demands of the project. Workers learn to focus their individual efforts and collective resources on the work that needs doing, changing as that changes."[24]

Chapter Review

Summary

1. In any organization, work has to be divided into manageable units and ultimately into jobs that can be performed by employees. The process of organizing work into tasks that are required to perform a specific job is known as job design. The term *job* means a group of tasks and duties, and several employees may have the same job. The collection of tasks and responsibilities performed by one person is known as a *position*.

2. Industrial engineering is concerned with analyzing work methods; making work cycles more efficient by modifying, combining, rearranging, or eliminating tasks; and establishing time standards. Behavioural scientists focus on identifying various job dimensions that would simultaneously improve the efficiency of organizations and job satisfaction of employees. Effective job design must also take physiological needs and health and safety issues into account.

Human engineering, or ergonomics, seeks to integrate and accommodate the physical needs of workers into the design of jobs.

3. Job analysis involves six steps: (1) determine the use to which the information will be put, (2) collect background information, (3) select the representative positions and jobs to be analyzed, (4) collect data, (5) review the information collected with the incumbents and their supervisors, and (6) develop the job descriptions and job specifications.

4. Four narrative techniques are used to gather job analysis data: interviews, questionnaires, direct observation, and participant logs. Quantitative job analysis techniques include the position analysis questionnaire (PAQ), functional job analysis (FJA), and the *National Occupational Classification* (NOC).

5. A job description is a written statement of what the jobholder actually does, how he or she does it, and under what conditions the job is performed. The job specification involves examining the duties and responsibilities and answering the question: "What human traits and experience are required to do this job?"

6. The concept of a "job" is changing because many employees are increasingly expected to adapt to organizational changes, such as reduced hierarchical structure, blurred boundaries, working in teams, more focus on organizational goals than rules, and continual change. Work has become more cognitively complex, more team-based and collaborative, more dependent on social skills, more dependent on technological competence, more time pressured, more mobile, and less dependent on geography. Employees therefore need to be flexible and responsive to changes in what they do and how they do it.

Key Terms

diary/log   *(p. 93)*
functional job analysis (FJA)   *(p. 95)*
human engineering (ergonomics)   *(p. 85)*
industrial engineering   *(p. 82)*
job   *(p. 82)*
job analysis   *(p. 87)*
job description   *(p. 87)*
job design   *(p. 82)*
job enlargement (horizontal loading)   *(p. 83)*
job enrichment (vertical loading)   *(p. 83)*
job rotation   *(p. 83)*
job specification   *(p. 87)*
National Occupational Classification (NOC)   *(p. 97)*
occupation   *(p. 97)*
organization chart   *(p. 80)*
organizational structure   *(p. 80)*
physical demands analysis   *(p. 103)*
position   *(p. 82)*
position analysis questionnaire (PAQ)   *(p. 95)*
process chart   *(p. 89)*
team   *(p. 85)*
team-based job design   *(p. 85)*
work simplification   *(p. 82)*

Review and Discussion Questions

1. Explain work simplification. In what situations is this approach to job design appropriate?

2. Differentiate among job enlargement, job rotation, and job enrichment, and provide an example of each.

3. What is involved in the human-engineering approach to job design? Why is it becoming increasingly important?

4. Several methods for collecting job analysis data are available—interviews, the position analysis questionnaire, and so on. Compare and contrast these methods, explaining what each is useful for and listing the pros and cons of each.

5. Although not legally required, having job descriptions is highly advisable. Why? How can firms ensure that their job specifications are legally defensible?

Critical Thinking Questions

1. Why isn't it always desirable or appropriate to use job enrichment or include the five core dimensions when designing jobs? How would you determine how enriched an individual employee's job should be?

2. Assume that you are the job analyst at a bicycle manufacturing company in British Columbia, and have been assigned responsibility for preparing job descriptions (including specifications) for all the supervisory and managerial positions. One of the production managers has just indicated that he will not complete the job analysis questionnaire you have developed. (a) How would you handle this situation?

(b) What arguments would you use to attempt to persuade him to change his mind? (c) If your persuasion efforts failed, how would you go about obtaining the job analysis information you need to develop the job description for his position?

3. Because the top job in a firm (such as president, executive director, or CEO) is by nature broader in scope than any other job, is there less need for a job description for the president? Why or why not?

4. Create guidelines for a "mental demands analysis" for service economy jobs that would parallel the traditional physical demands analysis.

Application Exercises

Running Case: LearnInMotion.com

Who Do We Have to Hire?

As the excitement surrounding the move into their new offices wound down, the two principal owners of LearnInMotion.com, Pierre and Jennifer, turned to the task of hiring new employees. In their business plan they'd specified several basic goals for the venture capital funds they'd just received, and hiring a team topped the list. They knew their other goals—boosting sales and expanding the Web site, for instance—would be unreachable without the right team.

They were just about to place their ads when Pierre asked a question that brought them to a stop: "What kind of people do we want to hire?" It seemed they hadn't really considered this. They knew the answer in general terms, of course. For example, they knew they needed at least two salespeople, a programmer, a Web designer, and several content management people to transform the incoming material into content they could post on their site. But it was obvious that job titles alone really didn't provide enough guidance. For example, if they couldn't specify the exact duties of these positions, how could they decide whether they needed experienced employees? How could they decide exactly what sorts of experiences and skills they had to look for in their candidates if they didn't know exactly

what these candidates would have to do? They wouldn't even know what questions to ask.

And that wasn't all. For example, there were obviously other tasks to do, and these weren't necessarily included in the sorts of things that salespeople, programmers, Web designers, or content management people typically do. Who was going to answer the phones? (Jennifer and Pierre had originally assumed they'd put in one of those fancy automated call directory and voice-mail systems—until they found out it would cost close to $10 000.) As a practical matter, they knew they had to have someone answering the phones and directing callers to the proper extension. Who was going to keep track of the monthly expenses and compile them for the accountants, who'd then produce monthly reports for the venture capitalist? Would the salespeople generate their own leads? Or would LearnInMotion.com have to hire Web surfers to search and find the names of people for the sales staff to call or e-mail? What would happen when the company had to purchase supplies, such as fax paper or computer disks? Would the owners have to do this themselves, or should they have someone in house do it for them? The list, it seemed, went on and on.

It was obvious, in other words, that the owners had to get their managerial act together and draw up the sorts of documents they'd read about as business majors—job descriptions, job specifications, and so forth. The trouble was, it had all seemed a lot easier when they read the textbook. Now they want you, their management consultant, to help them actually do it. Here's what they want you to do for them.

Questions

1. Draft a job description for the salesperson and for the Web designer. You may use whatever sources you want, but preferably search the Internet and relevant Web sites; you want job descriptions and lists of duties that apply specifically to dot-com firms.

2. Next, using sources similar to those in Question 1—and whatever other sources you can think of—draw up a job specification for these two jobs (salesperson and Web designer), including such things as desirable work habits, skills, education, and experience.

3. Next, keeping in mind that this company is on a tight budget, how should it accomplish the other activities it requires, such as answering the phones, compiling sales leads, producing monthly reports, and purchasing supplies?

Case Incident

TEAM FUN!

Tony has been director of human resources at TEAM FUN!, a sporting goods manufacturer and retailer, for three months. He is constantly amazed that the company does so well, considering that everything is so loose. Nothing is documented about job roles and responsibilities. People apparently have been hired because Kenny and Norton, the owners and founders, liked them or their relatives. Tony is lunching with Mary, a friend from college who now manages the human resource function for a large financial investor. Tony tells Mary, "I don't know if I should quit or what. They both got mad at me last week when I suggested smart cards for security. The employee handbook looks like a scrapbook from their kids' high school football days . . . no, *their* high school football days. No one has a job description. I don't get it. Everyone likes working there. The job gets done. Am I the one with the problem?"

Mary replies, "Couldn't be you! It does sound like a great place to work. Has it grown fast in the past few years?"

"Unbelievably," Tony says. "It had 25 employees five years ago, now we have nearly 150."

"That's probably part of it," Mary answers. "Remember how Dr. Smith said in his class that you could get by without a formal human resource structure up to about 100 employees?"

"Yeah. That was a great class. I met my wife in that class! We did lots of team exercises and projects," Tony sighs.

Mary nods. "Anyway, maybe you could start with writing your own job description. That would be a start."

"Then I could talk about the formal job analysis process." Tony cheers up. "That's a great idea."

Questions

1. Help Tony write his job description.
2. What techniques should he use to gather data?
3. How should he conduct the job analysis?
4. What should he say to Kenny and Norton to ensure their buy-in on this project?
5. How will job descriptions change the organization?

Source: D.A. DeCenzo and S.P. Robbins, *Fundamentals of Human Resource Management,* 8th ed. Hoboken NJ: John Wiley & Sons, 2005, pp. 141–142. Copyright © 2005 John Wiley & Sons. Reprinted with permission of John Wiley & Sons.

Experiential Exercises

1. Use organization chart software to draw an organization chart to accurately depict the structure of the organization in which you are currently employed or one with which you are thoroughly familiar. Once you have completed this task, form a group with several of your classmates. Taking turns, each member is to show his or her organization chart to the group, briefly describe the structure depicted, explain whether or not the structure seems to be appropriate to him or her, and identify several advantages and disadvantages he or she experienced working within this structure.

2. Working individually or in groups, obtain a copy of the *National Occupational Classification* and/or the *NOC Career Handbook* (2nd ed.) from your library or nearest HRSDC office. Find the descriptions for any two occupations with which you have some familiarity. Compare the Employment Requirements and/or the Profile Summaries. Based on what you know about these occupations, does the material provided seem accurate? Why or why not? What changes would you recommend, if any?

3. Working individually, prepare a job description (including job specifications) for a position that you know well, using the job analysis questionnaire in this chapter. Once you have done so, exchange job descriptions with someone else in the class. Critique your colleague's job description and provide specific suggestions regarding any additions/deletions/revisions that you would recommend to ensure that the job description accurately reflects the job and is legally defensible.

CHAPTER 5

HUMAN RESOURCES PLANNING

REQUIRED PROFESSIONAL CAPABILITIES

- Maintains an inventory of HR talent for the use of the organization

- Identifies potential sources of qualified candidates

- Identifies potential sources and the markets in which the organization competes for qualified candidates

LEARNING OUTCOMES

AFTER STUDYING THIS CHAPTER, YOU SHOULD BE ABLE TO

Define human resources planning (HRP), and **discuss** its strategic importance.

Describe four quantitative and two qualitative techniques used to forecast human resources demand.

Briefly **discuss** four strategies used to forecast internal human resources supply and four types of market conditions assessed when forecasting external human resources supply.

Describe the ways in which a surplus of human resources can be handled.

Explain how organizations deal with a shortage of human resources.

THE STRATEGIC IMPORTANCE OF HUMAN RESOURCES PLANNING

human resources planning (HRP)
The process of reviewing human resources requirements to ensure that the organization has the required number of employees, with the necessary skills, to meet its goals.

Human resources planning (HRP) is the process of reviewing human resources requirements to ensure that the organization has the required number of employees, with the necessary skills, to meet its goals. HRP is a proactive process, which both anticipates and influences an organization's future by systematically forecasting the demand for and supply of employees under changing conditions, and by developing plans and activities to satisfy these needs. Effective HRP helps an organization to achieve its strategic goals and objectives, achieve economies in hiring new workers, make major labour market demands more successfully, anticipate and avoid shortages and surpluses of human resources, and control and/or reduce labour costs.

As illustrated in **Figure 5.1**, key steps in the HRP process include forecasting demand for labour, analyzing the labour supply, and planning and implementing

FIGURE 5.1   Human Resources Planning Model

Step 1: Forecast Demand for Labour

Considerations
- Organizational strategic plans
- Organizational tactical plans
- Economic conditions
- Market and competitive trends
- Government and legislative issues
- Social concerns
- Technological changes
- Demographic trends

Techniques Utilized
- Trend analysis
- Ratio analysis
- Scatter plot
- Regression analysis
- Nominal group technique
- Delphi technique
- Managerial judgment
- Staffing tables

Step 2: Analyze Supply

Internal Analysis
- Markov analysis
- Skills inventories
- Management inventories
- Replacement charts and development tracking
- Replacement summaries
- Succession planning

External Analysis
- General economic conditions
- Labour market conditions (national and local)
- Occupational market conditions

Step 3: Implement Human Resources Programs to Balance Supply and Demand

Labour Shortage
- Overtime
- Hire temporary employees
- Subcontract work
- Recruitment
- Transfer
- Promotion

Labour Surplus
- Hiring freeze
- Attrition
- Buyouts and early retirement programs
- Job sharing
- Part-time work
- Work sharing
- Reduced workweek
- Alternative jobs within the organization
- Layoffs (reverse seniority or juniority)
- Supplemental unemployment benefits (SUBs)
- Termination
- Severance pay
- Outplacement assistance

FIGURE 5.2   Balancing Supply and Demand Considerations

Conditions and Possible Solutions

A. When labour demand exceeds labour supply
- Scheduling overtime hours
- Hiring temporary workers
- Subcontracting
- External recruitment
- Internal promotions and transfers
- *Performance management, training and retraining, and career development play a critical role.*

B. When labour supply exceeds labour demand
- Hiring freeze: reassigning current workers to job openings
- Attrition: standard employee resignation, retirement, or death
- Incentives to leave the organization: buyouts or early retirement programs
- Job sharing
- Reducing positions to part-time
- Work sharing and reduced workweek
- Finding employees alternative jobs within the organization
- Employee layoffs
- Termination of employment
- *Evaluating the effectiveness of layoffs and downsizing is critical, as is managing "survivor sickness."*

C. When labour demand equals labour supply
- Vacancies are filled internally through transfers or promotions, or externally by hiring new employees
- *Performance management, training, and career development are critical in achieving balance.*

An Ethical Dilemma

Is it ethical to hire and/or promote underqualified target group members simply to meet established employment equity goals and timetables?

HR programs to balance supply and demand. As illustrated in **Figure 5.2**, there are many alternative techniques to manage labour surpluses and labour shortages.

Lack of or inadequate human resources planning within an organization can result in significant costs when unstaffed positions create costly inefficiencies and when severance pay is required for large numbers of employees being laid off. It can also create situations in which one department is laying off employees while another is hiring individuals with similar skills, which can reduce morale and productivity and cause turnover. Perhaps most importantly, ineffective HRP can lead to the inability to accomplish short-term operational plans and/or long-range strategic plans.

The Relationship between HRP and Strategic Planning

Strategic plans are created and carried out by people. Thus, determining whether or not people will be available is a critical element of the strategic planning process. For example, plans to enter new businesses, build new plants, or reduce the level of activities all influence the number and types of positions to be filled. At the same time, decisions regarding how positions will be filled must be integrated with other aspects of the firm's HR plans, for instance, those pertaining to training current and new employees, appraising performance, and terminating, transferring, or promoting staff members.

In their HR planning, employers closely monitor trends, such as the availability of entry-level labour.

Although production, financial, and marketing plans have long been recognized as important cornerstones in the strategic planning process, more and more firms are realizing that HR plans are another essential component. It is becoming clear that HRP and strategic planning become effective when a reciprocal and interdependent relationship exists between them.[1]

Failure to integrate HRP and strategic planning can have very serious consequences. Despite the fact that the Canadian Nurses Association (CNA) warned governments in 1998 that an aging workforce and an inability to attract and retain nurses could leave the system short 113 000 nurses by 2011—a prediction now believed to be too low—it is clear that a long-term nationwide HR plan for nurses is still needed.[2] The shortage is having a direct impact on nurses' physical and mental health. They are reporting higher rates of absenteeism, emotional exhaustion, and higher injury claim rates than workers in other professions. And because of the inaction to date, the next time Canada faces a communicable disease outbreak, the health system may not be able to cope.[3]

The Importance of Environmental Scanning

Environmental scanning is a critical component of HRP and strategic planning processes; the most successful organizations are prepared for changes before they occur. The external environmental factors most frequently monitored include

- economic conditions (general, regional, and local)
- market and competitive trends
- new or revised laws and the decisions of courts and quasi-judicial bodies

- social concerns related to health care, childcare, and educational priorities
- technological changes
- demographic trends

Economic conditions affect supply and demand for products and services, which in turn affect the number and types of employees required. In the severe recession of the 1990s, for example, both private- and public-sector organizations restructured or downsized. Today, the most significant environmental factor relates to the dramatic demographic changes in labour force composition. By 2008, one in three Canadians will be age 50 or older, and many employers will see one-third to one-half of their management and professional employees reach early retirement thresholds in that year.[4] By 2026, it is predicted that for every 13 people who leave the workforce, only 10 will enter. Thus, a severe labour shortage is likely to occur over the next two decades as the baby boomers retire and there are not enough Generation X and Generation Y employees to replace them all.[5]

A shortage of even one worker can dramatically affect small businesses, as described in the Entrepreneurs and HR box.

Steps in HRP

Once the human resources implications of the organization's strategic plans have been analyzed, three subsequent processes are involved in HRP:

1. forecasting future human resources needs (demand)
2. forecasting the availability of internal and external candidates (supply)
3. planning and implementing HR programs to balance supply and demand

Entrepreneurs and HR

Help Wanted: Long-Term Vacancies a Major Small Business Challenge

A 2006 research report by the Canadian Federation of Independent Business (CFIB) states that over the past decade, the concern among small- and medium-sized business owners about the shortage of labour has grown considerably. Today, fully half of the small-business sector in Canada ranks the shortage of labour as a priority issue. Other CFIB research reveals that although there is a shortage of certain skills in some areas of the country, other firms are encountering a general shortage of labour (including unskilled workers), or a combination of skills and general labour shortages.

Although exacerbated by Canada's healthy economy, this problem appears far from temporary. The aging population and limited labour force growth suggests this problem will be with us for some time—perhaps worsening in the years ahead. It should also be noted that although the shortage of labour is particularly acute in some parts of the country (particularly western Canada) and in some sectors (such as construction), no region or industry is unaffected.

CFIB estimates that 233 000 positions in the small- and medium-sized business sector were left unfilled for at least four months in 2005. In addition, although larger firms are understandably more likely to have at least one vacancy, the vacancy rate is far higher in the smallest of businesses. Far from an academic problem, one longer-term vacancy in a five-person operation can have a crippling effect on the firm's ability to get its products and services to market.

Small firms recognize that there is no single solution to this problem and understand they play a role in helping to address the situation. Indeed, CFIB is planning further research on potential solutions, including tapping underrepresented pools of labour, such as Aboriginal, older, and new immigrant workers, and those with disabilities.

Source: Excerpt adapted from A. Bourgeois and A. Debus, *Help Wanted: Long-Term Vacancies a Major Small Business Challenge*, CFIB Research, April 2006. Used with the permission of the Canadian Federation of Independent Business.

STEP 1: FORECASTING FUTURE HUMAN RESOURCES NEEDS (DEMAND)

A key component of HRP is forecasting the number and type of people needed to meet organizational objectives. Managers should consider several factors when forecasting such requirements. From a practical point of view, the demand for the organization's product or service is paramount. Thus, in a manufacturing firm, sales are projected first. Then, the volume of production required to meet these sales requirements is determined. Finally, the staff needed to maintain this volume of output is estimated. In addition to this "basic requirement" for staff, several other factors should be considered, including

1. *projected turnover* as a result of resignations or terminations
2. *quality and nature of employees* in relation to what management sees as the changing needs of the organization
3. *decisions to upgrade* the quality of products or services *or enter into new markets,* which might change the required employee skill mix
4. *planned technological and administrative changes aimed at increasing productivity and reducing employee headcount,* such as the installation of new equipment or introduction of a financial incentive plan
5. the *financial resources* available to each department: for example, a budget increase may enable managers to pay higher wages and/or hire more people; conversely, a budget crunch might result in wage freezes and/or layoffs

In large organizations, needs forecasting is primarily quantitative in nature and is the responsibility of highly trained specialists. *Quantitative techniques* for determining human resources requirements include trend analysis, ratio analysis, scatter plot analysis, regression analysis, and computerized forecasting. *Qualitative approaches* to forecasting range from sophisticated analytical models to informal expert opinions about future needs, such as a manager deciding that the cost of overtime in his or her department is beginning to outweigh that involved in hiring an additional staff member, and then making plans to amend his or her staff complement during the next budget year.

Quantitative Approaches

Trend Analysis

trend analysis The study of a firm's past employment levels over a period of years to predict future needs.

Trend analysis involves studying the firm's employment levels over the last five years or so to predict future needs. For example, the number of employees in the firm at the end of each of the last five years—or perhaps the number in each subgroup (such as sales, production, and administration)—might be computed. The purpose is to identify employment trends that might continue into the future.

Trend analysis is valuable as an initial estimate only, since employment levels rarely depend solely on the passage of time. Other factors (like changes in sales volume and productivity) will also affect future staffing needs.

Ratio Analysis

ratio analysis A forecasting technique for determining future staff needs by using ratios between some causal factor (such as sales volume) and the number of employees needed.

Another approach, **ratio analysis**, involves making forecasts based on the ratio between (1) some causal factor (such as sales volume) and (2) the number of employees required (e.g., number of salespeople). For example, suppose a salesperson traditionally generates $500 000 in sales and that plans call for increasing the firm's sales by $3 million next year. Then, if the sales revenue–salespeople ratio remains the same, six new salespeople would be required (each of whom produces an extra $500 000 in sales).

Ratio analysis can also be used to help forecast other employee requirements. For example, a salesperson–secretary ratio could be computed to determine how many new secretaries will be needed to support the extra sales staff.

Like trend analysis, ratio analysis assumes that productivity remains about the same—for instance, that each salesperson can't be motivated to produce much more than $500 000 in sales. If sales productivity were to increase or decrease, then the ratio of sales to salespeople would change. A forecast based on historical ratios would then no longer be accurate.

The Scatter Plot

scatter plot A graphical method used to help identify the relationship between two variables.

A **scatter plot** is another option. Scatter plots can be used to determine whether two factors—a measure of business activity and staffing levels—are related. If they are, then when the measure of business activity is forecast, HR requirements can also be estimated.

An example to illustrate follows. Legislative changes to the health-care system require that two 500-bed Canadian hospitals be amalgamated. Both previously had responsibility for acute, chronic, and long-term care. The government's plan is for one facility to specialize in acute care while the other assumes responsibility for chronic and long-term care. In general, providing acute care requires staffing with registered nurses (RNs), while chronic and long-term care facilities can be staffed primarily with registered practical nurses (RPNs).

By the end of the calendar year, 200 beds at Hospital A must be converted from chronic and long-term care beds to facilities for acute patients. At the same time, Hospital A's 200 chronic and long-term patients must be transferred to Hospital B. In a joint meeting, the directors of nursing and HR decide that a good starting point in the planning process would be to calculate the relationship between hospital size (in terms of number of acute beds) and the number of RNs required. After placing telephone calls to their counterparts at eight hospitals in larger centres across the country, they obtain the following information:

Size of Hospital (Number of Acute Beds)	Number of Registered Nurses
200	240
300	260
400	470
500	500
600	620
700	660
800	820
900	860

To determine how many RNs would be needed, they use the data obtained to draw the scatter plot shown in **Figure 5.3**, in which hospital size is shown on the horizontal axis and number of RNs is shown on the vertical axis. If the two factors are related, then the points will tend to fall along a straight line, as they do in this case. Carefully drawing a line that minimizes the distances between the line and each of the plotted points (the line of best fit) permits an estimate of the number of nurses required for hospitals of various sizes. Thus, since Hospital A will now have 500 acute-care beds, the estimated number of RNs needed is 500.

FIGURE 5.3   Determining the Relationship between Hospital Size and Number of Nurses

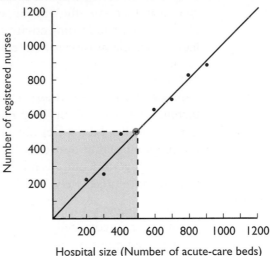

Note: After fitting the line, the number of employees needed, given the projected volume, can be extrapolated (projected).

Regression Analysis

regression analysis A statistical technique involving the use of a mathematical formula to project future demands based on an established relationship between an organization's employment level (dependent variable) and some measurable factor of output (independent variable).

Regression analysis is a more sophisticated statistical technique to determine the line of best fit. It involves the use of a mathematical formula to project future demands based on an established relationship between an organization's employment level (dependent variable) and some measurable factor of output (independent variable), such as revenue, sales, or production level. When there are several dependent and/or independent variables, multiple regression analysis is used.

Qualitative Approaches

In contrast to quantitative approaches, which utilize statistical formulas, qualitative techniques rely solely on expert judgments. Two approaches used to gather such opinions in order to forecast human resources demand (or supply) are the nominal group and Delphi techniques.

Nominal Group Technique

nominal group technique A decision-making technique that involves a group of experts meeting face to face. Steps include independent idea generation, clarification and open discussion, and private assessment.

The **nominal group technique** involves a group of experts (such as first-line supervisors and managers) meeting face to face. Although one of its uses is human resources demand forecasting, this technique is used to deal with issues and problems ranging from identifying training needs to determining safety program incentives. The steps involved are as follows:[6]

1. Each member of the group independently writes down his or her ideas on the problem or issue (in this case, the causes of demand).

2. Going around the table, each member then presents one idea. This process continues until all ideas have been presented and recorded, typically on a flipchart or chalkboard. No discussion is permitted during this step.

3. Clarification is then sought, as necessary, followed by group discussion and evaluation.

4. Finally, each member is asked to rank the ideas. This is done independently and in silence.

The advantages of this technique include involvement of key decision makers, a future focus, and the fact that the group discussion involved in the third step can facilitate the exchange of ideas and greater acceptance of results. Drawbacks include subjectivity and the potential for group pressure to lead to less accurate assessment than could be obtained through other means.

The Delphi Technique

Delphi technique A judgmental forecasting method used to arrive at a group decision, typically involving outside experts as well as organizational employees. Ideas are exchanged without face-to-face interaction and feedback is provided and used to fine-tune independent judgments until a consensus is reached.

Although short-term forecasting is generally handled by managers, the **Delphi technique** is useful for long-range forecasting and other strategic planning issues. It typically involves outside experts as well as company employees, based on the premise that outsiders may be able to assess changes in economic, demographic, governmental, technological, and social conditions and their potential impact more objectively. The Delphi technique involves the following steps:[7]

1. The problem is identified (in this case, the causes of demand) and each group member is requested to submit a potential solution by completing a carefully designed questionnaire. Direct face-to-face contact is not permitted.

2. After each member independently and anonymously completes the initial questionnaire, the results are compiled at a centralized location.

3. Each group member is then given a copy of the results.

4. If there are differences in opinion, each individual uses the feedback from other experts to fine-tune his or her independent assessment.

5. The third and fourth steps are repeated as often as necessary until a consensus is reached.

As with the nominal group technique, the advantages include involvement of key decision makers and a future focus. The Delphi technique permits the group to critically evaluate a wider range of views, however. Drawbacks include the fact that judgments may not efficiently use objective data, the time and costs involved, and the potential difficulty in integrating diverse opinions.

Managerial Judgment

Although managerial judgment is central to qualitative forecasting, it also plays a key role when quantitative techniques are used. It's rare that any historical trend, ratio, or relationship will continue unchanged into the future. Judgment is thus needed to modify the forecast based on anticipated changes.

Summarizing Human Resources Requirements

The end result of the forecasting process is an estimate of short-term and long-range HR requirements. Long-range plans are general statements of potential staffing needs and may not include specific numbers.

staffing table A pictorial representation of all jobs within the organization, along with the number of current incumbents and future employment requirements (monthly or yearly) for each.

Short-term plans—although still approximations—are more specific and are often depicted in a **staffing table**. As illustrated in **Figure 5.4**, a staffing table is a pictorial representation of all jobs within the organization, along with the number of current incumbents and future employment requirements (monthly or yearly) for each.

FIGURE 5.4   A Sample Staffing Table

Job Title (As on Job Description)	Department	Anticipated Openings												
		Total	Jan.	Feb.	Mar.	Apr.	May	June	July	Aug.	Sept.	Oct.	Nov.	Dec.
General Manager	Administration	1					1							
Director of Finance	Administration	1												1
Human Resources Officer	Administration	2	1					1						
Collection Clerk	Administration	1		1										
Groundskeeper	Maintenance	4						1	1					2
Service and Maintenance Technician	Maintenance	5	1			2					2			
Water Utility Engineer	Operations	3									2			1
Apprentice Lineperson	Operations	10	6						4					
Water Meter Technician	Operations	1												1
Engineering Technician	Operations	3			2							1		
Field Technician	Operations	8						8						
Senior Programmer/ Analyst	Systems	2				1				1				
Programmer/Operator	Systems	4		2						1			1	
Systems Operator	Systems	5					2						3	
Customer Service Representative	Sales	8	4					3				1		

Springbrook Utilities Commission Staffing Table
Date compiled:_____

STEP 2: FORECASTING THE AVAILABILITY OF INTERNAL AND EXTERNAL CANDIDATES (SUPPLY)

Short-term and long-range HR demand forecasts only provide half of the staffing equation by answering the question "How many employees will we need?" The next major concern is how projected openings will be filled. There are two sources of supply:

1. *internal*—present employees who can be transferred or promoted to meet anticipated needs
2. *external*—people in the labour market not currently working for the organization, including those who are employed elsewhere and those who are unemployed

Forecasting the Supply of Internal Candidates

Before estimating how many external candidates will need to be recruited and hired, management must determine how many candidates for projected openings will likely come from within the firm. This is the purpose of forecasting the supply of internal candidates.

Markov Analysis

Estimating internal supply involves much more than simply calculating the number of employees. Some firms use the **Markov analysis** technique to track

Markov analysis A method of forecasting internal labour supply that involves tracking the pattern of employee movements through various jobs and developing a transitional probability matrix.

FIGURE 5.5　Hypothetical Markov Analysis for a Manufacturing Operation

2007 ↓ → 2008	Plant Manager	Foreperson	Team Leader	Production Worker	Exit
Plant Manager (n = 5)	80% / 4				20% / 1
Foreperson (n = 35)	8% / 3	82% / 28			10% / 4
Team Leader (n = 110)		11% / 12	70% / 77	7% / 8	12% / 13
Production Worker (n = 861)			6% / 52	72% / 620	22% / 189
Projected Supply	7	40	129	628	

Percentages represent transitions (previous year's actuals).
Actual numbers of employees are shown as whole numbers in each block
(projections for 2008 based on current staffing).

the pattern of employee movements through various jobs and develop a transitional probability matrix for forecasting internal supply by specific categories, such as position and gender. As illustrated in **Figure 5.5**, such an analysis shows the actual number (and percentage) of employees who remain in each job from one year to the next, as well as the proportions promoted, demoted, transferred, and leaving the organization. These proportions (probabilities) are used to forecast human resources supply.

In addition to such quantitative data, the skills and capabilities of current employees must be assessed and skills inventories prepared. From this information, replacement charts and/or summaries and succession plans can be developed.

Skills Inventories and Management Inventories

Skills inventories contain comprehensive information about the capabilities of current employees. Data gathered for each employee include name, age, date of employment, current position, present duties and responsibilities, educational background, previous work history, skills, abilities, and interests. Information about current performance and readiness for promotion is generally included as well. Data pertaining to managerial staff are compiled in **management inventories**. Records summarizing the background, qualifications, interests, and skills of management employees, as well as information about managerial responsibilities and management training, are used to identify internal candidates eligible for promotion opportunities.

To be useful, skills and management inventories must be updated regularly. Failure to do so can lead to present employees being overlooked for job openings.

skills inventories　Manual or computerized records summarizing employees' education, experience, interests, skills, and so on, which are used to identify internal candidates eligible for transfer and/or promotion.

management inventories　Records summarizing the qualifications, interests, and skills of management employees, along with the number and types of employees supervised, duties of such employees, total budget managed, previous managerial duties and responsibilities, and managerial training received.

REQUIRED PROFESSIONAL CAPABILITIES

Maintains an inventory of HR talent for the use of the organization

replacement charts Visual representations of who will replace whom in the event of a job opening. Likely internal candidates are listed, along with their age, present performance rating, and promotability status.

Canadian Career Partners
www.career-partners.com

Updating every two years is generally adequate if employees are encouraged to report significant qualifications changes (such as new skills learned and/or courses completed) to the HR department as they occur.

Replacement Charts and Replacement Summaries

Replacement charts are typically used to keep track of potential internal candidates for the firm's most important positions. As can be seen in **Figure 5.6**, such charts typically indicate the age of potential internal candidates (which cannot be used as a criterion in making selection or promotion decisions but which is necessary to project retirement dates), the current performance level of the employee, and his or her promotion potential. The latter is based on the employee's future career aspirations and a supervisory assessment of readiness for promotion.

To provide a more objective estimate of future potential, this information may be supplemented by results of psychological tests, interviews with HR specialists, and other selection techniques.

Although replacement charts provide an excellent quick reference tool, they contain very little information. For that reason, many firms prefer to use

FIGURE 5.6 Management Replacement Chart

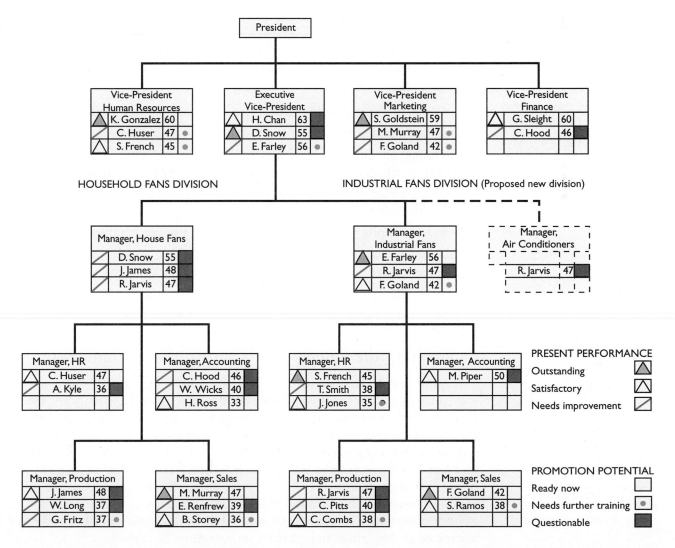

replacement summaries Lists of likely replacements for each position and their relative strengths and weaknesses, as well as information about current position, performance, promotability, age, and experience.

succession planning The process of ensuring a suitable supply of successors for current and future senior or key jobs, so that the careers of individuals can be effectively planned and managed.

REQUIRED PROFESSIONAL CAPABILITIES

Identifies potential sources of qualified candidates

Tips for the Front Line

replacement summaries. Such summaries list likely replacements for each position and their relative strengths and weaknesses, as well as information about current position, performance, promotability, age, and experience. These additional data can be extremely helpful to decision makers, although caution must be taken to ensure that no discrimination occurs on the basis of age, sex, and so on.

Succession Planning

Forecasting the availability of inside candidates is particularly important in succession planning. In a nutshell, **succession planning** refers to the plans a company makes to fill its most important executive positions. In the days when companies were hierarchical and employees tended to remain with the firm for years, executive succession was often straightforward: staff climbed the ladder one rung at a time, and it wasn't unusual for someone to start on the shop floor and end up in the president's office. Although that kind of ascent is still possible, employee turnover and flatter structures mean that the lines of succession are no longer as direct. For example, potential successors for top positions might be routed through the top jobs at several key divisions, as well as overseas, and sent through a university graduate-level, advanced management program.

Succession planning is extremely important today, as more than half of senior executives and 40 percent of second-level executives in the government, education, health, and primary industry sectors will be eligible to retire by 2011. The result of the limited attention paid to succession planning over the last several decades is that now, for every two senior executives, there is only one job-ready successor.[8]

Because succession planning requires balancing the organization's top-management needs with the potential and career aspirations of available candidates, it includes these activities:

- analysis of the demand for managers and professionals in the company
- audit of existing executives and projection of likely future supply
- planning of individual career paths based on objective estimates of future needs, performance appraisal data, and assessments of potential
- career counselling and performance-related training and development to prepare individuals for future roles
- accelerated promotions, with development targeted at future business needs
- planned strategic recruitment, aimed at obtaining people with the potential to meet future needs, as well as at filling current openings[9]

It should be noted that replacement charts, replacement summaries, and succession plans are considered highly confidential in most organizations.

Forecasting the Supply of External (Outside) Candidates

Some jobs cannot be filled with internal candidates, such as entry-level jobs and jobs for which no current employees are qualified. In these situations, the firm looks for external candidates. Employer growth is primarily responsible for the number of entry-level openings. Although there are some higher-level jobs that require such unique talents and skills that they are impossible to fill internally, and some jobs are vacated unexpectedly, a key factor in determining the number of positions that must be filled externally is the effectiveness of the organization's training and development and career-planning initiatives. If employees are not encouraged to expand their capabilities, they may not be ready to fill vacancies as they arise, and external sources must be tapped.

To project the supply of outside candidates, employers assess general economic conditions, national labour market conditions, local labour market conditions, and occupational market conditions.

General Economic Conditions

The first step is to forecast general economic conditions and the expected unemployment rate. The national unemployment rate provides an estimate of how difficult it is likely to be to recruit new employees in the immediate future. In general terms, the lower the rate of unemployment, the smaller the labour supply and the more difficult it will be to recruit employees. It is important to note, though, that even when unemployment rates are high, some positions will still be difficult to fill, because unemployment rates vary by occupation and geographic location.

National Labour Market Conditions

Demographic trends have a significant impact on national labour market conditions. Fortunately, a wealth of labour market information is available from Statistics Canada and other government and private sources.

A crucial reality is that Canada's population is aging as the baby boom cohort approaches retirement. As noted earlier, by 2008 one in three Canadians will be 50 years of age or older.[10] Currently, two-thirds of all Canadian workers retire before the age of 65, and the average age of retirement (currently 61) has been steadily declining.[11] Thus, large numbers of Canadian workers are approaching the age of retirement, and over the next 15 years the rate of workforce growth will approach zero. Soon after, Canada's workforce will begin to shrink, leading to a severe worker and skills shortage.[12] To further compound the problem, relatively fewer young workers will be entering the labour pool, as the portion of the population under the age of 25 has declined.[13] Thus, the supply of labour in Canada will be dramatically lowered over the next two decades.

Highly educated immigrants are the predominant drivers of growth in the Canadian labour pool.[14] Because of Canada's aging population and declining birth rate, it is expected that by 2011 almost all labour force growth will be made up by immigrant workers. Unfortunately, up to 550 000 immigrants have education and experience that are going unrecognized, according to a Conference Board of Canada report entitled *Brain Gain*, and 40 percent of professional and skilled immigrants leave Canada within ten years of arriving.[15] According to Gord Nixon, president and CEO of RBC Financial Group, it is clear that more talented immigrants will be part of Canada's response to the coming labour shortage, and employers will have to stop overlooking immigrants in their HR plans, start hiring immigrants to work at the level at which they were trained, and work harder at integrating immigrant workers into the workforce.[16] As indicated in the Workforce Diversity box, some employers are rethinking their strategies and programs, with the overall aim to make the best use of immigrant talent.[17]

Local Labour Market Conditions

Local labour markets are affected by many conditions, including community growth rates and attitudes. Communities that do not support existing businesses may experience declining population as residents move away to find jobs, which then makes it difficult to attract new business, because potential employers fear future local HR supply shortages. The end result is that there are fewer and

Statistics Canada
www.statcan.ca

REQUIRED PROFESSIONAL CAPABILITIES

Identifies potential sources and the markets in which the organization competes for qualified candidates

Workforce Diversity

Hiring Immigrants Makes Good Business Sense

Hiring newcomers to Canada is good business, say several leading Canadian companies that employ large numbers of skilled immigrants. "We see immigrant labour as a vital source for us," says Norm Hemfelt, vice-president of HR and administration for SNC Lavalin, a global engineering giant based in Montreal.

Logie Bruce-Lockhart, recruitment manager for engineering at Husky Injection Molding Systems Ltd. in Bolton, Ontario, says, "We did a review of our recruitment practices back in 2002. And, as a result, instead of screening people out for their lack of Canadian experience, we began screening people for their qualifications and skills, no matter where they had gained their experience." Because of this "screening-in" process, 40 percent of Husky's development engineers employed in Canada have at least one foreign degree.

ATI Technologies in Markham, Ontario, was started by an immigrant in his garage, and it has grown into a major tech firm, with 3800 employees around the world. "We compete worldwide for world-class talent," says ATI's Michel Cadieux, senior vice-president of corporate services. "So hiring skilled immigrants that are already here is critical to our strategy for growth."

Source: Adapted from A. Shaw, "Hiring Immigrants Makes Good Business Sense," *Canadian HR Reporter*, May 22, 2006. Reproduced by permission of *Canadian HR Reporter*, Carswell, One Corporate Plaza, 2075 Kennedy Road, Scarborough, ON M1T 3V4.

fewer jobs and more and more people leaving the local labour market—a vicious downward spiral. Conversely, one reason growing cities are attractive to employers is the promise of large future labour markets. Chambers of Commerce and provincial/local development and planning agencies can be excellent sources of local labour market information.

Occupational Market Conditions

Human Resources and Social Development Canada
www.hrsdc.gc.ca

In addition to looking at the overall labour market, organizations also generally want to forecast the availability of potential candidates in specific occupations (engineers, drill press operators, accountants, and so on) for which they will be recruiting. The ongoing shortage of nurses was discussed earlier in the chapter. Alberta is already facing a severe labour shortage of workers in the oil and gas sector.[18] The Conference Board of Canada estimates that there could be a shortage of 1 million skilled trades workers by 2020.[19] Shortages of civil service workers, accountants, lawyers, engineers, meteorologists, funeral directors (to bury the baby boomers!), hospitality industry workers, and information technology workers are also expected.[20]

Research ⊳
Insight

Forecasts for various occupations are available from a number of sources, including Human Resources and Social Development Canada (HRSDC). These forecasts are useful for determining whether any projected imbalances will be self-correcting or will require specific intervention on the part of governments and/or private-sector organizations.

A 2006 Conference Board of Canada study found that Canadian employers, unfortunately, are doing little to tackle the impending labour shortage from a strategic perspective.[21] The combination of competing organizational priorities and the lack of an imminent threat has discouraged organizations from preparing and implementing a strategic organizational response, as shown in **Figure 5.7**.

Physiotherapy is a skills-shortage occupation: the demand for physiotherapists exceeds the supply.

FIGURE 5.7   Preparation for Workforce Aging

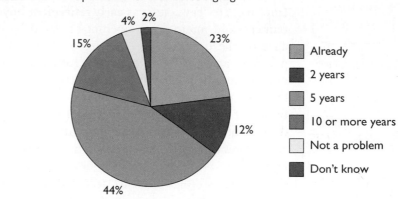

Note: Percentages add to more than 100 because of rounding.

Source: O. Parker, "Too Few People: Too Little Time: The Employer Challenge of an Aging Workforce," Conference Board Executive Action Series (July 2006), 2. Reprinted by permission of The Conference Board of Canada, Ottawa.

STEP 3: PLANNING AND IMPLEMENTING HR PROGRAMS TO BALANCE SUPPLY AND DEMAND

Once the supply and demand of human resources have been estimated, program planning and implementation commence. To successfully fill positions internally, organizations must manage performance and careers. Performance is managed through effectively designing jobs and quality of working life initiatives; establishing performance standards and goals, coaching, measuring, and evaluating; and implementing a suitable reward structure (compensation and benefits).

To manage careers effectively, policies and systems must be established for recruitment, selection and placement (including transfer, promotion, retirement, and termination), and training and development. Policies and systems are also required for job analysis, individual employee assessment, replacement and succession planning, and career tracking, as well as career planning and development.

Specific strategies must be formulated to balance supply and demand considerations. As was illustrated in Figure 5.2 (see page 114), there are three possible scenarios:

- labour supply exceeds demand (surplus)
- labour demand exceeds supply (shortage)
- expected demand matches supply

Labour Surplus

hiring freeze   A common initial response to an employee surplus. Openings are filled by reassigning current employees, and no outsiders are hired.

attrition   The normal separation of employees from an organization because of resignation, retirement, or death.

A labour surplus exists when the internal supply of employees exceeds the organization's demand. Most employers respond initially by instituting a **hiring freeze**, which means that openings are filled by reassigning current employees, and no outsiders are hired. The surplus is slowly reduced through **attrition**, which is the normal separation of employees because of resignation, retirement, or death. When employees leave, the ensuing vacancies are not filled, and the staffing level decreases gradually without any involuntary terminations. In addition to the time it takes, a major drawback of this approach is that the firm has no control over who stays and who leaves.

early retirement buyout programs
Strategies used to accelerate attrition, which involve offering attractive buyout packages or the opportunity to retire on full pension, with an attractive benefits package.

job sharing A strategy that involves dividing the duties of a single position between two or more employees.

work sharing Employees work three or four days a week and receive EI benefits on their non-workday(s).

reduced workweek Employees work fewer hours and receive less pay.

layoff The temporary withdrawal of employment to workers for economic or business reasons.

supplemental unemployment benefits (SUBs) A top-up of EI benefits to bring income levels closer to what an employee would receive if on the job.

termination Permanent separation from the organization for any reason.

severance package A lump-sum payment, continuation of benefits for a specified period of time, and other benefits that are provided to employees who are being terminated.

Some organizations attempt to accelerate attrition by offering incentives to employees to leave, such as **early retirement buyout programs**. Staffing levels are reduced and internal job openings created by offering attractive buyout packages or the opportunity to retire on full pension, with an attractive benefits package, at a relatively early age (often 50 or 55). To be successful, buyouts must be handled very carefully. Selection criteria should be established to ensure that key people who cannot be easily replaced do not leave the firm. A drawback of buyouts and early retirement packages is that they often require a great deal of money up-front. Care must also be taken to ensure that early retirement is voluntary, since forced early retirement is a contravention of human rights legislation.

Another strategy used to deal with an employee surplus involves reducing the total number of hours worked. **Job sharing** involves dividing the duties of a single position between two or more employees. Reducing full-time positions to *part-time work* is sometimes more effective, especially if there are peak demand periods. Creating a job-share position and/or offering part-time employment can be win–win strategies, since layoffs can be avoided. Although the employees involved work fewer hours and thus have less pay, they are still employed, and they may enjoy having more free time at their disposal. The organization benefits by retaining good employees.

Twenty-five years ago, the federal government introduced a **work-sharing** scheme, a layoff-avoidance strategy that involves employees working three or four days a week and receiving Employment Insurance (EI) benefits on their non-workday(s). Similar to work sharing, but without a formal arrangement with government regarding EI benefits, is a **reduced workweek**. Employees simply work fewer hours and receive less pay. The organization retains a skilled workforce, lessens the financial and emotional impact of a full layoff, and reduces production costs. The only potential drawback is that it is sometimes difficult to predict in advance, with any degree of accuracy, how many hours of work should be scheduled each week.

Another strategy used to manage an employee surplus is a **layoff**, the temporary withdrawal of employment to workers for economic or business reasons. Layoffs may be short in duration, as when plants close for brief periods to adjust inventory levels or to retool for a new product line, but can last months or even years if caused by a major change in the business cycle. Layoffs are not easy for either managers or workers, but they are sometimes necessary if attrition will take too long to reduce the number of employees to the required level.

To ease the financial burden of layoffs, some organizations offer **supplemental unemployment benefits (SUBs)**, which are a top-up of EI benefits to bring income levels of temporarily laid-off workers closer to their regular pay on the job. SUB programs are generally negotiated through collective bargaining. Benefits are payable until the pool of funds set aside has been exhausted.

When employees are no longer required, the employment relationship may be severed. **Termination** is a broad term that encompasses permanent separation from the organization for any reason. In situations in which employment is terminated involuntarily, employees with acceptable or better performance ratings are often offered severance pay and outplacement assistance.

A **severance package** is typically provided when employees are being terminated through no fault of their own, in order to avoid wrongful dismissal lawsuits. Severance pay is legally required in certain situations, such as mass layoffs. In addition to pay, severance packages often include the continuation of

Research
Insight ▷

An Ethical Dilemma

How much time, effort, and money should firms devote to helping "surviving" employees deal with downsizing? With mergers and acquisitions?

survivor sickness   A range of negative emotions experienced by employees remaining after a major restructuring initiative, which can include feelings of betrayal or violation, guilt, and detachment, and can result in stress symptoms, including depression, proneness to errors, and reduced productivity.

transfer   Movement of an employee from one job to another that is relatively equal in pay, responsibility, and/or organizational level.

promotion   Movement of an employee from one job to another that is higher in pay, responsibility, and/or organizational level, usually based on merit, seniority, or a combination of both.

benefits for a specified period. In determining the appropriate package, employers should take salary, years of service, the employee's age, and his or her likelihood of obtaining another job into consideration.[22] Executives may be protected by a *golden parachute clause* in their contract of employment, a guarantee by the employer to pay specified compensation and benefits in the case of termination because of downsizing or restructuring. To soften the blow of termination, *outplacement assistance,* generally offered by an outside agency, can assist affected employees in finding employment elsewhere.

Although restructuring initiatives ranging from layoffs to mergers and acquisitions were prevalent in the 1990s, the consequences were not as positive as anticipated. In a study of 6418 workforce reductions in Fortune 500 firms over 18 years (1982 to 2000), researchers found no consistent evidence that downsizing led to improved financial performance.[23]

As those firms discovered, a high cost associated with downsizing is **survivor sickness**, a range of emotions that can include feelings of betrayal or violation, guilt, and detachment. The remaining employees, anxious about the next round of terminations, often suffer stress symptoms including depression, increased errors, and reduced performance.

Labour Shortage

A labour shortage exists when the internal supply of human resources cannot meet the organization's needs. Scheduling overtime hours is often the initial response. Employers may also subcontract work on a temporary or permanent basis. Another short-term solution is to hire temporary employees.

As vacancies are created within the firm, opportunities are generally provided for employee transfers and promotions, which necessitate performance management, training (and retraining), and career development. Of course, internal movement does not eliminate a shortage, which means that recruitment will be required. It is hoped, though, that resultant vacancies will be for entry-level jobs, which can be filled more easily externally.

A **transfer** involves a lateral movement from one job to another that is relatively equal in pay, responsibility, and/or organizational level. Transfers can lead to more effective utilization of human resources, broaden an employee's skills and perspectives, and help make him or her a better candidate for future promotions. Transfers also offer additional technical and interpersonal challenges and increased variety of work, which may enhance job satisfaction and motivation.

A **promotion** involves the movement of an employee from one job to another that is higher in pay, responsibility, and/or organizational level. Such a move may be based on merit, seniority, or a combination of both. Merit-based promotions are awarded in recognition of a person's outstanding performance in his or her present job, or as an assessment of his or her future potential.

Looming Labour Shortage in Canada

Today, Canada faces a long-term labour shortage. Over the next 20 years, the vast majority of baby boomers will transition from working life to retirement, creating a critical undersupply of labour.[24] Watson Wyatt predicts a labour shortage of 1 million people by 2016 and possibly close to 3 million by 2026.[25] As a result, many employers are seeking strategies to increase the workforce participation of older Canadians, setting aside the stereotypes and prejudices that older workers are less productive, resistant to change, and hard to get along with. Instead, employers are seizing the opportunity to retain a wealth of knowledge and maturity. Although many older workers leave the workforce because of health problems, those who remain are in very good or excellent physical and mental condition.[26] The Strategic HR box describes how five Canadian companies are preparing for the looming labour shortage.

Other strategies include increasing the number of Aboriginal employees (Nunavut is setting up a trade school in Rankin Inlet) and visible minority employees, increasing the number of female employees in male-dominated workplaces (Yukon College is encouraging women to train in the trades), expanding apprenticeship programs (Ontario and British Columbia have already done so), aggressive recruiting of workers from other provinces (Calgary put a 20-page insert in the *Winnipeg Sun*), and offering high-quality jobs with challenging work and opportunities for skills development.[27]

Strategic HR

Stemming the Loss of Knowledge

A number of companies are fully aware of the coming labour shortage and are preparing for it with innovative programs and policies that will both retain their existing talent bank and attract more individuals with a lifetime of knowledge.

IBM

By talking to employees approaching retirement, IBM found that work/life balance is very important to this group. Employees don't want to leave work behind; they want to leave the stress behind. So IBM lets people work from home and allows them to manage their own time. IBM has also introduced a retiree "on-call" program, whereby interested retirees make themselves available for up to 1200 hours a year on a contract basis. The hours are flexible.

Direct Energy

Facing a serious shortage of skilled trades people, Direct Energy implemented a two-year apprenticeship program to train service technicians. The company is also aggressively recruiting people over 50 to fill sales and service positions. They find that employees in their 50s and 60s are just as motivated, often more so, than younger workers. The company encourages older workers to set their own hours, work from home, and "downshift" or gradually reduce their workloads as they approach retirement.

Home Depot

Almost one-quarter of Home Depot's workforce is over 50. The company has made a conscious effort to hire older workers. Many have chosen this job as a second career, others just to keep busy with a part-time job. Home Depot's experience has been that older workers are reliable and flexible, and tend to stay with the company. The company also finds that older workers want flexible work schedules, less physical work, and opportunities to learn new skills.

City of Calgary

This municipality recently found that one-third of its employees were over age 50, and it was facing the loss of 50 percent of its workforce over the next ten years. The city responded by introducing two new programs directed at retired and retiring staff. The first was to ask individuals with knowledge critical to the smooth operation of their division or department to return on a one-year contract to mentor their successor. The second was to establish a database of retirees willing to return for part-time, seasonal, contract, or backfill positions.

Merck Frosst

This Montreal-based pharmaceutical giant retains close ties with employees who have retired. The company launched a mentoring program where employees can request a retiree or older employee as a mentor to provide career guidance and the benefit of their wisdom and knowledge. The company has found that eldercare is a big issue for older workers and has responded by offering flexible work arrangements to reduce stress by enabling Sandwich Generation employees in their 40s and 50s to take time off to attend to the needs of their families.

Source: Adapted from M. Potter, "Stemming the Loss of Knowledge," *HR Professional*, June/July 2006, pp. 21–26. Reprinted by permission of the Human Resources Professionals Association of Ontario.

One of the more innovative ways to manage the coming labour shortage is through the use of flexible work arrangements. Many older workers are expected to respond to flexible options that will bridge work and retirement.[28]

Flexible Work Arrangements

Employees of all ages are increasingly demanding flexible work arrangements. Younger workers want time to have a "life" outside work and time to balance work with their family responsibilities. A recent study of 1439 young associate lawyers at major Canadian law firms found that 62 percent of the females and almost half of the males plan to change jobs within five years (costing law firms $315 000 each to replace them) to find an environment that is more supportive of their family and personal commitments and that provides them with more control over their work schedules.[29]

Older workers want less stress and more time for recreational and leisure activities. Work is the number one cause of stress in the lives of Canadians.[30] In between is the Sandwich Generation with both childcare and eldercare responsibilities, which comprises about 25 percent of the workforce.[31]

Time has become the new currency for compensating employees, and is increasingly seen by employees as necessary for success both at work and at home. Employers must be aware of the value of flexible schedules for attracting and retaining talent, as labour becomes increasingly scarce.[32]

Although flexible work arrangements have traditionally been associated with improving work/life balance, they are increasingly seen as part of a business strategy,[33] because they can assist organizations in meeting customer needs when and where they need to be met. For example, one B.C. firm used flexible work arrangements to enhance customer service by offering employees the option to start work at 6:00 a.m. Pacific Time in order to deal with customers at 9 a.m. Eastern Time.

Scotiabank is one Canadian employer that offers flexible work arrangements as part of its philosophy regarding its 70 percent female workforce.[34] At IBM Canada, flexible work arrangements help keep employees committed to the workplace.[35] Efforts to assist workers in adapting to ongoing societal and demographic changes can also help organizations to achieve a competitive advantage through increased productivity and lower costs.[36]

There are many different flexible work options, and we'll describe some of the most commonly used ones here. **Flextime** is a plan whereby employees' flexible workdays are built around a core of midday hours, such as 11 a.m. to 2 p.m. Workers determine their own flexible starting and stopping hours. For example, they may opt to work from 7 a.m. to 3 p.m. or from 11 a.m. to 7 p.m. In practice, most employers who use flextime give employees only limited freedom regarding the hours that they work. Typical schedules dictate the earliest starting time, latest starting time, and core periods. Employers often prefer a schedule that is fairly close to the traditional 9 a.m. to 5 p.m. workday. For example, starting times may be between 7 a.m. and 10 a.m., and the core time from 10 a.m. to 3 p.m. The effect of flextime for many employees is to have about an hour or two of leeway before 9 a.m. or after 5 p.m.

Telecommuting (or *teleworking*) is a common flexible work arrangement. Here, employees work at home, using their computers and fax machines to transmit completed work to the office. Increasingly, wireless technology and even satellite connections are being used. For employees, telecommuting reduces travel time, permits the employee to work whenever he or she is most productive, and

flextime   A plan whereby employees build their workday around a core of midday hours.

An Ethical Dilemma

Is it ethical for an employer to deny employees the right to flexible work arrangements just because managers are concerned about the additional communication required and about losing control over their employees?

provides flexibility for dealing with family responsibilities. Organizations using this virtual work approach report stunning improvements in cost savings, productivity, and employee morale.[37] Many managers are not comfortable supervising telecommuters, fearing a loss of control. Successful telecommuting requires that mutual trust be established between an employee and his or her supervisor. Successful telecommuters are highly motivated and have the self-discipline to work independently.[38]

As we mentioned earlier in the chapter, *job sharing* is a strategy that allows two or more employees to share a single full-time job. For example, two people may share a 40-hour-per-week job, with one working mornings and the other working afternoons, or one person working Monday through Wednesday noon, and the other from Wednesday noon through Friday. A *reduced workweek* is another option for employees who want to reduce their overall work hours. Cara Flight Kitchen recently negotiated a reduced workweek of three or four days for employees aged 50 or over.[39]

The most common **compressed workweek** arrangement involves employees working four ten-hour days instead of the more usual five eight-hour days. Compressed workweek plans have been fairly successful as they have several advantages. Productivity seems to increase since there are fewer startups and shutdowns. Workers are also more willing to work some evenings and weekends as part of these plans. The compressed workweek is generally effective in terms of reducing paid overtime, reducing absenteeism, and improving efficiency. Furthermore, workers also gain; there is a 20 percent reduction in commuter trips and an additional day off per week. Additional savings (e.g., in childcare expenses) may also result. However, there has not been a lot of experience with shortened workweeks, and it is possible that the improvements are short-lived. Fatigue is a potential drawback of the four-day workweek. (Note that fatigue was a main reason for adopting eight-hour workdays in the first place.)

Other employers, especially in Europe, are switching to a plan that they call **flexyear**. Under this plan, employees can choose (at six-month intervals) the number of hours that they want to work each month over the next year. A full-timer, for instance, might be able to work up to 173 hours a month. In a typical flexyear arrangement, an employee who wants to average 110 hours a month might work 150 hours in January (when the children are at school and the company needs extra help to cope with January sales). In February, the employee may work only 70 hours because he or she wants to go skiing. This arrangement may be particularly attractive to older employees or those who have already retired but are willing to work for part of the year.

Labour Supply Matches Labour Demand

When the expected supply matches the demand, organizations replace employees who leave the firm with individuals transferred or promoted from inside or hired from outside. As in shortage situations, performance management, training, and career development play crucial roles.

compressed workweek An arrangement that most commonly allows employees to work four ten-hour days instead of the more usual five eight-hour days.

flexyear A work arrangement under which employees can choose (at six-month intervals) the number of hours that they want to work each month over the next year.

Chapter Review

Summary

1. Human resources planning (HRP) is the process of reviewing HR requirements to ensure that the organization has the required number of employees with the necessary skills to meet its strategic goals. Forecasting future labour demand and supply is a critical element of the strategic planning process. HRP and strategic planning become effective when a reciprocal and interdependent relationship exists between them.

2. Four quantitative techniques for forecasting future HR demand are trend analysis, ratio analysis, scatter plots, and regression analysis. Two qualitative techniques used to forecast demand are the nominal group technique and the Delphi technique.

3. Four strategies used to forecast internal HR supply are Markov analysis, skills and management inventories, replacement charts and summaries, and succession planning. Forecasting external HR supply requires an assessment of general economic conditions, national labour market conditions, local labour market conditions, and occupational labour market conditions.

4. Strategies to manage a labour surplus include a hiring freeze; downsizing through attrition; early retirement buyout programs; reduced hours through job sharing, part-time work, work sharing, or reduced workweeks; and termination of employment.

5. Strategies to manage a human resources shortage include hiring temporary employees, subcontracting work, employee transfers and promotions, and flexible work arrangements to increase work/life balance.

Key Terms

attrition *(p. 127)*
compressed workweek *(p. 132)*
Delphi technique *(p. 120)*
early retirement buyout programs *(p. 128)*
flextime *(p. 131)*
flexyear *(p. 132)*
hiring freeze *(p. 127)*
human resources planning (HRP) *(p. 113)*
job sharing *(p. 128)*
layoff *(p. 128)*
management inventories *(p. 122)*
Markov analysis *(p. 121)*
nominal group technique *(p. 119)*
promotion *(p. 129)*
ratio analysis *(p. 117)*
reduced workweek *(p. 128)*
regression analysis *(p. 119)*
replacement charts *(p. 123)*
replacement summaries *(p. 124)*
scatter plot *(p. 118)*
severance package *(p. 128)*
skills inventories *(p. 122)*
staffing table *(p. 120)*
succession planning *(p. 124)*
supplemental unemployment benefits (SUBs) *(p. 128)*
survivor sickness *(p. 129)*
termination *(p. 128)*
transfer *(p. 129)*
trend analysis *(p. 117)*
work sharing *(p. 128)*

Review and Discussion Questions

1. Describe the costs associated with a lack of or inadequate HRP.

2. After analyzing the human resources implications of the organization's strategic plans, what are the three subsequent processes involved in HRP?

3. Differentiate between replacement charts and replacement summaries, and explain why replacement summaries are generally preferred.

4. Discuss various methods of easing the burden of a layoff or termination.

5. Differentiate between the seniority and merit-based approaches to promotion and describe the advantages and disadvantages associated with each.

6. Describe several flexible work arrangements that can help employers retain employees.

Critical Thinking Questions

1. A number of quantitative and qualitative techniques for forecasting human resources demand were discussed in this chapter. Working in groups, identify which strategies would be most appropriate for (a) small versus large companies, (b) industries undergoing rapid change, and (c) businesses/industries in which there are seasonal variations in HR requirements.

2. Suppose that it has just been projected that, because of a number of technological innovations, your firm will need 20 percent fewer clerical employees within the next five years. What actions would you take to try to retain your high-performing clerical staff members?

3. Suppose that you are the HR manager at a firm at which a hiring freeze has just been declared. The plan is to downsize through attrition. What steps would you take to ensure that you reap the advantages of this strategy while minimizing the disadvantages?

4. Work/life balance is important for both older workers and the younger generations in the workforce. What are some of the operational issues that need to be managed in implementing widespread flexible work arrangements?

Application Exercises

Running Case: LearnInMotion.com

To Plan or Not to Plan?

One aspect of HRM that Jennifer and Pierre studied at university was HR planning. Their professor emphasized its importance, especially for large organizations. Although LearnInMotion.com was certainly small at this point, with only a few employees, they were planning to expand, and it seemed that detailed HRP should be an essential part of their plans. There is no succession plan—after all, they have just started the business! But they both knew that the market for technology workers, in general, was competitive. Jennifer and Pierre have asked for some assistance with the following questions.

Questions

1. In what ways might HRP benefit LearnInMotion.com?

2. Should they decide to proceed with HRP, what steps should Jennifer and Pierre take?

3. What HRP techniques would be appropriate for them to use?

4. What other issues would have to be addressed to make HRP worthwhile?

Case Incident

How Much Work Schedule Flexibility Is Too Much Flexibility?

Jasmine Khan, operations manager at John's Grocery Store, is facing several scheduling problems with her cashiers. Julie Brown is on maternity leave. She is due to come back to work next week but has been unable to find acceptable daycare for her new daughter because of the baby's special medical needs. Julie wants to extend her leave. Al Fraser has just requested at least two weeks off to attend to his mother, who is in the early stages of Alzheimer's disease and needs to have homecare and other services organized.

The newest cashier, Bill Bradley, has requested that he only work shifts that finish by 4:30 p.m. so that he can pick up his kids from their daycare centre, which closes at 5 p.m. His cousin, who had been taking care of the children between 4:30 p.m. and whenever Bill finished his shift, will be moving to another city shortly and Bill doesn't know anyone else in town whom he would trust with his children.

Jasmine's best cashier, Sophia Chan, who has the potential to take over from the current head cashier who will be retiring next year, has recently told Jasmine that she is going back to university next month to finish her degree in business and will only be able to work part-time for the next eight months. To make matters worse, the head cashier, Shirley Trudeau, has a daughter who is about to become a single mother, and she wants to take three weeks off to help her daughter adjust to the demands of caring for an infant.

John's Grocery Store recently adopted a policy that it would be as flexible as possible to accommodate work–family conflict, which means that Jasmine can't just let cashiers go when they can't work regularly, as she has been able to do in the past. But Jasmine is wondering how can she do that and still operate the store—after all, customers don't care

about staffing issues; most just want to buy their groceries and be on their way as quickly as possible.

So far, the other five cashiers are available to work regular shifts. Jasmine is considering a variety of flexible work options, including regular part-time, temporary part-time, job sharing, compressed workweeks, flextime, and leaves of absence.

Questions

1. What difficulties might Jasmine face if she tries to accommodate all of these requests for flexible work arrangements to cope with work–family issues?

2. Should any of these requests be turned down?

3. How can the remaining requests be accommodated? Make recommendations on how to handle each of them.

Experiential Exercises

1. Develop a realistic, hypothetical staffing table for a department or organization with which you are familiar.

2. Contact the HR manager at a firm in your area and find out whether or not the firm uses any of the following: (a) skills/management inventories, (b) replacement charts or summaries, and (c) a succession plan. Prepare a brief summary of the information gathered. Once you have completed these tasks, form a group with several of your classmates. Share your findings with the group members. Were there similarities across firms? Did company size seem to make a difference in terms of strategies used for forecasting the supply of internal candidates? Can you identify any other factors that seem to play a role in the choice of forecasting techniques used?

3. This assignment requires working within teams of five or six. Half of the teams are to assume the role of management at a firm that is about to undergo major downsizing. The other half of the teams are to assume the roles of employees— some of whom will be affected and others of whom will remain. Each management team is paired with an employee team and must prepare a realistic simulation. Managers should work toward minimizing the negative impact on those who will be affected, as well as on those who will remain. Individuals in employee roles are asked to envision what their thoughts and feelings would be (if they have never actually been in this situation, that is) and to portray them as realistically as possible.

2   *Charlie Catchpaugh and The Outlet*

It is expected that there will be a lot of activity around persuading older workers to continue working past retirement age once the approaching labour shortage hits. Although the average age of retirement has been slowly decreasing, some workers enjoy their work so much that they continue on for years after most others have chosen to retire.

Charlie Catchpaugh is the editor, chief reporter, and photographer for *The Outlet*, a monthly newspaper for Anglo-Canadians of the Eastern Townships of Quebec. Catchpaugh has been cranking out this paper for 25 years and only lately, at the age of 76, has he taken on some part-time help. Obviously a labour of love for Charlie, *The Outlet* is a mix of neighbourhood church news, local gossip, corny jokes, and outrageous political comment. Charlie refuses to abandon his dwindling constituency of 4500 readers and wants to help keep the Anglo community alive in his area.

Questions

1. Why does Charlie choose to continue to work at the age of 76?
2. What are Charlie's strengths as an older employee?
3. Is Charlie's business facing any problems because of his age?

Source: Based on "Magog Town Crier," *CBC The National* (March 17, 2004).

CHAPTER 6

RECRUITMENT

THE STRATEGIC IMPORTANCE OF RECRUITMENT

recruitment The process of searching out and attracting qualified job applicants, which begins with the identification of a position that requires staffing and is completed when résumés and/or completed application forms are received from an adequate number of applicants.

Recruitment is the process of searching out and attracting qualified job applicants. It begins with the identification of a position that requires staffing and is completed when résumés and/or completed application forms are received from an adequate number of applicants.

The individuals recruited by the organizations are potential employees. If selected, they will be responsible for implementing, and in some cases creating, the organization's strategy. Therefore, recruitment is an important strategic activity because it directly affects the attainment of strategic objectives. Overall, the quality of an organization's human resources and human capital begins with a strategic perspective in the management of recruiting activities. Watson Wyatt's 2005 Human Capital Index study found that organizations with superior recruiting practices financially outperform those with less effective programs and that successful recruiting is a strong indicator of higher shareholder value.[1]

Recruiters Café
www.recruiterscafe.com

recruiter A specialist in recruitment, whose job it is to find and attract capable candidates.

Authority for recruitment is generally delegated to HR staff members, except in small businesses, where line managers usually recruit their own staff. In large organizations where recruiting is done on a continual basis, the HR team typically includes specialists, known as **recruiters**, whose job it is to find and attract qualified applicants.

THE RECRUITMENT PROCESS

As illustrated in **Figure 6.1**, the recruitment process has a number of steps:

REQUIRED PROFESSIONAL CAPABILITIES

Implements and monitors processes for attracting qualified candidates

1. *Job openings are identified* through HR planning (based on the organization's strategic plan) or manager request. HR plans play a vital role in the identification process, because they indicate present and future openings and specify which should be filled internally and which externally. Openings do arise unexpectedly, however, in which case managers request that a new employee be hired.

2. *The job requirements are determined*. This step involves reviewing the job description and the job specification and updating them, if necessary. Manager comments may also prove helpful in identifying requirements.

3. *Appropriate recruiting source(s) and method(s) are chosen*. There is no single, best recruiting technique, and the most appropriate for any given position depends on a number of factors, which will be discussed next.

4. *A pool of qualified recruits is generated.*

REQUIRED PROFESSIONAL CAPABILITIES

Implements deployment procedures, ensuring necessary compensation and benefit changes and education plans are addressed

A recruiter must be aware of constraints affecting the recruitment process in order to be successful in his or her job. Constraints arise from organizational policies, such as *promote-from-within policies*, which means that a recruiter cannot start recruiting externally for a specified period, even if he or she is aware that there are no suitable internal candidates. Constraints also arise from

FIGURE 6.1   An Overview of the Recruitment Process

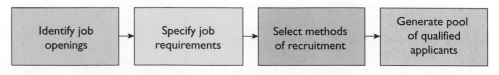

Identify job openings → Specify job requirements → Select methods of recruitment → Generate pool of qualified applicants

compensation policies since they influence the attractiveness of the job to potential applicants. If there is an *employment equity plan*, it will specify goals for increasing recruitment from the designated groups. Monetary and nonmonetary *inducements offered by competitors* impose a constraint, since recruiters must try to meet the prevailing standards or use alternative inducements.

Perhaps the biggest constraint on recruiting activity at this time is the emerging labour shortage, which makes recruiting more difficult. One survey by Hewitt Associates found that recruitment practices will have to undergo "enormous change" over the next several years.[2] Some initiatives are already underway to attract foreign recruits, as explained in the Global HRM box.

Global HRM

Manitoba Renews Program to Recognize Foreign-Trained Engineers

The Labour and Immigration Department of the Manitoba government sponsors a 12-month Internationally Educated Engineers Qualification program. The program is delivered at the University of Manitoba's Faculty of Engineering with the support of the Association of Professional Engineers and Geoscientists. The program features an academic component and a paid, work-experience placement with an employer in the participant's engineering discipline. Successful completion of the program means the participant's combined engineering education is recognized as equivalent to Canadian education standards. The one-year program is designed to shorten the typical three-year period a foreign-educated engineer would take to meet Canadian standards.

Since the program started in 2003, 15 internationally educated engineers have successfully completed the program requirements, resulting in 14 becoming employed in the engineering field and one entering into graduate studies. Another 13 participants will graduate in 2006. The target enrollment for the program for the next three years is 12 participants per year, for a total of 36.

"We are sending a very positive message to potential immigrants that Manitoba welcomes them and their skills," said Labour and Immigration Minister Nancy Allan.

Source: Adapted from *Manitoba Renews Program to Recognize Foreign-Trained Engineers,* Government of Manitoba News Release, March 17, 2006. www.gov.mb.ca/chc/press/top/2006/03/2006-03-17-04.html (August 8, 2006).

RECRUITING WITHIN THE ORGANIZATION

Although recruiting often brings job boards and employment agencies to mind, current employees are generally the largest source of recruits. Filling open positions with inside candidates has several advantages:

- Employees see that competence is rewarded, thus enhancing commitment, morale, and performance.

- Having already been with the firm for some time, insiders may be more committed to the company's goals and less likely to leave.

- Managers are provided with a longer-term perspective when making business decisions.

- It is generally safer to promote from within, because the firm is likely to have a more accurate assessment of the person's skills and performance level than would otherwise be the case.

- Inside candidates require less orientation than outsiders do.

Promotion from within also has a number of drawbacks, however:

- Employees who apply for jobs and don't get them may become discontented. Informing unsuccessful applicants as to why they were rejected and what remedial action they might take to be more successful in the future is thus essential.[3]
- Managers may be required to post all job openings and interview all inside candidates, even when they already know whom they want to hire, thus wasting considerable time and creating false hope on the part of those employees not genuinely being considered.
- Employees may be less satisfied and accepting of a boss appointed from within their own ranks than they would a newcomer.
- It is sometimes difficult for a newly chosen leader to adjust to no longer being "one of the gang."[4]
- There is a possibility of "inbreeding." When an entire management team has been brought up through the ranks, they may have a tendency to make decisions "by the book" and to maintain the status quo, when a new and innovative direction is needed.

Promotion from within requires the use of job posting, human resources records, and skills inventories.

Job Posting

job posting The process of notifying current employees about vacant positions.

Job posting is a process of notifying current employees about vacant positions. Most companies now use computerized job-posting systems, where information about job vacancies can be found on the company's intranet. This involves a notice outlining the job title, duties (as listed in the job description), qualifications (taken from the job specification), hours of work, pay range, posting date, and closing date, as shown in **Figure 6.2**. Not all firms use intranets. Some post jobs on bulletin boards or in employee publications. As illustrated in **Figure 6.3**, there are advantages and disadvantages to using job postings to facilitate the transfer and promotion of qualified internal candidates.

Human Resources Records

Human resources records are often consulted to ensure that qualified individuals are notified, in person, of vacant positions. An examination of employee files, including résumés and application forms, may uncover employees who are working in jobs below their education or skill levels, people who already have the requisite KSAs, or persons with the potential to move into the vacant position if given some additional training.

Skills Inventories

Skills inventories are an even better reference tool. Although such inventories may be used instead of job postings, they are more often used as a supplement. Whether computerized or manual, referring to such inventories ensures that qualified internal candidates are identified and considered for transfer or promotion when opportunities arise.

Limitations of Recruiting from Within

It is rarely possible to fill all non-entry-level jobs with current employees. Middle- and upper-level jobs may be vacated unexpectedly, with no internal

An Ethical Dilemma

Suppose a manager has already made up his or her mind about who will be selected for an internal position. But an internal job posting and subsequent interviews have shown another equally qualified candidate. Who should be offered the position?

FIGURE 6.2   Sample Job Posting

Fire Alarm Technician/Electrician

Toronto, Ontario, Canada
Posted: April 13, 2006
Vacancy Type: Vacancy Notice
Start: ASAP
Department: Campus Planning and Facilities   **Position:** 480416_MT_03
Grade: Electrician/Fire Alarm Technician   **Salary Scale:** $24.31
Hours of Work: 40 hours per week

Responsibilities
- Maintains the fire alarm and electrical systems operating in a safe, efficient, organized and serviceable condition on an ongoing basis.
- Performs preventative, demand and corrective maintenance; inspects, trouble-shoots, repairs, logs data and services fire alarm and electrical systems in University buildings in a manner meeting all applicable standards, codes and regulations of the NFPA, Ontario Fire Code, CSA and the Electrical Safety Authority of Ontario.
- Engages in work related to Plant Operations electrical requests.

Qualifications
- Successful completion of an Ontario Secondary School Diploma (OSSD) or equivalent, preferably in a technical program. Applicants must possess a current Ontario Fire Alarm Technicians Certificate and be licensed as a Journeyman Electrician both in construction and maintenance.
- Minimum of three (3) years of work experience as a capable Fire Alarm Technician and Licensed Journeyman Electrician performing fire alarm system maintenance, preferably with extensive experience in Edwards and Simplex fire alarm panels and related equipment.
- Electrical maintenance and repair experience in a complex industrial, commercial or institutional facility with low voltage and 13.8 kV substations with their switchgear, transformers, circuit breakers, panels, buss and wire distribution systems extending from 24V to 600V AC single and three-phase services for a wide range of equipment including fans motors, furnaces, electronic equipment, synchronized clock systems, fire alarm and enunciator systems, security surveillance systems and a variety of electronic/electric or electro-pneumatic control systems of the heating and ventilating systems.
- Proven ability to read and interpret specifications and drawings for building electrical services and fire alarm systems and to interpret code requirements.
- Must be capable of the heavy lifting and other strenuous physical activity such as: kneeling; climbing ladders; working on the back, sides and above shoulder/head for extended periods of time; working in confined spaces; working on scaffolds, air lifts or elevated equipment and in areas where excessive cold or heat may occur.
- Must be willing and able to wear and use protective clothing including (not an exclusive list) hard hat, safety boots, face masks, and breathing apparatus such as air helmet and respirator.
- Must demonstrate a commitment to client services, specifically students, staff and faculty.

Note:
The selection process may normally include the following: Candidates may be asked to demonstrate qualifications through occupational test and an interview conducted by a panel of at least 3 management representatives. Candidates must have a record of dependability/reliability and a commitment to maintain confidentiality. A review of the employee's official personnel file, job performance and reference checks may be conducted.

Deadline to Apply: Friday May 5, 2006
Ryerson University has an employment equity program and encourages applications from all qualified individuals, including Aboriginal peoples, persons with disabilities, members of visible minorities and women. Members of designated groups are encouraged to self-identify. All qualified candidates are encouraged to apply, however, Canadians and permanent residents will be given priority.

Source: Careers @ Ryerson: External Applicant Postings, Ryerson University. www.ryerson.ca (August 5, 2006). Reprinted with permission of Ryerson University, Human Resources Department.

FIGURE 6.3   Advantages and Disadvantages of Job Posting

Advantages

- Provides every qualified employee with a chance for a transfer or promotion.
- Reduces the likelihood of special deals and favouritism.
- Demonstrates the organization's commitment to career growth and development.
- Communicates to employees the organization's policies and guidelines regarding promotions and transfers.
- Provides equal opportunity to all qualified employees.

Disadvantages

- Unsuccessful job candidates may become demotivated, demoralized, discontented, and unhappy if feedback is not communicated in a timely and sensitive manner.
- Tensions may rise if it appears that a qualified internal candidate was passed over for an equally qualified or less qualified external candidate.
- The decision about which candidate to select may be more difficult if there are two or more equally qualified candidates.

replacements yet qualified or ready for transfer or promotion; or the jobs may require such specialized training and experience that there are no potential internal replacements. Even in firms with a policy of promoting from within, potential external candidates are increasingly being considered in order to meet strategic objectives. Hiring someone from outside may be preferable in order to acquire the latest knowledge and expertise or gain new ideas and revitalize the department or organization.[5]

RECRUITING OUTSIDE THE ORGANIZATION

Unless there is a workforce reduction, even in firms with a promote-from-within policy, a replacement from outside must eventually be found to fill the job left vacant once all eligible employees have been given the opportunity for transfer and/or promotion. In addition, most entry-level positions must be filled by external candidates. The advantages of external recruitment include

- generation of a larger pool of qualified candidates, which may have a positive impact on the quality of the selection decision
- availability of a more diverse applicant pool, which can assist in meeting employment equity goals and timetables
- acquisition of skills or knowledge not currently available within the organization and/or new ideas and creative problem-solving techniques
- elimination of rivalry and competition caused by employees jockeying for transfers and promotions, which can hinder interpersonal and interdepartmental cooperation
- potential cost savings resulting from hiring individuals who already have the skills, rather than providing extensive training

Planning External Recruitment

When choosing external recruitment method(s), in addition to the constraints mentioned earlier, several factors should be considered. The type of job to be filled has a major impact on the recruitment method selected. For example, most

FIGURE 6.4   Recruiting Yield Pyramid

firms normally rely on professional search firms for recruiting executive-level employees. In contrast, local newspaper advertising is commonly used for recruiting other salaried employees.

Yield ratios help to indicate which recruitment methods are the most effective at producing qualified job candidates. A **yield ratio** is the percentage of applicants that proceed to the next stage of the selection process. A recruiting yield pyramid, such as that shown in **Figure 6.4**, can be devised for each method by calculating the yield ratio for each step in the selection process.

The firm in this example typically hires 50 entry-level accountants each year. The firm has calculated that using this method leads to a ratio of offers made to actual new hires of two to one (about half of the candidates to whom offers are made accept). The firm also knows that the ratio of candidates interviewed to offers made is three to two, while the ratio of candidates invited for interviews to candidates actually interviewed is generally four to three. Finally, the firm knows that the ratio between leads generated and candidates selected for interviews is six to one. In other words, of six leads generated through college/ university recruiting efforts, one applicant is invited to attend an interview. Given these ratios, the firm knows that, using this particular recruitment method, 1200 leads must be generated in order to hire 50 new accountants.

The average number of days from when the company initiates a recruitment method to when the successful candidate begins to work is called *time-lapse data*. Assume that the accounting company in the above example found the following: six days elapsed between submission of application forms and résumés to invitation for an interview; five days then passed from invitation to actual interview; five days from interview to job offer; six days from job offer to acceptance; and 23 days from acceptance of job offer to commencement of work. These data indicate that, using on-campus recruiting, the firm must initiate recruitment efforts at least 45 days before the anticipated job opening date. Calculating time-lapse data for each recruitment method means that the amount of lead time available can be taken into account when deciding which strategy or strategies would be most appropriate.

Figure 6.5 provides the results of a recent survey of Canadian HR professionals regarding the effectiveness of various recruitment methods.

External Recruitment Methods

Many methods of recruiting from the external labour market are in use, but online recruiting has quickly become the most popular for many jobs. Several of the most common external recruitment methods will now be reviewed.

yield ratio   The percentage of applicants that proceed to the next stage of the selection process.

REQUIRED PROFESSIONAL CAPABILITIES

Evaluates recruiting effectiveness

FIGURE 6.5   Effectiveness of External Recruitment Methods

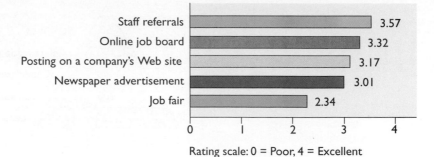

Rating scale: 0 = Poor, 4 = Excellent

Source: Chart 1, *Canadian HR Reporter* (May 23, 2005), R2. Reproduced by permission of *Canadian HR Reporter*, Carswell, One Corporate Plaza, 2075 Kennedy Road, Scarborough, ON M1T 3V4.

Online Recruiting

online recruitment The use of the Internet to aid in recruiting.

The majority of companies now use **online recruitment**, and a majority of Canadian workers use the Internet to research prospective employers, review job postings, complete online applications, and send their résumés via e-mail.[6] The online recruitment industry in Canada has grown to an estimated $40 million annually.[7]

The Internet provides recruiters with a large audience for job postings and a vast talent pool.[8] Online recruiting can involve accessing one or more Internet job boards, using a corporate Web site for external recruiting, and using an application service provider's recruitment software.

Recruiting Online
www.Jobster.com

Acti-Job Canada
www.actijob.com

Canadajobs.com
www.canadajobs.com

Canjobs.com
www.canjobs.com

Monster Board Canada
www.monster.ca

Workopolis.com
www.workopolis.com

HotJobs.com
www.hotjobs.com

CareerBuilder
www.careerbuilder.ca

Internet Job Boards   Online job boards are fast, easy, and convenient and allow recruiters to search for candidates for positions in two ways. First, for a fee, companies can post a job opening online and customize it by using corporate logos and adding details about the company benefits and culture. One job board is even offering employers the opportunity to advertise on television, as described in the Strategic HR box. Job seekers can search through the job postings, often by job type, region, or other criterion, and apply for the position online through the job board. The popularity of Internet job boards among job seekers is high because of the number of job postings available on one site—Monster.ca has an average of 25 000 Canadian job postings available at any given time.

Strategic HR

Lights, Camera, Recruitment

The Internet is a powerful forum for recruiters and job seekers alike, but in a tight labour market, employers have to pull out all the stops to attract the best candidates. Workopolis, an online career resource with job postings from across the country, is now offering employers a creative new way to sell themselves to potential recruits. In October 2005, Workopolis launched a 30-minute show, Workopolis TV, on Report on Business Television featuring career advice. The show features employers talking about what makes their companies great places to work as they highlight available positions.

A call-in segment will let jobseekers get more information about the company, the position, and how to apply. This ten-minute "career matching" segment will serve as a means of employment branding—a way to market to potential job candidates the same way a company markets its brand to consumers.

Source: Adapted from S. Klie, "Lights, Camera, Recruitment," *Canadian HR Reporter*, December 19, 2005, pp. 1, 14. Reproduced by permission of *Canadian HR Reporter*, Carswell, One Corporate Plaza, 2075 Kennedy Road, Scarborough, ON M1T 3V4.

Second, job seekers can post their résumés on job boards, and firms can search the database. Canada has hundreds of job boards, ranging from the largest one, Workopolis.com, with an average of 31 000 job postings daily, and Monster.ca, with a database of more than 2 million résumés and more than 3 million visitors per month, to many smaller job boards serving specific fields, from tourism to medicine.[9] Job board meta-crawlers, such as actualjobs.com and Toronto's 411jobs.ca, enable job seekers to search multiple job boards with one query.

One problem with Internet job boards is their vulnerability to privacy breaches. Fake job postings can lead to identity theft from submitted résumés, and résumés are sometimes copied onto competing job boards or other sites.[10]

Corporate Web Sites   With the overabundance of applicants now found on most online job boards, employers are now using their own corporate Web sites to recruit. Career pages provide a single platform for recruitment that promotes the corporate brand, educates the applicant about the company, captures data about the applicant, and provides an important link to job boards where a company's positions may be advertised.[11]

Using the company's Web site for recruiting has many advantages. It has been estimated that this recruitment strategy can reduce time to hire by weeks and save companies at least 30 percent on costs per hire. By targeting star candidates and acting immediately, firms can gain competitive advantage.[12] Another advantage is that company recruiters at one location can mine the candidate database and share résumés and candidate profiles with hiring managers and/or recruiters at other sites. Most software enables recruiters to track individual candidates through the recruitment and selection processes and permits candidates to keep their profiles up to date.

Corporate Web sites can help the company create a pool of candidates who have already expressed interest in the organization.[13] The company can also initiate ongoing communication via e-mail with candidates with whom the company feels it would be beneficial to keep in touch.

Using prescreening strategies is essential, however. The volume of résumés definitely does not diminish when the firm accepts them online. At Hewlett Packard, for example, more than 1 million online applications are received each year.[14] One way of coping with this volume is to generate automatic replies acknowledging receipt of applications. An automatic reply is an excellent public relations tool and also helps to avoid numerous follow-up e-mails and/or telephone calls.[15] At Montreal-based Bombardier Aerospace, for example, the Web site doesn't just provide a mechanism for e-mailing a résumé or filling in an application. The prescreening starts on the spot with a series of click-to-answer questions designed to determine the fit between the applicant and job specifications.

It is important that online recruiting be consistent with the company's overall marketing strategy and convey the same image and atmosphere as the organization itself. Recruitment is a two-way street, and having a world-class Web site provides an opportunity to sell the company and jobs to prospective applicants. To be effective, though, such Web sites must be user-friendly.[16]

Active job seekers are not the only potential future employees who visit corporate Web sites. Customers, investors, and competitors also visit corporate Web sites.[17] Many of those visiting career Web sites are "happily employed" individuals (known as "passive" job seekers) who are likely to arrive at the career site after browsing the company's main pages for other reasons, such as research into products or services. Therefore, it is important that a firm have a prominently positioned link on the homepage leading directly to the careers section to make it easy for passive job seekers to pursue job opportunities within the company.[18]

Best practices for career Web sites include the following:

- Include candid information about the culture, career paths, and business prospects.
- Include third-party sources of information on your company, such as articles, rankings, and awards.
- Design separate sections for different types of job seekers, such as students and part-timers.
- Have a direct link from the homepage to the career page.
- Have a job search tool that allows applicants to search open job positions by location and job category.
- Have a standardized application or résumé builder to allow for easy applicant screening.
- Use "e-mail to a friend" options for visitor referrals.[19]

Application Service Providers   Many firms use Web-enabled applicant tracking system providers, generically known as application service providers (ASPs), to power their career Web sites. ASP firms provide applicant screening tools to their subscribers, such as a standardized application or résumé builder, for candidates to fill out online. Standardized applicant information can then be sorted by using automated search, screening, and ranking to profile and verify a candidate's qualifications based on the job's specifications. Online applications can incorporate prescreening questions to assess the match between the candidate's skills, credentials, and experience and the requirements of a particular position. The use of applicant screening tools enables a firm's recruiter to create a short list of candidates for personal interviews.

The advantage of using ASP software is that the company does not have to worry about maintaining, updating, or administering recruiting software, allowing the HR department to focus on strategic recruitment efforts. Essentially, when applicants reach the career section of a company career page, they are moved to the ASP Web site.[20]

Print Advertising

Despite the advent of online recruiting, traditional advertising in newspapers and other print media is still a very common method of recruiting.[21] For advertising to bring the desired results, two issues must be addressed: the media to be used and the construction of the ad.[22] The selection of the best medium—whether it is the local newspaper, a national newspaper, a technical journal, or even a billboard—depends on the types of positions for which the organization is recruiting. Reaching individuals who are already employed and not actively seeking alternative employment requires a different medium than is appropriate to attract those who are unemployed.

To achieve optimum results from an advertisement, the following four-point guide, called *AIDA*, should be kept in mind as the ad is being constructed:

1. The ad should attract *attention*. The ads that stand out have borders, a company logo or picture, and effective use of empty white space. To attract attention, key positions should be advertised in display ads, rather than classified ads.

2. The ad should develop *interest* in the job. Interest can be created by the nature of the job itself, by pointing out the range of duties and/or the amount of challenge or responsibility involved. Sometimes other aspects of the job, such as its location or working conditions, are useful in attracting interest. To ensure that the individuals attracted are qualified, the job specifications should always be included.

3. The ad should create a *desire* for the job. This may be done by capitalizing on the interesting aspects of the job itself and by pointing out any unique benefits or opportunities associated with it, such as the opportunity for career development or travel. Desire may also be created by stressing the employer's commitment to employment equity. The target audience should be kept in mind as the ad is being created.

4. The ad should instigate *action*. To prompt action, ads often include a closing date and a statement such as "Call today," "Send your résumé today," "Check out our Web site for more information," or "Go to the site of our next job fair."

When properly constructed, advertisements can be an effective instrument for recruiting, as well as for communicating the organization's corporate image to the general public. A newspaper ad incorporating the AIDA guidelines is shown in **Figure 6.6**.

There are two general types of newspaper advertisements: want ads and blind ads. **Want ads** describe the job and its specifications, the compensation package, and the hiring employer. Although the content pertaining to the job, specifications, and compensation is identical in **blind ads**, such ads omit the identity and address of the hiring employer. Although many job seekers do not like responding to blind ads, because there is always the danger of unknowingly

---

RecruitAd
www.recruitad.com

want ad   A recruitment ad describing the job and its specifications, the compensation package, and the hiring employer. The address to which applications and/or résumés should be submitted is also provided.

blind ad   A recruitment ad in which the identity and address of the employer are omitted.

FIGURE 6.6   Recruitment Advertisement Illustrating AIDA Principles

Source: Reproduced with the permission of Anapharm.

sending a résumé to the firm at which they are currently employed, such ads do result in the opening remaining confidential (which may be necessary if the position is still staffed).

Many factors make advertising a useful recruiting method. Employers can use advertisements to reach and attract potential job applicants from a diverse labour market in as wide or narrow a geographical area as desired. To meet employment equity goals and timetables, ads can be placed in publications read by designated group members, such as a minority-language newspaper or the newsletter of a nonprofit agency assisting individuals who have a particular mental or physical disability.

Private Employment Agencies

Private employment agencies are often called on to provide assistance to employers seeking clerical staff, functional specialists, and technical employees. The "staffing" business has grown into a $6 billion industry that places hundreds of thousands of job seekers each year.[23] Generally, it is the employer who pays the agency fee. It is not uncommon for employers to be charged a fee equal to 15 to 30 percent of the first year's salary of the individual hired through agency referral. This percentage may vary depending on the volume of business provided by the client and type of employee sought.

These agencies take an employer's request for recruits and then solicit job seekers, relying primarily on Internet job boards, advertising, and walk-ins/write-ins. Employment agencies serve two basic functions: (1) expanding the applicant pool and (2) performing preliminary interviewing and screening. Specific situations in which an employment agency might be used for recruiting include the following:

- The organization does not have an HR department or does not have anyone with the requisite time and/or expertise.

- The firm has experienced difficulty in generating a pool of qualified candidates for the position or a similar type of position in the past.

- A particular opening must be filled quickly.

- There is a desire to recruit a greater number of designated group members than the firm has been able to attract on its own.

- The recruitment effort is aimed at reaching individuals who are currently employed and might therefore feel more comfortable answering ads placed by and dealing with an employment agency.

Tips for the Front Line

It should be noted, though, that the amount of service provided varies widely, as does the level of professionalism and the calibre of staff. Although most agencies carefully screen applicants, some simply provide a stream of applicants and let the client's HR department staff do the screening. Agency staff are usually paid on a commission basis, and their desire to earn a commission may occasionally compromise their professionalism (e.g., encouraging job seekers to accept jobs for which they are neither qualified nor suited).

Executive Search Firms

Employers retain executive search firms to fill critical positions in a firm, usually middle- to senior-level professional and managerial employees. Such firms often specialize in a particular type of talent, such as executives, sales, scientific, or middle-management employees. They typically know and understand the marketplace, have many contacts, and are especially adept at contacting qualified candidates who are employed and not actively looking to change jobs (which is why they have been given the nickname "headhunters"). Generally, one-third of the fee is payable as a retainer at the outset. Compared with the value of the time savings realized by the client firm's executive team, however, such a fee often turns out to be insignificant.

Using this recruitment method has some potential pitfalls.[24] Executive search firms cannot do an effective job if they are given inaccurate or incomplete information about the job and/or the firm. It is therefore essential for employers to explain in detail the type of candidate required—and why. A few headhunters are more salespeople than professionals, and they are more interested in persuading the employer to hire a candidate than in finding one who really meets the job specifications. Some firms have also been known to present an unpromising candidate to a client simply to make their one or two other prospects look that much better. The Association of Canadian Search, Employment and Staffing Services (ACSESS) sponsors the Certified Personnel Consultant (CPC) designation, which signifies that recruiters have met specific educational and testing requirements and confirms an individual's commitment to the best industry practices.[25]

Association of Canadian Search, Employee and Staffing Services (ACSESS)
www.acsess.org

Walk-Ins and Write-Ins

Individuals who go to organizations in person to apply for jobs without referral or invitation are called *walk-ins*. People who submit unsolicited résumés to organizations are known as *write-ins*. Walk-ins and write-ins are an inexpensive recruitment method. Their résumés are generally screened by the HR department and if an applicant is considered suitable, his or her résumé is retained on file for three to six months or passed on to the relevant department manager if there is an immediate or upcoming opening for which the applicant is qualified. Some organizations, such as RBC Financial Group, are using computer databases to store the information found on the résumés and application forms of walk-in and write-in candidates. Whether the original document is paper-based or submitted online, it can be scanned and stored on databases for fast, easy access using a few key words.[26]

Employee Referrals

Some organizations encourage applications from friends and relatives of current employees by mounting an employee referral campaign. Openings are announced in the company's intranet or newsletter, along with a request for referrals. Cash awards or prizes may be offered for referrals that culminate in a new hire. Because no advertising or agency fees are involved, paying bonuses still represents a low recruiting cost.

The disadvantages associated with employee referrals include the potential for inbreeding and **nepotism** to cause morale problems and dissatisfaction among employees whose referrals are not hired. Perhaps the biggest drawback, however, is that this method may result in systemic discrimination.

nepotism A preference for hiring relatives of current employees.

Educational Institutions

Recruiting at educational institutions is extremely effective when candidates require formal training but have relatively little full-time work experience. High schools can provide recruits for clerical and some blue-collar jobs. For example, EnCana, an oil-and-gas company headquartered in Calgary, is facing an ongoing shortage of skilled workers. It has started a program called "Oil and Gas

Many companies take recruitment campaigns into high schools to sell careers to a younger generation. This type of recruitment helps a variety of industries meet future recruitment demands. Here, students learn how to work on a car.

Production Field Operator Career Pathway," which offers high school students an opportunity to earn credits while learning about field production work. Beginning in grade 10, students in participating high schools can sign up for a distance-learning course supplied by Calgary-based Southern Alberta Institute of Technology (SAIT). Students who progress through the course in all three years will graduate with a production field operation certificate from SAIT. Students will have a chance of getting one of at least six paid internship positions with EnCana that last through eight weeks in the summer following each year.[27]

Most high schools, colleges, and universities have counselling centres that provide job-search assistance to students through such activities as skills assessment testing and workshops on résumé preparation and interview strategies. Sometimes they arrange for on-site job fairs, at which employers set up displays outlining the types of job opportunities available. The Halifax Joint Career Fair, a partnership among three of Nova Scotia's universities and colleges, is the foremost recruiting event in Atlantic Canada. Every year, the event attracts about 70 companies from across the country and 1500 students.[28]

Cooperative (co-op) education and field placement programs have become increasingly popular in Canada. These programs require students to spend a specified time working in organizations as an integral part of their academic program, thereby gaining some hands-on skills in an actual work setting. Co-op programs are offered in some high schools, as well as in colleges and universities.

Summer *internship programs* hire college and/or university students to complete summer projects between their second-last and final year of study. Their performance is assessed, and those who are judged to be superior are offered permanent positions following graduation. Other firms offer internship opportunities to graduates, thereby enabling them to acquire hands-on skills to supplement their education. As with student internships, outstanding performers

Career Edge
www.careeredge.org

Job Postings (Student Job Magazine)
www.jobpostings.ca

Student Connection Program
www.scp-ebb.com

are often offered full-time employment at the end of the program. It is now possible for firms to recruit graduate interns online through Career Edge, an organization committed to helping university, college, and high-school graduates gain essential career-related experience through internships. Career Edge uses the Internet as its sole means of bringing companies and youth together. More than 6500 young Canadians have started their careers through the program in more than 900 organizations. Within a few months of completing their internship, nearly 80 percent of interns have found permanent employment with competitive salaries and nearly 60 percent of the interns are hired by host organizations on a full-time basis.[29]

Internship, co-op, and field placement programs can produce a win–win result. The employer is provided with an inexpensive opportunity to assess potential employees while benefiting from the current knowledge and enthusiasm of bright, talented individuals. Because co-op students and interns have been exposed to the organization, they are less likely to leave shortly after permanent hire than recruits with no previous exposure to the firm.[30] Recognizing these benefits has made such programs a major recruitment method in many organizations.

Human Resources and Social Development Canada (HRSDC)

Job Bank
www.jobbank.gc.ca

Work Search
www.worksearch.gc.ca

CA Source
www.casource.com

Through various programs, including those for youth, Aboriginals, and persons with disabilities, HRSDC helps unemployed individuals to find suitable jobs and employers to locate qualified candidates to meet their needs—at no cost to either party. The Job Bank is the largest Web-based network of job postings available to Canadian employers free of charge, and it provides access to 700 000 new jobs each year, to more than 40 000 jobs at any given time, and up to 2000 new jobs posted every day. HRSDC also operates Job Match, a Web-based recruitment tool that can match employers' skill requirements with individuals' skill sets. Job seekers receive a list of employers with a matching job vacancy and employers receive a list of qualified candidates.[31]

Professional and Trade Associations

Professional and trade associations can be extremely helpful when recruiters are seeking individuals with specialized skills in such fields as IT, engineering, HR, and accounting, particularly if experience is a job requirement. Many such associations conduct ongoing placement activities on behalf of their members, and most regularly send their members newsletters or magazines in which organizations can place job advertisements. Such advertising may attract individuals who hadn't previously thought about changing jobs, as well as those actively seeking employment. For example, the Human Resources Professionals Association of Ontario (HRPAO) has an employment service called the Hire Authority. For a nominal fee, employers can post HR-related employment opportunities on the HRPAO Web site, where they can be viewed by HRPAO members. Additionally, employers can pay for access to an online database of member résumés and can search, sort, and prescreen qualified candidates for vacant positions.[32]

Labour Organizations

Some firms, particularly in the construction industry, obtain recruits through union hiring halls. The union maintains a roster of members (typically skilled trades people, such as carpenters, pipe fitters, welders, plumbers, and electricians), whom it sends out on assignment as requests from employers are received. Once the union members have completed their contracted work at one firm, they notify the union of their availability for another assignment.

Military Personnel

Military reservists are also potential recruits. The Canadian Forces Liaison Council (CFLC) is responsible for promoting the hiring of reservists by civilian employers. The CFLC also encourages civilian employers to give reservists time off for military training. Reserve force training develops skills and attributes sought after in the civilian workforce, such as leadership, planning, coordination, and teamwork.[33] Many organizations—such as Home Depot Canada and Énergie New Brunswick Power—have recognized the value of such leave and have joined the 4700 organizations in Canada that have signed a Statement of Support for the Reserve Forces with the CFLC.[34] The CFLC's Reserve Employment Assistance Program (REAP) allows employers to place job postings for skilled personnel at more than 300 military units across the country at no charge.[35]

Open Houses and Job Fairs

Another popular recruitment method involves holding an *open house*. Common in retail firms looking to staff a new store from the ground up, open houses have also been the choice of corporations trying to draw out scarce talent in an ultra-tight job market. A similar recruitment method involves holding a *job fair* on-site. At such events, recruiters share information about the organization and job opportunities with those attending in an informal, relaxed setting. Some organizations are now holding job fairs online (known as virtual job fairs) in order to connect with a wider geographical audience. Top prospects are invited to visit the firm or to return at a later date for a more in-depth assessment.

Recruiting Nonpermanent Staff

In recent years, many companies have increased their use of contingent workers in order to attain labour flexibility and to acquire employees with special skills on an as-needed basis. In these firms, recruiters are spending more time seeking temporary (term, seasonal, casual) and contract workers and less time recruiting permanent staff.[36] Three sources of nonpermanent staff are temporary help agencies, contract workers, and employee leasing.

Temporary Help Agencies

Temporary help agencies, such as Kelly Services and Office Overload, exist in all major cities in Canada. They specialize in providing temporary workers to cover for employees who are ill, on vacation, or on a leave of absence. Firms also use temporary employees to handle seasonal work, peak workloads, and special projects for which no current employees have the time and/or expertise. Temporary workers are agency employees and are reassigned to another employer when their services are no longer required.

Temps provide employers with three major benefits:

1. They cost much less than permanent employees, as they generally receive less compensation than permanent staff. There are also savings related to the hiring and training costs associated with permanent employees. In fact, training has become the central investment in the business strategy of many temporary employment agencies. For example, Accountemps invests in the skills and training of employees after they have worked for a specified amount of time. This training includes online tutoring in software they may use on the job and tuition reimbursement for skills training.[37]

2. If a temp performs unsatisfactorily, a substitute can be requested immediately. Generally, a suitable replacement is sent to the firm within one business day.

3. Individuals working as temps who are seeking full-time employment are often highly motivated, knowing that many firms choose full-time employees from the ranks of their top-performing temps.

Contract Workers

contract workers   Employees who develop work relationships directly with the employer for a specific type of work or period of time.

Contract workers are employees who develop work relationships directly with the employer for a specific type of work or period of time.[38] For example, Parc Aviation is a major supplier of contract workers to the airline industry. Airline organizations benefit from the services of contract engineers by having them cover seasonal or unplanned peaks in business, carry out special tasks or projects, and reduce the necessity for airlines to downsize permanent staff during cyclical downturns.[39]

Many professionals with specialized skills become contract workers, including project managers, accountants, and lawyers. Some have consciously made a decision to work for themselves; others have been unable to obtain full-time employment in their field of expertise or have found themselves out of a full-time job because of cutbacks. Thus, some want to remain self-employed; others work a contract while hoping to obtain a full-time position eventually. Some firms hire former employees (such as retirees) on a contract basis.

Employee Leasing

employee leasing   An arrangement that typically involves a company transferring specific employees to the payroll of an employee leasing firm/professional employer organization (PEO) in an explicit joint-employment relationship.

Employee leasing arrangements typically involve a company transferring specific employees to the payroll of an employee leasing firm/professional employer organization (PEO) in an explicit joint-employment relationship. These employees then become employees of the PEO, which leases these individuals back to the client company on a permanent basis. The PEO maintains the HR files for the leased employees, handles the administration of their pay and benefits, and performs most of the other functions normally handled by a firm's HR department staff members. In return, the PEO receives a placement fee.[40] Not all leasing arrangements are based on the transfer of staff from the client organizations to a PEO. Some leasing companies also hire workers themselves and then lease them out to client organizations.

National Association of Professional Employer Organizations (NAPEO) www.napeo.org

> **An Ethical Dilemma**
>
> Is it ethical to keep extending the contracts of contract workers rather than hiring them as permanent employees in order to avoid the cost of employee benefits?

RECRUITING A MORE DIVERSE WORKFORCE

Recruiting a diverse workforce is not just socially responsible—it's a necessity. As noted previously, the composition of Canada's workforce is changing dramatically. Trends of particular significance include the increasing necessity of hiring older employees, a decrease in the availability of young workers, and an increase in the number of women, visible minorities, Aboriginal people, and persons with disabilities in the workforce.

Attracting Older Workers

Prime50 www.prime50.com

Many employers, recognizing the fact that the workforce is aging, are encouraging retirement-age employees to stay with the company or are actively recruiting employees who are at or beyond retirement age. For example, 20 percent of Home Depot Canada's workforce is over age 50.[41] Hiring and retaining older employees has significant benefits. These workers typically have high job satisfaction, a strong sense of loyalty and organizational commitment, a strong work ethic, good people skills, and willingness to work in a variety of roles, including part-time.[42]

To make a company attractive to older workers, it is important to deal with stereotypical attitudes toward older workers through education, ensure that HR policies do not discourage recruitment of older workers, develop flexible work arrangements, and redesign jobs to accommodate decreased dexterity and strength. A 2005 research study by the Conference Board of Canada concluded that employers should take action to retain and recruit older workers. The retiring baby boomers represent a large, underutilized, skilled labour pool, and so far little effort has been made to attract these people.[43]

Attracting Younger Employees

Many firms are recognizing the benefits of a multigenerational workforce and not only are trying to attract older workers but also are taking steps to address the pending shortage of younger employees. Although older employees have comparatively wider experience and wisdom, the young bring energy, enthusiasm, and physical strength to their positions.

Successful organizations balance these different kinds of experience. McDonald's Restaurants of Canada Ltd. (one of the largest employers of youth in the country and an active recruiter of seniors) feels that it is critical for organizations in the service industry to have employees who mirror their customer base. Its experience is that each member of the multi-age teams brings a particular strength, which leads to synergy, respect, and team-building.[44]

Younger members of the workforce are part of the Generation X and Generation Y cohorts. To appeal to Generation Xers, it is important to stress that they will be able to work independently and that work/life balance is supported. They will be attracted by learning and development opportunities. Potential employees from Generation Y will want to know that they will be working with experts from across the organization and that they will have a variety of experiences. They will be attracted by organizations that value social responsibility, diversity, and creativity.[45]

Recruiting Designated Group Members

Aboriginal Human Resource Development Council of Canada
www.ahrdcc.com

Canadian Council for Rehabilitation and Work
www.ccrw.org

WORKink
www.workink.com

Ontario Ministry of Community and Social Services—Paths to Equal Opportunity
www.equalopportunity.on.ca

Most of the recruitment methods discussed previously can be used to attract designated group members, provided that the employer's commitment to equity and diversity is made clear to all involved in the recruitment process—whether it is employees asked for referrals or private employment agencies. This can also be stressed in all recruitment advertising. Alternative publications targeted at designated group members should be considered for advertising, and linkages can be formed with organizations and agencies specializing in assisting designated group members. Specific examples follow:

- The Aboriginal Human Resource Development Council of Canada, headquartered in Saskatoon, Saskatchewan, sponsors the Aboriginal Inclusion Network (iN), which offers a job board, résumé database, and other tools to hire, retain, and promote Aboriginal talent. The iN is linked to 350 Aboriginal employment centres across Canada.[46]

- WORKink is Canada's most powerful online career development and employment portal for Canadians with disabilities. The WORKink site offers a full complement of employment and recruitment resources and services for job seekers with disabilities and for employers looking to create an inclusive workplace. WORK*ink* is sponsored by the Canadian Council on Rehabilitation and Work. Employers can post job openings free of charge, browse résumés of people with disabilities, or access information on how to adapt the work environment to accommodate people with disabilities in their region.[47]

- The Society for Canadian Women in Science and Technology (SCWIST) is a nonprofit, volunteer organization aimed improving attitudes and stereotypes about, and assisting, women in scientific, technological, and engineering careers. Employers can access valuable information about resources, such as Web sites, employment agencies, and publications, to attract professional women for employment opportunities in industries where they generally have a low representation.[48]

- The Ontario Ministry of Community and Social Services sponsors a program called *Paths to Equal Opportunity* intended to provide links to information on removing and preventing barriers so that people with disabilities can work, learn, and play to their fullest potential. In conjunction with the Canadian Abilities Foundation, the program publishes a resource booklet called *Abilities @ Work*, which provides specific information to (1) employers who want to find out about recruiting, interviewing, hiring, and working with people with disabilities, and (2) employees and jobseekers with disabilities who want information on looking for work, accommodation in the workplace, and maintaining employment.

Another useful tool is the guidebook *Tapping the Talents of People with Disabilities: A Guidebook for Employers*, which is available through the Conference Board of Canada. More information on hiring people with disabilities is provided in the Workforce Diversity box.

Workforce Diversity

The Disconnect in Recruiting People with Disabilities

The good news is that employers want to hire people with disabilities, and qualified candidates are available. But putting employers and jobseekers together needs improved coordination to create more success stories. Employers have bottom-line reasons for building workforce diversity. Inclusiveness is a competitive advantage that lets an organization better connect with a diverse community and customer base. Inclusiveness provides access to a larger pool of strong job candidates in a time of skills shortages and enhances an organization's reputation as an employer of choice.

So why aren't more employers tapping into the wealth of human potential in people with disabilities? After all, as a group they make up some 13 percent of the working-age population. That is precisely what the

Canadian Abilities Foundation set out to determine in its recently completed *Neglected or Hidden* study, the findings of which may surprise employers.

Likely the most revealing finding that illustrates the need for a new employment strategy for people with disabilities is the disconnect that exists among employers, people with disabilities, and the service providers who help these individuals enter the workforce.

With few exceptions, these stakeholders just don't seem to know how to communicate with one another, if they are fortunate enough to find one another in the first place. The commitment and passion of workers with disabilities and those assisting them is sound. Meanwhile, hundreds and hundreds of disability-related organizations across Canada provide some level of employment support to these clients. The *Neglected or Hidden* study suggests that the number of Canadian employers willing to hire people with disabilities should be more than adequate to meet the availability of disabled jobseekers.

continued

The good news is that a small number of disability organizations have made significant inroads in their regions by using employer partnerships. One example is the Dartmouth Work Activity Society in Nova Scotia, which started its new approach with just a single employer "partner," who was highly satisfied with the services provided. EmployAbilities, a full-time service agency serving Edmonton and northern Alberta for more than 30 years, has also launched a partnership-building strategy. A unique feature of the agency's approach is its partnership with the local chamber of commerce through which it offers advice on disability issues to employers.

Source: Adapted from A. Prost, "Successful Recruiting from an Untapped Source," *Canadian HR Reporter*, January 16, 2006, pp. 11–12. Reproduced by permission of *Canadian HR Reporter*, Carswell, One Corporate Plaza, 2075 Kennedy Road, Scarborough, ON M1T 3V4.

DEVELOPING AND USING APPLICATION FORMS

For most employers, completion of an application form is the last step in the recruitment process. An application form provides an efficient means of collecting verifiable historical data from each candidate in a standardized format; it usually includes information about education, prior work history, and other job-related skills.

A completed application form can provide the recruiter with information on the applicant's education and experience, a brief overview of the applicant's career progress and growth, and information that can be used to predict whether or not the candidate will succeed on the job. Even when detailed résumés have been submitted, most firms also request that a standardized company application form be completed. There are many reasons for this practice:

> **Tips for the Front Line**

- Candidate comparison is facilitated because information is collected in a uniform manner.

- The information that the company requires is specifically requested, rather than just what the candidate wants to reveal.

- Candidates are typically asked to complete an application form while on the company premises, and thus it is a sample of the candidate's own work. (Obtaining assistance with résumés is common, given that many job boards offer online résumé building options.)

- Application forms typically ask the candidate to provide written authorization for reference checking.

- Candidates are asked to acknowledge that the information provided is true and accurate, which protects the company from applicants who falsify their credentials.

- Many application forms today have an optional section regarding designated group member status. An example is provided in **Figure 6.7**. The data collected are used for employment equity tracking purposes.

Human Rights Legislation and Application Forms

Application forms cannot ask questions that would directly or indirectly classify candidates on the basis of any of the prohibited grounds under human rights legislation, such as asking for a photograph; information about illnesses, disabilities, or workers' compensation claims; or information that could lead to direct, intentional discrimination, such as age, gender, sexual

Most firms require that a standardized company application form be completed, even if a résumé has been submitted.

FIGURE 6.7 Self-Identification for Employment Equity Purposes

Employee Self-Identification Form

(Confidential when completed)

- This form is designed to collect information on the composition of the Public Service workforce to comply with legislation on employment equity and to facilitate the planning and implementation of employment equity activities. Your response is voluntary and you may identify in more than one designated group.

- The information you provide will be used in compiling statistics on employment equity in the federal Public Service. With your consent (see Box E), it may also be used by the employment equity coordinator of your department for human resource management purposes. This includes referral for training and developmental assignments and, in the case of persons with disabilities, facilitating appropriate accommodation in the workplace.

- Employment equity information will be retained in the Employment Equity Data Bank (EEDB) of the Treasury Board Secretariat and its confidentiality is protected under the *Privacy Act*. You have the right to review and correct information about yourself and can be assured that it will not be used for unauthorized purposes.

- If you need more information or require assistance in completing this form, please contact _____ at _____. This form is also available in Braille, large print and on diskette and audio-cassette.

Step 1: Complete boxes A to E. In boxes B, C and D, refer to the definitions provided.

Step 2: Sign and date the form and return it in the attached envelope

Thank you for your cooperation.

TBS/PPB 300-02432
TBS/SCT 330-78 (Rev. 1999–02)

A.

Family Name	Given Name and Initial

Department or Agency/Branch

( )	
Telephone # (office)	Personal Record Identifier (PRI)

○ Female   ○ Male

B. A person with a disability (i) has a long-term or recurring physical, mental, sensory, psychiatric, or learning impairment and

a) considers himself/herself to be disadvantaged in employment by reason of that impairment, or

b) believes that an employer or potential employer is likely to consider him/her to be disadvantaged in employment by reason of that impairment, and includes persons whose functional limitations owing to their impairment have been accommodated in their current job or workplace.

ARE YOU A PERSON WITH A DISABILITY?

○ No

○ Yes, check all that apply

11 ○ Coordination or dexterity (difficulty using hands or arms, for example, grasping or handling a stapler or using a keyboard)

12 ○ Mobility (difficulty moving around, for example, from one office to another or up and down stairs)

16 ○ Blind or visual impairment (unable to see or difficulty seeing)

19 ○ Deaf or hard of hearing (unable to hear or difficulty hearing)

13 ○ Speech impairment (unable to speak or difficulty speaking and being understood)

continued

23 ○ Other disability (including learning disabilities, developmental disabilities and all other types of disabilities)

(Please specify) _____

C. An Aboriginal person is a North American Indian or a member of the First Nation, a Métis, or Inuit. North American Indians or members of a First Nation include status, treaty or registered Indians, as well as non-status and non-registered Indians.

ARE YOU AN ABORIGINAL PERSON?

○ No

○ Yes, check the appropriate circle

03 ○ North American Indian/First Nation

02 ○ Métis

01 ○ Inuit

D. A person in a visible minority in Canada is someone (other than an Aboriginal person as defined in C above) who is non-white in colour/race, regardless of place of birth.

ARE YOU IN A VISIBLE MINORITY GROUP?

○ No

○ Yes, check the circle which best describes your visible minority group or origin

41 ○ Black

45 ○ Chinese

51 ○ Filipino

47 ○ Japanese

48 ○ Korean

56 ○ South Asian/East Indian (including Indian from India; Bangladesh; Pakistani; East Indian from Guyana; Trinidad; East Africa; etc.)

58 ○ Southeast Asian (including Burmese; Cambodian; Laotian; Thai; Vietnamese; etc.)

57 ○ Non-White West Asian, North African and Arab (including Egyptian; Libyan; Lebanese; Iranian; etc.)

42 ○ Non-White Latin American (including indigenous persons from Central and South America, etc.)

44 ○ Persons of Mixed Origin (with one parent in one of the visible minority groups listed above)

59 ○ Other Visible Minority Group

(Please specify) _____

E. 99○ The information in this form may be used for human resources management.

_____   _____

29 Signature   Date (DD/MM/YY)

Modified: 2003–02-19

Source: Employee Self-identification Form, www.hrma-agrh.gc.ca/ee/survey-sondage/form-formulaire_e.asp. Reproduced courtesy of Public Service Human Resources Management Agency of Canada, and with permission of the Minister of Public Works and Government Services, 2007.

orientation, marital status, maiden name, date of birth, place of origin, number of dependants, and so on.

If an application form has any illegal questions, an unsuccessful candidate may challenge the legality of the entire recruitment and selection processes. In such case, the burden of proof is on the employer. Thus, taking human rights legislative requirements into consideration when designing application forms is imperative. The *Guide to Screening and Selection in Employment* in the Appendix to Chapter 7 (see page 193) provides helpful hints. Specific guidelines regarding questions that can and cannot be asked on application forms are available through the human rights commissions in each jurisdiction. **Figure 6.8,** a sample application form developed by the Ontario Human Rights Commission, illustrates the types of information that can legally be requested.

FIGURE 6.8   Sample Application Form

Sample Application for Employment

Position being applied for _____   Date available for work _____

PERSONAL DATA

Last name _____   Given name(s) _____

Address _____   Apt. No. _____

Home Telephone Number _____

City _____   Province _____   Postal Code _____

Business Telephone Number _____

Are you legally eligible to work in Canada?   Yes ☐   No ☐

Are you 18 years or more and less than 65 years of age?   Yes ☐   No ☐

Are you willing to relocate in Ontario?   Yes ☐   No ☐

Preferred Location _____

To determine your qualification for employment, please provide below and on the reverse, information related to your academic and other achievements including volunteer work, as well as employment history. Additional information may be attached on a separate sheet.

EDUCATION

SECONDARY SCHOOL ☐

BUSINESS OR TRADE SCHOOL ☐

Highest grade or level completed _____   Name of program _____

Length of program _____

Diploma, certificate or licence awarded?

Yes ☐   No ☐   Honours ☐   Type: _____

COMMUNITY COLLEGE ☐   UNIVERSITY ☐

Major subject _____   Name of program _____

Length of program _____

Degree, diploma or certificate awarded?

Yes ☐   No ☐   Honours ☐

Type: _____

Other courses, workshops, seminars, Licences, Certificates, Degrees

WORK-RELATED SKILLS

Describe any of your work-related skills, experience, or training that relate to the position being applied for.

EMPLOYMENT

Name of present/last employer _____   Job title _____

TYPE OF BUSINESS

Period of employment (includes leaves of absence related to maternity/parental leave, Workers' Compensation claims, handicap/disability, or human rights complaints)

From _____   To _____   Salary _____

continued

Reason for leaving (do not include leaves of absence related to maternity/parental leave, Workers' Compensation claims, handicap/disability, or human rights complaints)

Functions/Responsibilities _____

_____

Name of previous employer _____   Job title _____

TYPE OF BUSINESS

Period of employment (includes leaves of absence related to maternity/parental leave, Workers' Compensation claims, handicap/disability, or human rights complaints)

From _____   To _____   Salary _____

Reason for leaving (do not include leaves of absence related to maternity/parental leave, Workers' Compensation claims, handicap/disability, or human rights complaints)

Functions/Responsibilities _____

_____

Name of previous employer _____   Job title _____

TYPE OF BUSINESS

Period of employment (includes leaves of absence related to maternity/parental leave, Workers' Compensation claims, handicap/disability, or human rights complaints)

From _____   To _____   Salary _____

Reason for leaving (do not include leaves of absence related to maternity/parental leave, Workers' Compensation claims, handicap/disability, or human rights complaints)

Functions/Responsibilities _____

_____

For employment references may we approach:

Your present/last employer?   Yes ☐   No ☐

Your former employer(s)?   Yes ☐   No ☐

List references if different from above on a separate sheet. _____

_____

PERSONAL INTEREST AND ACTIVITIES (civic, athletic, etc.) _____

_____

I hereby declare that the foregoing information is true and complete to my knowledge. I understand that a false statement may disqualify me from employment, or cause my dismissal.

Have you attached an additional sheet?

Yes ☐   No ☐

Signature _____   Date _____

Source: Sample Application for Employment, from *Human Rights at Work* (Toronto: Ontario Human Rights Commission, 2005). © Queen's Printer for Ontario, 2005. Reproduced with permission.

Using Application Forms to Predict Job Performance

Some firms use application forms to predict which candidates will be successful and which will not, in much the same way that employers use tests for screening.

One approach involves designing a **weighted application blank (WAB)**. Statistical studies are conducted to find the relationship between (1) responses on the application form and (2) measures of success on the job. A scoring system is subsequently developed by weighting the different possible responses to those particular items. By scoring an applicant's response to each of those questions and then totalling the scores obtained, a composite score can be calculated for each applicant. Although studies have shown that WABs can be highly valid predictors, and they can be developed fairly easily, such forms are used by relatively few organizations.

Another type of application form that can be used to predict performance is a **biographical information blank (BIB)**, also known as a biodata form.[49] Essentially, it is a more detailed version of an application form, focusing on

weighted application blank (WAB) A job application form on which applicant responses have been weighted based on their statistical relationship to measures of job success.

biographical information blank (BIB) A detailed job application form requesting biographical data found to be predictive of success on the job, pertaining to background, experiences, and preferences. As with a WAB, responses are scored.

biographical data found to be predictive of job success. Candidates respond to a series of questions about their background, experiences, and preferences, including willingness to travel and leisure activities, as shown in **Figure 6.9**. Because

FIGURE 6.9   Example of a Biographical Information Blank

Personal Information

Name _____   _____
                            Last   First

Mailing Address _____
                                        Street, City, Province, Postal Code

How long have you lived at your current address? _____

Do you consider your net worth to be low _____   moderate _____   or high _____?

Have you ever been turned down for a loan?   Yes _____   No _____

How many credit cards do you have? _____

Education and Training

Highest level of education completed:

High School _____   Vocational _____   College _____   University _____   Postgraduate _____

What educational degrees do you have? Diploma/Certificate _____   B.A. _____   B.Sc. _____
B.Comm. _____   M.B.A. _____   Master's _____   Other (Identify) _____

What subjects did you major in? _____

What was your grade-point average in college or university?   A _____   B _____   C _____   D _____

Did you graduate with honours?   Yes _____   No _____

Did you receive any awards for academic excellence?   Yes _____   No _____

Did you receive any scholarships?   Yes _____   No _____

List the extracurricular activities you participated in during school:

_____

Information about You

Did you find school stimulating _____   boring _____?

Did you hold a job while attending school?   Yes _____   No _____

How did you pay for your post-high-school training? (Check as many as appropriate)

Parents paid _____   Loans _____   Scholarships _____   Paid own way _____

Have you ever held a job where you earned commissions on sales?   Yes _____   No _____

If "Yes," were your commissions low _____   moderate _____   high _____?

Five years from now, what do you expect your salary to be? _____

Do you enjoy meeting new people?   Yes _____   No _____

How many social phone calls do you receive a week? _____

Do people count on you to "cheer up" others?   Yes _____   No _____

How many parties do you go to in a year? _____

Do you enjoy talking to people?   Yes _____   No _____

Rate your conversational skills:

Excellent _____   Very Good _____   Good _____   Fair _____   Poor _____

How often do you introduce yourself to other people you don't know?

Always _____   Sometimes _____   Never _____

Do you enjoy social gatherings?   Yes _____   No _____

Do you go to social gatherings out of a sense of duty?   Yes _____   No _____

How many times a year do you go out to dinner with friends? _____

Do you enjoy talking to people you don't know?   Yes _____   No _____

What are your hobbies?

_____

What sports, recreational, or physical activities do you engage in?

_____

How confident are you in your ability to succeed?

Very Confident _____   Confident _____   Somewhat Confident _____

Source: From *Recruitment and Selection in Canada*, Third Canadian Edition, by Catano/Cronshaw, 2005. Reprinted with permission of Nelson, a division of Thomson Learning: www.thomsonrights.com. Fax 800-730-2215.

biographical questions rarely have right or wrong answers, BIBs are difficult to fake. The development of a BIB requires that the items that are valid predictors of job success be identified and that weights be established for different responses to these items. By totalling the scores for each item, it is possible to obtain a composite score for each applicant.

Chapter Review

Summary

1. Recruitment is the process of searching out and attracting qualified job applicants. It begins with the identification of a position that requires staffing and is completed when résumés and/or completed application forms are received. The individuals recruited by the organizations are potential employees. If selected, they will be responsible for implementing, and in some cases creating, the organization's strategy. Therefore, recruitment is an important strategic activity because it directly affects the attainment of strategic objectives.

2. The recruitment process has four steps. First, job openings are identified through HR planning or manager request. Second, the job description and job specification are then reviewed to determine the job requirements. Third, appropriate recruiting source(s) and method(s) are chosen. Fourth, using these strategies, a pool of qualified candidates is generated.

3. Job posting is the process of notifying existing employees about vacant positions. Human resources records may indicate appropriate applicants for vacant positions. Skills inventories may provide even better information.

4. External recruitment methods include online recruiting, print advertising, private employment agencies, executive search firms, walk-ins/write-ins, employee referrals, educational institutions, HRSDC, professional and trade associations, labour organizations, military personnel, and open houses/job fairs.

5. Three strategies for obtaining nonpermanent staff include using temporary help agencies, hiring contract workers, and leasing employees.

6. Recruiting a diverse workforce is a necessity, given the shrinking labour force. In particular, recruiters are trying to attract older workers, younger workers, women, visible minorities, Aboriginal people, and people with disabilities.

7. Application forms are important because they provide information on the applicant's education and experience, a brief overview of the applicant's career progress, and information that can be used to predict whether an applicant will succeed on the job.

Key Terms

biographical information blank (BIB)   *(p. 160)*
blind ad   *(p. 147)*
contract workers   *(p. 153)*
employee leasing   *(p. 153)*
job posting   *(p. 140)*
nepotism   *(p. 149)*
online recruitment   *(p. 144)*
recruiter   *(p. 138)*
recruitment   *(p. 138)*
want ad   *(p. 147)*
weighted application blank (WAB)   *(p. 160)*
yield ratio   *(p. 143)*

Review and Discussion Questions

1. Discuss the advantages and disadvantages of recruiting within the organization.

2. List the advantages of external recruitment.

3. Explain the difference between an Internet job board and a corporate career Web site.

4. Describe the AIDA guidelines for print advertising.

5. Under what circumstances should a private employment agency be used?

6. Describe three ways to recruit designated group members.

Critical Thinking Questions

1. What potential problems could be created by offering referral bonuses to existing employees?

2. Compare and contrast the advantages and disadvantages of traditional and virtual career fairs.

3. As the labour supply gets tighter and tighter, would you be in favour of loosening requirements for foreign-trained professionals to become qualified in Canada?

4. What are some of the specific reservations that a 30-year-old candidate might have about applying for a job that requires managing a workforce that is on average ten years older than he or she is?

Application Exercises

Running Case: LearnInMotion.com

Getting Better Applicants

If Jennifer and Pierre were asked what the main problem was in running their business, their answer would be quick and short: hiring good people. They were simply astonished at how hard it was to attract and hire good candidates. After much debate, they decided to post openings for seven positions: two salespeople, one Web designer, two content management people, one office manager, and one Web surfer.

Their first approach was to design and place a large display ad in two local newspapers. The display ad listed all the positions available. Jennifer and Pierre assumed that by placing a large ad with the name of the company prominently displayed and a bold border around the ad, it would draw attention and therefore generate applicants. For two consecutive weekends, the ad cost the fledgling company close to $1000, but it produced only a handful of applicants. After speaking with them by phone, Jennifer and Pierre rejected three outright; two said they weren't interested; and two scheduled interviews but never showed up.

The owners therefore decided to change their approach. They used different recruiting methods for each position. In the paper, they placed ads for the salespeople under "Sales" and for the office manager under "Administrative."

They advertised for a Web designer by placing an ad on Monster.ca. And for the content managers and Web surfer, they placed neatly typed help wanted ads in the career placement offices of a technical college and a community college about ten minutes away from their office. They also used this job posting approach to find independent contractors they could use to deliver courses physically to users' homes or offices.

The results were disappointing. Over a typical weekend, literally dozens of want ads for experienced salespeople appear, as well as almost as many for office managers. The ad for salespeople generated about three calls, one of whom Jennifer and Pierre felt might be a viable candidate, although the person wanted a much higher salary than they had planned to pay. One possible candidate emerged for the office manager position.

They decided to change the positioning of the sales ad (since the job involved entirely inside phone sales) in the newspaper from "Salespersons Wanted" to "Phone Sales," which is a separate category. Many of the calls they got (not all of them, but many) were from salespeople who were used to working in what some people called "boiler-room" operations. In other words, they sit at the phone all day making cold calls from lists provided by their employers, selling anything from burglar alarms to investments, all under very high-pressure conditions. They weren't interested in LearnInMotion, nor was LearnInMotion interested in them.

They fared a little better with the Web designer ad, which produced four possible applicants. They got no phone calls from the local college job postings; when they called to ask the placement offices why, they were told that their posted salary of $8 per hour was "way too low." They went back and replaced the job postings with $10 hourly rates.

"I just don't understand it," Jennifer finally said. Especially for the sales job, Jennifer and Pierre felt that they were offering perfectly acceptable compensation packages, so the lack of applicants surprised them. "Maybe a lot of people just don't want to work for dot-coms anymore," said Pierre, thinking out loud. "When the bottom fell out of the dot-com market, a lot of good people were by working for a series of two or three failed dot-coms. Maybe they've just had enough of the wired world."

Question

1. Tell Jennifer and Pierre what they're doing wrong.

2. Provide a detailed list of recommendations concerning how they should go about increasing their pool of acceptable job applicants, so they no longer have to hire almost anyone who walks in the door. (Recommendations should include completely worded advertisements and suggestions regarding any other recruiting strategies you would suggest they use.)

Case Incident

Expansion at Ontario Engineering Works

Ontario Engineering Works is considering a major expansion. Management expects the number of employees to increase by almost 30 percent in the next few years to meet the needs of expansion. The company has been keeping records of its experiences with recruiting methods in the recent past. **Figure 6.10** shows a summary of relevant data for the production and sales workforce.

Question

1. Make your recommendation on the best recruitment method(s) for each type of workforce.

FIGURE 6.10   Details of Past Recruitment Outcomes

	Walk-In	Write-In	HRSDC	Ads	Employee Referrals	Campus Recruiting	Internet
Total number of applications							
Production	90	70	40	230	30	30	410
Sales	30	60	130	420	20	40	300
Total yield (%)*							
Production	9	17	4	23	3	3	41
Sales	3	6	13	42	2	4	30
Ratio (%) of acceptance to applications							
Production	30	40	20	50	50	60	8
Sales	30	80	25	50	40	50	12
Ratio (%) of acceptance to job offers							
Production	50	60	70	75	60	75	50
Sales	70	80	80	50	50	60	40
Cost of recruiting per person hired ($)							
Production	20	40	12	110	20	20	40
Sales	20	30	9	140	20	30	30
Employee turnover within a two-year period							
Production	14	15	10	12.5	4	7.5	20
Sales	10	5	7.5	15	9	14	18

*Yield denotes the percentage of total applications emerging from this method.

Source: Adapted from H. Das, *Recruitment, Selection, and Deployment of Human Resources*, Toronto, ON: Pearson Education Canada, 2007, p. 197. Reproduced with permission of Pearson Education Canada.

Experiential Exercises

1. Examine classified and display ads appearing in the help-wanted section of a recent newspaper. Choose three ads and, using the AIDA guidelines presented in this chapter, analyze the effectiveness of each one.

2. Go to your university's or college's career centre and gather information on all the services they provide. How many companies come to recruit students through the centre each year? What services does the centre provide to employers seeking to hire graduating students? Employers seeking to hire summer students? Employers seeking to hire students for internships?

CHAPTER 7

SELECTION

REQUIRED PROFESSIONAL CAPABILITIES

- Analyzes position requirements to establish selection criteria

- Establishes screening and assessment procedures

- Establishes appointment procedures

LEARNING OUTCOMES

AFTER STUDYING THIS CHAPTER, YOU SHOULD BE ABLE TO

Define selection, and **discuss** its strategic importance.

Define reliability and validity, and **explain** their importance in selection techniques.

Describe at least four types of testing used in selection, and **analyze** the conflicting legal concerns related to alcohol and drug testing.

Describe the major types of selection interviews by degree of structure, type of content, and manner of administration.

Explain the importance of reference checking, **describe** strategies to make such checking effective, and **analyze** the legal issues involved.

THE STRATEGIC IMPORTANCE OF EMPLOYEE SELECTION

selection The process of choosing among individuals who have been recruited to fill existing or projected job openings.

Selection is the process of choosing among individuals who have been recruited to fill existing or projected job openings. Whether considering current employees for a transfer or promotion, or outside candidates for a first-time position with the firm, information about the applicants must be collected and evaluated.

The selection process has important strategic significance. More and more managers have realized that the quality of the company's human resources is often the single most important factor in determining whether the firm is going to survive and be successful in reaching the objectives specified in its strategic plan. Those individuals selected will be implementing strategic decisions and, in some cases, creating strategic plans. Thus, the successful candidates must fit with the strategic direction of the organization. For example, if the organization is planning to expand internationally, language skills and international experience will become important selection criteria.

When a poor selection decision is made and the individual selected for the job is not capable of acceptable performance in the job, strategic objectives will not be met. In addition, when an unsuccessful employee must be terminated, the recruitment and selection process must begin all over again, and the successor must be properly oriented and trained. The "hidden" costs are frequently even higher, including internal disorganization and disruption, and customer alienation. For example, the City of Waterloo was forced to fire its new chief administrative officer after three weeks on the job in 2004 when it was found that he had provided inaccurate and misleading information to city council in a previous job.[1]

There are also legal implications associated with ineffective selection. *Human rights* legislation in every Canadian jurisdiction prohibits discrimination in all aspects, terms, and conditions of employment on such grounds as race, religion or creed, colour, marital status, gender, age, and disability. Firms must ensure that all their selection procedures are free of both intentional and systemic discrimination (see Appendix 7.1, which provides the Canadian Human Rights Commission's *Guide to Screening and Selection in Employment*). Organizations required by law to implement an employment equity plan must ensure that all their employment systems, including selection, are bias-free and do not have an adverse impact on members of the four designated groups— women, visible minorities, Aboriginals, and persons with disabilities.

An Ethical Dilemma

As the company recruiter, how would you handle a request from the CEO that you hire her son for a summer job, knowing that, given current hiring constraints, the sons and daughters of other employees will not be able to obtain such positions?

Another legal implication is employer liability for *negligent or wrongful hiring*. Courts are increasingly finding employers liable when employees with unsuitable backgrounds are hired and subsequently engage in criminal activities falling within the scope of their employment. British Columbia has a law that requires schools, hospitals, and employers of childcare workers to conduct criminal record checks for all new employees.[2]

Suggested guidelines for avoiding negative legal consequences, such as human rights complaints, liability for negligent hiring, and wrongful dismissal suits, include

Hints to Ensure Legal Compliance

1. ensuring that all selection criteria and strategies are based on the job description and the job specification

2. adequately assessing the applicant's ability to meet performance standards or expectations

3. carefully scrutinizing all information supplied on application forms and résumés

4. obtaining written authorization for reference checking from prospective employees, and checking references very carefully

5. saving all records and information obtained about the applicant during each stage of the selection process

6. rejecting applicants who make false statements on their application forms or résumés

Supply Challenges

selection ratio   The ratio of the number of applicants hired to the total number of applicants.

Although it is desirable to have a large, qualified pool of recruits from which to select applicants, this is not always possible. The emerging labour supply shortage situation in Canada will result in increasingly small selection ratios. A **selection ratio** is the ratio of the number of applicants hired to the total number of applicants available, as follows:

$$\frac{\text{Number of Applicants Hired}}{\text{Total Number of Applicants}} = \text{Selection Ratio}$$

A small selection ratio, such as 1:2, means that there are a limited number of applicants from which to select, and it may also mean low-quality recruits. If this is the case, it is generally better to start the recruitment process over again, even if it means a hiring delay, rather than taking the risk of hiring an employee who will be a marginal performer at best.

The Selection Process

multiple-hurdle strategy   An approach to selection involving a series of successive steps or hurdles. Only candidates clearing the hurdle are permitted to move on to the next step.

Most firms use a sequential selection system involving a series of successive steps—a **multiple-hurdle strategy**. Only candidates clearing a "hurdle" (selection techniques including prescreening, testing, interviewing, and background/reference checking) are permitted to move on to the next step. Clearing the hurdle requires meeting or exceeding the minimum requirements established for that hurdle. Thus, only candidates who have cleared all of the previous hurdles remain in contention for the position at the time that the hiring decision is being made.

To assess each applicant's potential for success on the job, organizations typically rely on a number of sources of information. The number of steps in the selection process and their sequence vary with the organization. The types of selection instruments and screening devices used are also not standardized across organizations. Even within a firm, the number and sequence of steps often vary with the type and level of the job, as well as the source and method of recruitment. **Figure 7.1** illustrates the steps commonly involved.

At each step in the selection process, carefully chosen selection criteria must be used to determine which applicants will move on to the next step. It is through job analysis that the duties, responsibilities, and human requirements for each job are identified. By basing selection criteria on these requirements, firms can create a legally defensible hiring system.[3] Individuals hired after thorough screening against these carefully developed selection criteria (based directly on the job description and job specification) learn their jobs readily, are productive, and generally adjust to their jobs with a minimum of difficulty.

REQUIRED PROFESSIONAL CAPABILITIES

Analyzes position requirements to establish selection criteria

FIGURE 7.1   Typical Steps in the Selection Process

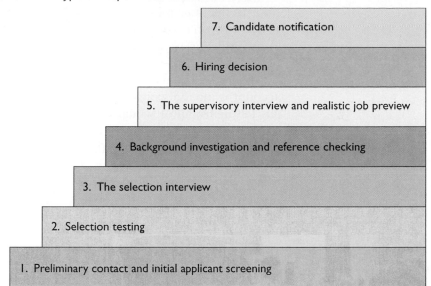

7. Candidate notification

6. Hiring decision

5. The supervisory interview and realistic job preview

4. Background investigation and reference checking

3. The selection interview

2. Selection testing

1. Preliminary contact and initial applicant screening

PRELIMINARY STEPS IN SELECTION

Initial applicant screening is generally performed by members of the HR department. Application forms and résumés are reviewed, and those candidates not meeting the essential selection criteria are eliminated first. Then, the remaining applications are examined and those candidates who most closely match the remaining job specifications are identified and given further consideration.

The use of technology is becoming increasingly popular to help HR professionals improve the initial screening process. An increasing number of firms, such as Blockbuster and Home Depot, are using technological applications to help screen large numbers of candidates and generate short-lists of individuals who will move on to the next step in the selection process.

SELECTION TESTING

REQUIRED PROFESSIONAL CAPABILITIES

Establishes screening and assessment procedures

Selection testing is a common screening device used by approximately two-thirds of Canadian organizations to assess specific job-related skills, as well as general intelligence, personality characteristics, mental abilities, interests, and preferences.[4] Testing techniques provide efficient, standardized procedures for screening large numbers of applicants. Several thousand psychological and personality tests are on the market.[5]

The Importance of Reliability and Validity

Tests and other selection techniques are only useful if they provide reliable and valid measures.[6] All reputable tests will provide information to users about the reliability and validity of the test.

Reliability

reliability   The degree to which interviews, tests, and other selection procedures yield comparable data over time; in other words, the degree of dependability, consistency, or stability of the measures used.

The degree to which interviews, tests, and other selection procedures yield comparable data over time is known as **reliability**. Reliability is the degree of dependability, consistency, or stability of the measures used. For example, a test that results in widely variable scores when it is administered on different occasions to the same individual is unreliable. Reliability also refers to the extent to which two or more methods (such as tests and reference checking) yield the same results or are consistent, as well as the extent to which there is agreement between two or more raters (inter-rater reliability).

When dealing with tests, another measure of reliability that is taken into account is internal consistency. For example, suppose a vocational interest test has ten items, all of which were supposed to measure, in one way or another, the person's interest in working outdoors. To assess internal reliability, the degree to which responses to those ten items vary together would be statistically analyzed. (That is one reason that tests often include questions that appear rather repetitive.) Reliability is also diminished when questions are answered randomly, the test setting is noisy or uncomfortable, and when the applicant is tired or unwell.

Validity

validity The accuracy with which a predictor measures what it is intended to measure.

Validity, in the context of selection, is an indicator of the extent to which data from a selection technique, such as a test or interview, are related to or predictive of subsequent performance on the job. Separate validation studies of selection techniques should be conducted for different subgroups, such as visible minorities and women, in order to assess **differential validity**. In some cases, the technique may be a valid predictor of job success for one group (such as white males) but not for other applicants, thereby leading to systemic discrimination.

differential validity Confirmation that the selection tool accurately predicts the performance of all possible employee subgroups, including white males, women, visible minorities, persons with disabilities, and Aboriginal people.

Three types of validity are particularly relevant to selection: criterion-related, content, and construct validity.

Criterion-Related Validity   The extent to which a selection tool predicts or significantly correlates with important elements of work behaviour is known as **criterion-related validity**. Demonstrating criterion-related validity requires proving that those who do well on a test or in an interview, for example, also do well on the job, and that individuals who do poorly on the test or in the interview receive low job-performance ratings.

criterion-related validity The extent to which a selection tool predicts or significantly correlates with important elements of work behaviour.

Content Validity   When a selection instrument, such as a test, adequately samples the knowledge and skills needed to perform the job, **content validity** is assumed to exist. The closer the content of the selection instrument is to actual samples of work or work behaviour, the greater the content validity. For example, asking a candidate for a secretarial position to demonstrate word processing skills, as required on the job, has high content validity.

content validity The extent to which a selection instrument, such as a test, adequately samples the knowledge and skills needed to perform the job.

Construct Validity   The extent to which a selection tool measures a theoretical construct or trait deemed necessary to perform the job successfully is known as **construct validity**. Intelligence, verbal skills, analytical ability, and leadership skills are all examples of constructs. Measuring construct validity requires demonstrating that the psychological trait or attribute is related to satisfactory job performance, as well as showing that the test or other selection tool used accurately measures the psychological trait or attribute.

construct validity The extent to which a selection tool measures a theoretical construct or trait deemed necessary to perform the job successfully.

Professional standards for psychologists require that tests be used as supplements to other techniques, such as interviews and background checks; that tests be validated in the organization where they will be used; that a certified psychologist be used to choose, validate, administer, and interpret tests; and that private, quiet, well-lit, and well-ventilated settings be provided to all applicants taking the test.[7]

Tests of Cognitive Abilities

Included in the category of test of cognitive abilities are tests of general reasoning ability (intelligence), tests of emotional intelligence, and tests of specific thinking skills, like memory and inductive reasoning.

Intelligence Tests

intelligence (IQ) tests   Tests that measure general intellectual abilities, such as verbal comprehension, inductive reasoning, memory, numerical ability, speed of perception, spatial visualization, and word fluency.

Intelligence (IQ) tests are tests of general intellectual abilities. They measure not a single "intelligence" trait, but rather a number of abilities, including memory, vocabulary, verbal fluency, and numerical ability. An IQ score is actually a *derived* score, reflecting the extent to which the person is above or below the "average" adult's intelligence score. Intelligence is often measured with individually administered tests, such as the Stanford-Binet Test or the Wechsler Test. Other IQ tests, such as the Wonderlic, can be administered to groups of people.

Emotional Intelligence Tests

emotional intelligence (EI) tests   Tests that measure ability to monitor one's own emotions and the emotions of others and use that knowledge to guide thoughts and actions.

Emotional Quotient Inventory
www.eiconsortium.org

Emotional intelligence (EI) tests measure ability to monitor one's own emotions and the emotions of others and use that knowledge to guide thoughts and actions. Someone with a high emotional quotient (EQ) is self-aware, can control his or her impulses, motivates himself or herself, and demonstrates empathy and social awareness. Many people believe that EQ, which can be modified through conscious effort and practice, is actually a more important determinant of success than a high IQ. Self-assessment EI tests include the Emotional Quotient Inventory (EQi), the EQ Map, the Mayer Salovey Caruso Emotional Intelligence Test (MSCEIT), and the Emotional Intelligence Questionnaire (EIQ). The Emotional Competence Inventory (ECI) is a 360-degree assessment in which several individuals evaluate one person to get a more complete picture of the individual's emotional competencies.[8]

Specific Cognitive Abilities

aptitude tests   Tests that measure an individual's aptitude or potential to perform a job, provided he or she is given proper training.

Microsoft Online Aptitude Testing
www.microsoft.com/skills2000

There are also measures of specific thinking skills, such as inductive and deductive reasoning, verbal comprehension, memory, and numerical ability. Tests in this category are often called **aptitude tests**, since they purport to measure the applicant's aptitudes for the job in question, that is, the applicant's potential to perform the job once given proper training. An example is the test of mechanical comprehension illustrated in **Figure 7.2**. It tests the applicant's understanding of basic mechanical principles. It may therefore reflect a person's aptitude for jobs—like that of machinist or engineer—that require mechanical comprehension. Multidimensional aptitude tests commonly used in applicant selection include the General Aptitude Test Battery (GATB).

Tests of Motor and Physical Abilities

To assess the traits on which job success depends, many firms, such as those that rely on computer literacy, administer a skills assessment test before hiring.

There are many *motor abilities* that a firm might want to measure. These include finger dexterity, manual dexterity, speed of arm movement, and reaction time. The Crawford Small Parts Dexterity Test, as illustrated in **Figure 7.3**, is an example. It measures the speed and accuracy of simple judgment, as well as the speed of finger, hand, and arm movements. Other tests include the Stromberg Dexterity Test, the Minnesota Rate of Manipulation Test, and the Purdue Peg Board.

FIGURE 7.2   Two Problems from the Test of Mechanical Comprehension

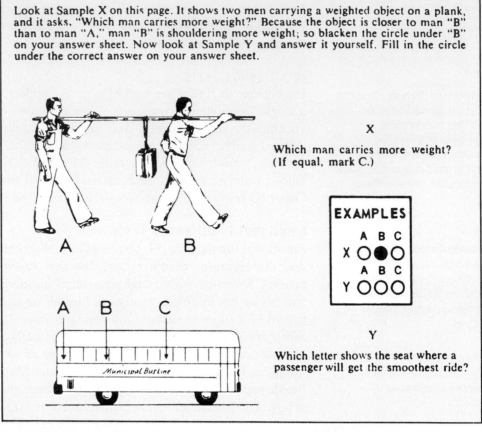

Look at Sample X on this page. It shows two men carrying a weighted object on a plank, and it asks, "Which man carries more weight?" Because the object is closer to man "B" than to man "A," man "B" is shouldering more weight; so blacken the circle under "B" on your answer sheet. Now look at Sample Y and answer it yourself. Fill in the circle under the correct answer on your answer sheet.

X

Which man carries more weight?
(If equal, mark C.)

EXAMPLES

A B C
X ○●○
A B C
Y ○○○

Y

Which letter shows the seat where a passenger will get the smoothest ride?

Note: 1969 is latest copyright on this test, which is still most commonly used for this purpose.

Source: Reproduced by permission. Copyright 1967, 1969 by The Psychological Corporation, New York, NY. All rights reserved.

FIGURE 7.3   Crawford Small Parts Dexterity Test

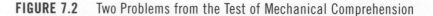

Source: The Psychological Corporation.

Tests of physical abilities may also be required.[9] For example, some firms are now using Functional Abilities Evaluations (FAE) to assist with placement decisions. An FAE, which measures a whole series of physical abilities—ranging from lifting, to pulling and pushing, sitting, squatting, climbing, and carrying—is particularly useful for positions with a multitude of physical demands, such as firefighter and police officer.[10] Ensuring that physical abilities tests do not violate human rights legislation requires basing such tests on job duties identified through job analysis and a physical demands analysis, ensuring that the tests duplicate the actual physical requirements of the job, developing and imposing such tests honestly and in good faith, ensuring that those administering the tests are properly trained and administer the tests in a consistent manner, and ensuring that testing standards are objectively related to job performance.[11]

Measuring Personality and Interests

A person's mental and physical abilities are seldom sufficient to explain his or her job performance. Other factors such as the person's motivation and interpersonal skills are important too. Personality and interest inventories are sometimes used as predictors of such intangibles.

personality tests Instruments used to measure basic aspects of personality, such as introversion, stability, motivation, neurotic tendency, self-confidence, self-sufficiency, and sociability.

Personality tests can measure basic aspects of an applicant's personality, such as introversion, stability, and motivation. The use of such tests for selection assumes that it is possible to find a relationship between a measurable personality trait (such as conscientiousness) and success on the job.[12] Many of these tests are *projective*. In the Thematic Apperception Test, an ambiguous stimulus (like an inkblot or clouded picture) is presented to the test taker, and he or she is asked to interpret or react to it. Because the pictures are ambiguous, the person's interpretation must come from within—he or she supposedly *projects* into the picture his or her own emotional attitudes about life. Thus, a security-oriented person might describe the woman in **Figure 7.4** as "my mother worrying about what I will do if I lose my job."

Myers-Briggs Type Indicator
www.psychometrics.com

The Myers-Briggs instrument, which has been in use for more than 50 years, is believed to be the most widely used personality inventory in the world. More than 2 million assessments are administered annually in the United States alone.[13] Another example of a common personality test is the Minnesota Multiphasic Personality Inventory (MMPI), which taps traits like hypochondria and paranoia.

FIGURE 7.4   Sample Picture from Thematic Apperception Test

How do you interpret this picture?

Research
I n s i g h t ▷

Research studies confirm that personality tests can help companies to hire more effective workers. For example, industrial psychologists often talk in terms of the "Big Five" personality dimensions as they apply to employment testing: *extroversion, emotional stability, agreeableness, conscientiousness,* and *openness to experience.*[14] One study focused on the extent to which these dimensions predicted performance (in terms of job and training proficiency, for example) for professionals, police officers, managers, sales workers, and skilled/semi-skilled workers. Conscientiousness showed a consistent relationship with all performance criteria for every occupation. Extroversion was a valid predictor of performance for managers and sales employees—the two occupations involving the most social interaction. Both openness to experience and extroversion predicted training proficiency for all occupations.[15] Another study involving a sample of 89 university employees concluded that absenteeism was inversely related to extroversion and conscientiousness.[16]

interest inventories   Tests that compare a candidate's interests with those of people in various occupations.

Interest inventories compare a candidate's interests with those of people in various occupations. Thus, a person taking the Strong-Campbell Inventory would receive a report comparing his or her interests with those of people already in occupations such as accountant, engineer, manager, or medical technologist. Interest inventories have many uses. One is career planning, since people generally do better in jobs involving activities in which they have an interest. Another is selection. If the firm can select people whose interests are roughly the same as those of high-performing incumbents in the jobs for which it is hiring, the new employees are more likely to be successful.[17]

Achievement Tests

achievement tests   Tests used to measure knowledge and/or proficiency acquired through education, training, or experience.

An **achievement test** is basically a measure of what a person has learned. Most of the tests taken in school are achievement tests. They measure knowledge and/or proficiency in such areas as economics, marketing, or HRM. Achievement tests are also widely used in selection. For example, the Purdue Test for Machinists and Machine Operators tests the job knowledge of experienced machinists with such questions as "What is meant by 'tolerance'?" Other tests are available for electricians, welders, carpenters, and so forth. In addition to job knowledge, achievement tests measure the applicant's abilities; a keyboarding test is one example.

Work Sampling

Work samples focus on measuring job performance directly and thus are among the best predictors of job performance. In developing a work-sampling test, experts first list all the possible tasks that jobholders would be required to perform. Then, by listing the frequency of performance and relative importance of each task, key tasks are identified. Each applicant then performs the key tasks, and his or her work is monitored by the test administrator, who records the approach taken. Finally, the work-sampling test is validated by determining the relationship between the applicants' scores on the work samples and their actual performance on the job. Then, once it is shown that the work sample is a valid predictor of job success, the employer can begin using it for selection.[18]

Management Assessment Centres

management assessment centre   A strategy used to assess candidates' management potential that uses a combination of realistic exercises, management games, objective testing, presentations, and interviews.

In a two- to three-day **management assessment centre**, the management potential of 10 or 12 candidates is assessed by expert appraisers who observe them

A management game or simulation is a typical component in a management assessment centre.

International Congress on Assessment Center Methods
www.assessmentcenters.org
Assessment Tools
www.behaviourworks.com

performing realistic management tasks. The centre may be a plain conference room, but it is often a special room with a one-way mirror to facilitate unobtrusive observations. Examples of the types of activities and exercises involved include the following:

1. *An in-basket exercise.* Each candidate is faced with an accumulation of reports, memos, messages from incoming phone calls, letters, and other materials collected in the in-basket of the simulated job that he or she is to take over and is required to take appropriate action. For example, he or she must write letters, return phone calls, and prepare meeting agendas. The trained evaluators then review the results.

2. *A leaderless group discussion.* A leaderless group is given a discussion question and told to arrive at a group decision. The raters evaluate each candidate's interpersonal skills, acceptance by the group, leadership ability, and individual influence.

3. *Management games.* Participants engage in realistic problem solving, usually as members of two or more simulated companies that are competing in the marketplace. Decisions might have to be made about such issues as how to advertise and manufacture and how much inventory to keep in stock.

4. *Individual presentations.* During oral presentations on an assigned topic, each participant's communication skills and persuasiveness are evaluated.

5. *Objective tests.* Candidates may be asked to complete paper-and-pencil or computer-based personality, aptitude, interest, and/or achievement tests.

6. *An interview.* Most centres also require an interview between at least one of the expert assessors and each participant to evaluate interests, background, past performance, and motivation.

Situational Testing

situational tests Tests in which candidates are presented with hypothetical situations representative of the job for which they are applying and are evaluated on their responses.

In **situational tests**, candidates are presented with hypothetical situations representative of the job for which they are applying (often on video) and are evaluated on their responses.[19] Several of the assessment centre exercises described previously are examples. In a typical test, a number of realistic scenarios are presented and each is followed by a multiple-choice question with several possible courses of action, from which candidates are asked to select the "best" response, in their opinion.[20] The level of each candidate's skills is then evaluated, and an assessment report can be easily generated, making the simulation easier and less expensive to administer than other screening tools. Simulations also provide a realistic job preview by exposing candidates to the types of activities that they will encounter on the job.

Research
I n s i g h t

Interactive employment tests administered on the computer are becoming popular as screening devices at many firms.

A research study of situational testing on 160 civil service employees demonstrated the validity of the situational test in predicting overall job performance as well as three performance dimensions: core technical proficiency, job dedication, and interpersonal facilitation. The situational test provided valid predictive information over and above cognitive ability tests, personality tests, and job experience.[21]

Micro-assessments

micro-assessment A series of verbal, paper-based, or computer-based questions and exercises that a candidate is required to complete, covering the range of activities required on the job for which he or she is applying.

An entirely performance-based testing strategy that focuses on individual performance is a **micro-assessment**. In a micro-assessment, each applicant completes a series of verbal, paper-based, or computer-based questions and exercises that cover the range of activities required on the job for which he or she is applying. In addition to technical exercises, participants are required to solve a set of work-related problems that demonstrate their ability to perform well within the confines of a certain department or corporate culture. Exercises are simple to develop because they are taken directly from the job.

Physical Examination and Substance Abuse Testing

The use of medical examinations in selection has decreased, in part because of the loss of physically demanding manufacturing and natural resource jobs. Before 1980, 25 percent of new hires underwent a medical exam, but by 2001, only 11 percent were required to do so.[22] Three main reasons that firms may include a medical examination as a step in the selection process are (1) to determine that the applicant *qualifies for the physical requirements* of the position and, if not, to document any *accommodation* requirements; (2) to establish a *record and baseline* of the applicant's health for the purpose of future insurance or compensation claims; and (3) to *reduce absenteeism and accidents* by identifying any health issues or concerns that need to be addressed, including communicable diseases of which the applicant may have been unaware. Medical exams are only permitted after a written offer of employment has been extended (except in the case of bona fide occupational requirements, as for food handlers).

The purpose of pre-employment substance abuse testing is to avoid hiring employees who would pose unnecessary risks to themselves or others and/or perform below expectations. However, in Canada, employers are not permitted to screen candidates for substance abuse. Alcohol and drug addiction is considered to be a disability under human rights codes, and an employee cannot be discriminated against during the selection process based on a disability.[23]

THE SELECTION INTERVIEW

selection interview A procedure designed to predict future job performance on the basis of applicants' oral responses to oral inquiries.

The interview is used by virtually all organizations for selecting job applicants. The **selection interview**, which involves a process of two-way communication between the interviewee(s) and the interviewer(s), can be defined as "a procedure designed to predict future job performance on the basis of applicants' oral responses to oral inquiries."[24]

Interviews are considered to be one of the most important aspects of the selection process and generally have a major impact on both applicants and interviewers. Interviews significantly influence applicants' views about the job and organization, enable employers to fill in any gaps in the information provided on application forms and résumés, and supplement the results of any tests administered. They may also reveal entirely new types of information.

A major reason for the popularity of selection interviews is that they meet a number of the objectives of both interviewer and interviewee. Interviewer objectives include assessing applicants' qualifications and observing relevant aspects of applicants' behaviour, such as verbal communication skills, degree of self-confidence, and interpersonal skills; providing candidates with information about the job and expected duties and responsibilities; promoting the organization and highlighting its attractiveness; and determining how well the applicants would fit into the organization. Typical objectives of job applicants include presenting a positive image of themselves; selling their skills and marketing their positive attributes to the interviewer(s); and gathering information about the job and the organization so that they can make an informed decision about the job, career opportunities in the firm, and the work environment.[25]

Types of Interviews

Selection interviews can be classified according to the degree of structure, their content, and the way in which the interview is administered.

The Structure of the Interview

First, interviews can be classified according to the degree to which they are structured. In an **unstructured interview**, questions are asked as they come to mind. Interviewees for the same job thus may or may not be asked the same or similar questions, and the interview's unstructured nature allows the interviewer to ask questions based on the candidate's last statements and to pursue points of interest as they develop. Unstructured interviews have low reliability and validity.[26]

The interview can also be structured. In the classical **structured interview**, the questions and acceptable responses are specified in advance and the responses are rated for appropriateness of content.[27] In practice, however, most structured interviews do not involve specifying and rating responses in advance. Instead, each candidate is asked a series of predetermined, job-related questions, based on the job description and specification. Such interviews are generally high in validity and reliability. However, a totally structured interview does not provide the flexibility to pursue points of interest as they develop, which may result in an interview that seems quite mechanical to all concerned.

Between these two extremes is the **mixed (semi-structured) interview**, which involves a combination of preset, structured questions based on the job description and specification, and a series of preset candidate-specific, job-related questions based on information provided on the application form and/or résumé. The questions asked of all candidates facilitate candidate comparison, while the job-related, candidate-specific questions make the interview more conversational. A realistic approach that yields comparable answers and in-depth insights, the mixed interview format is extremely popular.

A study of 92 real employment interviews found that the interviewers using high levels of structure in the interview process evaluated applicants less favourably than those who used semi-structured or unstructured interviews, and those applicants who were evaluated using a semi-structured interview were rated slightly higher than those evaluated by unstructured interviews. Additionally, the study found that significant differences occur in the way that female and male interviewers evaluate their applicants. Although male interviewers' ratings were unaffected by the interview structure, female interviewers' ratings were substantially higher in unstructured and semi-structured interviews than in highly structured interviews.[28]

The Content of the Interview

Interviews can also be classified according to the content of their questions. A **situational interview** is one in which the questions focus on the individual's

---

unstructured interview An unstructured, conversational-style interview. The interviewer pursues points of interest as they come up in response to questions.

structured interview An interview following a set sequence of questions.

mixed (semi-structured) interview An interview format that combines the structured and unstructured techniques.

Research Insight ▷

situational interview A series of job-related questions that focus on how the candidate would behave in a given situation.

behavioural or behaviour description interview (BDI) A series of job-related questions that focus on relevant past job-related behaviours.

ability to project what his or her *future* behaviour would be in a given situation.[29] The underlying premise is that intentions predict behaviour. For example, a candidate for a supervisory position might be asked how he or she would respond to an employee coming to work late three days in a row. The interview can be both *structured* and *situational*, with predetermined questions requiring the candidate to project what his or her behaviour would be. In a structured situational interview, the applicant could be evaluated, say, on whether he or she would try to determine if the employee was experiencing some difficulty in getting to work on time or would simply issue a verbal or written warning to the employee.

The **behavioural interview**, also known as a **behaviour description interview (BDI)**, involves describing various situations and asking interviewees how they behaved *in the past* in such situations.[30] The underlying assumption is that the best predictor of future performance is past performance in similar circumstances. The BMO Financial Group uses behaviour-based interviewing, as described in the Strategic HR box.

Administering the Interview

Interviews can also be classified based on how they are administered: one on one or by a panel of interviewers; sequentially or all at once; and computerized, videotaped, or conducted entirely in person. Most interviews are administered *one on one*. Most selection processes are sequential. In a *sequential interview* the

Strategic HR

How BMO Financial Selects Employees

Since the early 1990s, BMO Financial Group has used behavioural-focused interviewing to help assess candidates and ensure the best fit in the hiring process. When a position is posted, external résumés start pouring in. The first step that BMO takes is entering them into Recruit-Soft, a system used to filter applications. RecruitSoft looks for keywords in the résumé. For example, if BMO is looking for call centre staff, the system might scan for the phrase "cold calls." The candidate pool is determined through this efficient and time-saving process.

Next, the candidate pool is given to Hewitt Associates, the consulting firm used by BMO as external recruiters. Hewitt assesses the list to determine if there are sufficient candidates and whether or not all the critical information is there. Hewitt conducts an initial behaviour-focused interview. If the candidate is selected to move on, the next step is an interview with the hiring manager at BMO, who also uses behaviour-focused interview techniques.

Examples of the behavioural interview questions are

- "Tell me about the most challenging assignment you managed in the past year and what you did to meet this challenge."

- "Tell me about a crisis or emergency and how you handled it."

- "Give me an example of a particularly difficult situation involving an external client and how you handled it."

Hiring managers are specially trained to conduct interviews effectively and to use the behaviour-focused interview techniques. The purpose of the course for hiring managers is to equip them to make thoughtful hiring decisions and to try to make them as consistently as possible. The training puts a lot of emphasis on preparing for the interview. It is believed that a hiring manager who has done some legwork will be able to conduct a much better interview than one who just stops what he or she is doing when the candidate comes in.

Managers in the past were not as prepared for interviews as they are now. After this course, there is a lot more onus on managers to effectively prepare the interview and to conduct the interview so the potential employee is faced with someone who has done his or her homework. The feedback managers get from candidates suggests that this makes potential employees feel very valued right from the start. The company has used this technique to staff its 34 000 positions.

Source: Adapted from T. Humber, "How BMO Financial Selects Employees," *Canadian HR Reporter*, December 6, 2004. Reproduced by permission of *Canadian HR Reporter*, Carswell, One Corporate Plaza, 2075 Kennedy Road, Scarborough, ON M1T 3V4.

A panel interview is an efficient and cost-effective way of permitting a number of qualified persons to assess a candidate's KSAs.

applicant is interviewed by several persons in sequence before a selection decision is made. In an *unstructured sequential interview* each interviewer may look at the applicant from his or her own point of view, ask different questions, and form an independent opinion of the candidate. Conversely, in a *structured sequential* (or serialized) interview, each interviewer rates the candidate on a standard evaluation form, and the ratings are compared before the hiring decision is made.[31]

A **panel interview** involves the candidate being interviewed simultaneously by a group (or panel) of interviewers, including an HR representative, the hiring manager, and potential co-workers, superiors, and/or reporting employees. The key advantages associated with this technique are increased likelihood that the information provided will be heard and recorded accurately; varied questions pertaining to each interviewer's area of expertise; minimized time and travel/accommodation expenses as each interviewee only attends one interview; reduced likelihood of human rights/employment equity violations since an HR representative is present; and less likelihood of interviewer error, because of advance planning and preparation.

A more stressful variant of the panel interview is the *mass interview*, which involves a panel simultaneously interviewing several candidates. The panel poses a problem to be solved and then sits back and watches which candidate takes the lead in formulating an answer.

panel interview An interview in which a group of interviewers questions the applicant.

Interviewing and the Law

As a selection procedure, interviews must comply with human rights legislation. Doing so requires keeping the following guidelines in mind:

1. Interviewers cannot ask questions that would violate human rights legislation, either directly or indirectly. Questions cannot be asked about candidates' marital status, childcare arrangements, ethnic background, or workers' compensation history, for example.

2. All interviewees must be treated in the same manner. An interviewer cannot ask only female factory position applicants to demonstrate their lifting abilities, for example, or question female sales applicants about their willingness to travel but not ask male candidates.

Hints to Ensure Legal Compliance

3. Cutting short an interview based on preconceived notions about the gender or race of the "ideal" candidate should also be avoided, because this is another example of illegal differential treatment.

4. A helpful phrase to keep in mind when designing interview questions is "This job requires . . . ." Interviewers who focus on the job description and job specification can gather all the information required to assess applicants, without infringing on the candidates' legal rights.

Common Interviewing Mistakes

Several common interviewing errors that can undermine the usefulness of interviews are discussed below.

Poor Planning

Many selection interviews are simply not carefully planned and may be conducted without having prepared written questions in advance. Lack of planning often leads to a relatively unstructured interview, in which whatever comes up is discussed. The end result may be little or no cross-candidate job-related information. The less structured the interview is, the less reliable and valid the evaluation of each candidate will be.[32]

Snap Judgments

One of the most consistent literature findings is that interviewers tend to jump to conclusions—make snap judgments—during the first few minutes of the interview or even before the interview begins, based on the candidates' test scores or résumé data. Thus, it is important for a candidate to start off on the right foot with the interviewer.

Negative Emphasis

Interviewers seem to have a consistent negative bias. They are generally more influenced by unfavourable than favourable information about the candidate. Also, their impressions are much more likely to change from favourable to unfavourable than vice versa.

Halo Effect

It is also possible for a positive initial impression to distort an interviewer's rating of a candidate, because subsequent information is judged with a positive bias. This is known as the **halo effect**. An applicant who has a pleasant smile and firm handshake, for example, may be judged positively before the interview even begins. Having gained that positive initial impression, the interviewer may not seek contradictory information when listening to the candidate's answers to the questions posed.

Poor Knowledge of the Job

Interviewers who do not know precisely what the job entails, and what sort of candidate is best suited for it, usually make their decisions based on incorrect stereotypes about what a good applicant is. Interviewers who have a clear understanding of what the job entails conduct more effective interviews.

Contrast (Candidate-Order) Error

Contrast or candidate-order error means that the order in which applicants are seen can affect how they are rated. In one study, managers were asked to evaluate

halo effect A positive initial impression that distorts an interviewer's rating of a candidate, because subsequent information is judged with a positive bias.

contrast or candidate-order error An error of judgment on the part of the interviewer because of interviewing one or more very good or very bad candidates just before the interview in question.

a candidate who was "just average" after first evaluating several "unfavourable" candidates. The average candidate was evaluated more favourably than he or she might otherwise have been, because, in contrast to the unfavourable candidates, the average one looked better than he or she actually was.

Influence of Nonverbal Behaviour

Interviewers are also influenced by the applicant's nonverbal behaviour, and the more eye contact, head moving, smiling, and other similar nonverbal behaviours, the higher the ratings. These nonverbal behaviours often account for more than 80 percent of the applicant's rating. This finding is of particular concern since nonverbal behaviour is tied to ethnicity and cultural background. An applicant's attractiveness and gender also play a role. Research has shown that those rated as being more physically attractive are also rated as more suitable for employment, well ahead of those rated average looking and those regarded as physically unattractive. Although this bias is considered to be unconscious, it may have serious implications for aging employees.[33]

Telegraphing

Some interviewers are so anxious to fill a job that they help the applicants to respond correctly to their questions by telegraphing the expected answer. An obvious example might be a question like: "This job calls for handling a lot of stress. You can do that, can you not?" The telegraphing is not always so obvious. For example, favourable first impressions of candidates tend to be linked to use of a more positive interview style. This can translate into sending subtle cues regarding the preferred response, such as a smile or nod.[34]

Too Much/Too Little Talking

If the applicant is permitted to dominate the interview, the interviewer may not have a chance to ask his or her prepared questions and often learns very little about the candidate's job-related skills. At the other extreme, some interviewers talk so much that the interviewee is not given enough time to answer questions. One expert suggests using the 30/70 rule: During a selection interview, encourage the candidate to speak 70 percent of the time, and restrict the interviewer speaking to just 30 percent of the time.[35]

Similar-to-Me Bias

Interviewers tend to provide more favourable ratings to candidates who possess demographic, personality, and attitudinal characteristics similar to their own.[36]

Designing an Effective Interview

Problems like those just described can be avoided by designing and conducting an effective interview. Combining several of the interview formats previously discussed enables interviewers to capitalize on the advantages of each.[37] To allow for probing and to prevent the interview from becoming too mechanical in nature, a semi-structured format is recommended. Given their higher validity in predicting job performance, the focus should be on situational and behavioural questions.

Designing an effective interview involves composing a series of job-related questions to be asked of all applicants for a particular job, as well as a few job-related candidate-specific questions. Doing so involves the following five steps, the first two of which should occur before recruitment.[38]

must criteria   Requirements that are absolutely essential for the job, include a measurable standard of acceptability or are absolute, and can be screened initially on paper.

want criteria   Those criteria that have been culled from the must list. They represent qualifications that cannot be screened on paper or are not readily measurable, as well as those that are highly desirable but not critical.

The first step is to decide who will be involved in the selection process and to *develop selection criteria*. Specifying selection criteria involves clarifying and weighting the information in the job description and job specification, and holding discussion among the interview-team members, especially those most familiar with the job and co-workers.

The second step is to *specify "musts" and "wants" and weight the "wants."* Once agreed on, the selection criteria should be divided into two categories: musts and wants.[39] **Must criteria** are those that are absolutely essential for the job, include a measurable standard of acceptability, or are absolute. There are often only two musts: a specific level of education (or equivalent combination of education and work experience) and a minimum amount of prior, related work experience. The **want criteria** include skills and abilities that cannot be screened on paper (such as verbal communication skills) or are not readily measurable (such as leadership ability, teamwork skills, and enthusiasm), as well as qualifications that are desirable but not critical.

The third step is to determine assessment strategies and to *develop an evaluation form*. Once the must and want criteria have been identified, appropriate strategies for learning about each should be specified. For some qualifications, especially those that are critically important, the team may decide to use several assessment strategies. For example, leadership skills might be assessed through behavioural questions, situational questions, a written test, and an assessment centre. Once all want criteria have been agreed on and weighted, they become the basis for candidate comparison and evaluation, as illustrated in **Figure 7.5**.

The fourth step is to *develop interview questions* to be asked of all candidates. Questions should be developed for each KSA to be assessed during the interview. *Job-knowledge questions* and *worker-requirements questions* to gauge the applicants' motivation and willingness to perform under prevailing working conditions, such as shift work or travel, should also be included.

The fifth and final step is to *develop candidate-specific questions*. A few open-ended, job-related questions that are candidate-specific should be planned, based on each candidate's résumé and application form.

Conducting an Effective Interview

Although the following discussion focuses on a semi-structured panel interview, the steps described apply to all selection interviews.[40]

Planning the Interview

Before the first interview, agreement should be reached on the procedure that will be followed. Sometimes all members of the team ask a question in turn; in other situations, only one member of the team asks questions and the others serve as observers. Sitting around a large table in a conference room is much more appropriate and far less stressful than having all panel members seated across from the candidate behind a table or desk, which forms both a physical and a psychological barrier. Special planning is required when assessing candidates with disabilities. An example is provided in the Workforce Diversity box on page 184.

Establishing Rapport

The main reason for an interview is to find out as much as possible about the candidate's fit with the job specifications, something that is difficult to do if the individual is tense and nervous. The candidate should be greeted in a friendly manner and put at ease.

FIGURE 7.5 Worksheet—Comparison of Candidates for a Secretarial Position

Criteria		Alternatives											
		A Smith				**B** Brown				**C** Yuill			
Must		Info	Go/No			Info	Go/No			Info	Go/No		
Education — Office Admin. diploma or equivalent experience (3 years' clerical/secretarial experience)		Office admin. diploma	Go			Office admin. diploma	Go			No diploma, 1 year related experience	No Go		
Experience — At least 2 years' secretarial/clerical experience		3 years' experience	Go			2 years' experience	Go						
Wants	Wt.	Info	Sc.	Wt. Sc.		Info	Sc.	Wt. Sc.		Info	Sc.	Wt. Sc.	
Keyboarding/word processing	10	Word processing test	9	90		Word processing test	10	100					
Good oral communication	9	Interview assessment	9	81		Interview assessment	9	81					
Good spelling/grammar	9	Test results	8	72		Test results	9	81					
Organizational ability	9	Interview questions/simulation/ reference checking	8	72		Interview questions/simulation/ reference checking	9	81					
Initiative	8	Interview questions/simulation/ reference checking	7	56		Interview questions/simulation/ reference checking	8	64					
High ethical standards	7	Interview questions/simulation/ reference checking	7	49		Interview questions/simulation/ reference checking	7	49					
Shorthand skills (or speed writing)	4	Interview question and test results	4	16		Interview question and test results	0	0					
Designated group member, other than white female	2	Application form	2	4		Application form	0	0					
				440				456					
								TOP CANDIDATE					

Workforce Diversity

Listening to the Needs of the Deaf

Given the impending labour shortage, hiring a diverse workforce (including people with disabilities) is not only legally required and good public relations—it is a necessity. For many deaf, deafened, or hard-of-hearing people, lack of career education and career support services lead to fewer student work experiences and fewer leadership and volunteer opportunities during their student years. These challenges are heightened by reduced expectation and misconceptions of employers regarding the employability and capability of people with hearing disabilities. In spite of the fact that numerous people with hearing impairments are successfully employed in a wide variety of fields, serious underemployment of deaf individuals continues. In Ontario, 85 percent of deaf people are underemployed and/or unemployed. This may be a result of deep-rooted discrimination and a lack of understanding.

Accommodating deaf individuals through a selection process or at a job is not very difficult or expensive. Some applicants who are deaf may have difficulty reading and comprehending written applications, especially those that are heavily loaded with complicated English phrases or unfamiliar terms. Appropriate accommodations may include such strategies as allowing the person to take an application and obtain his or her own assistance in filling it out, allowing more time for completion, or providing a sign language interpreter.

Accommodations may also be required during selection interviews. Interviews should be sensitive to the range of communication abilities of people who have hearing impairments. Simple accommodation may include conducting the interview in a quiet, well-lit environment that minimizes visual distractions. The interviewer must be willing to use the interviewee's assistive listening device, if one is used. The interviewer should talk at a normal pace and at a normal volume. If asked, the interviewer must be willing to repeat questions, converse at a different pace or volume, or try other strategies, like note writing. The interviewer should avoid sitting in front of bright lights or windows that make it difficult for a person to read speech.

Source: Excerpt adapted from Valerie Bernard, *Youth Dynamic: An Employment Services Guide for Working with Deaf, Deafened and Hard of Hearing Youth* (Toronto: Ontario Association of Youth Employment Centres with the assistance of The Canadian Hearing Society and The Counselling Foundation of Canada, 2004). Reprinted with permission of the OAYEC.

Asking Questions

The questions written in advance should then be asked in order. Interviewers should listen carefully, encourage the candidate to express his or her thoughts and ideas fully, and record the candidate's answers briefly but thoroughly. Taking notes increases the validity of the interview process, since doing so (1) reduces the likelihood of forgetting job-relevant information and subsequently reconstructing forgotten information in accordance with biases and stereotypes; (2) reduces the likelihood of making a snap judgment and helps to prevent the halo effect, negative emphasis, and candidate-order errors; and (3) helps to ensure that all candidates are assessed on the same criteria.[41]

The rapport established with a job applicant not only puts the person at ease but also reflects the company's attitude toward its public.

Closing the Interview

Toward the end of the interview, time should be allocated to answer any questions that the candidate may have and, if appropriate, to advocate for the firm and position.

Evaluating the Candidate

Immediately following each interview, the applicant's interview performance should be rated by each panel member independently, based on a review of his or her notes. Since interviews are only one step in the process, and a final decision cannot be reached until all assessments (including reference checking) have been completed, these evaluations should not be shared at this time.

BACKGROUND INVESTIGATION AND REFERENCE CHECKING

Background investigation and reference checking are used to verify the accuracy of the information provided by candidates on their application forms and résumés. In an ideal world, every applicant's story would be completely accurate, but in real life, this is often not the case. At least one-third of applicants lie—overstating qualifications or achievements, attempting to hide negative information, or being deliberately evasive or untruthful.[42] Even executives lie, "embellishing" their résumés, as illustrated in **Figure 7.6**.

Unfortunately, some employers do not check references, which can have grave consequences. Recent cases in Canada have included a nurse who practised in a Toronto hospital for almost two years without a registered nurse qualification, a manufacturing plant payroll officer who embezzled almost $2 million, and a teacher arrested for possessing child pornography.[43] Background checks are thus necessary to avoid negligent hiring lawsuits when others are placed in situations of unnecessary and avoidable risk.[44]

Surveys indicate that at least 90 percent of Canadian organizations conduct background checks.[45] Many firms use reference-checking services or hire a consultant to perform this task, as shown in **Figure 7.7**. Obtaining such assistance may be a small price to pay to avoid the time and legal costs associated with the consequences.

Inline Reference Check
www.inlinereference.com

Kroll Background America
www.krollworldwide.com

FIGURE 7.6   Most Common Executive Résumé Embellishments

More than 300 executive recruiters from Korn/Ferry International were asked, "Which types of information are most frequently fabricated or exaggerated by executive candidates?" Respondents were asked to pick the top three.

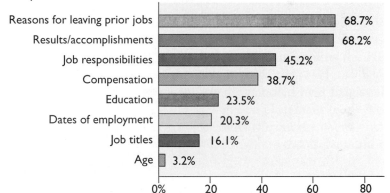

Source: Korn/Ferry International, Press Release, "Reason for Leaving a Prior Job Is the Information Most Frequently Fabricated ..." May 26, 2004. Reproduced with the permission of Korn/Ferry International.

FIGURE 7.7   Outsources of Recruitment and Collection

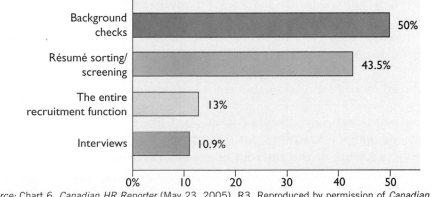

Source: Chart 6, *Canadian HR Reporter* (May 23, 2005), R3. Reproduced by permission of *Canadian HR Reporter*, Carswell, One Corporate Plaza, 2075 Kennedy Road, Scarborough, ON M1T 3V4.

Whether requesting reference information in writing or asking for such information over the telephone, questions should be written down in advance. **Figure 7.8** is an example of a form used for written reference checking. If enough

FIGURE 7.8   Form Requesting Written Reference Information

We are in the process of considering James Ridley Parrish (SIN Number: 123-456-789) for a sales position in our firm. In considering him/her, it would be helpful if we could review your appraisal of his/her previous work with you. For your information, we have enclosed a statement signed by him/her authorizing us to contact you for information on his/her previous work experience with you. We would certainly appreciate it if you would provide us with your candid opinions of his/her employment. If you have any questions or comments you would care to make, please feel free to contact us at the number listed in the attached cover letter. At any rate, thank you for your consideration of our requests for the information requested below. As you answer the questions, please keep in mind that they should be answered in terms of your knowledge of his/her previous work with you.

1. When was he/she employed with your firm? From _____ to _____
2. Was he/she under your direct supervision?   ☐ Yes   ☐ No
3. If not, what was your working relationships with him/her? _____
4. How long have you had an opportunity to observe his/her job performance? _____
5. What was his/her last job title with your firm? _____
6. Did he/she supervise any employees?   ☐ Yes   ☐ No   If so, how many?
7. Why did he/she leave your company? _____

Below is a series of questions that deal with how he/she might perform at the job for which we are considering him/her. Read the question and then use the rating scale to indicate how you think he/she would perform based on your previous knowledge of his/her work.

8. For him/her to perform best, how closely should he/she be supervised?
    ☐ Needs no supervision
    ☐ Needs infrequent supervision
    ☐ Needs close, frequent supervision
9. How well does he/she react to working with details?
    ☐ Gets easily frustrated
    ☐ Can handle work that involves some details but works better without them
    ☐ Details in a job pose no problems at all
10. How well do you think he/she can handle complaints from customers?
    ☐ Would generally refuse to help resolve a customer complaint
    ☐ Would help resolve a complaint only if a customer insisted
    ☐ Would feel the customer is right and do everything possible to resolve a complaint
11. In what type of sales job do you think he/she would be best?
    ☐ Handling sales of walk-in customers
    ☐ Traveling to customer locations out-of-town to make sales
12. With respect to his/her work habits, check all of the characteristics below that describe his/her work situation:
    ☐ Works best on a regular schedule
    ☐ Works best under pressure
    ☐ Works best only when in the mood
    ☐ Works best when there is a regular series of steps to follow for solving a problem
13. Do you know of anything that would indicate if he/she would be unfit or dangerous (for example, in working with customers or co-workers or in driving an automobile) in a position with our organization?   ☐ Yes   ☐ No
    If "yes" please explain. _____
14. If you have any additional comments, please make them on the back of this form.

Your Name: _____

Your Title: _____

Address: _____
                              City   Province   Postal Code

Company: _____

Telephone: _____

Thank you for your time and help. The information you provided will be very useful as we review all application materials.

Note: This form is completed by the reference giver.

Source: From *Human Resource Selection*, 5th ed., by Gatewood/Field. © 2001. Reprinted with permission of South-Western, a division of Thomson Learning: www.thomsonrights.com. Fax 800-730-2215.

time is taken and the proper questions are asked, such checking is an inexpensive and straightforward way of verifying factual information about the applicant. This may include current and previous job titles, salary, dates of employment, and reasons for leaving, as well as information about the applicant's fit with the job and organizational culture.

Information to Be Verified

A basic background check includes a criminal record check, independent verification of educational qualifications, verification of at least five years' employment, together with checks of three performance-related references from past supervisors. For financially sensitive positions, a credit check may also be included.

Obtaining Written Permission

Written permission is required not only for credit checking. As a legal protection for all concerned, applicants should be asked to indicate, in writing, their willingness for the firm to check with current and/or former employers and other references. There is generally a section on the application form for this purpose. Many employers will not give out any reference information until they have received a copy of such written authorization.

Making Reference Checks More Effective

Several things can be done to make reference checks more effective. One is to use a structured form to ensure that important questions are not overlooked. Another suggestion is to use the references offered by the applicant as a source for other references who may know of the applicant's performance. Thus, each of the applicant's references might be asked, "Could you please give me the name of another person who might be familiar with the applicant's performance?" In that way, information may be obtained from references who are more objective because they weren't referred directly by the applicant. Making reference checks productive also requires persistence.

Providing References

In providing reference information, the concept of *qualified privilege* is important. Generally speaking, if comments are made in confidence for a public purpose, without malice, and are honestly believed, the defence of "qualified privilege" exists. Thus, if honest, fair, and candid references are given by an individual who is asked to provide confidential information about the performance of a job applicant, then the doctrine of qualified privilege generally protects the reference giver, even if negative information is imparted about the candidate.

Nevertheless, with the fear of civil litigation increasing, more Canadian companies are adopting a "no reference" policy regarding previous employees or are only willing to confirm the position held and dates of employment—especially in the case of discharged employees.[46]

> **An Ethical Dilemma**
>
> As the HR manager, how would you balance your ethical responsibilities to those providing reference information and to the job applicant in a situation in which a candidate is being eliminated from a competition based on negative reference information from a number of sources?

FINAL STEPS IN SELECTION

The final steps in the selection process are the supervisory interview and realistic job preview, the hiring decision, and candidate notification.

Supervisory Interview

The two or three top candidates typically return for an interview with the immediate supervisor, who usually makes the final selection decision. The supervisory interview is important because the supervisor knows the technical aspects of the job, is most qualified to assess the applicants' job knowledge and skills, and is best equipped to answer any job-specific questions from the candidate. Also, the immediate supervisor generally has to work closely with the selected individual and must feel comfortable with that person. The selected individual must fit with the current members of the hiring department, something that the supervisor is often best able to assess. When a supervisor makes a hiring recommendation, he or she is usually committed to the new employee's success and will try to provide assistance and guidance. If the new hire is not successful, the supervisor is more likely to accept some of the responsibility.

realistic job preview (RJP)   A strategy used to provide applicants with realistic information—both positive and negative—about the job demands, the organization's expectations, and the work environment.

A **realistic job preview (RJP)** should be provided at the time of the supervisory interview. The purpose of an RJP is to create appropriate expectations about the job by presenting realistic information about the job demands, the organization's expectations, and the work environment.[47] Studies have reported that RJPs lead to improved employee job satisfaction, reduced voluntary turnover, and enhanced communication.[48] Although some candidates may choose not to accept employment with the firm after an RJP, those individuals probably would not have remained with the firm long had they accepted the job offer.[49]

The Hiring Decision

REQUIRED PROFESSIONAL CAPABILITIES

Establishes appointment procedures

To make the hiring decision, information from the multiple selection techniques used must be combined, and the applicant who is the best fit with the selection criteria must be identified. HR department staff members generally play a major role in compiling all the data. It is the immediate supervisor who is usually responsible for making the final hiring decision, however. Firms generally make a subjective evaluation of all the information gleaned about each candidate and arrive at an overall judgment. The validity and reliability of these judgments can be improved by using tests that are objectively scored and by devising a candidate-rating sheet based on the weighted want criteria.

statistical strategy   A more objective technique used to determine to whom the job should be offered that involves identifying the most valid predictors and weighting them through statistical methods, such as multiple regression.

Another approach involves combining all the pieces of information according to a formula and giving the job to the candidate with the highest score. Research studies have indicated that this approach, called a **statistical strategy**, is generally more reliable and valid than is a subjective evaluation.[50]

Regardless of collection methodology, all information used in making the selection decision should be kept in a file, including interview notes, test results, reference checking information, and so on. In the event of a human rights challenge, negligent hiring charge, or union grievance about the selection decision, such data are critical.

An Ethical Dilemma

As the HR manager, how much feedback should you provide to those individuals not selected for a position?

Candidate Notification

Once the selection decision has been made, a job offer is extended to the successful candidate. Often, the initial offer is made by telephone, but it should be followed up with a written employment offer that clearly specifies important terms and conditions of employment, such as starting date, starting salary, probation period, and so on.

Candidates should be given a reasonable length of time in which to think about the offer and not be pressured into making an immediate decision. If there are two candidates who are both excellent and the first-choice candidate declines the offer, the runner-up can then be offered the job.

Chapter Review

Summary

1. Selection is the process of choosing among individuals who have been recruited to fill existing or projected job openings. The purpose of selection is to find the "best" candidate. Because the quality of the company's human resources is often a competitive advantage in achieving the company's strategic objectives, selection of those employees has considerable strategic importance. Those individuals selected will be implementing strategic decisions and, in some cases, creating strategic plans. Thus, the successful candidates must fit with the strategic direction of the organization.

2. Reliability (the degree to which selection techniques are dependable, consistent, and stable) and validity (which relates to accuracy) are critically important for effective selection of the best candidate and to satisfy legal requirements.

3. The different types of tests used for selection include intelligence tests, emotional intelligence tests, aptitude tests, tests of motor and physical abilities, personality tests, interest inventories, achievement tests, the work-sampling technique, management assessment centres, situational testing, micro-assessments, and medical examinations. Pre-employment substance abuse testing is not permitted under human rights legislation.

4. Selection interviewing can be unstructured, structured, or semi-structured. The content varies between situational interviews (focus on future behaviour) and behavioural interviews (focus on past behaviour). Interviews can be administered on a one-on-one basis, sequentially, or by using a panel.

5. Reference checking is a very important source of information about job candidates. To make reference checks more effective, written permission should be obtained from each applicant, a structured form should be used, references offered by the applicant should be used as a source for other references, and staff checking references must be persistent. Failure to check references can lead to negligent or wrongful hiring lawsuits. The legal concept of qualified privilege means that if honest, fair, and candid references are given, the reference-giver is protected from litigation, even if negative information is imparted about the candidate. Nevertheless, the fear of civil litigation is increasing, and more Canadian companies are adopting a policy of "no references" or will only confirm the position held and dates of employment.

Key Terms

achievement tests   *(p. 174)*
aptitude tests   *(p. 171)*
behavioural or behaviour description interview (BDI)   *(p. 178)*
construct validity   *(p. 170)*
content validity   *(p. 170)*
contrast or candidate-order error   *(p. 180)*
criterion-related validity   *(p. 170)*
differential validity   *(p. 170)*
emotional intelligence (EI) tests   *(p. 171)*
halo effect   *(p. 180)*
intelligence (IQ) tests   *(p. 171)*
interest inventories   *(p. 174)*
management assessment centre   *(p. 174)*
micro-assessment   *(p. 176)*
mixed (semi-structured) interview   *(p. 177)*
multiple-hurdle strategy   *(p. 168)*
must criteria   *(p. 182)*
panel interview   *(p. 179)*
personality tests   *(p. 173)*
realistic job preview (RJP)   *(p. 188)*
reliability   *(p. 169)*
selection   *(p. 167)*
selection interview   *(p. 176)*
selection ratio   *(p. 168)*
situational interview   *(p. 177)*
situational tests   *(p. 175)*
statistical strategy   *(p. 188)*
structured interview   *(p. 176)*
unstructured interview   *(p. 176)*
validity   *(p. 170)*
want criteria   *(p. 182)*

Review and Discussion Questions

1. Explain the differences among criterion-related validity, content validity, and construct validity.

2. Describe three common personality tests.

3. Describe any four activities involved in a management assessment centre.

4. Explain the difference between situational and behavioural interviews. Give examples of situational and behavioural interview questions.

5. Briefly discuss any five common interviewing mistakes and explain how such errors can be avoided.

6. Why is the supervisory interview so important in the selection process?

Critical Thinking Questions

1. If you were asked to design an effective selection process for retail sales representatives working on a 100 percent commission basis, which of the steps described in this chapter would you include and why? Justify the omission of any steps and explain why the quality of the selection decision will not be compromised by their elimination.

2. Assume that you have just been hired as the employment manager in a firm that has never done any selection testing. Write a memorandum to the CEO describing the types of tests that you would recommend the firm consider using in the future, some of the legal and ethical concerns pertaining to such testing and how such concerns can be overcome, and the benefits to the firm of using the recommended testing.

3. Describe strategies that you could use to (a) establish rapport with an extremely nervous candidate, (b) get an interviewee who is rambling "back on track," (c) clarify a statement made by an applicant during an interview, and (d) obtain detailed reference information from an individual who seems reluctant to say much.

4. Alberta oil and gas companies are using pre-employment substance abuse testing even though it is prohibited. Their argument is that because they have multibillion-dollar projects underway with a lot of potential for accidents, environmental damage, and so on, they want to be sure that they are not hiring employees who have substance abuse problems. They know that their young, transient, and relatively wealthy oil sands workforce commonly abuses drugs and alcohol. How could this situation be resolved in the spirit of the law on accommodating disabilities?

Application Exercises

Running Case: LearnInMotion.com

The Better Interview

Like virtually all the other HR-related activities at LearnInMotion.com, the company has no organized approach to interviewing job candidates. Three people, Jennifer, Pierre, and Greg (from the board of directors), interview each candidate, and the three then get together for a discussion. Unfortunately, they usually reach strikingly different conclusions. For example, Greg thought a particular candidate was "stellar" and would not only be able to sell but also eventually assume various administrative responsibilities to take the load off Jennifer and Pierre. Pierre thought this particular candidate was hopeless: "I've been selling for eight years and have hired many salespeople, and there's no way this person's going to be a closer," he said. Jennifer, noting that a friend of her mother had recommended this particular candidate, was willing to take a wait-and-see attitude: "Let's hire her and see how she does," she said. Pierre replied that this was no way to hire a salesperson, and, in any case, hiring another administrator was pretty far down their priority list. "I wish Greg would stick to the problem at hand, namely hiring a 100 percent salesperson."

Jennifer was sure that inadequate formal interviewing practices, procedures, and training accounted for at least some of the problems they were having in hiring and keeping good salespeople. They did hire one salesperson whom they thought was going to be terrific, based on the praise provided by her references and on what they understood her previous sales experience had been; she stayed for a month and a half, sold hardly anything, cost the company almost $10 000 of its precious cash, and then left for another job.

The problem wasn't just with the salespeople. For one thing, they hired a programmer largely based on his assertion that he was expert in various Web-related programming, including HTML, XML, and Java script. They followed up with one of his references, who was neutral regarding the candidate's programming abilities. But, being desperate, Jennifer and Pierre hired him anyway—only to have him leave three weeks later, more or less by mutual consent.

"This is a total disaster," said Jennifer, and Pierre could only agree. It was obvious that in some respects their interviews were worse than not interviewing at all: for example, if they didn't have interviews, perhaps they would have used more caution in following up with the candidates' references. In any case, they now want you, their management consultant, to tell them what to do. Here's what they want you to do for them.

Questions

1. Tell Pierre and Jennifer what they're doing wrong.

2. In general, what can LearnInMotion.com do to improve its employee interviewing practices? Should the company develop interview forms that list questions for their various jobs? If so, what format should these take?

3. What are five questions they should ask salespeople candidates and five questions they should ask programmer candidates?

Case Incident

If We Knew Then What We Know Now

Pinpoint Networks, a promising Internet search engine company, had everything going for it. Its two teenage founders, Judson Bowman and Taylor Brockman, had taken the company far since its founding just two years earlier. Together, they had raised more than $5 million in venture capital and had made significant contacts with some big players in the telecommunications industry. But these two entrepreneurs knew they needed help to move the company forward. Although well prepared to perform the work that would take Pinpoint to the next level, they needed an executive running the company—someone who could obtain more venture capital as well as expand and nurture contacts in the telecommunications industry. Bowman and Brockman needed to hire a CEO.

An executive search firm helped identify several potential candidates. One, Anthony Blake, appeared to be the perfect choice. He had been involved in some of the industry's biggest initiatives. Blake, CEO of ObjectStream in California, indicated that he desired to leave his company because he was selling it to WorldCom. He had contacts and he had a vision. In quick order, he was hired as Pinpoint's CEO.

But shortly after hiring Blake, the excitement started to wane. Blake wanted no publicity surrounding his hiring as CEO. Several of his "friends in the business" had never head of Blake. The sale of ObjectStream to WorldCom was never announced, nor would it be from WorldCom's perspective. It appeared Blake had exaggerated his career success, his industry contacts, and even his age!

Just 13 weeks into Blake's tenure with Pinpoint, he and the company parted ways. This short association ran Pinpoint into some difficulty. Cash flow was hurting—they had at best, six to seven months left before the cash ran out. To help ease this situation, the company laid off one-third of its workforce. Two years later, the company has had a remarkable turnaround—with Bowman at the helm!

Interestingly, when the search firm had been contacted about the names they recommended to Pinpoint, a difference of opinion occurred. The search firm claimed they simply presented potential candidates without recommending any one in particular. The search firm claimed that Pinpoint was so excited with Blake's résumé that they proceeded too quickly and failed to leave ample time for anyone to verify the information with proper due diligence.

The search firm regarded this as an absolute must, as the year earlier, in conducting 70 background checks for people potentially placed in executive level positions, they found that 39 percent had serious problems—from insurance fraud to securities violations—never revealed on the résumé!

Questions

1. What are the background investigation implications of the Pinpoint Networks case?

2. Do you believe the search firm had a responsibility for checking candidates' references before giving Pinpoint its recommendations? Explain your position.

3. What role does the company play in reference checking—even if it uses a search firm?

Source: D.A. DeCenzo and S.P. Robbins, *Fundamentals of Human Resource Management*, 8th ed. New York: John Wiley & Sons, 2005, p. 193. Copyright © 2005 John Wiley & Sons. Reprinted with permission of John Wiley & Sons.

Experiential Exercises

1. Design a semi-structured interview questionnaire for a position with which you are extremely familiar, basing the candidate-specific questions on your own résumé. Ensure that behavioural, situational, job-knowledge, and worker-requirements questions are included. Once you have done so, select a partner. Role-play two selection interviews—one based on your questionnaire and the other based on your partner's questionnaire. The individual who wrote the questions is to play the role of interviewee, with his or her partner serving as the interviewer. Do not forget to build rapport, ask the questions in order, take effective notes, and bring the interview to a close. Once you have completed the two role-plays, critically evaluate each interview questionnaire.

2. Create an offer of employment for a successful customer-service representative at a call centre, outlining the terms and conditions of employment. Keep in mind that a copy of the letter should be signed and returned by the new hire and that a signed letter of offer becomes an employment contract.

A Guide to Screening and Selection in Employment

Subject	Avoid Asking	Preferred	Comment
Name	about name change: whether it was changed by court order, marriage, or other reason maiden name		ask after selection if needed to check on previously held jobs or educational credentials
Address	for addresses outside Canada	ask place and duration of current or recent address	
Age	for birth certificates, baptismal records, or about age in general	ask applicants whether they are eligible to work under Canadian laws regarding age restrictions	if precise age required for benefits plans or other legitimate purposes, it can be determined after selection
Sex	males or females to fill in different applications about pregnancy, child bearing plans, or child care arrangements	ask applicant if the attendance requirements can be met	during the interview or after selection, the applicant, for purposes of courtesy, may be asked which of Dr., Mr., Mrs., Miss, Ms. is preferred
Marital Status	whether the applicant is single, married, divorced, engaged, separated, widowed, or living common-law whether an applicant's spouse may be transferred about spouse's employment	if transfer or travel is part of the job, the applicant can be asked if he or she can meet these requirements ask whether there are any circumstances that might prevent completion of a minimum service commitment	information on dependants can be determined after selection if necessary
Family Status	number of children or dependants about child care arrangements	if the applicant would be able to work the required hours and, where applicable, overtime	contacts for emergencies and/or details on dependants can be determined after selection
National or Ethnic Origin	about birthplace, nationality of ancestors, spouse, or other relatives whether born in Canada for proof of citizenship	since those who are entitled to work in Canada must be citizens, permanent residents, or holders of valid work permits, applicants can be asked if they are legally entitled to work in Canada	documentation of eligibility to work (papers, visas, etc.) can be requested after selection
Military Service	about military service in other countries	inquire about Canadian military service where employment preference is given to veterans by law	
Language	mother tongue where language skills obtained	ask whether applicant understands, reads, writes, or speaks languages required for the job	testing or scoring applicants for language proficiency is not permitted unless job related
Race or Colour	about race or colour, including colour of eyes, skin, or hair		

continued

Subject	Avoid Asking	Preferred	Comment
Photographs	for photo to be attached to applications or sent to interviewer before interview	photos for security passes or company files can be taken after selection	
Religion	whether applicant will work a specific religious holiday about religious affiliation, church membership, frequency of church attendance for references from clergy or religious leader	explain the required work shift, asking whether such a schedule poses problems for the applicant	reasonable accommodation of an employee's religious beliefs is the employer's duty
Height and Weight			no inquiry unless there is evidence they are genuine occupational requirements
Disability	for list of all disabilities, limitations, or health problems whether applicant drinks or uses drugs whether applicant has ever received psychiatric care or been hospitalized for emotional problems whether applicant has received workers' compensation		the employer should: – disclose any information on medically-related requirements or standards early in the application process – then ask whether the applicant has any condition that could affect his or her ability to do the job, preferably during a pre-employment medical examination a disability is only relevant to job ability if it: – threatens the safety or property of others – prevents the applicant from safe and adequate job performance even when reasonable efforts are made to accommodate the disability
Medical Information	whether currently under a physician's care name of family doctor whether receiving counselling or therapy		medical exams should be conducted after selection and only if an employee's condition is related to job duties offers of employment can be made conditional on successful completion of a medical exam
Pardoned Conviction	whether applicant has ever been convicted whether applicant has ever been arrested whether applicant has a criminal record	if bonding is a job requirement, ask whether the applicant is eligible	inquiries about criminal record or convictions are discouraged unless related to job duties

continued

Subject	Avoid Asking	Preferred	Comment
Sexual Orientation	about the applicant's sexual orientation		contacts for emergencies and/or details on dependants can be determined after selection
References			the same restrictions that apply to questions asked of applicants apply when asking for employment references

Source: Canadian Human Rights Commission, *A Guide to Screening and Selection in Employment*. www.chrc-ccdp.ca/publications/ screening_employment-en.asp. Reproduced with the permission of the Ministry of Public Works and Government Services, 2006.

CHAPTER 8

ORIENTATION AND TRAINING

REQUIRED PROFESSIONAL CAPABILITIES

LEARNING OUTCOMES
AFTER STUDYING THIS CHAPTER, YOU SHOULD BE ABLE TO

Explain how to develop an orientation program.

Describe the five-step training process.

Discuss two techniques used for assessing training needs.

Explain at least five traditional training techniques.

Describe the three types of e-learning.

Describe how to evaluate the training effort.

Explain several common types of training for special purposes.

- Develops orientation policies and procedures for new employees

- Ensures legislated training obligations are met within the organization

- Ensures the application of appropriate development methods and techniques based on general accepted principles of adult learning

- Using a variety of methods, facilitates the delivery of development programs to groups and individuals

- Conducts training needs assessments by identifying individual and corporate learning requirements

- Establishes priority of responses to needs assessment results

- Identifies and accesses external sources of training funding available to employees

- Recommends the most appropriate way to meet identified learning needs (e.g., courses, secondments, and on-the-job activities)

- Participates in course design and selection/delivery of learning materials via various media

- Develops training budgets, monitors expenditures, and documents activities associated with training

- Ensures arrangements are made for training schedules, facilities, trainers, participants, and equipment and course material

- Conducts an evaluation of the program

- Compiles, analyzes, and documents evaluation data based on feedback

- Documents participant feedback to evaluate effectiveness of program delivery

- Ensures participant and organizational feedback is documented and evaluated

ORIENTING EMPLOYEES

Once employees have been recruited and selected, the next step is orienting them to their new company and their new job. A strategic approach to recruitment and retention of employees includes a well-integrated orientation program both before and after hiring.[1]

Purpose of Orientation Programs

employee orientation   A procedure for providing new employees with basic background information about the firm and the job.

Employee orientation provides new employees with basic background information about the employer and specific information that they need to perform their jobs satisfactorily. At the Law Society of Upper Canada, any time a new employee walks through the door, the organization acts quickly to help the person get started on the right foot. The Law Society views orientation as an investment in the retention of talent. The essence of the orientation program is to introduce people to the culture, give them a common bond, teach the importance of teamwork in the workplace, and provide the tools and information to be successful at the Law Society.[2]

socialization   The ongoing process of instilling in all employees the prevailing attitudes, standards, values, and patterns of behaviour that are expected by the organization.

Orientation is actually one component of the employer's new-employee socialization process. **Socialization** is the ongoing process of instilling in all employees the prevailing attitudes, standards, values, and patterns of behaviour that are expected by the organization.[3]

Orientation helps the employee to perform better by providing necessary information about company rules and practices. It helps to clarify the organization's expectations of an employee regarding his or her job, thus helping to reduce the new employee's first-day jitters and **reality shock**—the discrepancy between what the new employee expected from his or her new job and the realities of it.

reality shock   The state that results from the discrepancy between what the new employee expects from his or her new job, and the realities of it.

An important part of any effective orientation program is sitting down and deciding on work-related goals with the new employee. These goals provide the basis for early feedback and establish a foundation for ongoing performance management.[4] Orientation is the first step in helping the new employee manage the learning curve; it helps new employees to become productive more quickly than they might otherwise. In the long term, a comprehensive orientation can lead to reductions in turnover, increased morale, fewer instances of corrective discipline, and fewer employee grievances. It can also reduce the number of workplace injuries, particularly for young workers.[5]

Some organizations commence orientation activity before the first day of employment. At Ernst & Young, the firm keeps in touch with people who have been hired but have not yet started work by sending them internal newsletters, inviting them to drop by for chats, and hosting dinners for them.[6] Others use orientation as an ongoing "new-hire development process" and extend it in stages throughout the first year of employment, in order to improve retention levels and reduce the overall costs of recruitment.[7]

Content of Orientation Programs

Orientation programs range from brief, informal introductions to lengthy, formal programs. In the latter, the new employee is usually given (over an extended time)

- a handbook that covers matters like company history and current mission; working hours and attendance expectations; vacations and holidays; payroll, employee benefits, and pensions; and work regulations and policies

- a tour of the company facilities and introductions to the employee's supervisor and co-workers
- an explanation of job procedures, duties, and responsibilities
- a summary of training to be received (when and why)
- an explanation of performance appraisal criteria, including the estimated time to achieve full productivity

As illustrated in **Figure 8.1**, other information typically includes HR policies, strategic objectives, company organization and operations, and safety measures and regulations. At Ernst & Young, after a review of best practices, both internally and externally, the orientation program was redesigned to include[8]

- a presentation providing an overview of the firm
- an administrative checklist of tasks to be conducted before a new employee's start date and during the first three months of employment
- a binder explaining the firm's vision, values, strategies, and structures
- computer and voice-mail training
- a form for employee feedback
- an intranet site with information about the firm

<table>
<tr><td>

Hints to Ensure Legal Compliance

</td></tr>
</table>

Note that some courts have found employee handbook contents to represent a contract with the employee. Therefore, disclaimers should be included that make it clear that statements of company policies, benefits, and regulations do not constitute the terms and conditions of an employment contract, either express or implied. Firms should think twice before including such statements in the handbook as "No employee will be terminated without just cause," or statements that imply or state that employees have tenure; they could be viewed as legal and binding commitments.

Responsibility for Orientation

The first day of the orientation usually starts with the HR specialist, who explains such matters as working hours and vacation. The employee is then introduced to his or her new supervisor, who continues the orientation by explaining the exact nature of the job, introducing the person to his or her new colleagues, and familiarizing the new employee with the workplace. Sometimes, another employee at a peer level will be assigned as a "buddy" or mentor for the newly hired employee for the first few weeks or months of employment. It is a good idea for the HR department to follow up with each new employee about three months after the initial orientation to address any remaining questions.

In an orientation, the supervisor explains the exact nature of the job, introduces new colleagues, and familiarizes new employees with the workplace.

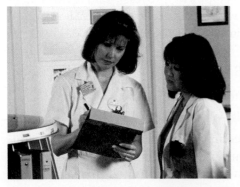

Special Orientation Situations

Diverse Workforce

In an organization that has not had a diverse workforce in the past, orienting new employees from different backgrounds poses a special challenge. The values of the organization may be new to them if these values were not part of their past experience. New employees should be advised to expect a variety of reactions from current employees to someone from a different background and be given some tips on how to deal with these reactions. In particular, they need to know which

FIGURE 8.1   Orientation Checklist—Government of Alberta

First day of employment

☐ Introduce new employee to co-workers in their section.

☐ Review hours of work, coffee, and lunch breaks.

☐ Assist in offering options for parking.

☐ Familiarize employee with lunchrooms, washrooms, supplies, storage, and appropriate equipment (e.g., photocopiers, fax machines, etc.).

☐ Explain branch norms to employee (e.g., coffee fund).

☐ Review the appropriate dress attire with employee.

☐ Assist new employee with activating voice mail.

☐ Ensure employee will have passwords set up for computer use.

☐ Demonstrate access to Departmental Intranet and *New Employee Web Site*—online orientation.

☐ Review all safety regulations and procedures, including:
    ☐ Accident and incident reports
    ☐ Security
    ☐ First Aid
    ☐ Evacuation procedures in case of emergency

☐ Explain function of the Division, Branch, and Section.

☐ Give employee a copy of their job description, review job duties and accountabilities with the employee.

☐ Provide a copy of an organizational chart for the appropriate area.

☐ Identify reporting relationships.

☐ Commencement administration:
    ☐ Payroll
    ☐ Benefits information and registration
    ☐ Employee status regarding Union membership
    ☐ Complete all commencement paperwork
    ☐ Oath of Office
    ☐ Arrange for departmental identification card

To be completed in the first weeks of employment

☐ Explain timesheets, absence and overtime reporting procedures, how attendance is recorded.

☐ Access to MyAGent for pay, benefits, vacation, and to review personal information.

☐ Provide access to, and explain departmental business plan, and how employee's role fits into the plan.

☐ Review Departmental Performance Management System.

☐ Set performance goals in collaboration with employee.

☐ Create a Learning Plan.

☐ Identify training opportunities.

☐ Provide employee with "high-level" organizational chart showing DM and reporting structures.

☐ Ensure employee has reviewed Government Business Plan.

☐ Employees should familiarize themselves with the structure of Government and how it works:
    ☐ Code of Conduct & Ethics
    ☐ Sexual & Workplace Harassment Policy
    ☐ Claiming Expenses
    ☐ Internet/E-mail Policy for the Government of Alberta
    ☐ Master and Subsidiary Agreements

☐ Follow-up to ensure employee has all applicable orientation tools and materials.

Source: "New Employee Orientation Checklist." Government of Alberta, Personnel Administration Office. Copyright © 2005. www.pao.gov.ab/orientation/basics/orientation-checklist.htm (July 19, 2006). Reproduced with permission.

reactions are prohibited under human rights legislation and how to report these, should they occur.

Mergers and Acquisitions

Employees hired into a newly merged company need to receive information about the details of the merger or acquisition as part of the information on company history. They also need to be made aware of any ongoing, as-yet-unresolved difficulties regarding day-to-day operational issues related to their work. A further orientation issue arises with respect to the existing employees at the time of the merger or acquisition: a new company culture will evolve in the merged organization, and everyone will experience a resocialization process. This presents an opportunity for the merged organization to emphasize the new organizational values and beliefs, in order to reinforce corporate culture and further the new organization's business objectives.[9]

Union versus Non-union Employees

New employees in unionized positions need to be provided with a copy of the collective agreement and be told which information relates specifically to their particular job. They also need to be introduced to their union steward, have payroll deduction of union dues explained, and be informed of the names of union executive members. New employees, both unionized and non-unionized, need to be made aware of which jobs are unionized and which ones are not.

Multi-location Organizations

New employees in a multi-location company need to be made aware of where the other locations are and what business functions are performed in each location. The Ontario Ministry of Education and Training is one such organization, and it uses a Web-based online orientation to deliver corporate-level information.[10] All employees have equal access regardless of their location, and the same message is delivered to each one. Updates can be made instantaneously, and employees can view the information at their own pace.

Problems with Orientation Programs

A number of potential problems can arise with orientation programs. Often, *too much information* is provided in a short time (usually one day) and the new employee is overwhelmed. New employees commonly find themselves inundated with forms to fill out for payroll, benefits, pensions, and so on. Another problem is that *little or no orientation* is provided, which means that new employees must personally seek answers to each question that arises and work without a good understanding of what is expected of them. This is a common problem for part-time and contract workers. Finally, the orientation information provided by the HR department can be *too broad* to be meaningful to a new employee, especially on the first day, whereas the orientation information provided by the immediate supervisor may be *too detailed* to realistically expect the new employee to remember it all.

Evaluation of Orientation Programs

Orientation programs should be evaluated to assess whether they are providing timely, useful information to new employees in a cost-effective manner. Three approaches to evaluating orientation programs are as follows:

1. *Employee reaction.* Interview or survey new employees for their opinion on the usefulness of the orientation program.
2. *Socialization effects.* Review new employees at regular intervals to assess progress toward understanding and acceptance of the beliefs, values, and norms of the organization.

3. *Cost/benefit analysis.* Compare (1) orientation costs, such as printing handbooks and time spent orienting new employees by HR staff and immediate supervisors; and (2) benefits of orientation, including reduction in errors, rate of productivity, efficiency levels, and so on.

Executive Integration

Typically, executives do not participate in formal orientation activities, and there is little planning regarding how they will be integrated into their new position and company. The common assumption is that the new executive is a professional and will know what to do, but full executive integration can take up to 18 months.[11] To make things even more difficult, executives are often brought in as change agents, in which case they can expect to face considerable resistance. Thus, a lack of attention to executive integration can result in serious problems with assimilation and work effectiveness. It is common to perceive executive integration as an orientation issue, but integration at senior levels in the organization requires an ongoing process that can continue for months as the new executive learns about the unspoken dynamics of the organization that are not covered in orientation programs, such as how decisions are really made and who holds what type of power.[12]

Executive integration is of critical importance to a productive relationship between a new executive and his or her organization, and it is important to review previous successes and failures at executive integration on an ongoing basis. Key aspects of the integration process include

- identifying position specifications (particularly the ability to deal with and overcome jealousy)
- providing realistic information to job candidates and providing support regarding reality shock
- assessing each candidate's previous record at making organizational transitions
- announcing the hiring with enthusiasm
- stressing the importance of listening as well as demonstrating competency, and promoting more time spent talking with the boss
- assisting new executives who are balancing their work to change cultural norms while they themselves are part of the culture itself[13]

THE TRAINING PROCESS

training   The process of teaching employees the basic skills/ competencies that they need to perform their jobs.

Training employees involves a learning process in which workers are provided with the information and skills that they need to successfully perform their jobs. Training might thus mean showing a production worker how to operate a new machine, a new salesperson how to sell the firm's product, or a new supervisor how to interview and appraise employees. Whereas *training* focuses on skills and competencies needed to perform employees' current jobs, *development* is training of a long-term nature. Its aim is to prepare current employees for future jobs within the organization.

It is important to ensure that business and training goals are aligned and that training is part of an organization's strategic plan.[14] A training professional in today's business world has to understand the organization's business, speak its language, and demonstrate the business value of training investment.[15] Purolator, one of Canada's largest courier services, has 13 000 employees, and Stephen Gould, senior vice-president of HR, says it's critical to the success of the business that the company's trainers understand the business strategy.[16]

In today's service-based economy, highly knowledgeable workers can be the company's most important assets. Thus, it is important to treat training as a strategic investment in human capital.[17] A recent federal government report concluded that

> To remain competitive and keep up with the accelerating pace of technological change, Canada must continuously renew and upgrade the skills of its workforce. We can no longer assume that the skills acquired in youth will carry workers through their active lives. Rather, the working life of most adults must be a period of continuous learning.[18]

Already, a skills crisis has arisen in the manufacturing sector, where lack of qualified personnel is a major problem. Skills in greatest need of improvement are problem solving, communications, and teamwork.[19] Training is therefore moving to centre stage as a necessity for improving employers' competitiveness. The federal government has called for businesses to increase spending on training, and business has asked the government to expand programs for professional immigrants to get Canadian qualifications in their fields. In response, the Canadian Council on Learning was created by the federal government to promote best practices in workplace learning. The Quebec government has legislated that all firms with a payroll of more than $250 000 must spend 1 percent of payroll on employee training (or else pay tax in the same amount).[20]

Another benefit of increased training is the fact that training can strengthen employee commitment. It implies faith in the future of the company and of the individual. Few things can better illustrate a firm's commitment to its employees than continuing developmental opportunities to improve themselves, and such commitment is usually reciprocated.[21] This loyalty is one reason that a high-commitment firm like the Bank of Montreal provides seven days of training per year for all employees, at a cost of $1800 per employee—more than double the national average.[22]

Training and Learning

Training is essentially a learning process. To train employees, therefore, it is useful to know something about how people learn. For example, people have three main learning styles: *auditory*, learning through talking and listening; *visual*, learning through pictures and print; and *kinesthetic*, tactile learning through a whole-body experience. Training effectiveness can be enhanced by identifying learning styles and personalizing the training accordingly.[23]

Research
Insight ▷

First, it is easier for trainees to understand and remember material that is meaningful. At the start of training, provide the trainees with an overall picture of the material to be presented. When presenting material, use as many visual aids as possible and a variety of familiar examples. Organize the material so that it is presented in a logical manner and in meaningful units. Try to use terms and concepts that are already familiar to trainees.

Second, make sure that it is easy to transfer new skills and behaviours from the training site to the job site. Maximize the similarity between the training situation and the work situation, and provide adequate training practice. Give trainees the chance to use their new skills immediately on their return to work.

Train managers first and employees second in order to send a message about the importance of the training, and control contingencies by planning rewards for trainees who successfully complete and integrate the new training.[24]

Third, motivate the trainee. Motivation affects training outcomes independently of any increase in cognitive ability. Training motivation is affected by individual characteristics, such as conscientiousness, and by the training climate.[25] Therefore, it is important to try to provide as much realistic practice as possible. Trainees learn best when correct responses are immediately reinforced, perhaps with a quick "Well done." Finally, trainees learn best at their own pace, so, if possible, let trainees pace themselves.

Fourth, effectively prepare the trainee. Research evidence shows that the trainee's pre-training preparation is a crucial step in the training process. It is important to create a perceived need for training in the minds of participants.[26] Also, provide preparatory information that will help to set the trainees' expectations about the events and consequences of actions that are likely to occur in the training environment (and, eventually, on the job). For example, trainees learning to become first-line supervisors might face stressful conditions, high workload, and difficult employees. Studies suggest that the negative impact of such events can be reduced by letting trainees know ahead of time what might occur.[27]

Legal Aspects of Training

Under human rights and employment equity legislation, several aspects of employee training programs must be assessed with an eye toward the program's impact on designated group members.[28] For example, if relatively few women or visible minorities are selected for the training program, there may be a requirement to show that the admissions procedures are valid—that they predict performance on the job for which the person is being trained. It could turn out that the reading level of the training manuals is too advanced for many visible minority trainees, which results in their doing poorly in the program, quite aside from their aptitude for the jobs for which they are being trained. The training program might then be found to be unfairly discriminatory.

Negligent training is another potential problem. *Negligent training* occurs when an employer fails to train adequately, and an employee subsequently harms a third party. Also, employees who are dismissed for poor performance or disciplined for safety infractions may claim that the employer was negligent in that the employee's training was inadequate. Precautions here include[29]

- confirming claims of skill and experience for all applicants

- reducing the risks of harm by extensively training employees who work with dangerous equipment, materials, or processes

- ensuring that the training includes procedures to protect third parties' health and safety (including that of other employees)

- evaluating the training activity to determine its effectiveness in reducing negligence risks

The Five-Step Training Process

A typical training program consists of five steps, as summarized in **Figure 8.2**. The purpose of the *needs analysis* step is to identify the specific job performance skills needed, to analyze the skills and needs of the prospective trainees, and to

FIGURE 8.2   The Five Steps in the Training and Development Process

1. NEEDS ANALYSIS

- Identify specific job performance skills needed to improve performance and productivity.
- Analyze the audience to ensure that the program will be suited to their specific levels of education, experience, and skills, as well as their attitudes and personal motivations.
- Use research to develop specific measurable knowledge and performance objectives.

2. INSTRUCTIONAL DESIGN

- Gather instructional objectives, methods, media, description of and sequence of content, examples, exercises, and activities. Organize them into a curriculum that supports adult learning theory and provides a blueprint for program development.
- Make sure all materials (such as video scripts, leaders' guides, and participants' workbooks) complement each other, are written clearly, and blend into unified training geared directly to the stated learning objectives.
- Carefully and professionally handle all program elements—whether reproduced on paper, film, or tape—to guarantee quality and effectiveness.

3. VALIDATION

- Introduce and validate the training before a representative audience. Base final revisions on pilot results to ensure program effectiveness.

4. IMPLEMENTATION

- When applicable, boost success with a train-the-trainer workshop that focuses on presentation-knowledge and skills in addition to training content.

5. EVALUATION AND FOLLOW-UP

- Assess program success according to
  REACTION—Document the learners' immediate reactions to the training.
  LEARNING—Use feedback devices or pre- and post-tests to measure what learners have actually learned.
  BEHAVIOUR—Note supervisors' reactions to learners' performance following completion of the training. This is one way to measure the degree to which learners apply new skills and knowledge to their jobs.
  RESULTS—Determine the level of improvement in job performance and assess needed maintenance.

Source: These are adapted from Mary D. Carolan, "Today's Training Basics: Some New Golden Rules," *HR Focus*, April 1993, p. 18. Used with permission of IOMA Inc.

develop specific, measurable knowledge and performance objectives. (Managers must make sure that the performance deficiency is amenable to training rather than caused by, say, poor morale because of low salaries.) In the second step, *instructional design*, the actual content of the training program is compiled and produced, including workbooks, exercises, and activities. Next, there may be a third step, *validation*, in which the bugs are worked out of the training program by presenting it to a small representative audience. Fourth, the training program is *implemented*, using techniques like those discussed in this chapter and the

Training and Development
www.ipmaac.org

next (such as on-the-job training and programmed learning). Fifth, there should be an *evaluation* and follow-up step in which the program's successes or failures are assessed.

STEP 1: TRAINING NEEDS ANALYSIS

REQUIRED PROFESSIONAL CAPABILITIES

Conducts training need assessments by identifying individual and corporate learning requirements

Establishes priority of responses to needs assessment results

task analysis   A detailed study of a job to identify the skills and competencies it requires so that an appropriate training program can be instituted.

performance analysis   Verifying that there is a performance deficiency and determining whether that deficiency should be rectified through training or through some other means (such as transferring the employee).

The first step in training is to determine what training is required, if any. The main task in assessing the training needs of new employees is to determine what the job entails and break it down into subtasks, each of which is then taught to the new employee. Assessing the training needs of current employees can be more complex, because it involves the added task of deciding whether or not training is the solution. For example, performance may be down not because of lack of training but because the standards are not clear or because the person is not motivated.

Task analysis and performance analysis are the two main techniques for identifying training needs. **Task analysis**—an analysis of the job's requirements—is especially appropriate for determining the training needs of employees who are *new* to their jobs. **Performance analysis** appraises the performance of *current* employees to determine whether training could reduce performance problems (such as excess scrap or low output). Other techniques used to identify training needs include supervisors' reports, HR records, management requests, observations, tests of job knowledge, and questionnaire surveys.[30]

Whichever technique is used—task analysis, performance analysis, or some other—employee input is essential. It is often true that no one knows as much about the job as the people actually doing it, so soliciting employee input is usually wise.[31]

Task Analysis: Assessing the Training Needs of New Employees

Task analysis—identifying the broad competencies and specific skills required to perform job-related tasks—is used for determining the training needs of employees who are new to their jobs. Particularly with entry-level workers, it is common to hire inexperienced people and train them.[32] Thus, the aim is to develop the skills and knowledge required for effective performance—like soldering (in the case of an assembly worker) or interviewing (in the case of a supervisor).

The job description and job specification are helpful here. These list the specific duties and skills required on the job and become the basic reference point in determining the training required to perform the job.

Task Analysis Record Form

Some employers supplement the current job description and specification with a task analysis record form. This consolidates information regarding the job's required tasks and skills in a form that is especially helpful for determining training requirements. As illustrated in **Table 8.1**, a task analysis record form contains six types of information:

1. *Column 1, Task List.* Here, the job's main tasks and subtasks are listed.
2. *Column 2, When and How Often Performed.* Here, the frequency with which the task and subtasks are performed is indicated.
3. *Column 3, Quantity and Quality of Performance.* Here, the standards of performance for each task and subtask are described in measurable terms, like "±tolerance of 0.007 in.," or "Within two days of receiving the order," for instance.

TABLE 8.1   Task Analysis Record Form

Task List	When and How Often Performed	Quantity and Quality of Performance	Conditions Under Which Performed	Competencies and Specific Knowledge Required	Where Best Learned
1. Operate paper cutter	4 times per day		Noisy press room: distractions		
1.1 Start motor					
1.2 Set cutting distance		± tolerance of 0.007 in.		Read gauge	On the job
1.3 Place paper on cutting table		Must be completely even to prevent uneven cut		Lift paper correctly	On the job
1.4 Push paper up to cutter				Must be even	On the job
1.5 Grasp safety release with left hand	100% of time, for safety			Essential for safety	On the job but practise first with no distractions
1.6 Grasp cutter release with right hand				Must keep both hands on releases	On the job but practise first with no distractions
1.7 Simultaneously pull safety release with left hand and cutter release with right hand					
1.8 Wait for cutter to retract	100% of time, for safety			Must keep both hands on releases	On the job but practise first with no distractions
1.9 Retract paper				Wait till cutter retracts	On the job but practise first with no distractions
1.10 Shut off	100% of time, for safety				On the job but practise first with no distractions
2. Operate printing press					
2.1 Start motor					
.					
.					
.					

Note: Task analysis record form showing some of the tasks and subtasks performed by a right-handed printing press operator.

4. *Column 4, Conditions under Which Performed.* This column indicates the conditions under which the tasks and subtasks are to be performed.

5. *Column 5, Competencies and Specific Knowledge Required.* This is the heart of the task analysis form. Here, the competencies and specific skills or knowledge required for each task and subtask are listed, specifying exactly what knowledge or skills must be taught. Thus, for the subtask "Set cutting distance," the trainee must be taught how to read the gauge.

6. *Column 6, Where Best Learned.* The decision as to whether the task is learned best on or off the job is based on several considerations. Safety is one: for example, prospective jet pilots must learn something about the plane off the job in a simulator before actually getting behind the controls.

Once the essential skills involved in doing the job are determined, new employees' proficiency in these skills can be assessed and training needs identified for each individual.

Performance Analysis: Determining the Training Needs of Current Employees

Performance analysis means verifying whether there is a significant performance deficiency and, if so, determining whether that deficiency should be rectified through training or some other means (such as transferring the employee). The first step is to appraise the employee's performance, because to improve it, the firm must first compare the person's current performance with what it should be. Examples of specific performance deficiencies follow:

- "Salespeople are expected to make ten new contacts per week, but John averages only six."
- "Other plants our size average no more than two serious accidents per month; we are averaging five."

<table>
<tr><td>Tips **for the Front Line**</td></tr>
</table>

Distinguishing between *can't do* and *won't do* problems is at the heart of performance analysis. First, the firm must determine whether it is a *can't do* problem and, if so, its specific causes. For example, the employees do not know what to do or what the standards are; there are obstacles in the system (such as a lack of tools or supplies); job aids are needed; poor selection has resulted in hiring people who do not have the skills to do the job; or training is inadequate. Conversely, it might be a *won't do* problem. In this case, employees *could* do a good job if they wanted to. If so, the reward system might have to be changed, perhaps by implementing an incentive program.

Training Objectives

REQUIRED PROFESSIONAL CAPABILITIES

Identifies and accesses external sources of training funding available to employees

Once training needs have been identified, training objectives can be established. Concrete, measurable training objectives should be set after training needs have been analyzed. Objectives specify what the trainee should be able to accomplish after successfully completing the training program. They thus provide a focus for the efforts of both the trainee and the trainer, and provide a benchmark for evaluating the success of the training program. A training program can then be developed and implemented, with the intent to achieve these objectives. These objectives must be accomplished within the organization's training budget.

STEP 2: INSTRUCTIONAL DESIGN

After the employees' training needs have been determined, and training objectives have been set, the training program can be designed. Descriptions of the most popular traditional training techniques, and more recent e-learning techniques, follow.

Traditional Training Techniques

On-the-Job Training

On-the-job training (OJT) involves having a person learn a job by actually performing it. Virtually every employee—from mailroom clerk to company president—gets some on-the-job training when he or she joins a firm. In many companies, OJT is the only type of training available. It usually involves assigning new employees to experienced workers or supervisors who then do the actual training.[33]

OJT has several advantages: it is relatively inexpensive, trainees learn while producing, and there is no need for expensive off-job facilities, like classrooms or manuals. The method also facilitates learning, since trainees learn by actually doing the job and get quick feedback about the quality of their performance.

Apprenticeship Training

More employers are going "back to the future" by implementing apprenticeship-training programs, an approach that began in the Middle Ages. Apprenticeship training basically involves having the learner/apprentice study under the tutelage of a master craftsperson.

Apprentices become skilled workers through a combination of classroom instruction and on-the-job training. Apprenticeships are widely used to train individuals for many occupations, including those of electrician and plumber. In Canada, close to 170 established trades have recognized apprenticeship programs.[34]

Apprenticeship training is critical today as more than half of skilled trades workers are expecting to retire by 2020. Federal, provincial, and territorial governments are increasing their funding of apprenticeship training programs in order to meet this growing need for more tradespeople.[35]

Informal Learning

About two-thirds of industrial training is not "formal" at all, but rather results from day-to-day unplanned interactions between the new worker and his or her colleagues. Informal learning may be defined as "any learning that occurs in which the learning process is not determined or designed by the organization."[36] This approach is often used in family businesses, as described in the Entrepreneurs and HR box.

On-the-job training is structured and concrete. Here, a supervisor teaches an employee to use a drumforming machine.

Entrepreneurs and HR

Family Business Training

Family businesses usually have a hard start but, once established, they tend to look at smooth growth for the next couple of years. However, if the growth in a family business slows down, either because the owners are aging or the market for their products and services has matured, the company often has to rely on a new generation to bring about change and drive new strategies.

Parents who hope to see their company led by a well motivated, well-prepared next generation should begin early to nurture the necessary skills. The notion of training young successors to be entrepreneurs may, in fact, be overstated. It is more important to teach successors how to build "a culture of interpreneurship"—in which family leaders revive their company's entrepreneurial spirit with the approach of a generational transition.

Instead of burdening successors to come up with all new ideas to improve business, parents should encourage them to see themselves as leaders whose job is to encourage, stimulate, and facilitate new ideas and entrepreneurial thinking throughout the organization. At the same time, a certain amount of conflict is healthy and should be welcomed during the period before and following a transition in leadership. The new, younger leaders who are eager to make their mark and rejuvenate the company with new ideas and strategies will inevitably clash in the short term with the older generation, whose business ideas were formed in different time. The successors need courage and persistence for the struggle and should be encouraged.

In later generations of a family business, a gulf opens up between the managers who must deal with business realities and other more passive shareholders. To overcome this tension, the leaders must educate shareholders on the necessity of change and work toward unity and support of the chosen strategy among shareholders.

Source: Adapted from H. Muson, "Growing a Family Company: An Exercise in Patience," *The Conference Board Executive Action Series*, June 2006, No. 196. Reprinted by permission of The Conference Board of Canada, Ottawa.

Job Instruction Training

job instruction training (JIT) The listing of each job's basic tasks, along with key points, in order to provide step-by-step training for employees.

Many jobs consist of a logical sequence of steps and are best taught step by step. This step-by-step process is called **job instruction training (JIT)**. To begin, all necessary steps in the job are listed, each in its proper sequence. Alongside each step, a corresponding "key point" (if any) should be noted. The steps show *what* is to be done, while the key points show *how* it is to be done, and *why*. Here is an example of a job instruction training sheet for teaching a right-handed trainee how to operate a large, motorized paper cutter:

Steps	Key Points
1. Start motor	None
2. Set cutting distance	Carefully read scale—to prevent wrong-sized cut
3. Place paper on cutting table	Make sure paper is even—to prevent uneven cut
4. Push paper up to cutter	Make sure paper is tight—to prevent uneven cut
5. Grasp safety release with left hand	Do not release left hand—to prevent hand from being caught in cutter
6. Grasp cutter release with right hand	Do not release right hand—to prevent hand from being caught in cutter
7. Simultaneously pull cutter and safety releases	Keep both hands on corresponding releases—to avoid hands being on cutting table
8. Wait for cutter to retract	Keep both hands on releases—to avoid having hands on cutting table
9. Retract paper	Make sure cutter is retracted; keep both hands away from releases
10. Shut off motor	None

In today's service economy, job instruction training for step-by-step manual work is being superseded by behaviour modelling for service workers. Behaviour modelling is discussed in the next chapter.

Lectures

Classroom training continues to be the primary method of providing corporate training in Canada, and lectures are a widely used method of classroom training delivery. Lecturing has several advantages. It is a quick and simple way of providing knowledge to large groups of trainees, as when the sales force must be taught the special features of a new product. Although written material like books and manuals could be used instead, they may involve considerable printing expense, and they do not permit the give and take of questioning that lectures do.

Audiovisual Techniques

Audiovisual techniques (videotapes and CDs) can be very effective and are widely used. Audiovisuals are more expensive than conventional lectures but offer some advantages. Trainers should consider using them in the following situations:

1. *When there is a need to illustrate how a certain sequence should be followed over time*, such as when teaching wire soldering or telephone repair. The stop-action, instant-replay, or fast- or slow-motion capabilities of audiovisuals can be useful.

2. *When there is a need to expose trainees to events not easily demonstrable in live lectures*, such as a visual tour of a factory or open-heart surgery.

3. *When the training is going to be used organization-wide* and it is too costly to move the trainers from place to place.

There are three options when it comes to audiovisual material: buying an existing product, making one, or using a production company. Dozens of businesses issue catalogues that list audiovisual programs on topics ranging from applicant interviewing to zoo management.

videoconferencing Connecting two or more distant groups by using audiovisual equipment.

Videoconferencing, in which an instructor is televised live to multiple locations, is now a common method for training employees. It has been defined as "a means of joining two or more distant groups using a combination of audio and visual equipment."[37] Videoconferencing allows people in one location to communicate live with people in another city or country, or with groups in several other cities. It is particularly important to prepare a training guide ahead of time, as most or all of the learners will not be in the same location as the trainer. It is also important for the trainer to arrive early and test all equipment that will be used.

Programmed Learning

programmed learning A systematic method for teaching job skills that involves presenting questions or facts, allowing the person to respond, and giving the learner immediate feedback on the accuracy of his or her answers.

Whether the programmed instruction device is a textbook or a computer, **programmed learning** consists of three functions:

1. presenting questions, facts, or problems to the learner

2. allowing the person to respond

3. providing feedback on the accuracy of his or her answers

The main advantage of programmed learning is that it reduces training time by about one-third.[38] In terms of the principles of learning listed earlier, programmed instruction can also facilitate learning because it lets trainees learn at their own pace, provides immediate feedback, and (from the learner's point of view) reduces the risk of error. However, trainees do not learn much more from programmed learning than they would from a traditional textbook. Therefore, the cost of developing the manuals and/or software for programmed instruction has to be weighed against the accelerated but not improved learning that should occur.

Vestibule or Simulated Training

Vestibule or simulated training is a technique by which trainees learn on the actual or simulated equipment that they will use on the job, but they are trained off the job. Therefore, it aims to obtain the advantages of on-the-job training without actually putting the trainee on the job. Vestibule training is virtually a necessity when it is too costly or dangerous to train employees on the job. Putting new assembly-line workers right to work could slow production, for instance, and when safety is a concern—as with pilots—vestibule training may be the only practical alternative.

Vestibule training may just place a trainee in a separate room with the equipment that he or she will actually be using on the job; however, it often involves the use of equipment simulators. In pilot training, for instance, the main advantages of flight simulators are safety, learning efficiency, and cost savings (on maintenance costs, pilot cost, fuel cost, and the cost of not having the aircraft in regular service).[39]

E-Learning

Electronic training techniques have been developed that allow training professionals to provide learning in a more flexible, personalized, and cost-effective manner. **E-learning** is the delivery and administration of learning opportunities and support via computer, networked, and Web-based technology, to enhance employee performance and development. Canadian employers are using e-learning to become more productive and innovative, and to create self-directed, lifelong learners of their employees.[40]

Effective e-learning requires good instructional design. It is critical to motivate learners by describing the benefits they will gain from the training, providing content designed to the learner's specific needs, and offering interactivity, such as application of the material to common problems in the context of the learner's workplace and intrinsic feedback.[41]

A 2006 review of e-learning by the Canadian Society for Training and Development found that e-learning is generally as effective as other forms of learning, at a reduced cost. The primary users of e-learning in Canada are professional and technical employees; clerical, service, and support employees; and managers. Interestingly, learners are more satisfied when Web-based learning involves high levels of human interaction. One future possibility is the use of mobile devices, such as personal digital assistants (PDAs), for e-learning.[42]

There are three major types of e-learning: computer-based training, online training, and electronic performance support systems (EPSS).

Computer-Based Training

In computer-based training (CBT), the trainee uses a computer-based system to interactively increase his or her knowledge or skills. Computer-based training almost always involves presenting trainees with integrated computerized simulations and the use of multimedia (including video, audio, text, and graphics) to help the trainee to learn how to do the job.[43]

Vestibule training simulates flight conditions at NASA headquarters.

vestibule or simulated training Training employees on special off-the-job equipment, as in airplane pilot training, whereby training costs and hazards can be reduced.

e-learning Delivery and administration of learning opportunities and support via computer, networked, and Web-based technology, to enhance employee performance and development.

A new generation of simulations has been developed to simulate role-play situations designed to teach behavioural skills and emotional intelligence. Body language, facial expressions, and subtle nuances are programmed in. These new simulations offer authentic and relevant scenarios involving pressure situations that tap users' emotions and force them to act.[44]

A higher percentage of Canadian firms use CBT compared with American firms, primarily because of Canada's geography. CBT is often more cost-effective than traditional training methods, which require instructors and/or trainees to travel long distances to training sites.[45] Alberta Pacific Forest Industries (AL-Pac) had such good results from using CBT as a staple of its training program that it launched a new component to enable employees to learn the skills of another trade. Employees benefit from having training that is accessible 24 hours a day, which addresses shift work and different learning styles. This training program also helps to keep non-union staff members satisfied, as the multi-skilling resulting from CBT enables many employees to rotate jobs.[46]

CBT programs can be very beneficial. Advantages include instructional consistency (computers, unlike human trainers, do not have good days and bad days), mastery of learning (if the trainee does not learn it, he or she generally cannot move on to the next step in the CBT), flexibility for the trainee, and increased trainee motivation (resulting from the responsive feedback of the CBT program).

Online Training

Web-based training is now commonly used by Canadian organizations. It is generally estimated that Web-based training costs about 50 percent less than traditional classroom-based training. Also, Web-based learning is ideal for adults, who learn what they want, when they want, and where they want. Online training is often the best solution for highly specialized business professionals, who have little time available for ongoing education. Students (the workers of tomorrow) thrive in online learning environments. They do not find it to be an isolated or lonely experience, and they find that they have more time to reflect on the learning material, which leads to livelier interaction.[47] Further, online training is ideal for global organizations that want consistent training for all employees worldwide. Alcan Inc. is using this approach to standardize its training programs for 72 000 employees in 55 countries.[48]

However, critics point out that content management, sound educational strategy, learner support, and system administration should receive more attention, as they are often the critical determining factors in successful training outcomes. In the last few years, "learner content management systems" have been developed to deliver personalized content in small "chunks" or "nuggets" of learning. These systems complement "learning management systems" that are focused on the logistics of managing learning. Together, they form a powerful combination for an e-learning platform. This development is considered to be part of the "second wave" of e-learning, involving greater standardization and the emergence of norms. Another problem is that the freedom of online learning means that unless learners are highly motivated, they may not complete the training. It is estimated that learners don't complete 50 to 90 percent of Web-based courses. In general, it is important to seek "blended learning," including both personal interaction and online training tools.[49]

Electronic Performance Support Systems (EPSS)

electronic performance support systems (EPSS) Computer-based job aids, or sets of computerized tools and displays that automate training, documentation, and phone support.

Electronic performance support systems (EPSS) are computer-based job aids, or sets of computerized tools and displays that automate training, documentation, and phone support. EPSS provides support that is faster, cheaper, and more effective than traditional paper-based job aids, such as manuals. When a customer calls a Dell Computer service representative about a problem with a new computer, the representative is probably asking questions prompted by an EPSS, which takes the service representative and the customer through an analytical sequence, step by step. Without the EPSS, Dell would have to train its service representatives to memorize an unrealistically large number of solutions. Learners say that EPSS provides significant value in maximizing the impact of training. If a skill is trained but the trainees don't need to use it until several weeks or months later, the learning material is always available through the EPSS.[50]

STEPS 3 AND 4: VALIDATION AND IMPLEMENTATION

Validation of the training program that has been designed is an often-overlooked step in the training process. In order to ensure that the program will accomplish its objectives, it is necessary to conduct a pilot study, or "run through," with a representative group of trainees. The results of the pilot study are used to assess the effectiveness of the training.

Revisions to the program can be made to address any problems encountered by the pilot group of trainees in using the training material and experiences provided to them. Testing at the end of the pilot study can measure whether or not the program is producing the desired improvement in skill level. If the results fall below the level of the training objectives, then more work must be undertaken to strengthen the instructional design.

Once the program has been validated, it is ready to be implemented by professional trainers. In some cases, a train-the-trainer workshop may be required to familiarize trainers with unfamiliar content or with unique and innovative new methods for presenting the training content.

STEP 5: EVALUATION OF TRAINING

transfer of training   Application of the skills acquired during the training program into the work environment, and the maintenance of these skills over time.

It is important to assess the return on investment in human capital made through training by determining whether the training actually achieved the objectives. **Transfer of training** is the application of the skills acquired during the training program into the work environment and the maintenance of these skills over time. A number of actions can be taken before, during, and after a training program to enhance transfer of training.[51]

Before training, potential trainees can be assessed on their level of ability, aptitude, and motivation regarding the skill to be taught, and those with higher levels can be selected for the training program. Trainees can be involved in designing the training, and management should provide active support at this stage.

During the training, it is important to provide frequent feedback, opportunities for practice, and positive reinforcement. After the training program, trainees can use goal-setting and relapse-prevention techniques to increase the likelihood of applying what they have learned. Management can enhance transfer of training by providing opportunities to apply new skills and by continuing to provide positive reinforcement of the new skills while being tolerant of errors.

After trainees complete their training (or at planned intervals during the training), the program should be evaluated to see how well its objectives have been met and the extent to which transfer of training has occurred. Thus, if assemblers should be able to solder a junction in 30 seconds, or a photocopier technician repair a machine in 30 minutes, then the program's effectiveness should be measured based on whether these objectives are attained. For example, are trainees learning as *much* as they can? Are they learning as *fast* as they can? Is there a *better method* for training them? These are some of the questions that are answered by properly evaluating training efforts.

Overall, there is little doubt that training and development can be effective. Formal studies of training programs substantiate the potential positive impact of such programs. Profitable companies spend the most on training, and those rated as being among the 100 best companies to work for in Canada spend the most per employee on training.[52] The value of the TD Bank's $50 million annual spending on training is measured very carefully, as illustrated in the Strategic HR box.

There are two basic issues to address when evaluating a training program. The first is the design of the evaluation study and, in particular, whether controlled experimentation will be used. The second is the training effect to be measured.

controlled experimentation
Formal methods for testing the effectiveness of a training program, preferably with a control group and with tests before and after training.

Controlled experimentation is the best method to use in evaluating a training program. A controlled experiment uses both a training group and a control group (that receives no training). Data (e.g., on quantity of production or quality of soldered junctions) should be obtained both before and after the training effort in the training group, and before and after a corresponding work period in the control group. In this way, it is possible to determine the extent to which any change in performance in the training group resulted from the training itself, rather than from some organization-wide change like a raise in pay, which would likely have affected employees in both groups equally.

Training Effects to Measure

Four basic categories of training outcomes can be measured:[53]

1. *Reaction*. First, evaluate trainees' reactions to the program. Did they like the program? Did they think it worthwhile? One expert suggests at least using an evaluation form like the one shown in **Figure 8.3** to evaluate reaction to the training program.[54]

Strategic HR

Measuring Effectiveness at TD Bank

Connie Karlsson is head of Learning Outcomes, a unit of six people inside the learning and development department at TD Bank Financial Group. The unit's job is to measure the value of the bank's training. The group started out by picking an evaluation model that would work. Six Sigma was eliminated because banking is a sales and service environment, and a return on investment model was rejected because it was not simple enough. The group wanted to institutionalize the measurement of training value.

The questionnaire the group developed for learners to fill out at the end of each training session was unique in that it went after indications of all four levels of measurement outlined in the classic training evaluation model—reaction, learning, behaviour, results. Karlsson sees the questionnaire as a reinforcement tool: it reminds trainees that they are being trained to affect their performance and to affect their ability to contribute to the achievement of business goals.

In working with business units within the bank to assess the results of training on business objectives, Karlsson says, "We've become business analysts. We've created partnerships. The people on my team are not perceived as training designers or facilitators. They're treated as business partners in helping the business align their business reporting with training. That was the real business win."

Source: Adapted from U. Vu, "Numbers-Cruncher Makes Impact on Training Culture at TD," *Canadian HR Reporter*, July 12, 2004, pp. 1–2. Reproduced by permission of *Canadian HR Reporter*, Carswell, One Corporate Plaza, 2075 Kennedy Road, Scarborough, ON M1T 3V4.

FIGURE 8.3   Sample Training Evaluation Form

PROGRAM NAME: _____   DATE: _____

YOUR NAME (Optional): _____   FACILITATOR(S): _____

OVERALL PROGRAM RATING	Poor		Fair		Good		Excellent
	1	2	3	4	5	6	7

What did you like **best** about the program?	What did you like **least** about the program?	What would you like to have spent **more** time on?

Please complete this form to help us assess how well this program met your needs and our objectives. Your feedback is important to us and will be used in our continuous efforts to improve the quality and usefulness of this program. Circle the number that best expresses your reaction to each Item.

	Strongly Disagree		Disagree		Agree		Strongly Agree
1. The program was well-organized:	1	2	3	4	5	6	7
2. The sequence of material presented was logical:	1	2	3	4	5	6	7
3. The content of the program was understandable:	1	2	3	4	5	6	7
4. The program activities were effective in helping me learn the concepts and skills presented:	1	2	3	4	5	6	7
5. The objectives of the program were clear:	1	2	3	4	5	6	7
6. The program met its stated objectives:	1	2	3	4	5	6	7
7. The facilitator(s) grasped the material and activities they presented:	1	2	3	4	5	6	7
8. The knowledge and skills learned in this program will help me do my job better:	1	2	3	4	5	6	7

9. The length of the program   was appropriate   should be shorter   should be longer

Thank you for your participation and feedback!

Source: CCH Ultimate HR Manual (Training and Development par. 15187), 2005, p. 19116. Copyright © 2005 Metrix Group. Used with permission.

2. *Learning.* Second, test the trainees to determine whether they learned the principles, skills, and facts that they were supposed to learn.

3. *Behaviour.* Next, ask whether the trainees' behaviour on the job changed because of the training program. For example, are employees in the store's complaint department more courteous toward disgruntled customers than previously? These measures determine the degree of transfer of training.

4. *Results.* Last, but probably most important, ask: "Did the number of customer complaints about employees drop? Did the rejection rate improve? Was turnover reduced? Are production quotas now being met?" and so on.

Improved results are, of course, especially important. The training program may succeed in terms of the reactions from trainees, increased learning, and even changes in behaviour, but if the results are not achieved, then in the final analysis, the training has not achieved its goals. If so, the problem may be related to inappropriate use of a training program. For example, training is ineffective when environmental factors are the cause of poor performance.

Although the four basic categories are understandable and widely used, there are several things to keep in mind when using them to measure training effects. First, there are usually only modest correlations among the four types of training criteria (i.e., scoring "high" on learning does not necessarily mean that behaviour or results will also score "high," and the converse is true as well). Similarly, studies show that "reaction" measures (e.g., "How well did you like the program?") may provide some insight into how they liked the program but probably will not provide much insight into what they learned or how they will behave once they are back on the job.

TRAINING FOR SPECIAL PURPOSES

Training increasingly does more than just prepare employees to perform their jobs effectively. Training for special purposes—increasing literacy and adjusting to diversity, for instance—is required too. The following is a sampling of such special-purpose training programs.

Literacy and Essential Skills Training

Functional illiteracy is a serious problem for many employers. As the Canadian economy shifts from goods to services, there is a corresponding need for workers who are more skilled, more literate, and better able to perform at least basic arithmetic. Not only does enhanced literacy give employees a better chance for success in their careers, but it also improves bottom-line performance of the employer—through time savings, lower costs, and improved quality of work.[55]

National Adult Literacy Database
www.nald.ca

The 2003 International Adult Literacy and Skills Survey included 23 000 Canadians and found that 48 percent scored below average in literacy and 55 percent scored below average in numeracy. The study also found a clear link between higher levels of literacy and higher levels of employment, as shown in **Figure 8.4**. There was a similar link between literacy and higher earnings, particularly for women. Research by University of Ottawa economists for Statistics Canada has shown that investments in essential skills training to improve literacy and numeracy pay off. For every increase of 1 percent in national literacy scores relative to the international average, a country will realize a 2.5 percent gain in productivity and a 1.5 percent increase in per capita GDP over the long term.[56]

Employers are responding to this issue in two main ways. Such organizations as diamond mining company BHP Billiton, steel giant Dofasco, the Construction Sector Council, and the Canadian Trucking Human Resources Council have implemented a training strategy with the objective of raising the essential skills of their workforce. Essential skills of workers can be measured with the Test of Workplace Essential Skills (TOWES), developed by Bow Valley College in Calgary. In 2005, the federal government made funding available for training professionals to develop Enhanced Language Training (ELT) to provide job-specific English instruction to help immigrants gain employment in their area of expertise.[57]

FIGURE 8.4   Literacy and Employment Levels in Canada

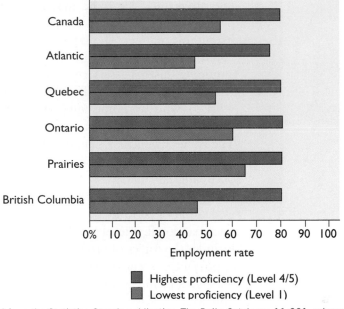

Employment rate among respondents at the highest and lowest levels of document proficiency, 2003

■ Highest proficiency (Level 4/5)
■ Lowest proficiency (Level I)

Source: Adapted from the Statistics Canada publication *The Daily*, Catalogue 11-001, release date: November 30, 2005, and also available from the Statistics Canada website at www.statcan.ca/Daily/English/051130/d051130b.htm.

Diversity Training

With increasingly diverse workforces and customers, there is a strong business case for implementing diversity-training programs. Diversity training enhances cross-cultural sensitivity among supervisors and nonsupervisors, with the aim of creating more harmonious working relationships among a firm's employees. It also enhances the abilities of salespeople to provide effective customer service.[58]

Two broad approaches to diversity training are cross-cultural communication training and cultural sensitivity training. *Cross-cultural communication training* focuses on workplace cultural etiquette and interpersonal skills. *Cultural sensitivity training* focuses on sensitizing employees to the views of different cultural groups toward work so that employees from diverse backgrounds can work together more effectively. All employees should be involved in managing diversity, and diversity initiatives should be planned and supported as any other business opportunity would be.[59]

Handidactis, a nonprofit organization in Montreal, provides sensitivity training to help people interact with those who have a disability, including those with a vision or hearing impairment, and individuals who have a physical or mental disability. The first step is to ask the person with the disability if he or she needs anything special to do the job. This practice is often overlooked as people jump in to help someone with a disability, which in effect takes away that person's independence. Furthermore, the person may not need help. The training also involves discovering what it is like to have a disability, through simulated blindness and speech impediments.[60]

Diversity Training Links
www.diversityatwork.com
www.diversitytraining.com

Customer-Service Training

More and more retailers are finding it necessary to compete based on the quality of their service, and many are therefore implementing customer-service training programs. The basic aim is to train all employees to (1) have excellent product knowledge, and (2) treat the company's customers in a courteous and hospitable manner. The saying "The customer is always right" is emphasized by countless service companies today. However, putting the customer first requires employee customer-service training.

The Canadian retail industry has struggled in the past with poorly trained workers who were not equipped to provide quality customer service. Retailers now understand that they need to make a serious investment in their employees.[61] The Retail Council of Canada offers a national customer service certification program for retail sales associates and retail first-level managers, based on national occupational standards and essential skills profiles for each group. Certification requires the completion of a workbook, a multiple-choice exam, an in-store evaluation-of-performance interview, and experience (600 hours for sales associates, one year for first-level managers). The certification program for sales associates includes the topics of professionalism, customer service and sales, inventory, store appearance, security and safety, and communication. Topics for first-level managers include professionalism, communication, leadership, human resources, operations, marketing, sales, customer service, administration, and planning.[62]

Training for Teamwork

An increasing number of firms today use work teams to improve their effectiveness. However, many firms find that teamwork does not just happen and that employees must be trained to be good team members.

Some firms use outdoor training—such as Outward Bound programs—to build teamwork. Outdoor training usually involves taking a group of employees out into rugged, mountainous terrain, where, by overcoming physical obstacles, they learn team spirit, cooperation, and the need to trust and rely on each other.[63] An example of one activity is the "trust fall." Here, an employee has to slowly lean back and fall backward from a height of, say, three metres into the waiting arms of five or ten team members. The idea is to build trust in one's colleagues.

Not all employees are eager to participate in such activities. Such firms as Outward Bound have prospective participants fill out extensive medical evaluations to make sure that participants can safely engage in risky outdoor activities. Others feel that the outdoor activities are too contrived to be applicable back at work. However, they do illustrate the lengths to which employers will go to build teamwork.

An Ethical
Dilemma

Is it ethical to require employees to participate in weekend and evening training programs, if they do not want to because it is going to take time that they would otherwise be spending on personal and family responsibilities?

Training for First-Time Supervisors

As baby boomers head into retirement, young employees are rising to positions of authority quickly and in large numbers. They are assuming supervisory roles at a much younger age than their counterparts were only 10 to 15 years ago. Along with the steep learning curve that all first-time supervisors face, the latest group faces generational diversity—supervising boomers, their own Generation Xers, and Generation Y (Nexters) following them. Generational diversity presents a challenge to today's younger bosses, as discussed in the Workforce Diversity box.

Workforce Diversity

Generational Diversity Leadership Challenges

Young supervisors today have to deal with the challenge of generational diversity in their workers. Four generations are working side by side: veterans, baby boomers, Xers, and Nexters (Generation Y).

Veterans (born 1922 to 1945) are a private, silent, generation of hard-working company loyalists. They prefer a command-and-control leadership style. To lead this generation, managers should respect their experience without being intimidated by it.

Boomers (born 1946 to 1965) have a strong work ethic that leads to struggles with work/life balance, and they are often considered to be competitive workaholics. They prefer collegial and consensual leadership styles, and they have problems dealing with conflict and change. To lead this generation, it is important to show an appreciation for their energy and hard work, and to provide support for work/life balance.

Xers (born 1966 to 1980) work to live, prefer a fun environment with few rules, and are unimpressed with authority. Former "latchkey kids," they are distrustful of institutions and disinterested in loyalty. Balance in their lives is extremely important. They struggle with social skills but are independent and adaptive to change. To lead this generation, tell them the truth, clearly identify boundaries, and offer learning opportunities and continual feedback.

Nexters (born after 1980) are a technologically savvy group with strong ties to family and friends. They see work as a learning opportunity. They are comfortable with structure in their lives and seek stability and security. Although their literacy levels are weaker than previous generations, they work well in teams. To lead this generation, provide them with clear, concise directions, feedback, and praise.

It is important to focus on the strengths that each generation can bring to a business. Veterans and boomers bring the wisdom of their long experience. Xers bring an ability to think outside the box with ease. Nexters bring their comfort with technology, innovation, and excitement. All employees have something to offer, and, ultimately, leaders must use generational diversity to create synergy and generate new opportunities.

Sources: M. Legault, "Caution: Mixed Generations at Work— Leading an Age Diverse Workforce," *Canadian HR Reporter,* December 1, 2003; M. Novakowski, "X-ploring X-pectations of Generation-X," *In Service:10-8* (Justice Institute of B.C.), April 2003, Vol. 3, No. 3, pp. 10–14; R. Berry, "Observations on Generational Diversity," *Profiles in Diversity Journal,* 2002, Vol. 4, No. 3, pp. 1–3.

New supervisors are often chosen for their technical ability, and their interpersonal and communication skills get overlooked. But it is precisely these skills that will determine success as a supervisor, which requires networking and the ability to get work done through other people. New supervisors also need to learn to define their personal supervisory style, how to give and receive feedback, and how to motivate others.[64]

This transition demands crucial training because first-time supervisors need to learn a new set of skills. Formal training is required, and higher-level managers need to coach, mentor, and provide performance feedback to new young supervisors.[65]

Training for Global Business

Firms competing in the global marketplace often implement special global training programs. The reasons for doing so include avoiding lost business because of cultural insensitivity, improving job satisfaction and retention of overseas staff, and enabling a newly assigned employee to communicate with colleagues abroad.[66]

Research
Insight

Recent research by Healthy Companies International has found that success in the global marketplace is predicted by developing leaders at all levels of business and by placing a high value on multicultural experience and competencies. The research identified four global literacies, or critical competencies, required to succeed in the global economy:

- personal literacy—understanding and valuing oneself
- social literacy—engaging and challenging other people
- business literacy—focusing and mobilizing the business
- cultural literacy—understanding and leveraging cultural differences[67]

Chapter Review

Summary

1. An orientation program is the joint responsibility of the HR department and the new employee's supervisor. HR should provide the new employee with general information on company history, work regulations, and employee benefits. The immediate supervisor should introduce the new employee to co-workers, conduct a tour of the company premises, and provide specific information on the job, performance criteria, and any training to be provided.

2. The basic training process consists of five steps: needs analysis, instructional design, validation, implementation, and evaluation.

3. Two techniques for assessing training needs are (1) task analysis to determine the training needs of employees who are new to their jobs, and (2) performance analysis to appraise the performance of current employees to determine whether training could reduce performance problems.

4. Traditional training techniques include on-the-job-training, apprenticeship training, informal learning, job instruction training, lectures, audiovisual techniques, programmed learning, and vestibule or simulated training.

5. Three types of e-learning are computer-based training, online training, and electronic performance support systems.

6. In evaluating the effectiveness of a training program, four categories of outcomes can be measured: reaction, learning, behaviour, and results.

7. Today's organizations often provide training for special purposes, including literacy training, diversity training, customer-service training, training for teamwork, training for first-time supervisors, and training for global business.

Key Terms

controlled experimentation   *(p. 214)*
electronic performance support systems
    (EPSS) *(p. 212)*
e-learning   *(p. 211)*
employee orientation   *(p. 197)*
job instruction training (JIT)   *(p. 209)*
performance analysis   *(p. 205)*
programmed learning   *(p. 210)*
reality shock   *(p. 197)*
socialization   *(p. 197)*
task analysis   *(p. 205)*
training   *(p. 201)*
transfer of training   *(p. 213)*
vestibule or simulated training   *(p. 211)*
videoconferencing   *(p. 210)*

Review and Discussion Questions

1. Prepare an orientation program checklist for your current or most recent job.

2. Choose a task with which you are familiar—such as mowing the lawn or using a chat room—and develop a job instruction training sheet for it.

3. Ali Khan is an undergraduate business student majoring in accounting. He has just failed the first accounting course, Accounting 101, and is understandably upset. Explain how you would use performance analysis to identify what, if any, are Ali's training needs.

4. Think about the jobs that you have had in the past. For which of these jobs could an electronic performance support system be used? Prepare an outline for such a system.

Critical Thinking Questions

1. "A well-thought-out orientation program is especially important for employees (like many recent graduates) who have had little or no work experience." Explain why you agree or disagree with this statement.

2. What do you think are some of the main drawbacks of relying on informal on-the-job training for teaching new employees their jobs?

3. This chapter points out that one reason for implementing special global training programs is to avoid business loss because of cultural insensitivity. What sort of cultural insensitivity do you think is referred to, and how might that translate into lost business? What sort of training programs would you recommend to avoid such cultural insensitivity?

4. Most training programs are not formally evaluated beyond a reaction measure. Why do you think employers do not measure the learning, behaviour, and results effects of training more often?

Application Exercises

Running Case: LearnInMotion.com

The New Training Program

"I just don't understand it," said Pierre. "No one here seems to follow instructions, and no matter how many times I've told them how to do things they seem to do them their own way." At present, LearnInMotion.com has no formal orientation or training policies or procedures. Jennifer believes this is one reason that employees generally ignore the standards that she and Pierre would like employees to adhere to.

Several examples illustrate this problem. One job of the Web designer (her name is Maureen) is to take customer copy for banner ads and adapt it for placement on LearnInMotion.com. She has been told several times not to tinker in any way with a customer's logo: Most companies put considerable thought and resources into logo design, and as Pierre has said, "Whether or not Maureen thinks the logo is perfect, it's the customer's logo, and she's to leave it as it is." Yet just a week ago, they almost lost a big customer when Maureen, to "clarify" the customer's logo, modified its design before posting it on LearnInMotion.com.

That's just the tip of the iceberg. As far as Jennifer and Pierre are concerned, it is the sales effort that is completely out of control. For one thing, even after several months on the job, it still seems as if the sales people don't know what they're talking about. For example, LearnInMotion has several co-brand arrangements with Web sites like Yahoo! This setup allows users on other sites to easily click through to LearnInMotion.com if they are interested in ordering educational courses or CDs. Jennifer has noticed that during conversations with customers, the two salespeople have no idea of which sites co-brand with LearnInMotion, or how to get to the LearnInMotion site from the partner Web site. The salespeople also need to know a lot more about the products themselves. For example, one salesperson was trying to sell someone who produces programs on managing call centres on the idea of listing its products under LearnInMotion's "communications" community. In fact, the "communications" community is for courses on topics like interpersonal communications and how to be a better listener; it has nothing to do with managing the sorts of call centres that, for instance, airlines use for handling customer inquiries. As another example, the Web surfer is supposed to get a specific e-mail address with a specific person's name for the salespeople to use, instead he often just comes back with an "information" e-mail address off a Web site. The list goes on and on.

Jennifer feels the company has had other problems because of the lack of adequate employee training and orientation. For example, a question came up recently when employees found they weren't paid for the Canada Day holiday. They assumed they would be paid, but they were not. Similarly, when a salesperson left after barely a month on the job, there was considerable debate about whether the person should receive severance pay and accumulated vacation pay. Other matters to cover during an orientation, says Jennifer, include company policy regarding lateness and absences; health and hospitalization benefits (there are none, other than workers' compensation); and matters like maintaining a safe and healthy workplace, personal appearance and cleanliness, personal telephone calls and e-mail, substance abuse, and eating on the job.

Jennifer believes that implementing orientation and training programs would help ensure that employees know how to do their jobs. She and Pierre further believe that it is only when employees understand the right way to do their jobs that there is any hope those jobs will in fact be carried out in the way the owners want them to be. Now they want you, their management consultant, to help them. Here's what they want you to do for them.

Questions

1. Specifically, what should be covered in the new employee orientation program, and how should this information be conveyed?

2. In the HR course Jennifer took, the book suggested using a task analysis record form to identify tasks performed by an employee. Should LearnInMotion use a form like this for the salespeople? If so, what, roughly speaking, should the completed, filled-in form look like?

3. Which specific training techniques should be used to train the salespeople, Web designer, and Web surfer, and why?

Case Incident

TPK Appliances

When TPK, a manufacturer of small appliances—electric kettles, toasters, and irons—automated its warehouse, the warehouse crew was reduced from 14 to four. Every one of the displaced stock workers was assigned to another department, as TPK had a history of providing stable employment.

Jacob Peters, a stock worker with more than 15 years of service, was transferred to the toaster assembly line to be retrained as a small-parts assembler. When he arrived to begin his new job, the supervisor said, "This may be only temporary, Jacob. I have a full staff right now, so I have nothing for you to do, but come on, I'll find you a locker." As there really was no job for him, Jacob did nothing for the first week except odd jobs such as filling bins. At the beginning of week two, Jacob was informed that a vacancy would be occurring the next day, so he reported for work eager to learn his new job.

The operation was depressingly simple. All Jacob had to do was pick up two pieces of metal, one in each hand, place them into a jig so that they were held together in a cross position, and press a button. The riveting machine then put a rivet through both pieces and an air jet automatically ejected the joined pieces into a bin.

"This job is so simple a monkey could do it," the supervisor told Jacob. "Let me show you how it's done," and he quickly demonstrated the three steps involved. "Now you do it," he said. Of course, Jacob did it right the first time. After watching him rivet two or three, the supervisor left Jacob to his work.

About three hours later, the riveter started to put the rivets in a little crooked, but Jacob kept on working. Finally, a fellow worker stopped by and said, "You're new here, aren't you?" Jacob nodded. "Listen, I'll give you a word of advice. If the supervisor sees you letting the rivets go in crooked like that, he'll give you hell. So hide these in the scrap over there." His new friend then showed Jacob how to adjust his machine.

Jacob's next problem began when the air ejection system started jamming. Four times he managed to clear it, but on the fifth try, he slipped and his elbow hit the rivet button. The machine put a rivet through the fleshy part of the hand, just below the thumb.

It was in the first aid station that the supervisor finally had the opportunity to see Jacob once again.

Questions

1. Comment on the strengths and weaknesses of Jacob's orientation and on-the-job training.

2. Outline how the process should have been conducted.

Source: From *Managing Performance Through Training and Development*, Third Edition, by Saks/Haccoun, 2004. Reprinted with permission of Nelson, a division of Thomson Learning: www.thomsonrights.com. Fax 800-730-2215. NOTE: This story is a fictional version of a real-life situation that existed at Canadian General Electric many years ago.

Experiential Exercises

1. Obtain a copy of an employee handbook from your employer or from some other organization. Review it and make recommendations for improvement.

2. Working individually or in groups, follow the steps in Figure 8.2 (page 204), and prepare a training program for a job that you currently hold or have had in the past.

3. In small groups of four to six students, complete the following exercise. JetBlue Airlines has asked you to quickly develop the outline of a training program for its new reservation clerks. Airline reservation clerks obviously need numerous skills to perform their jobs. You may want to start by listing the job's main duties, using the information provided below. In any case, please produce the requested training outline, making sure to be very specific about what you want to teach the new clerks and what methods and aids you suggest using to train them.

Duties of Airline Reservation Clerks: Customers contact airline reservation clerks to obtain flight schedules, prices, and itineraries. The reservation clerks look up the requested information on the airline's flight schedule systems, which are updated continuously. The reservation clerk must deal courteously and expeditiously with the customer, and be able to quickly find alternative flight arrangements in order to provide the customer with the itinerary that fits his or her needs. Alternative flights and prices must be found quickly, so that the customer is not kept waiting and so that the reservations operations group maintains its efficiency standards. It is often necessary to look under various routings, since there may be a dozen or more alternative routes between the customer's starting point and destination.

CHAPTER 9

CAREER DEVELOPMENT

REQUIRED PROFESSIONAL CAPABILITIES

LEARNING OUTCOMES
AFTER STUDYING THIS CHAPTER, YOU SHOULD BE ABLE TO

Explain what is involved in career planning and development.

Analyze the factors that affect career choices.

Explain how to make a new employee's first assignment more meaningful.

Recommend how to manage promotions and transfers more effectively.

Explain what management development is and why it is important.

Describe on-the-job and off-the-job management-development techniques.

- Interprets results of development programs in terms of contribution to organizational objectives, and does a post-development follow-up

- Monitors, documents, and reports on career development activities within the organization

- Provides the appropriate assessment tools for determining career development options for employees

- Develops deployment procedures (e.g., transfers, secondments, and reassignments)

- Facilitates the implementation of cross-functional development work experiences for employees

- Assesses and reports on the costs and benefits of engaging internal and external suppliers of development programs, given the organizational constraints and objectives

- Develops requests for proposals (RFPs) and reviews submissions by third parties

- Recommends the selection of external training consultants and contractors, such as public education institutions

- Facilitates coaching and post-training support activities to ensure transfer of learning to the workplace

CAREER PLANNING AND DEVELOPMENT

boundaryless career   A career that spans several organizations and/or industries.

career planning and development The deliberate process through which a person becomes aware of personal career-related attributes, and the lifelong series of activities that contribute to his or her career fulfillment.

Career planning has suddenly resumed its place as a critical strategic issue for organizations.[1] Through the 1990s and into the current decade, massive downsizings resulted in the death of job security and employee loyalty to employers. Employees learned to focus on transferable skills for employability in **boundaryless careers** spanning several organizations and/or industries.[2] However, the impending labour shortage has created a sense of urgency regarding the development of careers for the next generation of managers and executives needed to take responsibility for strategic leadership. Increasing competition for talent is expected to create a serious challenge for retaining high-potential employees.

Proactive organizations are taking action now to manage the coming labour shortage. The TD Bank is planning to become an "employer of choice" and is providing all its employees with opportunities for personal development, as described in the Strategic HR box.

HRM activities play an important role in **career planning and development**. Career-related programs help HR professionals to maintain employee commitment—an employee's identification with and agreement to pursue the company's or the unit's strategic goals. Most employees appreciate and respond well to having their skills and potential enhanced, and to knowing that they will be more marketable. Developmental activities, such as providing the educational and training resources required to help employees identify and develop their promotion and career potential, are also important. Career-oriented firms also stress career-oriented appraisals that link the employee's past performance, career preferences, and developmental needs in a formal career plan.

Strategic HR

Career Development a Huge Priority for TD Bank

Career development has become a huge priority at the TD Bank. The bank wants to become an "employer of choice" in order to attract new employees, as a large percentage of its workforce moves into retirement over the next five to ten years. TD has realized that part of becoming an employer of choice is striking a balance between organizational development (providing training that benefits the bank first and foremost) and personal development (offering training and development that benefits the employee).

Internal research showed that the number-one factor that made employees willing to give discretionary effort was skill development and career development. The bank spends between $50 million and $60 million per year on training, primarily to enhance organizational performance. Little attention was being paid to what it was doing for employees, and TD decided to put more time and money into employee career management.

The bank recognized that employees had assumed the responsibility for managing their own careers, and it wanted to find a way to help employees feel better about their career plans without being overly intrusive. TD decided on a career management self-service approach and partnered with Barbara Moses of BBM Human Resource Consultants Inc. to create a Web site that helps employees with all aspects of career management. The Career Advisor site provides help in the areas of self-awareness, choosing a career path, overcoming career distress, solving career-stage dilemmas, restoring work/life balance, and using career strategies, such as networking and mentoring.

Employee interest in the system has exceeded expectations. Managers find that they are having completely different conversations with employees, who are better able to articulate what they want and where they need to go to be happy and productive. They have a much better understanding of themselves and their sources of job satisfaction.

Source: Adapted from D. Brown, "TD Gives Employees Tool to Chart Career Paths," *Canadian HR Reporter*, June 20, 2005, pp. 11, 13. Reproduced by permission of *Canadian HR Reporter*, Carswell, One Corporate Plaza, 2075 Kennedy Road, Scarborough, ON M1T 3V4.

employee retention   The extent to which employees are retained by the organization over a relatively long time.

lifelong learning   Providing extensive continuing training throughout employees' careers.

Career Planning Exercises
www.careerstorm.com

Career Networking
www.careerkey.com

Career planning can play a significant role in retaining employees in the organization and reducing turnover of valued workers. The key factors in **employee retention** today are an organizational culture that values and nurtures talented employees, fair processes in "people" decisions, and managers who understand what motivates employees.[3] Employers and employees also recognize the need for **lifelong learning**. Retention can be strengthened by providing extensive, continuing training—from basic remedial skills to advanced decision-making techniques—throughout employees' careers.

Before proceeding, it would be useful to define some of the terms that will be used throughout this chapter.[4] A *career* is a series of work-related positions, paid or unpaid, that help a person to grow in job skills, success, and fulfillment. *Career development* is the lifelong series of activities (such as workshops) that contribute to a person's career exploration, establishment, success, and fulfillment. *Career planning* is the deliberate process through which someone becomes aware of personal skills, interests, knowledge, motivations, and other characteristics; acquires information about opportunities and choices; identifies career-related goals; and establishes action plans to attain specific goals.

Roles in Career Development

The individual, the manager, and the employer all have roles in the individual's career development. Ultimately, however, it is the *individual* who must accept responsibility for his or her own career. This requires an entrepreneurial, goal-oriented approach that uses four key skills: self-motivation, independent learning, effective time and money management, and self-promotion.[5] Networking is the foundation of active career management and is essential for accessing the most valuable career resource—people. Networking is an organized process whereby the individual arranges and conducts a series of face-to-face meetings with his or her colleagues and contacts, plus individuals they recommend (not cold calls). Networking does not involve asking for a job, and it is not a one-sided encounter where only one individual benefits, but rather a mutual sharing process. Its objectives are to let people know about background and career goals, and to exchange information, advice, and referrals.[6] A personal networking chart is shown in **Figure 9.1**.

Within the organization, the individual's *manager* plays a role, too. The manager should provide timely and objective performance feedback, offer developmental assignments and support, and participate in career-development discussions. The manager acts as a coach, an appraiser, an advisor, and a referral agent, for instance, listening to and clarifying the individual's career plans, giving feedback, generating career options, and linking the employee to organizational resources and career options.

Finally, the *employer* plays a career-development role. For example, an organization wanting to retain good employees should provide career-oriented training and development opportunities, offer career information and career programs, and give employees a variety of career options. Ultimately, employers need not and should not provide such career-oriented activities purely out of altruism. Most employees will ultimately grade their employers on the extent to which the organization allowed them to excel and to become the people they believed they had the potential to become. That will help to determine their overall job satisfaction and their commitment to their employers.[7]

FIGURE 9.1   Personal Networking Chart

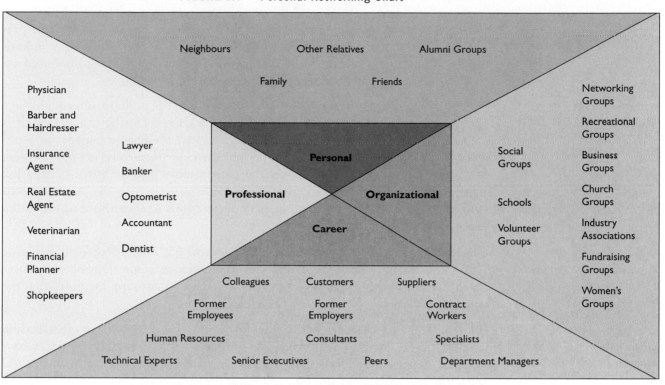

Factors That Affect Career Choices

The first step in planning a career is to learn as much as possible about the person's interests, aptitudes, and skills.

Identify Career Stage

Each person's career goes through stages, and the current stage will influence the employee's knowledge of and preference for various occupations. The main stages of this **career cycle** follow.[8]

Growth Stage   The **growth stage** lasts roughly from birth to age 14 and is a period during which the person develops a self-concept by identifying with and interacting with other people, such as family, friends, and teachers. Early in this period, role-playing is important, and children experiment with different ways of acting; this helps them to form impressions of how other people react to different behaviours and contributes to their developing a unique self-concept or identity. Toward the end of this stage, the adolescent (who by this time has developed preliminary ideas about what his or her interests and abilities are) begins to think realistically about occupational alternatives.

Exploration Stage   The **exploration stage** is the period (roughly from age 15 to 24) during which a person seriously explores various occupational alternatives. The person attempts to match these alternatives with what he or she has learned about them and about his or her own interests and abilities from school, leisure activities, and work. Tentative broad occupational choices are usually made

career cycle   The stages through which a person's career evolves.

growth stage   The period from birth to age 14, during which the person develops a self-concept by identifying with and interacting with other people, such as family, friends, and teachers.

exploration stage   The period from around age 15 to 24, during which a person seriously explores various occupational alternatives, attempting to match these alternatives with his or her interests and abilities.

during the beginning of this period. Toward the end of this period, a seemingly appropriate choice is made and the person tries out an entry-level job.

Probably the most important task that the person has in this and the preceding stage is to develop a realistic understanding of his or her abilities and talents. Similarly, the person must make sound educational decisions based on reliable sources of information about occupational alternatives.

establishment stage The period, roughly from age 24 to 44, that is the heart of most people's work lives.

Establishment Stage   The **establishment stage** spans the period from roughly age 24 to 44 and is the heart of most people's work lives. During this period, it is hoped that a suitable occupation is found and that the person engages in activities that help him or her to earn a permanent place in the chosen field. Often, and particularly in the professions, the person locks into a chosen occupation early. In most cases, however, this is a period during which the person is continually testing his or her capabilities and ambitions against those of the initial occupational choice.

maintenance stage The period from about age 45 to 65, during which the person secures his or her place in the world of work.

Maintenance Stage   Between the ages of 45 and 65, many people simply slide from the establishment stage into the **maintenance stage**. During this latter period, most efforts are now typically directed at maintaining the place that the person has created in the world of work.

decline stage The period during which many people are faced with the prospect of having to accept reduced levels of power and responsibility.

Decline Stage   As retirement age approaches, there may be a deceleration period known as the **decline stage**. Here, many people face the prospect of having to accept reduced levels of power and responsibility, and learn to accept and develop new roles as mentor and confidant for those who are younger. However, it is becoming more common for older workers, despite some decline in physical capabilities, to continue to work until normal retirement age and beyond. Following retirement, the person finds alternative uses for the time and effort formerly expended on his or her occupation.

Identify Occupational Orientation

occupational orientation The theory, developed by John Holland, that there are six basic personal orientations that determine the sorts of careers to which people are drawn.

Career-counselling expert John Holland says that a person's personality (including values, motives, and needs) determines his or her **occupational orientation**, which is another important factor in career choices. For example, a person with a strong social orientation might be attracted to careers that entail interpersonal rather than intellectual or physical activities and to such occupations as social work.

Based on research with his Vocational Preference Test (VPT), John Holland found six basic personality types or orientations:[9]

Research
I n s i g h t ▷

1. *Realistic orientation.* These people are attracted to occupations that involve physical activities requiring skill, strength, and coordination. Examples include forestry, farming, and agriculture.

2. *Investigative orientation.* Investigative people are attracted to careers that involve cognitive activities (thinking, organizing, and understanding) rather than affective activities (feeling, acting, or interpersonal and emotional tasks). Examples include biologists, chemists, and university professors.

3. *Social orientation.* These people are attracted to careers that involve interpersonal rather than intellectual or physical activities. Examples include clinical psychology, foreign service, and social work.

4. *Conventional orientation.* A conventional orientation favours careers that involve structured, rule-regulated activities, as well as careers in which it is expected that the employee subordinate his or her personal needs to those of the organization. Examples include accountants and bankers.

5. *Enterprising orientation.* Verbal activities aimed at influencing others are attractive to enterprising personalities. Examples include managers, lawyers, and public relations executives.

6. *Artistic orientation.* People here are attracted to careers that involve self-expression, artistic creation, expression of emotions, and individualistic activities. Examples include artists, advertising executives, and musicians.

Most people have more than one orientation (they might be social, realistic, and investigative, for example), and Holland believes that the more similar or compatible these orientations are, the less internal conflict or indecision a person will face in making a career choice.

Identify Skills and Aptitudes

Successful performance depends not just on motivation but also on ability. Someone may have a conventional orientation, but whether he or she has the skills to be an accountant, banker, or credit manager will largely determine the specific occupation ultimately chosen. Therefore, each individual's skills must be identified, based on his or her education and experience. In organizations using competency- or skill-based pay, a formal system for evaluating skills will already be in place.

For career-planning purposes, a person's aptitudes are usually measured with a test battery, such as the general aptitude test battery (GATB). This instrument measures various aptitudes, including intelligence and mathematical ability. Considerable work has been done to relate aptitudes, such as those measured by the GATB, to specific occupations.

Identify a Career Anchor

career anchor   A concern or value that you will not give up if a choice has to be made.

Edgar Schein says that career planning is a continuing process of discovery—one in which a person slowly develops a clearer occupational self-concept in terms of what his or her talents, abilities, motives, needs, attitudes, and values are. Schein also says that as you learn more about yourself, it becomes apparent that you have a dominant **career anchor**, a concern or value that you will not give up if a choice has to be made. Career anchors, as their name implies, are the pivots on which a person's career turns; a person becomes conscious of them as a result of learning about his or her talents and abilities, motives and needs, and attitudes and values. Based on his research, Schein believes that career anchors are difficult to predict ahead of time because they are evolutionary. Some people may not find out what their career anchors are until they have to make a major choice—such as whether to take the promotion to the headquarters staff or strike out on their own by starting a business. It is at this point that all the person's past work experiences, interests, aptitudes, and orientations converge into a meaningful pattern (or career anchor) that helps to show what is personally the most important in driving the person's career choices. Schein identified eight career anchors:[10]

1. *Technical/functional as a career anchor.* People who have a strong technical/functional career anchor tend to avoid decisions that would drive them toward general management. Instead, they make decisions that will enable them to remain and grow in their chosen technical or functional fields.

2. *Managerial competence as a career anchor.* Other people show a strong motivation to become managers, and their career experience convinces them that they have the skills and values required to rise to general-management positions. A management position of high responsibility is their ultimate goal. Qualifications for these jobs include (1) analytical competence (ability

to identify, analyze, and solve problems under conditions of incomplete information and uncertainty); (2) interpersonal competence (ability to influence, supervise, lead, manipulate, and control people at all levels); and (3) emotional competence (the capacity to be stimulated by emotional and interpersonal crises rather than exhausted or debilitated by them, and the capacity to bear high levels of responsibility without becoming paralyzed).

3. *Creativity as a career anchor.* People who become successful entrepreneurs have a need to build or create something that is entirely their own product—a product or process that bears their name, a company of their own, or a personal fortune that reflects their accomplishments. For example, one participant in Schein's research became a successful purchaser, restorer, and renter of townhouses in a large city; another built a successful consulting firm.

4. *Autonomy and independence as career anchors.* Some people seem driven to be on their own, free of the dependence that can arise when a person works in a large organization where promotions, transfers, and salary decisions make them subordinate to others. Many also have a strong technical/functional orientation. Instead of pursuing this orientation in an organization, however, they decide to become consultants, working either alone or as part of a relatively small firm. Others become professors of business, freelance writers, and proprietors of small retail businesses.

5. *Security as a career anchor.* Some people are mostly concerned with long-run career stability and job security. They seem willing to do what is required to maintain job security, a decent income, and a stable future in the form of a good retirement program and benefits. For those interested in *geographic security*, maintaining a stable, secure career in familiar surroundings is generally more important than pursuing superior career choices, if choosing the latter means injecting instability or insecurity into their lives by forcing them to move to another city. For others, security means *organizational security*. They are much more willing to let their employers decide what their careers should be.

6. *Service/dedication as a career anchor.* More and more people feel a need to do something meaningful in a larger context. Information technology has made global problems, such as the environment, overpopulation, and poverty, highly visible. New kinds of organizations and careers are being created to address these issues.

7. *Pure challenge as a career anchor.* A small group of people define their career in terms of overcoming impossible odds, solving the unsolved problems, and winning out over competitors. These people need to be active learners as the nature of these challenges will evolve rapidly with technological change.

8. *Lifestyle as a career anchor.* A growing number of people, particularly dual career couples, define their careers as part of a larger lifestyle integrating two careers and two sets of personal and family concerns. This group is more self-focused and preoccupied with lifestyle. Flexible work arrangements, such as job sharing, part-time work, sabbaticals, and other lifestyle support programs, are required to meet the needs of this group.

Responsibilities of the Organization

Along with the employee, the manager, employer, and HR staff all have career-management responsibilities. Some guidelines follow.

Avoid Reality Shock

Perhaps at no other stage in the person's career is it more important for the employer to be career development–oriented than at the initial entry stage, when the person is recruited, hired, and given a first assignment and a boss. This is (or should be) a period of *reality testing* during which his or her initial hopes and goals first confront the realities of organizational life and of the person's talents and needs.

For many first-time workers, this turns out to be a disastrous period, one in which their often-naïve expectations confront unexpected workplace realities, such as being relegated to an unimportant low-risk job where they "cannot cause any trouble while being tried out," interdepartmental conflict and politicking, or a boss who is neither rewarded for nor trained in the unique mentoring tasks needed to properly supervise new employees.[11]

Provide Challenging Initial Jobs

Most experts agree that one of the most important things is to provide new employees with challenging first jobs. In most organizations, however, providing such jobs seems more the exception than the rule. This imbalance, as one expert has pointed out, is an example of "glaring mismanagement" when one considers the effort and money invested in recruiting, hiring, and training new employees.[12]

Provide Realistic Job Previews

Providing recruits with realistic previews of what to expect should they be selected to work in the organization—previews that describe both the attractions and the possible pitfalls—can be an effective way of minimizing reality shock and improving employees' long-term performance.

Giving an employee responsibility for a major presentation to an important client is one way to front-load entry-level jobs with challenge and to foster employee commitment.

Be Demanding

There is often a "Pygmalion effect" in the relationship between a new employee and his or her boss.[13] In other words, the more the supervisor expects and the more confident and supportive he or she is, the better new employees will perform.

Provide Periodic Developmental Job Rotation and Job Pathing

The best way in which new employees can test themselves and crystallize their career anchors is to try out a variety of challenging jobs. By rotating to jobs in various specializations—from financial analysis to production to HR, for example—the employee gets an opportunity to assess his or her aptitudes and preferences. At the same time, the organization gets a manager with a broader, multifunctional view of the organization.[14] One extension of this is called **job pathing**, which means selecting carefully sequenced job assignments.[15]

job pathing Selecting carefully sequenced job assignments to enable employees to test their aptitudes and preferences.

Provide Career-Oriented Performance Appraisals

Supervisors must understand that valid performance appraisal information is, in the long run, more important than protecting the short-term interests of their staff.[16] Therefore, a supervisor needs concrete information regarding the employee's potential career path—information, in other words, about the nature of the future work for which he or she is appraising the employee, or which the employee desires.[17]

Provide Career-Planning Workshops

Employers should also take steps to increase their employees' involvement and expertise in planning and developing their own careers. One option here is to organize periodic career-planning workshops. A **career-planning workshop** has been defined as "a planned learning event in which participants are expected to be actively involved, completing career-planning exercises and inventories and participating in career-skills practice sessions."[18]

career-planning workshop A planned learning event in which participants are expected to be actively involved in career-planning exercises and career-skills practice sessions.

Such workshops usually contain a *self-assessment* activity in which individual employees actively analyze their own career interests, skills, and career anchors. There is then an *environmental assessment* phase in which relevant information about the company and its career options and staffing needs is presented. Finally, a career-planning workshop typically concludes with *goal setting and action planning* in which the individual sets career goals and creates a career plan.

A career-planning workbook may be distributed to employees either as part of a workshop or as an independent career-planning aid. This is "a printed guide that directs its users through a series of assessment exercises, models, discussions, guidelines, and other information to support career planning."[19] The workbook may also contain practical career-related information, such as how to prepare a résumé. Finally, career-planning workbooks usually contain guides for creating a career-development action plan. A career-planning workbook underlines the employee's responsibility to initiate the career-development process, whereas career workshops may reinforce the perception that the employer will do so.[20]

Provide Opportunities for Mentoring

mentoring An experienced individual (the mentor) teaching and training another person (the protégé) who has less knowledge in an area.

Mentoring has traditionally been defined as "the use of an experienced individual (the mentor) to teach and train someone [the protégé] with less knowledge in a given area." Through individualized attention, "the mentor transfers needed information, feedback, and encouragement to the protégé," and in that way, the opportunities for the protégé to optimize his or her career success are improved. Effective mentoring builds trust both ways in the mentor–protégé relationship. Mentoring provides benefits to both mentors, who demonstrate enhanced attitudes and job performance, and protégés, who become more self-confident and productive, and experience greater career satisfaction and faster career growth. Group mentoring is another option. A special mentor who offers insight and the wisdom of experience guides four to eight employees, and in addition, each employee's manager plays a key role in developing learning assignments and coaching the employee.[21]

Organizational mentoring may be formal or informal. Informally, of course, middle- and senior-level managers will often voluntarily take up-and-coming employees under their wings, not only to train them but also to give career advice and to help them steer around political pitfalls. However, many employers also establish formal mentoring programs. Here employers actively encourage mentoring relationships to take place and may pair protégés with potential mentors. Training may be provided to facilitate the mentoring process and, in particular, to aid both mentor and protégé in understanding their respective responsibilities in the mentoring relationship. A recent study on mentoring across Canada found interesting variations in the gender breakdown between male and female mentors and protégées, based on the type of mentoring program, as shown in **Figure 9.2**.

A recent study by Peer Resources, a nonprofit centre for mentoring in Victoria, B.C., found that mentoring is not being used to its full potential in Canadian workplaces. Almost one-third of Canadian organizations have no mentoring programs. This is surprising, given the emphasis on learning organizations and knowledge workers in today's businesses. Mentoring is one of the best and cheapest ways to transfer knowledge. Mentoring also keeps skilled employees motivated, loyal, and committed to the organization. Ultimately, an effective mentoring program supports corporate strategy by retaining future leaders.[22]

A new development in mentoring is *reverse mentoring* programs where younger employees provide guidance to senior executives on how to use the Web for messaging, buying products and services, finding new business opportunities, and so forth. General Motors, Procter & Gamble, General Electric, and the Wharton Business School are all using reverse mentoring. The relationship that develops often provides benefits to the young mentor when the Web-challenged older manager reciprocates in the form of career advice and guidance.[23]

Mentors—Peer Resources
www.mentors.ca

FIGURE 9.2   Male–Female Breakdown of Mentors and Protégées (Mentees)

Program Objectives	Mentor Male/Female Ratio	% Male	% Female	Mentee Male/Female Ratio	% Male	% Female
Entrepreneur development	1.1:1	52.2	47.8	0.5:1	35.4	64.5
Retention/succession leadership	1.7:1	63.3	36.7	2.1:1	67.3	32.7
Career entry/ settlement	1.4:1	58.7	41.3	1.4:1	58.5	41.5
Industry-specific mobility	0.1:1	8.7	91.3	0.004:1	3.7	96.3

Source: C. Cuerrier, ed., *Mentoring and the World of Work in Canada: Source Book of Best Practices.* Charlesbourg, QC: Fondation de l'entrepreneurship, 2003. Reprinted with permission of the publisher.

Become a Learning Organization

learning organization An organization focused on creating, acquiring, and transferring knowledge, and at modifying its behaviour to reflect new knowledge and insights.

Learning is a survival technique for both individuals and organizations. Today, employees at all levels know that they must engage in lifelong learning in order to remain employable and have a satisfying career. A **learning organization** "is an organization skilled at creating, acquiring, and transferring knowledge, and at modifying its behaviour to reflect new knowledge and insights."[24] The HR department is often the driving force behind ensuring that the training and development opportunities necessary to create a learning organization are in place, particularly in transferring knowledge, learning from experience, experimentation through searching for and testing new knowledge, learning from others, and systematic problem solving.

MANAGING PROMOTIONS AND TRANSFERS

Promotions and transfers are significant career-related decisions that managers make on an ongoing basis. These decisions have important career development implications for the promoted and/or transferred employee and substantial benefits for the organization in terms of creating a pool of potential future managers with broad experience throughout the firm.

Making Promotion Decisions

Employers must decide on the basis on which to promote employees, and the way that these decisions are made will affect the employees' motivation, performance, and commitment.

Decision 1: Is Seniority or Competence the Rule?

From the point of view of motivation, promotion based on competence is best. However, union agreements often contain a clause that emphasizes seniority in promotions, meaning that only *substantial differences in abilities* can be taken into account.[25]

Decision 2: How Is Competence Measured?

If promotion is to be based on competence, how will competence be defined and measured? Defining and measuring *past* performance are relatively straightforward matters, but promotion also requires predicting the person's *potential*; thus, there must be a valid procedure for predicting a candidate's future performance. Tests and assessment centres can be used to evaluate employees and identify those with executive potential.[26]

Decision 3: Is the Process Formal or Informal?

Many employers still depend on an informal system where the availability and requirements of open positions are kept secret. Key managers make promotion decisions among employees whom they know personally and who have impressed them.[27] The problem is that when employees are not made aware of the jobs that are available, the criteria for promotion, and how promotion decisions are made, the link between performance and promotion is severed, thereby diminishing the effectiveness of promotion as a reward. For this reason, many employers establish formal, published promotion policies and procedures that describe the criteria by which promotions are awarded. Skills inventories, replacement charts, and replacement summaries can be used to compile detailed information about the qualifications of hundreds or thousands of employees.

Hints **to Ensure**
Legal Compliance

The net effect of such actions is twofold: (1) an employer ensures that all qualified employees are considered for openings, and (2) promotion becomes more closely linked with performance in the minds of employees.

An Ethical Dilemma

Is it ethical for employers to keep promotion policies and procedures secret in an era of flattened organizations, where so many employees who aspire to higher positions will not get them but might achieve them elsewhere?

Decision 4: Vertical, Horizontal, or Other Career Path?

Finally, employers are increasingly facing the question of how to "promote" employees in an era of flattened organizations that have eliminated many of the higher-management positions to which employees might normally aspire.[28] Some firms have created two parallel career paths: one for managers and another for "individual contributors," such as engineers, who can move up to nonsupervisory but still more-senior positions, such as "senior engineer," with most of the perks and financial rewards attached to management-track positions at that level.[29] Another option is to provide career-development opportunities by moving the person horizontally, such as a production employee being moved horizontally to HR in order to give him or her an opportunity to develop new skills.

Managing Transfers

Employees may seek transfers into jobs that offer greater possibility for career advancement or opportunities for personal enrichment, or those that are more interesting or more convenient—better hours, location of work, and so on.[30]

Employers may transfer a worker in order to fill a vacant position or, more generally, to find a better fit for the employee within the firm. Transfers are thus increasingly used as a way to give employees opportunities for diversity of job assignment and, therefore, personal and career growth. Many organizations are recognizing that future leaders will need international experience to effectively manage their organizations in the increasingly globalized world of business, and they are providing international assignments as a career development experience, as outlined in the Global HRM box.

Global HRM

International Transfers at Siemens Canada

Terri Lynn Oliver, international HR advisor with Siemens Canada, notes that at Siemens, "the selection of high potentials (for assignment) is part of the overall corporate approach for succession planning and career development." With a global workforce of 420 000, of which 6600 are in Canada, there is no shortage of foreign opportunities. At Siemens the process for selection is quite structured and the company maintains a pool of potential talent to draw from as opportunities arise. The challenge from a corporate perspective, says Oliver, is managing the expectation and linking the move to a strategic objective. "People want to know, 'What position will I come back to?' In most situations it's impossible to give a guarantee about opportunities upon the completion of the assignment. And so people will often opt for the domestic promotion."

When it comes to individuals accepting an assignment, family and career issues dominate. "The spouse's career is a major consideration, particularly on a longer assignment," says Oliver. "Schooling is also a challenge and Siemens tries to be innovative for both its inpatriates and expatriates in finding workable solutions within budget."

Although family issues are the main barriers to individuals taking on a foreign assignment, safety is an escalating concern. Canada is a safe country in which to live and raise a family. Many of the countries where Canadians are working are becoming more dangerous with each passing day. Perhaps that's why Terri Lynn Oliver says, "flexibility to shorten an assignment and planning for the worst" are a key part in the development of any foreign assignment.

Source: Adapted from S. Cryne, "Foreign Assignments Increasing, Along with Employee Resistance," *Canadian HR Reporter*, September 27, 2004. Reproduced by permission of *Canadian HR Reporter*, Carswell, One Corporate Plaza, 2075 Kennedy Road, Scarborough, ON M1T 3V4.

Policies of routinely transferring employees from locale to locale, either to give their employees more exposure to a wide range of jobs or to fill open positions with trained employees, have fallen into disfavour, partly because of the cost of relocating employees, and partly because of the assumption that frequent transfers have a bad effect on an employee's family life. Companies are facing a record number of rejections of their relocation offers. About two-thirds of all transfer refusals are due to family or spousal concerns. Providing reassurances that relocation costs will be covered is often no longer enough to persuade employees to upset their lifestyles, their spouses' careers, and their children's activities. To overcome this problem, companies are offering spousal support in the form of career transition programs in order to encourage employees to accept transfers.[31]

MANAGEMENT DEVELOPMENT

management development Any attempt to improve current or future management performance by imparting knowledge, changing attitudes, or increasing skills.

Management development is any attempt to improve managerial performance by imparting knowledge, changing attitudes, or increasing skills. Management development is particularly important as baby boomers enter retirement and the next generation of managers assumes senior management responsibilities. The ultimate aim of management-development programs is to achieve business strategy. For this reason, the management-development process consists of (1) assessing the company's human resources needs to achieve its strategic objectives, (2) creating a talent pool, and then (3) developing the managers themselves.[32]

Some management-development programs are company-wide and involve all or most new (or potential) management recruits. The workers may be rotated through a programmed series of departmental assignments and educational experiences, the aim of which is to identify their management potential and provide the breadth of experience (in, say, production and finance) that will make the new managers more valuable in their first "real" assignment as group product leaders. Superior candidates may then be slotted onto a "fast track," a development program that prepares them more quickly to assume senior-level appointments.

Succession Planning

succession planning A process through which senior-level openings are planned for and eventually filled.

On the other hand, the management-development program may be aimed at filling a specific position, such as vice-president of finance. When it is an executive position to be filled, the process is usually called **succession planning**. Succession planning provides "a significant competitive advantage to companies that take it seriously—and serious risks to those that do not."[33]

Successful succession planning begins with CEO leadership and involvement in the following steps:[34]

1. establishing a strategic direction for the organization
2. identifying core leadership skills and competencies needed to achieve the strategy
3. identifying people inside the organization who have, or can acquire, those skills and providing them with developmental opportunities (being prepared to recruit externally as well)
4. implementing a succession plan

The HR department should work with the CEO on succession planning, but this process should not be delegated to HR. Succession planning can easily become an emotional issue for ambitious managers and can evoke political behaviour. It is often only the CEO who can manage these political and emotional issues.[35] HR staff can ensure that all the required information for effective succession planning is made available to those responsible in order to help ensure objectivity in the process. HR can also assume responsibility for providing the development activities required for employees identified in the succession plan.[36] Another important HR activity is anticipating the reaction of individuals who are not selected for the "fast track" in order to avoid alienating solid performers who are not chosen.

In today's fast-changing global world of business, the competition for talent is increasing rapidly. Succession planning for many organizations includes the identification of qualified candidates for all critical positions, both managerial and technical. When an organization loses a top salesperson or a talented engineer, the loss will not make headlines, but the impact on the bottom line could still be significant. A vacant position can mean that important decisions are delayed or made by other employees with less knowledge and expertise.[37]

A succession program typically takes place in stages. First, an *organization projection* is made; here, each department's management needs are anticipated based on strategic factors, like planned expansion or contraction. Next, the HR department reviews its *management-skills inventories* to identify the management talent now employed. These inventories contain data on things like education and work experience, career preferences, and performance appraisals. Next, *management-replacement charts* are drawn. These summarize potential candidates for each management slot, as well as each person's development needs. As shown in **Figure 9.3**, the development needs for a future divisional vice-president might include *job rotation* (to obtain more experience in the firm's finance and production divisions), *executive-development programs* (to provide training in strategic planning), and assignment for two weeks to the employer's *in-house management-development centre*.[38]

FIGURE 9.3   Management Replacement Chart Showing Development Needs of Future Divisional Vice-President

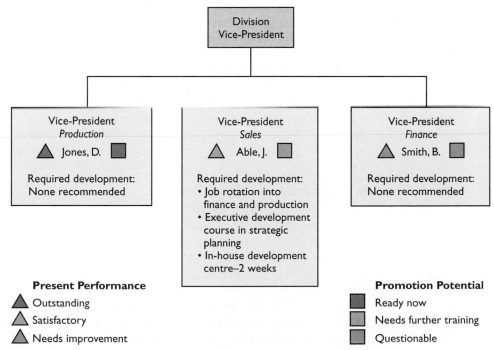

Employees should be encouraged to be proactive and accept responsibility for their own career, including seeking out opportunities for leadership training. Employees who feel empowered and motivated to be the initiators of their own management-development process may already be demonstrating leadership potential. Empowering employees in the organization to be part of a mutual succession-planning process increases the potential for its success.[39] However, it may be necessary to pay special attention to career development for older workers, as discussed in the Workforce Diversity box.

On-the-Job Management-Development Techniques

On-the-job training is one of the most popular development methods. Important techniques here include developmental job rotation, the coaching/understudy approach, and action learning.

Workforce Diversity

Career Development for Older Workers

If an employer doesn't pay attention to the career development of staff as they approach age 60, it won't have the benefit of their productivity during their second middle age. The "second middle age" is a term coined by Helen Harkness in the book *Don't Stop the Career Clock*. It refers to the 20-year period when an individual is between ages 60 and 80. It ought to be viewed as a time of potential and valuable contribution rather than as "the retirement years" or worse, "old age."

Here are practical career development strategies that will help keep employees fully engaged during their second middle age:

- *Adopt a new attitude.* Discard the stereotypes. Older workers are not necessarily closed-minded, reluctant to embrace change, risk averse, and focused on the past. Their views are grounded in years of hard-earned experience and many of them are open-minded, flexible, forward-thinking, and willing to take calculated risks.

- *Provide career counselling.* People want to do work that interests them, takes advantage of their knowledge, honours their values, and uses their key skills. These factors change for the individual over time, and often a person's career path takes him or her away from work that is truly enjoyed. Returning to an earlier role could be rejuvenating in second middle age or it might be feasible to launch into a completely new endeavour as an alternative to retirement. To help employees stay on a productive career track, it is crucial to provide good career counselling.

- *Invest in training and development.* Recent research debunks the myth of the inevitable decline of mental ability with age. Although slower processing and some memory loss are typical of aging, these are not necessarily signs of diminishing capacity in primary mental functions, such as verbal meaning, spatial orientation, inductive reasoning, numerical ability, or word fluency. These important mental competencies, which can remain intact well into someone's 90s in the absence of illness, make second middle-agers worthy candidates for training and development. It is easy to compensate for a slower mental pace and occasional memory lapse when intellectual capability is respected.

- *Honour the need for work/life balance.* After decades of commuting, working long hours, and taking short holidays, many people look forward to retirement as a welcome break from the unrelenting routine. The prospect of sleeping in seven days a week, taking an extended trip, or spending the winter in Florida can have a lot of appeal. Creative work arrangements could offer some of these perks to second middle-agers.

Second middle-agers could be organizational gold. Research has shown that they have lower rates of absenteeism, fewer accidents, higher levels of job satisfaction, and a stronger work ethic. Why wouldn't employers encourage them to develop their careers and remain productive in the workforce as long as possible?

Source: Adapted from M. Watters, "Career Development for Employees Heading into Their 'Second Middle Age,'" *Canadian HR Reporter*, February 13, 2006, p. 13. Reproduced by permission of *Canadian HR Reporter*, Carswell, One Corporate Plaza, 2075 Kennedy Road, Scarborough, ON M1T 3V4.

Developmental Job Rotation

developmental job rotation   A management-training technique that involves moving a trainee from department to department to broaden his or her experience and identify strong and weak points.

Developmental job rotation involves moving management trainees from department to department to broaden their understanding of all parts of the business.[40] The trainee—often a recent college or university graduate—may work for several months in each department; this not only helps to broaden his or her experience but also helps the trainee discover which jobs he or she prefers. TD Bank Financial Group provides MBA graduates with four customized six-month rotations within fast-paced and exciting areas throughout the organization.[41]

In addition to providing a well-rounded training experience for each person, job rotation helps to prevent stagnation through the constant introduction of new points of view in each department. It also tests the trainee and helps to identify the person's strong and weak points.[42] Job rotation is more appropriate for developing general line managers than functional staff experts.

Coaching/Understudy Approach

In the *coaching/understudy approach*, the trainee works directly with the person that he or she is to replace; the latter is, in turn, responsible for the trainee's coaching. Normally, the trainee relieves the executive of certain responsibilities and learns the job by doing it.[43] This helps to ensure that the employer will have trained managers to assume key positions.

To be effective, the executive has to be a good coach and mentor. His or her motivation to train the replacement will depend on the quality of the relationship between them.

Action Learning

action learning   A training technique by which management trainees are allowed to work full-time, analyzing and solving problems in other departments.

Action learning releases managers from their regular duties in order that they can work full-time on projects, analyzing and solving problems in departments other than their own. The trainees meet periodically with a project group of four or five people, with whom their findings and progress are discussed and debated. TD Bank Financial Group and Telus use this method.[44]

The idea of developing managers in this way has pros and cons. It gives trainees real experience with actual problems, and to that extent, it can develop skills like problem analysis and planning. Furthermore, working with the others in the group, the trainees can and do find solutions to major problems. The main drawback is that, in releasing trainees to work on outside projects, the employer loses the full-time services of a competent manager.

Action Learning
www.nestadt.com.au

Off-the-Job Management-Development Techniques

There are many techniques that are used to develop managers off the job, perhaps in a conference room at headquarters or off the premises entirely at a university or special seminar. These techniques are addressed next.

The Case Study Method

case study method   A development method in which a trainee is presented with a written description of an organizational problem to diagnose and solve.

The **case study method** presents a trainee with a written description of an organizational problem. The person then analyzes the case in private, diagnoses the problem, and presents his or her findings and solutions in a discussion with other trainees.[45] The case method approach is aimed at giving trainees realistic experience in identifying and analyzing complex problems in an environment in which their progress can be subtly guided by a trained discussion leader. Through the class discussion of the case, trainees learn that there are usually

Trainees participating in a case-study discussion

many ways to approach and solve complex organizational problems. Trainees also learn that their own needs and values often influence their solutions.

Several things can be done to increase the effectiveness of the case approach. If possible, the cases should be actual scenarios from the trainees' own firms; this will help to ensure that trainees understand the background of the case, as well as make it easier for trainees to transfer what they learn to their own jobs and situations. Instructors have to guard against dominating the case analysis and make sure that they remain no more than a catalyst or coach. Finally, they must carefully prepare the case discussion and let the participants discuss the case in small groups before class.[46]

Management Games

management game   A computerized development technique in which teams of managers compete with one another by making decisions regarding realistic but simulated companies.

In a computerized **management game**, trainees are divided into five- or six-person companies, each of which has to compete with the others in a simulated marketplace. Each company sets a goal (e.g., "maximize sales") and is told that it can make several decisions, such as (1) how much to spend on advertising, (2) how much to produce, (3) how much inventory to maintain, and (4) how many of which product to produce. As in the real world, each company usually cannot see what decisions the other firms have made, although these decisions do affect their own sales. For example, if a competitor decides to increase its advertising expenditures, it may end up increasing its sales at the expense of the other firms.[47] A board game called *Making Sense of Business: A Simulation* designed by Development Dimensions International provides participants with the opportunity to carry out strategic decision making and learn about the hard decisions and trade-offs that business leaders deal with every day.[48]

Development Dimensions International
www.ddiworld.com

Management games can be good development tools. People learn best by getting involved in the activity itself, and the games can be useful for gaining such involvement. They help trainees to develop their problem-solving skills and leadership skills, as well as foster cooperation and teamwork.

Outside Seminars

Niagara Institute
www.niagarainstitute.com

Many organizations offer special seminars and conferences aimed at providing skill-building training for managers. For example, the Niagara Institute in Niagara-on-the-Lake, Ontario, offers programs aimed at "developing the leaders of the

Adventure learning participants enhance their leadership skills, team skills, and risk-taking behaviour.

REQUIRED PROFESSIONAL CAPABILITIES

Assesses and reports on the costs and benefits of engaging internal and external suppliers of development programs, given the organizational constraints and objectives

Develops requests for proposals (RFPs) and reviews submissions by third parties

Recommends the selection of external training consultants and contractors, such as public education institutions

role-playing   A training technique in which trainees act the parts of people in a realistic management situation.

Queen's University School of Business Executive Program
http://business.queensu.ca/execdev/index.htm

future," and the Institute of Professional Management offers a professional accreditation program leading to the Canadian Management Professional (CMP) designation.[49] Outdoor experiential expeditions, or adventure learning experiences, are sometimes used to enhance leadership skills, team skills, and risk-taking behaviour.[50]

College/University-Related Programs

Colleges and universities provide three types of management-development activities. First, many schools provide *executive-development programs* in leadership, marketing, HRM, operations management, and the like. The programs use cases and lectures to provide senior-level managers with the latest management skills, as well as practice in analyzing complex organizational problems. Most of these programs take the executives away from their jobs, putting them in university-run learning environments for their entire stay.

Second, many colleges and universities also offer *individualized courses* in areas like business, management, and health-care administration. Managers can take these to fill gaps in their backgrounds. Thus, a prospective division manager with a gap in experience with accounting controls might sign up for a two-course sequence in managerial accounting.

Finally, many schools also offer *degree programs,* such as the MBA or Executive MBA. The latter is a Master of Business Administration degree program geared especially to middle managers and above, who generally take their courses on weekends and proceed through the program with the same group of colleagues.

The employer usually plays a role in university-related programs.[51] First, many employers offer *tuition refunds* as an incentive for employees to develop job-related skills. Thus, engineers may be encouraged to enroll in technical courses aimed at keeping them abreast of changes in their field. Supervisors may be encouraged to enroll in programs to develop them for higher-level management jobs. Employers are also increasingly granting technical and professional employees extended *sabbaticals*—periods of time off—to attend a college or university to pursue a higher degree or to upgrade skills.

Role-Playing

The aim of **role-playing** is to create a realistic situation and then have the trainees assume the parts (or roles) of specific people in that situation.[52] Roles that can be used in an employee discipline role-playing exercise are presented in **Figure 9.4**. When combined with the general instructions for the role-playing exercise, roles like these for all of the participants can trigger a spirited discussion among the role-players, particularly when they all throw themselves into the roles. The idea of the exercise is to solve the problem at hand and thereby develop trainees' skills in areas like leadership and delegation.

The role-players can also give up their inhibitions and experiment with new ways of acting. For example, a supervisor could experiment with both a considerate and an autocratic leadership style, whereas in the real world the person might not have this harmless avenue for experimentation. Role-playing also trains a person to be aware of and sensitive to the feelings of others.[53]

Role-playing has some drawbacks. An exercise can take an hour or more to complete, only to be deemed a waste of time by participants if the instructor does not prepare a wrap-up explanation of what the participants were to learn.

An Ethical Dilemma

Is it ethical to require employees to participate in role-playing exercises when they are uncomfortable in this situation?

FIGURE 9.4　Typical Roles in an Employee Discipline Role-Playing Exercise

Manager: Dale has failed to adapt to the new requirements for production planning. His/her plans are often incomplete or inadequate. Dale's attitude is defensive and he/she is often nasty to co-workers when they are working on their plans. Dale doesn't seem to understand the importance of the new planning procedure. You have given him/her two verbal warnings in the past. You need to get Dale to understand why production planning is so important in this business. You have just asked Dale to come into your office.

Employee: For 25 years in this job, you have never had any complaints about your work. However, in your performance appraisal last month your manager said that you needed to complete your production planning more quickly. Your manager is also very concerned about the accuracy of your production planning and has warned you a couple of times to be more careful. He/she has just asked you to come into his/her office, and you think it may be about your production planning work.

Some trainees also feel that role-playing is childish, while others who may be uncomfortable with acting are reluctant to participate at all. Knowing the audience and preparing a wrap-up are thus advisable.

Behaviour Modelling

behaviour modelling　A training technique in which trainees are first shown good management techniques, then asked to play roles in a simulated situation, and finally given feedback regarding their performance.

Behaviour modelling involves (1) showing trainees the right (or "model") way of doing something, (2) letting each person practise the right way to do it, and then (3) providing feedback regarding each trainee's performance.[54] It has been used to train first-line supervisors to better handle common supervisor–employee interactions; this includes giving recognition, disciplining, introducing changes, and improving poor performance. It has also been used to train middle managers to better handle interpersonal situations, such as performance problems and undesirable work habits. Finally, it has been used to train employees and their supervisors to take and give criticism, give and ask for help, and establish mutual trust and respect.

The basic behaviour-modelling procedure can be outlined as follows:

1. *Modelling.* First, trainees watch films or videotapes that show model persons behaving effectively in a problem situation. In other words, trainees are shown the right way to behave in a simulated but realistic situation. The film or video might thus show a supervisor effectively disciplining an employee, if teaching how to discipline is the aim of the training program.

2. *Role-playing.* Next, the trainees are given roles to play in a simulated situation; here they practise and rehearse the effective behaviours demonstrated by the models.

Tips for the Front Line

3. *Social reinforcement.* The trainer provides reinforcement in the form of praise and constructive feedback based on how the trainee performs in the role-playing situation.

REQUIRED PROFESSIONAL CAPABILITIES

Facilitates coaching and post-training support activities to ensure transfer of learning to the workplace

4. *Transfer of training.* Finally, trainees are encouraged to apply their new skills when they are back on their jobs.

In-House Development Centres

in-house development centre　A company-based method for exposing prospective managers to realistic exercises to develop improved management skills.

Some employers have **in-house development centres**, also called "corporate universities." These centres usually combine classroom learning (lectures and seminars,

for instance) with other techniques, like assessment centres, in-basket exercises, and role-playing, to help develop employees and other managers. The number of corporate universities in North America has grown exponentially over the last several years. One of the best-known centres in Canada is the BMO Financial Group's Institute for Learning.

Organization Development

Organization development (OD) is a method that is aimed at changing the attitudes, values, and beliefs of managers and other employees so that they can identify and implement organizational change. OD has several distinguishing characteristics. First, it is usually based on action research, which means collecting data about the organization and then feeding the data back to the employees to analyze and identify problems. Second, it applies behavioural science knowledge for the purpose of improving the organization's effectiveness. Third, it changes the attitudes, values, and beliefs of employees, so that the employees themselves can identify and implement the changes needed to improve the company's functioning. Fourth, it changes the organization in a particular direction—toward improved problem solving, responsiveness, quality of work, and effectiveness.[55]

The number and variety of OD techniques have increased substantially over the past few years. OD got its start with human-process interventions, which were aimed at understanding one's own and others' behaviour, in order to improve that behaviour for the benefit of the organization. Team building and survey feedback are two widely used human-process interventions.

1. Team Building   **Team building** refers to the process of improving team effectiveness. Data concerning the team's performance are collected and then fed back to the members of the group. The participants examine, explain, and analyze the data and develop specific action plans or solutions for solving the team's problems.

2. Survey Feedback   **Survey feedback** research requires that employees throughout the organization fill out attitude surveys. The data are then used as feedback to the work groups as a basis for problem solving and action planning. In general, such surveys are convenient for unfreezing an organization's management and employees by providing a comparative, graphic illustration of the fact that the organization does have problems that should be solved. The continuing popularity of employee attitude surveys reflects the view that there is validity in employee reports of their experiences. These reports can be very useful as diagnoses of the degree to which a new strategy is being implemented and the degree to which policies and practices are related to the achievement of strategic goals, like customer satisfaction and customer attention.[56]

The Bank of Montreal's Institute for Learning

BMO Financial Group
www.bmo.com

organization development (OD)   A method aimed at changing the attitudes, values, and beliefs of employees so that employees can improve the organization.

The Organization Development Institute
www.odinstitute.org

team building   Improving the effectiveness of teams through the use of consultants, interviews, and team-building meetings.

survey feedback   A method that involves surveying employees' attitudes and providing feedback so that problems can be solved by the managers and employees.

EXECUTIVE DEVELOPMENT

Canada is facing a shortage of leadership talent. The demand for leaders is increasing because of new opportunities being created by economic growth, global "brain drain," a decade of neglected succession planning, lack of organizational commitment to developing talent, and mixed success with external recruitment.[57] Bob Hedley, VP of Leadership at Maple Leaf Foods, says, "Where I lose sleep right now is we still don't have enough bench strength. One of the challenges is to acquire enough talent within the company and grow them fast enough so that we are ready to grow ourselves."[58]

Maple Leaf Foods believes that employees' success guarantees the success of the company. They call it the "Leadership Edge"—thousands of high-performing people, thriving in a high-performance culture. Employees are provided with ongoing feedback about their performance through a state-of-the-art performance assessment and development process. Employees receive recognition for both their accomplishments and their potential. This feedback is followed up with well-targeted developmental activities to ensure continued growth and development.[59]

The leadership development programs at the Banff Centre in Alberta focus on building leadership capability in five crucial areas that make up the leadership system. These are self, team, business unit, organization, and community/society. Leading in increasingly complex situations requires a systematic approach to successfully understand and navigate the interdependencies and linkages among all parts of the system, from the self through to the greater community. For this reason, the Banff Centre uses an integrated approach to develop leaders.[60] The Banff Centre believes that the three basic requirements of successful leadership are knowledge, competency, and character. **Figure 9.5** illustrates the Banff Centre

FIGURE 9.5   Banff Centre Competency Matrix Model

Source: Banff Centre Competency Matrix Model © 2006. Banff, AB: The Banff Centre 2006. www.banffcentre.ca/departments/leadership/assessment_tools/competency_matrix. Reproduced with permission of The Banff Centre.

Competency Matrix Model, based on six categories of competencies—self mastery, futuring (vision), sense making (thinking), design of intelligent action, aligning people to action (leading), and adaptive learning.

More emphasis on executive development today is essential in order for organizations to successfully cope with the coming exodus of "boomer" executives. New executive talent must be trained and ready to assume senior-level responsibilities if Canadian companies are to continue to compete successfully in the global economy.

Chapter Review

Summary

1. Career planning and development is the deliberate process through which a person becomes aware of personal career-related attributes, and the lifelong series of activities that contribute to his or her career fulfillment.

2. The first factor affecting career choice is to identify career stage. The main stages in a person's career are growth (roughly birth to age 14), exploration (roughly age 15 to 24), establishment (roughly age 24 to 44, the heart of most people's work lives), maintenance (45 to 65), and decline (pre-retirement). The next step is to identify occupational orientation: realistic, investigative, social, conventional, enterprising, and artistic. Then identify skills and aptitudes. Finally, identify career anchors: technical/functional, managerial competence, creativity, autonomy, security, service/dedication, pure challenge, or lifestyle.

3. An employee's first assignment can be made more meaningful by adhering to the following guidelines: avoid reality shock, provide challenging initial jobs, provide realistic job previews, be demanding, provide periodic developmental job rotation and job pathing, conduct career-oriented performance appraisals, provide career-planning workshops, provide opportunities for mentoring, and become a learning organization.

4. In making promotion decisions, firms have to (1) decide to promote based on seniority or competence, (2) decide how to measure competence, (3) choose between a formal or informal promotion system, and (4) determine whether career paths will be vertical, horizontal, or other. Transfers offer employees an opportunity for personal and career development, but they have become more difficult to manage because of spousal and family concerns. Thus career-transition programs for spouses are often provided.

5. Management development is any attempt to improve managerial performance and it is aimed at preparing employees for future jobs with the organization. When an executive position needs to be filled, succession planning is often involved. Management development is important because the majority of Canadian companies are facing a shortage of middle managers.

6. Managerial on-the-job training methods include developmental job rotation, coaching, and action learning. Basic off-the-job techniques include case studies, management games, outside seminars, college/university-related programs, role-playing, behaviour modelling, in-house development centres, and organizational development techniques such as team building and survey feedback.

Key Terms

action learning   *(p. 239)*
behaviour modelling   *(p. 242)*
boundaryless career   *(p. 225)*
career anchor   *(p. 229)*
career cycle   *(p. 227)*
career planning and development   *(p. 225)*
career-planning workshop   *(p. 232)*
case study method   *(p. 239)*
decline stage   *(p. 228)*
developmental job rotation   *(p. 239)*
employee retention   *(p. 226)*
establishment stage   *(p. 228)*
exploration stage   *(p. 227)*
growth stage   *(p. 227)*
in-house development centre   *(p. 242)*
job pathing   *(p. 232)*

learning organization   *(p. 234)*
lifelong learning   *(p. 226)*
maintenance stage   *(p. 228)*
management development   *(p. 236)*
management game   *(p. 240)*
mentoring   *(p. 232)*
occupational orientation   *(p. 228)*
organization development (OD)   *(p. 243)*
role-playing   *(p. 241)*
succession planning   *(p. 236)*
survey feedback   *(p. 243)*
team building   *(p. 243)*

Review and Discussion Questions

1. Briefly describe each of the five stages in a typical career.
2. What are the six main types of occupational orientation?
3. What is a career anchor? What are the five main types of career anchor?
4. Explain three different ways in which managers can assist in the career development of their employees.
5. Explain the four important decisions to be made in establishing a promotion policy.
6. Explain the three major on-the-job management development techniques.
7. Discuss the six competencies in the Competency Matrix Model.

Critical Thinking Questions

1. Do you think developmental job rotation is a good method to use for developing management trainees? Why or why not?
2. Would you tell high-potential employees that they are on the "fast-track"? How might this knowledge affect their behaviour? How might the behaviour of employees who are disappointed at not being included in management development activities be affected?
3. How do you think employees are going to respond to the new focus on career planning, given the emphasis in recent years on "being in charge of your own career"?
4. What steps could a company take to reduce political behaviour in the succession planning process?

Application Exercises

Running Case: LearnInMotion.com

What to Do about Succession?

In the second year of operation of LearnInMotion.com, Jennifer was involved in a serious car accident and spent two months in the hospital and another four months in rehabilitation before she was able to return to work. During this six-month period, Pierre had to manage the entire business on his own. It proved to be impossible. Despite some new training, the sales effort continued to falter and sales revenues declined by 25 percent. Staff turnover at LearnInMotion.com increased, as employees found it very frustrating to encounter so much trouble to have even a brief conversation with Pierre. Employees who left were not replaced, as the decline in sales meant that costs had to be reduced. Thus, Pierre was spared the difficult job of downsizing—at least for now.

The first day that Jennifer returned to work, Pierre said, "We have to have a succession plan. This business will not survive unless we have other employees who can take over from us temporarily now and permanently in the long term."

Jennifer agreed. "Yes, it was difficult for me being unable to work and knowing that you were overwhelmed with every problem throughout the entire company," she said. "And maybe employees' performance in their current jobs would be enhanced if they knew they had been identified as having management potential and were provided with specific development opportunities. We'll have to establish a management development program as well."

"I agree," said Pierre, "but we can't afford to spend much money on this." So Pierre and Jennifer would like your help in establishing a succession plan and a management development plan. Here's what they've asked you to do.

Questions

1. What is the best way for a small business like LearnInMotion.com to approach succession planning?

2. What on-the-job management development techniques would be most appropriate for LearnInMotion.com?

3. What off-the-job management development techniques, if any, would you recommend for LearnInMotion.com, given their financial constraints?

Case Incident

Family versus Career—and a Company Caught in the Middle

Dave and Nora live in the Vancouver area, where Dave works for a major software company. He is very motivated to put in whatever time and effort are needed to complete tasks and projects successfully. Top management recognizes his contributions as important, and his prospects at the company are excellent.

Nora has been married to Dave for five years and knows how devoted he is to his career. Both of them want to start a family and agree that Vancouver isn't where they want to raise their children. Nora, feeling that she can't wait forever to have kids, has been pressuring Dave to find a job in a smaller town.

Understanding Nora's concerns, Dave made a couple of discreet phone calls and was soon asked in for an interview by a company located in a town in Alberta. Dave didn't know what to say when the company made him an offer. The job pays less than his present job and offers fewer opportunities for advancement, but the area is the kind of environment he and Nora want. He knows Nora is thrilled at the prospect of the move, yet he can't help feeling sad. How can he simply walk away from all he has invested in his career at his present company?

Maybe there is more to life than his career, but he is already depressed and he hasn't even quit yet.

When Dave told his boss, Terri, about the new job offer, Terri was shocked. Dave is a central figure in the company's plans for the next couple of years, and his expertise is indispensable on a couple of important projects. Terri feels that Dave has blind-sided the company. Things will be a mess for a long time if he leaves. But what can the company do to keep him if money isn't the issue?

Questions

1. What preventive measures could Dave's company have taken to avoid the crisis it is faced with? What can the company do now?

2. Should Dave's company involve Nora in any of its attempts to retain Dave? If so, how?

3. Should Dave's company implement any career development programs after this crisis passes? If so, what kind would you recommend? Why?

Source: L.R. Gomez-Mejia, D.B. Balkin, R.L. Cardy, and D. Dimick, *Managing Human Resources*, Canadian Second Edition. Scarborough, ON: Pearson Education Canada, 2001, p. 254. Reprinted with permission of Pearson Education Canada.

Experiential Exercises

1. Review the Web site of a provider of management-development seminars, such as the Canadian Institute of Management. Obtain copies of recent listings of seminar offerings. At what levels of management are the seminar offerings aimed? What seem to be the most popular types of development programs? Why do you think that is the case?

2. Find an older person who is Web-challenged (perhaps a family friend or one of your professors who is having trouble setting up a Web site or getting full use of the e-mail system). Offer to reverse mentor him or her on using the Web for a short time (a few weeks) in return for some career mentoring for you. Prepare a short report on the benefits of this experience for both of you.

Career development workshops cover all sorts of the finer points required for top jobs, recognizing that one social misstep can derail careers and giant business deals. Today, it is particularly important to be confident in business etiquette in one's own culture before tackling social skills in more complicated cross-cultural situations. Business etiquette consultant Roz Usheroff coaches an MBA class at the Rotman School of Management at the University of Toronto on the art of small talk, handshakes, and looking people in the eye.

Questions

1. Why is training in business etiquette important for MBA students?
2. Why don't the MBA students in the video already know how to shake hands and look people in the eye?
3. Why is small talk important in business situations?

Source: Based on "Small Talk," *CBC Venture 887* (July 6, 2003).

CHAPTER 10

PERFORMANCE APPRAISAL
The Key to Effective Performance Management

LEARNING OUTCOMES

AFTER STUDYING THIS CHAPTER, YOU SHOULD BE ABLE TO

Explain what is meant by the term "performance management" and why it is important to effectively appraise performance.

Describe eight performance appraisal methods and the pros and cons of each.

Discuss the major problems inhibiting effective performance appraisals.

Discuss 360-degree appraisal from multiple sources.

Describe the three types of appraisal interview.

Discuss the future of performance management.

REQUIRED PROFESSIONAL CAPABILITIES

- Contributes to an environment that fosters effective working relationships

THE STRATEGIC IMPORTANCE OF PERFORMANCE MANAGEMENT

In any organization, achieving strategic objectives requires employee productivity above all else as organizations strive to create a high-performance culture by using a minimum number of employees. Thus, it has been suggested that better performance management represents a largely untapped opportunity to improve company profitability.[1] Many companies are still dealing with the reality that their performance management systems are ineffective—they need to downsize poor performers, but performance appraisal records indicate that all employees are performing adequately.

performance management   The process encompassing all activities related to improving employee performance, productivity, and effectiveness.

Performance management is a process encompassing all activities related to improving employee performance, productivity, and effectiveness. It includes *goal setting, pay for performance, training and development, career management,* and *disciplinary action.* The performance management system must provide an integrated network of procedures across the organization that will direct all work behaviour.[2]

The foundation of performance management is the *performance appraisal* process. Appraisals provide a concrete basis for analysis of an employee's work performance and for any action taken to maintain, enhance, or change it. The other aspects of performance management are discussed in other chapters of this text.

THE PERFORMANCE APPRAISAL PROCESS

Performance appraisal is of considerable strategic importance to today's organizations because the most effective way for firms to differentiate themselves in a highly competitive, service-oriented, global marketplace is through the quality of their employees.[3] The performance appraisal process should also link performance criteria to current strategic objectives and implementation plans.[4] A performance appraisal contains three steps:

1. *defining performance expectations* to make sure that job duties and job standards are clear to all

2. *appraising performance* by comparing an employee's actual performance with the standards that have been set, usually involving some type of rating form

3. *feedback sessions* where the employee's performance and progress are discussed and plans are made for any development that is required

Accurate performance appraisal information is important for many reasons. Appraisal results provide information with which *promotion and salary decisions* can be made. They also provide an opportunity for managers to *review* each employee's work-related behaviour, to reinforce the things that the employee is doing well, and to develop a plan for correction of any deficiencies that the appraisal might have identified. Finally, the appraisal should be central to a firm's *career-planning process* because it provides a good opportunity to review each employee's career plans in light of his or her exhibited strengths and weaknesses, and in light of the company's strategic plans.[5]

When appraisals are ineffective, it is for reasons that parallel the three steps—defining performance expectations, appraising performance, and providing feedback.[6] Some appraisals fail because employees are not told ahead of time exactly what is expected of them in terms of good performance. Even if performance standards are defined, they may be irrelevant, subjective, or unrealistic.[7] Others fail because of problems with the forms or procedures used to actually appraise

the performance; a lenient supervisor might rate all employees "high," for instance, although many are actually unsatisfactory. Still other problems arise during the feedback discussion, such as arguing and poor communications. Finally, failure to use evaluations in human resource decision making and career development negates the primary purpose of performance evaluations. Conducting effective appraisals thus begins with defining the job and its performance standards, which will now be discussed.

STEP 1: DEFINING PERFORMANCE EXPECTATIONS

Defining performance expectations is a critical step in understanding among employees of how their work makes a contribution to achieving business results. However, surveys indicate that this understanding is still limited for most employees.[8] Their "line of sight" from their own job duties to the achievement of strategic goals is blurred.[9] Most employees require much more clarification of their performance expectations and how these contribute to the organization's overall results.

In particular, the job description often is not sufficient to clarify what employees are expected to do and how their duties relate to strategic objectives. All sales associates in the firm might have the same job description, for instance, although each sales manager may have individual ideas about what his or her reporting sales associates are expected to do. For example, the job description may list such duties as "supervise support staff" and "be responsible for all customer liaisons." However, one particular sales associate may be expected to personally sell at least $600 000 worth of products per year by handling the division's two largest accounts, keep the sales assistants happy, and keep customers away from company executives.[10] With respect to strategic objectives, all the duties of sales associates contribute to increasing the revenue of the organization.

To clarify these expectations, measurable standards should be developed for each. The "personal selling" activity can be measured in terms of how many dollars of sales the associate is to generate personally. "Keeping the sales assistants happy" might be measured in terms of turnover (on the assumption that less than 10 percent of the sales assistants will quit in any given year if morale is high). "Keeping customers away from executives" can be measured with a standard of no more than ten customer complaints per year being the sales associate's target. In general, employees should always know ahead of time how and on what basis they will be appraised.

STEP 2: APPRAISING PERFORMANCE: COMMON METHODS

The appraisal itself is generally conducted with the aid of a predetermined and formal method, like one or more of those described in this section.

Graphic Rating Scale Method

graphic rating scale   A scale that lists a number of traits and a range of performance for each. The employee is then rated by identifying the score that best describes his or her level of performance for each trait.

The **graphic rating scale** is the simplest and most popular technique for appraising performance. **Figure 10.1** shows a typical rating scale. It lists traits (such as reliability) and a range of performance values (from unsatisfactory to outstanding) for each one. The supervisor rates each employee by circling or checking the score that best describes his or her performance for each trait. The assigned values are then totalled.

Instead of appraising generic traits or factors, many firms specify the duties to be appraised. For a payroll coordinator, these might include liaison with accounting

FIGURE 10.1   One Page of a Two-Page Graphic Rating Scale with Space for Comments

Performance Appraisal

Employee Name _____   Title _____

Department _____   Employee Payroll Number _____

Reason for Review: ☐ Annual   ☐ Promotion   ☐ Unsatisfactory Performance

☐ Merit   ☐ End Probation Period   ☐ Other _____

Date employee began present position _____/_____/_____

Date of last appraisal _____/_____/_____   Scheduled appraisal date _____/_____/_____

Instructions: Carefully evaluate employee's work performance in relation to current job requirements. Check rating box to indicate the employee's performance. Indicate N if not applicable. Assign points for each rating within the scale and indicate in the corresponding points box. Points will be totalled and averaged for an overall performance score.

RATING IDENTIFICATION

O–Outstanding–Performance is exceptional in all areas and is recognizable as being far superior to others.

V–Very Good–Results clearly exceed most position requirements. Performance is of high quality and is achieved on a consistent basis.

G–Good–Competent and dependable level of performance. Meets performance standards of the job.

I–Improvement Needed–Performance is deficient in certain areas. Improvement is necessary.

U–Unsatisfactory–Results are generally unacceptable and require immediate improvement. No merit increase should be granted to individuals with this rating.

N–Not Rated–Not applicable or too soon to rate.

GENERAL FACTORS	RATING	SCALE	SUPPORTIVE DETAILS OR COMMENTS
1. **Quality–**The accuracy, thoroughness, and acceptability of work performed.	O ☐ V ☐ G ☐ I ☐ U ☐	100–90 90–80 80–70 70–60 below 60	Points ____
2. **Productivity–**The quantity and efficiency of work produced in a specified period of time.	O ☐ V ☐ G ☐ I ☐ U ☐	100–90 90–80 80–70 70–60 below 60	Points ____
3. **Job Knowledge–**The practical/technical skills and information used on the job.	O ☐ V ☐ G ☐ I ☐ U ☐	100–90 90–80 80–70 70–60 below 60	Points ____
4. **Reliability–**The extent to which an employee can be relied upon regarding task completion and follow up.	O ☐ V ☐ G ☐ I ☐ U ☐	100–90 90–80 80–70 70–60 below 60	Points ____
5. **Availability–**The extent to which an employee is punctual, observes prescribed work break/meal periods, and the overall attendance record.	O ☐ V ☐ G ☐ I ☐ U ☐	100–90 90–80 80–70 70–60 below 60	Points ____
6. **Independence–**The extent of work performed with little or no supervision.	O ☐ V ☐ G ☐ I ☐ U ☐	100–90 90–80 80–70 70–60 below 60	Points ____

and benefits staff, continual updating of knowledge regarding relevant legislation, maintenance of payroll records, data entry and payroll calculations, and ongoing response to employees' inquiries regarding payroll issues.

FIGURE 10.2 Alternation Ranking Scale

ALTERNATION RANKING SCALE

For the Trait: _____

For the trait you are measuring, list all the employees you want to rank. Put the highest-ranking employee's name on line 1. Put the lowest-ranking employee's name on line 20. Then list the next highest ranking on line 2, the next lowest ranking on line 19, and so on. Continue until all names are on the scale.

Highest-ranking employee

1. _____   11. _____
2. _____   12. _____
3. _____   13. _____
4. _____   14. _____
5. _____   15. _____
6. _____   16. _____
7. _____   17. _____
8. _____   18. _____
9. _____   19. _____
10. _____   20. _____

Lowest-ranking employee

Alternation Ranking Method

alternation ranking method
Ranking employees from best to worst on a particular trait.

Ranking employees from best to worst on a trait or traits is another method for evaluating employees. Because it is usually easier to distinguish between the worst and best employees than to rank them, an **alternation ranking method** is most popular. First, list all employees to be rated, and then cross out the names of any not known well enough to rank. Then, on a form such as that in **Figure 10.2**, indicate the employee who is the highest on the characteristic being measured and also the one who is the lowest. Then choose the next highest and the next lowest, alternating between highest and lowest until all the employees to be rated have been ranked.

Paired Comparison Method

paired comparison method
Ranking employees by making a chart of all possible pairs of employees for each trait and indicating whom the better employee of the pair is.

The **paired comparison method** helps to make the ranking method more precise. For every trait (quantity of work, quality of work, and so on), every employee is paired with and compared with every other employee.

Suppose that five employees are to be rated. In the paired comparison method, a chart is prepared, as in **Figure 10.3**, of all possible pairs of employees for each trait. Then, for each trait, indicate (with a + or −) who is the better employee of the pair. Next, the number of times that an employee is rated better is added up. In Figure 10.3, employee Maria ranked highest (has the most + marks) for "quality of work," while Art was ranked highest for "creativity."

FIGURE 10.3   Ranking Employees by the Paired Comparison Method

FOR THE TRAIT "QUALITY OF WORK"						FOR THE TRAIT "CREATIVITY"					
	Employee Rated:						Employee Rated:				
As Compared with:	A Art	B Maria	C Chuck	D Diane	E José	As Compared with:	A Art	B Maria	C Chuck	D Diane	E José
A Art		+	+	−	−	A Art		−	−	−	−
B Maria	−		−	−	−	B Maria	+		−	+	+
C Chuck	−	+		+	−	C Chuck	+	+		−	+
D Diane	+	+	−		+	D Diane	+	−	+		−
E José	+	+	+	−		E José	+	−	−	+	
	↑ Maria Ranks Highest Here						↑ Art Ranks Highest Here				

Note: "+" means "better than" and "−" means "worse than." For each chart, add up the number of + signs in each column to get the highest-ranked employee.

Forced Distribution Method

The **forced distribution method** places predetermined percentages of ratees in performance categories. For example, it may be decided to distribute employees as follows:

- 15 percent high performers
- 20 percent high-average performers
- 30 percent average performers
- 20 percent low-average performers
- 15 percent low performers

Similar to bell-curve grading at school, this means that not everyone can get an A, and that one's performance is always rated relative to that of one's peers. This method has been criticized as being demotivating for the considerable proportion of the workforce that is classified as below average.[11]

Critical Incident Method

With the **critical incident method**, the supervisor keeps a log of desirable or undesirable examples or incidents of each employee's work-related behaviour. Then, every six months or so, the supervisor and employee meet to discuss the latter's performance by using the specific incidents as examples.

This method can always be used to supplement another appraisal technique, and in that role it has several advantages. It provides specific hard facts for explaining the appraisal. It also ensures that a manager thinks about the employee's appraisal throughout the year, because the incidents must be accumulated; therefore, the rating does not just reflect the employee's most recent performance. Keeping a running list of critical incidents should also provide concrete examples of what an employee can do to eliminate any performance deficiencies.

The critical incident method can be adapted to the specific job expectations laid out for the employee at the beginning of the year. Thus, in the example presented

TABLE 10.1   Examples of Critical Incidents for an Assistant Plant Manager

Continuing Duties	Targets	Critical Incidents
Schedule production for plant	Full utilization of employees and machinery in plant; orders delivered on time	Instituted new production scheduling system; decreased late orders by 10 percent last month; increased machine utilization in plant by 20 percent last month
Supervise procurement of raw materials and inventory control	Minimize inventory costs while keeping adequate supplies on hand	Let inventory storage costs rise 15 percent last month; overordered parts "A" and "B" by 20 percent; underordered part "C" by 30 percent
Supervise machinery maintenance	No shutdowns because of faulty machinery	Instituted new preventative maintenance system for plant; prevented a machine breakdown by discovering faulty part

in **Table 10.1,** one of the assistant plant manager's continuing duties is to supervise procurement and to minimize inventory costs. The critical incident shows that the assistant plant manager let inventory storage costs rise 15 percent; this provides a specific example of what performance must be improved in the future.

The critical incident method is often used to supplement a ranking technique. It is useful for identifying specific examples of good and poor performance and for planning how deficiencies can be corrected. It is not as useful by itself for comparing employees, nor, therefore, for making salary decisions.

Narrative Forms

Some employers use narrative forms to evaluate employees. For example, the form in **Figure 10.4** presents a suggested format for identifying a performance issue and presenting a *performance improvement plan*. The performance problem is described in specific detail, and its organizational impact is specified. The improvement plan identifies measurable improvement goals, provides directions regarding training and any other suggested activities to address the performance issue, and encourages the employee to add ideas about steps to be taken to improve performance. Finally, the outcomes and consequences, both positive and negative, are explicitly stated. A summary performance appraisal discussion then focuses on problem solving.[12]

Behaviourally Anchored Rating Scales

behaviourally anchored rating scale (BARS)   An appraisal method that aims to combine the benefits of narratives, critical incidents, and quantified ratings by anchoring a quantified scale with specific narrative examples of good and poor performance.

A **behaviourally anchored rating scale (BARS)** combines the benefits of narratives, critical incidents, and quantified ratings by anchoring a series of quantified scales, one for each performance dimension, with specific behavioural examples of good or poor performance. **Figure 10.5** provides an example of a BARS for one performance dimension, namely sales skill. The proponents of BARS claim that it provides better, more equitable appraisals than do the other tools that have been discussed.[13]

FIGURE 10.4 Performance Improvement Plan

PERFORMANCE IMPROVEMENT PLAN

Employee Name: Brent Goldman   **Department:** Purchasing
Date Presented: August 8, 2007   **Supervisor:** Paul Reisman

Incident Description and Supporting Details: Include the following information: Time, Place, Date of Occurrence, and Persons Present as well as Organizational Impact.

Brent,

On August 1, you conducted a telephone conversation with Morris Kirschenbaum, a wholesaler, regarding the price of switchplates for an upcoming sale. Specifically, you told Mr. Kirschenbaum that the best bid that you currently had was $.20 each for a lot. Another wholesaler, Fred Schiller, whom we've worked with for the past two and a half years, learned of your disclosure to Mr. Kirschenbaum. Mr. Schiller later refused to honor our original bid and consequently severed our working relationship because you disclosed confidential information to a third party.

This disclosure of confidential pricing information violates policy 3.01, "Confidential Information," which states: "All sales price bids are to be strictly confidential. Release of prior sales or present bids is strictly prohibited."

Performance Improvement Plan

1. Measurable/Tangible Improvement Goals. Brent, I expect you to abide by all established policies and procedures. I also expect that you will never again display such a serious lack of judgment or discretion by sharing bid prices in advance of a sale.

2. Training or Special Direction to Be Provided: Policy 3.01 is attached. Please read this policy immediately and see me with any questions that you may have.

3. Interim Performance Evaluation Necessary? No

4. Our Employee Assistance Program (EAP) Provider, Prime Behavioral Health Group, can be confidentially reached to assist you at (800) 555-5555. This is strictly voluntary. A booklet regarding the EAP's services is available from Human Resources.

5. In addition, I recognize that you may have certain ideas to improve your performance. Therefore, I encourage you to provide your own Personal Improvement Plan Input and Suggestions:

_____

_____

_____

(Attach additional sheets if needed.)

Outcomes and Consequences

Positive: If you meet your performance goals, no further disciplinary action will be taken regarding this issue. In addition, you will help our company remain profitable by ensuring that our bids are competitive and that our relationships with our vendors remain solid.

Negative: If you ever again divulge confidential company information regarding pricing, bids, or any other protected areas of information, disciplinary action up to and including dismissal may result. A copy of this document will be placed in your personnel file.

Scheduled Review Date: None

Employee Comments and/or Rebuttal

_____

_____

_____

(Attach additional sheets if needed.)

X_____
Employee Signature

FIGURE 10.5 Behaviourally Anchored Rating Scale

SALES SKILLS

Skilfully persuading customers to purchase products; using product benefits and opportunities effectively; closing skills; adapting sales techniques appropriately to different customers; effectively overcoming objections to purchasing products.

5 — If a customer insists on a particular brand name, the salesperson perseveres. Although products with this particular brand name are not available, the salesperson does not give up; instead, the salesperson persuades the customer that his or her needs could be better met with another product.

4 — The salesperson treats objections to purchasing the product seriously; works hard to counter the objections with relevant positive arguments regarding the benefits of the product.

3 — When a customer is deciding on which product to purchase, the salesperson tries to sell the product with the highest profit magin.

2 — The salesperson insists on describing more features of the product even though the customer wants to purchase it right now.

1 — When a customer states an objection to purchasing a product, the salesperson ends the conversation, assuming that the prospect must not be interested.

Developing a BARS typically requires five steps:[14]

Tips for the Front Line

1. *Generate critical incidents.* Persons who know the job being appraised (jobholders and/or supervisors) are asked to describe specific illustrations (critical incidents) of effective and ineffective performance.

2. *Develop performance dimensions.* These people then cluster the incidents into a smaller set of performance dimensions (say, five or ten). Each cluster (dimension) is then defined.

3. *Reallocate incidents.* Another group of people who also know the job then reallocate the original critical incidents. They are given the clusters' definitions and the critical incidents, and are asked to reassign each incident to the cluster that they think it best fits. Typically, a critical incident is retained if some percentage (usually 50 percent to 80 percent) of this second group assigns it to the same cluster as did the group in Step 2.

4. *Scale the incidents.* This second group is generally asked to rate the behaviour described in the incident as to how effectively or ineffectively it represents performance on the appropriate dimension (seven- or nine-point scales are typical).

5. *Develop final instrument.* A subset of the incidents (usually six or seven per cluster) is used as behavioural anchors for each dimension.

Advantages and Disadvantages

Developing a BARS can be more time-consuming than developing other appraisal tools, such as graphic rating scales. But BARS may also have important advantages:[15]

1. *A more accurate measure*. People who know the job and its requirements better than anyone else does develop BARS. The result should therefore be a good measure of performance on that job.

2. *Clearer standards*. The critical incidents along the scale help to clarify what is meant by extremely good performance, average performance, and so forth.

3. *Feedback*. The critical incidents may be more useful in providing feedback to appraisees than simply informing them of their performance rating and not providing specific behavioural examples.

4. *Independent dimensions*. Systematically clustering the critical incidents into five or six performance dimensions (such as "knowledge and judgment") should help to make the dimensions more independent of one another. For example, a rater should be less likely to rate an employee high on all dimensions simply because he or she was rated high in "conscientiousness."

5. *Consistency*. BARS evaluations also seem to be relatively consistent and reliable in that different raters' appraisals of the same person tend to be similar.[16]

Management by Objectives (MBO)

management by objectives (MBO)
Involves setting specific measurable goals with each employee and then periodically reviewing the progress made.

Stripped to its essentials, **management by objectives (MBO)** requires the manager to set specific measurable goals with each employee and then periodically discuss his or her progress toward these goals. A manager can implement a modest MBO program by jointly setting goals with employees and periodically providing feedback. However, the term *MBO* almost always refers to a comprehensive, *organization-wide, goal setting and appraisal program* that consists of six main steps:

1. *Set the organization's goals*. Establish an organization-wide plan for next year and set goals.

2. *Set departmental goals*. Here department heads and their superiors jointly set goals for their departments.

3. *Discuss departmental goals*. Department heads discuss the department's goals with all employees in the department (often at a department-wide meeting) and ask them to develop their own individual goals; in other words, how can each employee contribute to the department's attainment of its goals?

4. *Define expected results* (set individual goals). Here, department heads and employees set short-term performance targets.

5. *Performance reviews: Measure the results*. Department heads compare the actual performance of each employee with the expected results.

6. *Provide feedback*. Department heads hold periodic performance review meetings with employees to discuss and evaluate progress in achieving expected results.

Problems to Avoid

Using MBO has three problems. *Setting unclear, unmeasurable objectives* is the main one. Such an objective as "will do a better job of training" is useless.

Conversely, "will have four employees promoted during the year" is a measurable objective. Second, MBO is *time-consuming*. Taking the time to set objectives, to measure progress, and to provide feedback can take several hours per employee per year, over and above the time already spent doing each person's appraisal. Third, setting objectives with an employee sometimes turns into a *tug of war*, with the manager pushing for higher goals and the employee pushing for lower ones. It is thus important to know the job and the person's ability. To motivate performance, the objectives must be fair and attainable.

Mixing the Methods

Most firms combine several appraisal techniques. In addition, the use of computerized approaches for all performance appraisal methods is growing rapidly, as discussed in Chapter 3. An example of a form used to appraise the performance of managers in a large airline is shown in **Figure 10.6**. Note that it is basically a graphic rating scale with descriptive phrases included to define the traits being measured, but there is also a section for comments below each trait. This lets the rater jot down several critical incidents. The quantifiable ranking method permits comparisons of employees and is therefore useful for making salary, transfer, and promotion decisions. The critical incidents provide specific examples of good and poor performance.[17]

Performance Appraisal Problems and Solutions

Few of the things a manager does are fraught with more peril than appraising employees' performance. Employees in general tend to be overly optimistic about what their ratings will be, and they also know that their raises, career progress, and peace of mind may well hinge on how they are rated. Thus, an honest appraisal inevitably involves an emotional component, which is particularly difficult when managers are not trained in appraisal interview skills. The result is often dishonest appraisals or avoidance of appraisals.[18]

Even more problematic, however, are the numerous structural problems that can cast serious doubt on just how fair the whole process is. Fortunately, research shows that action by management to implement a more acceptable performance appraisal system can increase employee trust in management.[19] According to a 2004 study of 414 organizations conducted by Sibson Consulting, WorldatWork and Synygy, almost 60 percent of organizations view their performance management systems as ineffective. The study concluded that more focus on the execution of performance appraisal is required instead of searching for new techniques and methods.[20] Some of the main appraisal problems and how to solve them, as well as several other pertinent appraisal issues, will now be reviewed.

Validity and Reliability

Appraisal systems must be based on performance criteria that are valid for the position being rated and be reliable, in that their application must produce consistent ratings for the same performance. Employee concerns about appraisal fairness are influenced by these characteristics of the performance appraisal system.

Criteria used in performance appraisal must be accurate, or valid, in order to produce useful results. Criteria must be (1) relevant to the

Performance Measurement Resources
www.zigonperf.com/performance
.htm

This food service supervisor is conducting a feedback session about an employee's performance during today's major banquet, to keep communications open and build employee commitment.

FIGURE 10.6 One Page from a Typical Management Appraisal Form

MAJOR PERFORMANCE STRENGTHS/WEAKNESSES

Read the definitions of each management factor below and choose the ranking that most accurately describes the employee. If, after reading the definition, it is determined that the skill area was not demonstrated because of the nature of the employee's position, indicate as Non-Applicable (N/A). The evaluation on each of the management factors below should relate directly to the employee's actual performance on the job.

PLANNING SKILL – Degree to which incumbent:	Ranking Code	(CHECK ONE)	
– Assessed and established priorities of result areas.	5	Far exceeds requirements	
– Designed realistic short- and long-range plans.	4	Usually exceeds requirements	
– Formulated feasible timetables.	3	Fully meets requirements	
– Anticipated possible problems and obstacles toward reaching required results.	2	Usually meets requirements	
	1	Fails to meet requirements	

Comments: _____
_____
_____
_____

ORGANIZING SKILL – Degree to which incumbent:	Ranking Code	(CHECK ONE)	
– Grouped activities for optimal use of human and material resources in order to achieve goals.	5	Far exceeds requirements	
	4	Usually exceeds requirements	
– Clearly defined responsibilities and authority limits of employees.	3	Fully meets requirements	
– Minimized confusion and inefficiencies in work operations.	2	Usually meets requirements	
	1	Fails to meet requirements	

Comments: _____
_____
_____
_____

CONTROLLING SKILL – Degree to which incumbent:	Ranking Code	(CHECK ONE)	
– Established appropriate procedures to be kept informed of employee's work progress.	5	Far exceeds requirements	
	4	Usually exceeds requirements	
– Identified deviations in work goal progress.	3	Fully meets requirements	
– Adjusted to deviations in work to ensure that established goals were met.	2	Usually meets requirements	
	1	Fails to meet requirements	

Comments: _____
_____
_____
_____

Note: This is one page from a multipage form used to appraise managers.

job being appraised, (2) broad enough to cover all aspects of the job requirements, and (3) specific. For example, including a broad criterion, such as "leadership," may not be relevant to nonmanagement jobs and may be so vague that it can be interpreted in many different ways.

Effective appraisal criteria are precise enough to result in consistent measures of performance when applied across many employees by many different raters. This is difficult to achieve without quantifiable and measurable criteria.

Rating Scale Problems

Seven main problems can undermine appraisal tools such as graphic rating scales: unclear standards, the halo effect, central tendency, leniency or strictness, appraisal bias, the recency effect, and the similar-to-me bias.

unclear performance standards An appraisal scale that is too open to interpretation of traits and standards.

The problem of **unclear performance standards** is illustrated in **Table 10.2**. Although the graphic rating scale seems objective, it would probably result in unfair appraisals because the traits and degrees of merit are open to interpretation. For example, different supervisors would probably differently define "good" performance, "fair" performance, and so on. The same is true of traits, such as "quality of work" or "creativity." There are several ways in which to rectify this problem. The best way is to develop and include descriptive phrases that define each trait, as in Figure 10.1 (page 252) There, the form specified what was meant by "outstanding," "very good," and "good" quality of work. This specificity results in appraisals that are more consistent and more easily explained.

halo effect In performance appraisal, the problem that occurs when a supervisor's rating of an employee on one trait biases the rating of that person on other traits.

The **halo effect** means that the rating of an employee on one trait (such as "gets along with others") biases the way that the person is rated on other traits (such as "reliability"). This problem often occurs with employees who are especially friendly (or unfriendly) toward the supervisor. For example, an unfriendly employee will often be rated unsatisfactory for all traits rather than just for the trait "gets along well with others." Being aware of this problem is a major step toward avoiding it. Supervisory training can also alleviate the problem.[21]

central tendency A tendency to rate all employees in the middle of the scale.

Many supervisors have a **central tendency** when filling in rating scales. For example, if the rating scale ranges from one to seven, they tend to avoid the highs (six and seven) and lows (one and two) and rate most of their employees between three and five. If a graphic rating scale is used, this central tendency could mean that all employees are simply rated "average." Such a restriction can distort the evaluations, making them less useful for promotion, salary, or counselling purposes. Ranking employees instead of using a graphic rating scale can avoid this central tendency problem, because all employees must be ranked and thus cannot all be rated average.

strictness/leniency The problem that occurs when a supervisor has a tendency to rate all employees either high or low.

Some supervisors tend to rate all of their employees consistently high (or low), just as some instructors are notoriously high graders, and others are not. Fear of interpersonal conflict is often the reason for leniency.[22] Conversely, evaluators tend to give more weight to negative attributes than to positive ones.[23] This **strictness/leniency** problem is especially serious with graphic rating scales, since supervisors are not necessarily required to avoid giving all of their employees

TABLE 10.2   A Graphic Rating Scale with Unclear Standards

	Excellent	Good	Fair	Poor
Quality of work				
Quantity of work				
Creativity				
Integrity				

Note: For example, what exactly is meant by "good," "quantity of work," and so forth?

appraisal bias   The tendency to allow individual differences, such as age, race, and sex, to affect the appraisal ratings that these employees receive.

Canadian Human Rights Commission
www.chrc-ccdp.ca

high (or low) ratings. However, when ranking employees, a manager is forced to distinguish between high and low performers. Thus, strictness/leniency is not a problem with the ranking or forced distribution approaches.

Individual differences among ratees in terms of a wide variety of characteristics, such as age, race, and sex, can affect their ratings, often quite apart from each ratee's actual performance.[24] In fact, recent research shows that less than half of performance evaluation ratings are actually related to employee performance and that most of the rating is based on idiosyncratic factors.[25] This is known as **appraisal bias**. Not only does this bias result in inaccurate feedback, but it is also illegal under human rights legislation. Although age-related bias is typically thought of as affecting older workers, one study found a negative relationship between age and performance evaluation for entry-level jobs in public accounting firms.[26] A related issue is described in the Workforce Diversity box.

Interestingly, the friendliness and likeability of an employee have been found to have little effect on that person's performance ratings.[27] However, an employee's previous performance can affect the evaluation of his or her current performance.[28] The actual error can take several forms. Sometimes the rater

Workforce Diversity

Avoiding Racial Discrimination in Performance Appraisal

Studies on employment equity consistently show that racialized persons are still largely concentrated in lower-level positions within organizations and that upward mobility continues to be a problem. This issue is reflected in the number of human rights complaints that relate to promotion and advancement.

It is therefore important for organizations to be aware of how systems for promotion and advancement may result in obstacles for career progression. As with all other decision making, the use of informal guidelines rather than written or circulated policies is likely to attract concerns, even more so if informal approaches are applied inconsistently.

Barrier: Performance appraisals and progressive performance management are an important tool to avoiding issues of discrimination. However, it is also a good idea for organizations to be aware that in some instances they can pose a barrier. For example, some performance evaluation systems have the employee rate him- or herself and then discuss the rating with the manager. This practice may impact on some racialized persons, due to past experiences of discrimination or to cultural differences in selling oneself. As well, certain appraisals can inadvertently

have an impact on an employee later seeking promotion. For example, emphasizing an employee's "ability to follow instructions" may pose a barrier to a promotion where "ability to take initiative" is being sought.

Best Practice: All employees should be measured against the same criteria. Managers should be sensitive to whether the performance appraisal methodology or the specific evaluation given could be having an unintentional adverse impact.

Barrier: The clustering or concentration of racialized persons in certain jobs or categories, such as technical positions, can result in dead-ends to advancement, particularly into management. This problem can be compounded where subjective criteria, such as "communication skills," are emphasized in assessing suitability for a promotion.

Best Practice: Persons with strong technical skills should have the same opportunity to demonstrate the skills for other jobs. If necessary, training should be made available to bridge between technical and other jobs. An organization should acknowledge that there is more than one way to perform a job successfully and that requirements like "communication skills" may result in culturally non-neutral criteria being applied.

Source: From *Racism and Racial Discrimination Policy* (Toronto: Ontario Human Rights Commission, 2006). © Queen's Printer for Ontario, 2006. Reproduced with permission.

may systematically overestimate improvement by a poor worker or decline by a good worker, for instance. In some situations—especially when the change in behaviour is more gradual—the rater may simply be insensitive to improvement or decline. In any case, it is important to rate performance objectively. Such factors as previous performance, age, or race should not be allowed to influence results.

The **recency effect** occurs when ratings are based on the employee's most recent performance, whether good or bad. To the extent that this recent performance does not exemplify the employee's average performance over the appraisal period, the appraisal is biased.

If a supervisor tends to give higher ratings to employees with whom he or she has something in common, the **similar-to-me bias** is occurring. This bias can be discriminatory if it is based on similarity in race, gender, or other prohibited grounds.

recency effect The rating error that occurs when ratings are based on the employee's most recent performance rather than on performance throughout the appraisal period.

similar-to-me bias The tendency to give higher performance ratings to employees who are perceived to be similar to the rater in some way.

How to Avoid Appraisal Problems

There are at least three ways in which to minimize the impact of appraisal problems, such as bias and central tendency. First, raters must be familiar with the problems just discussed. Understanding the problem can help to prevent it.

Second, choose the right appraisal tool. Each tool, such as the graphic rating scale or critical incident method, has its own advantages and disadvantages. For example, the ranking method avoids central tendency but can cause ill feelings when employees' performances are in fact all "high" (see **Table 10.3**).

Third, training supervisors to eliminate rating errors, such as halo, leniency, and central tendency, can help them to avoid these problems.[29] In a typical training program, raters are shown a videotape of jobs being performed and are asked

TABLE 10.3　Important Advantages and Disadvantages of Appraisal Tools

	Advantages	Disadvantages
Graphic rating scale	Simple to use; provides a quantitative rating for each employee.	Standards may be unclear; halo effect, central tendency, leniency, and bias can also be problems.
Alternation ranking	Simple to use (but not as simple as graphic rating scale). Avoids central tendency and other problems of rating scales.	Can cause disagreements among employees and may be unfair if all employees are, in fact, excellent.
Forced distribution method	End up with a predetermined number of people in each group.	Appraisal results depend on the adequacy of the original choice of cutoff points.
Critical incident method	Helps specify what is "right" and "wrong" about the employee's performance; forces supervisor to evaluate employees on an ongoing basis.	Difficult to rate or rank employees relative to one another.
Behaviourally anchored rating scale	Provides behavioural "anchors." BARS is very accurate.	Difficult to develop.
Management by objectives	Tied to jointly agreed-upon performance objectives.	Time consuming.

to rate the worker. Ratings made by each participant are then placed on a flip chart and the various errors (such as leniency and halo) are explained. For example, if a trainee rated all criteria (such as quality, quantity, and so on) about the same, the trainer might explain that a halo error had occurred. Typically, the trainer gives the correct rating and then illustrates the rating errors made by the participants.[30] According to one study, computer-assisted appraisal training improved managers' ability to conduct performance appraisal discussions with their employees.[31]

Rater training is no panacea for reducing rating errors or improving appraisal accuracy. In practice, several factors—including the extent to which pay is tied to performance ratings, union pressure, employee turnover, time constraints, and the need to justify ratings—may be more important than training. This means that improving appraisal accuracy calls not only for training but also for reducing outside factors, such as union pressure and time constraints.[32] It has also been found that employee reaction to current performance reviews is affected by past appraisal feedback, which is beyond the control of the current manager.[33]

Legal and Ethical Issues in Performance Appraisal

Ethics should be the bedrock of a performance appraisal. Accurate, well-documented performance records and performance appraisal feedback are necessary to avoid legal penalties and to defend against charges of bias based on grounds prohibited under human rights legislation, such as age, sex, and so on. As one commentator puts it:

> The overall objective of high-ethics performance reviews should be to provide an honest assessment of performance and to mutually develop a plan to improve the individual's effectiveness. That requires that we tell people where they stand and that we be straight with them.[34]

Ashland Canada Ltd., an automotive products marketing company in British Columbia, was fined $20 000 for dismissing a sales employee based on an "unacceptable" performance rating even though the employee had exceeded his sales goals. The British Columbia Supreme Court found that the performance rating was unwarranted and undeserved, and criticized Ashland's human resources department for a "reprehensible and substantial departure" from good faith dealings with the employee.[35] In another case, a worker in a government mental health facility was terminated for unsatisfactory performance after ten years of work with no performance evaluations and no disciplinary record. An adjudicator determined that the employer had failed to establish that the worker's job performance was unsatisfactory, that she had not been given a chance to improve, and that the employer did not have just cause for termination. The employer was required to pay compensation in lieu of reinstatement.[36]

Guidelines for developing an effective appraisal process include the following: [37]

Hints to Ensure Legal Compliance

1. Conduct a job analysis to ascertain characteristics (such as "timely project completion") required for successful job performance. Use this information to create job-performance standards.

2. Incorporate these characteristics into a rating instrument. (The professional literature recommends rating instruments that are tied to specific job behaviours, that is, BARS.)

3. Make sure that definitive performance standards are provided to all raters and ratees.

4. Use clearly defined individual dimensions of job performance (like "quantity" or "quality") rather than undefined, global measures of job performance (like "overall performance").

5. When using a graphic rating scale, avoid abstract trait names (such as "loyalty," "honesty") unless they can be defined in terms of observable behaviours.

6. Employ subjective supervisory ratings (essays, for instance) as only one component of the overall appraisal process.

7. Train supervisors to use the rating instrument properly. Give instructions on how to apply performance appraisal standards ("outstanding," "satisfactory," and so on) when making judgments. Ensure that subjective standards are not subject to bias.

8. Allow appraisers regular contact with the employee being evaluated.

9. Whenever possible, have more than one appraiser conduct the appraisal, and conduct all such appraisals independently. This process can help to cancel out individual errors and biases.

10. Utilize formal appeal mechanisms and a review of ratings by upper-level managers.

11. Document evaluations and reasons for any termination decision.

12. Where appropriate, provide corrective guidance to assist poor performers in improving their performance.

Who Should Do the Appraising?

Who should actually rate an employee's performance? Several options exist.

Supervisor

Supervisors' ratings are still the heart of most appraisal systems. Getting a supervisor's appraisal is relatively easy and also makes a great deal of sense. The supervisor should be—and usually is—in the best position to observe and evaluate the performance of employees reporting to him or her and is responsible for their performance.

The best performance appraisal systems are those in which the supervisor or manager makes an ongoing effort to coach and monitor employees, instead of leaving evaluation to the last minute.

Peers

The appraisal of an employee by his or her peers can be effective in predicting future management success. There is a high correlation between peer and supervisor ratings.[38] Peers have more opportunity to observe ratees and to observe them at more revealing times than supervisors do.[39] From a study of military officers, for example, we know that peer ratings were quite accurate in predicting which officers would be promoted and which would not.[40] In another study that involved more than 200 industrial managers, peer ratings were similarly useful in predicting who would be promoted.[41] One potential problem is *logrolling*; here, all the peers simply get together to rate each other highly.

With more firms using self-managing teams, peer or team appraisals are becoming more popular. One study found that peer ratings had an immediate positive impact on perceptions of open communication, motivation, group cohesion, and satisfaction, and these were not dependent on the ratio of positive to negative feedback.[42] Thus, peer appraisals would appear to have great potential for work teams.

Committees

Many employers use rating committees to evaluate employees. These committees usually comprise the employee's immediate supervisor and three or four other supervisors. Using multiple raters can be advantageous. Although there may be a discrepancy in the ratings made by individual supervisors, the composite ratings tend to be more reliable, fair, and valid.[43] Several raters can help cancel out problems like bias and the halo effect on the part of individual raters. Furthermore, when there are variations in raters' ratings, they usually stem from the fact that raters often observe different facets of an employee's performance; the appraisal ought to reflect these differences.[44] Even when a committee is not used, it is common to have the appraisal reviewed by the manager immediately above the one who makes the appraisal.

Self

Employees' self-ratings of performance are sometimes used (generally in conjunction with supervisors' ratings). Employees value the opportunity to participate in performance appraisal more for the opportunity to be heard than for the opportunity to influence the end result.[45] Nevertheless, the basic problem with self-ratings is that employees usually rate themselves higher than they are rated by supervisors or peers.[46] In one study, for example, it was found that when asked to rate their own job performance, 40 percent of the employees in jobs of all types placed themselves in the top 10 percent ("one of the best"), while virtually all remaining employees rated themselves either in the top 25 percent ("well above average") or at least in the top 50 percent ("above average"). Usually no more than 1 percent or 2 percent will place themselves in a below-average category and then almost invariably in the top below-average category. However, self-ratings have been found to correlate more highly with performance measures if employees know that this comparison will be made and if they are instructed to compare themselves with others.[47]

Supervisors requesting self-appraisals should know that their appraisals and their employees' self-appraisals may accentuate appraiser–appraisee differences, and rigidify positions.[48] Furthermore, even if self-appraisals are not formally requested, each employee will enter the performance review meeting with his or her own self-appraisal in mind, and this will usually be higher than the supervisor's rating.

Subordinates

Traditionally, supervisors feared that being appraised by their employees would undermine their management authority. However, with today's flatter organizations and empowered workers, much managerial authority is a thing of the past, and employees are in a good position to observe managerial performance.[49] Thus, more firms today are letting employees anonymously evaluate their supervisors' performance, a process many call *upward feedback*.[50] When conducted throughout the firm, the process helps top managers to diagnose management styles, identify potential "people" problems, and take corrective action with individual managers as required. Such employee ratings are especially valuable when used for developmental rather than evaluative purposes.[51] Managers who receive feedback from employees who identify themselves view the upward appraisal process more positively than do managers who receive anonymous feedback; however, employees (not surprisingly) are more comfortable giving anonymous responses and those who have to identify themselves tend to provide inflated ratings.[52] Research comparing employee and peer ratings of managers found them to be comparable.[53]

Research
Insight

How effective is upward feedback from reporting employees in terms of improving the supervisor's behaviour? Considerably effective, to judge from the research evidence. One study examined data for 92 managers who were rated by one or more reporting employees in each of four administrations of an upward feedback survey over two and a half years. The reporting employees were asked to rate themselves and their managers in surveys that consisted of 33 behavioural statements. The feedback to the managers also contained results from previous administrations of the survey so that they could track their performance over time.

According to the researchers, "managers whose initial level of performance (defined as the average rating from reporting employees) was low improved between administrations one and two, and sustained this improvement two years later." Interestingly, the results also suggest that it is not necessarily the specific feedback that caused the performance improvement, because low-performing managers seemed to improve over time even if they did not receive any feedback. Instead, learning what the critical supervisory behaviours were (as a result of themselves filling out the appraisal surveys) and knowing that they might be appraised may have been enough to result in the improved supervisory behaviours. In a sense, therefore, it is the existence of the formal upward feedback program rather than the actual feedback itself that may signal and motivate supervisors to get their behaviours in line with what they should be.[54]

360-Degree Appraisal

360-degree appraisal   A performance appraisal technique that uses multiple raters including peers, employees reporting to the appraisee, supervisors, and customers.

Many Canadian firms are now using what is called **360-degree appraisal,** or "*multisource feedback*." Here, as shown in **Figure 10.7**, performance information is collected "all around" an employee, from his or her supervisors, subordinates, peers, and internal or external customers.[55] This feedback was originally used only for training and development purposes, but it has rapidly spread to the management of performance and pay.[56] The 360-degree approach supports the activities of performance feedback, coaching, leadership development, succession planning, and rewards and recognition.[57]

There are a number of reasons for the rapid growth of the 360-degree appraisal, despite the significant investment of time required for it to function successfully. Today's flatter organizations employ a more open communicative climate conducive to such an approach, and 360-degree appraisal fits closely with the goals of organizations committed to continuous learning, as highlighted in the Strategic HR box on page 269. A multiple-rater system is also more meaningful in today's reality of complex jobs, with matrix and team reporting relationships. A 360-degree appraisal can be perceived as a jury of peers, rather than the supervisor as a single judge, which enhances perceptions of fairness.[58]

Most 360-degree appraisal systems contain several common features. They are usually applied in a confidential and anonymous manner. Appropriate parties—peers, superiors, employees, and customers, for instance—complete survey questionnaires about an individual. The questionnaires must be custom-designed and linked to the organization's strategic direction, vision, and values.[59] All this information is then compiled into individualized reports. When the information is being used for self-development purposes only, the report is presented to the person being rated, who then meets with his or her own supervisor, and information pertinent for the purpose of developing a self-improvement plan is shared. When the information is being used for management of performance or pay, the information is also provided to the ratee's supervisor, and a supportive

FIGURE 10.7 360-Degree Performance Appraisals

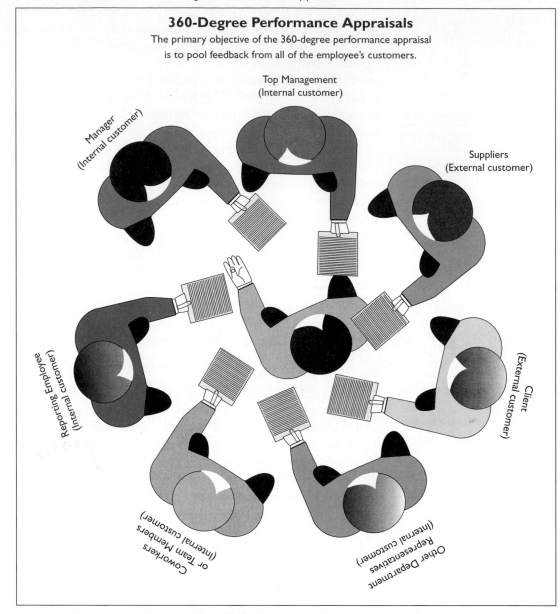

360-Degree Performance Appraisals

The primary objective of the 360-degree performance appraisal is to pool feedback from all of the employee's customers.

Top Management
(Internal customer)

Manager
(Internal customer)

Suppliers
(External customer)

Reporting Employee
(Internal customer)

Client
(External customer)

Coworkers
or Team Members
(Internal customer)

Other Department
Representatives
(Internal customer)

Source: J.F. Milliman, R.A. Zawacki, C. Norman, L. Powell, and J. Kerksey, "Companies Evaluate Employee from All Perspectives," *Personnel Journal*, November 1994, Vol. 73, No. 11, p. 100. Illustration by Tim Barker, copyright November 1994. Used with permission. All rights reserved.

and facilitative process to follow up is required to ensure that the behavioural change required for performance improvement is made.[60]

Research
Insight

There is a limited amount of research data on the effectiveness of 360-degree feedback. Some organizations have abandoned it for appraisal purposes because of negative attitudes from employees and inflated ratings.[61] Some studies have found that the different raters often disagree on performance ratings.[62] A recent study by researchers at Concordia University in Montreal found that 360-degree feedback is popular among Canadian employers, despite such problems as the amount of time and effort involved, lack of trust in the system by employees, and lack of fit with strategic goals and other HR practices. The results showed that organizations that successfully implemented 360-degree feedback were those that

Strategic HR

360-Degree Feedback at PACCAR of Canada Ltd.

The PACCAR of Canada Ltd. plant, located in Sainte-Thérèse, Quebec, is a truck assembly plant with 800 unionized production workers. The company's corporate values include mutual respect, communication, teamwork, and continuous improvement.

A few years ago, PACCAR decided to adopt a 360-degree feedback process for plant managers and coordinators, to be used strictly for development or skills improvement at the managerial level. The union was not comfortable with using this feedback for evaluative purposes.

Initially designed as an in-house feedback process, PACCAR later decided to hire industrial psychologists to manage the 360-degree feedback system. These consultants designed questions aligned with PACCAR's values, and established numerous precautions to protect the confidentiality of the evaluations. A psychologist now conducts development sessions with small groups of managers to explain their 360-degree feedback reports.

PACCAR developed an action plan for each manager to be assessed. The plan was submitted to his or her immediate superior in advance of a developmental meeting where opportunities for skills development were proposed. The superior then monitored the achievement of the action plan objectives and offered regular feedback during the year.

The 360-degree feedback process at PACCAR has been very successful. Managers were open to participating from the start because results were being used for development purposes only, not evaluative purposes. Now other employees have begun asking to be included. The process has facilitated the communication of corporate values to managers on a regular basis and has helped to align managers' behaviour and skills with these values. It has also facilitated opportunities for career management and development.

The HR department received a list of overall strengths and weaknesses attributed to the managers involved. Recently the feedback revealed that managers offered too little positive recognition to employees, and information sessions were held to assist managers in this regard.

The keys to successful 360-degree feedback to align managerial behaviour with corporate values at PACCAR have been confidentiality and anonymity; training of both assessors and the managers being evaluated; and customization of the program for PACCAR. In fact, PACCAR executives would like to implement a simplified version of 360-degree feedback with all plant employees.

Source: B. Bannille and S. St-Onge, "360-Degree Feedback at PACCAR of Canada Ltd.," from Human Resources and Social Development Canada, *Workplace Gazette* 7(2), Summer 2004, pp. 63–68. Reproduced with the permission of Her Majesty the Queen in Right of Canada 2006.

An Ethical Dilemma

Is it fair to factor in employee self-ratings in 360-degree performance appraisal, when we know that these appraisals tend to be inflated?

Tips for the Front Line

had the most clarity on what their initial objectives were. Organizations that rely exclusively on external consultants to establish 360-degree appraisal have less success than organizations that are more sensitive to contextual factors, such as the readiness of employees and the culture of the organization.[63]

Some experts suggest that 360-degree feedback be used for developmental purposes only.[64] In general, it is advisable to use 360-degree feedback for developmental/career-planning purposes initially, and then determine whether the organization is ready to use it for evaluative appraisal purposes. A pilot test in one department is often recommended. Once a decision to use 360-degree appraisal has been made, organizations should consider the following advice:[65]

- Have the performance criteria developed by a representative group that is familiar with each job.
- Be clear about who will have access to reports.
- Provide training for supervisors, raters, and ratees.
- Assure all raters that their comments will be kept anonymous.
- Plan to evaluate the 360-degree feedback system for fine-tuning.

Internet-based 360-degree feedback systems are now available, as described in Chapter 3.

STEP 3: PROVIDING FEEDBACK—THE APPRAISAL INTERVIEW

appraisal interview   An interview in which the supervisor and employee review the appraisal and make plans to remedy deficiencies and reinforce strengths.

The essence of a performance appraisal is the feedback provided in a one-on-one conversation called the **appraisal interview**. This is an interview in which the supervisor and employee review the appraisal and make plans to remedy deficiencies and reinforce strengths. A 2004 Conference Board of Canada survey found that only 40 percent of companies described their performance appraisal systems as effective or very effective. The survey results indicated that the execution of the systems is weak because managers are abdicating their responsibility for screening out poor performers.[66] This discussion is often avoided by supervisors and managers who have not been trained to provide constructive feedback and to deal with defensive employees. Ultimately, feedback should be ongoing, making the formal appraisal interview one of many performance discussions.

Types of Interviews

There are three basic types of appraisal interviews, each with its own objectives:[67]

Appraisal Interview Type	Appraisal Interview Objective
(1) Satisfactory performance— Promotable employee	(1) Make development plans
(2) Satisfactory performance— Unpromotable employee	(2) Maintain performance
(3) Unsatisfactory performance— Correctable	(3) Plan correction

If the employee's performance is unsatisfactory and the situation uncorrectable, there is usually no need for any appraisal interview because the person's performance is not correctable anyway. Either the person's poor performance is tolerated for now, or he or she is dismissed.

Satisfactory—Promotable

Here, the person's performance is satisfactory and there is a promotion ahead. This is the easiest of the three appraisal interviews. The objective is to discuss the person's career plans and to develop a specific action plan for the educational and professional development that the person needs in order to move to the next job.

Satisfactory—Not Promotable

This interview is for employees whose performance is satisfactory but for whom promotion is not possible. Perhaps there is no more room in the company. Some employees are also happy where they are and do not want a promotion.[68] The objective here is not to improve or develop the person, but to maintain satisfactory performance.

This situation is not easy. The best option is usually to find incentives that are important to the person and enough to maintain satisfactory performance. These might include extra time off, a small bonus, additional authority to handle a slightly enlarged job, and reinforcement, perhaps in the form of an occasional "Well done!"

Unsatisfactory—Correctable

When the person's performance is unsatisfactory but correctable, the interview objective is to lay out an *action plan* (as explained later) for correcting the unsatisfactory performance.

How to Prepare for the Appraisal Interview

There are three things to do in preparation for the interview.[69] First, assemble the data. Study the person's job description, compare the employee's performance to the standards, and review the files of the employee's previous appraisals. Next, prepare the employee. Give the employee at least a week's notice to review his or her own work, read over his or her job description, analyze problems he or she may be dealing with, and gather questions and comments for the interview. Finally, find a mutually agreeable time and place for the interview and allow a period long enough for the entire interview. Interviews with nonsupervisory staff should take no more than an hour. Appraising management employees often takes two or three hours. Be sure that the interview is done in a private place where there will be no interruptions.

How to Conduct the Interview

There are four things to keep in mind when conducting an appraisal interview:[70]

Tips for the Front Line

1. *Be direct and specific.* Talk in terms of objective work data. Use examples, such as absences, tardiness, quality records, inspection reports, scrap or waste, orders processed, productivity records, material used or consumed, timeliness of tasks or projects, control or reduction of costs, numbers of errors, costs compared with budgets, customers' comments, product returns, order processing time, inventory level and accuracy, accident reports, and so on.

2. *Do not get personal.* Do not say, "You are too slow in producing those reports." Instead, try to compare the person's performance with a standard ("These reports should normally be done within ten days"). Similarly, do not compare the person's performance with that of other people ("He is quicker than you are").

3. *Encourage the person to talk.* Stop and listen to what the person is saying; ask open-ended questions, such as, "What do you think we can do to improve the situation?" Use a phrase such as, "Go on," or "Tell me more." Restate the person's last point as a question, such as, "You do not think that you can get the job done?"

4. *Develop an action plan.* Do not get personal but do make sure that by the end of the interview you have (a) provided specific examples of performance that does and does not need attention or improvement, (b) made sure the person understands how you would like to see him or her improve his or her performance, (c) obtained an agreement from the person that he or she understands the reasons for your appraisal, and (d) developed an action plan that shows steps to achieving specified goals and the results you expect. Be sure you have included a timeline in your plan. **Figure 10.8** provides a good example of an action plan.

How to Handle Criticism and Defensive Employees

When criticism is required, it should be done in a manner that lets the person maintain his or her dignity and sense of worth. Specifically, criticism should be

FIGURE 10.8 Example of an Action Plan

ACTION PLAN

Date: May 18, 2007

For: John, Assistant Plant Manager

Problem: Parts inventory too high

Objective: Reduce plant parts inventory by 10% in June

Action Steps	*When*	*Expected Results*
Determine average monthly parts inventory	6/2	Establish a base from which to measure progress
Review ordering quantities and parts usage	6/15	Identify overstock items
Ship excess parts to regional warehouse and scrap obsolete parts	6/20	Clear stock space
Set new ordering quantities for all parts	6/25	Avoid future overstocking
Check records to measure where we are now	7/1	See how close we are to objective

provided constructively, in private, and immediately following poor performance. Provide examples of critical incidents and specific suggestions of what could be done and why. Finally, ensure that criticism is objective and free of any personal biases.

REQUIRED PROFESSIONAL CAPABILITIES

Contributes to an environment that fosters effective working relationships

When a person is accused of poor performance, the first reaction will often be denial. By denying the fault, the person avoids having to question his or her own competence. Others react to criticism with anger and aggression. This helps them to let off steam and postpones confronting the immediate problem until they are able to cope with it. Still others react to criticism by retreating into a shell.

Understanding and dealing with defensiveness is an important appraisal skill that requires the following:[71]

Tips for the Front Line

1. Recognize that defensive behaviour is normal.
2. Never attack a person's defences. Do not try to "explain someone" to himself or herself by saying things like, "You know the real reason you are using that excuse is that you cannot bear to be blamed for anything." Instead, try to concentrate on the act itself ("sales are down") rather than on the person ("you are not selling enough").
3. Postpone action. Sometimes it is best to do nothing at all. People frequently react to sudden threats by instinctively hiding behind their "masks." Given sufficient time, however, a more rational reaction usually takes over.
4. Recognize human limitations. Do not expect to be able to solve every problem that comes up, especially the human ones. More important, remember that a supervisor should not try to be a psychologist. Offering employees understanding is one thing; trying to deal with deep psychological problems is another matter entirely.

Ensuring That the Appraisal Interview Leads to Improved Performance

It is important to clear up performance problems by setting goals and a schedule for achieving them. However, even if you have obtained agreement from your employees about the areas for performance improvement, they may or may not be satisfied with their appraisal. In one study, researchers found that whether or not employees expressed satisfaction with their appraisal interview depended mostly on three factors: (1) not feeling threatened during the interview, (2) having an opportunity to present their ideas and feelings and to influence the course of the interview, and (3) having a helpful and constructive supervisor conduct the interview.[72]

In the end, it is not enough for employees to be satisfied with their appraisal interviews. The main objective is to get them to improve their subsequent performance. Legal experts suggest following these seven steps:

1. Let the employee know that his or her performance is unacceptable and explain your minimum expectations.
2. Ensure that your expectations are reasonable.
3. Let employees know that warnings play a significant role in the process of establishing just cause; employees must be warned and told that discharge will result if they continue to fail to meet minimum standards.
4. Ensure that you take prompt corrective measures when required; failure to do so could lead to a finding that you condoned your employee's conduct.
5. Avoid sending mixed messages, such as a warning letter together with a "satisfactory" performance review.
6. Provide the employee with a reasonable amount of time to improve performance.
7. Be prepared to provide your employees with the necessary support to facilitate improvement.[73]

How to Handle a Formal Written Warning

There will be times when an employee's performance is so poor that a formal written warning is required. Such written warnings serve two purposes: (1) they may serve to shake the employee out of his or her bad habits, and (2) they can help the manager to defend his or her rating of the employee, both to his or her boss and (if needed) to a court or human rights commission.

Written warnings should identify the standards under which the employee is judged, make it clear that the employee was aware of the standard, specify any violation of the standard, indicate that the employee has had an opportunity to correct his or her behaviour, and specify what the employee must now do to correct his or her behaviour.

Hints to Ensure Legal Compliance

THE FUTURE OF PERFORMANCE MANAGEMENT

Effective appraisals are the basis for successful performance management. Although performance appraisal is a difficult interpersonal task for managers, it cannot be eliminated.

Managers still need some way to review employees' work-related behaviour, and no one has offered any concrete alternative. Despite the difficulties involved, performance management is still the basis for fostering and managing employee skills and talents, and it can be a key component of improved organizational effectiveness. Performance management techniques in high- and low-performing organizations are essentially the same, but managers in high-performing organizations tend to conduct and implement appraisals and manage performance on a daily basis more effectively.[74]

Recent research indicates that effective performance management involves

- linking individual goals and business strategy
- showing leadership and accountability at all levels of the organization
- ensuring close ties among appraisal results, rewards, and recognition outcomes
- investing in employee development planning
- having an administratively efficient system with sufficient communication support[75]

The key success factor for effective performance appraisal that will lead to optimum employee performance is the quality of the performance appraisal dialogue between a manager and an employee.[76] Managers need to engage in training on an ongoing basis in order to ensure that they are in a position to engage in high-quality appraisal interviews.

Overall, the solution is to create more effective appraisals, as described in this chapter. Effective appraisals are essential to managing the performance required of an organization's employees in order to achieve that organization's strategic objectives.

Chapter Review

Summary

1. Performance management is a process encompassing all activities related to improving employee performance, productivity, and effectiveness. It includes goal setting, merit pay, pay for performance, training and development, career management, and disciplinary action. The foundation of performance management is the performance appraisal process. It is important to appraise performance effectively because appraisals provide the opportunity for managers to review each employee's work performance, which provides information for making promotion and salary decisions, and an opportunity to review each employee's career plans. Before the appraisal, the expected performance should be clarified so that each employee knows what he or she should be striving for. Employees need feedback regarding how they are doing; the appraisal provides an opportunity to give them that feedback on a formal basis.

2. There are a number of performance appraisal methods. Graphic rating scales are simple to use and facilitate comparison of employees, but the performance standards are often unclear, and bias can be a problem. Alternation ranking is a simple method that avoids central tendency, but it can be unfair if most employees are doing well. Paired comparison ensures that all employees are compared with each other, but it can also be unfair if most employees are performing similarly. Narrative forms provide concrete information to the employee but are time-consuming and can be subjective. The forced distribution method ensures differentiation of performance ratings but can be demotivating for employees classified as less than average. The critical incident method is very specific about the employee's strengths and weaknesses and forces the supervisor to evaluate employees on an ongoing basis, but it makes it difficult to compare employees. BARS is very accurate but is difficult and time-consuming to develop.

MBO ties performance ratings to jointly agreed-on performance objectives, but it is time-consuming to administer.

3. Appraisal problems to beware of include unclear standards, the halo effect, central tendency, leniency or strictness, appraisal bias, the recency effect, and the similar-to-me bias.

4. The use of 360-degree feedback has grown rapidly. Performance information is collected from the individual being appraised, his or her supervisor, other employees reporting to the person being appraised, and customers. This approach supports the activities of performance appraisal, coaching, leadership development, succession planning, and employee rewards and recognition.

5. There are three types of appraisal interview. When performance is unsatisfactory but correctable, the objective of the interview is to set out an action plan for correcting performance. For employees whose performance is satisfactory but for whom promotion is not possible, the objective of the interview is to maintain satisfactory performance. Finally, the satisfactory-and-promotable interview has the main objective of discussing the person's career plans and developing a specific action plan for the educational and professional development that the person needs in order to move on to the next job.

6. Although appraisals can be a difficult interpersonal task for managers, they cannot be eliminated. There is no alternative method for assessing employee performance, which is essential for talent management and improved organizational effectiveness. The key success factor is the quality of the performance appraisal dialogue between managers and employees. More training on how to effectively conduct these discussions is required.

Key Terms

alternation ranking method   (p. 253)
appraisal bias   (p. 262)
appraisal interview   (p. 270)
behaviourally anchored rating scale (BARS)   (p. 255)
central tendency   (p. 261)
critical incident method   (p. 254)
forced distribution method   (p. 254)
graphic rating scale   (p. 251)
halo effect   (p. 261)
management by objectives (MBO)   (p. 258)
paired comparison method   (p. 253)
performance management   (p. 250)
recency effect   (p. 263)
similar-to-me bias   (p. 263)
strictness/leniency   (p. 261)
360-degree appraisal   (p. 267)
unclear performance standards   (p. 261)

Review and Discussion Questions

1. Explain what is meant by the term "performance management."

2. Describe the three steps in appraising performance.

3. Explain how to ensure that the performance appraisal process is carried out ethically and without violating human rights laws.

4. Discuss the pros and cons of using different potential raters to appraise a person's performance.

5. What are the four key factors in conducting an appraisal interview?

6. Explain how to handle a defensive employee in a performance appraisal interview.

Critical Thinking Questions

1. Given the numerous problems with performance appraisal, and the negative consequences that often ensue, should performance appraisal be abolished?

2. How can the problem of inconsistency between managers who are rating workers be solved or at least diminished? Make two or more suggestions.

3. Given the difficulty with providing traditional performance standards for jobs that are quite flexible, what sort of "standards" could be developed for these flexible jobs?

4. BARS is not commonly used because it is so time-consuming to develop. How could the development steps be streamlined?

5. Do you agree with the use of forced rating scales? Why or why not?

6. How might a supervisor handle a situation in which negative appraisals in the past have caused an employee to undervalue his or her performance?

Application Exercises

Running Case: LearnInMotion.com

The Performance Appraisal

Jennifer and Pierre disagree over the importance of having performance appraisals. Pierre says it's quite clear whether any particular LearnInMotion.com employee is doing his or her job. It's obvious, for instance, if the salespeople are selling, if the Web designer is designing, if the Web surfer is surfing, and if the content management people are managing to get the customers' content up on the Web site in a timely fashion. Pierre's position, like that of many small-business managers, is that "we have 1000 higher-priority things to attend to," such as boosting sales and creating the calendar. And in any case, he says, the employees already get plenty of day-to-day feedback from him or Jennifer regarding what they're doing right and what they're doing wrong.

This informal feedback notwithstanding, Jennifer believes that a more formal appraisal approach is required. For one thing, they're approaching the end of the 90-day "introductory" period for many of these employees, and the owners need to make decisions about whether they should go or stay. And from a practical point of view, Jennifer simply believes that sitting down and providing formal, written feedback is more likely to reinforce what employees are doing right and to get them to modify things they may be doing wrong. "Maybe this is one reason we're not getting enough sales," she says. They've been debating this for about an hour. Now, they want you, their management consultant, to advise them on what to do. Here's what they want you to do for them.

Questions

1. Is Jennifer right about the need to evaluate the workers formally? Why or why not? If you think she's right, how do you explain away Pierre's arguments?

2. Develop a performance appraisal method for the salespeople, Web designer, or Web surfer. Please make sure to include any form you want the owners to use.

Case Incident

Objectives?

It was performance appraisal time again and Hans Funderburk knew that he would receive a low evaluation this time. Janet Stevens, Hans's boss, opened the appraisal interview with this comment, "The sales department had a good increase this quarter. Also, departmental expenses are down a good bit. But we have nowhere near accomplished the ambitious goals you and I set last quarter."

"I know," said Hans. "I thought we were going to make it though. We would have, too, if we had received that big Sears order and if I could have gotten us on the Internet a little earlier in the quarter."

"I agree with you, Hans," said Janet. "Do you think we were just too ambitious or do you think there was some way we could have made the Sears sale and sped up the Web page design?"

"Yes," replied Hans, "we could have gotten the Sears order this quarter. I just made a couple of concessions to Sears and their purchasing manager tells me he can issue the order next week. The delay with the Internet was my responsibility; I thought I knew what I was doing, but it was a little more complicated than I expected."

The discussion continued for about 30 minutes longer. Hans discovered that Janet was going to mark him very high in all areas despite his failure to accomplish the goals they had set.

Prior to the meeting, Janet had planned to suggest that the unattained goals for last period be set as the new goals for the coming quarter. After she and Hans had discussed matters, however, they both decided to establish new, somewhat higher goals. As he was about to leave the meeting, Hans said, "Janet, I feel good about these objectives, but I don't believe we have more than a 50 percent chance of accomplishing them."

"I believe you can do it," replied Janet. "If you knew for sure, though, the goals wouldn't be high enough."

"I see what you mean," said Hans, as he left the office.

Questions

1. What was wrong or right with Janet's appraisal of Hans's performance?

2. Should the new objectives be higher or lower than they are? Explain

Source: R.W. Mondy, R.M. Noe, S.R. Premeaux, and R.A. Knowles, *Human Resource Management*, Second Canadian Edition. Toronto, ON: Pearson Education Canada, 2001, p. 254. Reprinted with permission of Pearson Education Canada.

Experiential Exercises

1. Working individually or in groups, develop a graphic rating scale for a retail sales associate and a fast-food restaurant manager.

2. Working individually or in groups, develop, over a week, a set of critical incidents covering the classroom performance of one of your instructors.

CHAPTER 11

ESTABLISHING STRATEGIC PAY PLANS

REQUIRED PROFESSIONAL CAPABILITIES

- Performs a cost-benefit analysis of organizational and employee needs and preferences, including taxation consideration, legislative requirements, and funding requirements

- Establishes payroll guidelines based on relevant legislation, tax laws, company policy, and contractual pay requirements

- Ensures accurate and timely delivery of pay

- Determines the appropriateness of releasing confidential pay information

- Monitors the competitiveness of the compensation program relative to comparable organizations

- Ensures pay records are accurate and complete

LEARNING OUTCOMES
AFTER STUDYING THIS CHAPTER, YOU SHOULD BE ABLE TO

Explain the strategic importance of total rewards.

Explain in detail each of the five basic steps in establishing pay rates.

Discuss competency-based pay.

Describe the five basic elements of compensation for managers.

Define pay equity, and **explain** its importance today.

THE STRATEGIC IMPORTANCE OF TOTAL REWARDS

total rewards   An integrated package of all rewards (monetary and nonmonetary, extrinsic and intrinsic) gained by employees arising from their employment.

Compensation and rewards management is extremely important to every employee. **Total rewards** refers to an integrated package of all rewards (monetary and nonmonetary, extrinsic and intrinsic) gained by employees arising from their employment. Total rewards encompasses everything that employees value in the employment relationship.[1]

The total rewards approach, as opposed to the previous approach of managing different elements of compensation in isolation, has arisen from the changing business environment of the last several decades. The economies of developed nations, such as Canada, have evolved from a largely industrialized base to become far more virtual, knowledge-based, and service-based, where employees are increasingly regarded as drivers of productivity. A total rewards approach considers individual reward components as part of an integrated whole in order to determine the best mix of rewards that are aligned with business strategy and provide employee value, all within the cost constraints of the organization. Alignment is the extent to which rewards support outcomes that are important to achieving the organization's strategic objectives. For example, when competitive advantage relies on relentless customer service, this behaviour should be reinforced. Employee value is created when rewards are meaningful to employees and influence their affiliation with the organization.[2]

Originally, total rewards were conceptualized as having three broad categories: compensation, benefits, and work experience. Recently, research conducted by WorldatWork has clarified the work experience category by splitting it into three parts—work/life programs, performance and recognition, and development and career opportunities—resulting in five categories of total rewards, as shown in **Figure 11.1**.

FIGURE 11.1 The Total Rewards Model

Source: Total Rewards: WorldatWork Introduces a New View 2006. Reprinted with permission of WorldatWork, Scottsdale, AZ. www.worldatwork.org.

The Five Components of Total Rewards

1. *Compensation.* This category includes direct financial payments in the form of wages, salaries, incentives, commissions, and bonuses. Wages and salaries are discussed in this chapter and other direct financial payments are discussed in Chapter 12.

2. *Benefits.* This category includes indirect payments in the form of financial benefits, like employer-paid insurance and vacations. It also includes employee services, as discussed in Chapter 13.

3. *Work/life programs.* This category of rewards relates to programs that help employees do their jobs effectively, such as flexible scheduling, telecommuting, childcare, and so on. These programs are discussed in Chapter 4 and Chapter 13.

4. *Performance and recognition.* This category includes pay-for-performance and recognition programs. These programs are discussed in Chapter 12.

5. *Development and career opportunities.* This category of reward focuses on planning for the advancement and/or change in responsibilities to best suit individual skills, talents, and desires. Tuition assistance, professional development, sabbaticals, coaching and mentoring opportunities, succession planning, and apprenticeships are all examples of career-enhancing programs.

Different types of rewards appeal to employees at different stages of their lives, as discussed in the Workforce Diversity box.

Workforce Diversity

Rewards for Generation Y

Jean-Phillippe Naud, an organizational psychologist with AON Consulting in Montreal, says "Generation Y is a big talent pool organizations will have to attract if they want to be successful and want to compete." Pensions and benefits aren't generally on their radar screens.

"Under age 30, they're looking for a competitive base salary, great work environment, and good opportunities to learn and grow. And that's about it," says Jim Murta, a principal with Towers Perrin in Calgary. "You wouldn't have anyone doing an awful lot of comparison between what they might get in benefits at one place versus what they might get at another place."

Elaine Noel-Bentley agrees. She's Senior Director, Total Compensation with Petro-Canada in Calgary. The company has 4700 employees worldwide, the majority of whom are in Canada. It conducts annual recruitment drives at some Canadian universities. New graduates, she says, just aren't that interested in pensions and benefits.

"We don't do anything around benefits to attract new grads," she says. "We have to have a competitive package but, after that, pensions and benefits aren't the primary factor for taking on a job or not."

So what is this generation looking for when it comes to the working world? Generally, it looks for interesting work, ethical organizations, and flexibility. "New grads are very interested in not only competitive compensation packages but also the nature of the work, and that it's a reputable organization with appropriate practices," says Noel-Bentley. "So we have to make sure we document who we are, what we are, what we do, and how we do it."

Work/life balance also appears to be more important to younger workers. "You get a lot in that 18 to 29 age group who are willing to work very hard while they're at work, but they also want time away from work," says Murta. "You can have someone quite willing to put in a 50-hour work week, but they want four weeks of vacation."

Source: Adapted from A. Davis, "How to DEAL," *Benefits Canada*, October 2005, pp. 39–41. Reprinted with permission of *Benefits Canada* Magazine and the author.

Impact of Rewards

Towers Perrin
www.towersperrin.com

The purposes of rewards are to attract, retain, and motivate/engage employees. *Engagement* refers to a positive emotional connection to the employer and a clear understanding of the strategic significance of the job, which results in discretionary effort on the part of the employee. The *2005 Global Workforce Study* by Towers Perrin consultants found that, for Canadians, competitive base pay was the number one factor in attracting employees to an organization; belief that the organization cares about talent management by retaining high-calibre people and providing opportunities to learn and develop new skills was the most important factor in retaining employees; and senior management's interest in employee well-being, improvement of personal skills and capabilities, and the reputation of the organization as a good employer were the top factors influencing employee engagement. The results also showed that employees do not have favourable perceptions regarding what their employers are doing with respect to providing competitive base salaries (30 percent favourable) and retaining high-calibre people (34 percent favourable), or their interest in employee well-being (39 percent favourable).[3]

Pay and benefits are transactional rewards and are often relatively consistent across competing organizations. However, relational work experiences, such as work/life programs, performance and recognition, and development and career opportunities, can differ dramatically and can be difficult for competitors to duplicate.[4] Midwest Surveys of Calgary is one company that uses both transactional and relational rewards to compete for labour in the Alberta market, as discussed in the Strategic HR box.

Strategic HR

Total Rewards Becoming More Critical

Brent Gordon, Manager of HR for Midwest Surveys Inc. (a Calgary-based oil and gas surveyor with 425 employees that was recently named one of the top 50 employers in Canada), says organizations would be foolhardy to ignore the concept of total rewards.

Alberta is feeling the labour shortage more than any other part of the country, and companies need to brand themselves as an "employer of choice" to stay competitive, he says. And they can't lose sight of the fact that compensation itself is just one small piece of the total rewards puzzle. The less tangible aspects of total rewards are just as important and need to be communicated, he said.

"Trust, honesty, input, appreciation, and recognition are equally valuable, assuming employees are aware they're being fairly compensated," said Gordon. And

employers need to get a grasp on what drives their workers and build programs to meet those needs.

"There are definitely generational differences," he said. "You've got to make sure everyone is able to pick up on what's important to them. Maybe for the Generation Yer, money is the driver. Maybe for boomers it's not the money but the challenge of the work. You need to look at the whole picture."

Gordon says his HR department usually tries to highlight certain benefits at different times of the year. For example, after the holidays it puts the spotlight on the employee assistance plan: "After Christmas, people might be short on the financial end and things are tight at home, so that might be kind of a downer," he said. "So it's just a reminder that we have a program available for people who have issues financially, relationship issues, or whatever."

Source: Adapted from T. Humber, "Total Rewards Becoming More Critical," *Canadian HR Reporter*, January 30, 2006, pp. 22–23. Reproduced by permission of *Canadian HR Reporter*, Carswell, One Corporate Plaza, 2075 Kennedy Road, Scarborough, ON M1T 3V4.

BASIC CONSIDERATIONS IN DETERMINING PAY RATES

Four basic considerations influence the formulation of any pay plan: legal requirements, union issues, compensation policy, and equity.

Legal Considerations in Compensation

A number of laws affect compensation in Canada. These laws vary among the provinces and territories, and similar laws at the federal level cover employees in interprovincial operations (including highway, rail, and air transportation; pipelines; telecommunications; banking; federal Crown corporations; and others). Federal government employees are covered under yet another law (the Public Service Staff Relations Act). Thus, HR managers must pay careful attention to which legislation affects their employees. Further, these laws are constantly changing and require continual monitoring to ensure compliance. Legislation affecting compensation administration is discussed below.

Employment/Labour Standards Acts (Canada Labour Code)

Labour Code laws set minimum standards regarding pay, including minimum wage, maximum hours of work, overtime pay, paid vacation, paid statutory holidays, termination pay, record keeping of pay information, and more. There are variations in some of the minimum standards for students, trainees, domestics, nannies, seasonal agricultural workers, and others. Executive, administrative, and professional employees are generally exempt from the overtime pay requirements.

Pay Equity Acts

Pay equity legislation has been enacted in all Canadian jurisdictions other than the Northwest Territories and Nunavut. These laws apply to public-sector employees only, except in Ontario, Quebec, British Columbia, and the federal jurisdiction, where the laws cover employees in both the public and the private sectors. Pay equity laws were enacted to redress the historical undervaluation of "women's work" by providing equal pay for work of equal (or comparable) value performed by men and women. Employers are required to identify male- and female-dominated jobs, and then use a gender-neutral job evaluation system based on specific compensable factors (such as skill, effort, responsibility, and working conditions) to evaluate the jobs. Pay for female-dominated jobs that are equivalent in value to male-dominated jobs must be increased to the pay level of the comparable male-dominated job.

Human Rights Acts

All jurisdictions have enacted human rights laws to protect Canadians from discrimination on a number of grounds in employment and other areas. These grounds differ somewhat among jurisdictions, but most prohibit discrimination on the basis of age, sex, colour, race/ancestry/place of origin, religion/creed, marital/family status, and physical or mental disability.

Canada/Quebec Pension Plan

All employees and their employers must contribute to the Canada/Quebec Pension Plan throughout the employee's working life. Pension benefits based on the employee's average earnings are paid during retirement. Details of these and other benefits are provided in Chapter 13.

Association of Workers'
Compensation Boards of Canada
www.awcbc.org

Other Legislation Affecting Compensation

Each province and territory, as well as the federal government, has its own *workers' compensation laws*. The objective of these laws is to provide a prompt, sure, and reasonable income to victims of work-related accidents and illnesses. The *Employment Insurance Act* is aimed at protecting Canadian workers from total economic destitution in the event of employment termination that is beyond their control. Employers and employees both contribute to the benefits provided by this act. This act also provides up to 45 weeks of compensation for workers unemployed through no fault of their own (depending on the unemployment rate in the claimant's region and other factors). Maternity leave, parental leave, and compassionate care leave benefits are also provided under the Employment Insurance Act.[5]

Union Influences on Compensation Decisions

Unions and labour relations laws also influence how pay plans are designed. Historically, wage rates have been the main issue in collective bargaining. However, other issues—including time off with pay, income security (for those in industries with periodic layoffs), cost-of-living adjustments, and pensions—are also important.[6]

The Canada Labour Relations Board and similar bodies in each province and territory oversee employer practices and ensure that employees are treated in accordance with their legal rights. Their decisions underscore the need to involve union officials in developing the compensation package.

Union Attitudes toward Compensation Decisions

Several classic studies shed light on union attitudes toward compensation plans and on commonly held union fears.[7] Many union leaders fear that any system (like a time and motion study) used to evaluate the worth of a job can become a tool for management malpractice. They tend to believe that no one can judge the relative value of jobs better than the workers themselves. In addition, they believe that management's usual method of using several compensable factors

Work stoppages may reflect employee dissatisfaction with pay plans and other forms of compensation, such as benefits.

(like "degree of responsibility") to evaluate and rank the worth of jobs can be a manipulative device for restricting or lowering the pay of workers. One implication seems to be that the best way in which to gain the cooperation of union members in evaluating the worth of jobs is to get their active involvement in this process and in assigning fair rates of pay to these jobs. However, management has to ensure that its prerogatives—such as the right to use the appropriate job evaluation technique to assess the relative worth of jobs—are not surrendered.

Compensation Policies

REQUIRED PROFESSIONAL CAPABILITIES

Establishes payroll guidelines based on relevant legislation, tax laws, company policy, and contractual pay requirements

An employer's compensation policies provide important compensation guidelines regarding the wages and benefits that it pays. One consideration is whether the organization wants to be a leader or a follower regarding pay. Other important policies include the basis for salary increases, promotion and demotion policies, overtime pay policy, and policies regarding probationary pay and leaves for military service, jury duty, and holidays. Compensation policies are usually written by the HR or compensation manager in conjunction with senior management.[8]

Equity and Its Impact on Pay Rates

REQUIRED PROFESSIONAL CAPABILITIES

Ensures accurate and timely delivery of pay

A crucial factor in determining pay rates is the need for equity, specifically *external equity* and *internal equity*. Research has indicated that employee perceptions of fairness are one of the three key conditions for effective reward programs.[9] Externally, pay must compare favourably with rates in other organizations or an employer will find it hard to attract and retain qualified employees. Pay rates must also be equitable internally: each employee should view his or her pay as equitable given other pay rates in the organization.

ESTABLISHING PAY RATES

In practice, the process of establishing pay rates, while ensuring external and internal equity, requires five steps:

1. Determine the worth of each job within the organization through job evaluation (to ensure internal equity).
2. Group similar jobs into pay grades.
3. Conduct a wage/salary survey of what other employers are paying for comparable jobs (to help ensure external equity).
4. Price each pay grade by using wage curves.
5. Fine-tune pay rates.

Each of these steps will now be explained in turn.

Step 1: Determine the Worth of Each Job through Job Evaluation

job evaluation A systematic comparison to determine the relative worth of jobs within a firm.

Job evaluation is aimed at determining a job's relative worth. It is a formal and systematic comparison of jobs within a firm to determine the worth of one job relative to another, and it eventually results in a job hierarchy. The basic procedure is to compare the content of jobs in relation to one another, for example in terms of their effort, responsibility, skills, and working conditions. Once the compensation

benchmark job A job that is critical to the firm's operations or commonly found in other organizations that is used to anchor the employer's pay scale and that acts as a reference point around which other jobs are arranged in order of relative worth.

compensable factor A fundamental, compensable element of a job, such as skill, effort, responsibility, and working conditions.

specialist knows (based on salary survey data and compensation policies) how to price key **benchmark jobs**, and can use job evaluation to determine the worth of all the other jobs in the firm relative to these key jobs, he or she is well on the way to being able to pay all jobs in the organization equitably.

Compensable Factors

Two basic approaches are used for comparing jobs. The first is an intuitive approach. It might be decided that one job is "more important" or "of greater value or worth" than another without digging any deeper into why in terms of specific job-related factors.

As an alternative, jobs can be compared by focusing on certain basic factors that they have in common. In compensation management, these basic factors are called **compensable factors**. They are the factors that determine the definition of job content, establish how the jobs compare with one another, and set the compensation paid for each job.

Some employers develop their own compensable factors. However, most use factors that have been popularized by packaged job evaluation systems or by legislation. For example, most of the pay equity acts in Canada focus on four compensable factors: *skill, effort, responsibility,* and *working conditions.* As another example, the job evaluation method popularized by the Hay Group consulting firm focuses on four compensable factors: *know-how, problem solving, accountability,* and *working conditions.* Often, different job evaluation systems are used for different departments, employee groups, or business units.

Identifying compensable factors plays a pivotal role in job evaluation. All jobs in each employee group, department, or business unit are evaluated *using the same compensable factors.* An employer thus evaluates the same elemental components for each job within the work group and is then better able to compare jobs—for example, in terms of the degree of skill, effort, responsibility, and working conditions present in each.[10]

Preparation for Job Evaluation

Job evaluation is largely a judgmental process and one that demands close cooperation among supervisors, compensation specialists, and the employees and their union representatives. The main steps involved include identifying the need for the program, getting cooperation, and choosing an evaluation committee; the committee then carries out the actual job evaluation.[11] *Identifying the need for job evaluation* should not be difficult. Employee dissatisfaction with the inequities of paying employees different rates for similar jobs may be reflected in high turnover, work stoppages, or arguments.[12] Managers may express uneasiness about an existing informal way of assigning pay rates to jobs, accurately sensing that a more systematic means of assigning pay rates would be more equitable and make it easier to justify compensation practices.

Next, since employees may fear that a systematic evaluation of their jobs may actually reduce their wage rates, *getting employee cooperation* for the evaluation is a second important step. Employees can be told that as a result of the impending job evaluation program, wage rate decisions will no longer be made just by management whim: job evaluation will provide a mechanism for considering the complaints that they have been expressing, and no present employee's rate will be adversely affected as a result of the job evaluation.[13]

The next step is *choosing a job evaluation committee.* There are two reasons for doing so. First, the committee should bring to bear the points of view of several people who are familiar with the jobs in question, each of whom may have a different perspective regarding the nature of the jobs. Second, assuming that the committee includes at least some employees, the committee approach can help to ensure greater employee acceptance of the job evaluation results.

The group usually consists of about five members, most of whom are employees. The presence of managers can be viewed with suspicion by employees, but an HR specialist can usually be justified on the grounds that he or she has a more impartial image than other managers do and can provide expert assistance in the job evaluation. The HR specialist may serve in a nonvoting capacity. Union representation is also desirable and may be required by pay equity legislature. In some cases, the union's position is that it is accepting job evaluation only as an initial decision technique and is reserving the right to appeal the final pay decisions through grievance or bargaining channels.

The evaluation committee performs three main functions. First, the members usually identify 10 or 15 key benchmark jobs. These will be the first jobs to be evaluated and will serve as the anchors or benchmarks against which the relative importance or value of all other jobs can be compared. Next, the committee may select compensable factors (although the human resources department will usually choose these as part of the process of determining the specific job evaluation technique to be used). Finally, the committee turns to its most important function—actually evaluating the worth of each job. For this, the committee will probably use one of the following job evaluation methods: the ranking method, the job classification method, the point method, or the factor comparison method.

Ranking Method of Job Evaluation

The simplest job evaluation method ranks each job relative to all other jobs, usually based on some overall factor like "job difficulty." The job **ranking method** has several steps:

1. *Obtain job information.* Job analysis is the first step. Job descriptions for each job are prepared, and these are usually the basis on which the rankings are made.

2. *Group the jobs to be rated.* It is often not practical to make a single ranking of all jobs in an organization. The more usual procedure is to rank jobs by department or in "clusters" (such as factory or clerical workers). This eliminates the need for having to compare directly, say, factory jobs and clerical jobs.

3. *Select compensable factors.* In the ranking method, it is common to use just one factor (such as job difficulty) and to rank jobs on the basis of the whole job. Regardless of the number of factors chosen, it is advisable to explain the definition of the factor(s) to the evaluators carefully so that they evaluate the jobs consistently.

4. *Rank jobs.* Next the jobs are ranked. The simplest way is to give each rater a set of index cards, each of which contains a brief description of a job. These cards are then ranked from lowest to highest. Some managers use an "alternation ranking method" for making the procedure more accurate. Here, the committee members arrange the cards by first choosing the highest and the lowest, then the next highest and next lowest, and so forth until all of the cards have been ranked. A job ranking is illustrated in **Table 11.1**. Jobs in this small health facility are ranked from cleaner up to director of operations. The corresponding pay scales are shown on the right.

5. *Combine ratings.* It is usual for several raters to rank the jobs independently. Then the rating committee (or employer) can simply average the rankings.

ranking method The simplest method of job evaluation, which involves ranking each job relative to all other jobs, usually based on overall difficulty.

TABLE 11.1   Job Ranking by Olympia Health Care

Ranking Order	Annual Pay Scale
1. Director of operations	$60 000
2. Head nurse	54 000
3. Accountant	50 000
4. Nurse	40 000
5. Cook	26 000
6. Nurse's aide	24 000
7. Cleaner	20 000

After ranking, it becomes possible to slot additional jobs between those already ranked and to assign an appropriate wage rate.

This job evaluation method is the simplest, as well as the easiest to explain, and it usually takes less time to accomplish than other methods. Some of its drawbacks derive more from how it is used than from the method itself. For example, there is a tendency to rely too heavily on "guesstimates." Similarly, ranking provides no yardstick for measuring the value of one job relative to another. For example, the highest-ranked job may in fact be five times "more valuable" than the second highest-ranked job, but with the ranking system one only knows that one job ranks higher than the other. Ranking is often used by small organizations that are unable to afford the time or expense of developing a more elaborate system.

Another potential drawback relates to legal compliance requirements. The "whole job" approach to ranking, just described, cannot be used by employers covered by pay equity legislation. Instead, separate rankings must be completed for each of four compensable factors (skill, effort, responsibility, and working conditions) and judgment must be used to combine the results. Furthermore, pay equity legislation requires that jobs be ranked across clusters or departments, not separately.

Classification (or Grading) Evaluation Method

The **classification (or grading) method** is a simple, widely used method in which jobs are categorized into groups. The groups are called **classes** if they contain similar jobs or **grades** if they contain jobs that are similar in difficulty but otherwise different.

The federal government's UT (University Teaching) job group is an example of a job class because it contains similar jobs involving teaching, research, and consulting. Conversely, the AV (Audit, Commerce, and Purchasing) job group is an example of a job grade because it contains dissimilar jobs, involving auditing, economic development consulting, and purchasing.

There are several ways in which to categorize jobs. One is to draw up class descriptions (similar to job descriptions) and place jobs into classes based on their correspondence to these descriptions. Another is to draw up a set of classifying rules for each class (for instance, the amount of independent judgment, skill, physical effort, and so on, that the class of jobs requires). Then the jobs are categorized according to these rules.

The usual procedure is to choose compensable factors and then develop class or grade descriptions that describe each class in terms of amount or level of compensable factor(s) in jobs. The federal government's classification system, for example, employs different compensable factors for various job groups.

Hints to Ensure Legal Compliance

classification (or grading) method A method for categorizing jobs into groups.

classes Groups of jobs based on a set of rules for each class, such as amount of independent judgment, skill, physical effort, and so forth. Classes usually contain similar jobs—such as all secretaries.

grades Groups of jobs based on a set of rules for each grade, where jobs are similar in difficulty but otherwise different. Grades often contain dissimilar jobs, such as secretaries, mechanics, and firefighters.

grade/group description A written description of the level of compensable factors required by jobs in each grade. Used to combine similar jobs into grades or classes.

point method The job evaluation method in which a number of compensable factors are identified, the degree to which each of these factors is present in the job is determined, and an overall point value is calculated.

Based on these compensable factors, a **grade/group description** (like that in **Figure 11.2**) is written. Then, the evaluation committee reviews all job descriptions and slots each job into its appropriate class or grade.

The job classification method has several advantages. The main one is that most employers usually end up classifying jobs anyway, regardless of the job evaluation method that they use. They do this to avoid having to work with and price an unmanageable number of jobs; with the job classification method, all jobs are already grouped into several classes. The disadvantages are that it is difficult to write the class or grade descriptions and that considerable judgment is required in applying them. Yet many employers (including the Canadian government) use this method with success.

Point Method of Job Evaluation

The **point method** (also known as the point factor method) is widely used. It requires identifying several compensable factors, each with several degrees. A

FIGURE 11.2 Example of Group Definition in the Federal Government

Correctional Services (CX) Group Definition

The Correctional Services Group comprises positions that are primarily involved in the custody, control and correctional influence of inmates in the institutions of Correctional Service Canada and the training of staff engaged in custodial and correctional work at a Staff College of Correctional Service Canada.

Inclusions

Notwithstanding the generality of the foregoing, for greater certainty, it includes positions that have as their primary purpose, responsibility for one or more of the following activities:

1. the custody and control of inmates and the security of the institution;
2. the correctional influence of inmates with the continuing responsibility to relate actively and effectively to inmates;
3. the admission and discharge of inmates, and the control of inmate visits and correspondence;
4. the organization and implementation of recreational activities, the surveillance and control of inmates engaged in these activities and the custody and issue of recreational equipment;
5. the leadership of any of the above activities.

Exclusions

Positions excluded from the Correctional Services Group are those whose primary purpose is included in the definition of any other group or those in which one or more of the following activities is of primary importance:

1. the operation of heating plant, sewage facilities and water supplies and the provision of maintenance services;
2. the provision of patient care that requires the application of a comprehensive knowledge of or specialized expertise in physical and mental health care;
3. the provision of services and supplies to inmates; and
4. the instruction of inmates in workshops, crafts and training programs.

Source: Correctional Services (CX) Classification Standard, www.hrma-agrh.gc.ca/classification/tools/maps/mapsothergroup/ex_e.asp. Reproduced courtesy of Public Service Human Resources Management Agency of Canada, and with permission of the Minister of Public Works and Government Services Canada, 2007.

different number of points is then assigned for each degree of each factor. Next the extent/degree to which each factor is present in the job is evaluated. Once the degree to which each factor is present in the job is determined, all that remains is to add up the corresponding number of points for each factor and arrive at an overall point value for the job. Here are the steps:

1. *Determine clusters of jobs to be evaluated.* Because jobs vary widely by department, the same point-rating plan is not usually used for all jobs in the organization. Therefore, the first step is usually to cluster jobs, for example, into shop jobs, non-union jobs, and so forth. Then, the committee will generally develop a point plan for one group or cluster at a time.

2. *Collect job information.* Perform a job analysis and write job descriptions and job specifications.

3. *Select and define compensable factors.* Select compensable factors, like mental requirements, physical requirements, or skill. Each compensable factor must be carefully defined to ensure that the evaluation committee members will apply the factors with consistency. Examples of definitions are presented in **Figure 11.3**. The definitions are often drawn up or obtained by a human resources specialist.

FIGURE 11.3 Sample Definitions of Three Factors Used in Factor Comparison Method

1. Mental Requirements

Either the possession of and/or the active application of the following:

A. (inherent) Mental traits, such as intelligence, memory, reasoning, facility in verbal expression, ability to get along with people, and imagination.

B. (acquired) General education, such as grammar and arithmetic; or general information as to sports, world events, etc.

C. (acquired) Specialized knowledge such as chemistry, engineering, accounting, advertising, etc.

2. Skill

A. (acquired) Facility in muscular coordination, as in operating machines, repetitive movements, careful coordinations, dexterity, assembling, sorting, etc.

B. (acquired) Specific job knowledge necessary to the muscular coordination only; acquired by performance of the work and not to be confused with general education or specialized knowledge. It is very largely training in the interpretation of sensory impressions.

Examples

1. In operating an adding machine, the knowledge of *which* key to depress for a subtotal would be skill.

2. In automobile repair, the ability to determine the significance of a certain knock in the motor would be skill.

3. In hand-firing a boiler, the ability to determine from the appearance of the firebed how coal should be shoveled over the surface would be skill.

3. Physical Requirements

A. Physical effort, such as sitting, standing, walking, climbing, pulling, lifting, etc.; both the amount exercised and the degree of the continuity should be taken into account.

B. Physical status, such as age, height, weight, sex, strength, and eyesight.

Source: Jay L. Otis and Richard H. Leukart, *Job Evaluation: A Basis for Sound Wage Administration*, p. 181. © 1954, revised 1983. Reprinted by permission of Prentice Hall, Upper Saddle River, NJ.

4. *Define factor degrees.* Next, definitions of several degrees for each factor are prepared so that raters can judge the amount or degree of a factor existing in a job. Thus, the factor "complexity" might have six degrees, ranging from "job is repetitive" through "requires initiative." (Definitions for each degree are shown in Figure 11.3.) The number of degrees usually does not exceed five or six, and the actual number depends mostly on judgment. Thus, if all employees work either in a quiet, air-conditioned office or in a noisy, hot factory, then two degrees would probably suffice for the factor "working conditions." It is not necessary to have the same number of degrees for each factor, and degrees should be limited to the number necessary to distinguish among jobs.

5. *Determine factor weights.* The next step is to decide how much weight (or how many total points) to assign to each factor. This is important because, for each cluster of jobs, some factors are bound to be more important than others. Thus, for executives, the "mental requirements" factor would carry far more weight than would the "physical requirements." The opposite might be true of factory jobs.

   The relative values or weights to be assigned to each of the factors can now be determined. Assigning factor weights is generally done by the evaluation committee. The committee members carefully study factor and degree definitions and then determine the relative value of the factors for the cluster of jobs under consideration. For example,

Skill	30 percent
Effort	30 percent
Responsibility	30 percent
Working Conditions	10 percent
	100 percent

6. *Assign point values to factors and degrees.* Now, points are assigned to each factor, as in **Table 11.2**. For example, suppose that it is decided to use a total number of 500 points in the point plan. Then, since the factor "skill" had a weight of 30 percent, it would be assigned a total of 30 percent of 500 = 150 points.

   Thus, it was decided to assign 150 points to the skill factor. This automatically means that the highest degree for the skill factor would also carry 150 points. Then, points are assigned to the other degrees for this factor, in equal amounts from the lowest to the highest degree. This step is repeated for each factor (as in Table 11.2).

7. *Write the job evaluation manual.* Developing a point plan like this usually culminates in a job evaluation manual. This simply consolidates the factor and degree definitions and point values into one convenient manual.

TABLE 11.2   Evaluation Points Assigned to Factors and Degrees

Factor	First-Degree Points	Second-Degree Points	Third-Degree Points	Fourth-Degree Points	Fifth-Degree Points
Skill	30	60	90	120	150
Effort	30	60	90	120	150
Responsibility	30	60	90	120	150
Working conditions	10	20	30	40	50

8. *Rate the jobs.* Once the manual is complete, the actual evaluations can begin. Raters (usually the committee) use the manual to evaluate jobs. Each job, based on its job description and job specification, is evaluated factor by factor to determine the number of points that should be assigned to it. First, committee members determine the degree (first degree, second degree, and so on) to which each factor is present in the job. Then, they note the corresponding points (see Table 11.2) that were previously assigned to each of these degrees (in Step 6 above). Finally, they add up the points for all factors, arriving at a total point value for the job. Raters generally start by rating key jobs and obtaining consensus on these, and then they rate the rest of the jobs in the cluster.

Point systems have their advantages, as their wide use suggests. They involve a quantitative technique that is easily explained to and used by employees. However, it can be difficult and time-consuming to develop a point plan and to effectively train the job evaluation user group. This is one reason that many organizations opt for a plan developed and marketed by a consulting firm. In fact, the availability of a number of ready-made plans probably accounts in part for the wide use of point plans in job evaluation.

Factor Comparison Job Evaluation Method

factor comparison method A method of ranking jobs according to a variety of skill and difficulty factors, adding these rankings to arrive at an overall numerical rating for each given job, and then incorporating wage rates.

The **factor comparison method** is the most complex job evaluation method. It is actually a refinement of the ranking method. Each benchmark job is ranked several times—once for each compensable factor chosen. For example, jobs might be ranked first in terms of the factor "skill." Then they are ranked according to their "mental requirements." Next they are ranked according to their "responsibility," and so forth. Then the wage rate for each job is distributed by factor, and a job-comparison scale is constructed, as shown in **Table 11.3**. The scale is then used by slotting all the other jobs to be evaluated, factor by factor, into the job-comparison scale.

This method has two main advantages: first, it is an accurate, systematic method. Second, jobs are compared with other jobs to determine a relative value. Thus, it enables the determination of how much more of each compensable factor is required in one job versus all the others. This type of calibration is not possible with the ranking or classification methods. Complexity is probably the most serious disadvantage of the factor comparison method.

A study assessing the reliability of four job evaluation methods—ranking, classification, factor comparison, and point—found that ratings from the point method and the job classification method were most consistent, taking overall job evaluation ratings and individual job ratings into account.[14]

Research Insight ▷

The job evaluation step often takes the longest time. Once it has been completed, the next step is to group similar jobs into pay grades.

Step 2: Group Similar Jobs into Pay Grades

If the committee used the ranking, point, or factor comparison methods, it could assign pay rates to each individual job. For a larger employer, however, such a pay plan would be difficult to administer, since there might be different pay rates for hundreds or even thousands of jobs. Even in smaller organizations, there is a tendency to try to simplify wage and salary structures as much as possible. Therefore, the committee will probably want to group similar jobs (in terms of their ranking or number of points, for instance) into grades for pay purposes. Then, instead of having to deal with hundreds of pay rates, it might only have to focus on, say, 10 or 12.

TABLE 11.3   Factor Comparison Scale

$	Mental Requirements	Physical Requirements	Skill Requirements	Responsibility	Working Conditions
.25	....	....	....	....	Data Entry Clerk
.30	....	....	....	....	Security Guard
.40					
.50	....	....	....	....	Crane Operator
.60					
.70					
.75					
.80					
.90	....	....	....	....	Nurse
1.00	....	Crane Operator			Welder
1.10	....	....	Security Guard		
1.20					
1.30					
1.40					
1.50	Data Entry Clerk	....	....	Data Entry Clerk	
1.60					
1.70	Security Guard	Security Guard			
1.80					
1.90					
2.00	Crane Operater	Data Entry Clerk	Data Entry Clerk	Crane Operator	
2.25	....	....	Crane Operator		
2.40	....	....	....	Security Guard	
2.50					
2.80					
3.00	Welder	Nurse	Welder	Welder	
3.20					
3.40					
3.50	....	Welder			
3.80					
4.00	Nurse	....	Nurse	Nurse	
4.20					
4.40					
4.60					
4.80					

pay grade   A pay grade comprises jobs of approximately equal value.

A **pay grade** comprises jobs of approximately equal value or importance as determined by job evaluation. If the point method was used, the pay grade consists of jobs falling within a range of points. If the ranking plan was used, the grade consists of all jobs that fall within two or three ranks. If the classification system was used, then the jobs are already categorized into classes or grades. If the factor comparison method was used, the grade consists of a specified range of pay rates. Ten to 16 grades per logical grouping, such as factory jobs, non-union jobs, and so on, are common in large organizations. The next step is to obtain information on market pay rates by conducting a wage/salary survey.

Step 3: Conduct a Wage/Salary Survey

wage/salary survey   A survey aimed at determining prevailing wage rates. A good salary survey provides specific wage rates for comparable jobs. Formal written questionnaire surveys are the most comprehensive.

Compensation or **wage/salary surveys** play a central role in the pricing of jobs. Virtually every employer therefore conducts such surveys for pricing one or more jobs.[15]

An employer may use wage/salary surveys in three ways. First, survey data are used to price benchmark jobs that serve as reference points, which are used to anchor the employer's pay scale and around which other jobs are then slotted based on their relative worth to the firm. Second, an increasing number of positions are being priced directly in the marketplace (rather than relative to the firm's benchmark jobs), based on a formal or an informal survey of what similar firms are paying for comparable jobs.[16] As a result of the current shift away from long-term employment, compensation is increasingly shaped by the market wage and less by how it fits into the hierarchy of jobs in one organization. Finally, surveys also collect data on benefits, like insurance, sick leave, and vacation time, and so provide a basis on which to make decisions regarding employee benefits.

There are many ways to conduct a salary survey, including

- informal communication with other employers
- reviewing newspaper and Internet job ads
- surveying employment agencies
- buying commercial or professional surveys
- reviewing online compensation surveys
- conducting formal questionnaire-type surveys with other employers.

Data from the Hay Group consulting firm indicate that large organizations participate in an average of 11 compensation surveys and use information from 7 of them to administer their own compensation practices.[17]

Upward bias can be a problem regardless of the type of compensation survey. At least one compensation expert argues that the way in which most surveys are constructed, interpreted, and used leads almost invariably to a situation in which firms set higher wages than they otherwise might. For example, "Companies like to compare themselves against well-regarded, high-paying, and high-performing companies," so that baseline salaries tend to be biased upward. Similarly, "companies that sponsor surveys often do so with an implicit (albeit unstated) objective: to show the company [is] paying either competitively or somewhat below the market, so as to justify positive corrective action." For these and similar reasons, it is probably wise to review survey results with a skeptical eye and to acknowledge that upward bias may exist and should perhaps be adjusted for.[18]

Whatever the source of the survey, the data must be carefully assessed for accuracy before they are used to make compensation decisions. Problems can arise when the organization's job descriptions only partially match the descriptions contained in the survey, the survey data were collected several months before the time of use, the participants in the survey do not represent the appropriate labour market for the jobs being matched, and so on.[19]

Formal and Informal Surveys by the Employer

Most employers rely heavily on formal or informal surveys of what other employers are paying.[20] Informal telephone surveys are good for collecting data on a relatively small number of easily identified and quickly recognized jobs, such as when a bank's HR director wants to determine the salary at which a newly opened customer service representative's job should be advertised. Informal discussions among human resources specialists at regular professional association meetings are other occasions for informal salary surveys. Some employers use formal questionnaire surveys to collect compensation information from other employers, including things like number of employees, overtime policies, starting salaries, and paid vacations.

REQUIRED PROFESSIONAL CAPABILITIES

Determines the appropriateness of releasing confidential pay information

Monitors the competitiveness of the compensation program relative to comparable organizations

Tips for the Front Line

Commercial, Professional, and Government Salary Surveys

Many employers also rely on surveys published by various commercial firms, professional associations, or government agencies. For example, Statistics Canada provides monthly data on earnings by geographic area, by industry, and by occupation. **Table 11.4** provides an example of earnings data by industry and occupation.

The Toronto Board of Trade conducts five compensation surveys annually, covering executive; management; professional, supervisory, and sales; information technology; and administrative and support positions. In all, the surveys include information from small, medium, and large employers in the Greater Toronto Area, for more than 270 positions. A separate survey of employee benefits and employment practices is also conducted.

Private consulting and/or executive recruiting companies, like Watson Wyatt, Mercer Human Resources Consulting, and Hewitt Associates, annually publish data covering the compensation of senior and middle managers and members of boards of directors. Professional organizations, like the Certified General Accountants Association and Professional Engineers Ontario, conduct surveys of compensation practices among members of their associations.

Monster.ca Salary Centre
http://salary.monster.ca

For some jobs, salaries are determined directly based on formal or informal salary surveys. In most cases, though, surveys are used to price benchmark jobs, around which other jobs are then slotted based on their relative worth, as determined through job evaluation. Now all the information necessary to move to the next step—constructing wage curves—has been obtained.

TABLE 11.4   Average Weekly Earnings by Industry 2001–2005

	2001	2002	2003	2004	2005
All industries excluding unclassified enterprises	$ 667.27	$ 680.93	$ 690.57	$ 706.03	$ 728.17
Forestry, logging, and support	830.84	852.47	867.64	887.54	925.75
Mining and oil and gas extraction	1153.12	1168.01	1182.06	1248.93	1309.65
Utilities	1038.83	1058.31	1068.89	1061.59	1065.65
Construction	800.80	806.03	826.40	845.18	878.43
Manufacturing	808.10	830.30	842.67	859.57	884.76
Wholesale trade	774.87	778.70	790.79	803.13	829.78
Retail trade	431.06	434.18	444.13	453.94	470.52
Transportation and warehousing	741.69	764.37	761.92	756.87	775.78
Information and cultural industries	798.88	821.09	819.39	832.30	881.42
Finance and insurance	852.32	852.78	879.96	904.13	935.19
Real estate and rental and leasing	611.35	610.58	604.37	625.15	648.60
Professional, scientific, and technical services	886.09	899.14	914.05	929.94	952.96
Management of companies and enterprises	839.66	846.25	859.07	863.11	907.21
Administrative and support, waste management and remediation services	532.94	537.21	542.07	560.69	578.74
Educational services	694.06	724.24	745.68	776.65	805.57
Health care and social assistance	581.34	605.07	612.86	637.47	655.40
Arts, entertainment, and recreation	428.51	435.18	419.79	416.16	421.10
Accommodation and food services	286.00	292.02	279.47	294.14	311.60
Public administration	791.95	833.44	858.10	873.47	900.00
Other services	521.44	530.05	526.48	545.54	564.50

Source: Adapted from Statistics Canada CANSIM database http://cansim2.statcan.ca Table 281-0027 and Statistics Canada publication Catalogue No. 72-002, last modified May 29, 2006.

Step 4: Price Each Pay Grade by Using Wage Curves

The next step is to assign pay rates to each pay grade. (Of course, if jobs were not grouped into pay grades, individual pay rates would have to be assigned to each job.) Assigning pay rates to each pay grade (or to each job) is usually accomplished with a **wage curve**.

wage curve   A graphic description of the relationship between the value of the job and the average wage paid for this job.

The wage curve graphically depicts the pay rates currently being paid for jobs in each pay grade, relative to the points or rankings assigned to each job or grade by the job evaluation committee. An example of a wage curve is presented in **Figure 11.4**. Note that pay rates are shown on the vertical axis, while the pay grades (in terms of points) are shown along the horizontal axis. The purpose of the wage curve is to show the relationship between (1) the value of the job as determined by one of the job evaluation methods and (2) the current average pay rates for each job or grade.

The pay rates on the graph are traditionally those now paid by the organization. If there is reason to believe that the present pay rates are substantially out of step with the prevailing market pay rates for these jobs, then benchmark jobs within each pay grade are chosen and priced via a compensation survey. These new market-based pay rates are then used to plot a new wage curve.

There are several steps in pricing jobs with a wage curve using grades. First, *find the average pay for each pay grade*, since each of the pay grades consists of several jobs. Next, *plot the pay rates* for each pay grade, as was done in Figure 11.4. Then fit a line (called a *wage line*) through the points just plotted. This can be done either freehand or by using a statistical method known as regression analysis. Finally, *price jobs*. Wages along the wage line are the target wages or salary rates for the jobs in each pay grade. If the current rates being paid for any of the jobs or grades fall well above or well below the wage line, that rate may be "out of line"; raises or a pay freeze for that job may be in order. The next step, then, is to fine-tune the pay rates.

An Ethical Dilemma

What should employers do when there is a shortage of a certain type of skills and they cannot attract any workers unless they pay a market rate above the maximum of their salary range for that job? How should other jobs in the same salary range be paid?

FIGURE 11.4   Plotting a Wage Curve

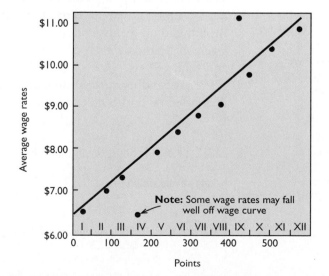

Note: The average pay rate for jobs in each grade (Grade I, Grade II, Grade III, etc.) is plotted, and the wage curve is fitted to the resulting points.

Step 5: Fine-Tune Pay Rates

Fine-tuning involves correcting out-of-line rates and (usually) developing rate ranges.

Developing Rate Ranges

rate ranges A series of steps or levels within a pay grade, usually based on years of service.

Most employers do not just pay one rate for all jobs in a particular pay grade. Instead, they develop **rate ranges** for each grade so that there might, for instance, be ten levels or "steps" and ten corresponding pay rates within each pay grade. This approach is illustrated in **Table 11.5**, which shows the pay rates and levels for some of the federal government pay grades. As of the time of this pay schedule, for instance, employees in positions that were classified in grade CX-1 could be paid annual salaries between $50 562 and $63 834, depending on the level at which they were hired into the grade, the amount of time they were in the grade, and their merit increases (if any). Another way to depict the rate ranges for each grade is with a wage structure, as in **Figure 11.5**. The wage structure graphically depicts the range of pay rates (in this case, per hour) to be paid for each grade.

The use of rate ranges for each pay grade has several benefits. First, the employer can take a more flexible stance with respect to the labour market. For example, it makes it easier to attract experienced, higher-paid employees into a pay grade where the starting salary for the lowest step may be too low to attract such experienced people. Rate ranges also allow employers to provide for performance differences between employees within the same grade or between those with differing seniority. As in Figure 11.5, most employers structure their rate ranges to overlap a bit so that an employee with greater experience or seniority may earn more than an entry-level person in the next higher pay grade.

The rate range is usually built around the wage line or curve. Some employers allow the rate range for each grade to become wider for the higher pay ranges, reflecting the greater demands and performance variability inherent in these more complex jobs.

Broadbanding

broadbanding Reducing the number of salary grades and ranges into just a few wide levels or "bands," each of which then contains a relatively wide range of jobs and salary levels.

The trend today is for employers to reduce their salary grades and ranges from ten or more down to three to five, a process that is called **broadbanding**. Broadbanding means collapsing salary grades and ranges into just a few wide levels or "bands," each of which then contains a relatively wide range of jobs and salary levels.

Broadbanding a pay system involves several steps. First, the number of bands is decided on and each is assigned a salary range. The bands usually have wide

TABLE 11.5   Federal Government Pay Schedules CX-1 and CX-2*

Grade	Rate Levels within Grade				
	1	2	3	4	5
CX-1	$50 562	53 596	56 812	60 220	63 834
CX-2	$53 658	56 878	60 290	63 907	67 740

Source: Treasury Board of Canada Secretariat, *Agreement between the Treasury Board and the Union of Canada Correctional Officers*, Appendix A, 2001. www.tbs-sct.gc.ca/pubs_pol/hrpubs/coll_agre/cx/cx08_e .asp. Reproduced with the permission of the Minister of Public Works and Government Services, 2007.

FIGURE 11.5 Wage Structure

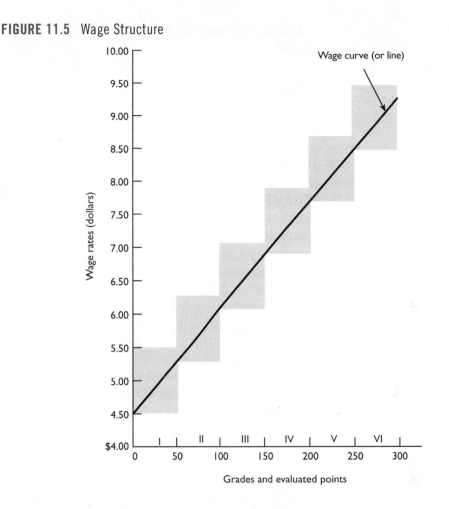

salary ranges and also overlap substantially. As a result, there is much more flexibility to move employees from job to job within bands and less need to "promote" them to new grades just to get them higher salaries.

The bands are then typically subdivided into either specific jobs or skill levels (see **Figure 11.6**). For example, a band may consist of a number of jobs each assigned a market value. More often, bands are subdivided into several skill levels. With this approach, workers are not paid above market value just for doing a job well or for having seniority. Instead, they must increase their competencies, such as skills, knowledge, and abilities.[21]

Broadbanding's basic advantage is that it injects greater flexibility into employee compensation.[22] Broadbanding is especially sensible where firms flatten their hierarchies and organize around self-managing teams. The new, broad salary bands can include both supervisors and those reporting to them, and can also facilitate moving employees slightly up or down along the pay scale without accompanying promotional raises or demotional pay cuts.

Broadbanding also facilitates less specialized, boundaryless jobs and organizations. Less specialization and more participation in cross-departmental processes generally mean enlarged duties or capabilities and more possibilities for alternative career tracks.

Correcting Out-of-Line Rates

The actual wage rate for a job may fall well off the wage line or well outside the rate range for its grade, as shown in Figure 11.5. This means that the average pay

FIGURE 11.6 Broadbanding

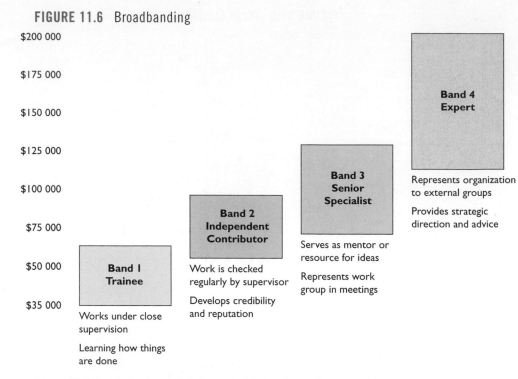

Source: H. Risher, "Planning a 'Next Generation' Salary System," *Compensation and Benefits Review*, November/December 2002, p. 16. © 2002. Reprinted with permission of Sage Publications, Inc.

red circle pay rate A rate of pay that is above the pay range maximum.

competencies Individual knowledge, skills, and behaviours that are critical to successful individual or corporate performance.

for that job is currently too high or too low, relative to other jobs in the firm. If a point falls well below the line, a pay raise for the job may be required. If the plot falls well above the wage line, pay cuts or a pay freeze may be required.

Underpaid employees should have their wages raised to the minimum of the rate range for their pay grade, assuming that the organization wants to retain the employees and has the funds. This can be done either immediately or in one or two steps.

Pay rates of overpaid employees are often called **red circle pay rates,** and there are several ways to cope with this problem. One is to freeze the rate paid to employees in this grade until general salary increases bring the other jobs into line with it. A second alternative is to transfer or promote some or all of the employees involved to jobs for which they can legitimately be paid their current pay rates. The third alternative is to freeze the rate for six months, during which time attempts are made to transfer or promote the overpaid employees. If this is not possible, then the rate at which these employees are paid is cut to the maximum in the pay range for their grade.

COMPETENCY-BASED PAY

Competency-based pay (also called skill-based pay for manufacturing jobs) pays employees for the range, depth, and types of knowledge that they are capable of using, rather than for the job that they currently hold. **Competencies** are individual knowledge, skills, and behaviours that are critical to successful individual or corporate performance based on their relation to the organization's visions, values, and business strategy.[23]

Core competencies describe knowledge and behaviours that employees throughout the organization must exhibit for the organization to succeed, such

Construction workers today are often compensated for their work through the method of skill-based pay.

as "customer service orientation" for all hotel employees. *Functional competencies* are associated with a particular organizational function, such as "negotiation skills" for salespeople, or "safety orientation" for pilots. *Behavioural competencies* are expected behaviours, such as "always walking a customer to the product they are looking for rather than pointing."[24]

A competency-based pay program should include the following:

- Competencies and skills—directly important to job performance—that can be defined in measurable and objective terms.
- Competencies that employees apply on the job to gain desirable job performance objectives. Employers should pay for performance, not training.
- New and different competencies that replace obsolete competencies or competencies that no longer are important to job performance. If additional competencies are needed, the obsolete competency should be removed from the program.
- On-the-job training, not "in the classroom." Those who possess the competencies should teach them. Also include on-the-job assessment, which can be supplemented by paper-and-pencil exams administered on the job, as well.[25]

As an example, in a manufacturing plant setting, workers would be paid based on their attained skill levels. In a three-level plan,

1. Level 1 would indicate limited ability, such as knowledge of basic facts and ability to perform simple tasks without direction.
2. Level 2 would mean that the employee has attained partial proficiency and could, for instance, apply technical principles on the job.
3. Level 3 would mean that the employee is fully competent in the area and could, for example, analyze and solve production problems.

Increased workforce flexibility is one of the most significant advantages of competency-based pay. Employees rotate between different jobs or production areas to encourage the learning of new competencies and skills. This process fosters flexibility by encouraging workers to learn multiple competencies and skills and willingly switch tasks.[26]

Experience has shown that competency-based pay is more efficient in the first years of its existence. The greatest challenge is measurement of skills, abilities, and competencies. As time goes on, employees often become dissatisfied if these measurements are not valid, or if the people responsible for assessing competencies are considered incompetent or biased. Another major employee concern is that pay be linked sufficiently to performance as well as competencies. Some compensation consultants suggest that firms should not pay for competencies at the exclusion of rewards for high-performance results. For example, competencies could be linked to the determination of base salary, combined with bonuses that are based on performance.[27]

Experts predict that the viewpoint that people, rather than jobs, provide advantage to organizations will continue to grow in popularity. They foresee the emergence of new pay systems combining competencies and market values.[28]

PAY FOR MANAGERIAL AND PROFESSIONAL JOBS

Developing a compensation plan to pay executive, managerial, and professional employees is similar in many respects to developing a plan for other employees.[29] The basic aims of the plan are the same in that the goal is to attract good employees and maintain their commitment. Yet for managerial and professional jobs, job evaluation provides only a partial answer to the question of how to pay these employees. Managers and professionals are almost always paid based on their performance as well as on the basis of static job demands, like working conditions. Developing compensation plans for managers and professionals, therefore, tends to be relatively complex, and job evaluation, while still important for determining base salary, usually plays a secondary role to incentives based on performance appraisal results and organizational performance.

Compensating Managers

There are five elements in a manager's compensation package: salary, benefits, short-term incentives, long-term incentives, and perquisites.[30] The amount of salary that managers are paid usually depends on the value of the person's work to the organization and how well the person is discharging his or her responsibilities. The value of the manager's work is often determined through job evaluation and salary surveys and the resulting fine-tuning of salary levels. Salary is the cornerstone of executive compensation, because it is the element on which the others are layered, with benefits, incentives, and perquisites often awarded in some proportion to the manager's base pay.

Executive compensation tends to emphasize performance incentives more than other employees' pay plans do, since organizational results are likely to reflect the contributions of executives more directly than those of other employees.

The heavy incentive component of executives' compensation can be illustrated by using some of Canada's best-paid executives.[31] In 2005, Hank Swartout, CEO of Precision Drilling Trust, received a base salary of $840 000, an annual bonus of $3 360 000, and long-term incentives of $70 624 333, for a total of $74 824 331. Hunter Harrison, CEO of Canadian National Railway, received a base salary of $1 665 950, an annual bonus of $4 664 660, and long-term incentives of $49 888 884. Mike Zafirovski, CEO of Nortel Networks, received a base salary of $305 785, no annual bonus (given the company's continuing struggles), and long-term incentives of $37 235 512.

Research
I n s i g h t

A major review of the results of many previous studies of CEO pay determined that firm size accounts for 40 percent in the variance of total CEO pay, while firm performance accounts for less than 5 percent of the variance.[32]

There has been considerable debate regarding whether top executives are worth what they are paid. Some argue that the job of an executive is increasingly difficult. The stakes are high and job tenure is often short. Expectations are getting higher, the questions from shareholders are more direct, and the challenge of navigating an organization through difficult economic times has never been so great. However, shareholder activism regarding executive pay has attempted to tighten the restrictions on what firms pay their top executives.

Some believe that pay for performance is taking hold, with companies now making stronger links between company performance and CEO total compensation. Others believe that linking pay to performance is still inadequate in the majority of companies. Most agree that better disclosure of executive pay is required, and such groups as the Canadian Securities Administrators and the Canadian Coalition for Good Governance are pressing for dramatic changes in executive compensation disclosure.[33]

Compensating Professional Employees

Compensating nonsupervisory professional employees, like engineers and scientists, presents unique problems. Analytical jobs require creativity and problem solving, compensable factors not easily compared or measured. Furthermore, the professional's economic impact on the firm is often related only indirectly to the person's actual efforts; for example, the success of an engineer's invention depends on many factors, like how well it is produced and marketed.

In theory, the job evaluation methods explained previously can be used for evaluating professional jobs.[34] The compensable factors here tend to focus on problem solving, creativity, job scope, and technical knowledge and expertise. The job classification method is commonly used—a series of grade descriptions are written, and each position is slotted into the grade having the most appropriate definition.

In practice, traditional methods of job evaluation are rarely used for professional jobs since it is so difficult to identify compensable factors and degrees of factors that meaningfully capture the value of professional work. "Knowledge and the skill of applying it," as one expert notes, "are extremely difficult to quantify and measure."[35]

As a result, most employers use a *market-pricing approach* in evaluating professional jobs. They price professional jobs in the marketplace to the best of their ability to establish the values for benchmark jobs. These benchmark jobs and the employer's other professional jobs are then slotted into a salary structure. Specifically, each professional discipline (like mechanical engineering or electrical engineering) usually ends up having four to six grade levels, each of which requires a fairly broad salary range. This approach helps ensure that the employer remains competitive when bidding for professionals whose attainments vary widely and whose potential employers are found literally worldwide.[36]

PAY EQUITY

Historically, the average pay for Canadian women has been considerably lower than that for men. In 1967, women's average wages were 46.1 percent of men's average wages. This "wage gap" of 53.9 percent meant that for every dollar earned by a man, a woman earned 46.1 cents. **Table 11.6** shows the most recent wage gap statistics. Some of this gap is due to the fact that women do more part-time work than men, but even when full-year, full-time workers are compared, the gap has stalled at approximately 30 percent since 1995. The wage gap is narrower for single women than for those who are married, and for younger women compared with those who are older.[37]

Moreover, the gap persists even when women have the same qualifications and do the same type of work as men. A 2004 study showed that two years after graduation, female university graduates in the Maritime provinces working full-time earned 78 percent of the weekly wage of males, even after accounting for differences in field of study, occupation, location, and hours worked.[38]

Although such factors as differences in hours worked, experience levels, education levels, and level of unionization contribute to the wage gap, systemic discrimination is also present.[39] The purpose of pay equity legislation is to redress systemic gender discrimination in compensation for work performed by employees in female-dominated job classes. **Pay equity** requires that equal wages be paid for jobs of equal value or "worth" to the employer, as determined by gender-neutral (i.e., free of any bias based on gender) job evaluation techniques.

pay equity   Providing equal pay to male-dominated job classes and female-dominated job classes of equal value to the employer.

The legal process involved can be lengthy. A final decision is still pending in a pay equity complaint filed against Canada Post in 1983 claiming that six thousand clerical workers had been subjected to systemic discrimination. In 2006, the Supreme Court of Canada ruled against a Canadian Human Rights Tribunal decision that female Air Canada flight attendants' jobs could not be compared with those of mainly male mechanics and pilots, and sent the case back to the tribunal. The Court condemned Air Canada's use of legal technicalities to delay the case, which began in 1991.[40]

Six provinces (Ontario, Quebec, Manitoba, Nova Scotia, New Brunswick, and Prince Edward Island) have created separate proactive legislation that specifically requires that pay equity be achieved. Ontario and Quebec require pay equity in

TABLE 11.6   Male/Female Average Earnings Ratio* for Full-Year, Full-Time Workers

Year	Women ($)	Men ($)	Earnings Ratio (%)
1995	35 500	49 100	72.4
1996	34 900	48 300	72.3
1997	34 600	50 700	68.3
1998	37 100	51 700	71.9
1999	35 700	52 200	68.4
2000	36 900	52 200	70.6
2001	37 200	53 300	69.9
2002	37 500	53 400	70.2
2003	37 300	53 200	70.2
2004	38 400	54 900	69.9

*Earnings stated in constant year 2004 dollars.

Source: Adapted from Statistics Canada CANSIM Database www.cansim2.statca.ca Table 202-0102.

Saskatchewan workers demonstrate for pay equity.

both the public and the private sectors, whereas the legislation in the remaining provinces applies only to the public sector. In the federal jurisdiction, Yukon (public sector only), and British Columbia, human rights legislation requires equal pay for work of equal value, determined by comparing skill, effort, responsibility, and working conditions (and knowledge in B.C.). In Newfoundland and Labrador and Saskatchewan, a requirement for equal pay for males and females doing substantially similar work, determined by assessing skill, effort, and responsibility, is incorporated into the human rights legislation (similar wording is included in Yukon's Employment Standards Act). Although Newfoundland and Labrador and Saskatchewan do not have specific pay equity legislation, both provinces have formally implemented pay equity in the public sector. There is currently no requirement for pay equity in Alberta, the Northwest Territories, or Nunavut.[41]

To date, pay equity has reduced the wage gap in Ontario to some extent. However, although pay equity legislation has narrowed the wage gap, it has not eliminated it, and there is still no explanation other than systemic discrimination for much of the 30 percent gap that still persists.[42]

In 2001, the federal government set up a task force to study its legislation, which was introduced in 1977, and to propose changes to improve the effectiveness of the legislation in ensuring pay equity. The task force concluded in 2004 that the complaint-based model currently in place had not proved to be an effective means of achieving the goal of equal pay for work of equal value, and recommended that new pay equity legislation be enacted to require employers to develop a pay equity plan. No legislative changes have resulted to date.[43]

Implications

The Pay Equity Commission (Ontario)
www.payequity.gov.on.ca

One of the reasons that many female Generation X employees are experiencing career disappointment and leaving the workforce is the gender wage gap.[44] In the long term, the best way to remove the portion of the wage gap resulting from systemic discrimination is to eliminate male- and female-dominated jobs by ensuring that women have equal access to, and are equally represented in, all jobs.

To avoid pay equity problems, questions to ask include the following:

Hints to Ensure Legal Compliance

1. Are job duties and responsibilities clearly documented, either by a job analysis questionnaire or by a job description? Are they reviewed and updated annually?

2. Is the pay system clearly documented in a salary administration manual? If not, the credibility and defensibility of pay practices are ripe for challenge.

3. When was the pay system last reviewed? If more than three years have passed, serious inequities could exist. Maintenance of pay equity is a requirement of pay equity legislation.

4. Are the pay equity laws being monitored and adhered to in each province/ territory in which the organization has employees? There are differences in the legislation among jurisdictions.

Chapter Review

Summary

1. A total rewards approach considers individual reward components as part of an integrated whole in order to determine the best mix of rewards that are aligned with business strategy and provide employee value, all within the cost constraints of the organization. Alignment is the extent to which rewards support outcomes that are important to achieving the organization's strategic objectives. For example, when competitive advantage relies on relentless customer service, this behaviour should be reinforced. Employee value is created when rewards are meaningful to employees and influence their affiliation with the organization.

2. Establishing pay rates involves five steps: evaluating jobs, developing pay grades, conducting a salary survey, using wage curves, and fine-tuning pay rates. Job evaluation is aimed at determining the relative worth of jobs within a firm. It compares jobs with one another based on their content, which is usually defined in terms of compensable factors, such as skill, effort, responsibility, and working conditions. Most managers group similar jobs into wage or pay grades for pay purposes. These comprise jobs of approximately equal value or importance as determined by job evaluation. Salary surveys collect data from other employers in the marketplace who are competing for employees in similar kinds of positions. The wage curve (or line) shows the average target wage for each pay grade (or job). It illustrates what the average wage for each grade should be, and whether any present wages or salaries are out of line.

3. Competency-based pay plans provide employee compensation based on the skills and knowledge that they are capable of using, rather than the job that they currently hold.

4. The five basic elements of compensation for managers are salary, benefits, short-term incentives, long-term incentives, and perquisites.

5. Pay equity is intended to redress systemic gender discrimination as measured by the wage gap, which indicates that full-time working women make about 70 cents for every dollar made by full-time working men. Pay equity requires equal pay for female-dominated jobs of equal value to male-dominated jobs (where value is determined through job evaluation).

Key Terms

benchmark job　*(p. 285)*
broadbanding　*(p. 296)*
classes　*(p. 287)*
classification (or grading) method　*(p. 287)*
compensable factor　*(p. 285)*
competencies　*(p. 298)*
factor comparison method　*(p. 291)*
grade/group description　*(p. 288)*
grades　*(p. 287)*
job evaluation　*(p. 284)*
pay equity　*(p. 302)*
pay grade　*(p. 292)*
point method　*(p. 288)*
ranking method　*(p. 286)*
rate ranges　*(p. 296)*
red circle pay rate　*(p. 298)*
total rewards　*(p. 279)*
wage curve　*(p. 295)*
wage/salary survey　*(p. 292)*

Review and Discussion Questions

1. What are the five components of total rewards?

2. Describe what is meant by the term "benchmark job."

3. What are the pros and cons of the following methods of job evaluation: ranking, classification, factor comparison, point method?

4. Explain the term "competencies," and explain the differences among core, functional, and behavioural competencies.

5. Explain what is meant by the market-pricing approach in evaluating professional jobs.

6. Explain what pay equity legislation is intended to accomplish, what action is required by the legislation in order to accomplish it, and how effective the legislation has been in accomplishing its objectives.

Critical Thinking Questions

1. Do you think that transactional or relational rewards have more impact on overall organizational performance?

2. Why do companies pay for compensation surveys where job matching may be difficult rather than conducting their own surveys?

3. It was recently reported in the news that the average pay for most university presidents was around $200 000 per year but that a few earned closer to $500 000 per year. What would account for such a disparity in the pay of university CEOs?

4. Do you agree with paying people for competencies and skills that they are rarely required to use on the job?

5. What are some of the potential reasons that gender-based pay discrimination is so hard to eradicate?

Application Exercises

Running Case: LearnInMotion.com

The New Pay Plan

LearnInMotion.com does not have a formal wage structure, nor does it have rate ranges or use compensable factors. Jennifer and Pierre base wage rates almost exclusively on those prevailing in the surrounding community, and they temper these by trying to maintain some semblance of equity among what workers with different responsibilities are paid. As Jennifer says, "Deciding what to pay dot-com employees is an adventure: wages for jobs like Web designer and online salesperson are always climbing dramatically, and there's not an awful lot of loyalty involved when someone else offers you 30 percent or 40 percent more than you're currently making." Jennifer and Pierre are therefore continually scanning various sources to see what others are paying for positions like theirs. They peruse the want ads almost every day and conduct informal surveys among their friends in other dot-coms. Once or twice a week, they also check compensation Web sites, like Monster.ca.

Although the company has taken a somewhat unstructured, informal approach to establishing its compensation plan, the firm's actual salary schedule is guided by several basic pay policies. For one thing, the difficulty they had recruiting and hiring employees caused them to pay salaries 10 to 20 percent above what the market would seem to indicate. Jennifer and Pierre write this off to the need to get and keep good employees. As Jennifer says, "If you've got ten Web designers working for you, you can afford to go a few extra weeks without hiring another one, but when you need one designer and you have none, you've got to do whatever you can to get that one designer hired." Their somewhat informal approach has also led to some potential inequities. For example, the two salespeople—one a man, the other a woman—are earning different salaries, and the man is making about 30 percent more. If everything were going fine—for instance, if sales were up, and the calendar was functional—perhaps they wouldn't be worried. However, the fact is that the two owners are wondering if a more structured pay plan would be a good idea. Now they want you, their management consultant, to help them decide what to do. Here's what they want you to do for them.

Questions

1. Is the company at the point where it should be setting up a formal salary structure complete with job evaluations? Why or why not?

2. Is the company's policy of paying more than the prevailing wage rates a sound one? What do you base that on?

3. Is the salespersons' male–female differential wise? If not, why not?

4. What would you suggest Jennifer and Pierre do now?

Case Incident

Salary Inequities at Acme Manufacturing

Joe Blackenship was trying to figure out what to do about a problem salary situation that he had in his plant. Blackenship recently took over as president of Acme Manufacturing. The founder, Bill George, had been president for 35 years. The company is family-owned and located in a small eastern Manitoba town. It has approximately 250 employees and is the largest employer in the community. Blackenship is a member of the family that owns Acme, but he had never worked for the company prior to becoming president. He has an MBA and a law degree, plus 15 years of management experience with a large manufacturing organization, where he was senior vice-president of human resources when he made his move to Acme.

A short time after joining Acme, Blackenship started to notice that there was considerable inequity in the pay structure for salaried employees. A discussion with the HR director led him to believe that salaried employees' pay was very much a matter of individual bargaining with the past president. Hourly paid factory workers were not part of the problem, because they were unionized and their wages were set by collective bargaining. An examination of the salaried payroll showed that there were 25 employees, whose pay ranged from that of the president to that of the receptionist. A closer examination showed that 14 of the salaried employees were female. Three of these were front-line factory supervisors, and one was the HR director. The rest were nonmanagement employees.

This examination also showed that the HR director appeared to be underpaid, and that the three female supervisors were paid somewhat less than any of the male supervisors. However, there were no similar supervisory jobs in which there were both male and female incumbents. When asked, the HR director said that she thought the female supervisors may have been paid at a lower rate mainly because they were women, and perhaps George did not think that women needed as much money because they had working husbands. However, she added the thought that they might be paid less because they supervised lesser-skilled employees than did male supervisors. Blackenship was not sure that this was true.

The company from which Blackenship had moved had a good job evaluation system. Although he was thoroughly familiar and capable with this compensation tool, Blackenship did not have time to make a job evaluation study at Acme. Therefore, he decided to hire a compensation consultant from a nearby university to help him. Together, they decided that all 25 salaried jobs should be in the same job evaluation cluster, that a modified ranking system of job evaluation should be used, and that the job descriptions recently completed by the HR director were current, accurate, and usable in the study.

The job evaluation showed that there was no evidence of serious inequities or discrimination in the nonmanagement jobs, but that the HR director and the three female supervisors were being underpaid relative to comparable male salaried employees.

Blackenship was not sure what to do. He knew that if the underpaid supervisors took their case to the local pay equity commission, the company could be found guilty of sex discrimination and then have to pay considerable back wages. He was afraid that if he gave these women an immediate salary increase large enough to bring them up to where they should be, the male supervisors would be upset and the female supervisors might comprehend the total situation and want back pay. The HR director told Blackenship that the female supervisors had never complained about pay differences, and they probably did not know the law to any extent.

The HR director agreed to take a sizable salary increase with no back pay, so this part of the problem was solved. Blackenship believed that he had four choices relative to the female supervisors:

- to do nothing
- to increase the female supervisors' salaries gradually
- to increase their salaries immediately
- to call the three supervisors into his office, discuss the situation with them, and jointly decide what to do

Questions

1. What would you do if you were Blackenship?
2. How do you think the company got into a situation like this in the first place?
3. Why would you suggest that Blackenship pursue your suggested alternative?

Source: Based on a case prepared by Professor James C. Hodgetts of the Fogelman College of Business and Economics at the University of Memphis. All names are disguised. Used with permission.

Experiential Exercises

1. Working individually or in groups, conduct salary surveys for the positions of entry-level accountant and entry-level chemical engineer. What sources did you use, and what conclusions did you reach? If you were the HR manager for a local engineering firm, what would you recommend that each job be paid?

2. Obtain information on the pay grades and rate ranges for each grade at your college or university. Do they appear to be broad bands? If not, propose specific broad bands that could be implemented.

CHAPTER 12

PAY-FOR-PERFORMANCE AND FINANCIAL INCENTIVES

REQUIRED PROFESSIONAL CAPABILITIES

- Monitors the competitiveness of the compensation program relative to comparable organizations

LEARNING OUTCOMES

AFTER STUDYING THIS CHAPTER, YOU SHOULD BE ABLE TO

Discuss how piecework, standard hour, and team or group incentive plans are used.

Explain how to use short-term and long-term incentives for managers and executives.

Analyze the main advantages and disadvantages of salary plans and commission plans for salespeople.

Explain why money is somewhat less important as an incentive for professional employees than it is for other employees.

Compare the three types of organization-wide incentive plans.

Explain under what conditions it is best to use an incentive plan.

Analyze the emerging emphasis on employee recognition.

MONEY AND MOTIVATION

Frederick Taylor University
www.ftu.edu

variable pay   Any plan that ties pay to productivity or profitability.

The use of financial incentives—financial rewards paid to workers whose production exceeds some predetermined standard—is not new; it was popularized by Frederick Taylor in the late 1800s. As a supervisory employee of the Midvale Steel Company, Taylor had become concerned with the tendency of employees to work at the slowest pace possible and produce at the minimum acceptable level. What especially intrigued him was the fact that some of these same workers still had the energy to run home and work on their cabins, even after a 12-hour day. Taylor knew that if he could find some way to harness this energy during the workday, huge productivity gains would be achieved.

Today's efforts to achieve the organization's strategy through motivated employees include financial incentives, pay-for-performance, and variable compensation plans. These types of compensation are now commonly called **variable pay**, meaning any plan that links pay with productivity, profitability, or some other measure of organizational performance. Employers continue to increase their use of variable pay plans while holding salary increases to modest levels. More than 85 percent of Canadian employers have one or more types of variable pay plans in place.[1] Of those, many have more than one type of plan, as shown in **Figure 12.1**.

Variable pay facilitates management of total compensation costs by keeping base pay inflation controlled. The fundamental premise of variable pay plans is that top performers must get top pay in order to secure their commitment to the organization. Thus, *accurate performance appraisal or measurable outcomes is a precondition of effective pay-for-performance plans*. Another important prerequisite for effective variable pay plans is "line of sight," or the extent to which an employee can relate his or her daily work to the achievement of overall corporate goals. Employees need to understand corporate strategy and how their work as individual employees is important to the achievement of strategic objectives.[2]

The entire thrust of such programs is to treat workers like partners and get them to think of the business and its goals as their own. It is thus reasonable to pay them more like partners, too, by linking their pay more directly to performance. For example, the owners of a Surrey, B.C.–based trucking company handed out bonus cheques totalling more than $400 000 to more than 400 employees in August 2005. Over the preceding five years, the owners had grown

FIGURE 12.1   Variable Pay Programs, 2005
(*n* = 283, percent among those with at least one annual variable pay plan in place)

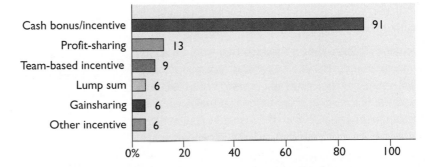

Note: Figures do not add to 100% because some respondents have more than one plan.

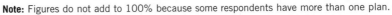

Source: C. Baarda, *Compensation Planning Outlook 2006*. Ottawa: Conference Board of Canada, 2005, p. 6. Reprinted by permission of The Conference Board of Canada, Ottawa.

Coastal Pacific Xpress (CPX) by 500 percent and decided to reward their employees for their hard work. In the future, CPX will give out bonuses every year that the company makes a profit.[3]

Types of Incentive Plans

spot bonus A spontaneous incentive awarded to individuals for accomplishments not readily measured by a standard.

There are several types of incentive plans. *Individual incentive programs* give income over and above base salary to individual employees who meet a specific individual performance standard. **Spot bonuses** are awarded, generally to individual employees, for accomplishments that are not readily measured by a standard, such as "to recognize the long hours that this employee put in last month," or "to recognize exemplary customer service this week." *Group incentive programs* are like individual incentive plans, but they give pay over and above base salary to all team members when the group or team collectively meets a specified standard for performance, productivity, or other work-related behaviour. *Profit-sharing plans* are generally organization-wide incentive programs that provide employees with a share of the organization's profits in a specified period. *Gainsharing programs* are organization-wide pay plans designed to reward employees for improvements in organizational productivity. They generally include employee suggestion systems and focus on reducing labour costs through employee suggestions and participation.[4]

It is important to ensure that whatever incentive is being provided is appealing to the individual receiving it. Demographic factors can have an impact on what is appealing, as discussed in the Workforce Diversity box.

Workforce Diversity

Targeting Incentives for Life Stage

In developing incentive programs, which are targeted to job function and performance level, employers should also consider the demographics of their workforce. For instance, what motivates a Generation X employee may not have an impact on a baby boomer in the same company. Understanding each employee's life stage will help employers determine the most effective incentive program approach, which results in a workforce that is satisfied, engaged, and more likely to perform better and remain with the company.

Traditionalists (1922–1946): Rewards that work for traditionalists include flexible schedules that allow them to work seasonally or as time permits; health and fitness rewards that help them enjoy this life stage; and entertainment rewards that they would not purchase for themselves, such as computers and cellphones.

Boomers (1946–1965): Rewards that work for boomers include recognition and being appreciated for their work; travel rewards, such as adventure travel; and luxury and health-related awards, such as spas, high-end fitness equipment, and personal chefs.

Generation X (1966–1980): Rewards that work for this generation include gadgets and high-tech rewards that are state-of-the-art technology; work/life balance rewards, such as extra vacation days and onsite daycare; and flexibility to allow time for family, friends, and meaningful life experiences.

Generation Y (1981+): Rewards that work for this group include relationship enhancers, such as electronic communications equipment, home entertainment items, and dining experiences; personalized rewards where they can choose colours and accessories; and charitable rewards, like time off to volunteer for non-profit organizations and charitable donations made in their names.

Motivation is highly personal. Companies that provide rewards and recognition that are meaningful to employees based on their life cycle will be more successful in creating the right environment for maximum performance.

Source: Adapted from R. Stotz, "Targeting Employee Incentives for Maximum Performance," *workspan*, June 2006, pp. 46–48. Reprinted with permission of WorldatWork, Scottsdale, AZ. www.worldatwork.org.

For simplicity, we will discuss these plans as follows: incentives for operations employees; incentives for senior managers and executives; incentives for salespeople; incentives primarily for other managers and professional employees (merit pay); and organization-wide incentives.

INCENTIVES FOR OPERATIONS EMPLOYEES

Piecework Plans

piecework   A system of pay based on the number of items processed by each individual worker in a unit of time, such as items per hour or items per day.

Several incentive plans are particularly well suited for use with operations employees, such as those doing production work. **Piecework** is the oldest incentive plan and still the most commonly used. Earnings are tied directly to what the worker produces; the person is paid a *piece rate* for each unit that he or she produces. Thus, if Tom Smith gets $0.40 per piece for stamping out door jambs, then he would make $40 for stamping out 100 a day and $80 for stamping out 200.

Developing a workable piece-rate plan requires both job evaluation and (usually) industrial engineering. Job evaluation enables firms to assign an hourly wage rate to the job in question. The crucial issue in piece-rate planning is the production standard, however, and this standard is usually developed by industrial engineers. Production standards are stated in terms of a standard number of minutes per unit or a standard number of units per hour. In Tom Smith's case, the job evaluation indicated that his door-jamb stamping job was worth $8 per hour. The industrial engineer determined that 20 jambs per hour was the standard production rate. Therefore, the piece rate (for each door jamb) was $8.00 ÷ 20 = $0.40 per door jamb.

straight piecework plan   A set payment for each piece produced or processed in a factory or shop.

With a **straight piecework plan**, Tom Smith would be paid on the basis of the number of door jambs that he produced; there would be no guaranteed minimum wage. However, after passage of employment/labour standards legislation, it became necessary for most employers to guarantee their workers a minimum wage. With a **guaranteed piecework plan**, Tom Smith would be paid the minimum wage whether or not he stamped out the number of door jambs required to make minimum wage—for example, 11 pieces if minimum wage is $4.40 per hour. As an incentive he would, however, also be paid at the piece rate of $0.40 for each unit that he produced over the number required to make minimum wage.

guaranteed piecework plan   The minimum hourly wage plus an incentive for each piece produced above a set number of pieces per hour.

Piecework generally implies straight piecework, a strict proportionality between results and rewards regardless of the level of output. Thus, in Smith's case, he continues to get $0.40 apiece for stamping out door jambs, even if he stamps out many more than planned (say, 500 per day). Other types of piecework incentive plans call for a sharing of productivity gains between worker and employer such that the worker does not receive full credit for all production above normal.[5]

Advantages and Disadvantages

Piecework incentive plans have several advantages. They are simple to calculate and easily understood by employees. Piece-rate plans appear equitable in principle, and their incentive value can be powerful since rewards are directly tied to performance.

Piecework also has some disadvantages. A main one is its somewhat unsavoury reputation among many employees, based on some employers' habits of arbitrarily raising production standards whenever they found their workers earning "excessive" wages. In addition, piece rates are stated in monetary terms (like $0.40 per piece). Thus, when a new job evaluation results in a new hourly wage rate, the piece rate must also be revised; this can be a big clerical chore. Another disadvantage is more subtle: since the piece rate is quoted on a per-piece basis, in workers' minds production standards become tied inseparably to the amount of money earned. When an attempt is made to revise production standards, it meets considerable worker resistance, even if the revision is fully justified.[6]

In fact, the industrial-engineered specificity of piecework plans represents the seeds of piecework's biggest disadvantage these days. Piecework plans tend to be tailor-made for relatively specialized jobs in which employees do basically the same narrow set of tasks over and over again many times a day. This, in turn, fosters a certain rigidity: employees become preoccupied with producing the number of units needed and are less willing to concern themselves with meeting quality standards or switching from job to job (since doing so could reduce the person's productivity).[7] Employees tend to be trained to perform only a limited number of tasks. Similarly, attempts to introduce new technology or innovative processes may be more likely to fail, insofar as they require major adjustments to engineered standards and negotiations with employees. Equipment tends not to be as well maintained, since employees are focusing on maximizing each machine's output.

Such problems as these have led some firms to drop their piecework plans (as well as their standard hour plans, discussed next) and to substitute team-based incentive plans or programs, such as gainsharing, which will also be discussed later in this chapter.

Standard Hour Plan

standard hour plan A plan by which a worker is paid a basic hourly rate plus an extra percentage of his or her base rate for production exceeding the standard per hour or per day. It is similar to piecework payment but is based on a percentage premium.

The **standard hour plan** is like the piece-rate plan, with one major difference. With a piece-rate plan, the worker is paid a particular rate for each piece that he or she produces. With the standard hour plan, the worker is rewarded by a *premium that equals the percentage by which his or her performance exceeds the standard*. The plan assumes the worker has a guaranteed base rate.

As an example, suppose that the base rate for Smith's job is $8 per hour. (The base rate may, but need not, equal the hourly rate determined by the job evaluation.) Assume also that the production standard for Smith's job is 20 units per hour, or 3 minutes per unit. Suppose that in one day (8 hours) Smith produces 200 door jambs. According to the production standard, this should have taken Smith 10 hours (200 divided by 20 per hour); instead it took him 8 hours. He produced at a rate that was 25 percent (40 divided by 160) higher than the standard rate. The standard rate would be 8 hours times 20 (units per hour) = 160: Smith actually produced 40 more, or 200. He will, therefore, be paid at a rate 25 percent above his base rate for the day. His base rate was $8 per hour times 8 hours, which equals $64, so he will be paid 1.25 times 64, or $80 for the day.

The standard hour plan has most of the advantages of the piecework plan and is fairly simple to compute and easy to understand. The incentive is expressed in units of time instead of in monetary terms (as it is with the piece-rate system). Therefore, there is less tendency on the part of workers to link their production standard with their pay. Furthermore, the clerical job of re-computing piece rates whenever hourly wage rates are re-evaluated is avoided.[8]

Team or Group Incentive Plans

team or group incentive plan A plan in which a production standard is set for a specific work group, and its members are paid incentives if the group exceeds the production standard.

There are several ways in which to implement **team or group incentive plans**.[9] One is to set work standards for each member of the group and maintain a count of the output of each member. Members are then paid based on one of three formulas: (1) all members receive the pay earned by the highest producer; (2) all members receive the pay earned by the lowest producer; or (3) all members receive payment equal to the average pay earned by the group.

The second approach is to set a production standard based on the final output of the group as a whole; all members then receive the same pay, based on the piece rate that exists for the group's job. The group incentive can be based on either the piece rate or standard hour plan, but the latter is somewhat more prevalent.

A third option is to choose a measurable definition of group performance or productivity that the group can control. For instance, broad criteria, such as total labour-hours per final product, could be used: piecework's engineered standards are thus not necessarily required here.[10]

There are several reasons to use team incentive plans. Sometimes, several jobs are interrelated, as they are on project teams. Here, one worker's performance reflects not only his or her own effort but that of co-workers as well; thus, team incentives make sense. Team plans also reinforce group planning and problem solving and help to ensure that collaboration takes place. In Japan, employees are rewarded as a group in order to reduce jealousy, make group members indebted to one another (as they would be to the group), and encourage a sense of cooperation. There tends to be less bickering among group members over who has "tight" production standards and who has loose ones. Group incentive plans also facilitate on-the-job training, since each member of the group has an interest in getting new members trained as quickly as possible.[11]

A group incentive plan's chief disadvantage is that each worker's rewards are no longer based solely on his or her own effort. To the extent that the person does not see his or her effort leading to the desired reward, a group plan may be less effective at motivating employees than an individual plan is.

Research Insight ▷

Group incentive plans have been found to be more effective when there are high levels of communication with employees about the specifics of the plan and strong worker involvement in the plan's design and implementation, and when group members perceive the plan as fair.[12]

INCENTIVES FOR SENIOR MANAGERS AND EXECUTIVES

Most employers award their senior managers and executives a bonus or an incentive because of the role they play in determining divisional and corporate profitability.[13]

Short-Term Incentives: The Annual Bonus

annual bonus Plans that are designed to motivate the short-term performance of managers and are tied to company profitability.

More than 90 percent of firms in Canada with variable pay plans provide an **annual bonus**.[14] Unlike salaries, which rarely decline with reduced performance, short-term incentive bonuses can easily result in an increase or decrease of 25 percent or more in total pay relative to the previous year. Three basic issues should be considered when awarding short-term incentives: eligibility, fund-size determination, and individual awards.

Eligibility

Eligibility is usually decided in one of three ways. The first criterion is *key position*. Here, a job-by-job review is conducted to identify the key jobs (typically only line jobs) that have a measurable impact on profitability. The second approach to determining eligibility is to set a *salary-level* cutoff point; all employees earning over that threshold amount are automatically eligible for consideration for short-term incentives. Finally, eligibility can be determined by *salary grade*. This is a refinement of the salary cutoff approach and assumes that all employees at a certain grade or above should be eligible for the short-term incentive program. The simplest approach is just to use salary level as a cutoff.[15]

The size of the bonus is usually greater for top-level executives. Thus, an executive earning $150 000 in salary may be able to earn another 80 percent of his or her salary as a bonus, while a manager in the same firm earning $80 000 can earn only another 30 percent. Similarly, a supervisor might be able to earn up to 15 percent of his or her base salary in bonuses. Average bonuses range from a low of 10 percent to a high of 80 percent or more: a typical company might establish a plan whereby executives could earn 45 percent of base salary, managers 25 percent, and supervisors 12 percent.

How Much to Pay Out (Fund Size)

Next, a decision must be made regarding the fund size—the total amount of bonus money that will be available—and there are several formulas to do this. Some companies use a *nondeductible formula*. Here a straight percentage (usually of the company's net income) is used to create the short-term incentive fund. Others use a *deductible formula* on the assumption that the short-term incentive fund should begin to accumulate only after the firm has met a specified level of earnings.

In practice, what proportion of profits is usually paid out as bonuses? There are no hard-and-fast rules, and some firms do not even have a formula for developing the bonus fund. One alternative is to reserve a minimum amount of the profits, say 10 percent, for safeguarding shareholders' investments, and then to establish a fund for bonuses equal to 20 percent of the corporate operating

Frank Stronach, CEO of Magna Corp., receives very high bonuses in addition to his regular compensation.

profit before taxes in excess of this base amount. Thus, if the operating profits were $100 000, then the management bonus fund might be 20 percent of $90 000, or $18 000. Other illustrative formulas used for determining the executive bonus fund are as follows:

- 10 percent of net income after deducting 5 percent of average capital invested in the business
- 12.5 percent of the amount by which net income exceeds 6 percent of shareholders' equity
- 12 percent of net earnings after deducting 6 percent of net capital[16]

Determining Individual Awards

The third issue is determining the *individual awards* to be paid. In some cases, the amount is determined on a discretionary basis (usually by the employee's boss), but typically a target bonus is set for each eligible position and adjustments are then made for greater or less than targeted performance. A maximum amount, perhaps double the target bonus, may be set. Performance ratings are obtained for each manager and preliminary bonus estimates are computed. Estimates for the total amount of money to be spent on short-term incentives are thereby made and compared with the bonus fund available. If necessary, the individual estimates are then adjusted.

A related question is whether managers will receive bonuses based on individual performance, team performance, corporate performance, or some combination of these. Keep in mind that there is a difference between a profit-sharing plan and a true, individual incentive bonus. In a profit-sharing plan, each person gets a bonus based on the company's results, regardless of the person's actual effort. With a true individual incentive, it is the manager's individual effort and performance that are rewarded with a bonus.

Here, again, there are no hard-and-fast rules. Top-level executive bonuses are generally tied to overall corporate results (or divisional results if the executive is, say, the vice-president of a major division). The assumption is that corporate results reflect the person's individual performance. However, as one moves further down the chain of command, corporate profits become a less accurate gauge of a manager's contribution. For supervisory staff or the heads of functional departments, the person's individual performance, rather than corporate results, is a more logical determinant of his or her bonus.

Many experts argue that, in most organizations, managerial and executive-level bonuses should be tied to both organizational and individual performance, and there are several ways to do this.[17] Perhaps the simplest is the *split-award method*, which breaks the bonus into two parts. Here, the manager actually gets two separate bonuses, one based on his or her individual effort and one based on the organization's overall performance. Thus, a manager might be eligible for an individual performance bonus of up to $10 000 but receive an individual performance bonus of only $8000 at the end of the year, based on his or her individual performance evaluation. In addition, though, the person might also receive a second bonus of $8000 based on the company's profits for the year. Thus, even if there were no company profits, the high-performing manager would still get an individual performance bonus.

One drawback to this approach is that it pays too much to the marginal performer, who, even if his or her own performance is mediocre, at least gets that second, company-based bonus. One way to get around this problem is to use the

Tips for the Front Line

An Ethical Dilemma

Is it ethical to provide potentially large bonuses to managers and executives on a purely discretionary basis, not necessarily related to performance?

multiplier method. For example, a manager whose individual performance was "poor" might not even receive a company-performance-based bonus, on the assumption that the bonus should be a *product* of individual *and* corporate performance. When either is very poor, the product is zero.

Whichever approach is used, outstanding performers should get substantially larger awards than do other managers. They are people that the company cannot afford to lose, and their performance should always be adequately rewarded by the organization's incentive system. Conversely, marginal or below-average performers should never receive awards that are normal or average, and poor performers should be awarded nothing. The money saved on those people should be given to above-average performers.[18]

Long-Term Incentives

The Conference Board of Canada
www.conferenceboard.ca

Long-term incentives are intended to motivate and reward top management for the firm's long-term growth and prosperity, and to inject a long-term perspective into executive decisions. If only short-term criteria are used, a manager could, for instance, increase profitability by reducing plant maintenance; this tactic might, of course, reduce profits over two or three years. Approximately 50 percent of Canadian organizations provide long-term incentives.[19]

This issue of long- versus short-term perspective has received considerable attention in the past few years as shareholders have become increasingly critical of management focus on short-term returns at the expense of long-term increase in stock price. Long-term incentives are intended also to encourage executives to stay with the company by giving them the opportunity to accumulate capital (in the form of company stock) based on the firm's long-term success. Long-term incentives or **capital accumulation programs** are most often reserved for senior executives but have more recently begun to be extended to employees at lower organizational levels.[20]

capital accumulation programs Long-term incentives most often reserved for senior executives. Six popular plans include stock options, book value plans, stock appreciation rights, performance achievement plans, restricted stock plans, and phantom stock plans.

There are six popular long-term incentive plans (for capital accumulation) in Canada: stock options, book value plans, stock appreciation rights, performance achievement plans, restricted stock plans, and phantom stock plans.[21] The popularity of these plans changes over time because of economic conditions and trends, internal company financial pressures, changing attitudes toward long-term incentives, and changes in tax law, as well as other factors. **Figure 12.2** illustrates the popularity of various long-term incentive plans.

Stock Options

stock option   The right to purchase a stated number of shares of a company stock at today's price at some time in the future.

The **stock option** is the most popular long-term incentive in Canada, but its use is decreasing. Fifty-seven percent of organizations using long-term incentives provided stock options in 2005, compared with 58 percent in 2004 and 72 percent in 2002.[22] A stock option is the right to purchase a specific number of shares of company stock at a specific price during a period of time. Sometimes a vesting (waiting) period is required to ensure that the employee has contributed to any increase in stock price. The executive thus hopes to profit by exercising his or her option to buy the shares in the future but at today's price. The assumption is that the price of the stock will go up, rather than going down or staying the same. As shown in **Figure 12.3**, if shares provided at an option price of $20 per share are exercised (bought) later for $20 when the market price is $60 per share, and sold on the stock market when the market price is $80 per share, a cash gain of $60 per share results. Often, part of the gain is

FIGURE 12.2 Long-Term Incentive Plans*, 2005
(*n* = 168, percent based on organizations with at least one LTIP in place)

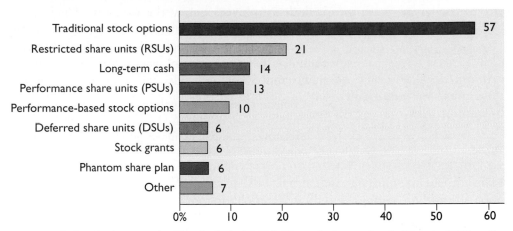

Source: C. Baarda, *Compensation Planning Outlook 2006.* Ottawa: Conference Board of Canada, 2005, p. 8. Reprinted by permission of The Conference Board of Canada, Ottawa.

FIGURE 12.3 Stock Options

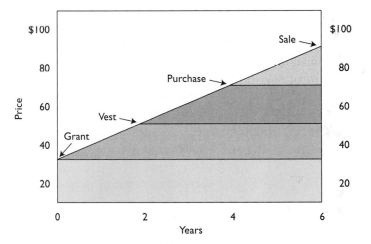

Source: B.R. Ellig, "Executive Pay: A Primer," *Compensation and Benefits Review,* January/February 2003, p. 48. © 2003. Reprinted with permission of Sage Publications, Inc.

needed to meet income tax liabilities that are triggered when the options are exercised. Stock options are attractive from a taxation perspective in Canada, as only 75 percent of the gain on exercising the options is taxable. Thus, stock option plans are often seen as a cash windfall with no downside risk but unlimited upside potential.[23]

Unfortunately, stock price depends to a significant extent on considerations outside the executive's control, such as general economic conditions and investor sentiment. An executive performing valiantly in a declining market or troubled industry may receive nothing, since stock options are worthless if share prices don't rise. This is a particularly important concern in today's volatile stock market.[24] However, stock price is affected relative to the overall stock market by the firm's profitability and growth, and to the extent that the executive can affect these factors, the stock option can be an incentive.

One of the interesting trends in stock options as long-term incentives is that, increasingly, they are not just for high-level managers and executives—or even just managers and executives—anymore. Pepsico, Starbucks, the Gap, Telus, Corel, and many other companies have broad-based stock option plans that include employees below the executive level. The trend toward broad-based plans is aimed at providing support for the competitive strategies being pursued by many firms today. Such companies have been asking more from employees than ever before, but employees often feel that they are corporate "partners" in name only, working harder but receiving little in return. In response,

> Companies are increasingly interested in drawing employees into the new deal by implementing broad-based stock option plans. By giving stock options to non-executives, companies make good the promise of letting employees share in the company's success.[25]

In the post-Enron world, stock options have come under attack as the motive for short-term managerial focus and questionable accounting practices. Proposals have been made to require that stock options be shown as an expense on company financial statements because the excessive issuing of options dilutes share values for shareholders and creates a distorted impression of the true value of a company. The Canada Pension Plan Investment Board stated in its *2006 Proxy Voting Principles and Guidelines,*

> Stock options are a less effective and less efficient form of compensation than direct share ownership in aligning the interests of directors with those of shareholders, (and) it does not motivate the executive to enhance long-term corporate performance. Stock-based compensation is superior to option-based compensation plans for three broad reasons:
> - It provides better alignment of interest of employees with shareholders (across a wide range of future share prices),
> - It is more efficient form of compensation (in terms of the perceived value received by the executive), and
> - It alters the capital structure in a more predictable way (with less potential dilution and more straightforward accounting treatment).[26]

Some organizations have done so voluntarily. Others are considering individual performance in eligibility for stock options. In addition, other forms of capital accumulation plans are becoming more prominent as some companies look for alternatives to stock options. However, the use of stock options persists, as companies continue to cope with the importance of attracting and retaining human capital in the face of fluctuating economic conditions.[27]

Book Value Plan
A book value plan is one alternative to stock options. Here, managers are permitted to purchase stock at current book value, a value anchored in the value of the company's assets. Executives can earn dividends on the stock they own and, as the company grows, the book value of their shares may grow too. When these employees leave the company, they can sell the shares back to the company at the new higher book value.[28] The book value approach avoids the uncertainties of the stock market, emphasizing instead a company's growth. Book value plans are used by privately held companies, as publicly traded companies cannot issue book value stock.

Other Plans
There are several other popular long-term incentive plans. *Stock appreciation rights* (SARs) are usually combined with stock options; they permit the recipient either to exercise the regular stock option (by buying the stock) or to take any

appreciation in the stock price in cash, stock, or some combination of these. A *performance achievement plan* awards shares of stock for the achievement of predetermined financial targets, such as profit or growth in earnings per share. A variation on this plan is to provide stock options that are only exercisable after a performance target has been achieved. With *restricted stock plans*, shares are usually awarded without cost to the executive but with certain restrictions that are imposed by the employer. For example, there may be a risk of forfeiture if an executive leaves the company before the specified time limit elapses. Finally, under *phantom stock plans*, executives receive not shares but "units" that are similar to shares of company stock. Then, at some future time, they receive an amount (usually in cash) equal to the appreciation of the "phantom" stock that they own.[29] Some phantom stock plans even provide the full original unit value plus the amount of appreciation.

Performance Plans

The need to tie executives' pay more clearly to the firm's performance while building in more risk has led many firms to institute *performance plans*. Performance plans "are plans whose payment or value is contingent on financial performance measured against objectives set at the start of a multi-year period."[30] The executive may be granted "performance units" similar to an annual bonus but with a measurement period of longer than a year. For example, an executive might be granted $100 000 in units valued at $50 per unit, in proportion to his or her success in meeting assigned financial goals. In Canada, these plans are usually limited to three years because of income tax rules.

Relating Strategy to Executive Compensation

Executive compensation is more likely to be effective if it is appropriately linked to corporate strategy.[31] Few HR practices have as much connection to strategy as does how the company crafts its long-term incentives. Whether expanding sales through joint ventures abroad, consolidating operations and downsizing the workforce, or some other tactic, few strategies can be accomplished in just one or two years. As a result, the long-term signals that are sent to executives regarding the results and activities that will (or will not) be rewarded can have an impact on whether or not the firm's strategy is implemented effectively. For example, a strategy to boost sales by expanding abroad might suggest linking incentives to increased sales abroad. A cost-reduction strategy might instead emphasize linking incentives to improved profit margins.

Compensation experts therefore suggest defining the strategic context for the executive compensation plan before creating the compensation package itself, as follows:[32]

1. Define the internal and external issues that face the company and its business objectives—boosting sales abroad, downsizing, and so on.

2. Based on the strategic aims, shape each component of the executive compensation package and then group the components into a balanced whole. Include a stock option plan to give the executive compensation package the special character it needs to meet the unique needs of the executives and the company.

3. Check the executive compensation plan for compliance with all legal and regulatory requirements and for tax effectiveness.

4. Install a process for reviewing and evaluating the executive compensation plan whenever a major business change occurs.

INCENTIVES FOR SALESPEOPLE

Sales Compensation
www.davekahle.com/article/getem
.htm

Sales compensation plans have typically relied heavily on incentives (sales commissions), although this varies by industry. In the real estate industry, for instance, salespeople are paid entirely via commissions, while in the pharmaceutical industry, salespeople tend to be paid a salary. However, the most prevalent approach is to use a combination of salary and commissions to compensate salespeople.[33]

The widespread use of incentives for salespeople is due to three factors: tradition, the unsupervised nature of most sales work, and the assumption that incentives are needed to motivate salespeople. The pros and cons of salary, commission, and combination plans follow.

Salary Plan

In a salary plan, salespeople are paid a fixed salary, although there may be occasional incentives in the form of bonuses, sales contest prizes, and the like. There are several reasons to use straight salary. It works well when the main sales objective is prospecting (finding new clients) or when the salesperson is mostly involved in account servicing, such as developing and executing product training programs for a distributor's sales force or participating in national and local trade shows.[34] Jobs like these are often found in industries that sell technical products. This is one reason why the aerospace and transportation equipment industries have a relatively heavy emphasis on salary plans for their salespeople.

There are advantages to paying salespeople on a straight salary basis. Salespeople know in advance what their income will be, and the employer also has fixed, predictable sales force expenses. Straight salary makes it simple to switch territories or quotas or to reassign salespeople, and it can develop a high degree of loyalty among the sales staff. Commissions tend to shift the salesperson's emphasis to making the sale rather than to prospecting and cultivating long-term customers. A long-term perspective is encouraged by straight salary compensation.

The main disadvantage is that salary plans do not depend on results.[35] In fact, salaries are often tied to seniority rather than to performance, which can be demotivating to potentially high-performing salespeople who see seniority—not performance—being rewarded.

Commission Plan

Commission plans pay salespeople in direct proportion to their sales: they pay for results and only for results. The commission plan has several advantages. Salespeople have the greatest possible incentive, and there is a tendency to attract high-performing salespeople who see that effort will clearly lead to rewards. Sales costs are proportional to sales rather than fixed, and the company's selling investment is reduced. The commission basis is also easy to understand and compute.

The commission plan also has drawbacks, however. Salespeople focus on making a sale and on high-volume items; cultivating dedicated customers and working to push hard-to-sell items may be neglected. Wide variances in income between salespeople may occur; this can lead to a feeling that the plan is inequitable. More serious is the fact that salespeople are encouraged to neglect other duties, like servicing small accounts. In addition, pay is often excessive in boom times and very low in recessions.

An Ethical Dilemma

Is it fair to compensate sales employees on a 100-percent commission basis with no financial security?

Recent research evidence presents further insights into the impact of sales commissions. One study addressed whether paying salespeople on commission "without a financial net" might induce more salespeople to leave. The participants in this study were 225 field sales representatives from a telecommunications company. Results showed that paying salespersons a commission accounting for 100 percent of pay was the situation with by far the highest turnover of salespersons. Turnover was much lower in the situation in which salespersons were paid a combination of a base salary plus commissions.[36] These findings suggest that although 100 percent commissions can drive higher sales by focusing the attention of strong-willed salespeople on maximizing sales, without a financial safety net, it can also undermine the desire of salespeople to stay.

The effects on the salesperson of a commission pay plan could also depend on that person's personality. A second study investigated 154 sales representatives who were responsible for contacting and renewing existing members and for identifying and adding new members. A number of the sales reps in this study were more extroverted than were the others—they were more sociable, outgoing, talkative, aggressive, energetic, and enthusiastic.[37] It might be expected that extroverted salespeople would usually generate higher sales than less extroverted ones, but in this study, extroversion was positively associated with higher performance (in terms of percentage of existing members renewing their memberships and the count of new members paying membership fees) *only when the salespeople were explicitly rewarded for accomplishing these tasks*. Thus, being extroverted did not always lead to higher sales; extroverts only sold more than those less extroverted when their rewards were contingent on their performance.

Research Insight ▷

Combination Plan

There has been a definite movement away from the extremes of straight commission or fixed salary to combination plans for salespeople. Combination plans provide some of the advantages of both straight salary and straight commission plans, and also some of their disadvantages. Salespeople have a floor to their earnings. Furthermore, the company can direct its salespeople's activities by detailing what services the salary component is being paid for, while the commission component provides a built-in incentive for superior performance.

However, the salary component is not tied to performance, and the employer is therefore trading away some incentive value. Combination plans also tend to become complicated, and misunderstandings can result. This might not be a problem with a simple "salary plus commission" plan, but most plans are not so simple. For example, there is a "commission plus drawing account" plan, whereby a salesperson is paid basically on commissions but can draw on future earnings to get through low sales periods. Similarly, in the "commission plus bonus" plan, salespeople are again paid primarily on the basis of commissions. However, they are also given a small bonus for directed activities, like selling slow-moving items.

An example can help to illustrate the complexities of the typical combination plan. In one company, for instance, the following three-step formula is applied:

- Step 1: Sales volume up to $18 000 a month. Base salary plus 7 percent of gross profits plus 0.5 percent of gross sales.
- Step 2: Sales volume from $18 000 to $25 000 a month. Base salary plus 9 percent of gross profits plus 0.5 percent of gross sales.
- Step 3: Sales volume more than $25 000 a month. Base salary plus 10 percent of gross profits plus 0.5 percent of gross sales.

In all cases, base salary is paid every two weeks, while the earned percentage of gross profits and gross sales is paid monthly. It should be remembered that setting sales goals or targets is complex and requires careful planning and analysis. Answers to such questions as why $18 000 and $25 000 were chosen as break points must be available.[38]

Tips for the Front Line

The sales force also may get various special awards. Trips, home stereos, TVs, DVD players, and video cameras are commonly used as sales prizes. Access to the latest technology (such as notebook computers with customer and product databases, portable printers, digital cellphones, and so on) can also have a strong behavioural impact on field sales staff.[39]

Sales Compensation in the E-commerce Era

Traditional product-based sales compensation focuses on the amount of product sold. In the Internet age, an integrated team of individuals works together to position the company with prospects, make sales, and service accounts. All sales team members work to deepen customer relationships. This new approach is due to the fact that for customers who know what they want, rapid low-cost purchases can be made over the Internet. Face-to-face sales are now reserved for high-volume customers and higher-margin services.

In the future, sales incentive plans will have to encourage the sales force to focus on the customer, integrate with e-commerce, and support rapid change. Cross-selling incentives (making multiple sales of different product lines to the same customer) will be more important, as will incentives for relationship management and customer satisfaction. Experts recommend setting sales salaries at 50 to 75 percent of total expected compensation, plus incentives. A portion of the incentive should be tied to team-based sales results, in order to encourage sharing, handoffs, and peer pressure.[40]

INCENTIVES FOR OTHER MANAGERS AND PROFESSIONALS

merit pay (merit raise) Any salary increase awarded to an employee based on his or her individual performance.

Merit pay or a **merit raise** is any salary increase that is awarded to an employee based on his or her individual performance. It is different from a bonus in that it usually represents a continuing increment, whereas the bonus represents a one-time payment. Although the term *merit pay* can apply to the incentive raises given to any employees—office or factory, management or nonmanagement— the term is more often used with respect to white-collar employees and particularly professional, office, and clerical employees.

Merit pay has both advocates and detractors and is the subject of much debate.[41] Advocates argue that only pay or other rewards tied directly to performance can motivate improved performance. They contend that the effect of awarding pay raises across the board (without regard to individual performance) may actually detract from performance by showing employees that they will be rewarded the same regardless of how they perform.

Conversely, merit pay detractors present good reasons why merit pay can backfire. One is that the usefulness of the merit pay plan depends on the validity of the performance appraisal system, because if performance appraisals are viewed as unfair, so too will the merit pay that is based on them. Second, supervisors often tend to minimize differences in employee performance when computing merit raises. They give most employees about the same raise, either because of a reluctance to alienate some employees, or a desire to give everyone

Stephanie Kwolek, a DuPont scientist, received the company's highest award, the Lavoisier Medal for Technical Achievement.

a raise that will at least help them to stay even with the cost of living. A third problem is that almost every employee thinks that he or she is an above-average performer; being paid a below-average merit increase can thus be demoralizing.

However, although problems like these can undermine a merit pay plan, there seems to be little doubt that merit pay can and does improve performance. It is critical, however, that performance appraisals be carried out effectively.[42]

Traditional merit pay plans have two basic characteristics: (1) merit increases are usually granted to employees at a designated time of the year in the form of a higher base salary (or *raise*); and (2) the merit raise is usually based exclusively on individual performance, although the overall level of company profits may affect the total sum available for merit raises.[43] In some cases, merit raises are awarded in a single lump sum once a year, without changing base salary. Occasionally, awards are tied to both individual and organizational performance.

Incentives for Professional Employees

Professional employees are those whose work involves the application of learned knowledge to the solution of the employer's problems. They include lawyers, doctors, economists, and engineers. Professionals almost always reach their positions through prolonged periods of formal study.[44]

Pay decisions regarding professional employees involve unique problems. One is that, for most professionals, money has historically been somewhat less important as an incentive than it has been for other employees. This is true partly because professionals tend to be paid well anyway, and partly because they are already driven—by the desire to produce high-calibre work and receive recognition from colleagues.

However, that is not to say that professionals do not want financial incentives. For example, studies in industries like pharmaceuticals and aerospace consistently show that firms with the most productive research and development groups have incentive pay plans for their professionals, usually in the form of bonuses. However, professionals' bonuses tend to represent a relatively small portion of their total pay. The time cycle of the professionals' incentive plans also tends to be longer than a year, reflecting the long time spent in designing, developing, and marketing a new product.

There are also many nonsalary items that professionals must have to do their best work. Not strictly incentives, these items range from better equipment and facilities and a supportive management style to support for professional journal publications.

ORGANIZATION-WIDE INCENTIVE PLANS

Many employers have incentive plans in which virtually all employees can participate. These include profit sharing, employee stock ownership, and Scanlon plans.

Profit-Sharing Plans

profit-sharing plan A plan whereby most or all employees share in the company's profits.

In a **profit-sharing plan**, most or all employees receive a share of the company's profits. Fewer than 20 percent of Canadian organizations offer profit sharing plans.[45] These plans are easy to administer and have a broad appeal to employees and other company stakeholders. The weakness of profit-sharing plans regards "line of sight." It is unlikely that most employees perceive that they personally have the ability to influence overall company profit. It has been found that these plans produce a one-time productivity improvement, but no change thereafter. Another weakness of these plans is that they typically provide an annual payout, which is not as effective as more frequent payouts.[46]

There are several types of profit-sharing plans. In *cash plans*, the most popular, a percentage of profits (usually 15 to 20 percent) is distributed as profit shares at regular intervals. One example is Atlas-Graham Industries Limited in Winnipeg. A profit-sharing pool is calculated by deducting 2 percent of sales from pre-tax profit, and then taking 30 percent of the result. The pool is distributed equally among all employees. Other plans provide cash and deferred benefits. Fisheries Products International Limited in St. John's, Newfoundland, contributes 10 percent of pre-tax income to a profit-sharing pool that is divided up, just before Christmas, based on each employee's earnings. The first 75 percent of each employee's share is paid in cash, and the remaining 25 percent is allocated to pension plan improvements.[47]

There are also *deferred profit-sharing plans*. Here, a predetermined portion of profits is placed in each employee's account under the supervision of a trustee. There is a tax advantage to such plans, since income taxes are deferred, often until the employee retires and is taxed at a lower rate.

Employee Share Purchase/Stock Ownership Plan

employee share purchase/stock ownership plans (ESOPs) A trust is established to hold shares of company stock purchased for or issued to employees. The trust distributes the stock to employees on retirement, separation from service, or as otherwise prescribed by the plan.

Employee share purchase/stock ownership plans (ESOPs) are in place at approximately 60 percent of Canadian organizations with publicly traded stock.[48] A trust is established to purchase shares of the firm's stock for employees by using cash from employee (and sometimes employer) contributions. Employers may also issue treasury shares to the trust instead of paying cash for a purchase on the open market. The trust holds the stock in individual employee accounts and distributes it to employees, often on retirement or other separation from service. Some plans distribute the stock to employees once a year.

The corporation receives a tax deduction equal to the fair market value of the shares that are purchased by the trustee by using employer contributions but not for any treasury shares issued. The value of the shares purchased with employer contributions, and of any treasury shares issued, is a taxable benefit to the employees in the year of purchase of the shares. This tax treatment can create two problems. First, if the plan requires employees to complete a certain period of service before taking ownership of the shares and the employee leaves before being eligible for ownership, the employee has paid tax on the value of shares that he or she never owns. Therefore, most plans have immediate vesting.[49] Second, if the value of the shares drops, employees may have paid tax on a greater amount than they receive when they eventually sell the shares.

ESOPs can encourage employees to develop a sense of ownership in and commitment to the firm, particularly when combined with good communication, employee involvement in decision making, and employee understanding of the business and the economic environment.[50] For example, Creo Products, a digital products company in Burnaby, British Columbia, has become an international success story. It experienced accelerated revenue growth of about 40 percent a year between 1996 and 2000. Employee ownership helped the small entrepreneurial firm to avoid the high failure rate typical of such companies, retain valuable employees, attract investors, and expand rapidly during the early stages of its growth curve and life cycle. As one Creo employee said, "It's not just the shares. It's the way of thinking. I'm extremely happy here."[51]

Scanlon Plan

Few would argue with the fact that the most powerful way of ensuring commitment is to synchronize the organization's goals with those of its employees. Many techniques have been proposed for obtaining this idyllic state, but few have been implemented as widely or successfully as the **Scanlon plan**, an incentive plan developed in 1937 by Joseph Scanlon, a United Steelworkers Union official.[52]

The Scanlon plan is remarkably progressive, considering that it was developed about 70 years ago. As currently implemented, Scanlon plans have the following basic features. The first is the *philosophy of cooperation* on which it is based. This philosophy assumes that managers and workers have to rid themselves of the "us" and "them" attitudes that normally inhibit employees from developing a sense of ownership in the company. A pervasive philosophy of cooperation must exist in the firm for the plan to succeed.[53]

A second feature of the plan is what its practitioners refer to as *identity*. This means that to focus employee involvement, the company's mission or purpose must be clearly articulated and employees must fundamentally understand how the business operates in terms of customers, prices, and costs, for instance.

Competence is a third basic feature. The plan assumes that hourly employees can competently perform their jobs as well as identify and implement improvements, and that supervisors have leadership skills for the participative management that is crucial to a Scanlon plan.

The fourth feature of the plan is the *involvement system*.[54] Productivity-improving suggestions are presented by employees to the appropriate departmental-level committees, the members of which transmit the valuable ones to the executive-level committee. The latter group then decides whether to implement the suggestion.

The fifth element of the plan is the *sharing of benefits formula*. Basically, the Scanlon plan assumes that employees should share directly in any extra profits resulting from their cost-cutting suggestions. If a suggestion is implemented and successful, all employees usually share in 75 percent of the savings. For example, assume that the normal monthly ratio of payroll costs to sales is 50 percent. (Thus, if sales are $600 000, payroll costs should be $300 000.) Assume that suggestions are implemented and result in payroll costs of $250 000 in a month when sales were $550 000 and payroll costs would otherwise have been $275 000 (50 percent of sales). The saving attributable to these suggestions is $25 000 ($275 000 − $250 000). Workers would typically share in 75 percent of this ($18 750), while $6250 would go to the firm. In practice, a portion, usually one-quarter of the $18 750, is set aside for the months in which labour costs exceed the standard.

The Scanlon plan has been quite successful at reducing costs and fostering a sense of sharing and cooperation among employees. Yet Scanlon plans do fail, and there are several conditions required for their success. They are usually more effective when there is a relatively small number of participants, generally fewer than 1000. They are more successful when there are stable product lines and costs, since it is important that the labour costs/sales ratio remain fairly

Scanlon plan An incentive plan developed in 1937 by Joseph Scanlon and designed to encourage cooperation, involvement, and sharing of benefits.

constant. Good supervision and healthy labour relations also seem essential. In addition, it is crucial that there be strong commitment to the plan on the part of management, particularly during the confusing phase-in period.[55]

Gainsharing Plans

gainsharing plan An incentive plan that engages employees in a common effort to achieve productivity objectives and share the gains.

The Scanlon plan is actually an early version of what today is known as a **gainsharing plan,** an incentive plan that engages many or all employees in a common effort to achieve a company's productivity objectives; any resulting incremental cost-saving gains are shared among employees and the company.[56] In addition to the Scanlon plan, other popular types of gainsharing plans include the Rucker and Improshare plans.

The basic difference among these plans is in the formula used to determine employee bonuses.[57] The Scanlon formula divides payroll expenses by total sales. The Rucker formula uses sales value minus materials and supplies, all divided into payroll expenses. The Improshare plan creates production standards for each department. The Scanlon and Rucker plans include participative management systems that use committees. Improshare does not include a participative management component but instead considers participation an outcome of the bonus plan.

The financial aspects of a gainsharing program can be quite straightforward. Assume that a supplier wants to boost quality. Doing so would translate into fewer customer returns, less scrap and rework, and therefore higher profits. Historically, $1 million in output results in $20 000 (2 percent) scrap, returns, and rework. The company tells its employees that if next month's production results in only 1 percent scrap, returns, and rework, the 1 percent saved would be a gain, to be split 50/50 with the workforce, less a small amount for reserve for months in which scrap exceeds 2 percent. Awards are often posted monthly but allocated quarterly.[58]

Gainsharing works well in stable organizations with predictable goals and measures of performance, but is less flexible and useful in dynamic industries that require rapid business adjustment. In general, most of their cost savings are generated in the early years.[59] For example, in 2005 the Canadian National Railway Company and its unionized employees negotiated a gainsharing plan whereby 20 percent of productivity gains would be distributed to employees, to a maximum of 4 percent of their base salary.[60]

DEVELOPING EFFECTIVE INCENTIVE PLANS

There are two major practical considerations in developing an effective incentive plan—when to use it and how to implement it.

When to Use Incentives

Before deciding to implement an incentive plan, it is important to remember several points:

1. *Performance pay cannot replace good management.* Performance pay is supposed to motivate workers, but lack of motivation is not always the culprit. Ambiguous instructions, lack of clear goals, inadequate employee selection and training, unavailability of tools, and a hostile workforce (or management) are just a few of the factors that impede performance.

2. *Firms get what they pay for.* Psychologists know that people often put their effort where they know they will be rewarded. However, this can backfire. An incentive plan that rewards a group based on how many pieces are produced could lead to rushed production and lower quality. Awarding a plant-wide incentive for reducing accidents may simply reduce the number of reported accidents.

3. *"Pay is not a motivator."*[61] Psychologist Frederick Herzberg makes the point that money only buys temporary compliance; as soon as the incentive is removed the "motivation" disappears too. Instead, Herzberg says, employers should provide adequate financial rewards and then build other motivators, like opportunities for achievement and psychological success, into their jobs.

4. *Rewards rupture relationships.* Incentive plans have the potential for reducing teamwork by encouraging individuals (or individual groups) to blindly pursue financial rewards for themselves.

5. *Rewards may undermine responsiveness.* Since the employees' primary focus is on achieving some specific goal, like cutting costs, any changes or extraneous distractions mean that achieving that goal will be harder. Incentive plans can, therefore, mediate against change and responsiveness.

Research
Insight

Nelson Motivation Inc.
www.nelson-motivation.com

Recent research by two professors at the University of Alberta focused on resolving a longstanding debate about whether extrinsic rewards can backfire by reducing intrinsic motivation, or whether extrinsic rewards boost performance and enhance intrinsic motivation. The authors concluded that *careful* management of rewards does enhance performance. Common problem areas to be avoided include not tying rewards to performance, not delivering on all rewards initially promised, and delivering rewards in an authoritarian style or manner.[62]

Potential pitfalls like these do not mean that financial incentive plans cannot be useful or should not be used. They do suggest, however, that goals need to be reasonable and achievable but not so easily attained that employees view incentives as entitlements.[63] In general, any incentive plan is more apt to succeed if implemented with management support, employee acceptance, and a supportive culture characterized by teamwork, trust, and involvement at all levels.[64] This probably helps to explain why some of the longest-lasting incentive plans, like the Scanlon and Rucker plans, depend heavily on two-way communication and employee involvement in addition to incentive pay.

Therefore, in general, it makes more sense to use an incentive plan when units of output can be measured, the job is standardized, the workflow is regular, and delays are few or consistent. It is also important that there be a clear relationship between employee effort and quantity of output, that quality is less important than quantity, or, if quality is important, that it is easily measured and controlled.[65]

How to Implement Incentive Plans

There are several specific common-sense considerations in establishing any incentive plan. Of primary importance is "line of sight." The employee or group must be able to see their own impact on the goals or objectives for which incentives are being provided.[66]

Recent research indicates that there are seven principles that support effective implementation of incentive plans that lead to superior business results:[67]

1. Pay for performance—and make sure that performance is tied to the successful achievement of critical business goals.

2. Link incentives to other activities that engage employees in the business, such as career development and challenging opportunities.

3. Link incentives to measurable competencies that are valued by the organization.

4. Match incentives to the culture of the organization—its vision, mission, and operation principles.

5. Keep group incentives clear and simple—employee understanding is the most important factor differentiating effective from ineffective group incentive plans.

6. Overcommunicate—employees become engaged when they hear the message that they are neither faceless nor expendable.

7. Remember that the greatest incentive is the work itself. For example, highly skilled engineers at MacDonald Detweiler and Associates Ltd. in Richmond, B.C., feel valued and appreciated when they are chosen by their peers to work on project teams, to work on the Canada space arm, or to work on a project to save the rainforest, and they don't require large financial incentives to work hard.

EMPLOYEE RECOGNITION PROGRAMS

Although appreciated at the time of receipt, monetary rewards are quickly spent and offer no lasting symbol of recognition. There is a growing awareness that, in competitive times, when organizations need all the skill and talents of all their people, demonstrating appreciation of employees' achievements is more important than ever. Why? Because lack of recognition and praise is the number-one reason that employees leave an organization. The traditional role of recognition plans has been to reward employees for long service. Today, employees value being appreciated by an employer even more than the reward itself.[68]

Some companies, such as RBC Financial Group, have embedded recognition into their culture, as explained in the Strategic HR box. An employee's introduction to a corporate recognition culture needs to start on the day he or she is hired. For example, have a welcome note, a nameplate ready made, and a personalized gift pack that includes a company t-shirt and coffee mug. These things are all very easy to do, and they send a very clear message to a new employee.[69]

Employees consistently say that they receive little recognition. One study found that only 50 percent of managers give recognition for high performance, and that up to 40 percent of workers feel that they never get recognized for outstanding performance. Nurses are one group of employees that has long suffered from lack of respect. They feel ignored and undervalued as subservient assistants to doctors. The shortage of nurses in Canada has forced employers to consider treating nurses with the respect and recognition they deserve as invaluable contributors of knowledge and skills to the health-care system.[70]

Some believe that this lack of recognition occurs because expressing generous appreciation means talking about feelings in public, which may make managers feel vulnerable. However, when lack of recognition and praise is resulting in the loss of valued employees, managers need to confront such apprehension and start recognizing their employees for their achievements. Why? Because employees favour recognition from supervisors and managers by a margin of two-to-one over recognition from other sources.[71]

Recognition is also cost-effective. It takes 5 to 15 percent of pay to have an impact on behaviour when a cash reward is provided, but only 3 to 5 percent when a noncash form of reward is used (such as recognition and modest gifts).[72] The most common recognition awards are shown in **Figure 12.4**.

Recognition Plus
www.recognitionplusinc.com
National Association for Employee Recognition
www.recognition.org
O.C. Tanner Recognition Co.
www.octanner.com

Strategic HR

Recognition at RBC Financial Group

There probably aren't many people in Canada doing what Steve Richardson does. His full-time job at the RBC Financial Group is to manage recognition—to make sure the elements that compose the RBC recognition strategy are running smoothly and effectively, and to reward RBC's more than 60 000 employees when they go above and beyond for the good of the bank.

There is a very different rewards and recognition philosophy at RBC, says Richardson. Since the late 1980s, the bank has endeavoured to make recognition and rewards an integral part of everything it does—to embed it in the culture of the company. As a former president made it very clear many years ago, recognition would not be something that came and went with the tide. The company has stayed true to that commitment, keeping the recognition budget almost unchanged for more than 15 years.

But meaningful "R and R" programs, as Richardson calls them, have little correlation to the size or value of the actual reward, he says. The important element is

the recognition done by the manager. Everyone has heard horror stories of employees doing extraordinary work and getting nothing more than an e-mail from the manager to go along with the gift or reward, he says. In those cases the intended advantage of a recognition program is lost and employees are left wondering what they have to do to receive the manager's appreciation.

And although recognition is an essential plank in the bank's human resources management strategy, it is not an HR responsibility, says Richardson. It is important for employees to make that distinction.

When recognition is thought of as something HR does, it becomes associated with compensation and employees start to form expectations. "We all expect to get paid every week or expect that our benefits are there, but recognition shouldn't be an expected event. Recognition is really something that should be done when it is warranted, not like salary," he says.

Source: Adapted from D. Brown, "RBC's Recognition Department Oversees Rewarding Culture," *Canadian HR Reporter*, March 14, 2005, pp. 7, 9. Reproduced by permission of *Canadian HR Reporter*, Carswell, One Corporate Plaza, 2075 Kennedy Road, Scarborough, ON M1T 3V4.

FIGURE 12.4   Common Recognition Awards

Certificates and plaques continue to be the most common form of recognition to employees, according to a survey of 614 North American organizations by WorldatWork and the National Association for Employee Recognition in 2005. Nearly nine out of every ten organizations (89 percent) offer some form of recognition to staff. Below is a list of various items and the percentage of respondents that offer them.

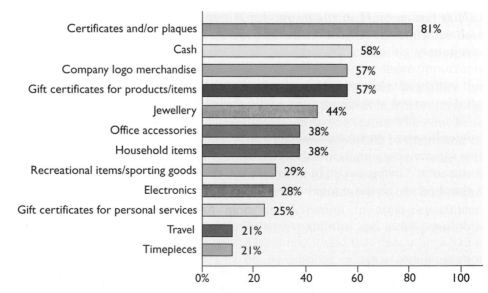

Source: WorldatWork's Trends in Employee Recognition 2005. Reprinted with permission of WorldatWork, Scottsdale, AZ. www.worldatwork.org.

Making time to recognize the individual in front of his or her colleagues is critical to the success of the program. Personal attention and public celebration create recognition that is personal in nature and that addresses the deep needs that we all have for belonging and contributing to something worthwhile. Effective recognition is sincere, immediate, meaningful, consistent, and visible. If it is memorable, it will continue to evoke emotion and make the employee feel that his or her individual effort made a difference. Company DNA, an incentives provider, offers an online points system where recognition points can be spent on merchandise with merchant partners, such as Eddie Bauer, La Senza, Canadian Tire, and Future Shop.[73]

Recognition programs are more effective than cash in achieving improved employee attitudes, increased workloads and hours of work, and productivity (speed of work/intensity of work). They can build confidence, create a positive and supportive environment, build a sense of pride in accomplishments, inspire people to increase their efforts, and help people feel valued. Recognition can act as a strategic change effort if recognition criteria are aligned with business strategy, employee input is solicited regarding program design and implementation, and a recognition culture is created.[74]

Recognition is also important for high performers, who focus on what needs to be done to exceed expectations. These employees are driven by internal motivation, and look to reward programs to add fuel to their achievements. Recognition satisfies "wants" rather than "needs" (where cash bonuses often go); such programs eliminate guilt about owning luxury items, provide bragging rights, and create a lasting impression in the employees' memory.[75]

Finally, recognition programs are key corporate communication tools that can achieve several goals—saying thank you, encouraging good workers, and encouraging good behaviour.[76] RBC Financial Group, Stikeman Elliott law firm, Research In Motion, Procor Limited, Avis car rentals, Minto Developments Inc., Alberta Milk, Southland Transportation, and Snow Valley Edmonton are just some of the Canadian companies that are reaping the benefits of employee recognition programs.[77]

Chapter Review

Summary

1. Piecework is the oldest type of incentive plan. Here, a worker is paid a piece rate for each unit that he or she produces. The standard hour plan rewards workers by a premium that equals the percentage by which their performance is above standard. Group incentive plans are useful when the workers' jobs are highly interrelated.

2. Most management employees receive a short-term incentive, usually in the form of an annual bonus linked to company or divisional profits. Long-term incentives are intended to motivate and reward top management for the firm's long-term growth and prosperity, and to inject a long-term perspective into executive decisions.

3. Salary plans for salespeople are effective when the main sales objective is finding new clients or servicing accounts. The main disadvantage of salary plans is that pay is not tied to performance. Commission plans attract high-performing salespeople who see that performance will clearly lead to rewards. The problem with straight commission plans is that there is a tendency to focus on "big-ticket" or "quick-sell" items and to disregard long-term customer relationships.

4. Money is somewhat less important as an incentive for professional employees than it is for other employees, because professionals are already driven by the desire to produce high-calibre work, and because the time cycle of professionals' incentive plans tends to be longer

than one year, reflecting time for research, design, and development of new products and services. Professionals seek recognition and support in the form of the latest equipment and support for journal publications.

5. Profit-sharing plans, employee share purchase/stock ownership plans, and gainsharing plans, such as the Scanlon plan, are examples of organization-wide incentive plans. Profit-sharing plans provide a share of company profits to all employees in the organization. The problem with such plans is that sometimes the link between a person's efforts and rewards is unclear. Stock purchase plans provide a vehicle for employees to purchase company stock with their own and sometimes employer contributions. Gainsharing plans engage employees in a common effort to achieve a company's productivity objectives, and incremental cost-savings are shared among employees and the company. All these plans are intended to increase employee commitment to the organization and motivate workers.

6. Incentive plans are particularly appropriate when units of output are easily measured, employees can control output, the effort–reward relationship is clear, work delays are under employees' control, and quality is not paramount.

7. Employee recognition plans are growing in popularity as a cost-effective method of retaining employees by praising their achievements. Recognition has the most impact when it is sincerely and meaningfully provided by the supervisor in a public presentation format.

Key Terms

annual bonus   *(p. 313)*
capital accumulation programs   *(p. 316)*
employee share purchase/stock ownership plans   *(p. 324)*
gainsharing plan   *(p. 326)*
guaranteed piecework plan   *(p. 311)*
merit pay (merit raise)   *(p. 322)*
piecework   *(p. 311)*
profit-sharing plan   *(p. 323)*
Scanlon plan   *(p. 325)*
spot bonus   *(p. 310)*
standard hour plan   *(p. 312)*
stock option   *(p. 316)*
straight piecework plan   *(p. 311)*
team or group incentive plan   *(p. 313)*
variable pay   *(p. 309)*

Review and Discussion Questions

1. What are two prerequisites for effective pay-for-performance plans?

2. Describe the three basic issues to be considered when awarding short-term management bonuses.

3. Explain how stock options work. What are some of the reasons that stock options have been criticized in recent years?

4. When and why should a salesperson be paid a salary? A commission? Salary and commission combined?

5. What is a Scanlon plan? What are the five basic features of these plans?

6. Explain five reasons why incentive plans fail.

7. Why are recognition plans useful for motivating high performers?

Critical Thinking Questions

1. A university recently instituted a "Teacher Incentive Program" (TIP) for its faculty. Basically, faculty committees within each of the university's colleges were told to award $5000 raises (not bonuses) to about 40 percent of their faculty members based on how good a job they did in teaching undergraduates, and how many of these students they taught per year. What are the potential advantages and pitfalls of such an incentive program? How well do you think it was accepted by the faculty? Do you think that it had the desired effect?

2. Do you think that it is a good idea to award employees with merit raises? Why or why not? If not, what approach would you take to incentive compensation?

3. In this chapter, we listed a number of reasons that experts give for not instituting a pay-for-performance plan in a vacuum (such as "rewards rupture relationships"). Do you think that these points (or any others) are valid? Why or why not?

4. Recognition can take many forms. Prepare a list of some forms of recognition that would be particularly motivational for Generation Y employees, and explain why you have chosen them.

Application Exercises

Running Case: LearnInMotion.com

The Incentive Plan

Of all its HR programs, those relating to pay for performance and incentives are LearnInMotion.com's most fully developed. For one thing, the venture capital firm that funded it was very explicit about reserving at least 10 percent of the company's stock for employee incentives. The agreement with the venture capital firm also included very explicit terms and conditions regarding LearnInMotion.com's stock option plan. The venture fund agreement included among its 500 or so pages the specific written agreement that LearnInMotion.com would have to send to each of its employees, laying out the details of the company's stock option plan.

Although there was some flexibility, the stock option plan details came down to this:

- Employees would get stock options (the right to buy shares of LearnInMotion.com stock) at a price equal to 15 percent less than the venture capital fund paid for those shares when it funded LearnInMotion.com.

- The shares will have a vesting schedule of 36 months, with one-third of the shares vesting once the employee has completed 12 full months of employment with the company, and one-third vesting on successful completion of each of the following two full 12-month periods of employment.

- If an employee leaves the company for any reason before his or her first full 12 months with the firm, the person is not eligible for stock options.

- If the person has stock options and leaves the firm for any reason, he or she must exercise the options within 90 days of the date of leaving the firm, or lose the right to exercise them.

The actual number of options an employee gets depends on the person's bargaining power and on how much Jennifer and Pierre think the person brings to the company. The options granted generally ranged from options to buy 10 000 shares for some employees up to 50 000 shares for others, but this has not raised any questions to date. When a new employee signs on, he or she receives a letter of offer. This provides minimal details regarding the option plan; after the person has completed the 90-day introductory period, he or she receives the five-page document describing the stock option plan, which Jennifer or Pierre, as well as the employee, signs.

Beyond that, the only incentive plan is the one for the two salespeople. In addition to their respective salaries, both salespeople receive about 20 percent of any sales they bring in, whether those sales are from advertising banners or course listing fees. It's not clear to Jennifer and Pierre whether this incentive is effective. Each salesperson gets a base salary regardless of what he or she sells (one gets about $50 000, the other about $35 000). However, sales have simply not come up to the levels anticipated. Jennifer and Pierre are not sure why. It could be that Internet advertising has dried up. It could be that their own business model is no good, or there's not enough demand for their company's services. They may be charging too much or too little. It could be that the salespeople can't do the job because of inadequate skills or inadequate training. Or, of course, it could be the incentive plan. ("Or it could be all of the above," as Pierre somewhat dejectedly said late one Friday evening.) They want to try to figure out what the problem is. They want you, their management consultant, to help them figure out what to do. Here's what they want you to do for them.

Questions

1. Up to this point they've awarded only a tiny fraction of the total stock options available for distribution. Should they give anyone or everyone additional options? Why or why not?

2. Should they put other employees on a pay-for-performance plan that somehow links their monthly or yearly pay to how well the company is doing sales-wise? Why or why not? If so, how should the company do it?

3. Is there another incentive plan you think would work better for the salespeople? What is it?

4. On the whole, what do you think the sales problem is?

Case Incident

Loafers at Interlake Utility Company

Interlake Utility Company provides electrical power to a district with 50 000 households. Pamela Johnson is the manager in charge of all repair and installation crews. Each crew consists of approximately seven employees who work closely together to respond to calls concerning power outages, fires caused by electrical malfunctions, and installation of new equipment or electrical lines.

Fourteen months ago, Johnson decided to implement a team-based incentive system in which an annual bonus would be provided to each crew that met certain performance criteria. Performance measures included such indicators as average length of time needed to restore power, results of a customer satisfaction survey, and number of hours required to complete routine installation assignments successfully. At the end of the first year, five crews received an average cash bonus of $12 000 each, with the amount divided equally among all crew members.

Soon after Johnson announced the recipients of the cash bonus, she began to receive a large number of complaints. Some teams not chosen for the award voiced their unhappiness through their crew leader. The two most common complaints were that the teams working on the most difficult assignments were penalized (because it was harder to score higher on the evaluation) and that crews unwilling to help out other crews were being rewarded.

Ironically, members of the crews that received the awards also expressed dissatisfaction. A surprisingly large number of confidential employee letters from the winning teams reported that the system was unfair because the bonus money was split evenly among all crew members. Several letters named loafers who received "more than their share" because they were frequently late for work, took long lunches and frequent smoking breaks, and lacked initiative. Johnson is at a loss about what to do next.

Questions

1. What major issues and problems concerning the design and implementation of pay-for-performance systems does this case illustrate? Explain.

2. Are team-based incentives appropriate for the type of work done by Johnson's crews?

3. Might it be desirable to use a combination of team-based and individual incentives at Interlake Utility Company? How might such a plan be structured?

Source: L. Gomez-Mejia, D.B. Balkin, R.L. Cardy and D. Dimick, *Managing Human Resources*, Canadian Second Edition, Scarborough, ON: Prentice-Hall Canada, 2000, pp. 342–343. Reprinted with permission of Pearson Education Canada.

Experiential Exercises

1. Working individually or in groups, develop an incentive plan for each of the following positions: Web designer, hotel manager, and used-car salesperson. What factors had to be taken into consideration?

2. Explain why employee recognition plans are growing in popularity. How would you go about recognizing your favourite professor?

3. Express Automotive, an automobile mega-dealership with more than 600 employees that represents 22 brands, has just received a very discouraging set of survey results. It seems its customer satisfaction scores have fallen for the ninth straight quarter. Customer complaints included the following:

   • It was hard to get prompt feedback from mechanics by phone.

   • Salespeople often did not return phone calls.

   • The finance people seemed "pushy."

   • New cars were often not properly cleaned or had minor items that needed immediate repair or adjustment.

   • Cars often had to be returned to have repair work redone.

   The following table describes Express Automotive's current compensation system.

The class is to be divided into five groups. Each group is assigned to one of the five teams in column one. Each group should analyze the compensation package for its team. Each group should be able to identify the ways in which the current compensation plan (1) helps company performance and/or (2) impedes company performance. Once the groups have completed their analyses, the following questions are to be discussed as a class:

(a) In what ways might your group's compensation plan contribute to the customer service problems?

(b) Are rewards provided by your department that impede the work of other departments?

(c) What recommendations would you make to improve the compensation system in a way that would likely improve customer satisfaction?

Team	Responsibility	Current Compensation Method
Sales force	Persuade buyers to purchase a car.	Very small salary (minimum wage) with commissions; commission rate increases with every 20 cars sold per month.
Finance office	Help close the sale; persuade customer to use company finance plan.	Salary, plus bonus for each $10 000 financed with the company.
Detailing	Inspect cars delivered from factory, clean and make minor adjustments.	Piecework paid on the number of cars detailed per day.
Mechanics	Provide factory warranty service, maintenance, and repair.	Small hourly wage, plus bonus based on (1) number of cars completed per day and (2) finishing each car faster than the standard estimated time to repair.
Receptionists/ phone service personnel	Act as primary liaison between customer and sales force, finance, and mechanics.	Minimum wage.

CHAPTER 13

EMPLOYEE BENEFITS AND SERVICES

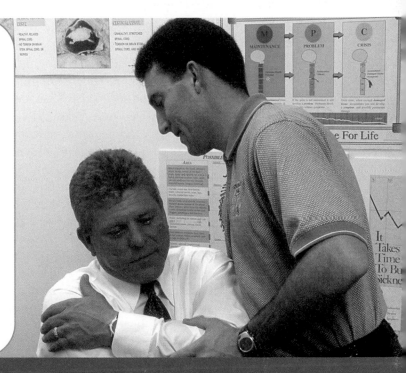

REQUIRED PROFESSIONAL CAPABILITIES

- Ensures compliance with legally required programs
- Establishes sound operational practices to ensure confidentiality of employee information and compliance with regulatory requirements
- Develops specifications for the acquisition and day-to-day management of employee benefit programs
- Integrates the basic benefits program with disability management
- Develops specifications for the acquisition or redesign of pension plans and their administration
- Reviews pension proposals submitted by third parties and evaluates the information received
- Recommends the pension plan most suited to organizational objectives

- Performs a cost-benefit analysis of organizational and employee needs and preferences relative to benefit plans, including taxation considerations and funding requirements
- Administers the reporting, funding, and fiduciary aspects of the plan
- Ensures the effectiveness of benefit programs by providing information, ensuring accessibility of the program, and minimizing the cost of the program
- Manages the transition to new plans, including communications, employee counselling, training, and discarding redundant practices
- Provides necessary information and counselling to pension plan participants
- Manages the transition to new or revised plans by providing information to plan participants and providing appropriate training for administrative staff

THE STRATEGIC ROLE OF EMPLOYEE BENEFITS

employee benefits Indirect financial payments given to employees. They may include supplementary health and life insurance, vacation, pension, education plans, and discounts on company products, for instance.

Employee benefits and services can be defined as all the indirect financial payments that an employee receives during his or her employment with an employer.[1] Benefits are generally available to all of a firm's employees and include such things as time off with pay, supplementary health and life insurance, and employee assistance plans. Employee services, traditionally a minor aspect of compensation, are becoming more sought after by today's employees in the post-job-security era. Research indicates that benefits do matter to employees and that if they are aligned with business strategy, they can help to attract and retain the right people to achieve business objectives.[2]

Employee benefits are an important part of most employees' compensation, particularly given today's reality of modest salary increases.[3] For the aging workforce, health-care benefits are becoming increasingly important. Employee benefits are in the midst of an evolution, based on the aging population, the looming labour shortage in Canada, and advances in health care. Each of these factors is expected to increase the cost of benefits, which are already at an all-time high.[4]

Administering benefits today represents an increasingly specialized task because workers are more financially sophisticated and demanding, and because benefit plans must comply with a wide variety of laws. Providing and administering benefits is also an increasingly expensive task. Benefits as a percentage of payroll (for public and private sectors combined) are about 37 percent today (compared with about 15 percent in 1953). That translates to around $17 500 in total annual benefits per employee.[5] Most employees do not realize the market value and high cost to the employer of their benefits, so prudent employers list the benefits' true costs on each employee's pay stub.

Most Canadian companies provide some form of employee benefits. Almost all employers provide group life insurance, and most provide health and dental care insurance and retirement benefits. In the remainder of this chapter, we will describe government-sponsored benefits, voluntary employer-sponsored benefits, employee services, flexible benefits, and benefits administration.

Benefits Interface
www.benefits.org
Employee Benefit Research Institute
www.ebri.org
Benefits Link
www.benefitslink.com
Benefits Canada
www.benefitscanada.ca

GOVERNMENT-SPONSORED BENEFITS

Canada has one of the world's finest collections of social programs to protect its citizens when they cannot earn income. Employers and employees provide funding for these plans, along with general tax revenues.

Employment Insurance (EI)

employment insurance A federal program that provides income benefits if a person is unable to work through no fault of his or her own.

Employment insurance is a federal program that provides weekly benefits if a person is unable to work through no fault of his or her own. It does not apply to workers who are self-employed. EI provides benefits for employees who are laid off, terminated without just cause, or who quit their job for a justifiable reason, such as harassment. EI benefits are not payable when an employee is terminated for just cause—for example, for theft of company property—or when an employee quits for no good reason. Workers may also be eligible for special EI benefits in cases of illness, injury, or quarantine where the employer has no sickness or disability benefits (or once such benefits have been exhausted), and for maternity/parental leaves.

To receive benefits, an employee must first have worked a minimum number of hours during a minimum number of weeks called a *qualifying period* (the number of hours and weeks varies among regions of the country). Then there is a waiting period from the last day of work until benefits begin. The waiting period varies but is often two weeks. If the employee was provided with severance pay or holiday pay at the time of losing the job, these payments must run out before the waiting period begins.

The EI benefit is generally 55 percent of average earnings during the last 14 to 26 weeks of the qualifying period, depending on the regional unemployment rate. The benefit is payable for up to 45 weeks, depending on the regional unemployment rate and other factors. To receive EI benefits, individuals must demonstrate that they are actively seeking work. Claimants are encouraged to work part-time, as they can earn up to 25 percent of their EI benefit amount before these earnings will be deducted from the benefit. Compassionate care benefits are payable for up to six weeks, illness benefits for up to 15 weeks, and maternity/parental leave benefits can be taken by one or split between both parents for up to 50 weeks.[6]

The EI program is funded by contributions from eligible employees and their employers. Employee contributions are collected by payroll deduction, and employers pay 1.4 times the employee contribution. Employer contributions can be reduced if the employer provides a wage loss replacement plan for employee sick leave.

A supplemental unemployment benefit (SUB) plan is an agreement between an employer and the employees (often the result of collective bargaining) for a plan that enables employees who are eligible for EI benefits to receive additional benefits from an SUB fund created by the employer. The purpose of an SUB plan is to supplement EI benefits so that employees can better maintain their standard of living during periods of unemployment resulting from a variety of circumstances (including layoffs, maternity/parental leave, and illness) by receiving a combined benefit closer to their actual working wage. One Canadian study found that 80 percent of employers who provide SUBs do so for maternity leaves. SUBs are often found in heavy-manufacturing operations, such as the auto and steel industries, where layoffs are common. The amount of the SUB benefit is usually determined based on length of service and wage rate. Eighty percent of Canadian SUBs provide benefits of 90 percent of the working wage or greater.[7] Work-sharing programs are a related arrangement in which employees work a reduced workweek and receive EI benefits for the remainder of the week. The EI Commission must approve SUB plans and work-sharing programs.

Canada/Quebec Pension Plan (C/QPP)

The Canada/Quebec Pension Plans (C/QPP) were introduced in 1966 to provide working Canadians with a basic level of financial security on retirement or disability. Four decades later, these benefits do indeed provide a significant part of most Canadians' retirement income. Almost all employed Canadians between the ages of 18 and 65 are covered, including self-employed individuals. Casual and migrant workers are excluded, as are people who are not earning any employment income, such as homemakers. The benefits are portable, meaning that pension rights are not affected by changes in job or residence within Canada. Both contributions and benefits are based only on earnings up to the "Year's Maximum Pensionable Earnings" (intended to approximate the average industrial wage) as defined in the legislation. Benefits are adjusted based on inflation each year in line with the consumer price index. Contributions made by employees (4.95 percent of pensionable earnings) are matched by employers.

Income Security Programs
www.hrsdc.gc.ca/en/gateways/nav
/top_nav/program/isp.shtml

REQUIRED PROFESSIONAL CAPABILITIES

Ensures compliance with legally required programs

Hints to Ensure Legal Compliance

Canada/Quebec Pension Plan (C/QPP)   Programs that provide three types of benefits: retirement income; survivor or death benefits payable to the employee's dependants regardless of age at time of death; and disability benefits payable to employees with disabilities and their dependants. Benefits are payable only to those individuals who make contributions to the plans and/or available to their family members.

Canada Pension Plan
www.cpp-rpc.gc.ca

Three types of benefits are provided: retirement pensions, disability pensions, and survivor benefits. The *retirement pension* is calculated as 25 percent of the average earnings (adjusted for inflation up to the average inflation level during the last five years before retirement) over the years during which contributions were made. Plan members can choose to begin receiving benefits at any time between the ages of 60 and 70. Benefits are reduced on early retirement before age 65 and are increased in the case of late retirement after age 65. *Disability benefits* are only paid for severe disabilities that are expected to be permanent or to last for an extended period. The disability benefit is 75 percent of the pension benefit earned at the date of disability, plus a flat-rate amount per child. *Survivor benefits* are paid on the death of a plan member. A lump sum payment is made to survivors, and a monthly pension is also payable to the surviving spouse.

Workers' Compensation

workers' compensation Workers' compensation provides income and medical benefits to victims of work-related accidents or illnesses and/or their dependants, regardless of fault.

Workers' compensation laws are aimed at providing sure, prompt income and medical benefits to victims of work-related accidents or illnesses and/or their dependants, regardless of fault. Every province and territory, and the federal jurisdiction, has its own workers' compensation law. These laws impose compulsory collective liability for workplace accidents and work-related illnesses. This means that employees and employers cannot sue each other regarding the costs of workplace accidents or illnesses. Workers' compensation is, in effect, a "no fault" insurance plan designed to help injured or ill workers get well and return to work. For an injury or illness to be covered by workers' compensation, one must only prove that it arose while the employee was on the job. It does not matter that the employee may have been at fault; if he or she was on the job when the injury or illness occurred, he or she is entitled to workers' compensation. For example, suppose all employees are instructed to wear safety goggles when working at their machines, and one does not and is injured. Workers' compensation benefits will still be provided. The fact that the worker was at fault in no way waives his or her claim to benefits.

Employers collectively pay the full cost of the workers' compensation system, which can be an onerous financial burden for small businesses. The amount of the premiums (called assessments) varies by industry and by actual employer costs. Employer premiums are tax-deductible. Workers' Compensation Boards (WCB); Workplace Safety and Insurance Board in Ontario; WorkSafe BC in British Columbia; the Workplace Health, Safety and Compensation Commission in New Brunswick and in Newfoundland and Labrador; and the Commission de la santé et de la sécurité du travail in Quebec) exist in each jurisdiction to determine and collect assessments from employers, determine rights to compensation, and pay workers the amount of benefit to which they are entitled under the legislation in their jurisdiction. Employers and employees have some representation on these boards, but usually both parties believe they should have more control.

Workers' compensation benefits include payment of expenses for medical treatment and rehabilitation, and income benefits during the time in which the worker is unable to work (temporarily or permanently) because of his or her disability (partial or total). Survivor benefits are payable if a work-related death occurs. All benefits are nontaxable.

Although safety gear is always recommended, failure to wear it does not invalidate an employee's claim for benefits under workers' compensation laws.

Controlling Workers' Compensation Costs

In most provinces, workers' compensation costs skyrocketed during the 1980s and 1990s. Unfunded liabilities for future pensions across the country reached more than $15 billion. As a result, a number of provinces amended their workers' compensation legislation to reduce benefit levels, limit benefit entitlements for stress-related illnesses and chronic pain, reduce inflation indexing of benefits, and put more emphasis on rehabilitation and return to work. Several provinces followed the lead of Alberta in using sound business principles and practices to streamline the large administrative bureaucracies that had developed and to eliminate unfunded liabilities while still providing the benefits required by law and generating surplus funds to return to employers.

All parties agree that a renewed focus on accident prevention is the best way to manage workers' compensation costs over the long term. Minimizing the number of workers' compensation claims is an important goal for all employers. Although the Workers' Compensation Board pays the claims, the premiums for most employers depend on the number and amount of claims that are paid. Minimizing such claims is thus important.

In practice, there are two basic approaches to reducing workers' compensation claims. First, firms try to reduce accident- or illness-causing conditions in facilities by instituting effective *safety and health programs* and complying with government safety standards. Second, since workers' compensation costs increase the longer an employee is unable to return to work, employers have become involved in instituting *rehabilitation programs* for injured or ill employees. These include physical therapy programs and career counselling to guide such employees into new, less strenuous or stressful jobs to reintegrate recipients back into the workforce. Workers are required to cooperate with return-to-work initiatives, such as modified work.[8] When Purolator's workers' compensation costs came to $13 million in 2005, it decided to use both of these approaches to reduce costs. The company hired occupational nurses, conducted physical demands analysis of many of its jobs, strengthened its return-to-work program, tied injury reduction to managers' bonuses, and increased its interaction with doctors.[9]

Vacations and Holidays

Labour/employment standards legislation sets out a minimum amount of paid vacation that must be provided to employees, usually two weeks per year, but the requirements vary by jurisdiction. The actual number of paid employee vacation days also varies considerably from employer to employer. Even within the same organization, the number of vacation days usually depends on how long the employee has worked at the firm. Thus, a typical vacation policy might call for

- two weeks for the first 5 years of service
- three weeks for 6 to 10 years of service
- four weeks for 11 to 15 years of service
- five weeks for 16 to 25 years of service
- six weeks after 25 years of service

The average number of annual vacation days is generally greater in European countries. For example, employees in Sweden and Austria can expect 30 vacation days; in France, 25 days; and in the United Kingdom, Spain, Norway, Finland, and Belgium, 20 to 25 days. There is some pressure from younger Canadian employees to increase vacation time, to assist with work/life balance.[10]

The number of paid holidays similarly varies considerably from one jurisdiction to another, from a minimum of five to a maximum of nine. The most common paid holidays include New Year's Day, Good Friday, Canada Day, Labour Day, Thanksgiving Day, and Christmas Day. Other common holidays include Victoria Day, Remembrance Day, and Boxing Day. Additional holidays may be observed in each province, such as Saint Jean-Baptiste Day in Quebec and the Alberta Family Day.

Leaves of Absence

All the provinces and territories, and the federal jurisdiction, require unpaid leaves of absence to be provided to employees in certain circumstances. Maternity/pregnancy leave is provided in every jurisdiction, and each has one or more of paternity, parental, and adoption leave available as well. The amount of maternity leave is 17 or 18 weeks in each jurisdiction (usually after one year of service), but parental and adoption leaves range from 8 to 52 weeks. Employees who take these leaves of absence are guaranteed their old job or a similar job when they return to work.

REQUIRED PROFESSIONAL CAPABILITIES

Establishes sound operational practices to ensure confidentiality of employee information and compliance with regulatory requirements

Bereavement leave on the death of a family member is provided for employees in some, but not all, jurisdictions. The amount of time off varies by jurisdiction and depends on the closeness of the relationship between the employee and the deceased. Bereavement leave is usually unpaid, but in some cases it can be partially or fully paid. All jurisdictions except Alberta and the Northwest Territories provide compassionate care leave for employees who are caring for a dying relative (six weeks of employment insurance is payable during these leaves).[11]

Having a clear procedure for any leave of absence is essential. An application form, such as the one in **Figure 13.1**, should be the centrepiece of any such procedure. In general, no employee should be given a leave until it is clear what the leave is for. If the leave is for medical or family reasons, medical certification should be obtained from the attending physician or medical practitioner. A form like this also places on record the employee's expected return date and the fact that, without an authorized extension, his or her employment may be terminated.

Although these leaves are unpaid, it is incorrect to assume that the leave is costless to the employer. For example, one study concluded that the costs associated with recruiting new temporary workers, training replacement workers, and compensating for the lower level of productivity of these workers could represent a substantial expense over and above what employers would normally pay their full-time employees.[12]

Pay on Termination of Employment

Employment/labour standards legislation requires that employees whose employment is being terminated by the employer be provided with termination pay when they leave. The amount to be paid varies among jurisdictions and with the circumstances, as follows.

Pay in Lieu of Notice

An employee must be provided with advance written notice if the employer is going to terminate his or her employment (unless the employee is working on a short-term contract or is being fired for just cause). The amount of advance notice that is required increases with the length of employment of the employee

FIGURE 13.1   Sample Application for Leave of Absence

APPLICATION FOR LEAVE OF ABSENCE WITHOUT PAY

NAME:			
	Surname	*First Name*	*Initial*

I.D #

WORK LOCATION:
☐ King Edward Campus   ☐ City Centre Campus
☐ Other: _____
Please specify

DEPARTMENT:

EMPLOYEE GROUP:
☐ Support Staff (CUPE)   ☐ VCCFA Instructors
☐ Administrators   ☐ VCCFA Health Nurses

PERIOD OF LEAVE REQUESTED (Includes Weekends):

FROM (First Calendar Day of Leave):

Day   Month   Year

TO (Last Calendar Day of Leave):

Day   Month   Year

If period of Leave requested is 15 (fifteen) calendar days or less, you must complete this section:

Number of Duty Days on Leave: _____

Total Number of Hours on Leave: _____

Working under Compressed Work Week Schedule: ☐ Yes   ☐ No

If Leave Is One Duty Day or Less, Indicate Hours of Leave: _____

For Faculty Members:

This unpaid Leave of Absence will not count as "duty days" for the purpose of regularization of appointment nor for the purpose of time-status increase.

REASON FOR REQUEST:

☐ **PERSONAL**   ☐ **ILLNESS** (Exhaustion of Sick Leave Credits) _____
First Date of Absence

☐ **MATERNITY** (Please attach Doctor's note indicating Expected Date of Confinement)

☐ **OTHER** _____
Please Specify

EMPLOYEE'S SIGNATURE:	DATE:	
APPROVAL—DEPARTMENT HEAD:	DATE:	
APPROVAL—HUMAN RESOURCES:	DATE:	
THIS SECTION FOR PAYROLL USE:		

The information on this form is collected under the authority of the Collective Agreement between the College and its bargaining units. The information provided will be used to process your leave. If you have any questions about the collection and use of this information, please contact the Department of Human Resources.

Completed "Original" Form to be Forwarded to the Department of Human Resources for Processing

Source: Human Resources Department, Vancouver Community College. © 2003. Reproduced with permission.

(often one week per year of employment to a specified maximum) and varies among jurisdictions. Many employers do not provide advance written notice. Instead, they ask the employee to cease working immediately and provide the employee with a lump sum equal to their pay for the notice period. This amount is called "pay in lieu of notice."

Severance Pay

Employees in Ontario and the federal jurisdiction may be eligible for severance pay in addition to pay in lieu of notice in certain termination situations. In Ontario, employees with five or more years of service may be eligible for severance pay if (1) the employer's annual Ontario payroll is $2.5 million or more, or (2) the employer is closing down the business and 50 or more employees will be losing their jobs within a six-month period. The amount of the severance pay is one week's pay for each year of employment (maximum 26 weeks). In the federal jurisdiction, employees who have been employed for 12 months or more receive the greater of (1) two days' wages per year of employment and (2) five days' wages.

Pay for Mass Layoffs

The provinces of British Columbia, Manitoba, Ontario, New Brunswick, and Newfoundland and Labrador require that additional pay be provided when a layoff of 50 or more employees occurs. In Nova Scotia and Saskatchewan, additional pay is required if 10 or more employees are being laid off. The amount of additional pay ranges from 6 weeks to 18 weeks, depending on the province and the number of employees being laid off.

VOLUNTARY EMPLOYER-SPONSORED BENEFITS

Although they are not required to do so, employers often provide many other employee benefits. Several of the most common types of employee benefits will now be described.

Life Insurance

group life insurance Insurance provided at lower rates for all employees, including new employees, regardless of health or physical condition.

Virtually all employers provide **group life insurance** plans for their employees. As a group, employees can obtain lower rates than if they bought such insurance as individuals. In addition, group plans usually contain a provision for coverage of all employees—including new ones—regardless of health or physical condition.

In most cases, the employer pays 100 percent of the base premium, which usually provides life insurance equal to about two years' salary. Additional life insurance coverage is sometimes made available to employees, on an optional, employee-paid basis. *Accidental death and dismemberment* coverage provides a fixed lump-sum benefit in addition to life insurance benefits when death is accidental. It also provides a range of benefits in case of accidental loss of limbs or sight and is often paid for by the employer.

Critical illness insurance provides a lump-sum benefit to an employee who is diagnosed with and survives a life-threatening illness. This benefit bridges the gap between life insurance and disability insurance by providing immediate funds to relieve some the financial burden associated with the illness (such as paying for out-of-country treatment or experimental treatment) or enabling employees to enjoy their remaining time by pursuing activities that would normally be beyond their financial means.[13]

REQUIRED PROFESSIONAL CAPABILITIES

Develops specifications for the acquisition and day-to-day management of employee benefit programs

Supplementary Health-Care/Medical Insurance

Most employers provide their employees with supplementary health-care/medical insurance (over and above that provided by provincial health-care plans). Along with life insurance and long-term disability, these benefits form the cornerstone of almost all benefit programs.[14] Supplementary health-care insurance is aimed at providing protection against medical costs arising from off-the-job accidents or illness.

Most supplementary health insurance plans provide insurance at group rates, which are usually lower than individual rates and are generally available to all employees—including new ones—regardless of health or physical condition. Supplementary health-care plans provide major medical coverage to meet medical expenses not covered by government health-care plans, including prescription drugs, private or semi-private hospital rooms, private duty nursing, physiotherapy, medical supplies, ambulance services, and so on. In most employer-sponsored drug plans, employees must pay a specified amount of **deductible** expense (typically $25 or $50) per year before plan benefits begin. Many employers also sponsor health-related insurance plans that cover expenses like vision care, hearing aids, and dental services, often with deductibles. In a majority of cases, the participants in such plans have their premiums paid for entirely by their employers.[15]

deductible The annual amount of health/dental expenses that an employee must pay before insurance benefits will be paid.

Reducing Health Benefit Costs

Dramatic increases in health-care costs are the biggest issue facing benefits managers in Canada today. **Figure 13.2** shows how increases in medical and dental plan costs have escalated since 1990. The main reasons for these increases are increased use of expensive new drugs, rising drug utilization by an aging population, and reductions in coverage under provincial health-care plans. Despite government health-care plans, Canadian employers pay about 30 percent of all health-care expenses in Canada, most of this for prescription drugs. The latest research from the Canadian Life and Health Insurance Association shows that annual employer health benefit payments total $12.5 billion.[16]

Many Canadian managers now find controlling and reducing health-care costs topping their to-do lists. The simplest approach to reducing health-benefit costs (and most common, as shown in **Table 13.1**) is to *increase the amount of health-care costs paid by employees.* This can be accomplished by increasing employee premiums, increasing deductibles, reducing company **coinsurance** levels, instituting

Tips for the Front Line

coinsurance The percentage of expenses (in excess of the deductible) that are paid for by the insurance plan.

FIGURE 13.2 Health Plan Costs versus Inflation

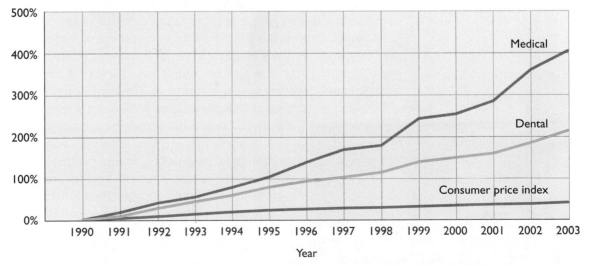

Source: Jason Billard, "Communicating Can Ease the Pain of Rising Benefits Costs," *Canadian HR Reporter,* June 17, 2002, pp. G3, G11. Reproduced by permission of *Canadian HR Reporter,* Carswell, One Corporate Plaza, 2075 Kennedy Road, Scarborough, ON M1T 3V4.

TABLE 13.1   Initiatives to Control Rising Health-Care Costs

Initiative	Number of Respondents	Percentage*
Cost-sharing	58	31
Review	40	21
Plan redesign	38	20
Caps/maximums	26	14
Communication/education	25	13
Implementation/considering flexible benefit plans	22	12
Cuts (including cuts to dependants' coverage)	14	7
Negotiating with provider; finding new provider	11	6
Wellness initiatives	9	5
Negotiating with union	5	3

Source: N. Wassink and J.L. MacBride-King, *Beyond Band-Aid Solutions: Managing Organizations' Health Benefit Costs.* Ottawa: Conference Board of Canada, May 2004, p. 3. Reprinted by permission of The Conference Board of Canada, Ottawa.

or lowering annual maximums on some services, or even eliminating coverage for spouses, private hospital rooms, and other benefits. An Angus Reid poll of 1500 Canadians found that three-quarters of the respondents were willing to pay higher premiums to cover the high cost of prescription drugs.[17]

Another cost-reduction strategy is to publish a *restricted list of the drugs* that will be paid for under the plan, to encourage the use of generic rather than more expensive brand-name drugs. New drugs may not be covered if equally effective, cheaper alternatives are available. This approach should be combined with employee education to effectively manage the demand for drugs.[18]

A third approach is *health promotion*. In-house newsletters can caution workers to take medication properly and advertise programs on weight management, smoking cessation, exercise classes, on-site massage therapy, nutrition counselling, and other wellness programs. After ten years of providing an on-site exercise program for employees, Canada Life Insurance Company found that absenteeism dropped 24 percent for employees who exercised two to three times per week.[19] Employee assistance programs can help to combat alcohol and drug addiction, and provide stress-management counselling. Enbridge has used the health-promotion approach, as described in the Strategic HR box.

A fourth approach is to implement *risk-assessment* programs. Such programs are being used by the Canadian Imperial Bank of Commerce and other companies. A third party conducts a confidential survey of the health history and lifestyle choices of employees in order to identify common health risk factors, such as those associated with heart disease or mental health, so that problem-specific programs can be implemented.[20]

Finally, *health services spending accounts* are offered by more than 90 percent of Canadian employers, either alone or in combination with a standard health-care plan. The employer establishes an annual account for each employee containing a certain amount of money (determined by the employer). This provides cost control for the employer. Then the employee can spend the money on health-care costs as he or she wants. This provides flexibility for the employee. These accounts are governed by the Income Tax Act, which allows expenses not normally covered under employer-sponsored health-care plans

Canadian Health Network
www.canadian-health-network.ca

An on-site employee fitness centre

Strategic HR

Proactive Enbridge Reduces Health Care Costs

In the spring of 2003, Enbridge Consumers Gas, a natural gas distribution company that employs 1800 people, decided to combat escalating benefit costs—particularly prescription drug costs. As a first step, the human resources team asked the company's benefits carrier to review prescription claims for the previous year and to provide a list of the most frequently used drugs, on an aggregate basis. Those most used were cholesterol-lowering, cardiovascular, stomach acid reduction, anti-depressant, and anti-inflammatory drugs—all associated with chronic conditions.

Armed with this information, human resources staff worked with colleagues in the Enbridge Health Centre to design activities that specifically targeted health conditions underlying the employees' prescription drug use. The Health Centre, a long-standing part of the organization's Employee Health and Safety group, was already providing preventative and rehabilitative services, as well

as counselling for the management of health conditions. However, it relied primarily on employees to take the initiative to use these services. By carrying out such activities as blood pressure checking and cholesterol testing in high-traffic areas, such as the organization's lobby, HR and Health Centre staff were able to increase employees' awareness of these services and reach a larger number of employees.

Health Centre staff worked with the cafeteria to promote "heart-healthy" food choices, snacking guidelines, and "lunch 'n' learn" sessions on lifestyle change. They also made themselves available for 20- to 30-minute presentations on health-related topics, as part of regular departmental meetings. In addition, Enbridge gave out prizes to promote its on-site fitness centre and walking programs. Not only did these actions aim to keep down prescription drug costs, but they also supported the goals of improving workplace health and reducing absenteeism.

Source: Adapted from N. Wassink and J.L. MacBride-King, *Beyond Band-Aid Solutions: Managing Organizations' Health Benefit Costs.* Ottawa: The Conference Board of Canada, 2004. Reprinted by permission of The Conference Board of Canada, Ottawa.

(such as laser eye surgery) and defines dependants more broadly than most employer plans.[21]

> **An Ethical Dilemma**
>
> Should it be the employer's responsibility to cover health-care costs for early retirees until they become eligible for government health-care benefits at age 65?

Retiree Health Benefits

Another concern is the cost of health benefits provided to retirees. These benefits typically include life insurance, drugs, and private/semi-private hospital coverage. Some continue coverage to a surviving spouse. Retiree benefit costs are already exceeding the costs for active employees in some organizations, in part because many early retirees between the ages of 50 and 65 are not yet eligible for government health benefits that start at age 65. Employers are required to disclose liabilities for retiree benefits in their financial statements. These liabilities are not required to be prefunded and thus are at risk in the case of business failure.[22]

As members of the baby boom generation retire with long life expectancies, these costs will increase rapidly. Employers can cut costs by increasing retiree contributions, increasing deductibles, tightening eligibility requirements, and reducing maximum payouts.[23]

Short-Term Disability Plans and Sick Leave Plans

short-term disability and sick leave   Plans that provide pay to an employee when he or she is unable to work because of a non-work-related illness or injury.

Short-term disability plans (also known as salary continuation plans) provide a continuation of all or part of an employee's earnings when the employee is absent from work because of non-work-related illness or injury. Usually a medical certificate is required if the absence extends beyond two or three days. These plans typically provide full pay for some period (often two or three weeks) and then gradually reduce the percentage of earnings paid as the period of absence lengthens. The benefits cease when the employee returns to work or when the employee qualifies for long-term disability. These plans are sometimes provided through an insurance company.

Sick leave plans operate quite differently from short-term disability plans. Most sick leave policies grant full pay for a specified number of permissible sick days—usually up to about 12 per year (often accumulated at the rate of one day per month of service). Newfoundland and Labrador, Yukon, Quebec, and the federal jurisdiction require sick leave (unpaid), as a minimum standard. Sick leave pay creates difficulty for many employers. The problem is that although many employees use their sick days only when they are legitimately sick, others simply use their sick leave as extensions to their vacations, whether they are sick or not. Also, seriously ill or injured employees get no pay once their sick days are used up.

Employers have tried several tactics to eliminate or reduce the problem. Some now buy back unused sick leave at the end of the year by paying their employees a daily equivalent pay for each sick leave day not used. The drawback is that the policy can encourage legitimately sick employees to come to work despite their illness. Others have experimented with holding monthly lotteries in which only employees with perfect monthly attendance are able to participate; those who participate are eligible to win a cash prize. Still others aggressively investigate all absences, for instance by calling the absent employees at their homes when they are off sick.

Long-Term Disability

Long-term disability insurance is aimed at providing income protection or compensation for loss of income because of long-term illness or injury that is not work-related. The disability payments usually begin when normal short-term disability or sick leave is used up and may continue to provide income to age 65 or beyond. The disability benefits usually range from 50 to 75 percent of the employee's base pay.

The number of long-term disability claims in Canada is rising sharply. This trend is expected to accelerate as the average age of the workforce continues to increase because the likelihood of chronic illness, such as arthritis, heart disease, and diabetes, increases with age. The average cost of one disability claim is $80 000 and includes production delays, product and material damage because of inexperienced replacement staff, clerical and administrative time, and loss of expertise, on top of the actual benefit payments. Therefore, disability management programs with a goal of returning workers safely back to work are becoming a priority in many organizations.[24]

Disability management is a proactive, employer-centred process that coordinates the activities of the employer, the insurance company, and health-care providers in an effort to minimize the impact of injury, disability, or disease on a worker's capacity to successfully perform his or her job. Maintaining contact with a worker who is ill or injured is imperative in disability management so that the worker can be involved in the return-to-work process from the beginning. Ongoing contact also allows the employer to monitor the employee's emotional well-being, which is always affected by illness and/or injury.[25]

Effective disability management programs include prevention, early assessment and intervention regarding employee health problems, monitoring and management of employee absences, and early and safe return-to-work policies.[26] In some cases, it may be necessary to consider diversity issues in return-to-work plans, as discussed in the Workforce Diversity box.

National Institute of Disability Management and Research
www.nidmar.ca

Canadian Council on Rehabilitation and Work
www.ccrw.org

disability management
A proactive, employer-centred process that coordinates the activities of the employer, the insurance company, and health-care providers in an effort to minimize the impact of injury, disability, or disease in a worker's capacity to successfully perform his or her job.

REQUIRED PROFESSIONAL CAPABILITIES

Integrates the basic benefits program with disability management

Workforce Diversity

Diversity Issues in Return-to-Work Plans

When an employee of the County of Oxford, near London, Ontario, injured her shoulder, her workplace developed a comprehensive return-to-work strategy for her. It included some special ergonomic equipment to save wear and tear on her shoulder. Puzzlingly, however, she chose not to use the equipment and her shoulder worsened. The employee health coordinator, Ann McKnight Duralia, finally determined that the employee had been upset when a co-worker challenged her disability and rather than report the incident to her supervisor, she just avoided the issue and didn't use the equipment. "In Canada, most women are taught to be assertive," McKnight Duralia says. "But this employee was from a different culture in which authority shouldn't be questioned. She had difficulty even making eye contact with the person."

It may be obvious that a worker is female and about 60 years old, but it may not be so apparent that she has arthritis. That young, bright, and enthusiastic supervisor might have lots of people skills with people his age. But he may be uncomfortable accommodating the needs of older workers, particularly those who remind him of his father, with whom he has a stormy relationship.

Cathy Gourley, HR coordinator at Canfor's Northwood Pulp Mill in Prince George, B.C., says that she is particularly sensitive to the desire of some workers to come back too soon or to take on too much too quickly: "Because they're guys and have that guy mentality, they may come back too soon." It may also be an issue with Asian workers, who tend to have a particularly strong work ethic.

In another case, a researcher who required a wheelchair was working too slowly. When no one knew what to do, a counsellor was brought in. The case was closed when the counsellor suggested that the researcher simply place her files on a table at the same height as her desk. This painless fix allowed the employee to double her output.

Source: Adapted from D. Gray-Grant, "Factoring Diversity in to Return-to-Work Plans," *Canadian HR Reporter*, July 14, 2003, p. 19. Reproduced by permission of *Canadian HR Reporter*, Carswell, One Corporate Plaza, 2075 Kennedy Road, Scarborough, ON M1T 3V4.

The three most common approaches to returning a worker with a disability to work are reduced work hours, reduced work duties, and workstation modification.[27] Evaluating the physical capabilities of the worker is an important step in designing work modifications to safely reintegrate injured workers. In many cases, the cost of accommodating an employee's disability can be quite modest.

Disability management programs in Canada have had dramatic results. Western Forest Products participated in a WCB program in British Columbia targeting companies with higher than average injury rates. Between 1998 and 2004, claims for the 90 employees in Western Forest's sawmill division decreased by more than 90 percent (from more than 30 claims per year to two). Their injury rate dropped dramatically, and absenteeism decreased by 86 percent (from 25 percent to 3.6 percent).[28]

Mental Health Benefits

Mental health issues continue to be the leading cause of short- and long-term disability claims in Canada. Psychiatric disabilities are the fastest growing of all occupational disabilities, with depression being the most common (even though only 32 percent of those afflicted seek treatment, as they do not want to admit it to their employer).[29]

Depression has been described as a "clear and present danger" to business, as it manifests itself in alcoholism, absenteeism, injury, physical illness, and lost productivity. Estimates suggest that an employee with depression who goes untreated costs the company twice what treatment costs per year. A Harvard University study projects that, by 2020, depression will become the biggest source of lost workdays in developed countries.[30] Young workers (15 to 24) are at most risk, as shown in **Figure 13.3.**

FIGURE 13.3   Employee Assistance Plan Accesses for Depression by Age

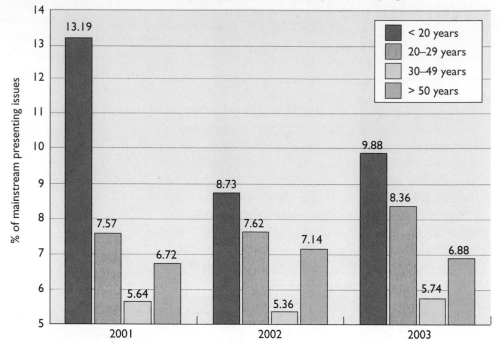

Source: Workplace Mental Health Indicators: An EAP's Perspective. Shepell-fgi Research Group, 2005, Series 1, Vol. 1, Issue 1. Reprinted with permission.

For Canadian employers, the cost of mental health benefits is about $33 billion annually. Despite the staggering costs, employers are unprepared to deal with stress, depression, and anxiety in the workplace, and only one-third of employers have implemented return-to-work programs specific to mental health. Such companies as Bell Canada, Alcan, and Superior Propane are trying to help reduce costs with prevention and early intervention programs, including psychiatric counselling and peer-support groups.[31]

Additional Leaves of Absence

Some employers provide full or partial pay for all or part of legally required unpaid leaves by "topping up" what employees receive from EI so the total amount they receive more closely matches their regular salary. For example, in some cases bereavement leave may be partially or fully paid by the employer.

A few employers provide sabbatical leaves for employees who want time off to rejuvenate or to pursue a personal goal. Sabbatical leaves are usually unpaid, but some employers provide partial or full pay. Sabbaticals can help to retain employees and to avoid employee burnout.

Additional Paid Vacations and Holidays

Many employers provide additional paid holidays and paid vacation over and above the amount required by law. For example, long-service employees typically receive more vacation time than legally required.

Retirement Benefits

pension plans Plans that provide income when employees reach a predetermined retirement age.

defined benefit pension plan A plan that contains a formula for determining retirement benefits.

defined contribution pension plan A plan in which the employer's contribution to the employees' retirement fund is specified.

Canadian Association for Retired Persons
www.fifty-plus.net

Benefits and Pensions Monitor
www.bpmmagazine.com

Association of Canadian Pension Management
www.acpm.com

deferred profit-sharing plan A plan in which a certain amount of company profits is credited to each employee's account, payable at retirement, termination, or death.

Employer-sponsored **pension plans** are intended to supplement an employee's government-sponsored retirement benefits, which on average make up 50 percent of the average Canadian's retirement income.[32] Unlike government-provided retirement benefits, employer-sponsored pension plans are prefunded. Money is set aside in a pension fund to accumulate with investment income until it is needed to pay benefits at retirement. Pension fund assets have grown rapidly over the past 40 years. Much of this money is invested in Canadian stocks and bonds, because of laws restricting the investment of these assets in foreign securities.

Pension plans fall into two categories—defined benefit pension plans and defined contribution pension plans. A **defined benefit pension plan** contains a formula for determining retirement benefits so that the actual benefits to be received are defined ahead of time. For example, the plan might include a formula, such as 2 percent of final year's earnings for each year of service, which would provide a pension of 70 percent of final year's earnings to an employee with 35 years of service. A **defined contribution pension plan** specifies what contribution the employer will make to a retirement fund set up for the employee. The defined contribution plan does not define the eventual benefit amount, only the periodic contribution to the plan. In a defined benefit plan, the employee knows ahead of time what his or her retirement benefits will be on retirement. With a defined contribution plan, the employee cannot be sure of his or her retirement benefits until retirement, when his or her share of the money in the pension fund is used to buy an annuity. Thus, benefits depend on both the amounts contributed to the fund and the retirement fund's investment earnings. The prevalence of these two types of plans is shown in **Table 13.2**.

There are two other types of defined contribution arrangements. Under a *group registered retirement savings plan (Group RRSP)*, employees can have a portion of their compensation (which would otherwise be paid in cash) put into an RRSP by the employer. The employee is not taxed on those set-aside dollars until after he or she retires (or removes the money from the plan). Most employers do not match all or a portion of what the employee contributes to the Group RRSP because employer contributions are considered taxable income to employees. Instead, the employer often establishes a **deferred profit-sharing plan** (DPSP), and contributes a portion of company profits into the DPSP fund, where an account is set up for each employee. No employee contributions to a DPSP are allowed under Canadian tax law. Group RRSP/DPSP combinations are popular in Canada because no tax is paid until money is received from the

TABLE 13.2   Registered Pension Plans

Type of Plan	Number of Plans	Percentage of Plans Registered	Number of Canadians Covered	Percentage of Total Plan Membership
Defined benefit	6 777	47.1	4 546 326	82.2
Defined contribution	7 347	51.1	835 826	15.1
Combination DB/DC	196	1.4	102 137	1.9
Other	56	0.4	43 288	0.8
Total	14 376	100.0	5 527 577	100.0

Source: Adapted from Statistics Canada publication *Pension Plans in Canada: Key Tables, 2003*, Catalogue No. 74-508, release date: September 22, 2004.

plans at the time of the employee's death or termination of employment (at retirement or otherwise).

The entire area of pension planning is complicated, partly because of the laws governing pensions. For example, companies want to ensure that their pension contributions are tax deductible and must, therefore, adhere to the Income Tax Act. Each province and the federal jurisdiction also have a law governing employer-sponsored pension plans. Sometimes the complicated and overlapping federal and provincial legislation can make employers question whether or not to sponsor a pension plan.[33] Legislation regarding pension plans varies around the world, as described in the Global HRM box.

When designing a pension plan, there are several legal and policy issues to consider:[34]

- *Membership requirements.* For example, at what minimum number of years of service do employees become eligible to join the plan?
- *Benefit formula* (defined benefits plans only). This usually ties the pension to the employee's final earnings, or an average of his or her last three to five years' earnings.

> **Hints to Ensure Legal Compliance**

Global HRM

Cultural Issues in Retirement Plans

Cultural differences can have an impact on international pension planning. The Asia Pacific region will expect a different level of pension planning because of a heightened level of respect for older people. Whereas government social security benefits in North America are provided on a defined benefit basis, many countries in the Asia Pacific region provide a *provident fund*, which is a defined contribution approach. The legislative environment in the region is also a bit more relaxed than in other parts in the world, with the exception of Japan, where the market is heavily regulated. Taiwan only recently passed a labour standards law.

In Europe, there is a greater sense of entitlement than in Asia or parts of Latin America. All of Europe has a sophisticated tax and financial system, with the exception of parts of Eastern Europe. Although the United Kingdom is changing from defined benefit to defined contribution, Germany is, by nature, a defined benefit culture. The continent as a whole is headed toward defined contribution plans. There are many ways to deliver defined contribution plans, and European countries, such as Spain, Italy, and the U.K., have recently passed legislation affecting the design of such plans.

In Latin America, the working population is much younger than in the rest of the world. The emphasis is less on retirement benefits and more on medical and life insurance benefits. In the 1990s, Chile revamped legislation on its social security policies that is known today as the Chilean model. It is a defined contribution model based on sound ideas; however, it was passed without any strict investment regulations, and Chile found its system in serious financial difficulty. New legislation now restricts the amount of commission that can be received on contributions from employees and guaranteed returns that must be met.

In Africa, different issues arise. For example, in Nigeria, a mandatory retirement age of 65 has been legislated for academic faculty. The monthly pension payable is 50 percent of the employee's basic pay, and a gratuity of 75 percent of monthly basic pay multiplied by the number of years of service is also payable. Despite this requirement, many Nigerian pensioners have suffered severe economic deprivation when they exit from the labour market. The nonpayment of gratuity at the time of retirement and frequent delays in the payment of monthly pensions to retired civil servants have influenced employees' attitudes toward retirement. There is now a general trend for prospective pensioners to falsify their birth records or make a new age declaration to circumvent the mandatory retirement age policy in the civil service.

Sources: R. Polak, "Finding a Path to Global Benefits," *Workspan,* February 2003, pp. 32–35; Y.B. Yehudah, "Nigerian Academic Faculty: Issues in Compensation and Retirement Benefits," *Compensation and Benefits Review,* November/December 2002, pp. 55–58.

- *Retirement age.* The normal retirement age in Canada is 65. However, some employer plans may permit early or late retirement, and plans covering employees in provinces that have outlawed mandatory retirement cannot require these employees to retire at age 65. Some plans call for "30 and out." This permits an employee to retire after 30 years of continuous service, regardless of the person's age.

- *Funding.* The question of how the plan is to be funded is another key issue. One aspect is whether the plan will be contributory or noncontributory. In the former, contributions to the pension fund are made by both employees and the employer. In a noncontributory fund, only the employer contributes.

vesting Provision that employer money placed in a pension fund cannot be forfeited for any reason.

- *Vesting.* Employee **vesting** rights is another critical issue in pension planning. Vesting refers to the money that the employer has placed in the pension fund that cannot be forfeited for any reason. The employees' contributions can never be forfeited. An employee is vested when he or she has met the requirements set out in the plan, whereby, on termination of employment, he or she will receive future benefits based on the contributions made to the plan by the *employer* on behalf of the employee. In most provinces, pension legislation requires that employer contributions be vested once the employee has completed two years of service. Plans may vest more quickly than required by law. If the employee terminates employment before being vested, he or she is only entitled to a refund of his or her own contributions, plus interest (unless the employer has decided to be more generous). Once an employee is vested, all contributions are "locked in" and cannot be withdrawn by the employee on termination of employment; that is, employees must wait until retirement to receive a pension from the plan. Most plans permit the employee to transfer the amount into a locked-in RRSP (see the discussion on portability below), but the money cannot be accessed until retirement.

> ## An Ethical
> ### Dilemma
> Should an employer with a pension plan that covers employees in several provinces give each group the minimum vesting and portability benefits for their province, or take the most generous of these and provide it to all employees?

portability A provision that employees who change jobs can transfer the lump-sum value of the pension they have earned to a locked-in RRSP or their new employer's pension plan.

- *Portability.* Canadian employers today are being required by pension legislation to make their pensions more "portable" for employees on termination of employment. **Portability** means that employees in defined contribution plans can take the money in their company pension account to a new employer's plan or roll it over into a locked-in RRSP. For defined benefit plans, the lump-sum value of the benefit earned can be transferred.

Recent Trends

Rapid Growth of Defined Contribution Plans It had long been expected that defined benefit plans will continue to be used in large organizations where long tenure is the norm. However, even those organizations are rethinking their commitment to defined benefit plans because of recent increases in unfunded liabilities arising from poor stock market returns and a major Supreme Court decision regarding the sharing of investment surpluses. The decision resulted in defined benefit plan sponsors in Ontario being held liable for funding deficits but not allowed to reap the benefits of a funding surplus.[35] The cost and complexity of sponsoring a defined benefit plan in an increasingly fragmented legislative environment is another reason that employers are increasingly switching to defined contribution plans. Defined contribution plans are often considered ideal for the growing number of today's businesses with a relatively young workforce of highly skilled professional and technical people who expect to work with several employers during their careers. Defined contribution plan sponsors benefit from predictable costs, and employees find the plan easier to understand.[36]

> **REQUIRED PROFESSIONAL CAPABILITIES**
>
> Develops specifications for the acquisition or redesign of pension plans and their administration
>
> Reviews pension proposals submitted by third parties and evaluates the information received
>
> Recommends the pension plan most suited to organizational objectives

Employees in defined contribution plans make decisions about the investment of the pension fund assets, which means that member communication is one of the most critical challenges facing defined contribution plan sponsors. Surveys show that many employees are not comfortable with making their own investment decisions, given their relative inexperience in that area. Fluctuating returns in the stock market over the last few years have highlighted the importance of sound investment decisions and of employers' responsibility for educating their employees about investment choices.[37]

Employers must pay careful attention to their obligation to educate and inform (but not advise) plan members about pension investments. There have been cases where plan members who were unhappy with the information provided by the employer and surprised by small benefits have sued their employers and won. Conversely, the University of Western Ontario plan converted to defined contribution in 1970, and faculty members are retiring with incomes greater than their working salaries.[38]

There has also been an increase in the number of employers offering "hybrid plans," which combine defined benefit and defined contribution features. For example, an employer-paid defined benefit plan can be offered with an employee-paid defined contribution component (which could have partial matching employer contributions).[39]

Phased Retirement   The looming labour shortage when baby boomers start retiring is resulting in employers seeking to retain older employees. At the same time, many Canadians often hope to retire at age 55 or 60, but they find that they are not in a financial position to do so and that they need to continue working to age 60, 65, or even later.[40]

The idea of **phased retirement**, whereby employees gradually ease into retirement using reduced workdays and/or shortened workweeks, has been in place in Europe for some time, and this approach is expected to increase in Canada as the labour shortage becomes more acute and employers want to retain older workers. Despite constraints under the Income Tax Act and pension legislation in some jurisdictions, phased retirement arrangements in which older workers are paid for their reduced hours and also collect some of their pension benefits have been arranged.[41]

Supplemental Employee Retirement Plans (SERPs)   Because the maximum benefit permissible under the Income Tax Act has remained essentially unchanged since 1976, many Canadians have their pension benefits capped at less than what the maximum allowable benefit formula (under income tax legislation) could provide. Originally this situation only created problems for highly paid executives, but in recent years, more and more employees have been affected. **Supplemental employee retirement plans** (SERPs) are intended to provide the difference in pension benefit and thus restore pension adequacy for high earners. Other objectives for SERPs are shown in **Figure 13.4**.

A 2004 Towers Perrin survey found that nearly three-quarters of employers provide SERPs (including about two-thirds of small employers with fewer than 500 employees). The survey also found that 53 percent of SERP sponsors cover employees below the executive level in "broad-based" plans. Most SERPs are "pay-as-you-go" plans; that is, they do not have a fund established to accumulate money to pay the benefits (because contributions are not tax-deductible). However, the security of SERP benefits has been improving, as 41 percent of plans are now secured in some manner.[42]

phased retirement   An arrangement whereby employees gradually ease into retirement by using reduced workdays and/or shortened workweeks.

supplemental employee retirement plans   Plans that provide the additional pension benefit required for employees to receive their full pension benefit in cases where their full pension benefit exceeds the maximum allowable benefit under the Income Tax Act.

FIGURE 13.4   Objectives of SERPs

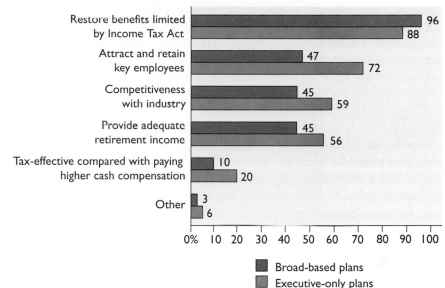

Source: Supplementary Pensions Under Pressure: Towers Perrin 2004 SERP Report. Toronto: Towers Perrin, 2004, p. 8. Reprinted with permission.

EMPLOYEE SERVICES

Although an employer's time off and insurance and retirement benefits account for the largest portion of its benefits costs, many employers also provide a range of services, including personal services (such as counselling), job-related services (such as childcare facilities), and executive perquisites (such as company cars and planes for executives).

Personal Services

First, many companies provide personal services that most employees need at one time or another. These include credit unions, counselling, employee assistance plans, and social and recreational opportunities.

Credit Unions

Credit unions are usually separate businesses established with the assistance of the employer. Employees usually become members of a credit union by purchasing a share of the credit union's stock for $5 or $10. Members can then deposit savings that accrue interest at a rate determined by the credit union's board of directors. Perhaps more important to most employees, loan eligibility and the rate of interest paid on the loan are usually more favourable than those found in banks and finance companies.

Counselling Services

Employers are also providing a wider range of counselling services to employees. These include *financial counselling* (e.g., in terms of how to overcome existing indebtedness problems), *family counselling* (for marital problems, etc.), *career counselling* (in terms of analyzing one's aptitudes and deciding on a career), *job placement counselling* (for helping terminated or disenchanted employees find new jobs), and *pre-retirement counselling* (aimed at preparing retiring employees for what many find is the trauma of retiring). Many employers also make available to employees a full range of *legal counselling* through legal insurance plans.[43]

Employee Assistance Plans (EAPs)

An **employee assistance plan (EAP)** is a formal employer program that provides employees (and very often their family members) with confidential counselling and/or treatment programs for problems such as mental health issues, marital/family problems, work/life balance issues, stress, legal problems, substance abuse, and other addictions such as gambling. They are particularly important for helping employees who suffer workplace trauma—ranging from harassment to physical assault. The number of EAPs in Canada is growing because they are a proactive way for organizations to reduce absenteeism and disability costs. A very general estimate is that 10 percent of employees use EAP services. With supervisory training in how to identify employees who may need an EAP referral, usage can be expanded to more employees who need help.[44]

EAP counsellors can be employed in-house, or the company can contract with an external EAP firm. It is important to assess the services provided by external EAP providers before using them, as quality levels vary. Whatever the model, an EAP provider should be confidential, accessible to employees in all company locations, and timely in providing service, and should offer highly educated counsellors and provide communication material to publicize the plan to employees. They should also provide utilization reports on the number of employees using the service and the types of services being provided, without compromising confidentiality.[45]

Other Personal Services

Finally, some employers also provide various social and recreational opportunities for their employees, including company-sponsored athletic events, dances, annual summer picnics, craft activities, and parties. In practice, the benefits offered are limited only by creativity in thinking up new benefits. For example, pharmaceutical giant Pfizer Inc. provides employees with free drugs made by the company, including Viagra![46]

Job-Related Services

Job-related services aimed directly at helping employees perform their jobs, such as educational subsidies and daycare centres, constitute a second group of services.

Subsidized Childcare

Large numbers of Canadian workers have children under six years old. Subsidized daycare is offered to assist in balancing these work and life responsibilities. Many employers simply investigate the daycare facilities in their communities and recommend certain ones to interested employees, but more employers are setting up company-sponsored daycare facilities themselves, both to attract young parents to the payroll and to reduce absenteeism. In this case, the centre is a separate, privately run venture, paid for by the firm. IKEA, Husky Injection Moldings, IBM, and the Kanata Research Park have all chosen this option. Where successful, the hours of operation are structured around parents' schedules, the daycare facility is close to the workplace (often in the same building), and the employer provides 50 to 75 percent of the operating costs. Two emerging benefits are daycare for mildly ill children and emergency backup childcare.[47]

---

employee assistance plan (EAP)
A company-sponsored program to help employees cope with personal problems that are interfering with or have the potential to interfere with their job performance, as well as issues affecting their well-being and/or that of their families.

Family Services Employee Assistance Programs
www.familyserviceseap.com

Warren Shepell
www.warrenshepell.com

Subsidizing daycare facilities for children of employees has many benefits for the employer, including lower employee absenteeism.

To date, the evidence regarding the actual effects of employer-sponsored childcare on employee absenteeism, turnover, productivity, recruitment, and job satisfaction is positive, particularly with respect to reducing obstacles to coming to work and improving workers' attitudes.[48]

Eldercare

With the average age of the Canadian population rising, eldercare is increasingly a concern for many employers and individuals. It is a complex, unpredictable, and exhausting process that creates stress for the caregiver, the family, and co-workers. Eldercare is expected to become a more common workplace issue than childcare as we progress through the twenty-first century. Almost 20 percent of Canadians over the age of 45 have taken on eldercare responsibilities. Of these, 54 percent are women, 46 percent are men, and most are married, urban dwellers.[49]

Company eldercare programs are designed to assist employees who must help elderly parents or relatives who are not fully able to care for themselves, up to and including palliative care of the dying. Eldercare benefits include flexible hours, support groups, counselling, free pagers, and adult daycare programs. Referral services to help employees connect with the wide variety of services for the elderly are particularly helpful for employees with eldercare responsibilities.[50]

Subsidized Employee Transportation

Some employers also provide subsidized employee transportation. An employer can negotiate with a transit system to provide free year-round transportation to its employees. Other employers facilitate employee car-pooling, perhaps by acting as the central clearinghouse to identify employees from the same geographic areas who work the same hours.

Food Services

Food services are provided in some form by many employers; they let employees purchase meals, snacks, or coffee, usually at relatively low prices. Even employers that do not provide full dining facilities generally make available food services, such as coffee wagons or vending machines, for the convenience of employees.

Educational Subsidies

Educational subsidies, such as tuition refunds, have long been a popular benefit for employees seeking to continue or complete their education. Payments range from all tuition and expenses to some percentage of expenses to a flat fee per year of, say, $500 to $600. Most companies pay for courses directly related to an employee's present job. Many also reimburse tuition for courses that are not job-related (such as a secretary taking an accounting class) that pertain to the company business and those that are part of a degree or diploma program. In-house educational programs include remedial work in basic literacy and training for improved supervisory skills.

Family-Friendly Benefits

One of the top drivers of workforce commitment in Canada is management's recognition of personal and family life. Ninety percent of responding employees in one survey said work/life benefits were "important" or "very important" to them.[51] Recognition of the pressures of balancing work and family life have led many employers to bolster what they call their "family-friendly" benefits.

Research
I n s i g h t   ▷

Although there is no single list of what does or does not constitute a "family-friendly" benefit, the family-friendly benefits at several companies are illustrative. Eddie Bauer, Inc. reportedly "believes its associates shouldn't confuse having a career with having a life." Over the last decade, Eddie Bauer has therefore introduced more than 20 new family-friendly benefits, ranging from on-site mammography to emergency childcare services. Also included in the firm's existing family-friendly benefits are a casual dress code, subsidies for liberal paid parental leave, alternative transportation options, a compressed workweek, and telecommuting.[52]

Family-friendly benefits are intended to reduce the extent to which work–family conflicts spill over to the employee's job and undermine the person's job satisfaction and performance. Research has found that "the relationship between job satisfaction and various [work–family] conflict measures is strong and negative across all samples; people with high levels of [work–family] conflict tend to be less satisfied with their jobs."[53] Similarly, there was a strong negative correlation between work–family conflict and measures of "life satisfaction"—in other words, the extent to which the employees were satisfied with their lives in general. Managers should therefore understand that providing their employees with family-friendly benefits can apparently have very positive effects on the employees, one of which is making them more satisfied with their work and their jobs.

Executive Perquisites

Perquisites (perks, for short) are usually given to only a few top executives. Perks can range from the substantial to the almost insignificant. A bank chairperson may have a chauffeur-driven limousine and use of a bank-owned property in the Caribbean. Executives of large companies often use a corporate jet for business travel. At the other extreme, perks may entail little more than the right to use a company car.[54]

**An Ethical
Dilemma**
Is it ethical for executive perquisites to continue if the company is facing financial problems?

A multitude of popular perks fall between these extremes. These include management loans (which typically enable senior officers to use their stock options); salary guarantees (also known as *golden parachutes*) to protect executives if their firms are the targets of acquisitions or mergers; financial counselling (to handle top executives' investment programs); and relocation benefits, often including subsidized mortgages, purchase of the executive's current house, and payment for the actual move. A potpourri of other executive perks include outplacement assistance, company cars, chauffeured limousines, security systems, company planes and yachts, executive dining rooms, legal services, tax assistance, liberal expense accounts, club memberships, season tickets, credit cards, and subsidized education for their children. Perks related to wellness and quality of life (such as physical fitness programs) are highly valued in today's stressful environment. An increasingly popular new perk offered at KPMG, Telus, and Ernst & Young is concierge service, intended to carry out errands, such as grocery shopping or organizing a vacation, for busy executives.[55] Employers have many ways of making their hard-working executives' lives as pleasant as possible!

FLEXIBLE BENEFITS PROGRAMS

Research conducted more than 30 years ago found that an employee's age, marital status, and sex influenced his or her choice of benefits.[56] For example, preference for pensions increased significantly with employee age, and preference for the family dental plan increased sharply as the number of dependants increased. Thus, benefits that one worker finds attractive may be unattractive to another. In the last few years in Canada, there has been a significant increase in **flexible benefits programs** that permit employees to develop individualized benefits packages for themselves by choosing the benefits options they prefer. In 1980, there were no flex plans in Canada, and in 2005, 41 percent of employers offered flex benefits plans. Benefit consultants Hewitt Associates report that 85 percent of Canadian employers either have a flex plan in place or expect to implement one at some point. Fifty-three percent either have a full flex plan now or will have one within two years.[57]

flexible benefits program Individualized benefit plans to accommodate employee needs and preferences.

REQUIRED PROFESSIONAL CAPABILITIES

Performs a cost-benefit analysis of organizational and employee needs and preferences relative to benefit plans, including taxation considerations and funding requirements

Employers derive several advantages from offering flexible benefit plans, the two most important being cost containment and the ability to meet the needs of an increasingly diverse workforce. Hewitt Associates' surveys have found that over the years, the most important advantage of implementing flexible benefits has been meeting diverse employee needs. However, in 2005, for the first time in survey history, the concern about containing benefit cost increases surpassed meeting diverse employee needs as the most significant reason to implement flexible plans. In the 2006 survey, 100 percent of respondents reported that their flex plans were meeting or exceeding their expectations regarding meeting employee needs, and the level of satisfaction with flex plans as a cost containment measure was 78 percent.[58]

Flexible benefits plans empower the employee to put together his or her own benefit package, subject to two constraints. First, the employer must carefully limit total cost for each total benefits package. Second, each benefit plan must include certain items that are not optional. These include, for example, Canada/Quebec Pension Plan, workers' compensation, and employment insurance. Subject to these two constraints, employees can pick and choose from the

Benefits Design Inc.
www.benefitsdesign.com

International Foundation of Employee Benefit Plans
www.ifebp.org

FIGURE 13.5 Advantages and Disadvantages of Flexible Benefit Programs

ADVANTAGES

1. Employees choose packages that best satisfy their unique needs.
2. Flexible benefits help firms meet the *changing* needs of a *changing* workforce.
3. Increased involvement of employees and families improves understanding of benefits.
4. Flexible plans make introduction of new benefits less costly. The new option is added merely as one among a wide variety of elements from which to choose.
5. Cost containment—the organization sets the dollar maximum. Employee chooses within that constraint.

DISADVANTAGES

1. Employees make bad choices and find themselves not covered for predictable emergencies.
2. Administrative burdens and expenses increase.
3. Adverse selection—employees pick only benefits they will use. The subsequent high benefit utilization increases its cost.

Source: G.T. Milkovich, J.M Newman, N.D. Cole *Compensation,* Canadian 1st ed. Toronto: McGraw Hill Ryerson, © 2005. Reproduced with permission of McGraw-Hill Ryerson Ltd.

available options. Thus, a young parent might opt for the company's life and dental insurance plans, while an older employee opts for an improved pension plan. The list of possible options that the employer might offer can include many of the benefits discussed in this chapter—vacations, insurance benefits, pension plans, educational services, and so on.

Advantages and disadvantages of flexible benefit programs are summarized in **Figure 13.5** on page 357. The flexibility is, of course, the main advantage. Although most employees favour flexible benefits, some do not like to spend time choosing among available options, and some choose inappropriate benefits. Communication regarding the choices available in a flexible plan is considered the biggest challenge for employers. A majority of flex plan sponsors provide a plan Web site. However, even with new technology, employers still find face-to-face communication is the preferred method for providing initial information about a new flex plan.[59] The recent rapid increase in the number of flexible plans in Canada indicates that the pros outweigh the cons.

BENEFITS ADMINISTRATION

Canadian Pension and Benefits Institute
www.cpbi-icra.ca

REQUIRED PROFESSIONAL CAPABILITIES

Administers the reporting, funding, and fiduciary aspects of the plan

Ensures the effectiveness of benefit programs by providing information, ensuring accessibility of the program, and minimizing the cost of the program

Manages the transition to new plans, including communications, employee counselling, training, and discarding redundant practices

Provides necessary information and counselling to pension plan participants

Manages the transition to a new or revised plan by providing information to plan participants and providing appropriate training for administrative staff

---

Whether it is a flexible benefits plan or a more traditional one, benefits administration is a challenge. Even in a relatively small company with 40 to 50 employees, the administrative problems of keeping track of the benefits status of each employee can be a time-consuming task as employees are hired and separated, and as they use or want to change their benefits. However, software is available to assist with this challenge. Many companies make use of some sort of benefits spreadsheet software to facilitate tracking benefits and updating information. Another approach is outsourcing benefits administration to a third-party expert. The major advantages are greater efficiency and consistency, and enhanced service.[60]

Keeping Employees Informed

Benefits communication, particularly regarding pension plans and flexible benefits, is increasingly important as a large number of people are approaching retirement. Correct information must be provided in a timely, clear manner. Pension legislation across Canada specifies what information must be disclosed to plan members and their spouses. Court challenges concerning information on benefits plans are on the rise, as people's awareness of their right to information grows.[61]

Increasingly, organizations are utilizing new technology, such as intranets, to ensure that up-to-date information is provided in a consistent manner. Some companies are now using real-time e-statements. At Hewlett Packard (Canada) Ltd., an electronic pension booklet is available on the company's intranet, and a pension-modelling tool can be accessed through the Web. The modelling software allows employees to fill in their personal information to calculate various "what if" scenarios.[62]

Chapter Review

Summary

1. The strategic importance of employee benefits is increasing in the post-job-security era. When benefits are aligned with business strategy, they can help to attract and retain the right people to achieve business objectives.

2. Six government-sponsored benefits are employment insurance, Canada/Quebec Pension Plan, workers' compensation, vacations and holidays, leaves of absence, and pay on termination of employment.

3. Health insurance costs are rising because of expensive new drugs, rising drug utilization by an aging population, and reductions in coverage under provincial health-care plans. These costs can be reduced by increasing the amount of health-care costs paid by employees, publishing a restricted list of the drugs that will be paid for under the plan, implementing health and wellness promotion plans, using risk assessment programs, and offering health services spending accounts.

4. Recent trends in retirement benefits include the rapid growth of defined contribution plans, growing interest in phased retirement, and the increasing use of supplemental employee retirement plans (SERPs).

5. Three types of personal employee services offered by many organizations include credit unions, counselling services, and employee assistance plans. Six types of job-related services offered by many employers include subsidized childcare, eldercare, subsidized employee transportation, food services, educational subsidies, and family-friendly benefits.

6. The flexible benefits approach allows the employee to put together his or her own benefit plan, subject to total cost limits and the inclusion of certain compulsory items. The employer first determines the total cost for the benefits package. Then a decision is made as to which benefits will be compulsory (such as Canada/Quebec Pension Plan, workers' compensation, and employment insurance). Then other benefits are selected for inclusion in the plan, such as life insurance, health and dental coverage, short- and long-term disability insurance, and retirement plans. Sometimes vacations and employee services are included as well. Then employees select the optional benefits they prefer with the money they have available to them under the total plan.

Key Terms

Canada/Quebec Pension Plan   *(p. 337)*
coinsurance   *(p. 343)*
deductible   *(p. 343)*
deferred profit-sharing plan   *(p. 349)*
defined benefit pension plan   *(p. 349)*
defined contribution pension plan   *(p. 349)*
disability management   *(p. 346)*
employee assistance plan (EAP)   *(p. 354)*
employee benefits   *(p. 336)*
employment insurance   *(p. 336)*
flexible benefits program   *(p. 357)*
group life insurance   *(p. 342)*
pension plans   *(p. 349)*
phased retirement   *(p. 352)*
portability   *(p. 351)*
sick leave   *(p. 345)*
short-term disability   *(p. 345)*
supplemental employee retirement plans   *(p. 352)*
vesting   *(p. 351)*
workers' compensation   *(p. 338)*

Review and Discussion Questions

1. Explain two main approaches to reducing workers' compensation claims.

2. Explain the difference between sick leave plans and short-term disability plans.

3. Why are long-term disability claims increasing so rapidly in Canada?

4. Outline the kinds of services provided by EAPs.

Critical Thinking Questions

1. You are applying for a job as a manager and are at the point of negotiating a salary and benefits. What questions would you ask your prospective employer concerning benefits? Describe the benefits package that you would try to negotiate for yourself.

2. What are pension "vesting" and "portability"? Why do you think these are (or are not) important to a recent university or college graduate?

3. You are the HR consultant to a small business with about 40 employees. Currently, the business offers only the legal minimum number of days for vacation and paid holidays, and legally mandated benefits. Develop a list of other benefits that you believe should be offered, along with your reasons for suggesting them.

4. If you were designing a retirement benefit for a mid-sized organization that had not previously offered one, what type of plan would you recommend to them and why?

Application Exercises

Running Case: LearnInMotion.com

The New Benefits Plan

LearnInMotion.com provides only legislatively required benefits for all its employees. These include participation in employment insurance, Canada Pension Plan, and workers' compensation. No employee services are provided.

Jennifer can see several things wrong with the company's policies regarding benefits and services. First, she wants to determine whether similar companies' experiences with providing health and life insurance benefits suggest it makes hiring easier and/or reduces employee turnover. Jennifer is also concerned that the company has no policy regarding vacations or for sick leave. Informally, at least, it is understood that employees get a one-week vacation after one year's work. However, the policy regarding pay for such days as New Year's and Thanksgiving has been inconsistent: Sometimes employees on the job only two or three weeks are paid fully for one of these holidays; sometimes employees who have been with the firm for six months or more get paid for only half a day. No one really knows what the company's chosen "paid" holidays are. Jennifer knows these policies must be more consistent.

She also wonders about the wisdom of establishing some type of retirement plan for the firm. Although everyone working for the firm is still in their 20s, she believes a defined contribution plan in which employees contribute a portion of their pretax salary, to be matched up to some limit by a contribution by LearnInMotion.com, would contribute to the sense of commitment she and Pierre would like to create among their employees. However, Pierre isn't so sure. His position is that if they don't get sales up pretty soon, they're going to burn through their cash. Now they want you, their management consultant, to help them decide what to do. Here's what they want you to do for them.

Questions

1. Draw up a policy statement regarding vacations, sick leave, and paid days off for LearnInMotion.com, based on such sources as those discussed in this chapter, as well as the previous two chapters.

2. What are the advantages and disadvantages to LearnInMotion.com of providing its employees with health insurance and disability programs?

3. In terms of competitors and any other information that you think is relevant, do you or do you not think it's a good idea for LearnInMotion.com to establish a defined contribution retirement plan for its employees? If Jennifer and Pierre were to establish such a plan, briefly summarize the plan as you see it.

Case Incident

Barrie Shipping Ltd.

Heath Proctor, Benefits Manager at Barrie Shipping Ltd., was faced with the task of redesigning the company's health-care plans. Costs had risen to an unacceptable level, largely due to prescription drug and dental plan costs. Two-thirds of employees were over age 45, and drug utilization had increased along with the average age of the workforce. The remaining employees, like their older counterparts, tended to be smokers, drinkers, and bar brawlers, who were unconcerned about their health—a common situation among workers in Great Lakes shipping companies.

The current prescription drug plan had an annual deductible of $20, and coinsurance of 100 percent. The dental plan had an annual deductible of $25, and coinsurance of 90 percent. Insurance company premiums were fully paid by Barrie Shipping. Retirees were also covered under these plans, but they paid 25 percent of the premiums.

Heath had proposed the idea of a flexible benefits plan in the past, but management had not seen any need to change from the standard benefit package they had offered for many years. Furthermore, none of their competitors had flexible plans, and the three large companies in the industry traditionally offered similar human resources programs.

Heath knew that the company had to cut drug costs immediately. He had read something about proactive measures that could be taken and wondered if any of these should be considered by Barrie Shipping in the longer term.

Heath's boss, Leo Santini, the vice-president of Human Resources, asked him to investigate different options for reducing health benefit costs and to prepare a short presentation describing each option and making some recommendations about which options might be most effective for Barrie Shipping.

Questions

1. What methods of health-care cost control should Heath include in his presentation? What are the advantages and disadvantages of each?

2. Should Barrie Shipping continue to provide health-care coverage to retirees? Why or why not?

3. What recommendations should Heath Proctor make to Leo?

Experiential Exercises

1. Working individually or in groups, compile a list of the perks available to the following individuals: the head of your local public utilities commission, the president of your college or university, and the president of a large company in your area. Do they all have certain perks in common? What do you think accounts for any differences?

2. Working individually or in groups, contact your provincial Workers' Compensation Board (or equivalent in your province) and compile a list of its suggestions for reducing workers' compensation costs. What seem to be the main recommendations?

4   Pension Promise

Employees in private companies that have gone bankrupt have found that their company pensions have been decimated, and that they have little recourse. Workers at bankrupt steel companies in Hamilton, Ontario, have been hit especially hard. Some are receiving less than half of the pension they had earned under their plan and have had to find new jobs to supplement their income. Steelworkers Union activists are trying to promote an NDP private member's bill in Ottawa that would move pensioners up from the bottom of the list of creditors when companies go bankrupt.

Defined benefit pension funds were in good shape in the later 1990s, but the 2001 stock market crash left 60 percent of plans seriously underfunded by 2004. Consulting actuary Ian Markham says that if the banks were elbowed out of their number one spot on the creditors list, they simply wouldn't lend to companies with defined benefit pension plans.

Questions

1. Why have the older workers shown in the video not received the full pension they had earned over their working life?
2. What laws could be introduced to prevent this situation?
3. If the workers had been in a defined contribution plan, would they be facing the same problem?

Source: Based on "Pension Promise," *CBC The National* (November 15, 2004).

CHAPTER 14

OCCUPATIONAL HEALTH AND SAFETY

LEARNING OUTCOMES

AFTER STUDYING THIS CHAPTER, YOU SHOULD BE ABLE TO

Analyze the responsibilities and rights of employees and employers under occupational health and safety legislation.

Explain WHMIS legislation.

Analyze in detail three basic causes of accidents.

Describe how accidents at work can be prevented.

Explain why employee wellness programs are becoming increasingly popular.

Discuss six major employee health issues at work, and **recommend** how they should be handled.

REQUIRED PROFESSIONAL CAPABILITIES

- Implements and evaluates practices in the areas of health, safety, security, and workers' compensation

- Ensures that security programs and policies minimize risks while considering the obligation of the employer and the rights of employees, union, and third parties

- Ensures due diligence and strict liability requirements are met (e.g., records are kept and formal procedures established

- Responds to any refusals to perform work believed to be unsafe

continued

- Provides input on matters related to the drafting and/or application of legislation or regulations related to health, safety, security, and workers' compensation

- Establishes a joint responsibility system as required by law (e.g., worker–management health and safety committees, investigations, audits, testing, and training), to ensure employee safety

- Ensures that the organization complies with legislated and contractual requirements for information management (e.g., records of hours worked and records of exposure to hazardous substances)

- Analyzes risk to the health and safety of employees and determines appropriate preventative measures, including training, provision of required safety equipment, and administrative practices

- Establishes effective programs for accident prevention, incident investigation, inspections, fire and emergency responses, and required training

- Ensures internal environmental concerns, such as quality of air and water, are addressed

- Provides information to employees and managers on available programs

- Contributes to and ensures that policies for required medical testing are in place and fall within the limits of statute and contract

- Ensures that mechanisms are in place for responding to crises in the workplace, including critical incident stress management

- Coordinates workers' compensation benefits with other employee benefits such as sick leave, long-term disability, and pension

- Establishes and implements strategies to minimize compensation costs

- Analyzes rate grouping costs, early intervention and return to work programs, claims management programs, and claims appeals

- Creates a strategy for effective liaison with the medical community

- Ensures compliance with legislated reporting requirements

- Ensures accommodation and graduated return to work programs are in place to meet the need of disabled employees

- Ensures that modifications to the work environment are consistent with the nature of worker disability (e.g., total versus partial and temporary versus permanent)

- Develops or provides for wellness and employee assistance programs to support organizational effectiveness

- Contributes to policy on the workplace environment (e.g., smoking, workplace violence, scent-free, communicable diseases, and addictions)

STRATEGIC IMPORTANCE OF OCCUPATIONAL HEALTH AND SAFETY

REQUIRED PROFESSIONAL CAPABILITIES

Implements and evaluates practices in the areas of health, safety, security, and workers' compensation

Health and safety initiatives are part of a strategic approach to human resources management. Service provided to clients and customers is a function of how employees are treated, and employee health, safety, and wellness management are important determinants of employee perceptions regarding fair treatment by the organization. Further, investment in disability management and proactive wellness programs create measurable bottom-line returns.[1]

Another reason that safety and accident prevention concern managers is that the work-related accident figures are staggering. According to the Association of Workers' Compensation Boards of Canada, in 2004 there were 928 deaths and 340 502 injuries resulting from accidents at work. Thus, on average, more than three Canadian workers die each working day. These deaths and injuries cost the economy more than $12 billion.[2] On April 28 each year, a day of mourning is observed for Canadian workers killed or injured on the job. These figures do not include minor injuries that do not involve time lost from work beyond the day of the accident. Moreover, these figures do not tell the full story. They do not reflect the human suffering incurred by injured or ill workers and their families.

Workplace health concerns are also widespread. A 2005 Ipsos-Reid poll conducted for WorkSafeBC and the Association of Workers' Compensation Boards of Canada found that 61 percent of Canadians believe that workplace accidents are inevitable.[3] This statistic is particularly disturbing, because workplace accidents can be prevented.

Ceremonies are held across Canada every April 28 to mark the National Day of Mourning for workers killed or injured on the job. In Moncton, New Brunswick, Pauline Farrell lays roses in memory of her husband Bill Kelly, who was killed more than 30 years ago.

BASIC FACTS ABOUT OCCUPATIONAL HEALTH AND SAFETY LEGISLATION

occupational health and safety legislation   Laws intended to protect the health and safety of workers by minimizing work-related accidents and illnesses.

All provinces, territories, and the federal jurisdiction have **occupational health and safety legislation** based on the principle of joint responsibility shared by workers and employers to maintain a hazard-free work environment and to enhance the health and safety of workers.[4]

Purpose

These laws fall into three categories: general health and safety rules, rules for specific industries (e.g., mining), and rules related to specific hazards (e.g., asbestos). In some jurisdictions, these are combined into one overall law with regulations for specific industries and hazards, while in others they remain separate. The regulations are very complex and cover almost every conceivable hazard in great detail, as shown in **Figure 14.1**. Provisions of occupational health and safety legislation differ significantly across Canada but most have certain basic features in common.

FIGURE 14.1   Ontario Occupational Health and Safety Act—Construction Regulations

> **O.REG.213/91**
>
> **68. A sign used to direct traffic,**
>
> (a) shall be diamond shaped, 450 millimetres wide and 450 millimetres long, with the diamond mounted at one corner on a pole 1.2 metres long; (b) shall be made of material that has at least the rigidity of six millimetres thick plywood; (c) shall be reflective fluorescent and coloured, (i) red-orange on one side with the corner areas coloured black, so that the red-orange area forms a regular eight-sided figure, with the word "STOP" written in legible white letters 150 millimetres high in a central position on the sign, and (ii) chartreuse on one side, with the word "SLOW" written in legible black letters 150 millimetres high in a central position on the sign; and (d) shall be maintained in a clean condition.

REQUIRED PROFESSIONAL CAPABILITIES

Ensures that security programs and policies minimize risks while considering the obligation of the employer and the rights of employees, union, and third parties

Ensures due diligence and strict liability requirements are met (e.g., records are kept and formal procedures established)

Responds to any refusals to perform work believed to be unsafe

Provides input on matters related to the drafting and/or application of legislation or regulations related to health, safety, security, and workers' compensation

Responsibilities and Rights of Employers and Employees

In all jurisdictions, employers are responsible for taking every reasonable precaution to ensure the health and safety of their workers. This is called the "due diligence" requirement. Specific duties of the employer include filing government accident reports, maintaining records, ensuring that safety rules are enforced, and posting safety notices and legislative information.[5]

Employees are responsible for taking reasonable care to protect their own health and safety and, in most cases, that of their co-workers. Specific requirements include wearing protective clothing and equipment, and reporting any contravention of the law or regulations. Employees have three basic rights under the joint responsibility model: (1) the right to know about workplace safety hazards, (2) the right to participate in the occupational health and safety process, and (3) the right to refuse unsafe work if they have "reasonable cause" to believe that the work is dangerous. "Reasonable cause" usually means that a complaint about a workplace hazard has not been satisfactorily resolved, or a safety problem places employees in immediate danger. If performance of a task would adversely affect health and safety, a worker cannot be disciplined for refusing to do the job.

Joint Health and Safety Committees

The function of joint health and safety committees is to provide a nonadversarial atmosphere where management and labour can work together to ensure a safe and healthy workplace. Most jurisdictions require a joint health and safety committee to be established in each workplace with a minimum number of workers (usually 10 or 20). In the other jurisdictions, the government has the power to require a committee to be formed. Committees are usually required to consist of between 2 and 12 members, at least half of whom must represent workers. In small workplaces, one health and safety representative may be required.

REQUIRED PROFESSIONAL CAPABILITIES

Establishes a joint responsibility system as required by law (e.g., worker–management health and safety committees, investigations, audits, testing, and training) to ensure employee safety

The committee is generally responsible for making regular inspections of the workplace in order to identify potential health and safety hazards, evaluate the hazards, and implement solutions. Hazard control can be achieved by addressing safety issues before an accident or injury happens, identifying ways in which a hazardous situation can be prevented from harming workers, and establishing procedures to ensure that a potential hazard will not recur. Health and safety committees are also responsible for investigating employee complaints, accident investigation,

This woman's loose hair creates an unsafe condition for use of the band saw.

Canadian Centre for Occupational Health and Safety
www.ccohs.ca

development and promotion of measures to protect health and safety, and dissemination of information about health and safety laws and regulations. In Ontario, at least one management and one labour representative must be certified in occupational health and safety through a provincial training program. Committees are often more effective if the company's health and safety manager acts as an independent expert rather than as a management representative.[6]

Enforcement of Occupational Health and Safety Laws

In all Canadian jurisdictions, occupational health and safety law provides for government inspectors to periodically carry out safety inspections of workplaces. Health and safety inspectors have wide powers to conduct inspections, and employers are required to assist them. Safety inspectors may enter a workplace at any time without a warrant or prior notification and may engage in any examination and inquiry that they believe necessary to ascertain whether the workplace is in compliance with the law. Safety inspectors may order a variety of actions on the part of employers and employees, including orders to stop work, stop using tools, install first aid equipment, and stop emission of contaminants. Governments have been criticized for weak enforcement of health and safety laws, and several provinces have recently strengthened their inspection services.[7]

Penalties consist of fines and/or jail terms. Governments across Canada are increasingly turning to prosecutions as a means of enforcing health and safety standards. A truck driver in Ontario was sentenced to 20 days' imprisonment for each of two violations of the Occupational Health and Safety Act that resulted in the death of a co-worker. Agricore United of Carman, Manitoba, was fined $50 000 for unsafe working conditions that led to the death of a worker, and in two Ontario cases, also relating to worker fatalities caused by unsafe working conditions, Woodbridge Foam Corporation was fined $175 000 and the Toronto District School Board was fined $150 000.[8]

Canadian corporate executives and directors may be held directly responsible for workplace injuries. In 2002, a corporate officer in Ontario was sentenced to 45 days in prison for health and safety violations that led to the serious injury of a young worker—the first time a corporate officer rather than a supervisor was convicted.[9] The Criminal Code was amended in 2004 to introduce a criminal offence commonly known as "corporate killing," which imposes criminal liability on "all persons" who direct the work of other employees and fail to ensure an appropriate level of safety in the workplace. This legislation arose from a public inquiry into the Westray mine explosion in Nova Scotia that killed 26 workers in 1992. Criminal Code convictions can be penalized by incarceration up to life in prison and unlimited fines. Unions have called for more charges to be laid under this law, but the supervisory behaviour must go beyond negligence to being deliberate for it to be considered criminal.[10]

Control of Toxic Substances

Most occupational health and safety laws require basic precautions with respect to toxic substances, including chemicals, biohazards (such as HIV/AIDS and

REQUIRED PROFESSIONAL CAPABILITIES

Ensures that the organization complies with legislated and contractual requirements for information management (e.g., records of hours worked and records of exposure to hazardous substances)

SARS), and physical agents (such as radiation, heat, and noise). An accurate inventory of these substances must be maintained, maximum exposure limits for airborne concentrations of these agents adhered to, the substances tested, and their use carefully controlled.

The **Workplace Hazardous Materials Information System (WHMIS)** is a Canada-wide legally mandated system designed to protect workers by providing crucial information about hazardous materials or substances in the workplace. WHMIS was the outcome of a cooperative effort among the federal, provincial, and territorial governments, together with industry and organized labour. The WHMIS legislation has three components:[11]

1. Labelling of hazardous material containers to alert workers that there is a potentially hazardous product inside (see **Figure 14.2** for examples of hazard symbols).

Workplace Hazardous Materials Information System (WHMIS) A Canada-wide legally mandated system designed to protect workers by providing information about hazardous materials in the workplace.

FIGURE 14.2 WHMIS Symbols

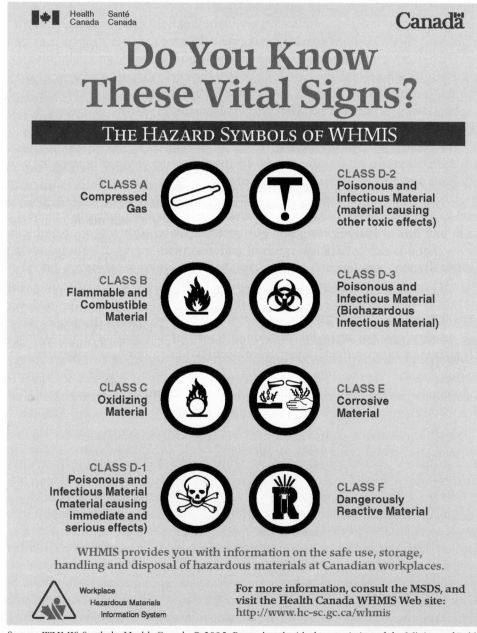

Source: WHMIS Symbols. Health Canada © 2005. Reproduced with the permission of the Minister of Public Works and Government Services Canada, 2007.

2. Material safety data sheets (MSDS) to outline a product's potentially hazardous ingredients and the procedures for safe handling of the product (see **Figure 14.3** for a sample MSDS).

WHMIS Training
www.whmis.net

3. Employee training to ensure that employees can identify WHMIS hazard symbols, read WHMIS supplier and workplace labels, and read and apply the information on an MSDS.

Occupational Health and Safety and Other Legislation

Health and safety, human rights, labour relations, and employment standards laws are in force in every jurisdiction in Canada in an interlaced web of legislation. Situations arise in which it is difficult to know which law is applicable, or which one takes precedence over another. For example, are the human rights of one employee to wear a ceremonial knife related to a religion more important than the safety of other employees? How much discipline is acceptable to labour arbitrators for health and safety violations? Should fights in the workplace be considered a safety hazard? Is sexual harassment a safety hazard? And how long does an employer have to tolerate poor performance from an alcoholic employee whose attempts at treatment fail? In Saskatchewan, human rights and occupational health and safety legislation overlap because sexual harassment is considered to be a workplace hazard.[12]

The Supervisor's Role in Safety

REQUIRED PROFESSIONAL CAPABILITIES

Analyzes risk to the health and safety of employees and determines appropriate preventative measures, including training, provision of required safety equipment, and administrative practices

Most jurisdictions impose a personal duty on supervisors to ensure that workers comply with occupational health and safety regulations, and they place a specific obligation on supervisors to advise and instruct workers about safety. Safety-minded managers must aim to instill in their workers the desire to work safely. Minimizing hazards (by ensuring that spills are wiped up, machine guards are adequate, and so forth) is important, but no matter how safe the workplace is, there will be accidents unless workers want to and do act safely. Of course, supervisors try to watch each employee closely, but most managers know that this will not work. In the final analysis, the best (and perhaps only) alternative is to get workers to want to work safely. Then, when needed, safety rules should be enforced.[13]

At DuPont, safety is the company's highest value, and its accident rate worldwide has been much lower than that of the chemical industry as a whole. As the DuPont safety philosophy states, "Safety management is an integral part of our business and is built on the belief that all injuries and occupational illnesses are preventable; that we are all responsible for our safety and also that of our fellow employees; and that managers are responsible for the safety of those in their organizations."[14]

Without full commitment at all levels of management, any attempts to reduce unsafe acts by workers will meet with little success. The first-line supervisor is a critical link in the chain of management. If the supervisor does not take safety seriously, it is likely that those under him or her will not either.

WHAT CAUSES ACCIDENTS?

Workplace accidents have three basic causes: (1) chance occurrences, (2) unsafe conditions, and (3) unsafe acts on the part of employees.

FIGURE 14.3 Material Safety Data Sheet (MSDS)

SECTION 1—CHEMICAL PRODUCT AND COMPANY IDENTIFICATION

Product Identifier	[WHMIS Classification]

Product Use

Manufacturer's Name	Supplier's Name
Street Address	Street Address

City	Province	City	Province
Postal Code	Emergency Telephone	Postal Code	Emergency Telephone

Date MSDS Prepared	MSDS Prepared by	Phone Number

SECTION 2—COMPOSITION/INFORMATION ON INGREDIENTS

Hazardous Ingredients (specific)	%	CAS Number	LD_{50} of Ingredients (specific species and route)	LD_{50} of Ingredients (specific species)

SECTION 3—HAZARDS IDENTIFICATION

Route of Entry   ☐ Skin Contact   ☐ Skin Absorption   ☐ Eye Contact   ☐ Inhalation   ☐ Ingestion

[Emergency Overview]

[WHMIS Symbols]

[Potential Health Effects]

SECTION 4—FIRST AID MEASURES

Skin Contact

Eye Contact

Inhalation

Ingestion

continued

Product Identifier

SECTION 5—FIRE FIGHTING MEASURES

Flammability ☐ Yes ☐ No	If yes, under which conditions?

Means of Extinction

Flashpoint (°C) and Method	Upper Flammable Limit *(% of volume)*	Lower Flammable Limit *(% of volume)*
Autoignition Temperature (°C)	Explosion Data—Sensitivity to impact	

Hazardous Combustion Products

[NFPA]

SECTION 6—ACCIDENTAL RELEASE MEASURES

Leak and Spill Procedures

SECTION 7—HANDLING AND STORAGE

Handling Procedures and Equipment

Storage Requirements

SECTION 8—EXPOSURE CONTROL/PERSONAL PROTECTION

Exposure Limits   ☐ ACGIH TLV   ☐ OSHA PEL   ☐ Other (specify)

Specific Engineering Controls *(such as ventilation, enclosed process)*

Personal Protective Equipment   ☐ Gloves   ☐ Respirator   ☐ Eye   ☐ Footwear   ☐ Clothing   ☐ Other

If checked, specify type

continued

Product Identifier

SECTION 9—PHYSICAL AND CHEMICAL PROPERTIES

Physical State	Odour and Appearance	Odour Threshold (ppm)
Specific Gravity	Vapour Density (air = 1)	Vapour Pressure (mmHg)
Evaporation Rate	Boiling Point (°C)	Freezing Point (°C)
pH	Coefficient of Water/Oil Distribution	[Solubility in Water]

SECTION 10—STABILITY AND REACTIVITY

Chemical Stability

Incompatibility with Other Substances

Reactivity, and under what conditions?

Hazardous Decomposition Products

SECTION 11—TOXICOLOGICAL INFORMATION

Effects of Acute Expusure

Effects of Chronic Exposure

Irritancy of Product

Skin Sensitization	Respiratory Sensitization
Carcinogenicity—IARC	Carcinogenicity—ACGIH
Reproductive Toxicity	Teratogenicty
Embryotoxicity	Mutagenicity

Name of Synergistic Products/Effects

continued

SECTION 12—ECOLOGICAL INFORMATION

[Aquatic Toxicity]

SECTION 13—DISPOSAL CONSIDERATIONS

Waste Disposal

SECTION 14—TRANSPORT INFORMATION

Special Shipping Information

	PIN
TDG	[DOT]
[IMO]	[ICAO]

SECTION 15—REGULATORY INFORMATION

[WHMIS CLASSIFICATION]	[OSHA]
[SERA]	[TSCA]

This product has been classified in accordance with the hazard criteria of the Controlled Products Regulations (CPR) and the MSDS contains all of the information required by CPR.

SECTION 16—OTHER INFORMATION

Safety Council
www.safety-council.org

Chance Occurrences

Chance occurrences (such as walking past a plate-glass window just as someone hits a ball through it) contribute to accidents but are more or less beyond management's control. We will therefore focus on *unsafe conditions* and *unsafe acts*.

Unsafe Conditions

Unsafe conditions are one main cause of accidents. They include such factors as

- improperly guarded equipment
- defective equipment
- hazardous procedures in, on, or around machines or equipment
- unsafe storage (congestion, overloading)
- improper illumination (glare, insufficient light)
- improper ventilation (insufficient air change, impure air source)[15]

The basic remedy here is to eliminate or minimize the unsafe conditions. Government standards address the mechanical and physical conditions that cause accidents. Furthermore, a checklist of unsafe conditions can be used to conduct a job hazard analysis. Common indicators of job hazards include increased numbers of accidents, employee complaints, poor product quality, employee modifications to workstations, and higher levels of absenteeism and turnover.[16]

In addition to unsafe conditions, three other work-related factors contribute to accidents: the *job itself*, the *work schedule*, and the *psychological climate* of the workplace. Certain *jobs* are inherently more dangerous than others. According to one study, for example, the job of crane operator results in about three times more accident-related hospital visits than does the job of supervisor. Similarly, some departments' work is inherently safer than others'. An accounting department usually has fewer accidents than a shipping department.

Work schedules and fatigue also affect accident rates. Accident rates usually do not increase too noticeably during the first five or six hours of the workday. Beyond that, however, the accident rate increases quickly as the number of hours worked increases. This is due partly to fatigue. It has also been found that accidents occur more often during night shifts.

Many experts believe that the *psychological climate* of the workplace affects the accident rate. For example, accidents occur more frequently in plants with a high seasonal layoff rate and those where there is hostility among employees, many garnished wages, and blighted living conditions. Temporary stress factors, such as high workplace temperature, poor illumination, and a congested workplace, are also related to accident rates. It appears that workers who work under stress, or who consider their jobs to be threatened or insecure, have more accidents than those who do not work under these conditions.[17]

Unsafe Acts

Most safety experts and managers know that it is impossible to eliminate accidents just by improving unsafe conditions. People cause accidents, and no one has found a sure-fire way to eliminate *unsafe acts* by employees, such as

- throwing materials
- operating or working at unsafe speeds (either too fast or too slow)

- making safety devices inoperative by removing, adjusting, or disconnecting them
- using unsafe equipment or using equipment unsafely
- using unsafe procedures in loading, placing, mixing, combining
- taking unsafe positions under suspended loads
- lifting improperly
- distracting, teasing, abusing, startling, quarrelling, and instigating horseplay

Such unsafe acts as these can undermine even the best attempts to minimize unsafe conditions.

Personal Characteristics

A model summarizing how personal characteristics are linked to accidents is presented in **Figure 14.4**. Personal characteristics (personality, motivation, and so on) can serve as the basis for certain "behaviour tendencies," such as the tendency to take risks, and undesirable attitudes. These behaviour tendencies in turn result in unsafe acts, such as inattention and failure to follow procedures. It follows that such unsafe acts increase the probability of someone having an accident.[18]

Years of research have failed to uncarth any set of traits that accident repeaters seemed to have in common. Instead, the consensus is that the person who is accident prone on one job may not be on a different job—that accident proneness is situational. For example, *personality traits* (such as emotional stability) may distinguish accident-prone workers on jobs involving risk; and *lack of motor skills* may distinguish accident-prone workers on jobs involving coordination. In fact, many human traits *have* been found to be related to accident repetition *in specific situations*, as the following discussion illustrates.[19]

FIGURE 14.4 How Personal Factors May Influence Employee Accident Behaviour

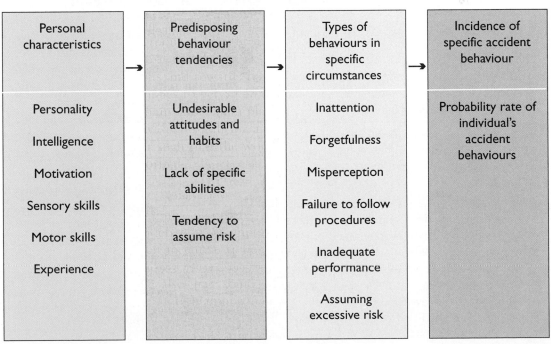

Personal characteristics	Predisposing behaviour tendencies	Types of behaviours in specific circumstances	Incidence of specific accident behaviour
Personality	Undesirable attitudes and habits	Inattention	Probability rate of individual's accident behaviours
Intelligence		Forgetfulness	
Motivation	Lack of specific abilities	Misperception	
Sensory skills		Failure to follow procedures	
Motor skills	Tendency to assume risk	Inadequate performance	
Experience		Assuming excessive risk	

Vision

Vision is related to accident frequency for many jobs. For example, passenger car drivers, intercity bus drivers, and machine operators who have high visual skills have fewer injuries than those who do not.[20]

Age

Managing Young Workers
www.youngworker.ca

Canadian LifeQuilt
www.youngworkerquilt.ca

Accidents are generally most frequent among people between the ages of 17 and 28, declining thereafter to reach a low in the late 50s and 60s. Although different patterns might be found with different jobs, this age factor repeats year after year. Across Canada, young workers between the ages of 15 and 24 (often students in low-paying summer jobs) represent about one-third of all workplace accidents.[21] Jared Diduck, age 19, died on November 9, 2001, while working on an oil rig near Chetwynd, British Columbia, when a one-ton piece of equipment crashed down, hitting him on the neck.[22] Many injuries and fatalities occur in the first few days of employment, which raises questions about the supervision and training of young workers. Suggestions regarding training of young workers are provided in the Workforce Diversity box.

Perceptual versus Motor Skills

If a worker's perceptual skill is greater than or equal to his or her motor skill, the employee is more likely to be a safe worker than another worker whose perceptual skill is lower than his or her motor skill.[23] In other words, a worker who reacts more quickly than he or she can perceive is more likely to have accidents.

In summary, these findings provide a partial list of the human traits that have been found to be related to higher accident rates, and they suggest that, for specific jobs, it seems to be possible to identify accident-prone individuals and to screen them out. Overall, it seems that accidents can have multiple causes. With that in mind, we now turn to a discussion of how to prevent accidents.

Workforce Diversity

Guiding Young Workers in Health and Safety

The Canadian Centre for Occupational Health and Safety suggests that in order to reduce the likelihood of accidents and injuries to young workers, the following basic steps should be observed:

1. *Assign suitable work.* Avoid assigning jobs that require long training times, a high degree of skill, a lot of responsibility, critical or risky tasks, or working alone.

2. *Understand young workers.* Young workers think differently than older and more experienced employees do. Young workers tend to take risks and are unrealistic about their own mortality; they may be reluctant to ask questions for fear of appearing unknowledgeable; and because of a lack of understanding, they may decide to make changes to the job in unexpected and possibly risky ways.

3. *Provide training.* Tell young workers not to perform any task until they have been properly trained; not to leave their work area unless they are told to do so, as other worksites may have special hazards; and to ask someone if they are unsure of anything. Make sure that any young worker who must use hazardous equipment is given detailed training on safety features. If young workers must wear protective equipment, make sure they know when they need to wear it, where to find it, how to use it, and how to care for it. Finally, provide training on what to do in case of emergency.

4. *Supervise.* Effective supervision of young workers requires that supervisors be qualified to organize and direct work; that they know the laws and regulations that apply to the job; and that they know the actual and potential hazards in the workplace.

Source: Adapted Canadian Centre for Occupational Health and Safety, *Employers: Guiding Young Workers in Health and Safety*, www.ccohs.ca/youngworkers/employers.html. Reproduced with the permission of CCOHS (2007).

HOW TO PREVENT ACCIDENTS

In practice, accident prevention involves reducing unsafe conditions and reducing unsafe acts.

Reducing Unsafe Conditions

Reducing unsafe conditions is an employer's first line of defence. Safety engineers should design jobs to remove or reduce physical hazards. In addition, supervisors and managers play a role in reducing unsafe conditions. A brief checklist can be used to identify and remove potential hazards. However, only 4 percent of accidents stem from unsafe working conditions, and therefore we will concentrate mainly on accident prevention methods that focus on changing behaviours.[24]

Reducing Unsafe Acts

Reducing unsafe acts is the second basic approach, and one way to do this is to screen out accident-prone persons before they are hired. The basic technique is to identify the human trait (such as visual skill) that might be related to accidents on the specific job, and then determine whether scores on this trait are related to accidents on the job.[25] For example,

- *Measures of muscular coordination.* Coordination is a predictor of safety for certain jobs.
- *Tests of visual skills.* Good vision plays a part in preventing accidents in many occupations, including operating machines and driving.
- *Employee reliability tests.* Several studies suggest that a test, such as the Employee Reliability Inventory (ERI), can help employers to reduce unsafe acts at work. The ERI measures reliability dimensions, such as emotional maturity, conscientiousness, safe job performance, and courteous job performance.
- *Behaviour-based interviewing.* Behavioural interviews and observations made in a test situation can also help to determine the likelihood that the candidate will be a safe worker.

Research
I n s i g h t ▷

A Canadian study conducted in a major industrial plant compared injury costs for a group of employees that was subjected to post-offer screening to assess their physical capability to perform job duties, and another group that did not receive post-offer screening. Injury costs over five years for the screened group were $6500 and for the nonscreened group were $2 073 000—a highly significant difference.[26]

Canadian human rights legislation has particular relevance for safety-related screening decisions. Many employers would like to inquire about applicants' workers' compensation history before hiring, in part to avoid habitual workers' compensation claimants and accident-prone individuals. However, inquiring about an applicant's workers' compensation injuries and claims can lead to allegations of discrimination based on disability. Similarly, applicants cannot be asked whether they have a disability nor can they be asked to take tests that tend to screen out those with disabilities.

Hints to Ensure Legal Compliance

Employers can ask each applicant whether he or she has the ability to perform the essential duties of the job and ask, "Do you know of any reason why you would not be able to perform the various functions of the job in question?"

Candidates can also be asked to demonstrate job-related skills, provided that every applicant is required to do so. Any selection test that duplicates the physical requirements of the job at realistic levels and type of work expected does not violate human rights law, as long as it is developed and imposed honestly and in good faith to test whether or not the applicant can meet production requirements.[27]

Industrial Accident Prevention Association
www.iapa.ca

Training and Education

Safety training is a third technique for reducing accidents. The Canadian Centre for Occupational Health and Safety and several safety associations, such as the Industrial Accident Prevention Association (IAPA), are available to partner in training efforts. All employees should be required to participate in occupational health and safety training programs, and opportunities for employee input into the content and design of such programs is advisable. The training should include instructions on safe work practices and procedures, warnings of potential hazards, the development of worker awareness about health and safety issues, and emphasis on commitment to responsible and appropriate workplace behaviour. It should include a practical evaluation process to ensure that workers are applying the acquired knowledge and following recommended safety procedures. Such training is especially appropriate for new employees. This training can be delivered through a variety of media, including classroom training, printed material, computer, videos, intranets, and the Internet.[28]

Safety posters can also help reduce unsafe acts. However, posters are no substitute for a comprehensive safety program; instead, they should be combined with other techniques, like screening and training, to reduce unsafe conditions and acts.[29] Posters with pictures may be particularly valuable for immigrant workers.

An Ethical Dilemma

Is it ethical to provide safety training in English to immigrant workers who speak little English, in order to reduce costs?

Positive Reinforcement

Safety programs based on positive reinforcement are a fourth strategy for improving safety at work. Employees often receive little or no positive reinforcement for performing safely. One approach is to establish and communicate a reasonable goal (in terms of observed incidents performed safely) so that workers know what is expected of them in terms of good performance. Employees are then encouraged to consider increasing their performance to the new safety goal, for their own protection and to decrease costs for the company. Next, various observers (such as safety coordinators and senior managers) should walk through the plant regularly, collecting safety data. The results can then be posted on a graph charting the percentage of incidents performed safely by the group as a whole, thus providing workers with feedback on their safety performance. Workers can thereby compare their current safety performance with their assigned goal. In addition, supervisors should praise workers when they perform selected activities safely.[30]

Top-Management Commitment

Studies consistently find that successful health and safety programs require a strong management commitment. This commitment, a fifth approach to accident reduction, manifests itself in senior managers: being personally involved in safety activities on a routine basis, giving safety matters high priority in company meetings and production scheduling, giving the company safety officer high rank and status, and including safety training in new workers' training. For example, linking managers' bonuses to safety improvements can reinforce a firm's commitment to safety and encourage managers to emphasize safety. HR managers have an important role to play in communicating the importance of health and safety to senior management, by demonstrating how it affects the bottom line.[31] Regina-based USF Water Group has had great success with this approach, as outlined in the Strategic HR box.

Monitoring Work Overload and Stress

Research studies have found that "role overload" (where the employee's performance is affected by inadequate time, training, and resources) is significantly associated with unsafe behaviours. Further, as work overload increases, workers are more likely to adopt more risky work methods.[32] Thus, a sixth approach to reducing unsafe acts is having employers and supervisors monitor employees (particularly those in relatively hazardous jobs) for signs of stress and overload.

Controlling Workers' Compensation Costs

Workers' compensation costs are often the most expensive benefit provided by an employer. For example, the average workplace injury in Ontario costs more than $59 000 in workers' compensation benefits. Indirect costs are estimated to be about four times the direct costs.[33] Employers' workers' compensation premiums are proportional to each firm's workers' compensation experience rate. Thus, the more workers' compensation claims a firm has, the more the firm will pay in premiums.

There are several steps in reducing workers' compensation claims.

Before the Accident

The appropriate time to begin "controlling" workers' compensation claims is before the accident happens, not after. This involves taking all the steps previously

---

Strategic HR

Safe Practices at USF Water Group

Gerald Mushka, environmental health and safety manager for USF Water Group, said employees have embraced the idea of a safety culture at the company's head office, which employs 80 manufacturing and 120 office staff.

"You can set up all the policies and all the discipline procedures to make sure people are following safe work procedures," said Mushka. "But those things historically have not had a lot of effect on incident rates."

What makes the program at USF successful is the fact that health and safety is constantly put in front of staff. When changes are made to the work environment, employees are given a say in how their workstations are set up. Once a month a safety package is sent out and employees meet with their supervisors to talk about what's in the package.

"They may talk about an incident that occurred last month or fire extinguisher use, or it may be something outside of work, like safe driving or Christmas tree light safety," Mushka says. "I'm a more safety-conscious person than I was 10 years ago. But to develop that attitude, that when you go home at night and you take out your skill saw and you put your safety glasses on and make sure you're not wearing cutoffs, of thinking about safety all the time, that takes a lot of time and effort."

One of the more creative initiatives the company is using is a health and safety bingo. Every day a bingo number is given out and employees keep track of the numbers and can win a variety of prizes. If there is a lost-time accident, the game board is erased and employees have to start over again. Prizes range from a free lunch or a gift certificate, up to a trip to Edmonton to see an NHL hockey game.

Mushka says that health and safety are a pretty easy sell to management simply because of the cost of an accident. Depending on a company's profit margin, an organization might have to make a $100 000 sale just to cover the cost of a $10 000 accident.

Source: Adapted from T. Humber, "WCBs, Lawmakers Tackle Rising Death Toll," *Canadian HR Reporter*, April 19, 2004, pp. 15, 19. Reproduced by permission of *Canadian HR Reporter*, Carswell, One Corporate Plaza, 2075 Kennedy Road, Scarborough, ON M1T 3V4.

summarized. For example, firms should remove unsafe conditions, screen out employees who might be accident-prone for the job in question (without violating human rights legislation), and establish a safety policy and loss control goals.

After the Accident

Association of Workers'
Compensation Boards of Canada
www.awcbc.org
Canadian Injured Workers Alliance
www.ciwa.ca

An occupational injury or illness can obviously be a traumatic event for the employee, and the employer's way of handling it can influence the injured worker's reaction to it. The employee is going to have specific needs and specific questions, such as where to go for medical help and whether he or she will be paid for any time off. Employers should provide first aid, make sure that the worker gets quick medical attention, make it clear that they are interested in the injured worker and his or her fears and questions, document the accident, file any required accident reports, and encourage a speedy return to work.[34]

Facilitate the Employee's Return to Work

According to one discussion of managing workers' compensation costs,

> Perhaps the most important and effective thing an employer can do to reduce costs is to develop an aggressive return-to-work program, including making light-duty work available. Surely the best solution to the current workers' compensation crisis, for both the employer and the employee, is for the worker to become a productive member of the company again instead of a helpless victim living on benefits.[35]

The National Institute of Disability Management and Research (NIDMAR) in Victoria, British Columbia, recommends following the three C's: (1) *commitment* to keeping in touch with the worker and ensuring his or her return to work; (2) *collaboration* among the parties involved, including medical, family, and workers' compensation; and (3) *creativity* in focusing on how to use the worker's remaining abilities on the job.[36]

Specific actions to encourage early return to work can be internal and/or external to the organization. Internally, an employer can set up rehabilitation committees to identify modified work, including relevant stakeholders, such as the employee and his or her colleagues, HR professionals, union representatives, and managers.

Functional abilities evaluations (FAEs) are an important step in facilitating the return to work. The FAE is conducted by a health-care professional, in order to

- improve the chances that the injured worker will be safe on the job
- help the worker's performance by identifying problem areas of work that can be addressed by physical therapy or accommodated through job modification
- determine the level of disability so that the worker can either go back to his or her original job or be accommodated[37]

Externally, the employer can work with the employee's family to ensure that they are supportive, mobilize the resources of the EAP to help the employee, ensure that physical and occupational therapists are available, and make the family physician aware of workplace accommodation possibilities.[38]

**Tips for the
Front Line**

REQUIRED PROFESSIONAL CAPABILITIES

Creates a strategy for effective liaison with the medical community

Ensures compliance with legislated reporting requirements

Ensures accommodation and graduated return to work programs are in place to meet the needs of employees with disabilities

Ensures that modifications to the work environment are consistent with the nature of worker disability (e.g., total versus partial and temporary versus permanent)

EMPLOYEE WELLNESS PROGRAMS

employee wellness program A program that takes a proactive approach to employee health and well-being.

There are three elements in a healthy workplace: the physical environment, the social environment, and health practices. **Employee wellness programs** take a proactive approach to all these areas of employee well-being (as opposed to EAPs,

Strength-Tek Fitness and Wellness
Consultants
www.strengthtek.com

Healthy Workplace Week
www.healthyworkplaceweek.ca

REQUIRED PROFESSIONAL CAPABILITIES

Develops or provides for wellness and employee assistance programs to support organizational effectiveness

which provide reactive management of employee health problems). Wellness should be viewed as a management strategy to achieve measurable outcomes related to increased levels of employee health, such as reduced health and safety costs, decreased absenteeism, lower workers' compensation costs, fewer long-term disability claims, reduced time off for short-term disability/sickness, increased morale, decreased health-care costs, and fewer employees in high-risk health categories (such as smokers).[39] Experience has shown that wellness programs are very effective; there is overwhelming evidence that money invested in a wellness program is returned many times over.[40]

For example, an innovative health partnership called "Tune Up Your Heart" was launched in 2003 at DaimlerChrysler's Windsor assembly plant in partnership with the Canadian Auto Workers, Pfizer Canada, and the local county health unit. The program was designed to assess and reduce the risks of heart disease among employees and retirees and to reduce health-care costs. The results were dramatic. Almost half of the participants lost an average of 7 kilograms and among those at highest cardiovascular risk, there was a 36 percent reduction in smoking. Overall, the participants reduced their ten-year cardiovascular risk from an average of "moderate" to an average of "low risk" in one year. An independent actuarial analysis calculated that these results could save more than $2 million in ten years if implemented across the company.[41]

One expert predicts that over the next 25 years, prevention and wellness will be the next great leap forward in health care, as employees become more broadly recognized as the most important assets of organizations. A focus on wellness will also be driven by the shrinking workforce, an increase in postponed retirement, increased awareness of mental health, and medical and technological advances.[42]

Wellness initiatives often include stress management, nutrition and weight management, smoking cessation programs, tai chi, heart health (such as screening cholesterol and blood pressure levels), physical fitness programs, and workstation wellness through ergonomics. Wellness and prevention efforts need to be understood and undertaken as a process—a long-term commitment to a holistic focus on the total person. B.C. Telus has a 50-year-old wellness program in which managers are held accountable—if absenteeism increases in their department, their bonus decreases![43] Telus believes that a focus on wellness and enhancing corporate competitiveness are one and the same. Its long-term experience has netted a savings of three dollars for every dollar spent on wellness.

Although wellness programs tend to be associated with large companies, smaller employers can also benefit from wellness programs, as outlined in the Entrepreneurs and HR box.

Almost 64 percent of Canadian organizations offer some form of wellness initiatives, such as smoking cessation programs, as shown in **Figure 14.5**. NCR Canada saved $600 000 in direct and indirect costs during the first year of its wellness program, and absenteeism was cut by more than half after 12 months and was still one-third lower after 36 months.[44] The National Quality Institute (NQI) gave its 2005 Healthy Workplace Award to Homewood Health Centre, a mental health and addiction treatment centre in Guelph,

DaimlerChrysler Canada is partnering with labour and local health units to promote wellness. The automaker's new workplace wellness program in Windsor, Ontario, includes a health risk assessment tool and various health promotion initiatives, such as health fairs.

Entrepreneurs and HR

Wellness at Bradford Progress Childcare Centres

Bradford Progress Childcare Centres operates five childcare locations in the Bradford/Newmarket area north of Toronto. They are a nonprofit organization with 50 full-time and 15 casual employees, all female. In this childcare environment, workplace wellness has become an integral part of their planning. Part of their goal is to minimize turnover of staff in order to maintain consistency for the children. To the extent that turnover is due to sick days and leaves of absence, they believe that a focus on wellness can help.

Their first step toward a wellness program was to get support from all their stakeholders, including the board of directors, staff, parents, and the communities around

them, by demonstrating to them the importance of wellness in the workplace and the potential benefits of a wellness program. They started working with their local County Workplace Wellness Committee, from whom they receive resources and support. Workplace wellness policies are incorporated into their personnel manuals and their general policy manual, and staff members are surveyed annually to address specific wellness issues.

Finally, to ensure that wellness issues are always on the table, their joint health and safety committees have incorporated wellness into all their meetings and continually address all issues that they come across. All these actions are intended to send the message that the organization intends to protect employees and promote their well-being.

Source: Adapted from *Local Success Stories,* Simcoe Muskoka District Health Unit. www.simcoehealth.org/resources_04/workplace/502_Success_Stories/success1.asp (May 18, 2006). Reprinted with permission.

Ontario. As an advocate for healthy and balanced living, Homewood offers many opportunities for employees to develop healthy lifestyles. These include walking trails, tennis courts, in-house recreation and fitness centre, on-site daycare, and other wellness initiatives, such as free noon-hour presentations.[45]

FIGURE 14.5 Corporate Wellness Initiatives

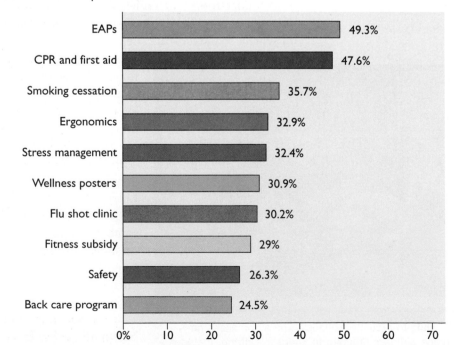

Source: Corporate Wellness Initiatives, Health Canada © 2002. Reproduced with the permission of the Minister of Public Works and Government Services Canada, 2007.

OCCUPATIONAL HEALTH AND SAFETY ISSUES AND CHALLENGES

A number of health-related issues and challenges can undermine employee performance at work.[46] These include alcoholism and substance abuse, stress and burnout, repetitive strain injuries, workplace toxins, smoking, and workplace violence.

Substance Abuse

The effects of substance abuse on the employee and his or her work are severe. Both the quality and quantity of work decline sharply. The problem is particularly severe in the manufacturing sector, where employees have substance abuse rates at nearly twice the national norm.[47]

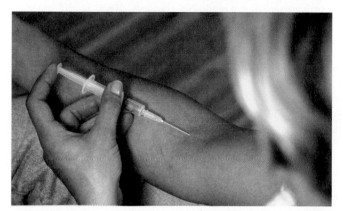

The use of drugs, especially in the workplace, is a growing concern for Canadian companies and has led to increased numbers of alcohol and drug abuse counselling programs.

The cost of substance abuse in Canada was estimated at $39.8 billion in 2002. Tobacco abuse cost $16 billion, alcohol abuse $14.6 billion, and illegal drug abuse $8.2 billion.[48] Employers can expect between 10 and 20 percent of their workforce to be problem drinkers and alcoholics, and 2 to 7 percent to have a problem with illicit drug use, according to the Centre for Addiction and Mental Health. Overall, about 30 percent of Canadian companies report having problems with drugs and alcohol in the workplace.[49]

Recognizing the substance abuser on the job can pose a problem. The early symptoms can be similar to those of other problems and thus hard to classify. Problems range from tardiness to prolonged unpredictable absences in later stages of addiction.[50] Supervisors should be the company's first line of defence in combating substance abuse in the workplace, but they should not try to be company detectives or medical diagnosticians. Guidelines that supervisors should follow include these:

- If an employee appears to be under the influence of drugs or alcohol, ask how the employee feels and look for signs of impairment, such as slurred speech. An employee judged to be unfit for duty may be sent home but not fired on the spot.

- Make a written record of observed behaviour and follow up each incident. In addition to issuing a written reprimand, managers should inform workers of the number of warnings that the company will tolerate before requiring termination. Regardless of any suspicion of substance abuse, concerns should be focused on work performance, expected changes, and available options for help.

- Troubled employees should be referred to the company's employee assistance program.

Traditional Techniques

The four traditional techniques for dealing with substance abuse are discipline, discharge, in-house counselling, and referral to an outside agency. Discharge is used to deal with alcoholism and drug problems only after repeated attempts at rehabilitation have failed.[51]

Tips for the Front Line

REQUIRED PROFESSIONAL CAPABILITIES

Contributes to policy on the workplace environment (e.g., smoking, workplace violence, scent-free, communicable diseases, and addictions)

Bellwood Health Services Inc.
www.bellwood.ca

In-house counselling can be offered by the employer's medical staff, the employee assistance plan, or agencies such as Alcoholics Anonymous.

In Grande Prairie, Alberta, a clinic was established by the Alberta Alcohol and Drug Abuse Commission as a result of requests from the business community for a treatment centre that could deal with workplace-specific issues. It offers quick enrollment in its 30-day alcohol treatment program, or the 50-day cocaine treatment program, for $175 per day, plus months of follow-up, helping 180 clients a year return to work as soon as possible.[52]

Workplace Substance Abuse and the Law

Because of the seriousness of the problem, most employers are taking additional steps to deal with alcohol and substance abuse on the job. This is difficult in Canada, because employers must balance conflicting legal obligations. On the one hand, under human rights laws, alcoholism and drug addiction are considered to be disabilities. On the other hand, under occupational health and safety legislation, employers are responsible for maintaining due diligence. As a result, employers worry that when they accommodate an employee with an addiction, they may not be ensuring a safe work environment for other employees.[53]

Drug and alcohol testing in Canada is only legal in situations where three conditions determined by the Supreme Court are met, as follows:

1. The test is rationally connected to the performance of the job.

2. The test is adopted in an honest and good-faith belief that it is necessary for the fulfillment of a legitimate work-related purpose.

3. The test is reasonably necessary to the accomplishment of the work-related purpose.[54]

Random drug tests do not measure actual impairment and are therefore unjustifiable. Arbitrary alcohol testing of one or more employees but not others is not usually justifiable, but for employees in safety-sensitive positions, such as airline pilots, it may be justifiable. "For cause" and "post-incident" testing for either alcohol or drugs may be acceptable in specific circumstances. Positive test results should generally result in accommodation of the employee. Immediate dismissal is not generally justifiable.[55]

Substance Abuse Policies

Centre for Addiction & Mental Health
www.camh.net

In general, a clear, well-communicated substance abuse policy that is reasonably and consistently enforced is the employer's best approach. The Centre for Addiction and Mental Health recommends that the policy components should include[56]

- the prohibition of alcohol and drug use (or coming to work drugged or drunk) during work hours and company special events, with clearly defined business circumstances, if any, in which alcohol consumption is considered appropriate

- clearly defined roles and responsibilities of workers and management in meeting company expectations regarding alcohol and drug use, and seeking help if problems arise

- disciplinary measures for infractions (these must meet human rights legal requirements that addictions be considered a disability)

- communication procedures to ensure that all employees know and understand the policy

**Hints to Ensure
Legal Compliance**

- preventive education to ensure that employees are knowledgeable about alcohol and drug abuse
- training to ensure that front-line supervisors and union stewards can identify employees with suspected substance abuse problems, complete thorough documentation of job performance problems, and refer the employees to a company-sponsored or external treatment program
- provision for confidential assistance and treatment programs for employees with drug and alcohol problems

Finally, organizations should remember that health promotion and drug education programs can help to prevent employee drug and alcohol problems from developing in the first place.

Job Stress

Workplace stress is a pervasive problem that is getting worse. A recent Canadian Mental Health Association survey found that half of employed Canadians list work as the biggest contributor to "serious stress" in their lives. Stress-related absenteeism is estimated to cost Canadian employers about $3.5 billion every year. The 2005 Labour Force Survey revealed a steady rising trend in both work absence and time lost for personal reasons (illness, family demands) between 1997 and 2002.[57]

Organizations begin to suffer when too many employees feel that the relent less pace of work life is neither sustainable nor healthy. Why is this happening? Downsizing has resulted in employees being asked to do more with less, creating work overload, increased time pressures, and tighter deadlines. Also, technology and the sheer volume of e-mail and voice mail are imposing terrific amounts of pressure and distraction on employees, taking a toll on their emotional equilibrium. Psychopathic bosses with no conscience, called "snakes in suits," can wreak havoc with other employees, and the result is a corporate climate characterized by fatigue, depression, and anxiety.[58]

Job stress has two main sources: environmental factors and personal factors. First, a variety of external, *environmental factors* can lead to job stress. The top ten sources of workplace stress are shown in **Table 14.1**. Two factors are particularly

TABLE 14.1   Top Ten Sources of Workplace Stress

1. Feeling of not contributing and having a lack of control.
2. Lack of two-way communication up and down the chain of command.
3. Being unappreciated.
4. Inconsistent performance management. Raises but no reviews. Positive feedback and then laid off with no understanding of why.
5. Career/job ambiguity. Things happen without employees knowing why.
6. Unclear company direction and policies.
7. Mistrust. Vicious office politics disrupts positive behaviour.
8. Doubt. Employees are uncertain about what is happening and where things are headed in their position, department or organization.
9. Random interruptions.
10. Treadmill syndrome. Too much to do at once, requires 24-hour workday.

Source: Adapted from *Top 10 Sources of Workplace Stress.* Toronto: Global Business and Economic Roundtable on Addiction and Mental Health, 2003. Available online at www.mentalhealthroundtable.ca/aug_round_pdfs/Top Ten Sources of Stress.pdf. Reprinted with the permission of Global Business and Economic Roundtable on Addiction and Mental Health.

stress-inducing. The first is a high-demand job, such as one with constant deadlines coupled with low employee control. The second is high levels of mental and physical effort combined with low reward in terms of compensation or acknowledgement.[59]

However, no two people react to the same job in an identical way, since *personal factors* also influence stress. For example, Type A personalities—people who are workaholics and who feel driven to always be on time and meet deadlines—normally place themselves under greater stress than do others. Similarly, one's patience, tolerance for ambiguity, self-esteem, health and exercise, and work and sleep patterns can also affect how one reacts to stress. Add to job stress the stress caused by non-job-related problems like divorce, postpartum depression, seasonal affective disorder, and work/family time conflict, and many workers are problems waiting to happen.

Job stress has serious consequences for both the employee and the organization. In Canada, the total cost of mental health problems approximates 17 percent of payroll, and the overall economic impact of work-related mental health problems is estimated to be $14.4 billion annually.[60] The human consequences of job stress include anxiety, depression, anger, and various physical consequences, such as cardiovascular disease, headaches, and accidents. Stress also has serious consequences for the organization, including reductions in productivity and increased absenteeism and turnover.[61]

Yet stress is not necessarily dysfunctional. Too little stress creates boredom and apathy. Performance is optimal at a level of stress that energizes but does not wear someone out.[62] Others find that stress may result in a search that leads to a better job or to a career that makes more sense, given the person's aptitudes. A modest level of stress may even lead to more creativity if a competitive situation results in new ideas being generated.

Reducing Job Stress

There are things that a person can do to alleviate stress, ranging from common-sense remedies, such as getting more sleep, eating better, and taking vacation time, to more exotic remedies, such as biofeedback and meditation. Finding a more suitable job, getting counselling through an EAP or elsewhere, and planning and organizing each day's activities are other sensible responses.[63]

The organization and its HR specialists and supervisors can also play a role in identifying and reducing job stress. One expert, Dr. John Yardley of the Brock University Wellness Institute, predicts that due diligence for health and safety could soon include an obligation for employers to ensure that employees are not faced with excessive amounts of stress.[64] A recent survey by Buffet Taylor and Associates, a Canadian health and wellness organization, found a mismatch between employers' health concerns and what they offer in their wellness programs—the number one concern of employers is employee stress management, yet stress management programs are the least commonly offered component of wellness programs.[65]

Offering an EAP is a major step toward alleviating the pressure on managers to try to help employees cope with stress. About 40 percent of EAP usage is related to stress at work. For the supervisor, important activities include monitoring each employee's performance to identify symptoms of stress, and then informing the person of the organizational remedies that may be available, such as EAPs, job transfers, or other counselling. Also important are fair treatment and permitting the employee to have more control over his or her job.[66] The HR

An Ethical Dilemma

Is it ethical for an organization to ignore the issue of job stress entirely?

specialist's role includes the use of attitude surveys to identify organizational sources of stress, refining selection and placement procedures to ensure effective person–job matches, and providing career planning aimed at ensuring that the employee moves toward a job that makes sense in terms of his or her aptitudes.

The Business and Economic Roundtable on Mental Health has recommended that HR executives take a more aggressive role in helping to combat workplace depression.[67] HR executives need to become advocates for employee health within the senior management team. Today's highly valued employees who are driving corporate productivity, innovation, and performance tend to be young knowledge workers, precisely the type of worker most prone to depression and stress, as illustrated in **Figure 14.6**. Unfortunately, there is still a stigma associated with mental illness, which drives a lot of it underground and leaves it unreported to employers or even health-care providers. The roundtable group is calling for stimulation of EAP usage and for the creation of special EAPs specifically targeting depression, which affects about 10 percent of the labour force. Some of the steps recommended by the roundtable group to eradicate depression and work-generated stress include creating a healthy work climate, reducing e-mail enslavement, creating special return-to-work strategies for employees with depression, taking an inventory of emotional work hazards (including office politics), and creating a plan to decrease the risks associated with them and to use work/life balance strategies.[68]

Research
Insight ▷

Giving employees more control over their job can also mediate the effects of job stress. This is illustrated by the results of a study in which the psychological strain caused by job stress was reduced by the amount of control that employees had over their job. The less stressful jobs did have high demands in terms of quantitative workload, the amount of attention that the employees had to pay

FIGURE 14.6   Percentage of Workforce with Depression

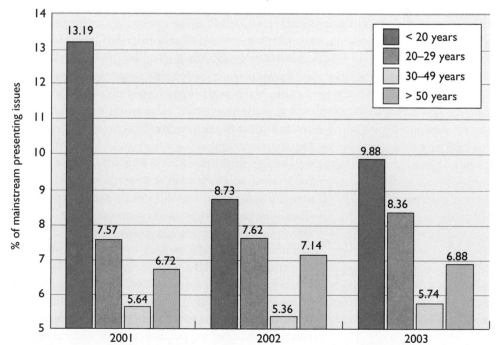

Source: Workplace Mental Health Indicators: An EAP's Perspective. Shepell-fgi Research Group, 2005, Series 1, Vol. 1, Issue 1. Reprinted with permission.

to their work, and work pressure. However, they also ranked high in task clarity, job control, supervisory support, and employee skill utilization. The researchers conclude that "to achieve a balanced system, that is, to reduce psychological strain, [job] demands and [ambiguity regarding the future of the job] need to be lowered, while skill utilization, task clarity, job control, and supervisor support need to be increased."[69]

Burnout

burnout The total depletion of physical and mental resources caused by excessive striving to reach an unrealistic work-related goal.

Many people fall victim to **burnout**—the total depletion of physical and mental resources—because of excessive striving to reach an unrealistic work-related goal. Burnout begins with cynical and pessimistic thoughts, and leads to apathy, exhaustion, withdrawal into isolation, and eventually depression.[70] Burnout is often the result of too much job stress, especially when that stress is combined with a preoccupation with attaining unattainable work-related goals. Burnout victims often do not lead well-balanced lives; virtually all of their energies are focused on achieving their work-related goals to the exclusion of other activities, leading to physical and sometimes mental collapse. This need not be limited to upwardly mobile executives: for instance, social-work counsellors caught up in their clients' problems are often burnout victims.

What can a candidate for burnout do? Here are some suggestions:

> **Tips for the Front Line**

- *Break patterns.* First, survey how you spend your time. Are you doing a variety of things, or the same thing over and over? The more well-rounded your life is, the better protected you are against burnout. If you have stopped trying new activities, start them again—for instance, travel or new hobbies.

- *Get away from it all periodically.* Schedule occasional periods of introspection during which you can get away from your usual routine, perhaps alone, to seek a perspective on where you are and where you are going.

- *Reassess goals in terms of their intrinsic worth.* Are the goals that you have set for yourself attainable? Are they really worth the sacrifices that you will have to make?

- *Think about work.* Could you do as good a job without being so intense or while also pursuing outside interests?

- *Reduce stress.* Organize your time more effectively, build a better relationship with your boss, negotiate realistic deadlines, find time during the day for detachment and relaxation, reduce unnecessary noise around your office, and limit interruptions.

Workers' Compensation and Stress-Related Disability Claims

All Canadian jurisdictions provide benefits for post-traumatic stress caused by a specific and sudden workplace incident. However, when it comes to chronic stress, there is very limited or no coverage, depending on the jurisdiction.[71] The rationale is that stress has multiple causes, including family situations and personal disposition. Research suggests, however, that a significant portion of chronic stress is often work-related. In particular, high-demand/low-control jobs (such as an administrative assistant with several demanding bosses) are known to be "psychotoxic." Consequently, employees who are denied workers' compensation benefits for chronic stress that they believe to be work-related are suing their employers. The courts are recognizing these claims and holding employers responsible for actions of supervisors who create "poisoned work environments" through harassment and psychological abuse. Courts are finding that a fundamental implied term of any employment relationship is that the employer will treat the employee fairly and with respect and dignity, and that the due diligence requirement includes protection of employees from psychological damage as well as physical harm.[72]

Repetitive Strain Injuries

repetitive strain injuries (RSIs) Activity-related soft-tissue injuries of the neck, shoulders, arms, wrist, hands, back, and legs.

RSI Clinic
www.rsiclinic.com

Human Systems Inc.
www.humansys.com

Human Factors and Ergonomics Society
www.hfes.org

Repetitive strain injuries (RSIs) are rapidly becoming the most prevalent work-related injury because of the increasing number of "knowledge" workers who use computers. RSI is an umbrella term for a number of "overuse" injuries affecting muscles, tendons, and nerves of the neck, back, chest, shoulders, arms, and hands. Typically arising as aches and pains, these injuries can progress to become crippling disorders that prevent sufferers from working and from leading normal lives. Warning signs of RSI include tightness or stiffness in the hands, elbow, wrists, shoulder, and neck; numbness and tingling in the fingertips; hands falling asleep; and frequent dropping of tools.[73]

A variety of workplace factors can play a role in the development of RSIs, including repetition, work pace, awkward or fixed positions, forceful movements, vibration, cold temperatures, and insufficient recovery time. RSIs are costly for employers in terms of compensation claims, overtime, equipment modification, retraining, and lost productivity. As with any other workplace safety issue, employers are required under occupational health and safety law to put controls in place to prevent RSIs. British Columbia has the most rigorous requirements regarding protection of workers against RSIs, and unions are calling for other provinces to follow suit. Employers must advise and train workers about the risk of RSIs from workplace activity, identify and assess job-related RSI risk factors, encourage workers to report RSI symptoms early, and use ergonomic interventions.[74]

Ergonomics

Poorly designed workstations, bad posture, and long periods of time working on computers are common conditions leading to RSIs, and these are easily preventable. **Ergonomics** is the art of fitting the workstation and work tools to the individual, which is necessary because there is no such thing as an average body. **Figure 14.7** illustrates ergonomic factors at a computer workstation. The most important preventive measure is to have employees take short breaks every half-hour or hour to do simple stretches at their workstations.[75]

ergonomics The art of fitting the workstation and work tools to the individual.

Ergonomically designed workstations have been found to increase productivity and efficiency, as well as reduce injuries. The Institute for Work and Health recently studied 200 tax collectors who were in sedentary, computer-intensive jobs. Workers who were given a highly adjustable chair combined with a 90-minute ergonomics training session reported less musculoskeletal pain over their workday, compared with workers who received just the training or nothing at all. Productivity increased nearly 18 percent because of the reduction in pain and more effective use of workspaces.[76]

Ergonomics will become more and more important as the workforce ages, and the physical demands of work will need to be adapted to accommodate some of the many physical changes typically associated with aging, including changes in muscular strength, hand function, cardiovascular capacity, vision, and hearing. In fact, a recent survey found that the workers most likely to suffer from ergonomically related problems are females over the age of 50 with a professional occupation who spend between 75 and 100 hours a week at their desk.[77]

Research
I n s i g h t ▷

FIGURE 14.7 Computer Ergonomics

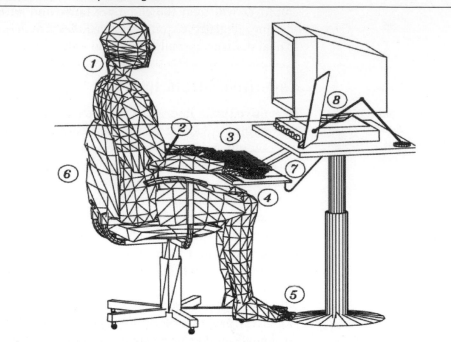

Note: This diagram is just an example. Workstation set ups will vary according to the particular desk style, monitor, tray mount or other accessories used.

1) The monitor should be set at a height so that your neck will be straight.

2) Your elbow joints should be at about 90 degrees, with the arms hanging naturally at the sides.

3) Keep your hands in line with the forearms, so the wrists are straight, not bending up, down or to either side.

4) Thighs should be roughly parallel to the floor, with your feet flat on the floor or footrest.

5) If necessary, use a footrest to support your feet.

6) Your chair should be fully adjustable (i.e., for seat height, backrest height and seat pan tilt, and, preferably, armrests). It should have a well-formed lumbar (lower back) support to help maintain the lumbar curve.

7) There should be enough space to use the mouse. Use a wrist rest or armrest so that your wrist is straight and your arm muscles are not overworked.

8) Use an adjustable document holder to hold source documents at the same height, angle and distance as the monitor.

Source: Computer Ergonomics: Workstation Layout and Lighting (Toronto: Ontario Ministry of Labour Health and Safety Guidelines, 2004). © Queen's Printer for Ontario, 2004. Reproduced with permission.

Video Display Terminals

The physical demands of new technologies have brought a new set of RSIs. The fact that many workers today must spend hours each day working with video display terminals (VDTs) is creating new health problems at work. Short-term eye problems, like burning, itching, and tearing, as well as eyestrain and eye soreness are common complaints among video display operators. Backaches and neck aches are also widespread among display users. These often occur because employees try to compensate for display problems like glare and immovable keyboards by manoeuvring into awkward body positions.

Researchers also found that employees who used VDTs and had heavy workloads were prone to psychological distress, like anxiety, irritability, and fatigue.

There is also a tendency for computer users to suffer from RSIs, such as *carpal tunnel syndrome* (a tingling or numbness in the fingers caused by the narrowing of a tunnel of bones and ligaments in the wrist) caused by repetitive use of the hands and arms at uncomfortable angles.[78]

General recommendations regarding the use of VDTs include giving employees rest breaks every hour, designing maximum flexibility into the workstation so that it can be adapted to the individual operator, reducing glare with devices, such as shades over windows and terminal screens, and giving VDT workers a complete pre-placement vision exam to ensure that vision is properly corrected to reduce visual strain.[79]

> **Tips for the Front Line**

Workplace Toxins

The leading cause of work-related deaths around the world is cancer, as shown in **Figure 14.8**. Hundreds of Canadian workers die from occupational cancer each year. There is an erroneous perception that cancer-causing agents in the workplace are disappearing. Employers often face significant costs in order to eliminate carcinogens in the workplace, and unions are often so preoccupied with wage and benefit increases that they don't bring the issue to the bargaining table. However, the Canadian Labour Congress launched an initiative in 2005 to reduce work-related cancers by releasing an information kit for workers on cancer-causing materials on the job.[80] In addition to known carcinogens, such as asbestos and benzene, new chemicals and substances are constantly

FIGURE 14.8 Deaths Attributed to Work Worldwide

According to the International Labour Organization, there were an estimated two million work-related deaths around the globe in the year 2000. Out of eight work-related diseases, cancer was cited as the number one cause of death.

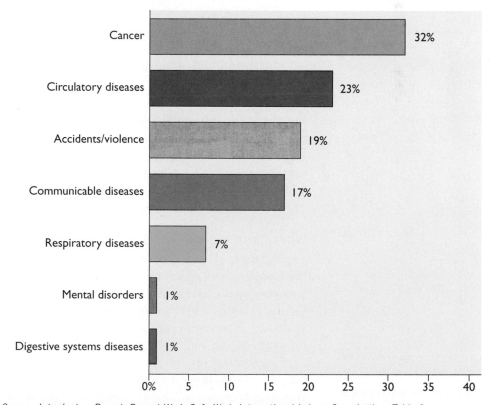

being introduced into the workplace without adequate testing.[81] In 2002, Manitoba's workers' compensation law was amended to provide benefits to firefighters who develop any of five specific job-related cancers. This new law could set a precedent for other occupations and other jurisdictions.[82]

Workplace Smoking

Smoking is a serious problem for employees and employers. Employers face higher costs deriving from higher supplementary health-care and disability insurance, as smoking is associated with numerous health problems. Smoking employees have reduced productivity and a significantly greater risk of occupational accidents than do nonsmokers. Employees who smoke also expose nonsmoking co-workers to toxic second-hand smoke. The May 2006 lung cancer death of Heather Crowe, a waitress who never smoked but was exposed to second-hand smoke on the job for 40 years, focused attention on the deadly effects of second-hand smoke in the workplace.[83]

Smokers who are also exposed to other carcinogens in the workplace, such as asbestos, have dramatically higher rates of lung cancer. The effects of on-the-job exposure to radon on lung cancer rates were found to last up to 14 years, and the cancer rates were greatly increased for smokers.[84]

Seven of Canada's 13 jurisdictions have banned smoking in workplaces. Health Canada is urging employers to implement smoking cessation programs for employees to achieve better health for employees, better business results, legislative compliance, increased employee satisfaction (especially for the 80 percent of Canadians who do not smoke), and avoidance of litigation.[85]

Violence at Work

Workplace violence is defined by the International Labour Organization (ILO) as incidents in which an employee is abused, threatened, or assaulted in circumstances relating to work, and it includes harassment, bullying, intimidation, physical threats, assaults, and robberies. Most workplace violence arises from members of the public—customers or strangers—rather than co-workers. Canada is the fourth-worst country in the world for workplace violence (the United States is seventh) according to ILO data.[86] Violence against employees at work is particularly prevalent for women in health-care professions. A 2004 study in British Columbia showed that health-care workers made up 10 percent of the workforce and 40 percent of WCB claims for violence.[87]

Workplace Violence and the Law

Legal safeguards against workplace violence in Canada are vague and fragmented. British Columbia and Saskatchewan have included workplace violence as an occupational hazard under occupational health and safety legislation. The federal labour code requires employers to take steps to protect employees from violence. Human rights laws across the country prohibit various forms of harassment and bullying.

Employers may be found vicariously liable for the violent acts of their employees on the basis that the employer negligently hired or negligently retained someone whom the employer should reasonably have known could cause the violent act, or when employers are aware of violent incidents and fail to respond.[88] In a 2005 Windsor, Ontario, case where Dr. Marc Daniel fatally

Hints to Ensure
Legal Compliance

Workplace Violence Research Institute
www.workviolence.com

Canadian Initiative on Workplace Violence
www.workplaceviolence.ca

stabbed Lori Dupont, a nurse with whom he had been romantically linked, the Dupont family sued the hospital for $13.5 million. Lori Dupont had complained to management about harassment by Dr. Daniel and told them that she feared for her safety. The hospital put Daniel and Dupont on different shifts and provided her with an escort to the parking lot but concluded that there was not sufficient evidence to fire Dr. Daniel.[89]

Prevention and Control of Workplace Violence

There are several concrete steps that employers can take to reduce the incidence of workplace violence. These include identifying jobs with high risk of violence, enhancing security arrangements, instituting a workplace violence policy, creating a healthy work environment, heightening security measures, training for violence reduction, and improving employee screening.

Identify Jobs with High Risk of Violence   Kevin Kelloway, a researcher at Saint Mary's University in Halifax, has identified job characteristics that are reliable predictors of workplace violence, shown in **Figure 14.9**. Identifying and redressing these hazards and risk factors, such as installing safety shields for taxi drivers and bus drivers, can help to reduce victimization.

Institute a Workplace Violence Policy   Firms should develop, support, and communicate a workplace violence policy that clearly communicates management's commitment to preventing violent incidents.

Create a Healthy Work Environment   According to Julian Barling, a researcher at Queen's University, a healthy work environment with professional supervision is the best way to reduce violence on the part of employees. Leaders, managers, and supervisors should express real concern for employees and treat people fairly.[90]

Heighten Security Measures   Security precautions to reduce the risk of workplace violence include improving external lighting, using drop safes to minimize cash on hand and posting signs noting that only a limited amount of cash is on hand, installing silent alarms and surveillance cameras, increasing the number of staff members on duty, and closing establishments during high-risk hours late

FIGURE 14.9 Job Characteristics That Increase the Risk of Workplace Violence

1. Being responsible for the physical/emotional care of others.
2. Making decisions that influence other people's lives/denying a service or request.
3. Working alone during the day/night/evening.
4. Handling valuables, guns, weapons, or dispensing drugs.
5. Exercising security functions of physical control of others.
6. Supervising/disciplining others.
7. Interacting with frustrated individuals.
8. Working evenings or nights.
9. Working in clients' homes.
10. Having contact with individuals under the influence of alcohol, illegal drugs, or medication.

Source: E.K. Kelloway, "Predictors and Outcomes of Workplace Violence," *HR Professional*, February/March 2003, p. 52. Reprinted by permission of the Human Resources Professionals Association of Ontario.

at night and early in the morning. In workplaces serving members of the public, some important precautions for employee safety include providing staff training in conflict resolution and defusing anger; having security staff to refuse admittance to anyone who appears intoxicated, visibly angry, or threatening; and instituting a recognizable "help" signal to alert other staff members that assistance is required.[91]

Provide Workplace Violence Training   Workplace violence training explains what workplace violence is, identifies its causes and signs, and offers tips on how to prevent it and what to do when it occurs. Supervisors can also be trained to identify the typical perpetrator—male, age 25 to 40, bad at handling stress, a constant complainer, has a tendency to make verbal threats and physical or verbal outbursts, harbours grudges, and brandishes weapons to gain attention.[92]

Improve Employee Screening   Screening out potentially violent applicants means instituting a sound pre-employment investigation of all information provided. Sample interview questions to ask might include, for instance, "What frustrates you?" and "Who was your worst supervisor and why?"[93] As sensible as it is to try to screen out potentially violent employees, doing so incurs the risk of liability and lawsuits. Human rights legislation limits the use of criminal records in hiring decisions.

Chapter Review

Summary

1. Employers and employees are held jointly responsible for maintaining the health and safety of workers, including participation on joint health and safety committees. Employers are responsible for "due diligence"—taking every reasonable precaution to ensure the health and safety of their workers. Employees are responsible for protecting their own health and safety and that of their co-workers. Employees have the right to know about workplace safety hazards, the right to participate in the occupational health and safety process, and the right to refuse unsafe work.

2. The Workplace Hazardous Materials Information System (WHMIS) law is a Canada-wide legally mandated system designed to protect workers by providing crucial information about hazardous materials and substances in the workplace. WHMIS requires labelling of hazardous material containers, material safety data sheets, and employee training.

3. There are three basic causes of accidents: chance occurrences, unsafe conditions, and unsafe acts on the part of employees. In addition, three other work-related factors (the job itself, the work schedule, and the psychological climate) also contribute to accidents.

4. One approach to preventing accidents is to reduce unsafe conditions by identifying and removing potential hazards. Another approach to improving safety is to reduce unsafe acts—for example, through selection and placement, education and training, positive reinforcement, top-management commitment, and monitoring work overload and stress.

5. Employee wellness programs aim to improve employees' health and reduce costs for sickness and disability claims, workers' compensation, and absenteeism. Wellness initiatives include physical fitness programs, smoking cessation programs, relaxation classes, and heart health monitoring.

6. Substance abuse is an important and growing health problem among employees. Techniques to deal with this challenge include disciplining, discharge, in-house counselling, and referrals to an outside agency. Stress, depression, and burnout are other potential health problems at work. Job stress can be reduced by ensuring

that employees take breaks each day, providing access to counselling, and giving employees more control over their jobs. Repetitive strain injuries occur as a result of repetitive movements, awkward postures, and forceful exertion. Ergonomics is very effective at reducing RSIs. Workplace toxins can be carcinogenic, and some governments are providing workers' compensation benefits to workers with job-related cancer. Employees who smoke have reduced productivity and greater health costs. Governments across Canada have increasingly banned workplace smoking. Violence against employees is a serious problem at work. Steps that can reduce workplace violence include improved security arrangements, better employee screening, and workplace violence training.

Key Terms

burnout   *(p. 388)*
employee wellness program   *(p. 380)*
ergonomics   *(p. 389)*
occupational health and safety legislation
   (p. 365)
repetitive strain injuries (RSIs)   *(p. 389)*
Workplace Hazardous Materials Information
   System (WHMIS)   *(p. 368)*

Review and Discussion Questions

1. Discuss the purpose of occupational health and safety legislation and how it is enforced.
2. Explain the supervisor's role in safety.
3. Explain what causes unsafe acts.
4. Describe how to reduce workers' compensation costs, both before and after an accident.
5. Explain the four traditional techniques for dealing with substance abuse.
6. Analyze the legal and safety issues concerning workplace toxins.
7. Explain how to reduce violence at work.

Critical Thinking Questions

1. What is your opinion on the question: "Is there such a thing as an accident-prone person?"
2. What guidelines would you suggest for determining the point at which to terminate an employee who shows signs of being prone to violence?
3. What do you think are the most important things to include in a wellness program, and why?
4. Given the disappointing progress in reducing workplace injuries and deaths, do you think that the "corporate killing" law should be used more aggressively?

Application Exercises

Running Case: LearnInMotion.com

The New Health and Safety Program

At first glance, a dot-com is one of the last places you would expect to find potential health and safety hazards—or so Jennifer and Pierre thought. There is no danger of moving machinery, no high-pressure lines, no cutting or heavy lifting, and certainly no forklift trucks. However, there are health and safety problems.

In terms of unsafe conditions, for instance, two things dot-com companies have lots of are cables and wires. There are cables connecting the computers to each other and to the servers, and in many cases separate cables running from some computers to separate printers. There are ten telephones in the office, all on five-metre phone lines that always seem to be snaking around chairs and tables. There is, in fact, an astonishing amount of cable considering that this is an office with fewer than ten employees. When the installation specialists wired the office (for electricity, high-speed DSL, phone lines, burglar alarms, and computers), they estimated that they used more than five kilometres of cable of one sort or another. Most of the cables are hidden in the walls or ceilings, but many of them snake their way from desk to desk, and under and over doorways.

Several employees have tried to reduce the nuisance of having to trip over wires whenever they get up by putting their plastic chair pads over the wires closest to them, However, that still leaves many wires unprotected. In other cases, they brought in their own packing tape, and tried to tape down the wires in those spaces where they are particularly troublesome, such as across doorways.

The cables and wires are one of the more obvious potential accident-causing conditions. The firm's programmer, before he left the firm, had tried to repair the main server while the unit was still electrically alive. To this day, they are not exactly sure where he stuck the screwdriver, but the result was that he was "blown across the room" as Pierre puts it. He was all right, but it was still a scare.

And although the company has not received any claims yet, every employee spends hours at his or her computer, so carpal tunnel syndrome is a risk, as are eyestrain and strained backs. One recent incident particularly scared them. The firm uses independent contractors to deliver the firm's book- and CD-ROM–based course in Toronto and two other cities. A delivery person was riding his bike at the corner of King and Bay Streets in Toronto, where he was struck by a car. Luckily he was not hurt, but the bike's front wheel was wrecked, and the close call got Pierre and Jennifer thinking about their lack of a safety program.

It's not just the physical conditions that concern the company's two owners. They also have some concerns about potential health problems such as job stress and burnout. Although the business may be (relatively) safe with respect to physical conditions, it is also relatively stressful in terms of the demands it makes in hours and deadlines. It is not at all uncommon for employees to get to work by 7:30 or 8 o'clock in the morning and to work through until 11 or 12 o'clock at night, at least five, and sometimes six or seven days per week. Just getting the company's new calendar fine-tuned and operational required 70-hour workweeks for three weeks from five of LearnInMotion.com's employees. The bottom line is that both Jennifer and Pierre feel quite strongly that they need to do something about implementing a health and safety plan. Now they want you, their management consultant, to help them to actually do it. Here's what they want you to do for them.

Questions

1. Based on your knowledge of health and safety matters, and your actual observations of operations that are similar to LearnInMotion.com, make a list of the potential hazardous conditions employees and others face at this company. Make specific recommendations to reduce the potential severity of the top five hazards.

2. Would it be advisable for the company to set up a procedure for screening out stress-prone or accident-prone individuals? Why or why not? If so, how should they be screened?

3. If a decision is made to screen applicants, what are the legal implications? Can they do this legally? How?

4. What specific topics should be included in their health and safety training program?

Case Incident

Introducing Ergonomics: What Went Wrong?

HR manager Roger Scanlon was flipping through a business magazine as he rode the train home one night when he read that the post office had recently saved more than $10 million with a new ergonomics program in its automated mail sorting system. Roger was impressed, and the next morning he began putting together a plan for research and training in ergonomics at his own firm, Harbour Office Supply. He told his boss that he was sure Harbour could realize financial savings and a reduction in absenteeism and turnover if the workplace could be made more ergonomically streamlined.

Roger knew that Harbour relied heavily on its many data entry clerks, particularly since several of the firm's major corporate customers had adopted stockless purchasing operations and now placed their office supply orders directly with Harbour's clerks. Over the last few years, as business increased, absenteeism rose as well, and various work-related health complaints seemed to be on the rise. Despite brighter lighting and posters reminding employees to take frequent short breaks, the clerks often reported headaches, backaches, eyestrain, and even some cases of carpal tunnel syndrome.

Roger began by surveying the data entry supervisors to learn their observations of worker behaviour. Were people wringing their wrists, stretching their necks and backs, or bringing pillows and backrests from home in their attempt to make their workstations more comfortable? He asked the supervisors to question employees about the kinds of problems that they were experiencing and to give him a tally of reported problems. Next, he researched the injury and illness records, looking for reasons for absenteeism and sick leave, and even for transfer requests and employee turnover.

It seemed to Roger that Harbour's records and the supervisors' reports indicated that there were several ways in which to improve the firm's ergonomic profile and achieve the promised improvements in cost and performance. He decided to implement a two-step program that would consist of training and some office renovation. With management's approval, he developed a two-hour training program for the entire staff that focused on showing employees how to correct their posture at their workstations, how to adjust the lighting around their computer screens, how to schedule regular breaks in their work, and how to use stretching and mild exercise to prevent stiffness and strain. Supervisors were given an extra training session on spotting potential health problems in their reporting employees that could be caused by excessively repetitive work, poor posture, and inadequate light and ventilation.

The second part of the program was to include training in ergonomic principles for the purchasing staff, and the purchase and installation of new ergonomic workstations, adjustable chairs, and accessories like slanted keyboards and screen filters. Roger had even arranged for the clerks' work areas to be redesigned to put more clerks near the windows. Before this part of the plan could be put into action, however, Roger discovered that instead of the decrease in complaints that he expected, the first few weeks after the training session had actually brought an increase in the rates of illness and injury reported by the clerks. Roger's boss told him that the CEO was now questioning whether to spend the money on the renovation and new equipment. She asked him to attend a meeting in which the three of them would discuss what had gone wrong.

Questions

1. What went wrong in this case?
2. What elements of Roger's plan could be improved?
3. What do you think accounts for the increase in reported illness and injury?
4. Given your answer to Question 3, do you think that Harbour should go ahead with the renovation?

Experiential Exercises

1. In a group of four to six students, spend about 30 to 45 minutes in and around one of the buildings on your campus identifying health and safety hazards. Research whether or not these unsafe conditions violate the applicable health and safety legislation.

2. Review a workplace violence consulting Web site and contact a workplace violence consultant. Gather information on what advice is provided to clients on preventing workplace violence, and ask for a sample workplace violence policy. Prepare a brief presentation to the class on your findings.

CHAPTER 15

FAIR TREATMENT
The Foundation of Effective Employee Relations

LEARNING OUTCOMES
AFTER STUDYING THIS CHAPTER, YOU SHOULD BE ABLE TO

Explain three techniques for building effective two-way communication in organizations.

Discuss the three foundations of a fair and just disciplinary process.

Define wrongful dismissal, and **explain** how to handle a wrongful dismissal lawsuit.

Explain the six steps in the termination interview.

Analyze important HR considerations in adjusting to downsizings and mergers.

REQUIRED PROFESSIONAL CAPABILITIES

- Builds constructive and supportive relationships
- Provides input into the development of employee feedback systems that support the organizational directions and cultures
- Develops and implements programs for employee involvement
- Establishes and maintains the trust and support of one's manager and subordinates
- Gathers and analyzes employee feedback to assist decision making
- Monitors application of HR policies
- Assesses requests for HR information in light of corporate policy, freedom of information legislation, evidentiary privileges, and contractual or other releases
- Contributes to the development of information security measures

THE STRATEGIC IMPORTANCE OF EFFECTIVE EMPLOYEE RELATIONS

The objectives of HRM include establishing and maintaining a harmonious employer–employee relationship and retaining productive employees. Today more than ever it is important to build a strategic competitive advantage through an organization's human resources. From an economic and practical standpoint, it is important to keep the employees that companies have spent time and money recruiting, selecting, and training continually motivated and engaged in pursuing the goals of the organization. To do this, organizations must also invest the time and money to establish programs that foster this commitment. They also need to ensure that employees are treated fairly, ethically and legally. Over 25 years of organizational research clearly indicates that employees are sensitive to the treatment they receive, particularly the perceived fairness of processes used to make decisions that affect them, and to the perceived fairness of the interpersonal treatment they receive at work.[1]

REQUIRED PROFESSIONAL CAPABILITIES

Builds constructive and supportive relationships

Although it is impossible to guarantee that every employee will perceive that he or she is being treated fairly, employers can take steps to move in that direction. As will be explained in this chapter, these steps include building two-way communication, implementing formal fair treatment programs, protecting employees' privacy, ensuring fairness in employee discipline and dismissals, and carefully managing layoffs, downsizing, and retirements.

EMPLOYEE COMMUNICATION AND FAIR TREATMENT PROGRAMS

Consider the following example of how difficult employee communication can be. When collective bargaining between Telus and its employees reached an impasse in 2005, the company sent out customized e-mails to employees describing the company's contract offer and how much each worker would get in annual raises and variable pay. The union considered this form of communication to be an unfair labour practice and filed a complaint with the Canadian Industrial Relations Board (CIRB). The CIRB had already found Telus guilty of unfair labour practices earlier for communicating company positions to employees in e-newsletters and town-hall meetings with senior management. In the unionized context, the line between permissible and impermissible communication is not very clear.[2]

Based on past court cases, an employer must be careful to avoid "negligent misrepresentation." An employer can be found liable of negligent misrepresentation if it is demonstrated that[3]

Hints to Ensure Legal Compliance

- the information provided to employees is "untrue, inaccurate, or misleading" or was misrepresented
- the employer was negligent in providing the information
- the information was relied on by the employee in a reasonable manner
- the employee suffered damages as a result of relying on the information provided by the employer
- the employer did not take reasonable care to ensure the accuracy of the information communicated to employees

REQUIRED PROFESSIONAL CAPABILITIES

Provides input into the development of employee feedback systems that support the organizational directions and culture

Treating employees fairly begins with good listening and effective two-way communication. What follows are four examples of such programs: *suggestion programs, employee opinion surveys, top-down communication programs*, and *fair treatment programs*.

Suggestion Programs

Employees can often offer well-informed, thoughtful, and creative suggestions regarding issues ranging from malfunctioning vending machines to unlit parking lots to a manager's spending too much of the department's money on travel. Dofasco Inc.'s suggestion program has been a success story for decades. Employees can receive cash awards of up to $50 000, depending on the savings realized by implementing the suggestion. Another organization with a successful suggestion plan is the Royal Bank of Canada. One suggestion for streamlining computer backup procedures and reducing the required amount of data storage equipment saved the bank almost $8 million over three years. Employees receive monetary rewards for suggestions that are implemented, but most of all, they say they want to improve operations and productivity for the bank and its customers.[4]

Suggestion programs like these have several benefits. They let management continually monitor employees' feelings and concerns, they make it clear that employees have several channels through which to communicate concerns and get responses, and the net effect is that there is less likelihood that small problems will grow into big ones.

Employee Opinion Surveys

employee opinion surveys
Communication devices that use questionnaires to ask for employees' opinions about the company, management, and work life.

Many firms also administer periodic anonymous **employee opinion surveys.** For maximum benefit, surveys should be conducted regularly and the results must be provided to participants.[5] **Figure 15.1** provides a list of survey "dos" and "don'ts."

A new employee satisfaction survey, called the Employee Feedback System (EFS), has been developed by the National Quality Institute and the Workplace Health Research Unit at Brock University.[6] The EFS examines 16 areas ranging from job satisfaction and co-worker cohesion to quality focus and employee commitment. The plan is to promote the EFS as a national standard for employee feedback surveys.

Very recently, employees have begun to use blogs to express opinions about their employers. Many companies initially reacted with concern about damage to their reputation and possible disclosure of confidential company information. However, other corporations, such as IBM, Cisco, and Sun Microsystems, have chosen to trust their employees and have suggested guidelines and specific tactics so that employees can blog without causing themselves or their employers any grief.[7]

Top-down Communication Programs

top-down communication programs Communication activities, including in-house television centres, electronic bulletin boards, and newsletters, that provide continuing opportunities for the firm to update employees on important matters.

It is hard for employees to feel committed when their boss will not tell them what is going on. Some firms, therefore, give employees extensive data on the performance of and prospects for their operations. Employers have used a number of **top-down communication programs** over the years. Traditionally, newsletters and verbal presentations were the methods used to disseminate information from the company to employees. More recently, organizations have utilized videos and high-tech communication using computers—e-mail, electronic bulletin boards, and intranets.[8]

Toyota's management works hard to share what it knows with every team member. There are three-times-per-shift, five-minute team information meetings at job sites, where employees get the latest news about the plant. There are monthly "roundtable" discussions between top management and selected non-

FIGURE 15.1 Survey Dos and Don'ts

Do	Don't
Create an effective team (two to 10 members) with representatives from corporate HR, corporate communication and business/front-line employees.	Announce really good news (everyone is getting a bonus) or really bad news (staff cutbacks) when handing out surveys.
Identify communication strategy and training needs.	Promise to listen and then don't.
Determine final project objectives: scope, timelines, deliverables, success measures, outcomes.	Say you will act on the findings and then don't.
Define key audiences (internal and external).	Promise anonymity or confidentiality and then break that promise.
Identify core survey content, as well as customized, business-specific content.	Make the survey too long, complicated and technical.
Finalize the method of survey administration.	Forget to add the due date and where to return the completed survey.
Distribute the survey according to pre-determined information needs: Do you survey the entire population or a sample?	Think you know how to analyze the data because you have mastered multiplication tables.
Have a communication plan—pre-survey, mid-survey and post-survey. Consider key messages and distribution channels.	Search the data until you find that nasty little tidbit you knew was there if you only looked hard enough.
Once the survey closes, determine the level of analysis required (simple descriptive statistics, predictive modelling, correlations).	Release write-in comments without figuring out what to do about any included names of employees, managers and leaders, foul language, slanderous remarks, serious workplace health and safety issues or harassing or discriminatory comments.

Source: J. Douglas, "Bad Surveys Beat Great Technology," *Canadian HR Reporter,* March 10, 2003, p. G3. Reproduced by permission of *Canadian HR Reporter,* Carswell, One Corporate Plaza, 2075 Kennedy Road, Scarborough, ON M1T 3V4.

supervisory staff, as well as a bi-monthly news bulletin reporting current events in Toyota worldwide, and a bi-weekly local newsletter. The firm's president is often in the plant—fielding questions, providing performance information, and ensuring that all in the company are aware of Toyota's goals and where the company is heading.

REQUIRED PROFESSIONAL CAPABILITIES

Monitors applications of HR policies

distributive justice Fairness of a decision outcome.

procedural justice Fairness of the process used to make a decision.

Fair Treatment Programs

Fairness is an integral part of what most people think of as "justice." A company that is "just" is equitable, fair, impartial, and unbiased in the ways it conducts its business. With respect to employee relations, experts generally define organizational justice in terms of its three components—distributive justice, procedural justice, and interactional justice. **Distributive justice** refers to the fairness and justice of the outcome of a decision (for instance, did I get an equitable pay raise?). **Procedural justice** refers to the fairness of the process (for instance, is the process

interactional justice Fairness in interpersonal interactions by treating others with dignity and respect.

fair treatment programs Employer programs aimed at ensuring that all employees are treated fairly, generally by providing formalized, well-documented, and highly publicized vehicles through which employees can appeal any eligible issues.

my company uses to allocate merit raises fair?). **Interactional justice** refers to the manner in which managers conduct their interpersonal dealings with employees and, in particular, to the degree to which they treat employees with dignity and respect as opposed to abuse or disrespect (for instance, does my supervisor treat me with respect?). Fair treatment tends to be more formalized in Europe, as illustrated in the Global HRM box.

There is always potential for employee grievances and discontent stemming from perceived unfairness. Discipline cases and seniority issues in promotions, transfers, and layoffs probably top the list. Others include grievances growing out of job evaluations and work assignments, overtime, vacations, incentive plans, and holidays. Whatever the source, many firms today (and virtually all unionized ones) give employees **fair treatment programs** through which to air grievances. A grievance procedure helps to ensure that every employee's grievance is heard and treated fairly, and unionized firms do not hold a monopoly on opportunities for such fair treatment.

The Strategic HR box provides details on how FedEx uses employee communication and fair treatment programs to create business success.

ELECTRONIC TRESPASSING AND EMPLOYEE PRIVACY

One relatively new and complex area of concern regarding fair treatment is employer reaction to misuse of company time and property arising from employee use of the Internet and e-mail at work for personal and possibly illegal uses, such as gambling, and visiting pornographic sites.[9] Some employees have resorted to electronic monitoring, which is becoming easier and less expensive as new software is developed that can track Web sites visited by workers and the time spent on each. Individuals are concerned with privacy—their control over information about themselves, and their freedom from unjustifiable interference

Global HRM

Employment Contracts in Europe

Businesses expanding abroad soon discover that hiring employees in Europe requires much more stringent communication than does hiring people in [Canada and] the United States. For example, the European Union (EU) has a directive that requires employers to provide employees with very explicit contracts of employment, usually within two months of their starting work.

How employers must comply with this law varies by country. For example, in the United Kingdom the employee must be given a written contract specifying, among other things, name of employer, grievance procedure, job title, rate of pay, disciplinary rules, pension plan, hours of work, vacation and sick leave policies, pay periods, and date when employment began. In Germany, the contracts need not be in writing, although they customarily are, given the amount of detail they must cover, including minimum

notice prior to layoff, wages, vacations, maternity/paternity rights, equal pay, invention rights, non-competition clause, and sickness pay. The contract need not be in writing in Italy, but again, it usually is. Items covered include start date, probationary period, working hours, job description, place of work, basic salary, and a non-competition clause. In France, the contract must be in writing, and specify information such as the identity of the parties, place of work, type of job or job descriptions, notice period, dates of payment, and work hours.

Although employment contract requirements differ from one European country to another, one thing can be said with certainty. When it comes to outlining the nature of the employment relationship, employers can't take fair treatment lightly, but instead must be very explicit about what the nature of the employer–employee relationship is to be.

Source: G. Dessler, Human Resource Management, 10th ed., © 2005, p. 519. Reprinted by permission of Pearson Education, Inc., Upper Saddle River, NJ.

Strategic HR

FedEx Attributes Success to People-First Philosophy

"To provide the level of service and quality necessary to become, and to remain, the leader in the air express cargo transportation industry, FedEx has developed a unique relationship with its employees, based on a people-first corporate philosophy. Founder and CEO Fred Smith was determined to make employees an integral part of the decision-making process, because of his belief that "when people are placed first they will provide the highest possible service, and profits will follow." Resulting from this principle is the FedEx corporate philosophy: People-Service-Profit. These three corporate goals form the basis for all business decisions."

Employee input is crucial to a people-first work environment.

The Survey Feedback Action (SFA) program at FedEx Canada includes an anonymous survey which allows employees to express opinions about the company and their managers, service, pay, and benefits. Each manager then has an opportunity to use the results to design a blueprint for improving work group engagement.

SFA has three phases. The survey is a standard, anonymous questionnaire given each year to every permanent employee. The second phase is a feedback session between the manager and his or her work group to discuss the survey results and to review areas of opportunity. The feedback meeting culminates with an action plan listing actions that the work group will take to address employees' concerns and boost results.

FedEx Canada's Guaranteed Fair Treatment Procedure (GFTP) goes beyond most grievance procedures: (1) special, easily available forms make filing the grievance easy; (2) employees are encouraged to use the system; and (3) the highest levels of top management are routinely involved in reviewing concerns.

Eligible Concerns

GFTP is available to all permanent FedEx Canada employees. It covers concerns regarding such matters as job promotion or disciplinary matters.

Procedure

The FedEx Guaranteed Fair Treatment procedure contains three steps:

1. *Management review.* The complainant contacts an employee representative from the HR department, who helps him or her to submit a written complaint to a member of management (manager or senior manager of the employee's department) within seven calendar days of the occurrence of the eligible issue. The decision to uphold, modify, or overturn management's action is communicated within ten calendar days of receipt of the complaint.

2. *Officer Review.* The complainant submits a written complaint to the managing director of his or her functional area within seven calendar days of the decision made in Step 1. The decision to uphold, overturn, or modify management's action, or initiate a review of the facts of the case is communicated to the complainant with copies to the department's HR representative and the complainant's manager within ten calendar days of receipt of the complaint.

3. *Executive appeals review.* The complainant submits a written complaint within seven calendar days of the Step 2 decision to the employee relations department, which investigates and prepares a GFTP case file for the international appeals board executive review. The appeals board—the president of FedEx Canada, the vice-president of human resources (Canada), and the employee's departmental vice-president—then makes a decision within 14 calendar days of receipt of the complaint either to uphold, overturn, or initiate a review of the facts of the case, or to take other appropriate action. The decision of the appeals board's is final.

Employees also have the option of entering into "Win-Win" mediation as a way to resolve issues they are having with either their manager, or a peer. This program enables employees to be solution oriented when problem solving and emphasizes individual ownership for these solutions.

Source: Adapted in part from *About FedEx: FedEx Attributes Success to People-First Philosophy,* FedEx Canada. www.fedex.com/no/about/overview/philosophy.html?link=4 (July 8, 2006). Used with permission of Federal Express Canada.

in their personal life. However, employers must maintain the ability to effectively manage their employees, and prevent liability to the company, as companies can be held legally liable for the actions of their employees.[10]

For example, in 2003, the Yukon Public Service Commission completed a massive investigation into allegations of computer misuse and disciplined 96 employees

Some employees may abuse company Internet and e-mail privileges.

for visiting offensive Web sites. The employees' union, the Public Service Alliance of Canada (PSAC), said that the investigation violated employees' right to privacy.[11] In an Ontario case, an employee was terminated for using his company computer and Internet service on a daily basis to operate a separate travel business.[12]

Today's employers are grappling with the problem of how to deal fairly with the issue of electronic trespassing and employee privacy. Modern technological advances have put employees' privacy rights on a potential collision course with their employers' access to and monitoring of information.[13] Research indicates that task performance declines when employees are being monitored unless they have control over the monitoring.[14] Nevertheless, employers want to monitor the use of computer-related activities in the workplace in order to eliminate time wastage (on Web surfing, playing computer games, and so on) and abuse of company resources.[15]

The issue boils down to the manner in which workers' privacy interests are balanced with the employer's "right to know." Potential justifications for access and/or monitoring include productivity measurement, harassment/defamation cases, activity involving obscenity and pornography, security issues, workplace investigations, and protection of confidentiality. For example, a supervisor at one of Linamar's auto parts manufacturing facilities in Guelph, Ontario, was caught in an undercover cross-border Internet child pornography sting. He was arrested by the Ontario Provincial Police and pled guilty to possession of child pornography. He was sentenced to three months in jail and lost his job.[16]

In general, courts in Canada have permitted electronic surveillance as long as there is proper balancing of opposing interests. Because Internet and e-mail usage occur over telephone lines, previous case law determining that cellphone conversations are not "private" because the transmission is being done through a device that can be intercepted by someone other than the intended recipient has been deemed to apply. Thus, at the present time, employers are given substantial leeway in monitoring their employees' use of the Internet and e-mail. Employers are in an even stronger position if there is a written policy in place. The policy should be updated regularly to reflect changes in technology and should address the use of equipment away from the employer's premises, such as laptops and PDAs.[17] **Figure 15.2** provides a sample company Internet and e-mail usage policy.

Video Surveillance

Some employers install video surveillance of employees to prevent theft and vandalism, and to monitor productivity. Employees must be made aware of the surveillance. Unions typically file grievances against video surveillance, and arbitrators have been reluctant to support this type of surveillance because of privacy concerns. They typically assess whether the surveillance was reasonable and whether there were reasonable alternatives available. Generally, they have decided that video surveillance is not reasonable and that other means could be used.[18]

Privacy Legislation

The Personal Information Protection and Electronic Documents Act (PIPEDA) governs the collection, use, and disclosure of personal information across Canada,

---

Hints to Ensure Legal Compliance

REQUIRED PROFESSIONAL CAPABILITIES

Assesses requests for HR information in light of corporate policy, freedom of information legislation, evidentiary privileges, and contractual or other releases

Contributes to the development of information security measures

Privacy Commission of Canada
www.privcom.gc.ca

Information and Privacy Commissioner of Ontario
www.ipc.on.ca

An Ethical Dilemma

Is it ethical to use video surveillance of employees?

FIGURE 15.2   Sample Company E-mail and Internet Usage Policy

E-mail System

The e-mail system is used to facilitate business-related communication throughout the company and field locations. Employees who use the e-mail system should keep the following in mind. The e-mail system is to be used primarily for company business as it relates to the application of your position. Information on the e-mail system is considered proprietary and belongs to the association and that the association reserves the right to review that material with or without employees' knowledge.

Extensive personal use of the e-mail system is discouraged to reduce the amount of e-mail traffic so that company business can take priority. At no time should the system be used to communicate opinions such as politics, social issues or personal biases.

E-mail users should understand that information on the system is not greatly protected and highly confidential and sensitive material should not be placed on the e-mail system; it should be communicated directly to the applicable parties by other means.

Internet Code of Conduct

Access to the Internet has been provided to staff members for the benefit of the organization and its customers. It allows employees to connect to information resources around the world. Every staff member has a responsibility to maintain and enhance the company's public image, and to use the Internet in a productive manner. To ensure that all employees are responsible, productive Internet users and are protecting the company's public image, the following guidelines have been established for using the Internet.

Acceptable Use of the Internet:

Employees accessing the Internet are representing the company. All communications should be for professional reasons. Employees are responsible for seeing that the Internet is used in an effective, ethical and lawful manner. Internet Relay Chat channels may be used to conduct official company business, or to gain technical or analytical advice. Databases may be accessed for information as needed. E-mail may be used for business contacts.

Unacceptable Use of the Internet:

1. The Internet should not be used for personal gain or advancement of individual views. Solicitation of non-company business, or any use of the Internet for personal gain is strictly prohibited. Use of the Internet must not disrupt the operation of the company network or the networks of other users. It must not interfere with your productivity.

2. Dialing into our network from home to access the Internet, except for a direct business purpose.

Communications:

Each employee is responsible for the content of all text, audio or images that they place or send over the Internet. Fraudulent, harassing or obscene messages are prohibited. All messages communicated on the Internet should have your name attached. No messages will be transmitted under an assumed name. Users may not attempt to obscure the origin of any message. Information published on the Internet should not violate or infringe upon the rights of others. No abusive, profane or offensive language is transmitted through the system. Employees who wish to express personal opinions on the Internet are encouraged to obtain their own usernames on other Internet systems.

continued

Software:

To prevent computer viruses from being transmitted through the system there will be no unauthorized downloading of any software. All software downloads will be scanned for viruses.

Copyright Issues:

Copyrighted materials belonging to entities other than this company may not be transmitted by staff members on the Internet. One copy of copyrighted material may be downloaded for your own personal use in research. Users are not permitted to copy, transfer, rename, add or delete information or programs belonging to other users unless given express permission to do so by the owner. Failure to observe copyright or licence agreements may result in disciplinary action from the company or legal action by the copyright owner.

Security:

All messages created, sent or retrieved over the Internet are the property of the company, and should be considered public information.

The company reserves the right to access and monitor all messages and files on the computer system as deemed necessary and appropriate.

Internet messages are public communication and are not private. All communications including text and images can be disclosed to law enforcement or other third parties without prior consent of the sender or the receiver.

Harassment:

Harassment of any kind is prohibited. No messages with derogatory or inflammatory remarks about an individual or a group's race, religion, national origin, physical attributes or sexual preference will be transmitted.

Violations:

Violations of any guidelines listed above may result in disciplinary action.

Source: Donna F. Dunn, "E-mail and Internet Usage," The Canadian Association, May 2004. www.axi.ca/TCA/may2004/policies and practices_1.shtml (September 21, 2006)

including employers' collection and dissemination of personal information about employees. Any information beyond name, title, business address, and telephone number is regarded as personal and private, including health-related information provided to insurers.[19] Employers must obtain consent from employees whenever personal information is collected, used, or disclosed. Employers need to establish a privacy policy, appoint a chief privacy officer, conduct a privacy audit, and develop detailed procedures about how the organization will protect personal information about employees.[20]

FAIRNESS IN DISCIPLINE AND DISMISSALS

Employee discipline and termination of employment are two of the most common situations in which employees perceive that they are treated unfairly. This reaction is not surprising given the negative ramifications in each case. Thus, it is very important for all managers and HR professionals to be aware of how to discipline employees fairly and how to ensure that employee terminations are conducted legally and fairly.

Employee Discipline

discipline A procedure intended to correct an employee's behaviour because a rule or procedure has been violated.

The purpose of **discipline** is to encourage employees to adhere to rules and regulations. Courts have repeatedly articulated the rights of employees to fair treatment, not only during the term of employment but also during the disciplinary and termination process.[21] A fair and just disciplinary process is based on three foundations: *rules and regulations*, a *system of progressive penalties*, and an *appeals process*.

A set of clear *rules and regulations* is the first foundation. These rules address matters such as theft, destruction of company property, drinking on the job, and insubordination. Examples of rules include

- Poor performance is not acceptable. Each employee is expected to perform his or her work properly and efficiently and to meet established standards of quality.

- Liquor and drugs do not mix with work. The use of either during working hours and reporting for work under the influence of either are both strictly prohibited.

- Safety rules must be followed at all times.

The purpose of these rules is to inform employees ahead of time as to what is and is not acceptable behaviour. Employees must be told, preferably in writing, what is not permitted. This is usually done during the employee's orientation. The rules and regulations are generally listed in the employee orientation handbook.

A *system of progressive penalties* is a second foundation of effective discipline. Penalties may range from verbal warnings to written warnings to suspension from the job to discharge. The severity of the penalty is usually a function of the type of offence and the number of times the offence has occurred. For example, most companies issue warnings for the first instance of unexcused lateness. However, for a fourth offence, discharge is the more usual disciplinary action.

Finally, there should be an *appeals process* as part of the disciplinary process; this helps to ensure that discipline is meted out fairly and equitably. Programs like FedEx's Guaranteed Fair Treatment Program help to ensure their employees have a real appeals process. Several important discipline guidelines are summarized in **Figure 15.3**.

Research has shown that there are six general components of fairness relating to a disciplinary discussion between a manager and an employee. Managers should do the following:[22]

1. Take a counselling approach to the problem.

2. Exhibit a positive nonverbal demeanour, not angry or anxious.

3. Provide the employee with some control over the disciplinary process and outcome.

4. Provide a clear explanation of the problem behaviour.

5. Ensure that the discussion occurs in private.

6. Ensure that the discipline is not arbitrary; that is, it is consistent with other similar situations.

Discipline without Punishment

Traditional discipline has two major potential flaws. First, although fairness guidelines like those previously mentioned can help, no one ever feels good about being punished. There may, therefore, be residual bad feelings among all involved. A second shortcoming is that forcing the rules on employees may gain their short-term compliance but not their active cooperation when supervisors are not on hand to enforce the rules.

Discipline without punishment (or nonpunitive discipline) is aimed at avoiding these disciplinary problems. This is accomplished by gaining the employees'

An Ethical Dilemma

Is it ethical to apply disciplinary action in cases of ongoing absenteeism and tardiness because of family responsibilities? What other approach could be used?

Research Insight ▷

FIGURE 15.3 Discipline Guidelines

- Make sure that the evidence supports the charge of employee wrongdoing. In one study, "the employer's evidence did not support the charge of employee wrongdoing" was the reason arbitrators gave most often for reinstating discharged employees or for reducing disciplinary suspensions.
- Ensure that the employee's due process rights are protected. Arbitrators normally reverse discharges and suspensions that are imposed in a manner that violates basic notions of fairness of employee due process procedures. For example, follow established progressive discipline procedures, and do not deny the employee an opportunity to tell his of her side of the story.
- Adequately warn the employee of the disciplinary consequences of his or her alleged misconduct.
- Ensure that the rule that allegedly was violated is "reasonably related" to the efficient and safe operation of the particular work environment (since employees are usually allowed by arbitrators to question the reason behind any rule or order).
- Management must fairly and adequately investigate the matter before administering discipline.
- Ensure that the investigation produces substantial evidence of misconduct.
- Apply rules, orders, or penalties even-handedly and without discrimination.
- Ensure that the penalty is reasonably related to the misconduct and to the employee's past work history.
- Maintain the employees' right to counsel. All union employees have the right to bring a union representative when they are called in for an interview that they reasonably believe might result in disciplinary action.
- Do not rob the employee of his or her dignity. Discipline employees in private (unless they request counsel).
- Remember that the burden of proof is on the employer. In our society, a person is always considered innocent until proven guilty.
- Get the facts. Do not base disciplinary decisions on hearsay evidence or on general impressions.
- Do not act while angry. Very few people can be objective and sensible when they are angry.

acceptance of the rules and by reducing the punitive nature of the discipline itself. Here is an example. Assume that there has been a breach of discipline (such as disregarding safety rules) or unsatisfactory work performance (such as carelessness in handling materials). In such a case, the following steps would constitute a typical nonpunitive approach to discipline:[23]

- *Step 1:* Issue an oral reminder. The goal here is to get the employee to agree to solve the problem by reminding the employee of (1) the reason for the rule, and (2) the fact that he or she has a responsibility to meet performance standards. Keep a written record of the incident in a separate working file in the supervisor's desk rather than in the employee's HR file.

- *Step 2:* Should another incident arise within six weeks, issue the employee a formal written reminder, a copy of which is placed in the HR file. In addition, privately hold a second discussion with the employee to express confidence in the person's ability to act responsibly at work. Should another such incident occur in the next six weeks, you may decide to hold a follow-up meeting to investigate the possibility that the person is ill-suited to or bored with the job. Usually, though, the next step after the written reminder would be a paid one-day leave.

- *Step 3:* The next step is a paid one-day "decision-making leave." If another incident occurs in the next six weeks or so after the written warning, tell the employee to take a one-day leave with pay, to stay home and consider whether or not the job is right for him or her and whether or not he or she wants to abide by the company's rules. The fact that the person is paid for the day is a final expression of the company's hope that the employee can and will act responsibly with respect to following the rules. When the employee returns to work, he or she should be asked to provide a decision regarding whether or not the rules will be followed. Assuming that there is a positive response, the supervisor should work out a brief action plan to help the person change his or her behaviour.
- *Step 4:* If no further incidents occur in the next year or so, the one-day paid suspension is purged from the person's file. If the behaviour is repeated, dismissal is required.

The process must, of course, be changed in exceptional circumstances. Criminal behaviour or in-plant fighting might be grounds for immediate dismissal, for instance. In addition, if several incidents occurred at very close intervals, Step 2—the written warning—might be skipped.

Nonpunitive discipline can be effective. Employees seem to welcome the less punitive aspects and do not seem to abuse the system by misbehaving to get a day off with pay. Grievances, sick leave usage, and disciplinary incidents all seem to drop in firms that use these procedures. However, there will still be times when dismissals will be required.

Managing Dismissals

dismissal Involuntary termination of an employee's employment.

Dismissal is the most drastic disciplinary step that can be taken toward an employee and one that must be handled with deliberate care. Specifically, the dismissal should be fair in that *sufficient cause* exists for it. Furthermore, the dismissal should occur only after *all reasonable steps* to rehabilitate or salvage the employee have failed. However, there are undoubtedly times when dismissal is required, and in these instances it should be carried out forthrightly.[24]

Grounds for Dismissal

There are four bases for dismissal: unsatisfactory performance, misconduct, lack of qualifications for the job, and changed requirements of (or elimination of) the job. *Unsatisfactory performance* may be defined as a persistent failure to perform assigned duties or to meet prescribed standards on the job.[25] Specific reasons here include excessive absenteeism or tardiness; a persistent failure to meet normal job requirements; or an adverse attitude toward the company, supervisor, or fellow employees. *Misconduct* can be defined as deliberate and willful violation of the employer's rules and may include stealing, rowdyism, and insubordination. The prevalence of theft behaviour is alarming. For example, a 2006 Ernst & Young study estimated that 47 percent of retail "inventory shrinkage" is attributable to employees, and the Retail Council of Canada estimates that employee theft costs Canadian businesses about $1 billion per year.[26] Air Canada estimates that it loses up to 9 percent of its cabin stock each year to employee theft, or about $9 per day per employee.[27] *Lack of qualifications* for the job is defined as an employee's incapability of doing the assigned work although the person is diligent. Since the employee in this case may be trying to do the job, it is especially important that every effort be made to salvage him or her. *Changed requirements of the job* may be defined as an employee's incapability of doing the assigned work after the nature of the job has been changed. Similarly, an employee may have to be dismissed when his or her job is eliminated. Here again, the employee may be industrious, so every effort should be made to retrain or transfer this person, if possible.

insubordination Willful disregard or disobedience of the boss's authority or legitimate orders; criticizing the boss in public.

Insubordination is a form of misconduct providing grounds for dismissal, although it may be relatively difficult to describe and to prove. To that end, it is important to communicate to employees that some acts are considered insubordinate whenever and wherever they occur. These generally include the following:[28]

1. Direct disregard of the boss's authority. At sea, this is called mutiny.

2. Flat-out disobedience of, or refusal to obey, the boss's orders—particularly in front of others.

3. Deliberate defiance of clearly stated company policies, rules, regulations, and procedures.

4. Public criticism of the boss. Contradicting or arguing with him or her is also negative and inappropriate.

5. Blatant disregard of the boss's reasonable instructions.

6. Contemptuous display of disrespect: making insolent comments, for example, and, more important, portraying these feelings in the attitude shown while on the job.

7. Disregard for the chain of command, shown by going around the immediate supervisor or manager with a complaint, suggestion, or political manoeuvre. Although the employee may be right, that may not be enough to save him or her from the charges of insubordination.

8. Participation in (or leadership of) an effort to undermine and remove the boss from power. If the effort does not work (and it seldom does), those involved will be "dead in the water."

Instituting clear policies against such behaviour and providing HR department support to supervisors and managers who are dealing with employees who are behaving in an insubordinate manner can go a long way to preventing this problem from escalating and ending up before a judge or arbitrator.[29] **Figure 15.4** provides guidelines on insubordination used by the Saskatchewan government to assist managers and supervisors in dealing with insubordination.

Arbitrators may find extenuating circumstances in insubordination. For example, a railway worker who had been on the job for more than 25 years cursed at his supervisor and told her to "f— off" during a heated exchange in May 2004. He was sent home and later fired. The arbitrator ordered the worker reinstated with full seniority but did not take the insubordination lightly, as his decision stipulated that the worker not be compensated for the time off work between being fired (June 2004) and being reinstated (February 2005). The arbitrator found the termination to be too harsh but believed that the lack of compensation would make it clear that profane and antagonistic language directed at supervisors would not be tolerated.[30]

Employment Contracts, Reasonable Notice, and Wrongful Dismissal

In Canada, the employer—employee relationship is governed by an employment contract—a formal agreement (in writing or based on mutual understanding)

FIGURE 15.4   Saskatchewan Public Service Commission Corrective Discipline
Guidelines for Insubordination

Saskatchewan Public Service Commission	**Human Resource Manual** www.gov.sk.ca/psc/hrmanual
	Section: PS 803-Guidelines
Corrective Discipline Guidelines Part E: Insubordination	Date issued: 1982 11 17 Revision date: 1990 09 30

The following sets out guidelines to assist managers and supervisors in dealing with the discipline situation.

1. **Insubordination - A Special Case**

   Insubordination is defined as the refusal of an employee to carry out the order of a supervisor. Employees are required, under the Public Service Employment Regulations Section 15.1, to carry out such orders. Employees may disagree with such orders. However, the proper employee response is to obey the order and seek redress via grievance action. The rule of "obey now - grieve later" is well founded in arbitration decisions.

   Note however, that the "obey now - grieve later" rule does not apply to all orders given by supervisors. Some exceptions are as follows:

   - where the order given is not related to work, e.g., deliver my personal mail as opposed to deliver departmental mail, etc. An employee may be directed and is required to perform work duties not found in his job description. However, the employee may later grieve the assignment of these duties.

   - where the employee has reasonable grounds for believing that obeying the order given would endanger health and/or safety.

   - where the order given is illegal.

   - where the order is given by someone without authority. Note however that all orders need not be given by one's immediate supervisor. Where the employee knows that the order is being given by his supervisor's superior, such orders must be followed.

   - where the order interferes with personal appearance or privacy, e.g., a search of one's personal effects where there is suspected theft, that one shave a beard, cut ones hair, wear certain clothes, etc. Note however that appearance or clothing rules may apply where they are a direct job requirement, e.g., uniforms for regulatory staff, cleanliness when preparing food, etc. The refusal of an employee to submit himself to a search of personal effects when management has reasonable grounds for such a request should be recorded. Inform the employee discipline action may be taken; consult with your personnel advisor on how to proceed.

   - where the employee has a reasonable personal excuse, e.g., the employee was provoked into refusing the order, where the employee has a legitimate and reasonable personal excuse and gives it at the time of refusal - personal illness, death in the family, etc. Note however that mere personal inconvenience is not acceptable, e.g., I'm on my break, it's my bowling night, etc.

continued

made between the two parties. If the contract is for a specific length of time, the contract ends at the expiration date, and the employee cannot be prematurely dismissed without just cause.

Employees are often hired under an implied contract where the understanding is that employment is for an indefinite period of time and may be terminated by either party only when *reasonable notice* is given.[31] Employers cannot hire and fire employees at will, as is the case in the United States. Canadian employers can only terminate an employee's employment without reasonable notice when just cause exists. If just cause is not present, then a termination without notice is considered **wrongful dismissal**.

Just cause is usually considered to include disobedience, incompetence, dishonesty, insubordination, fighting, and persistent absence or lateness.[32] However, just cause cannot be assessed in isolation and may vary depending on the possible

wrongful dismissal   An employee dismissal that does not comply with the law or does not comply with a written or implied contractual arrangement.

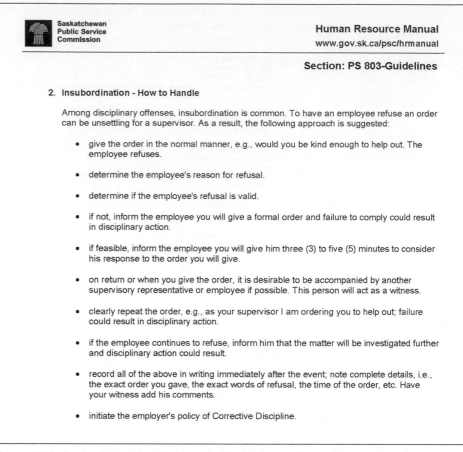

	Human Resource Manual
Saskatchewan Public Service Commission	www.gov.sk.ca/psc/hrmanual

Section: PS 803-Guidelines

2. Insubordination - How to Handle

Among disciplinary offenses, insubordination is common. To have an employee refuse an order can be unsettling for a supervisor. As a result, the following approach is suggested:

- give the order in the normal manner, e.g., would you be kind enough to help out. The employee refuses.

- determine the employee's reason for refusal.

- determine if the employee's refusal is valid.

- if not, inform the employee you will give a formal order and failure to comply could result in disciplinary action.

- if feasible, inform the employee you will give him three (3) to five (5) minutes to consider his response to the order you will give.

- on return or when you give the order, it is desirable to be accompanied by another supervisory representative or employee if possible. This person will act as a witness.

- clearly repeat the order, e.g., as your supervisor I am ordering you to help out; failure could result in disciplinary action.

- if the employee continues to refuse, inform him that the matter will be investigated further and disciplinary action could result.

- record all of the above in writing immediately after the event; note complete details, i.e., the exact order you gave, the exact words of refusal, the time of the order, etc. Have your witness add his comments.

- initiate the employer's policy of Corrective Discipline.

Source: Public Service Commission, Government of Saskatchewan, *Human Resource Manual*, www.gov.sk.ca/psc/hrmanual/appendices/ps803–ge.pdf (July 9, 2006). Used with permission.

consequences of the misconduct, the status of the employee, and the circumstances of the case. The burden of proof rests with the employer. In Canada, courts often do not accept the assertion of just cause by the employer, and unions almost never do—one union alleged that a death threat made by an employee to his supervisor was "mild insubordination."[33]

In any termination where just cause is not involved, the employer must provide *reasonable notice* to the employee (often three to four weeks per year of service). The employee sometimes continues to work during the period of notice given but usually ceases work at the time that the notice of termination is given. In the latter case, the employee receives a lump sum of money equal to his or her pay for the period of notice.

Often, the amount considered *"reasonable"* is beyond the minimum notice requirements of employment/labour standards legislation. The employee can accept the notice given or can sue for wrongful dismissal if the notice is considered unacceptable. The court will review the circumstances of the dismissal and make a final decision on the amount of notice to be provided. The courts generally award a period of notice based on their assessment of how long it will take the employee to find alternative employment, taking into account the employee's age, salary, length of service, the level of the job, and other factors. Rarely have notice periods exceeded 24 months.[34]

More recently, "bad-faith conduct" on the part of the employer in dismissing an employee has been added as another factor being considered by the courts in determining the period of reasonable notice.[35] At a minimum, employers are required to be candid, reasonable, honest, and forthright with their employees in the course of dismissal and should refrain from engaging in conduct that is unfair or in bad faith, such as being untruthful, misleading, or unduly insensitive. The resulting additional periods of notice (known as "Wallace damages") have been unpredictable, often about three to six months, no matter the context.[36] This has resulted in a few cases where the notice period has exceeded 24 months. It is clear that employers must treat employees with honesty and respect at all times, especially at the time of dismissal.[37]

In extreme cases, employers may also be ordered to pay punitive damages for harsh and vindictive treatment of an employee, and/or damages for aggravated or mental distress if the employee suffered undue distress from not being given adequate notice of termination.[38] In March 2005, the largest punitive damage award in Canadian history was handed down when Honda Canada was ordered to pay $500 000 in punitive damages to a terminated employee for its "outrageous mistreatment" of the employee, who suffered from chronic fatigue syndrome.[39]

Avoiding Wrongful Dismissal Suits

With the increased likelihood that terminated employees can and will sue for wrongful dismissal, it is wise for employers to protect themselves against wrongful dismissal suits. The time to do that is before mistakes have been made and suits have been filed.

One of the most important ways to avoid wrongful dismissal lawsuits is to avoid "luring" a new employee away from stable employment elsewhere and then having to terminate his or her employment because of a business downturn. For example, an information technology specialist who was employed at a salary of $300 000 in a large Canadian corporation was lured away to work for a U.S. software developer called Blue Pumpkin Software Inc. She was assured that this was a long-term opportunity and that her position was secure as long as she performed well, because Canada was going to be the company's fastest-growing market and because Blue Pumpkin was definitely committed to Canada for the estimated three to five years needed to establish itself in the market. The employee joined Blue Pumpkin and performed well but was dismissed six months later as part of a cost-cutting initiative aimed at avoiding bankruptcy. The employee sued for wrongful dismissal and was awarded 12 months' notice.[40]

Other steps to take in order to avoid wrongful dismissal suits are the following:[41]

Hints to Ensure Legal Compliance

1. Use employment contracts with a termination clause and with wording clearly permitting the company to dismiss without cause during the probationary period.

2. Document all disciplinary action.

3. Do not allege just cause for dismissal unless it can be proven.

4. Time the termination so that it does not conflict with special occasions, such as birthdays or holidays.

5. Use termination letters in all cases, clearly stating the settlement offer.

6. Schedule the termination interview in a private location at a time of day that will allow the employee to clear out belongings with a minimal amount of contact with other employees.

7. Include two members of management in the termination meeting.

Tips for the
Front Line

**An Ethical
Dilemma**

Is it ethical to "buy out" an undesirable employee with severance pay and a good letter of reference, in order to avoid prolonged wrongful dismissal litigation, even if you know the letter is misleading to potential future employers?

constructive dismissal   The employer makes unilateral changes in the employment contract that are unacceptable to the employee, even though the employee has not been formally terminated.

Restructuring Tips
www.hr.cch.com

If a wrongful dismissal suit is made against the company, the firm should[42]

- review the claim carefully before retaining an employment lawyer
- ask for a legal opinion on the merits of the case
- work with the lawyer and provide all relevant facts and documentation
- never allege cause if none exists
- investigate for other improper conduct
- avoid defamatory statements
- discuss any possible letter of reference with the lawyer
- offer to settle in order to save time and money
- consider mediation as an option

Constructive Dismissal

Constructive dismissal can be considered to occur when the employer makes unilateral changes in the employment contract that are unacceptable to the employee, even though the employee has not been formally terminated.[43] The most common changes in employment status that are considered to constitute constructive dismissal are demotion, reduction in pay and benefits, forced resignation, forced early retirement, forced transfer, and changes in job duties and responsibilities. An employee who believes that he or she has been constructively dismissed can sue the employer for wrongful dismissal. If the judge agrees that constructive dismissal occurred, he or she will determine a period of notice to be provided to the employee.

For example, two executives in an Alberta energy exploration company sued for constructive dismissal following a disagreement with the CEO regarding their desire to cash out their stock options. The three men effectively ran the company together. The CEO wrote hostile letters to the two executives questioning their integrity and professionalism, and advising them to seek legal advice as the company was considering whether the matter constituted cause for their dismissal. The court found that the CEO's letters questioning their integrity constituted the end of their working relationship and made it impossible for them to remain in their jobs, thus constituting constructive dismissal.[44]

Dismissal Procedures

In the event of a dismissal, a number of steps should be followed:

- Hold warning discussions before taking any final action. An employee must be made aware that he or she is not performing satisfactorily.
- Get written confirmation of the final warning.
- Prepare a checklist of all property that should be accounted for, including computer disks and manuals.
- Change security codes and locks previously used by discharged individuals.
- Always prepare for the possibility that the discharged individual may act irrationally or even violently, either immediately or in weeks to come.
- Decide beforehand how other employees will be informed about this person's dismissal. An informal departmental meeting of those directly involved with this person is usually sufficient.

Consider having a lawyer create an employee release form. Such releases are obtained from employees who have asserted claims against the company or who

Hints to Ensure
Legal Compliance

are the subject of employment actions, such as discharges and layoffs. They release the employer from claims by giving the employee something of value—"consideration" in legal terms.[45] Any such release should include (1) a general release of the employee's claims, (2) a covenant not to sue the employer, and (3) an indemnification and payback provision relating to breaches of the release and covenant-not-to-sue provisions.[46]

A recent study of 996 recently fired or laid-off workers found that wrongful dismissal claims were strongly correlated with the way workers felt they had been treated at the time of termination. They also found a "vendetta effect" where the instances of wrongful dismissal claims became stronger as negative treatment became extreme, as shown in **Figure** 15.5. The researchers concluded that many wrongful dismissal lawsuits could be avoided if effective human resource practices, specifically treating employees fairly, were employed. Providing clear, honest explanations of termination decisions and handling the termination in a way that treats people with dignity and respect can be especially effective.[47]

The Termination Interview

Dismissing an employee is one of the most difficult tasks that a manager will face at work.[48] The dismissed employee, even if warned many times in the past, will often still react with total disbelief or even violence. Guidelines for the **termination interview** itself are as follows.

termination interview The interview in which an employee is informed of the fact that he or she has been dismissed.

Step 1: Plan the Interview Carefully   According to experts at Hay Group, this means doing the following:

• Schedule the meeting on a day early in the week.

• Never inform an employee over the phone.

FIGURE 15.5 Fair Treatment and Wrongful Dismissal Claims: The Vendetta Effect

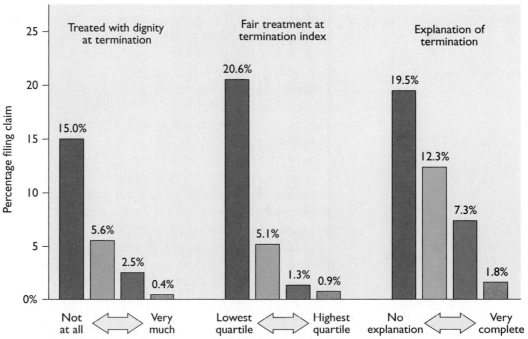

Source: E.A. Lind, J. Greenberg, K.S. Scott, and T.D. Welchans, "The Winding Road from Employee to Complainant: Situational and Psychological Determinants of Wrongful-Termination Claims," *Administrative Science Quarterly*, September 2000, p. 557–590. Reproduced by permission of *Administrative Science Quarterly*.

- Allow 10 to 15 minutes as sufficient time for the interview.
- Avoid Fridays, pre-holidays, and vacation times when possible.
- Use a neutral site, never your office.
- Have employee agreements, human resources file, and release announcement (internal and external) prepared in advance.
- Be available at a time after the interview in case questions or problems arise.
- Have phone numbers ready for medical or security emergencies.

Termination interviews are among the most difficult tasks that managers face, but there are guidelines for making them less painful for both parties.

Step 2: Get to the Point   As soon as the employee arrives, give the person a moment to get comfortable and then inform him or her of the decision.

Step 3: Describe the Situation   Briefly, in three or four sentences, explain why the person is being let go. For instance, "Production in your area is down 4 percent, and we are continuing to have quality problems. We have talked about these problems several times in the past three months and the solutions are not being followed through. We have to make a change."[49] Remember to describe the situation rather than attacking the employee personally.

Step 4: Listen   It is important to continue the interview until the person appears to be talking freely and reasonably calmly about the reasons for his or her termination and the severance package that he or she is to receive. Behavioural indications can be used to help gauge the person's reaction and to decide how best to proceed. Five major reactions often occur.

First, some employees will be *hostile and angry*, expressing hurt and disappointment. In such case, remain objective while providing information on any outplacement or career counselling to be provided, being careful to avoid being defensive or confronting the person's anger.

Second, some employees may react in a *defensive, bargaining* manner, based on their feelings of fear and disbelief. In this case, it is important to acknowledge that this is a difficult time for the employee, and then provide information regarding outplacement counselling without getting involved in any bargaining discussions.

Third, the employee may proceed in a *formal, controlled* manner, indicative of a suppressed, vengeful reaction, and the potential for legal action. In this case, allow the employee to ask any questions pertaining to his or her case (avoiding side issues) in a formal tone while leading into information about the outplacement counselling to be provided.

Fourth, some employees will maintain a *stoic* façade, masking their shock, disbelief, and numbness. In this case, communicate to the employee that his or her shock is recognized and that the details can be handled later if the employee prefers. Answer any questions arising at that point and provide information on outplacement counselling.

A fifth reaction is an *emotional* one involving tears and sadness, indicating grief and worry on the part of the employee. Allow the person to cry and provide tissues. When the person regains his or her composure, explain the outplacement-counselling process.

Step 5: Review All Elements of the Severance Package   Describe severance payments, benefits, and the way in which references will be handled. However, under no conditions should any promises or benefits beyond those already in the severance package be implied. The termination should be complete when the person leaves.

Step 6: Identify the Next Step   The terminated employee may be disoriented, so explain where he or she should go on leaving the interview. Remind the person whom to contact at the company regarding questions about the severance package or references.

Outplacement Counselling

outplacement counselling   A systematic process by which a terminated person is trained and counselled in the techniques of self-appraisal and securing a new position.

Outplacement counselling provides career counselling and job search skills training for terminated employees. The counselling itself is done either by the employer's in-house specialist or by outside consultants. The outplacement counselling is considered part of the terminated employee's severance package.[50]

Outplacement counselling is usually conducted by outplacement firms, such as Drake Beam Morin and Right Management. Middle- and upper-level managers who are let go will typically have office space and secretarial services that they can use at local offices of such firms, in addition to the counselling services.

MANAGING LAYOFFS AND DOWNSIZING

Research Insight ▷

Layoffs and downsizing are a fact of life in organizations in today's fast-changing business world. Fair treatment of employees whose jobs are lost in these situations is very important for both them and the "survivors" who continue to come to work in these difficult circumstances. Communicating the news of impending layoffs or downsizing is a difficult task. In recent years, there has been an increasing tendency for managers to do so quite impersonally through company-wide e-mail, the grapevine, or media press releases.

Recent research has found that employees who receive bad news delivered face to face feel more fairly treated and are more willing to accept the news than are employees who receive the same news through e-mail or word of mouth. The use of personal face-to-face communication lead to greater perceptions of fair treatment and acceptance of the news because the employees feel that they are being treated with dignity and respect, because of the genuine and sincere manner of the people who give them the bad news.[51]

group termination laws   Laws that require an employer to notify employees in the event that an employer decides to terminate a group of employees.

Group termination laws require employers who are terminating a large group of employees to give them more notice than that required on termination of an individual employee. The laws are intended to assist employees in situations of plant closings and large downsizings. Most jurisdictions in Canada require employers who are terminating a group of employees (some specify 10 or more, others 25 or more) within a short time to give advance notice to employees and sometimes to their union. The amount of notice varies by jurisdiction and with the number of employees being terminated, but it generally ranges from 6 weeks to 18 weeks.

Hints **to Ensure** Legal Compliance

The laws do not prevent the employer from closing down, nor do they require saving jobs. They simply give employees time to seek other work or retraining by giving them advance notice of the termination. The law is not clear about how the notice to employees must be worded. However, a letter to the individual employees to be terminated might include a paragraph toward the end of the letter as follows:

Please consider this letter to be your official notice, as required by law, that your current position with the company will end 60 days from today because of a (layoff or closing) that is now projected to take place on (date). After that day, your employment with the company will be terminated, and you will no longer be carried on our payroll records or be covered by any company benefit programs. Any questions concerning this notice will be answered in the HR office.[52]

Layoffs

layoff The temporary withdrawal of employment to workers for economic or business reasons.

A **layoff**, in which workers are sent home for a time, is a situation in which three conditions are present: (1) there is no work available for the employees, (2) management expects the no-work situation to be temporary and probably short term, and (3) management intends to recall the employees when work is again available.[53] A layoff is therefore not a termination, which is a permanent severing of the employment relationship. However, some employers do use the term *layoff* as a euphemism for discharge or termination.

Bumping/Layoff Procedures

Most such procedures have the following features in common:[54]

1. For the most part, seniority is the ultimate determinant of who will stay.
2. Seniority can give way to merit or ability but usually only when none of the senior employees is qualified for a particular job.
3. Seniority is usually based on the date the employee joined the organization, not the date he or she took a particular job.
4. Because seniority is usually company-wide, an employee in one job is usually allowed to bump or displace an employee in another job, provided that the more senior employee is able to do the job in question without further training.

> Tips **for the Front Line**

Alternatives to Layoffs

Many employers today recognize the enormous investments that they have in recruiting, screening, and training their employees. As a result, they are more hesitant to lay off employees at the first signs of business decline. Instead, they are using new approaches to either blunt the effects of the layoff or eliminate the layoffs entirely.

There are several alternatives to layoff. With the *voluntary reduction in pay plan*, all employees agree to reductions in pay in order to keep everyone working. Other employers arrange to have all or most of their employees accumulate their vacation time and to concentrate their vacations during slow periods. Other employees agree to take *voluntary time off*, which again has the effect of reducing the employer's payroll and avoiding the need for a layoff. Another way to avoid layoffs is the use of *contingent employees*. Temporary supplemental employees can be hired with the understanding that their work is of a temporary nature where they may be laid off at any time. Then, when layoffs come, the first group to be laid off is the cadre of contingent workers.[55] The use of contingent workers in Canada is growing and is expected to continue to increase.[56] Finally, the *Work Sharing Program* available through Human Resources and Social Development Canada allows employers to reduce the workweek by one to three days and for the time not worked, employees can claim employment insurance.

As more firms relocate their manufacturing plants to foreign countries in order to minimize costs, workers protest the signing of any free trade agreements, which they think encourage such actions.

Downsizing

downsizing Refers to the process of reducing, usually dramatically, the number of people employed by the firm.

Downsizing refers to the process of reducing, usually dramatically, the number of people employed by the firm. Although it is not clear why, most firms do not find that their operating earnings improve after major staff cuts are made. There are probably many ways to explain this anomaly, but declining employee morale as a result of downsizing is one plausible reason. Therefore, firms that are downsizing must also give attention to the remaining employees. Certainly those "downsized-out" should be treated fairly, but it is around the employees retained that the business will be built.

When dealing with the survivors immediately after the downsizing, one of two situations must be faced right away. First, if no further reductions are anticipated at that time, workers can be reassured accordingly. Second, if it is expected that more reductions will probably take place, be honest with those who remain, explaining that while future downsizings will probably occur, they will be informed of these reductions as soon as possible.

Specific Steps to Take

A critical responsibility of human resources managers in any downsizing is to ensure that the bad news is delivered in a humane manner.[57] Department managers need to be trained in how to deliver unwelcome news effectively (by participating in role-plays for practice) and in how to listen to and observe other managers. These managers also need to identify and recognize their own personal values that will anchor them during the difficult communication process. The responsibility for delivering tough news humanely, treating people with dignity and respect, and advising people of all support services available to them must be emphasized. It helps if managers work with a partner who acts as a coach when preparing for a termination interview, and debriefs them on the experience when it is over. Finally, every effort should be made to deliver downsizing news in a one-on-one manner and to anticipate the emotional reactions from everyone involved, including the manager.

Handling a Merger/Acquisition

About two-thirds of all corporate mergers fail to reach their forecasted goals of increased efficiency and cost-effectiveness.[58] The merging organizations often underestimate the difficulty involved in merging two distinct work cultures (and in many cases, ethnic cultures). A human resources department with credibility and strong two-way communication programs enabling it to assess morale in merger situations can find great opportunity to take on the responsibility for facilitating the change process.

Dismissals and downsizings in the case of mergers or acquisitions are usually one-sided. One company essentially acquires the other, and it is often the employees of the latter who find themselves out looking for new jobs. In such a situation, the employees in the acquired firm will be hypersensitive to mistreatment of their colleagues. Thus, managers should ensure that employees whose employment is terminated are treated with courtesy. Seeing former colleagues fired is bad enough for morale; seeing them fired under conditions that seem unfair can poison the relationship for years to come. As a rule, therefore, managers should[59]

- avoid the appearance of power and domination
- avoid win–lose behaviour
- remain businesslike and professional in all dealings

- maintain as positive a feeling about the acquired company as possible
- remember that the degree to which the organization treats the acquired group with care and dignity will affect the confidence, productivity, and commitment of those remaining

MANAGING THE RETIREMENT PROCESS

With Canada's rapidly aging population, retirement issues are becoming increasingly important and complex.[60] By 2025, more than 20 percent of the Canadian population will be over age 65, and the labour force will shrink dramatically. For many years, the trend has been toward earlier retirement—the average retirement age dropped from 65 in 1979 to 61 in 2005. However, with a labour shortage approaching as baby boomers retire over the next two decades, it is expected that this trend will reverse as organizations promote later retirement as a key strategy for dealing with the labour shortage.[61]

The Retirement Education Centre
www.iretire.org

Financial Knowledge Inc.
www.financialknowledgeinc.com

T.E. Financial Consultants
www.tefinancial.com

At any age, retirement for most employees is bittersweet. For some, it is the culmination of their careers, a time when they can relax and enjoy the fruits of their labour without worrying about the problems of work. For others, it is the retirement itself that is the trauma, as the once-busy employee tries to cope with suddenly being "nonproductive." For many retirees, in fact, maintaining a sense of identity and self-worth without a full-time job is the single most important task they will face. It is one that employers are increasingly trying to help their retirees cope with as a logical last step in the career management process.

Pre-retirement Counselling

pre-retirement counselling
Counselling provided to employees some months (or even years) before retirement, which covers such matters as benefits advice, second careers, and so on.

Most employers provide some type of formal **pre-retirement counselling** aimed at easing the passage of their employees into retirement.[62] Court decisions have confirmed that employers do have some legal responsibility to help employees prepare for retirement.[63] Retirement education and planning firms provide services to assist upcoming retirees with such issues as lifestyle goals (including part-time or volunteer work and/or moving to another country), financial planning, relationship issues, and health issues. Both individual and group transition counselling are offered in seminars and workshops featuring workbooks, questionnaires, discussions, group exercises, and software products. In the end, employees who are taking control of their retirement plans often have reduced absenteeism and health-care costs.[64]

An employee contemplating different retirement options

The Future of Retirement

A 2006 Statistics Canada report entitled *New Frontiers of Research on Retirement* identified some of the major changes expected in the management of the retirement process. First, there are gender differences in retirement patterns. Boomers are the first group to include a generation of women who have worked in the labour force for most of their lives, and they are expected to change retirement norms. Women are more likely to take early retirement for lifestyle reasons and they find the psychological transition to retirement easier than men do. These women will treat retirement as "amorphous and fluid," opting in and out of the workforce after retirement, based on caregiving demands. They are also more likely to seek out new experiences and challenges after retirement.

Second, joint retirement is becoming an issue for many dual-income couples. Retirement planning is becoming much more complex as two sets of financial and personal circumstances must be considered when making retirement decisions. Third, maintaining a standard of living in retirement will be a concern for those without substantial personal savings.

Finally, flexibility in retirement arrangements is expected to increase dramatically. Currently, many retirees return to paid work on a contract or part-time basis, and about half participate in volunteer activities. Later retirement and more gradual transitions to retirement may be encouraged by employers by making more flexible retirement options available to older workers. Reduced work schedules with continued pension accrual may be very attractive to retirement-age workers. HR policies that are older-worker-friendly and an end to age discrimination will be necessary for more flexible retirement options to succeed.[65]

Chapter Review

Summary

1. Three techniques for building effective two-way communication in organizations are suggestion programs, employee opinion surveys, and top-down communication programs.

2. A fair and just disciplinary process is based on three prerequisites: rules and regulations, a system of progressive penalties, and an appeals process.

3. Employees who are dismissed without just cause must be provided with reasonable notice. This means paying them for several weeks or months in addition to the legally required notice period on termination. If the employee does not believe that the period of notice is reasonable, he or she may file a wrongful dismissal lawsuit. To avoid wrongful dismissal suits, firms should avoid constructively dismissing employees by placing them in lower-paying jobs in hopes of a resignation, avoid promising permanent employment, document all disciplinary action, use employment contracts with a termination clause, and use termination letters that clearly state the settlement offer.

4. The six steps in the termination interview are plan the interview carefully, get to the point, describe the situation, listen until the person has expressed his or her feelings, discuss the severance package, and identify the next step.

5. HR considerations in adjusting to downsizings and mergers include avoiding the appearance of power and domination, avoiding win–lose behaviour, remaining businesslike and professional in all dealings, maintaining as positive a feeling about the acquired company as possible, and remembering that the degree to which the organization treats the acquired group with care and dignity will affect the confidence, productivity, and commitment of those remaining.

Key Terms

constructive dismissal   *(p. 414)*
discipline   *(p. 406)*
dismissal   *(p. 409)*
distributive justice   *(p. 401)*
downsizing   *(p. 419)*
employee opinion surveys   *(p. 400)*
fair treatment programs   *(p. 402)*
group termination laws   *(p. 417)*
insubordination   *(p. 410)*
interactional justice   *(p. 402)*
layoff   *(p. 418)*
outplacement counselling   *(p. 417)*
pre-retirement counselling   *(p. 420)*
procedural justice   *(p. 401)*
termination interview   *(p. 415)*
top-down communication programs   *(p. 400)*
wrongful dismissal   *(p. 411)*

Review and Discussion Questions

1. Explain the role of communication and fair treatment programs in establishing a foundation for effective employee relations.

2. Describe specific techniques that you would use to foster top-down communication in an organization.

3. Explain how fairness in employee discipline can be ensured, particularly the prerequisites to discipline, discipline guidelines, and the "discipline without punishment" approach.

4. Describe the four main reasons for dismissal.

5. What are the techniques that can be used as alternatives to layoffs?

6. Discuss some of the issues that should be covered in a pre-retirement counselling program.

Critical Thinking Questions

1. Describe the similarities and differences between such a program as FedEx Canada's guaranteed fair treatment program and a typical union grievance procedure.

2. Describe the similarities and differences between the "discipline without punishment" approach and a typical progressive discipline procedure.

3. Is it worth the time and expense to monitor employees' use of the Internet if employee performance is generally good? How is this any different from monitoring telephone usage for personal calls?

4. Should a company consider providing termination packages to employees who have ongoing disciplinary problems rather than taking the time and effort to go through the progressive discipline process?

Application Exercises

Running Case: LearnInMotion.com

Fair Treatment in Disciplinary Action

Because the employees used high-cost computer equipment to do their jobs, Jennifer and Pierre have always felt strongly about not allowing employees to eat or drink at their desks. Jennifer was therefore surprised to walk into the office one day to find two employees eating lunch at their desks. There was a large pizza in its box, and the two of them were sipping soft drinks and eating slices of pizza and submarine sandwiches from paper plates. Not only did it look messy, but there were also grease and soft drink spills on their desks and the office smelled of onions and pepperoni. In addition to looking unprofessional, the mess on the desks increased the possibility that the computers could be damaged. One of the employees continued to use his computer with greasy fingers between bites.

Although this was a serious matter, neither Jennifer nor Pierre believes that what the employees were doing is grounds for immediate dismissal, partly because there is no written policy on eating at the workstations. They just assumed that people would use their common sense. The problem is that they do not know what to do. It seems to them that the matter calls for more than just a warning but less than dismissal. As their management consultant, here's what they want you to do for them.

Questions

1. Advise Jennifer and Pierre whether there should be formal policies and rules regarding employee behaviour. What should these include?

2. Should a disciplinary system be established at LearnInMotion.com? Why or why not?

3. If such a system is introduced, what should it cover, and how should the company deal with employees who break the rules?

Case Incident

Fire My Best Salesperson?

Greg Johns, sales director for International Widget Industries (IWI), had a problem. He was just told that his top salesperson, Bob Pollock, was stealing from the company. Pollock had been inflating expense reports and exaggerating his sales (by double booking sales orders). He therefore got higher expense reimbursements and commissions than he deserved. The accounting department had proof that Pollock was stealing. IWI's CEO has told Johns to either rectify the situation or lose his own job. Johns is in a quandary about what to do. He doesn't want to lose his best salesperson, and he thinks perhaps there might be extenuating circumstances—such as family pressures—that explain Pollock's behaviour. The question is, what should Johns do now?

Questions

Assume you are Johns. Specifically,

1. What should you do now?
2. Why should you do it?
3. How would you do it?

Please answer that three-part question before moving on to see what actually happened, by reading the following:

In this case, there's no question of what to do. The company must terminate this salesperson. According to the people who are actually involved in this situation, no company can tolerate stealing on the part of its employees. If you cannot trust the salesperson, his presence with your company will have a corrosive effect on all that he deals with, including customers and co-workers.

The consensus is to confront him. First, confirm that the information is accurate. Show him the evidence, get his response, and assuming the accusations are true, have the person surrender all his company account information and leads in return for a quiet termination.

Now, knowing what IWI actually did, what do you think of their response? What, if anything, would you have done differently?

Source: Based on "What Would You Do?" *Sales & Marketing Management* 155 (January 2003), pp. 52–54.

Experiential Exercises

1. Working individually or in groups, obtain copies of the student handbook for a college or university and determine to what extent there is a formal process through which students can air grievances. Would you expect the process to be effective? Why or why not? Based on contacts with students who have used the grievance process, has it been effective?

2. Working individually or in groups, determine the nature of the academic discipline process in a college or university. Does it appear to be an effective one? Based on this chapter, should any modification be made to the student discipline process?

3. A computer department employee made an entry error that ruined an entire run of computer reports. Efforts to rectify the situation produced a second batch of improperly run reports. As a result of the series of errors, the employer

incurred extra costs of $2400, plus a weekend of overtime work by other computer department staffers. Management suspended the employee for three days for negligence and also revoked a promotion for which the employee had previously been approved.

Protesting the discipline, the employee stressed that she had attempted to correct her error in the early stages of the run by notifying the manager of computer operations of her mistake. Maintaining that the resulting string of errors could have been avoided if the manager had followed up on her report and stopped the initial run, the employee argued that she had been treated unfairly in being severely punished because the manager had not been disciplined at all even though he had compounded the problem. Moreover, citing her "impeccable" work record and management's acknowledgment that she had always been a "model employee," the employee insisted that the denial of her previously approved promotion was "unconscionable."

(a) In groups, determine what your decision would be if you were the arbitrator. Why? (Your instructor will inform you of the actual arbitrator's decision when you discuss this exercise in class.)

(b) Do you think that the employer handled the disciplinary situation correctly? Why? What would you have done differently?

CHAPTER 16

LABOUR RELATIONS

LEARNING OUTCOMES

AFTER STUDYING THIS CHAPTER, YOU SHOULD BE ABLE TO

Discuss the key elements of Canada's labour laws.

Outline the five steps in the labour relations process.

Describe the five steps in a union organizing campaign.

Outline the three ways to obtain union recognition.

Describe the three steps in the collective bargaining process.

Explain the typical steps in a grievance procedure.

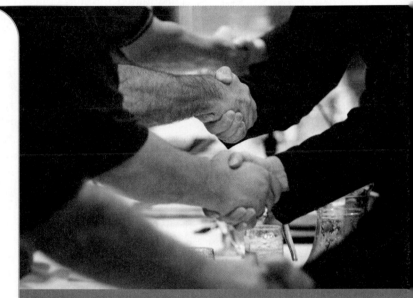

REQUIRED PROFESSIONAL CAPABILITIES

- Provides advice to clients on the establishment, continuation, and termination of bargaining rights

- Collects and develops information required for good decision making throughout the bargaining process

- Contributes to the communication plan during work disruptions

- Advises clients on matters related to interest arbitration

- Provides consultation and risk assessment in issues involving arbitration

INTRODUCTION TO LABOUR RELATIONS

labour union (union)   An officially recognized association of employees practising a similar trade or employed in the same company or industry, who have joined together to present a united front and collective voice in dealing with management.

labour–management relations   The ongoing interactions between labour unions and management in organizations.

collective agreement (union contract)   A formal agreement between an employer and the union representing a group of its employees regarding terms and conditions of employment.

collective bargaining   Negotiations between a union and an employer to arrive at a mutually acceptable collective agreement.

bargaining unit   The group of employees in a firm, a plant, or an industry that has been recognized by an employer or certified by a Labour Relations Board (LRB) as appropriate for collective bargaining purposes.

Canadian Labour and Business Centre
www.clbc.ca

Ontario Ministry of Labour, Labour Management Services
www.labour.gov.on.ca

Canada LabourWatch Association
www.labourwatch.com

A **labour union** (or **union**) is an officially recognized body representing a group of employees who have joined together to present a collective voice in dealing with management. The purposes of unionization are to influence HR policies and practices that affect bargaining unit members, such as pay and benefits; to achieve greater control over the jobs being performed, greater job security, and improved working conditions; and to increase job satisfaction and meet employees' affiliation needs. The term **labour–management relations** refers to the ongoing interactions between labour unions and management in organizations.

The presence of a labour union alters the relationship between employees and the firm. Managerial discretion and flexibility in dealing with employees and in implementing and administering HR policies and procedures are reduced. For example, union seniority provisions in the **collective agreement (union contract)**, negotiated through **collective bargaining**, govern the selection of employees for transfers, promotions, and training programs, and specify the order in which employees can be laid off and recalled. Many other terms and conditions of employment for **bargaining unit** members are determined and standardized through collective bargaining, rather than being left to management's discretion.

An organization's *labour relations (LR) strategy*, one component of its HR strategy, is its overall plan for dealing with unions, which sets the tone for its union–management relationship. The decision to accept or avoid unions is the basis of an organization's LR strategy.[1]

Managers in firms choosing a *union acceptance strategy* view the union as the legitimate representative of the firm's employees. Such a relationship can lead to innovative initiatives and win–win outcomes. Managers select a *union avoidance strategy* when they believe that it is preferable to operate in a non-unionized environment. Wal-Mart is well known for its preference to remain non-union (and has even closed stores that have attempted to unionize). To avoid unions, companies can either adopt a *union substitution approach*, in which they become so responsive to employees' needs that there is no incentive for them to unionize (as is the case at Dofasco), or adopt a *union suppression approach* when there is a desire to avoid a union at all costs.

When employees at the Wal-Mart in Jonquière, Quebec, unionized, Wal-Mart closed the store.

Canada's Labour Laws

Canadian labour laws have two general purposes:

1. to provide a common set of rules for fair negotiations
2. to protect the public interest by preventing the impact of labour disputes from inconveniencing the public

As with other employment-related legislation, there are 13 provincial/territorial jurisdictions, as well as federal labour relations legislation for employees subject to federal jurisdiction. There are a number of common characteristics in the LR legislation across Canada, which can be summarized as follows:

- procedures for the certification of a union
- the requirement that a collective agreement be in force for a minimum of one year
- procedures that must be followed by one or both parties before a strike or lockout is legal
- the prohibition of strikes or lockouts during the life of a collective agreement
- the requirement that disputes over matters arising from interpretation of the collective agreement be settled by final and binding arbitration
- prohibition of certain specified "unfair practices" on the part of labour and management
- establishment of a Labour Relations Board or the equivalent; Labour Relations Boards are tripartite—made up of representatives of union and management, as well as a neutral chair or a vice-chair, typically a government representative

Labour relations legislation attempts to balance employees' rights to engage in union activities with employers' rights to manage. For example, managers are prohibited from interfering with and discriminating against employees who are exercising their rights under the LR legislation. One restriction on unions is that they are prohibited from calling or authorizing an unlawful strike.

The Labour Movement in Canada Today

The primary goal of the labour unions active in Canada is to obtain economic benefits and improved treatment for their members. It may involve lobbying for legislative changes pertaining to these issues. This union philosophy, with its emphasis on economic and welfare goals, has become known as **business unionism**. Unions strive to ensure *job security* for their members and to attain *improved economic conditions* and *better* working conditions for their members. Most unions today also become involved in broader political and social issues affecting their members. Activities aimed at influencing government economic and social policies are known as **social (reform) unionism**. For example, unions have worked hard to support the rights of lesbian, gay, bisexual, and trans-gendered (LGBT) people, as outlined in the Workforce Diversity box.

Types of Unions

The labour unions in Canada can be divided according to the following:

1. *Type of worker eligible for membership.* All the early trade unions in Canada were **craft unions**—associations of persons performing a certain type of skill or trade (e.g., carpenters or bricklayers). Examples in today's workforce include the British Columbia Teachers' Federation and the Ontario Nurses' Association. An **industrial union** is a labour organization comprising all the workers eligible for union membership in a particular company or industry, irrespective of the type of work performed.

2. *Geographical scope.* Labour unions with their head offices in the United States that charter branches in both Canada and the United States are known as *international unions*. Labour unions that charter branches in Canada only and have their head office in this country are known as *national unions*. A small number of employees belong to labour unions that are purely *local* in geographical scope.

business unionism The activities of labour unions focusing on economic and welfare issues, including pay and benefits, job security, and working conditions.

social (reform) unionism Activities of unions directed at furthering the interests of their members by influencing the social and economic policies of governments at all levels, such as speaking out on proposed legislative reforms.

craft union Traditionally, a labour organization representing workers practising the same craft or trade, such as carpentry or plumbing.

industrial union A labour organization representing all workers eligible for union membership in a particular company or industry, including skilled tradespersons.

Construction Labour Relations
www.clra.org

International Labour News
www.labourstart.org

Workforce Diversity

May 17, 2006—National Day Against Homophobia

In 2005, we celebrated a significant step forward for lesbian, gay, bisexual and transgender communities when Canada legally recognized same-sex marriage. The Canadian trade union movement played an important role in winning this impressive victory. The Canadian Labour Congress will continue to do whatever we can to ensure that this beacon of equality is not lost.

We have reissued our solidarity buttons with the message: I Do! Support Equality. Last year, during the campaign for equal marriage union leaders and members across the country energetically supported this key human rights initiative. We stand ready to do so again if the Conservative government threatens to roll back the clock on these hard-won equality gains.

We recognize that winning legal rights is not the end of the struggle. Lesbian, gay, bisexual and transgender members of our communities still face the reality of homophobia and transphobia in their daily lives. Trade unionists know that an injury to one is an injury to all. We will continue to work together in solidarity against discrimination.

In this spirit, we support the National Day Against Homophobia May 17th and commit to continuing the fight for full equality for all.

The Canadian labour movement joins in the celebration of Pride again this year.

We strongly encourage our members to increase labour's participation in Pride events across the country and demonstrate our solidarity with our LGBT sisters and brothers in the ongoing struggle for equality and dignity.

Source: Canadian Labour Congress, "National Day Against Homophobia." http://canadianlabour.ca. Reprinted with permission of the CLC.

---

3. *Labour congress affiliation.* A third way of distinguishing among labour unions is according to affiliation with one or another central labour organization. These central organizations include

- *Canadian Labour Congress* (*CLC*). The CLC is the major central labour organization in Canada, and has approximately 3 million affiliated union members. Most international and national unions belong, as well as all directly chartered local unions, local/district labour councils, and provincial/territorial federations of labour.

- *Confédération des syndicats nationaux* (*CSN*)—in English, Confederation of National Trade Unions (CNTU). This organization is the Quebec counterpart of the CLC and has more than 275 000 members.

- *American Federation of Labor—Congress of Industrial Organizations* (*AFL-CIO*). The American counterpart of the CLC is the AFL–CIO. The two organizations operate independently, but since most international unions in the CLC are also members of the AFL–CIO, a certain degree of common interest exists.

The basic unit of the labour union movement in Canada is the **local,** formed in a particular location. For HR managers and front-line supervisors, the union locals are generally the most important part of the union structure. Key players within the local are the elected officials known as **union stewards,** who are responsible for representing the interests and protecting the rights of bargaining unit employees in their department or area.

Membership Trends

As of 2005, more than 30 percent of Canadian employees were unionized. The membership in unions as a percentage of the labour force has been slowly

Canadian Labour Congress (CLC)
www.clc-ctc.ca

Ontario Federation of Labour
www.ofl.ca

American Federation of Labor–Congress of Industrial Organizations (AFL–CIO)
www.aflcio.org

local   A group of unionized employees in a particular location.

union steward   A union member elected by workers in a particular department or area of a firm to act as their union representative.

decreasing since the 1980s. Various factors are responsible for membership decline, including a dramatic increase in service-sector and white-collar jobs, combined with a decrease in employment opportunities in the industries that have traditionally been highly unionized, such as manufacturing. More effective HR practices in non-unionized firms are another contributing factor.[2]

Current Challenges to the Canadian Labour Movement

As with employers, global competition and technological advances pose challenges for the union movement. Unions also have to deal with challenges pertaining to the privatization and the unionization of white-collar employees, managers, and professionals; and innovative work practices that have the potential to decrease employee interest in unionization.

Global Competition and Technological Change

A Conference Board of Canada research report *Industrial Relations Outlook 2006: Shifting Ground, Shifting Attitudes* concluded that

> Globalization is transforming the dynamics of labour relations in Canada. Faced with an onslaught of global competition, employers are becoming more militant, and unions are struggling to maintain their influence at the bargaining table. . . . Weakened at the bargaining table, some unions face the difficult choice of negotiating concessions or watching jobs go to lower-cost countries. . . . Many unions and employers are failing to work together to address fundamental business issues of importance to each side. Both parties will need to change their attitudes about how to conduct labour relations if they are to adjust to the shifting landscape wrought by globalization.[3]

Technology

Technological advances pose another challenge to unions.[4] In some cases, technology has decreased the effectiveness of strikes, because highly automated organizations can remain fully operational with minimal staffing levels during work stoppages. Improvements in technology have also lowered the demand for blue-collar workers, resulting in a decline in union membership in the auto, steel, and other manufacturing industries. E-commerce work (such as processing credit card claims) is highly portable and can be shifted, almost literally, at the touch of a button from one centre to another—even overseas.

Privatization and the Unionization of White-Collar Employees

Increasing difficulties in attempting to resolve grievances, combined with a lack of job security related to downsizing, as well as the privatization of services ranging from hydro to home care, has led to increased interest in unionization among white-collar workers.[5] Service sector workers, such as those in retail stores, fast-food chains, and government agencies, as well as managers and professionals (including university/college faculty), have been targeted for organizing campaigns. To attract white-collar employees, unions are now focusing more on work/family issues and the health and safety risks associated with white-collar jobs, such as the potential for repetitive strain injury from working at video display terminals.

Innovative Workplace Practices

In workplaces in which employees participate in decision making, have a high degree of autonomy and little supervision, and are paid based on their performance or the knowledge/skills they have attained, there may be less perceived need for a union. Some individuals argue that such innovative workplace practices as semi-autonomous work teams, skill-based pay, profit sharing, and employee stock ownership plans undermine union power by co-opting employees and aligning employee interests with those of management. However, in workplaces in which the unions have supported such changes, the end result may be better communication and more cooperation, a win–win situation.

THE LABOUR RELATIONS PROCESS

As illustrated in **Figure 16.1**, the labour relations process consists of five steps:

1. Employees decide to seek collective representation.
2. The union organizing campaign begins.
3. The union receives official recognition.
4. Union and management negotiate a collective agreement.
5. Day-to-day contract administration begins.

Each of these five steps will now be reviewed in detail.

Step 1: Desire for Collective Representation

Based on numerous research studies, a number of factors can clearly be linked to the desire to unionize:[6]

FIGURE 16.1   An Overview of the Labour Relations Process

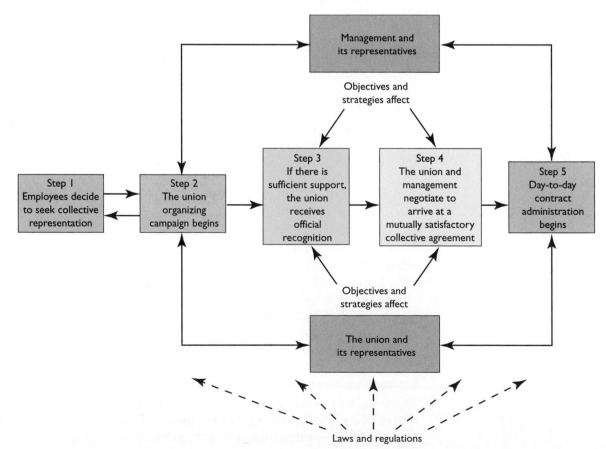

Research
Insight ▷

- job dissatisfaction, especially with pay, benefits, and working conditions
- lack of job security
- unfair or biased administration of policies and practices
- perceived inequities in pay
- lack of opportunity for advancement
- lack of a desired amount of influence or participation in work-related decisions
- the belief that unions can be effective in improving pay and working conditions.

Given the fact that unionized employees in Canada earn 8 percent more than non-unionized workers, these expectations seem quite justifiable.[7] Being a union member also has an impact on female workers' ability to achieve pay equity. On average, full-time female unionized workers earned 90 percent of the hourly wages of their male counterparts, and those working part-time earned 9 percent *more* than their male counterparts.[8]

However, research studies have made it clear that dissatisfaction alone will not lead to unionization. More important seems to be the employees' belief that it is only through unity that they can protect themselves from the arbitrary whims of management. *In other words, it is only when workers are dissatisfied and believe that they are without the ability to change the factors causing dissatisfaction, except through collective action, that they become interested in unionizing.*[9]

Promoting the benefits of unionization

Step 2: Union Organizing Campaign

Once interest in joining a union has been aroused, the union organizing process begins. There are five steps typically involved in this process:

1. *Employee/union contact.* A formal organizing campaign may be initiated by a union organizer or by employees acting on their own behalf. Most organizing campaigns are begun by employees who get in touch with an existing union.[10] However, large unions have a number of *union organizers* on staff, who are responsible for identifying organizing opportunities and launching organizing campaigns. During these initial discussions, employees investigate the advantages of union representation, and the union officials start to gather information about the employees' sources of dissatisfaction.

2. *Initial organizational meeting.* The union organizer then schedules an initial meeting with the individuals who first expressed an interest in unionization and co-workers who subsequently express their support. The aim is to identify employees who would be willing to help the organizer direct the campaign.

3. *Formation of an in-house organizing committee.* This committee comprises a group of employees who are dedicated to the goal of unionization and who are willing to assist the union organizer.

4. *The organizing campaign.* Members of the in-house committee then contact employees, present the case for unionization, and encourage as many employees as possible to sign an **authorization card** that indicates their willingness to be represented by the union in collective bargaining with their employer.

5. *The outcome.* There are a number of possible outcomes to a unionization campaign, including rejection by the majority of eligible employees. For a union to become the bargaining unit for a group of employees, it must be certified by an LRB or receive official recognition from the employer.

authorization card   A card signed by an employee that indicates his or her willingness to have the union act as his or her representative for purposes of collective bargaining.

Signs of Organizing Activity

Managers who suspect that a unionization attempt may be underway should watch for a number of the following signs:[11]

- disappearance of employee lists or directories
- more inquiries than usual about benefits, wages, promotions, and other HR policies and procedures
- questions about their opinions of unions
- an increase in the number or nature of employee complaints or grievances
- a change in the number, composition, and size of informal groups at lunch and coffee breaks
- the sudden popularity of certain employees (especially if they are the informal leaders)
- the sudden cessation of employee conversation when a member of management approaches or an obvious change in employees' behaviour toward members of management, expressed either formally or informally
- the appearance of strangers in the parking lot
- the distribution of cards, flyers, or pro-union buttons

Employer Response to an Organizing Campaign

If the employer prefers that the group seeking unionization retain its non-union status, a careful campaign is usually mounted to counteract the union drive. Normally, HR department staff members head up the campaign, although they may be assisted by a consultant or labour lawyer. Absolutely critical to the success of a company's counter-campaign is supervisory training. Supervisors need to be informed about what they can and cannot do or say during the organizing campaign, to ensure that they do not violate LR legislation and avoid actions that might inadvertently provide fuel for the union's campaign.

Labour Management Services
(Ontario)
www.labour.gov.on.ca

As much information about the union as possible should be obtained, pertaining to dues, strike record, salaries of officers, and any other relevant facts that might cause employees to question the benefits of unionization. Communication strategies can be planned, with the aim of reminding employees about the company's good points, pointing out disadvantages of unionization, and refuting any misleading union claims. The employer's case for remaining non-union should be presented in a factual, honest, and straightforward manner.

Under the law, employers are granted the right to do the following:

- Express their views and opinions regarding unions.
- State their position regarding the desirability of remaining non-union.
- Prohibit distribution of union literature on their own property on company time.
- Increase wages, make promotions, and take other HR actions, as long as they would do so *in the normal course of business*. In most jurisdictions, however, once an application for certification is received by the LRB, wages, benefits, and working conditions are frozen until the application is dealt with.
- Assemble employees during working hours to state the company's position, as long as employees are advised of the purpose of the meeting in advance, attendance is optional, and threats and promises are avoided (employers have no obligation to give the union the same opportunity).

Step 3: Union Recognition

A union can obtain recognition as a bargaining unit for a group of workers in three basic ways: (1) voluntary recognition, (2) the regular certification process, and (3) a pre-hearing vote. Bargaining rights can also be terminated in various ways.

Voluntary Recognition

An employer in every Canadian jurisdiction, except Quebec, can voluntarily recognize a union as the bargaining agent for a group of its employees. Although fairly rare, this may occur if an employer has adopted a union acceptance strategy and believes that employees want to be represented by that union.

Regular Certification

certification The procedure whereby a labour union obtains a certificate from the relevant LRB declaring that the union is the exclusive bargaining agent for a defined group of employees in a bargaining unit that the LRB considers appropriate for collective bargaining purposes.

The normal union **certification** procedure is for the union to present evidence of at least a minimum level of membership support for a bargaining unit that they have defined, in the form of signed authorization cards, to the appropriate LRB, along with an application for certification. The minimum level of support required to apply for certification varies by jurisdiction, from 25 percent of the bargaining unit in Saskatchewan to 65 percent in Manitoba.[12] The LRB then determines whether the bargaining unit defined by the union is appropriate for collective bargaining purposes.

In most jurisdictions, LRBs can grant *automatic certification* without a vote if the applicant union can demonstrate a high enough level of support for the proposed bargaining unit (generally 50 or 55 percent). Automatic certification may also be granted in some jurisdictions if the employer has engaged in unfair practices. If the level of support is not sufficient for automatic certification, but is above a specified minimum level (between 25 and 45 percent, depending on jurisdiction), the LRB will order and supervise a **representation vote**.[13] Eligible employees have the opportunity to cast a secret ballot, indicating whether or not they want the union to be certified. In some jurisdictions, to gain certification, the voting results must indicate that *more than 50 percent of the potential bargaining unit members* are in support of the union. In other jurisdictions, the standard is the support of *more than 50 percent of those voting*.[14] If the union loses, another election cannot be held among the same employees for at least one year. Only about 20 percent of certifications are the result of a vote—roughly four out of five certifications are the result of authorization cards alone.[15]

representation vote A vote conducted by the LRB in which employees in the bargaining unit indicate, by secret ballot, whether or not they want to be represented, or continue to be represented, by a labour union.

Pre-hearing Votes

pre-hearing vote An alternative mechanism for certification, used in situations in which there is evidence of violations of fair labour practices early in the organizing campaign.

In most jurisdictions, a **pre-hearing vote** may be conducted where there is evidence of violations of fair labour practices early in an organizing campaign. In such a case, the LRB may order a vote before holding a hearing to determine the composition of the bargaining unit. The intent is to determine the level of support for the union as quickly as possible, before the effect of any irregularities can taint the outcome. The ballot box is then sealed until the LRB determines whether the bargaining unit is appropriate and, if so, which employees are eligible for membership. If the bargaining unit is deemed appropriate by the LRB, only the votes of potential bargaining unit members are counted, and if the majority of the ballots cast support the union, it is certified.

Termination of Bargaining Rights

decertification The process whereby a union is legally deprived of its official recognition as the exclusive bargaining agent for a group of employees.

All LR acts provide procedures for workers to apply for the **decertification** of their unions. Generally, members may apply for decertification if the union has failed to negotiate a collective agreement within one year of certification, or if they are dissatisfied with the performance of the union. The LRB holds a secret-ballot vote, and if more than 50 percent of the ballots cast (or bargaining unit members, depending on jurisdiction) are in opposition to the union, the union will be decertified. A labour union also has the right to notify the LRB that it no longer wants to continue to represent the employees in a particular bargaining unit. This is known as "termination on abandonment." Once the LRB has declared that the union no longer represents the bargaining unit employees, any collective agreement negotiated between the parties is void.

Step 4: Collective Bargaining

Collective bargaining is the process by which a formal collective agreement is established between labour and management. The collective agreement is the cornerstone of the Canadian LR system. Both union and management representatives are required to bargain in good faith. This means that they must communicate and negotiate, that proposals must be matched with counterproposals, and that both parties must make every reasonable effort to arrive at an agreement.[16]

Steps typically involved in the collective bargaining process include (1) preparation for bargaining, (2) face-to-face negotiations, and (3) obtaining approval for the proposed contract. There are two possible additional steps. First, when talks break down, third-party assistance is required by law in every jurisdiction except Saskatchewan.[17] The second additional step is a strike/lockout or interest arbitration if the parties arrive at a bargaining impasse. Each of these steps will be described next.

Preparation for Negotiations

Good preparation leads to a greater likelihood that desired goals will be achieved. Preparation for negotiations involves planning the bargaining strategy and process and assembling data to support bargaining proposals. Both union and management will gather data on general economic trends, analyze other collective agreements and trends in collective bargaining, conduct an analysis of grievances, review the existing contract or the union's organizing campaign promises, conduct wage and salary surveys at competitor organizations, prepare cost estimates of monetary proposals, and make plans for a possible strike or lockout. In addition, management negotiators will obtain input from supervisors. Union negotiators will obtain input from union stewards, obtain the company's financial information (if it is a public company), gather demographic information on their membership, and obtain input from members.

Once these steps are completed, each side forms a negotiating team and an initial bargaining plan/strategy is prepared. Initial proposals are then finalized and presented for approval by either senior management or the union membership.

Face-to-Face Negotiations

Under LR legislation, representatives of either union or management can give written notice to the other party of their desire to bargain to negotiate a first collective agreement or renew an existing one. Early in the negotiating process, demands are exchanged—often before the first bargaining session. Then both negotiating teams can make a private assessment of the other team's demands. Usually, each team finds some items with which

Negotiating a collective agreement

they can agree quite readily and others on which compromise seems likely. Tentative conclusions are also made regarding which items, if any, are potential strike or lockout issues.

Location, Frequency, and Duration of Meetings   Negotiations are generally held at a neutral, off-site location, such as a hotel meeting room, so that there is no psychological advantage for either team and so that interruptions and work distractions can be kept to a minimum. Each side generally has another room in which intra-team meetings, known as **caucus sessions**, are held.

Generally, meetings are held as often as either or both parties consider desirable, and they last as long as progress is being made. Marathon bargaining sessions, such as those lasting all night, are not typical until conciliation has been exhausted and the clock is ticking rapidly toward the strike/lockout deadline.

Initial Bargaining Session   The initial meeting of the bargaining teams is extremely important in establishing the climate that will prevail during the negotiating sessions that follow. A cordial attitude, with occasional humour, can help to relax tension and ensure that negotiations proceed smoothly. Generally, the first meeting is devoted to an exchange of demands (if this has not taken place previously) and the establishment of rules and procedures that will be used during negotiations.

Subsequent Bargaining Sessions   In traditional approaches to bargaining, each party argues for its demands and resists those of the other at each negotiating session. At the same time, both are looking for compromise alternatives that will enable an agreement to be reached. Every proposal submitted must be either withdrawn temporarily or permanently, accepted by the other side in its entirety, or accepted in a modified form. Ideally, both sides should come away from negotiations feeling that they have attained many of their basic bargaining goals and confident that the tentative agreement reached will be acceptable to senior management and the members of the bargaining unit.

For each issue on the table to be resolved satisfactorily, the point at which agreement is reached must be within limits that the union and employer are willing to accept, often referred to as the **bargaining zone**. As illustrated in **Figure 16.2**, if the solution desired by one party exceeds the limits of the other party, then it is outside of the bargaining zone. Unless that party modifies its demands sufficiently to bring them within the bargaining zone, or the other party extends its limits to accommodate such demands, a bargaining deadlock is the inevitable result.[18]

caucus session   A session in which only the members of one's own bargaining team are present.

bargaining zone   The area defined by the bargaining limits (resistance points) of each side, in which compromise is possible, as is the attainment of a settlement satisfactory to both parties.

FIGURE 16.2 The Bargaining Zone and Characteristics of Distributive Bargaining

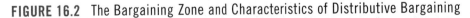
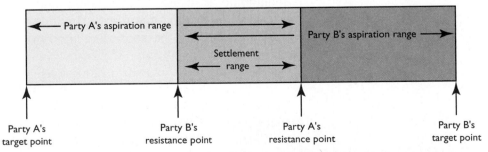
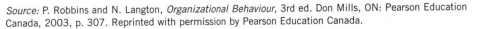

Source: P. Robbins and N. Langton, *Organizational Behaviour*, 3rd ed. Don Mills, ON: Pearson Education Canada, 2003, p. 307. Reprinted with permission by Pearson Education Canada.

distributive bargaining   A win–lose negotiating strategy, such that one party gains at the expense of the other.

Distributive bargaining is an approach often typified as "win–lose" bargaining, because the gains of one party are normally achieved at the expense of the other.[19] It is appropriately involved when the issues being discussed pertain to the distribution of things that are available in fixed amounts, such as wage increases and benefits improvements. However, it may also be used when there is a history of distrust and adversarial relations, even when dealing with issues on which a more constructive approach is possible.

As indicated in Figure 16.2, distributive bargaining is characterized by three distinct components: the initial point, the target point, and the resistance point. The initial point for the union is usually higher than what the union expects to receive from management. The union target point is next, and represents the negotiating team's assessment of what is realistically achievable from management. The union's bargaining zone limit is its resistance point, which represents its minimally acceptable level.

These points are essentially reversed for management. The management team's initial point is its lowest level, which is used at the beginning of negotiations. Next is its target point, the desired agreement level. Management's resistance point forms the other boundary of the bargaining zone.

integrative bargaining   A negotiating strategy in which the possibility of win–win, lose–win, win–lose, and lose–lose outcomes is recognized, and there is acknowledgement that achieving a win–win outcome will depend on mutual trust and problem solving.

Integrative bargaining is an approach that assumes that a win–win solution can be found but also acknowledges that one or both sides can be losers if the bargaining is not handled effectively.[20] Integrative bargaining strategies require that both management and union negotiators adopt a genuine interest in the joint exploration of creative solutions to common problems.

Issues pertaining to work rules, job descriptions, and contract language can often be handled effectively by using an integrative approach, in situations in which management negotiators are not intent on retaining management rights and both sides are committed to seeking a win–win solution. Wage rates and vacation entitlements are more likely to be fixed-sum issues that are handled by a distributive approach.

The objective of integrative bargaining is to establish a creative negotiating relationship that benefits labour and management. Becoming increasingly popular these days is a relatively new integrative approach, known as mutual gains or interest-based bargaining.

mutual gains (interest-based) bargaining   A win–win approach based on training in the fundamentals of effective problem solving and conflict resolution, in which the interests of all stakeholders are taken into account.

Mutual gains (interest-based) bargaining is another win–win approach to LR issues. All key union and management negotiators are trained in the fundamentals of effective problem solving and conflict resolution. Such training is often extended to other employees in order to ensure that the principles of mutual gains (interest-based) bargaining are incorporated into the organization's value system and that cooperation becomes a year-round corporate objective.[21]

Solutions must take the interests of each party into account. A joint sense of accountability is fostered and ongoing joint union/management initiatives can result from the negotiating process. In addition, the tools that are used at the bargaining table can be applied to the resolution of all workplace issues.[22] Although mutual gains (interest-based) bargaining has been put into practice in about 40 percent of Canadian negotiations, experts warn that implementation is difficult as it requires a grassroots culture change.[23]

Thus, the negotiating process is far more complex than it may appear to a casual observer. There are different types of bargaining strategies involved, and each side arrives at the bargaining table with political and organizational interests at stake.

The Contract Approval Process

memorandum of settlement
A summary of the terms and conditions agreed to by the parties that is submitted to the constituent groups for final approval.

ratification   Formal approval by secret-ballot vote of the bargaining unit members of the agreement negotiated between union and management.

As mentioned previously, collective agreements must be written documents. However, the parties do not normally execute a formal written document until some time after the bargaining process has been completed. Instead, the terms and conditions agreed to by the parties are usually reduced to a **memorandum of settlement** and submitted to the constituent groups for final approval.

Generally, final approval for the employer rests with the senior management team. In most cases, the union bargaining team submits the memorandum of settlement to the bargaining unit members for **ratification**. In some jurisdictions, ratification is required by law, and all members of the bargaining unit must be given ample opportunity to cast a secret-ballot vote indicating approval or rejection of the proposed contract. If the majority of bargaining unit members vote in favour of the proposal, it goes into effect. If the proposed collective agreement is rejected, union and management negotiators must return to the bargaining table and seek a more acceptable compromise. In such instances, third-party assistance is often sought.

Once approval has been received from the constituent groups, the bargaining team members sign the memorandum of settlement. Once signed, this memorandum serves as the collective agreement until the formal document is prepared and contract administration begins.

Third-Party Assistance and Bargaining Impasses

conciliation   The use of a neutral third party to help an organization and the union representing a group of its employees to come to a mutually satisfactory collective agreement.

Conciliation and Mediation
www.labour.gov.on.ca/english/lr/

mediation   The use (usually voluntary) of a neutral third party to help an organization and the union representing its employees to reach a mutually satisfactory collective agreement.

Legislation in all Canadian jurisdictions provides for conciliation and mediation services. Although the terms *conciliation* and *mediation* are often used interchangeably, they have quite distinct and different meanings.

Conciliation is the intervention of a neutral third party whose primary purpose is to bring the parties together and keep them talking to enable them to reach a mutually satisfactory collective agreement. The only means available to a conciliator to bring the parties to agreement is persuasion; he or she is not permitted to have any direct input into the negotiation process or to impose a settlement. Conciliation is typically requested after the parties have been negotiating for some time and are starting to reach a deadlock or after talks have broken down. The aim of conciliation is to try to help the parties avoid the hardship of a strike or lockout.

In all jurisdictions except Saskatchewan, strikes and lockouts are prohibited until third-party assistance has been undertaken. (Conciliation is required in all but two jurisdictions.) In most jurisdictions in which third-party assistance is mandatory, strikes/lockouts are prohibited until conciliation efforts have failed and a specified time period has elapsed.[24]

Mediation is the intervention of a neutral third party whose primary purpose is to help the parties to fashion a mutually satisfactory agreement. Mediation is usually a voluntary process, typically occurring during the countdown period prior to a strike or lockout or during the strike or lockout itself. The mediator's role is an active one. It often involves meeting with each side separately and then bringing them together in an attempt to assist them in bridging the existing gaps. He or she is allowed to have direct input into the negotiation process but cannot impose a settlement.

When the union and management negotiating teams are unable to reach an agreement, and once the conciliation process has been undertaken (where required), the union may exercise its right to strike or request interest arbitration, and the employer may exercise its right to lock out the bargaining unit members.

strike   The temporary refusal by bargaining unit members to continue working for the employer.

strike vote   Legally required in some jurisdictions, it is a vote seeking authorization from bargaining unit members to strike if necessary. A favourable vote does not mean that a strike is inevitable.

picket   Stationing groups of striking employees, usually carrying signs, at the entrances and exits of the struck operation to publicize the issues in dispute and discourage people from entering or leaving the premises.

boycott   An organized refusal of bargaining unit members and supporters to buy the products or use the services of the organization whose employees are on strike, in an effort to exert economic pressure on the employer.

lockout   Temporary refusal of a company to continue providing work for bargaining unit employees involved in a labour dispute, which may result in closure of the establishment for a time.

REQUIRED PROFESSIONAL CAPABILITIES

Contributes to the communication plan during work disruptions

Striking member of the Public Service Alliance of Canada

Alternatively, bargaining unit members may continue to work without a collective agreement once the old one has expired, until talks resume and an agreement is reached.

Strikes   A **strike** can be defined as a temporary refusal by bargaining unit members to continue working for the employer. When talks are reaching an impasse, unions will often hold a **strike vote**. Legally required in some jurisdictions, such a vote seeks authorization from bargaining unit members to strike if necessary. A favourable vote does not mean that a strike is inevitable. In fact, a highly favourable strike vote is often used as a bargaining ploy to gain concessions that will make a strike unnecessary. The results of a strike vote also help the union negotiating team members to determine their relative bargaining strength. Unless strike action is supported by a substantial majority of bargaining unit members, union leaders are rarely prepared to risk a strike and must therefore be more willing to compromise, if necessary, to avoid a work stoppage.

It should be noted that more than 95 percent of labour negotiations are settled without a work stoppage.[25] Since a strike can have serious economic consequences for bargaining unit members, the union negotiating team must carefully analyze the prospects for its success. Striking union members receive no wages and often have no benefits coverage until they return to work, although they may draw some money from the union's strike fund. Work stoppages are costly for employers as well. When employees at Inco Ltd. in Sudbury, Ontario, stopped working following the expiry of their collective agreement in 2003, the company's total production of nickel declined by 50 percent. The estimated cost of the strike for the company was US$20 million per month.[26]

When a union goes on strike, bargaining unit members often **picket** the employer. To ensure as many picketers as possible, the union may make strike pay contingent on picket duty. Picketers stand at business entrances, carrying signs advertising the issues in dispute, and attempt to discourage people from entering or leaving the premises.

Another economic weapon available to unions is a **boycott**, which is a refusal to patronize the employer. A boycott occurs when a union asks its members, other union members, the employer's customers/clients, and supporters in the general public not to patronize the business involved in the labour dispute. Such action can harm the employer if the union is successful in gaining a large number of supporters. As with a strike, a boycott can have long-term consequences if former customers/clients develop a bias against the employer's products or services or make a change in buying habits or service provider that is not easily reversed.

The duration and ultimate success of a strike depends on the relative strength of the parties. Once a strike is settled, striking workers return to their jobs. During a labour dispute many people are put under remarkable pressure, and relationships essential to effective post-settlement work dynamics can be tarnished—especially in firms that rely heavily on teamwork. Post-settlement work environments are often riddled with tension, derogatory remarks, and hostility.

Lockout   Although not a widely used strategy in Canada, a **lockout** is legally permissible. This involves the employer prohibiting the bargaining unit employees from entering the company premises, as a means of putting pressure on the union to agree to the terms and conditions being offered by management. Sometimes the employer chooses to close operations entirely, which means that nonstriking employees are also affected. Most employers try to avoid this

wildcat strike   A spontaneous walkout, not officially sanctioned by the union leadership, which may be legal or illegal, depending on its timing.

arbitration   The use of an outside third party to investigate a dispute between an employer and union and impose a settlement.

interest dispute   A dispute between an organization and the union representing its employees over the terms of a collective agreement.

interest arbitration   The imposition of the final terms of a collective agreement.

Arbitration
www.psab.gov.on.ca/english/psgb/
Arbitration.htm

union security clause   The contract provisions protecting the interests of the labour union, dealing with the issue of membership requirements and, often, the payment of union dues.

option, since doing so means that the well-being of innocent parties is threatened, and a lockout may damage the firm's public image. Employees at forest products company Stora Enso in Port Hawkesbury, Nova Scotia, were locked out in January 2006 after 20 months of bargaining when the union refused to accept a wage rollback of 10 percent, contracting out, and loss of seniority rights. An agreement was ratified five months later, just before the mill closure deadline set by the company.[27]

Unlawful Strikes and Lockouts   An unlawful strike is one that contravenes the relevant LR legislation and lays the union and its members open to charges and possible fines and/or periods of imprisonment if found guilty. For example, it is illegal for a union to call a strike involving employees who do not have the right to strike because of the essential nature of their services, such as nurses or police officers. In all jurisdictions, it is illegal to call a strike during the term of an existing collective agreement.

A **wildcat strike** is a spontaneous walkout, not officially sanctioned by the union leaders, that is illegal if it occurs during the term of a collective agreement. For example, in May 2006, 8500 Toronto Transit Commission workers staged a one-day illegal wildcat strike to protest lack of management action regarding driver safety concerns and shift assignments. Hundreds of thousands of commuters were affected.[28]

Interest Arbitration Arbitration involves the use of an outside third party to investigate a dispute between an employer and union, and impose a settlement. A sole arbitrator or three-person arbitration board may be involved. Arbitrators listen to evidence, weigh it impartially and objectively, and make a decision based on the law and/or the contract language. An arbitrator is not a judge, however. First, arbitration hearings tend to be much more informal than courtroom proceedings. Second, the arbitrator is not bound by precedents to the extent that a judge is usually held.[29] Third, both the law and court decisions have given the arbitration function considerable power and freedom. Arbitration decisions are final and binding and cannot be changed or revised.

Interest arbitration may be used to settle an **interest dispute** regarding the terms of a collective agreement by imposing the terms of the collective agreement. The right to interest arbitration is legally mandated for workers who are not permitted to strike, such as hospital and nursing home employees, police officers and firefighters in most jurisdictions, and some public servants.[30] Interest arbitration is also involved when special legislation is passed, ordering striking or locked-out parties back to work because of public hardship.

The Collective Agreement: Typical Provisions

The eventual outcome of collective bargaining, whether negotiated by the parties or imposed by an arbitrator, is a formal, written, collective agreement.

Union Recognition Clause   A *union recognition clause* clarifies the scope of the bargaining unit by specifying the employee classifications included therein or listing those excluded.

Union Security/Checkoff Clause   All Canadian jurisdictions permit the inclusion of a **union security clause** in the collective agreement to protect the interests of the labour union. This clause deals with the issue of membership requirements and, often, the payment of union dues. There are various forms of union security clauses:[31]

- A *closed shop* is the most restrictive form of union security. Only union members in good standing may be hired by the employer to perform bargaining unit work. This type of security clause is common in the construction industry.

- In a *union shop*, membership and dues payment are mandatory conditions of employment. Although individuals do not have to be union members at the time that they are hired, they are required to join the union on the day on which they commence work or on completion of probation.

- In a *modified union shop*, the individuals who were bargaining unit members at the time of certification or when the collective agreement was signed are not obliged to join the union, although they must pay dues, but all subsequently hired employees must do both.

- Under a *maintenance-of-membership arrangement*, individuals voluntarily joining the union must remain members during the term of the contract. Membership withdrawal is typically permitted during a designated period around the time of contract expiration. Dues payment is generally mandatory for all bargaining unit members.

An Ethical Dilemma

Given the fact that some workers have religious or other objections to unions, is the Rand formula ethical?

- The *Rand formula* is the most popular union security arrangement, as shown in **Table 16.1**. It does not require union membership, but it does require that all members of the bargaining unit pay union dues. It is a compromise arrangement that recognizes the fact that the union must represent all employees in the bargaining unit, and should therefore be entitled to their financial support, but also provides the choice to join or not join the union.

- An *open shop* is a type of security arrangement whereby union membership is voluntary and nonmembers are not required to pay dues.

No-Strike-or-Lockout Provision There must be a clause in every contract in Canada forbidding strikes or lockouts while the collective agreement is in effect. The intent is to guarantee some degree of stability in the employment relationship during the life of the collective agreement, which must be at least one year. Saskatchewan and Quebec are the only jurisdictions that impose a maximum duration of three years.[32] In general, the duration of collective agreements in Canada is increasing. In 1994, the average duration was 28.4 months, but by 2003 the average duration had risen to 35.7 months.[33] Halifax police accepted a 12-year agreement in 2003.[34]

Management Rights Clause The management rights clause clarifies the areas in which management may exercise its exclusive rights without agreement from the union and the issues that are not subject to collective bargaining. It typically refers to the rights of management to operate the organization, subject to the

TABLE 16.1   Union Security Provisions in Canada, 2004

	% of Agreements	% of Employees
Closed shop	10	10
Union shop	40	31
Modified union shop	14	15
Maintenance of membership	3	2
Rand formula	92	95

Source: Suzanne Payette, "Union Security Provisions," from Human Resources and Social Development Canada, *Workplace Gazette* 7(2), Summer 2004, p. 81. Reproduced with the permission of Her Majesty the Queen in Right of Canada 2006.

terms of the collective agreement. Any rights not limited by the clause are reserved to management.

Arbitration Clause All Canadian jurisdictions require that collective agreements contain a clause providing for the final and binding settlement, by arbitration, of all disputes arising during the term of a collective agreement. Such disputes may relate to the application, interpretation, or administration of that agreement, as well as alleged contraventions by either party.

Step 5: Contract Administration

After a collective agreement has been negotiated and signed, the contract administration process begins. Both union and management are required to abide by the contract provisions. It is also in day-to-day contract administration that the bulk of labour–management relations occurs. Regardless of the amount of time and effort put into the wording of the contract, it is almost inevitable that differences of opinion will arise regarding the application and interpretation of the agreement. Seniority and discipline issues tend to be the major sources of disagreement between union and management.

Seniority

seniority Length of service in the bargaining unit.

Unions typically prefer to have employee-related decisions determined by **seniority**, which refers to length of service in the bargaining unit. In many collective agreements, seniority is the governing factor in layoffs and recalls (the most senior employees are the last to be laid off and the first to be recalled), and a determining factor in transfers and promotions. In some collective agreements, seniority is also the determining factor in decisions pertaining to work assignments, shift preferences, allocation of days off, and vacation time.

Unions prefer the principle of seniority as an equitable and objective decision-making criterion, ensuring that there is no favouritism. Managers often prefer to place greater weight on ability or merit.

Discipline

Almost all collective agreements give the employer the right to make reasonable rules and regulations governing employees' behaviour and to take disciplinary action if the rules are broken. In every collective agreement, bargaining unit members are given the right to file a grievance if they feel that any disciplinary action taken was too harsh or without just cause.

Most collective agreements restrict an employer's right to discipline employees by requiring proof of just cause for the disciplinary action imposed. Since just cause is open to different interpretations, disciplinary action is a major source of grievances. Thus, disciplinary issues must be handled in accordance with the terms of the collective agreement and backed by carefully documented evidence. Even when disciplinary action is handled carefully, the union may argue that there were extenuating circumstances that should be taken into consideration. Supervisors have to strike a delicate balance between fairness and consistency.

When discipline cases end up at arbitration, two independent decisions are made. The first is whether the employee actually engaged in some form of misconduct. Then, if that question is answered in the affirmative, an assessment must be made of whether such misconduct warrants the particular discipline imposed, as well as whether such disciplinary action violated the collective agreement.

Grievance Resolution and Rights Arbitration

grievance A written allegation of a contract violation, filed by an individual bargaining unit member, the union, or management.

A **grievance** is a written allegation of a contract violation relating to a disagreement about its application or interpretation. When such alleged violations or disagreements arise, they are settled through the grievance procedure. A multi-step grievance procedure, the last step of which is final and binding arbitration, is found in virtually all collective agreements. Such procedures have been very effective in resolving day-to-day problems arising during the life of the collective agreement.

The primary purpose of the grievance procedure is to ensure the application of the contract with a degree of justice for both parties. Secondary purposes include providing the opportunity for the interpretation of contract language, such as the meaning of "sufficient ability"; serving as a communications device through which managers can become aware of employee concerns and areas of dissatisfaction; and bringing to the attention of both union and management those areas of the contract requiring clarification or modification in subsequent negotiations.

Steps in the Grievance Procedure   The grievance procedure involves systematic deliberation of a complaint at progressively higher levels of authority in the company and union, and most provide for arbitration as a final step. Grievances are usually filed by individual bargaining unit members. If the issue in contention is one that may affect a number of union members, either at that time or in the future, the union may file a *policy grievance*. Management also has the right to use the grievance procedure to process a complaint about the union, although such use is rare. Although the number of steps and people involved at each vary, **Figure 16.3** illustrates a typical grievance procedure.

As illustrated in Figure 16.3, the typical first step of the grievance procedure is the filing of a written complaint with the employee's immediate supervisor. If the problem is not resolved to the satisfaction of the employee at the first step, he or she may then take the problem to the next higher managerial level designated in the contract, and so on through all the steps available. Time limits are typically provided for resolution at each step. Failure to respond within the specified time limit may result in the grievance being automatically processed at the next step or being deemed to have been withdrawn or resolved. Ninety percent or more of all grievances are settled, abandoned, or withdrawn before arbitration.

rights dispute A disagreement between an organization and the union representing its employees regarding the interpretation or application of one or more clauses in the current collective agreement.

rights arbitration The process involved in the settlement of a rights dispute.

Rights Arbitration   Grievances relating to the interpretation or administration of the collective agreement are known as **rights disputes**. If these cannot be resolved internally, they must be referred to arbitration for a final and binding decision. The process involved in resolving such issues is known as **rights arbitration**.

A written arbitration award is issued at the conclusion of most rights arbitration cases, indicating that the grievance has been upheld or overturned. In disciplinary cases, it is also possible for an arbitration award to substitute a penalty that is more or less severe than the one proposed by union or management.

THE IMPACT OF UNIONIZATION ON HRM

Unionization results in a number of changes relating to HRM, all relating back to the requirements of the collective agreement. A union does have an impact on the way in which managers perform their HR responsibilities; when union leaders are treated as partners, they can provide a great deal of assistance with HR functions.

FIGURE 16.3   A Typical Grievance Procedure

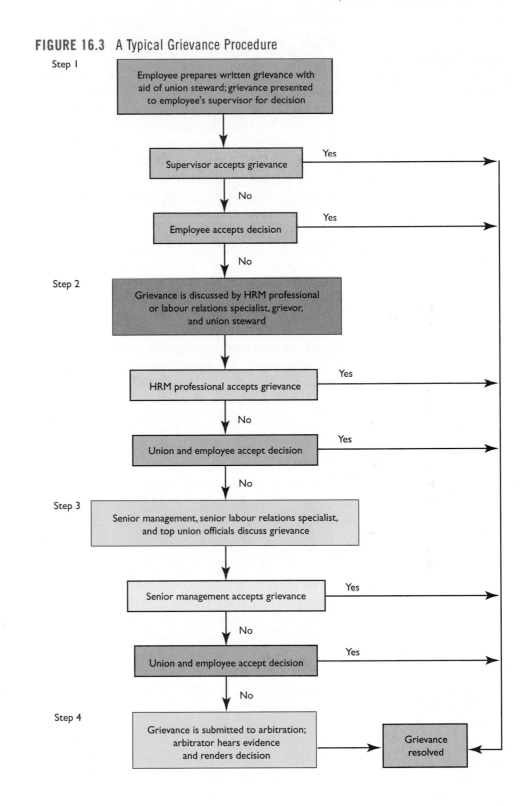

Organizational Structure

Once an organization is unionized, the HR department is typically expanded by the addition of an LR specialist or section. In a large firm with a number of bargaining units, human resources and labour relations may form two divisions within a broader department, often called industrial relations or labour relations.

Management Decision Making

In a unionized setting, management has less freedom to make unilateral decisions. This change may lead managers and supervisors to feel that they have lost some of their authority, which can cause resentment, especially since they inevitably find that unionization results in an increase in their responsibilities. Supervisors are often required to produce more written records than ever before, since documentation is critical at grievance and arbitration hearings.

Formulation of Policies and Procedures

All HR policies must be consistent with the terms of the collective agreement. Union representatives are often involved in the formulation of any policies that affect bargaining unit members—such as those pertaining to disciplinary rules and regulations—or are at least consulted as such policies are being drafted.

Centralization of Record Keeping

Unionization generally results in greater centralization of employee record keeping, which helps to ensure consistency and uniformity.

BUILDING EFFECTIVE LABOUR–MANAGEMENT RELATIONS

One of the biggest challenges to HRM in unionized organizations is to build a cooperative and harmonious working relationship between management and union leaders. The result can be a win–win situation. There are a number of ways to promote cooperation between management and labour that we'll discuss here.

Instituting an Open-Door Policy

When the key managers involved in labour–management relations welcome employees into their offices to discuss any problems or concerns, and employees feel comfortable in doing so, many issues can be resolved informally. For example, if the president of the local knows that he or she can approach the LR manager "off the record" and that anything discussed in such sessions will be kept strictly confidential, fewer grievances and a more trusting and harmonious relationship often result.

Extending the Courtesy of Prior Consultation

Although not every management decision requires union approval, if any actions that might affect union members are discussed with the union executive first, the likelihood of grievances is greatly reduced.

Demonstrating Genuine Concern for Employee Well-Being

When managers are genuinely concerned about employee well-being, and demonstrate that concern, mutual trust and respect are often established. This involves fair treatment and communication going well above and beyond the requirements of the collective agreement.

Forming Joint Committees

Forming labour–management committees to investigate and resolve complex issues can lead to innovative and creative solutions, as well as to a better relationship. An excellent example of such cooperation is described in the Strategic HR box.

Holding Joint Training Programs

When a contract is first signed, it can be beneficial to hold a joint training program to ensure that supervisors and union stewards are familiar with the terms and conditions specified therein and that they understand the intent of the negotiating teams. Such training can reduce misunderstandings and the likelihood of disagreement regarding interpretation of contract language.

Meeting Regularly

Whether required by the collective agreement or voluntarily instituted, regularly scheduled union–management meetings can result in more effective communication and the resolution of problems/concerns before they become formal grievance issues.

Using Third-Party Assistance

To build a better relationship, it is often beneficial to bring in a consultant or a government agency representative to help identify common goals and objectives and ways in which trust and communication can be strengthened.

Strategic HR

Labour–Management Partnership at the City of Saskatoon

The City of Saskatoon and its nine unions and employee associations worked together to take advantage of the federal government's Labour-Management Partnerships Program (LMPP), which funds a wide variety of pilot or demonstration projects involving labour–management cooperation. The City of Saskatoon addresses problems relating to the process for dealing with workplace harassment complaints.

A joint labour–management committee was set up to develop a new draft harassment policy. The key to the policy was to make sure that managers, supervisors, and union representatives had strong conflict management skills to solve problems earlier in the process. The committee created a conflict management training plan for managers, supervisors, and the union executive, as well as a communication plan for all employees.

Over the next several months, the committee members effectively communicated the new policy and process to all employees and provided two-day conflict resolution training sessions. Participants were very enthusiastic about the policy and the training sessions.

Source: Adapted from K. Burnett, "Management and Labour Can Work Together," *Canadian HR Reporter*, October 11, 2004. Reproduced by permission of *Canadian HR Reporter*, Carswell, One Corporate Plaza, 2075 Kennedy Road, Scarborough, ON M1T 3V4.

Chapter Review

Summary

1. Canada's labour laws provide a common set of rules for fair negotiations and ensure the protection of public interest by preventing the impact of labour disputes from inconveniencing the public. Tripartite Labour Relations Boards across the country administer labour relations laws. These laws try to balance employees' rights to engage in union activity with employers' management rights.

2. There are five steps in the LR process: (i) employees' decision to seek collective representation, (ii) the union organizing campaign, (iii) official recognition of the union, (iv) negotiation of a collective agreement, and (v) day-to-day contract administration.

3. The union organizing process involves five steps, which typically include (i) employee/union contact, (ii) an initial organizational meeting, (iii) the formation of an in-house organizing committee, (iv) an organizing campaign, and (v) the outcome—certification, recognition, or rejection.

4. There are three basic ways in which a union can obtain recognition as a bargaining unit for a group of workers: voluntary recognition, the regular certification process, and a pre-hearing vote.

5. The three steps in the collective bargaining process are preparation for negotiations, face-to-face negotiations, and obtaining approval for the proposed contract. Two possible additional steps are third-party assistance if talks break down and a strike/lockout or interest arbitration if the parties arrive at a bargaining impasse.

6. Typical steps in a grievance procedure involve presenting a written grievance to the worker's immediate supervisor, then to an HR/LR specialist, then to senior management, and finally to an arbitrator for final and binding rights arbitration.

Key Terms

arbitration   *(p. 439)*
authorization card   *(p. 431)*
bargaining unit   *(p. 426)*
bargaining zone   *(p. 435)*
boycott   *(p. 438)*
business unionism   *(p. 427)*
caucus session   *(p. 435)*
certification   *(p. 433)*

collective agreement (union contract)   *(p. 426)*
collective bargaining   *(p. 426)*
conciliation   *(p. 437)*
craft union   *(p. 427)*
decertification   *(p. 433)*
distributive bargaining   *(p. 436)*
grievance   *(p. 442)*
industrial union   *(p. 427)*
integrative bargaining   *(p. 436)*
interest arbitration   *(p. 439)*
interest dispute   *(p. 439)*
labour–management relations   *(p. 426)*
labour union (union)   *(p. 426)*
local   *(p. 428)*
lockout   *(p. 438)*
mediation   *(p. 437)*
memorandum of settlement   *(p. 437)*
mutual gains (interest-based) bargaining   *(p. 436)*
picket   *(p. 438)*
pre-hearing vote   *(p. 433)*
ratification   *(p. 437)*
representation vote   *(p. 433)*
rights arbitration   *(p. 441)*
rights dispute   *(p. 441)*
seniority   *(p. 441)*
social (reform) unionism   *(p. 427)*
strike   *(p. 438)*
strike vote   *(p. 438)*
union security clause   *(p. 439)*
union steward   *(p. 428)*
wildcat strike   *(p. 439)*

Review and Discussion Questions

1. Cite three examples of unfair labour practices on the part of management and three on the part of unions.

2. Explain three of the challenges facing the union movement in Canada today.

3. Describe five signs to which managers should be alert in order to detect an organizing campaign.

4. Explain the bargaining zone and draw a diagram to illustrate this concept.

5. Explain the six common forms of union security clause.

6. Explain how arbitration differs from conciliation and mediation, and differentiate between interest arbitration and rights arbitration.

Critical Thinking Questions

1. "If supervisors communicate effectively with employees, deal with their concerns, and treat them fairly, employees are far less likely to be interested in forming or joining a union." Do you agree or disagree with this statement? Why?

2. Two possible approaches to labour relations are union acceptance and union avoidance. Determine which of these strategies seems to have been adopted in a firm in which you have been employed or with which you are familiar. Provide evidence to back up your answer.

3. As the LR specialist, what steps would you take in order to prepare the firm and management team if you believed that a strike was a possible outcome of the upcoming negotiations?

4. Think of an organization with which you are familiar in which there is a harmonious labour–management relationship. Compare and contrast the steps taken to build such a relationship with the guidelines provided in this chapter.

Application Exercises

Running Case: LearnInMotion.com

The Grievance

When coming in to work one day, Pierre was surprised to be taken aside by Jason, one of their original employees, who met him as he was parking his car. "Jennifer told me I was suspended for two days without pay because I came in late last Thursday," said Jason. "I'm really upset, but around here Jennifer's word seems to be law, and it sometimes seems like the only way anyone can file a grievance is by meeting you like this in the parking lot."

Pierre was very disturbed by this revelation and promised the employee that he would discuss the situation with Jennifer. He began mulling over possible alternatives.

Questions

1. Do you think that it is important for LearnInMotion.com to have a formal grievance procedure? Why or why not?

2. Based on what you know about LearnInMotion.com, outline the steps that you think should be involved in the firm's grievance process, should they decide to implement one.

3. What else could Jennifer and Pierre do, other than implementing a grievance process, to ensure that complaints and grievances get expressed and handled?

Case Incident

Strategy

"They want what?" the mayor exclaimed.

"Like I said," the town clerk replied, "17 percent over two years."

"There is no way that the taxpayers will accept a settlement anywhere near that," reiterated the mayor. "I don't care if the garbage doesn't get collected for a century. We can't do more than 8 percent over the next two years."

The town clerk looked worried. "How much loss of service do you think the public will accept? Suppose they do go on strike? I'm the one who always gets the complaints. Then there's the health problem with rats running all over the place! Remember over in Neibringtown, when that little kid was bitten? There was a hell of an outcry."

The mayor agreed: "Garbage collectors always have strong bargaining power, but, if I don't fight this, I'll be voted out in the next election. I say we offer 6 percent over 18 months. Then we can go either way—6 percent over 12 months or 8 percent over two years."

"I wonder if we have any other options?" worried the town clerk.

"Well, we could threaten not to hire any more union personnel and to job out the collection service to private contractors if the union wasn't cooperative," mused the mayor.

"That's a good idea!" The town clerk sounded enthusiastic. "Also, we can mount a newspaper advertising campaign to get the public behind us. If we play on the fear of massive tax increases, the garbage collectors won't have much public sympathy."

"What about asking the union to guarantee garbage collection for old people during a strike? If they refuse, they'll look bad in the public eye; if they accept, we are rid of a major problem. Most people can bring their trash to a central collection point. Not all old people can," chuckled the mayor. "We can't lose on that issue!"

"Okay then," said the town clerk. "It looks like we have the beginning of a bargaining strategy here. Actually, I feel better now. I think we're in a rather strong position."

Questions

1. Discuss the plight of public sector unions faced with the reality of a limited tax base and public pressure to lower taxes.

2. Is the town clerk right? Is the town in a good bargaining position? Explain your answer.

3. What strengths does the union have in its position?

4. If you were a labour relations consultant, would you agree with the present strategy? What alternatives, if any, would you propose?

Source: R.W. Mondy, R.M. Noe, S.R. Premeux and R.A. Knowles, *Human Resource Management*, Second Canadian Edition, Toronto, ON: Pearson Education Canada, 2001, 386. Reprinted with permission of Pearson Education Canada.

Experiential Exercises

1. Assume that you are the vice-president of HR at a relatively new non-union firm that has been experiencing rapid growth. In view of the management team's desire to remain non-union, you have been asked to prepare a report to the other senior management team members, making specific recommendations regarding strategies that the firm should adopt to help to ensure that the employees will have no desire to unionize.

2. Working with two or three classmates, devise a management counter-campaign to a unionization attempt, ensuring that all recommended courses of action are legal.

3. Working with several of your classmates, use role-playing to differentiate between distributive and integrative bargaining.

4. Obtain a copy of two collective agreements. Compare and contrast the following provisions: union recognition, management rights, union security, grievance procedure, and arbitration clause.

Lakeside Packers

Lakeside Packers is a slaughterhouse in Brooks, Alberta, owned by Tyson Chicken of Arkansas. The plant processes four thousand cattle a day. Workers are fired if they complain or get sick, which is common practice in the slaughterhouse industry. Alberta is in the midst of an economic boom and job opportunities are plentiful.

Brooks is a "redneck" town, and most residents do not welcome unions. However, hundreds of Lakeside Packers workers are on strike to get their first contract. Hundreds of others have been willing to cross that line just to keep working. Since Alberta has no anti-scab legislation, strikers can only stop replacement workers for three minutes before letting them into the plant.

One-third of the workers are immigrants from poor countries making much more money than they could ever make at home, and they are not interested in striking. Residents of Brooks don't understand the strike—they think the workers should just quit and get another job if they are dissatisfied.

Questions

1. Why are workers striking when they could easily quit and get another job?

2. Why have so many workers decided to cross the picket line as "scabs"?

3. Why are the other people in Brooks so opposed to the strike?

Source: Based on "Brooks," *CBC: The National* (October 20, 2005).

CHAPTER 17

MANAGING HUMAN RESOURCES IN A GLOBAL BUSINESS

REQUIRED PROFESSIONAL CAPABILITIES

• Contributes to an environment that fosters effective working relationships

LEARNING OUTCOMES

AFTER STUDYING THIS CHAPTER, YOU SHOULD BE ABLE TO

Explain how intercountry differences have an impact on HRM.

Explain how to improve global assignments through employee selection.

Discuss the major considerations in formulating a compensation plan for overseas employees.

Describe the main considerations in repatriating employees from abroad.

Answer the question "Is it realistic for a company to try to institute a standardized HR system in all or most of its facilities around the world?"

THE GLOBALIZATION OF BUSINESS AND STRATEGIC HR

It is clear that global business is important to companies here and abroad. Huge companies like Noranda, Alcan, and Molson have long had extensive overseas operations. With the ongoing European market unification and the burgeoning economies of China and India, the vast majority of companies are finding that their success depends on their ability to market and manage overseas. Thousands of Canadian corporations with international operations are now relocating employees overseas on a regular basis—about 110 000 employees annually at a cost of around $1 billion.[1] Of course, to foreign companies like Toyota, Canada is "overseas," and thousands of foreign firms already have thriving operations in Canada.

As a result of this globalization, companies must increasingly be managed globally. Some of the most pressing challenges concern globalization's impact on an employer's HR management system and specifically the techniques used to recruit, select, train, compensate, and maintain the work/life quality of employees who are based abroad.[2] As shown in **Figure 17.1**, HR is one of the top three most important business functions for executing global strategy.

Strategic HR involvement in the design and implementation of a global expansion strategy is required right from the start. Extensive research may be required in regards to local hiring practices, the availability of skilled labour, and employment regulations. Relocation specialists are becoming a strategic

FIGURE 17.1 Value Added by HR in Executing Global Strategy

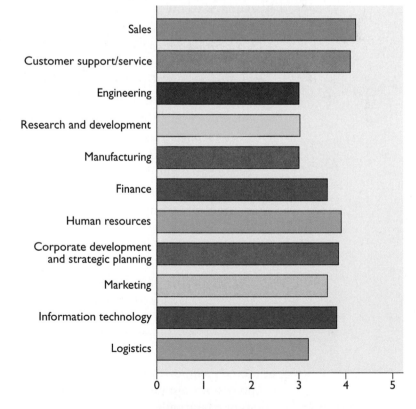

Rating scale: 0 = No value added, 5 = Value added

partner in determining the need for an assignment or relocation, identifying who is best suited to go, and making sure that all supports are in place to make that assignment a success.[3]

As companies have gone global, the number of their employees abroad has increased. Family issues rank as the number one concern when it comes to employee relocations. Employees who are considering an international assignment will also want to know how working and living in another country will affect their compensation, benefits, and taxes, and what kind of relocation assistance they will receive. There is a trend toward short-term global assignments instead of permanent relocations, because of the prevalence of dual-career families and a host of other issues.[4]

With more employees abroad, HR departments have had to tackle new global challenges. Three broad global HR challenges that emerged were as follows:

- *Deployment.* Easily getting the right skills to where they are needed in the organization regardless of geographical location.

- *Knowledge and innovation dissemination.* Spreading state-of-the art knowledge and practices throughout the organization regardless of where they originate.

- *Identifying and developing talent on a global basis.* Identifying who has the ability to function effectively in a global organization and developing these abilities.[5]

From a practical point of view, one has to address issues such as the following:

1. *Candidate identification, assessment, and selection.* In addition to the required technical and business skills, key traits to consider for global assignments include cultural sensitivity, interpersonal skills, and flexibility.

2. *Cost projections.* The average cost of sending an employee and family on an overseas assignment is reportedly between three and five times the employee's pre-departure salary; as a result, quantifying total costs for a global assignment and deciding whether to use an expatriate or a local employee are essential in the budgeting process.

3. *Assignment letters.* The assignee's specific job requirements and remuneration, vacation, home leave, and repatriation arrangements will have to be documented and formally communicated in an assignment letter.[6]

4. *Compensation, benefits, and tax programs.* There are many ways in which to compensate employees who are transferred abroad, given the vast differences in living expenses around the world. Some common approaches to international pay include home-based pay plus a supplement and destination-based pay.

5. *Relocation assistance.* The assignee will probably have to be assisted with such matters as maintenance of a home and automobiles, shipment and storage of household goods, and so forth. The average cost of a permanent international relocation for a Canadian employee is between $50 000 and $100 000.[7]

6. *Family support.* Cultural orientation, educational assistance, and emergency provisions are just some of the matters to be addressed before the family is shipped abroad.

The last two issues relate to the heightened focus on work/life balance that is so necessary in today's climate of relocation refusals because of concerns

International Association for Human Resource Information Management
www.ihrim.org

Mobility Services International
www.msimobility.com

Monster Board Moving
www.monstermoving.com/
International

about a mother-in-law's homecare, the children's education, a spouse's career, and the difficulty of adjusting to new surroundings while juggling family responsibilities at the same time as focusing on the job. According to the Canadian Employee Relocation Council's *2005 Employee Relocation Policy Survey*, a typical relocating employee is a male manager, aged 36 to 40 years, with a working spouse, an income of between $70 000 and $100 000, and most likely a home owner. An employee who rejects relocation will most likely do so because of concerns regarding children, compensation, and the spouse's career. Major work/life balance relocation challenges thus include career assistance for the spouse, and education and school selection assistance for the children.[8]

That is just the tip of the iceberg. Cross-cultural, technical, and language training programs will probably be required. Provisions for re-assimilating the expatriate when he or she returns home is another matter that must be addressed. All these issues are significant because the cost of "expatriate failure"—early return from an expatriate assignment—can result in costs in excess of three times the employee's salary. Companies that provide strong support to expatriate employees stand a higher chance of success.[9]

Sending employees abroad and managing HR globally is complicated by the nature of the countries into which many firms are expanding. Today's expatriates are heading to China (increasingly the most likely destination for a foreign assignment), India, Brazil, Russia, Mexico, Singapore, and Hong Kong.[10] Some of the issues involved in doing business in China are reviewed in the Global HRM box.

Global HRM

Doing Business in China Has Everything to Do with People

China now has the world's fastest-growing economy and is undergoing what has been described as a second industrial revolution. However, the traditional notions of collectivism and "saving face" remain important in Chinese society. In both personal and business interactions with Chinese people, it is therefore essential to honour and respect these cultural traditions in a very explicit way.

China has multiple layers of bureaucracy that can make doing business there extremely frustrating. Working with a local person who can be trusted and who can act as a translator and a facilitator is invaluable. Finding an official from a Canadian consulate or chamber of commerce can be very helpful. Because of the importance of rank, status, and hierarchy in China, being accompanied by an official of significant status and rank who is knowledgeable about the local community can open many doors.

Guanxi (the Chinese term for "relationship") plays an important part in how the business and personal world operates in China. Making good connections and maintaining them will enhance personal, family, and organizational status. Part of making and maintaining good connections is giving and returning favours. Strong trust relationships are central to developing stable and effective business dealings.

Rensia Melles of FGIWorld, a global human resources consulting firm, says, "The Chinese communication style tends to be very indirect. Even for Canadians, who are less direct than Americans, the challenge is, you need to take the time you need to build relationships, you need to learn to read the silences, the punctuation."

Olga Latour, coordinator of international mobility at Bombardier, says that communication is what often trips up expatriates. The company has had to bring a few people back from assignments in China when they became ineffective because of inappropriate interpersonal habits. She spoke of an employee who was perceived as arrogant by her Chinese colleagues. "When they don't have any respect for you, you get nothing done."

Sources: Adapted from U. Vu, "Doing Business in China Has Everything to Do with People," *Canadian HR Reporter*, September 26, 2005, pp. 5, 7; L. Kaminsky, "Preparing for Life, and Business, in China," *Canadian HR Reporter*, September 26, 2005, pp. 8–9. Reproduced by permission of *Canadian HR Reporter*, Carswell, One Corporate Plaza, 2075 Kennedy Road, Scarborough, ON M1T 3V4.

HOW INTERCOUNTRY DIFFERENCES AFFECT HRM

To a large extent, companies operating only within Canada's borders have the luxury of dealing with a relatively limited set of economic, cultural, and legal variables. Notwithstanding the range from liberal to conservative, for instance, Canada is basically a capitalist competitive society. In addition, although a multitude of cultural and ethnic backgrounds are represented in the Canadian workforce, various shared values (such as an appreciation for democracy) help to blur the otherwise sharp cultural differences.

A company that is operating multiple units abroad is generally not blessed with such relative homogeneity. For example, minimum legally mandated holidays may range from none in the United States to five weeks per year in Luxembourg. In addition, although there are no formal requirements for employee participation in Italy, employee representatives on boards of directors are required in companies with more than 30 employees in Denmark.

Another troubling issue is the need for tight security and terrorism awareness training for employees sent to such countries as Colombia, where kidnapping of foreign executives is commonplace.[11] And two-thirds of the world's nations are corrupt places to conduct business.[12] The point is that the management of the HR functions in multinational companies is complicated enormously by the need to adapt HR policies and procedures to the differences among countries in which each subsidiary is based. The following are some intercountry differences that demand such adaptation.[13]

Cultural Factors

Wide-ranging cultural differences from country to country demand corresponding differences in HR practices among a company's foreign subsidiaries. We might generalize, for instance, that the cultural norms of the Far East and the importance there of the patriarchal system will mould the typical Japanese worker's view of his or her relationship to an employer as well as influence how that person works. Japanese workers have often come to expect lifetime employment in return for their loyalty. As well, incentive plans in Japan tend to focus on the work group, while in the West the more usual prescription is still to focus on individual worker incentives.[14]

A well-known study by Professor Geert Hofstede underscores other international cultural differences. Hofstede says that societies differ first in *power distance*; in other words, they differ in the extent to which the less powerful members of institutions accept and expect that power will be distributed unequally.[15] He concluded that the institutionalization of such an inequality is higher in some countries (such as Mexico) than in others (such as Sweden).

His findings identified several other cultural differences. *Individualism versus collectivism* refers to the degree to which ties between individuals are normally loose rather than close. In more individualistic countries, "all members are expected to look after themselves and their immediate families."[16] Individualistic countries include Canada and the United States. Collectivist countries include Indonesia and Pakistan.

According to Hofstede, *masculinity versus femininity* refers to the extent to which a society values assertiveness ("masculinity") versus caring (what he called "femininity"). Japan and Austria ranked high in masculinity; Denmark and Chile ranked low.

Such intercountry cultural differences have several HR implications. First, they suggest the need for adapting HR practices, such as testing and pay plans, to local cultural norms. They also suggest that HR staff members in a foreign subsidiary are best drawn from host-country citizens. A high degree of sensitivity and empathy for the cultural and attitudinal demands of co-workers is always important when selecting employees to staff overseas operations. However, such sensitivity is especially important when the job is HRM and the work involves "human" jobs like interviewing, testing, orienting, training, counselling, and (if need be) terminating. As one expert puts it, "An HR staff member who shares the employee's cultural background is more likely to be sensitive to the employee's needs and expectations in the workplace—and is thus more likely to manage the company successfully."[17]

Economic Systems

Differences in economic systems among countries also translate into intercountry differences in HR practices. In free enterprise systems, for instance, the need for efficiency tends to favour HR policies that value productivity, efficient workers, and staff cutting where market forces dictate. Moving along the scale toward more socialist systems, HR practices tend to shift toward preventing unemployment, even at the expense of sacrificing efficiency.

Labour Cost Factors

Differences in labour costs may also produce differences in HR practices. High labour costs can require a focus on efficiency, for instance, and on HR practices (like pay for performance) aimed at improving employee performance. Along with differences in wages and salaries, wide gaps exist in hours worked. Thus, workers in Portugal average about 1980 hours of work annually, while workers in Germany average 1648 hours. Employees in Europe generally receive four to six weeks of vacation as compared with two or three weeks in Canada. Several European countries, including the United Kingdom and Germany, require substantial severance pay to departing employees, usually equal to at least two years' service in the United Kingdom and one year in Germany.[18] Since the fall of communism, wages in Eastern Europe have stagnated and now average only one-third of those in Western Europe.[19]

Industrial Relations Factors

Industrial relations, and specifically the relationship among the worker, the union, and the employer, vary dramatically from country to country and have an enormous impact on HRM practices. In Germany, for instance, *codetermination* is the rule. Here, employees have the legal right to a voice in setting company policies. In this and several other countries, workers elect their own representatives to the supervisory board of the employer, and there is also a vice-president for labour at the top management level.[20] Conversely, in many other countries, the state interferes little in the relations between employers and unions. In Canada, for instance, HR policies on most matters, such as wages and benefits, are set not by the government but by the employer, or by the employer in negotiations with its labour unions. In Germany, conversely, the various laws on codetermination largely determine the nature of HR policies in many German firms.

The European Union Parliament

The European Union (EU)

The EU is a common market for goods, services, capital, and even labour. The EU has 27 members, with three other countries waiting to join. Generally speaking, tariffs for goods across borders from one EU country to another no longer exist, and employees (with some exceptions) find it easier to move relatively freely between jobs in various EU countries. Also, the EU hopes that its unique blend of social and economic policy will provide a competitive advantage.[21]

However, some differences remain, such as minimum annual holidays. Social legislation by the EU's European Parliament and its administrative European Commission are slowly narrowing some gaps. However, HR practices will still vary from country to country. Even into the near future, in other words, and even just within Europe, managing human resources multinationally will present problems for HR managers.

Summary

In summary, intercountry variations in culture, economic systems, labour costs, and legal and industrial relations systems complicate the task of selecting, training, and managing employees abroad. These variations result in corresponding differences in management styles and practices from country to country, and such differences "may strain relations between headquarters and subsidiary personnel or make a manager less effective when working abroad than at home."[22] International assignments thus run a relatively high risk of failing unless special steps are taken in selecting, training, and compensating international assignees.

SELECTION FOR GLOBAL ASSIGNMENTS

Canadian companies have reported low failure rates for expatriates relative to other countries, particularly the United States, which has a failure rate of 40 to 50 percent.[23] A truism regarding selection for international assignments is that it is usually not inadequate technical competence but family and personal problems that undermine the international assignee.[24] As one expert puts it:

> The selection process is fundamentally flawed. Expatriate assignments rarely fail because the person cannot accommodate to the technical demands of the job. The expatriate selections are made by line managers based on technical competence. They fail because of family and personal issues and lack of cultural skills that haven't been part of the process.[25]

The Canadian experience is unique. Canadians may be more culturally adaptable than their foreign counterparts because they are already familiar with bilingualism and multiculturalism. In fact, Canadian executives are in demand across the globe. The country's diverse ethnic makeup has produced a generation of business leaders who mix easily with different cultures.[26]

Some organizations have moved away from full-scale relocation of an employee and his or her family to alternatives, such as frequent extended business trips with corresponding time spent back at home, short-term assignments of between three months and a year with frequent home leave (once every 12 weeks on average), and the dual household arrangement where the employee's family remains at home and the employee sets up a small household for himself or herself in the foreign country. Overall, relocation policies are becoming more flexible, as the majority of all services are provided on a case-by-case basis.[27] Often, firms neglect to prepare employees for short-term assignments in the same way as they do for the long-term variety, which leads to problems such as lack of cross-cultural awareness, extreme loneliness, and feeling undervalued on returning to the home office.[28] Best practices for foreign assignments are shown in **Figure 17.2**.

Sources of Managers

There are several ways in which to classify international managers. *Locals* are citizens of the countries where they are working. *Expatriates* are noncitizens of the countries in which they are working. *Home-country nationals* are the citizens of the country in which the multinational company's headquarters is based. *Third-country nationals* are citizens of a country other than the parent or the host country—for example, a British executive working in a Tokyo subsidiary of a Canadian multinational bank.[29]

Expatriates represent a minority of managers. Thus, most managerial positions are filled by locals rather than expatriates in both headquarters and foreign subsidiary operations. There are several reasons to rely on local, host-country management talent for filling the foreign subsidiary's management ranks. Many people simply prefer not to work in a foreign country, and in general the cost of using expatriates is far greater than the cost of using local management talent. The multinational corporation may be viewed locally as a "better citizen" if it uses local management talent, and indeed some governments actually press for the "nativization" of local management. There may also be a fear that expatriates, knowing that they are posted to the foreign subsidiary for only a few years, may overemphasize short-term projects rather than focus on perhaps more necessary long-term tasks.[30]

International Labour Organization
www.ilo.org

An Ethical Dilemma

How ethical is it for a multinational organization to recruit expatriate staff for managerial positions when similarly qualified staff can be identified in the host country?

FIGURE 17.2   Ten Best Practices for Foreign Assignments

- Recruit people with competencies for international assignments.
- Make assignments part of career development and succession planning.
- Pre-screening of individuals is key.
- Look beyond technical skills; people skills and progressive leadership styles are critical to a successful assignment.
- Screen for international readiness using behavioural testing methods.
- Provide cultural training for all family members.
- Outline a repatriation plan up front.
- Maintain a pool of pre-qualified individuals to draw from in responses to changes in business conditions.
- Communicate and involve expatriates in home company news and affairs on a regular basis.
- Be flexible and have contingency plans in place.

Source: Adapted from S. Cryne, "Foreign Assignments Increasing, Along with Employee Resistance," *Canadian HR Reporter*, September 27, 2004, p. 9. Reproduced by permission of *Canadian HR Reporter*, Carswell, One Corporate Plaza, 2075 Kennedy Road, Scarborough, ON M1T 3V4.

There are also several reasons for using expatriates—either home-country or third-country nationals—for staffing subsidiaries. The major reason is technical competence: in other words, employers may be unable find local candidates with the required technical qualifications.[31] Multinationals also increasingly view a successful stint abroad as a required step in developing top managers. Control is another important reason. Multinationals sometimes assign home-country nationals from their headquarters staff abroad on the assumption that these managers are more steeped in the firm's policies and culture and more likely to unquestioningly implement headquarters' instructions. A recent Hay Group study found that the most admired companies frequently use expatriates, as described in the Strategic HR box.

Global Staffing Policy

Canadian Employee Relocation Council
www.cerc.ca

Transition Dynamics
www.transition-dynamics.com

The Expatriate Group
www.expat.ca

Multinational firms' top executives are often classified as either ethnocentric, polycentric, or geocentric. In an *ethnocentric* corporation, the prevailing attitude is that home-country managers are superior to those in the host country. In the *polycentric* corporation, there is a belief that only host-country managers can understand the culture and behaviour of the host-country market; and therefore, foreign subsidiaries should have local managers. The *geocentric* approach, which

---

Strategic HR

Most-Admired Companies Use Expatriates

Conventional wisdom would suggest that expatriate assignments are often problematic for organizations. However, according to a new Hay Group study of the most-admired companies operating globally, this does not have to be the case. The study found that almost three-quarters of these companies have a strong track record of success with expatriates. This compares with a little more than half of the survey respondents from peer organizations.

One of the dominating trends in the Hay Group study was clarity, with these companies having very clear criteria for evaluating potential candidates for international assignments as well as well-developed training systems for preparing managers. They also have well-established procedures for determining both the total cost and the return on investment (ROI) associated with international assignments.

"The most-admired companies are far more effective in identifying talent on a global basis than their peers," said Hay Group vice-president Mel Stark. "These leaders devote a significant portion of their time to talent management and providing ongoing coaching to their people."

According to the Hay Group study findings, these global companies with top reputations are far more likely

to make use of planned career assignments to develop global experience. Also, these same organizations are more likely to have executive teams of members who have held positions outside their home countries and to have boards of directors that are diverse in terms of the members' nationalities.

"Companies such as Novartis in pharmaceuticals and Caterpillar in manufacturing make leadership development a top priority," said Murray Dalziel, group managing director of global practices for Hay Group. They devote significant resources beyond the HR department to talent management. This includes buy-in and involvement by the CEO and senior executives.

The study found that these companies are more likely than their peers to report that they have a global approach to performance management and a clearly defined global compensation strategy.

"Caterpillar evaluates and measures performance the same way around the world," notes Stuart L. Levenick, Caterpillar Group vice-president. "This is true for succession planning as well. Using the same performance measures we are able to assess our talent and place individuals in positions around the world that work for the company and the individuals' career growth."

Source: Adapted from "Most Admired Companies Frequently Utilizing Expatriate Assignments," *workspan,* July 2006, p. 18. Reprinted with permission of WorldatWork, Scottsdale, AZ. www.worldatwork.org.

is becoming more common, assumes that management candidates must be searched for globally, on the assumption that the best manager for any specific position anywhere on the globe may be found in any of the countries in which the firm operates.[32]

These three multinational attitudes translate into three international staffing policies. An ethnocentric staffing policy is one in which all key management positions are filled by parent-country nationals. At Royal Dutch Shell, for instance, virtually all financial controllers around the world are Dutch nationals. Reasons given for ethnocentric staffing policies include lack of qualified host-country senior management talent, a desire to maintain a unified corporate culture and tighter control, and the desire to transfer the parent firm's core competencies (e.g., a specialized manufacturing skill) to a foreign subsidiary more expeditiously.[33]

A polycentric-oriented firm would staff foreign subsidiaries with host-country nationals and its home-office headquarters with parent-country nationals. This may reduce the local cultural misunderstandings that expatriate managers may exhibit. It will also almost undoubtedly be less expensive. One expert estimates that an expatriate executive can cost a firm up to three times as much as a domestic executive because of transfer expenses and other expenses such as schooling for children, annual home leave, and the need to pay income taxes in two countries.[34]

A geocentric staffing policy "seeks the best people for key jobs throughout the organization, regardless of nationality."[35] This may allow the global firm to use its human resources more efficiently by transferring the best person to the open job, wherever he or she may be. It can also help to build a stronger and more consistent culture and set of values among the entire global management team. Team members here are continually interacting and networking with one another as they move from assignment to assignment around the globe and participate in global development activities.

Selecting Global Managers

There are common traits that managers to be assigned domestically and overseas will obviously share. Wherever a person is to be posted, he or she will need the technical knowledge and skills to do the job and the intelligence and people skills to be a successful manager.[36] In addition, foreign assignments make demands on expatriate assignees that are different from what the manager would face if simply assigned to a management post in his or her home country. There is the need to cope with a workforce and management colleagues whose cultural inclinations may be drastically different from one's own, and the considerable stress that being alone in a foreign land can bring to bear on the manager.

If the employee's spouse and children share the assignment, there are also the complexities and pressures that the family will have to confront, from learning a new language to shopping in strange surroundings, to finding new friends and attending new schools. Perceived organizational support and fairness regarding family issues can reduce intentions to return home early.[37]

Research
I n s i g h t ▷

Selecting managers for expatriate assignments, therefore, means screening them for traits that predict success in adapting to what may be dramatically new environments. A recent study of 338 international assignees from many countries and organizations identified five factors perceived by international assignees to contribute to success in a foreign assignment. They were job knowledge and motivation, relational skills, flexibility/adaptability, extracultural openness, and family situation. Specific items—including managerial ability, organizational ability, administrative skills, and creativity—were statistically combined into a single "job knowledge and motivation" factor. Respect, courtesy and tact, display of respect, and kindness were some of the items composing the "relational skills" factor. "Flexibility/adaptability" included such items as resourcefulness, ability to deal with stress, flexibility, and emotional stability. "Extracultural openness" included a variety of outside interests, interest in foreign countries, and openness. Finally, several items (including adaptability of spouse and family, spouse's positive opinion, willingness of spouse to live abroad, and stable marriage) compose the "family situation" factor.[38]

The five factors were not equally important in the foreign assignee's success, according to the responding managers. As the researchers conclude, "Family situation was generally found to be the most important factor, a finding consistent with other research on international assignments and transfers."[39] Therefore, although all five factors were perceived to be important to the foreign assignee's success, the company that ignores the candidate's family situation does so at its own peril.

Research
Insight ▷

A study of 838 managers from 6 international firms and 21 countries studied the extent to which personal characteristics (such as "sensitive to cultural differences") could be used to distinguish between managers who had high potential as international executives and those whose potential was not as high. Results showed that personal characteristics successfully distinguished the managers identified by their companies as "high potential." Consistent with such results as those mentioned previously, the characteristics—such as flexibility, integrity, the courage to take a stand, seeking and using feedback, business knowledge, bringing out the best in people, taking risks, and openness to criticism—reflect a blend of technical expertise, openness, and flexibility in dealing with people and getting things done.[40]

Adaptability Screening

Adaptability screening is generally recommended as an integral part of the expatriate selection process. Generally conducted by a professional psychologist or psychiatrist, adaptability screening aims to assess the family's probable success in handling the foreign transfer and to alert them to personal issues (such as the impact on children) that the foreign move may involve.[41]

Past experience is often the best predictor of future success, and some companies look for overseas candidates whose work and nonwork experience, education, and language skills already demonstrate a commitment to and facility in living and working with different cultures. Even several summers spent successfully travelling overseas or participating in foreign student programs would seem to provide some concrete basis for believing that the potential transferee can accomplish the required adaptation when he or she arrives overseas.

Realistic job previews at this point are also crucial. Again, both the potential assignee and his or her family require all the information that can be provided on the problems to expect in the new job (such as mandatory private schooling for the children), as well as any information obtainable about the cultural benefits, problems, and idiosyncrasies of the country in question. A pre-assignment visit to the new location by the employee and his or her family can provide an opportunity to make an informed decision about a potential relocation assignment. International HR managers speak about avoiding culture shock in much the same way as we discussed using realistic job previews to avoid reality shock among new employees.[42]

There are also paper-and-pencil tests that can be used to more effectively select employees for overseas assignments. The Overseas Assignment Inventory is one such assessment tool. Based on 12 years of research with more than seven thousand candidates, the test's publisher contends that it is useful in identifying characteristics and attitudes that such candidates should have.[43]

There is an increasing demand for background checks for overseas employees, given global security concerns. This can be problematic in many countries where access to information is limited. A routine practice in Asian countries is for potential employers to use their network of contacts to check on job candidates.[44]

MAINTAINING GLOBAL EMPLOYEES

Painstaking screening is just the first step in ensuring that the foreign assignee is successful. The employee may then require special training and, additionally, international HR policies must be formulated for compensating the firm's overseas managers and maintaining healthy labour relations.

Orienting and Training Employees for Global Assignments

When it comes to providing the orientation and training required for success overseas, the practices of most North American firms reflect more form than substance. One consultant says that, despite many companies' claims, there is generally little or no systematic selection and training for assignments overseas. One relevant survey concluded that a sample of company presidents and chairpersons agreed that international business was growing in importance and required employees to be firmly grounded in the economics and practices of foreign countries. However, few of their companies actually provided such overseas-oriented training to their employees. This is unfortunate, because a positive relationship exists between realistic expectations and cross-cultural adjustment.[45]

What sort of special training do overseas candidates need? One firm specializing in such programs prescribes a four-step approach. Level 1 training focuses on the impact of cultural differences, and on raising trainees' awareness of such differences and their impact on business outcomes. Even transfers to the United States from Canada can involve culture shock. Level 2 training focuses on attitudes and aims at getting participants to understand how attitudes (both negative and positive) are formed and how they influence behaviour. (For example, unfavourable stereotypes may subconsciously influence how a new manager responds to and treats his or her new foreign employees.) Finally, Level 3 training provides factual knowledge about the target country, while Level 4 provides skill building in areas like language and adjustment and adaptation skills. The depth of training is of the utmost importance. If firms are going to provide cross-cultural training, it needs to be in-depth and done with care. For example, language training must include nonverbal communication awareness, as it varies so widely across the world.[46]

Many organizations offer spousal assistance in the form of reimbursement for continuing education, job search assistance, résumé preparation, or recertification.[47]

Beyond these special training practices, there is also the need for more traditional training and development of

Orientation and training for international assignments can help employees (and their families) to avoid "culture shock" and better adjust to their new surroundings.

overseas employees. At IBM, for instance, such development includes the use of a series of rotating assignments that permits overseas IBM managers to grow professionally. At the same time, IBM and other major firms have established management development centres around the world where executives can go to hone their skills. Beyond that, classroom programs (such as those at the London Business School, or at INSEAD in France) provide overseas executives with the opportunities that they need to hone their functional skills.

In addition to honing functional skills, international management development often aims to foster improved control of global operations by building a unified corporate culture. The assumption here is that the firm should bring together managers from its far-flung subsidiaries and steep them for a week or two in the firm's cherished values and current strategy and policies. The managers should then be more likely to adhere consistently to these values, policies, and aims once they return to their assignments abroad.

International Compensation

The whole area of international compensation management presents some tricky problems. Compensation programs throughout a global firm must be integrated for overall effectiveness, yet differentiated to effectively motivate and meet the specific needs of the various categories and locations of employees. On the one hand, there is certain logic in maintaining company-wide pay scales and policies so that, for instance, divisional marketing directors throughout the world are all paid within the same narrow range. This reduces the risk of perceived inequities and dramatically simplifies the job of keeping track of disparate country-by-country wage rates. However, most multinational companies have recognized the need to make executive pay decisions on a global level, and executive pay plans are gradually becoming more uniform.[48]

Yet, the practice of not adapting pay scales to local markets can present an HR manager with more problems than it solves. The fact is that living in Tokyo is three times more expensive than living in Calgary, while the cost of living in Bangalore, India, is 30 percent lower than that in Toronto.[49] If these cost-of-living differences are not considered, it may be almost impossible to get managers to take "high-cost" assignments.

However, the answer is usually not just to pay, say, marketing directors more in one country than in another. For one thing, the firm could thereby elicit resistance when telling a marketing director in Tokyo who is earning $3000 per week to move to a division in Spain, where his or her pay for the same job (cost of living notwithstanding) will drop by half. One way to handle the problem is to pay a similar base salary company-wide and then add on various allowances according to individual market conditions.[50]

Determining equitable wage rates in many countries is no simple matter. There is a wealth of "packaged" compensation survey data already available in North America, but such data are not so easy to come by overseas. As a result, "one of the greatest difficulties in managing total compensation on a multinational level is establishing a consistent compensation measure among countries that builds credibility both at home and abroad." Compensation professionals must face the challenge of designing programs that motivate local employees in each country as well as internationally mobile employees of all nationalities. Some multinational companies deal with this problem for local managers by conducting their own annual compensation surveys. Others use a global career progression framework that includes the flexibility to accommodate local practices and still maintain organization-wide consistency.[51]

The Balance Sheet Approach

The most common approach to formulating expatriate pay is to equalize purchasing power across countries, a technique known as the *balance sheet approach*. The basic idea is that each expatriate should enjoy the same standard of living that he or she would have had at home. With the balance sheet approach, four main home-country groups of expenses—income taxes, housing, goods and services, and reserve—are the focus of attention. The employer estimates what each of these four expenses is for the expatriate's home country, and also what each is expected to be in the expatriate's host country. For example, a Canadian manager posted abroad may have to pay not only Canadian taxes but also income taxes to the country to which he or she is posted as well. Any differences—such as additional income taxes or housing expenses—are then paid by the employer.[52]

In practice, this usually boils down to building the expatriate's total compensation around five or six separate components. For example, *base salary* will normally be in the same range as the manager's home-country salary. In addition, however, there might be an *overseas or foreign service premium*. This is paid as a percentage of the executive's base salary, in part to compensate the manager for the cultural and physical adjustments that he or she will have to make.[53] There may also be several *allowances*, including a housing allowance and an education allowance for the expatriate's children.

Incentives

The incentive value of stock-based incentives for expatriates is highly suspect since the performance of the company's stock on a Canadian stock market may have little relevance to, say, a manager in a German subsidiary. This is particularly true because, regardless of size, a foreign subsidiary's influence on its parent company's stock price is more likely to result from exchange rate movements than from management action.[54]

The answer here, more multinationals are finding, is to formulate new long-term incentives specifically for overseas executives. Multinationals are thus devising performance-based long-term incentive plans that are tied more closely to performance at the subsidiary level. These can help to build a sense of ownership among key local managers while providing the financial incentives needed to attract and keep the people required for overseas operations.

International EAPs

EAPs are going global, helping expatriates to take care of their mental health, which is often affected by the stressful relocation process. The approach is to proactively contact employees before departure to explain the program's services; then about three months after arrival, families are contacted again. By this time, they have usually run into some challenges from culture shock and will welcome some assistance. The expatriates and their families have then established a connection with the EAP to use for ongoing support.[55]

Problems, such as homesickness, boredom, withdrawal, depression, compulsive eating and drinking, irritability, marital stress, family tension, and conflict, are all common reactions to culture shock. Employees on short-term assignment without their families can experience extreme loneliness. Treatment for psychiatric illnesses varies widely around the world, as do the conditions in government-run mental health institutions, and consultation with an EAP professional having extensive cross-cultural training may be critical in ensuring that appropriate medical treatment is obtained.[56]

Performance Appraisal of Global Managers

Several issues complicate the task of appraising an expatriate's performance.[57] For one thing, the question of who actually appraises the expatriate is crucial. Obviously, local management must have some input into the appraisal, but the appraisal may then be distorted by cultural differences. Thus, an expatriate manager in India may be evaluated somewhat negatively by his host-country bosses, who find his use of participative decision making inappropriate in their culture. However, home-office managers may be so geographically distanced from the expatriate that they cannot provide valid appraisals because they are not fully aware of the situation that the manager actually faces. This can be problematic: the expatriate may be measured by objective criteria, such as profits and market share, but local events, such as political instability, may undermine the manager's performance while remaining "invisible" to home-office staff.

Two experts make five suggestions for improving the expatriate appraisal process:[58]

1. Stipulate the assignment's difficulty level. For example, being an expatriate manager in China is generally considered to be more difficult than working in England, and the appraisal should take such difficulty-level differences into account.

2. Weight the evaluation more toward the on-site manager's appraisal than toward the home-site manager's distant perceptions of the employee's performance.

3. If, however (as is usually the case), the home-site manager does the actual written appraisal, he or she should use a former expatriate from the same overseas location to provide background advice during the appraisal process. This can help to ensure that unique local issues are considered during the appraisal process.

4. Modify the normal performance criteria used for that particular position to fit the overseas position and characteristics of that particular locale. For example, "maintaining positive labour relations" might be more important in Chile, where labour instability is more common, than it would be in Canada.

5. Attempt to give the expatriate manager credit for relevant insights into the functioning of the operation and specifically the interdependencies of the domestic and foreign operations. In other words, do not just appraise the expatriate manager in terms of quantifiable criteria, like profits or market share. His or her recommendations regarding how home-office/foreign-subsidiary communication might be enhanced, and other useful insights, should also affect the appraisal.

Cultural differences between on-site managers and their expatriate employees can affect the provision of performance feedback. **Table 17.1** provides an example of specific differences in approach to performance appraisal between the United States and Malaysia.

International Labour Relations

Firms opening subsidiaries abroad will find substantial differences in labour relations practices among the world's countries and regions. The following synopsis illustrates some of these differences by focusing on Europe. However, keep in mind that similarly significant differences would exist in South and Central America and Asia. Some important differences between labour relations practices in Europe and North America include the following:[59]

TABLE 17.1   Impact of Culture on Performance Feedback

The Characteristics of Performance Feedback Influenced	United States	Malaysia
Level of Achievement	**Individualistic** • Provide direct feedback to improve individual performance and self-identity	**Collectivistic** • Feedback should consider the individual's role in his or her group • Feedback should consider group harmony and relationship
Feedback Approach	**Low Power Distance** • Provide opportunity for individuals to participate in the performance evaluation • Encourage subordinate self-evaluation	**High Power Distance** • Focus mainly on top-down communication and control • Avoid perceptions of managerial weakness by encouraging too much participation
Performance Accountability	**Master of Nature** • Hold subordinates accountable for their own performance • Encourage the belief that the individual is empowered and can increase his or her own performance through greater effort	**Subjugated to Nature** • Consider external work factors as a source of individual work performance • Find consensus on areas where the individual was in control of his or her performance
Communication Style	**Low Cultural Context** • Communication should be direct and explicit • Follow up verbal feedback with written summary of evaluation	**High Cultural Context** • Consider the surrounding context of the feedback. • Avoid loud nonverbal gestures. Pay close attention to the body language of the individual. • Be indirect in conveying feedback ("read between the lines").

Source: J. Milliman, S. Taylor, and A.J. Czaplewski, "Cross-Cultural Performance Feedback in Multinational Enterprises: Opportunity for Organizational Learning," *Human Resource Planning,* 2002, Vol. 25, No. 3, p. 36. Copyright 2002 by The Human Resources Planning Society, 317 Madison Ave., Suite 1509, New York, NY 10017. Phone: (212) 490-6387, Fax: (212) 682-6851.

1. *Centralization.* In general, collective bargaining in Western Europe is likely to be industry-wide or regionally oriented, whereas North American collective bargaining generally occurs at the enterprise or plant level.

2. *Union structure.* Because collective bargaining is relatively centralized in most European countries, local unions in Europe tend to have much less autonomy and decision-making power than in North America, and they basically concentrate on administrative and service functions.

3. *Employer organization.* Because of the prevalence of industry-wide bargaining, the employer's collective bargaining role tends to be performed primarily by employer associations in Europe; individual employers in North America generally (but not always) represent their own interests when bargaining collectively with unions.

4. *Union recognition.* Union recognition for collective bargaining in Western Europe is much less formal than in North America. For example, in Europe there is no legal mechanism requiring an employer to recognize a particular union; even if a union claims to represent 80 percent of an employer's workers, another union can try to organize and bargain for the other 20 percent.

5. *Union security.* Union security in the form of formal closed-shop agreements is largely absent in continental Western Europe.

6. *Labour–management contracts.* As in North America, most European labour–management agreements are legally binding documents, except in Great Britain, where such collective agreements are viewed as "gentlemen's agreements" existing outside the law.

7. *Content and scope of bargaining.* North American labour–management agreements tend to focus on wages, hours, and working conditions. European agreements tend to be brief and simple and to specify minimum wages and employment conditions.

8. *Grievance handling.* In Western Europe, grievances occur much less frequently than in North America; when raised, they are usually handled by a legislated machinery outside the union's formal control.

9. *Strikes.* Generally speaking, strikes occur less frequently in Europe. This is probably due to industry-wide bargaining, which generally elicits less management resistance than in North America, where demands "cut deeper into the individual enterprise's revenues."[60]

10. *Government's role.* In Europe, governments generally do not regulate the bargaining process but are much more interested in directly setting the actual terms of employment than is the case in North America.

11. *Worker participation.* Worker participation has a long and relatively extensive history in Western Europe. In many countries in Western Europe, works councils are required. A *works council* is a committee in which plant workers consult with management about certain issues or share in the governance of the workplace.[61] Codetermination is a second form of worker participation in Europe. *Codetermination* means that there is mandatory worker representation on an enterprise's board of directors. It is especially prevalent in Germany.

In Eastern Europe, unionization rates have plummeted since the fall of the Iron Curtain, resulting in a competitive advantage, with wages averaging only one-third of those in Western Europe.[62]

Safety and Fair Treatment Abroad

Making provisions to ensure employee safety and fair treatment does not stop at a country's borders. Although Canada has often taken the lead with respect to such matters as occupational safety, other countries are also quickly adopting such laws, and, in any event, it is hard to make a legitimate case for being less safety conscious or fair with workers abroad than with those at home.

Having employees abroad does raise some unique safety and fair treatment issues, however. As one security executive at an oil company put it, "It's crucial for a company to understand the local environment, local conditions and what threat exists." For example, "kidnapping has become a way of life" in some countries in Central and South America, and can also be a problem in Africa and Asia-Pacific.[63]

Kidnap and ransom insurance is a rapidly growing benefit, given that between 10 000 and 15 000 kidnappings of foreigners for ransom occur each year, with about 80 percent in Latin America. The insurance policy usually covers

- ransom money and coverage on the money while in transit
- professional negotiators

- consultant to handle media, law, and family communications
- bodily injury of abductee
- security company fees
- extortion against company property, product contamination, and computer systems
- travel expenses for negotiator, family, and employee
- lost salary of abductee
- psychological counselling for employee and family[64]

Keeping business travellers out of crime's way is a specialty all its own but suggestions include the following:

- Provide expatriates with general training about travelling and living abroad, and specific information about the place that they are going to, so they are better oriented when they get there.
- Have travellers arrive at airports as close to departure time as possible and wait in areas away from the main flow of traffic where they are not as easily observed.
- Equip the expatriates' car and home with adequate security systems.
- Tell employees to vary their departure and arrival times and take different routes to and from work.
- Keep employees current on crime and other problems by regularly checking travel advisory service and consular information sheets; these provide up-to-date information on possible threats in almost every country of the world.
- Advise employees to remain confident at all times: body language can attract perpetrators, and those who look like victims often become victimized.[65]

Wages paid to foreign nonmanagement workers abroad are a well-publicized aspect of employee fair treatment today. For example, high-profile companies have recently received bad publicity for the working conditions, long hours, and low pay rates for their factory workers in developing countries. Many companies have therefore taken steps to increase wages for foreign workers.

REPATRIATION

Repatriation is often a bittersweet experience for the returning expatriate. *Repatriation*, the process of moving back to the parent company and country from the foreign assignment, means returning one's family to familiar surroundings and old friends. The returning employee all too often discovers, however, that in many respects his or her employer has ignored the manager's career and personal needs. Up to 25 percent of expatriates leave the company within one year of their return home. A recent survey found that although 85 percent of companies said reintegration of employees is important, only 20 percent believe they do it well. Among expatriate employees, 75 percent report integration is managed poorly, primarily because it is not clear about who is responsible for this process. Also, fewer than half of these employees were able to use their newly developed skills and capabilities in their roles on their return.[66]

Several repatriation problems are very common. One is the expatriate's fear that he or she has been "out of sight, out of mind" during an extended foreign stay and has thus lost touch with the parent firm's culture, top executives, and those responsible for the firm's management selection processes. Indeed, such fears can be well founded: Many repatriates are temporarily placed in mediocre or makeshift jobs. Ironically, the company often undervalues the cross-cultural skills acquired abroad, and the international posting becomes a career-limiting, rather than career-enhancing, move. Many are shocked to find that the executive trappings of the overseas job (private schools for the children and a company car and driver, for instance) are lost on return and that the executive is again just a small fish in a big pond. Perhaps more exasperating is the discovery that some of the expatriate's former colleagues have been more rapidly promoted while he or she was overseas. Even the expatriate's family may undergo a sort of reverse culture shock, as the spouse and children face the often-daunting task of picking up old friendships and habits or starting schools anew on their return. Expatriates who experience problems fitting back into the organization often leave, and the firm loses a valuable resource.[67]

Progressive multinationals anticipate and avoid these problems by taking a number of sensible steps. These can be summarized as follows:[68]

1. *Write repatriation agreements.* Many firms use repatriation agreements, which guarantee in writing that the international assignee will not be kept abroad longer than some period (such as five years) and that on return he or she will be given a mutually acceptable job.

2. *Assign a sponsor.* The employee should be assigned a sponsor/mentor (such as a senior manager at the parent firm's home office). This person's role is to look after the expatriate while he or she is away. This includes keeping the person apprised of significant company events and changes back home, monitoring his or her career interests, and nominating the person to be considered for key openings when the expatriate is ready to come home.

3. *Provide career counselling.* Provide formal career counselling sessions to ensure that the repatriate's job assignments on return will meet his or her needs.

4. *Keep communication open.* Keep the expatriate "plugged in" to home-office business affairs through management meetings around the world and frequent home leave combined with meetings at headquarters. Only 18 percent of companies in a 2006 Watson Wyatt global survey had a global communication plan in place to keep employees around the world informed about what the company was doing.

5. *Offer financial support.* Many firms pay real estate and legal fees and help the expatriate to rent or in some other way to maintain his or her residence, so that the repatriate and his or her family can actually return "home."

6. *Develop reorientation programs.* Finally, provide the repatriate and his or her family with a reorientation program to facilitate the adjustment back into the home culture.

7. *Build in return trips.* Expatriates can benefit from more frequent trips to the home country to ensure that they keep in touch with home-country norms and changes during their international assignment.

HOW TO IMPLEMENT A GLOBAL HR SYSTEM

Given cross-cultural differences like these in HR practices around the world, one could reasonably ask, "Is it realistic for a company to try to institute a standardized HR system in all or most of its facilities around the world?" A recent study suggests that the answer is "yes." It shows that the employer may have to defer to local managers on some specific issues. However, in general, the fact that there are currently global differences in HR practices doesn't mean that these differences are necessary or even advisable. The important thing is knowing how to create and implement the global HR system.

In this study, the researchers interviewed HR professionals from six global companies—Agilent, Dow, IBM, Motorola, Procter & Gamble, and Shell Oil—as well as international HR consultants.[69] Their overall conclusion was that employers who successfully implement global HR systems apply various international HR best practices in doing so. This enables them to create global HR systems that are globally *acceptable*, that they can *develop* more effectively, and that their HR staffs can then *implement* more effectively. Let's look at each of these objectives.

Making the Global HR System More Acceptable

First, employers engage in three best practices so that the global HR systems they eventually develop will be acceptable to their local managers around the world:

1. *Remember that global systems are more accepted in truly global organizations.* These companies and all their managers think of themselves as global in scope and perspective, and all or most functions and business units operate on a truly global basis. They are not simply aggregates of numerous more or less independent local entities. For example, truly global organizations require their managers to work on global teams, and they identify, recruit, and place the employees they hire globally. This makes it easier for managers everywhere to accept the global imperative for having a more standardized HR system.

2. *Investigate pressures to differentiate and determine their legitimacy.* HR managers seeking to standardize selection, training, appraisal, compensation, or other HR practices worldwide will always meet resistance from local managers who insist, "you can't do that here, because we are different culturally and in other ways." Based on their research, these investigators found that these "differences" are usually not persuasive. For example, when Dow wanted to implement an online employee recruitment and selection tool in a particular region abroad, the hiring managers there told Dow that there was no way their managers would use it. After investigating the supposed cultural roadblocks and then implementing the new system, "what we found is that the number of applicants went through the roof when we went online, and the quality of the applicants also increased."

   However, the operative word here is "investigate"—it does not mean ramming through a change without ascertaining whether there may in fact be some reason for using a more locally appropriate system. Carefully assess whether the local culture or other differences might in fact undermine the new system. Be knowledgeable about local legal issues, and be willing to differentiate where necessary. Then, market-test the new HR tool.

3. *Try to work within the context of a strong corporate culture.* A strong corporate culture helps override geographical differences. Companies that create a strong corporate culture find it easier to obtain agreement among far-flung employees when it comes time to implement standardized practices worldwide. For example, Procter & Gamble has a strong corporate culture. Because of how P&G recruits, selects, trains, and rewards them, its managers have a

A global HR team

strong sense of shared values. For instance, Procter & Gamble emphasizes orderly growth, and its culture therefore encourages a relatively high degree of conformity among managers. New recruits quickly learn to think in terms of "we" instead of "I." They learn to value thoroughness, consistency, self-discipline, and a methodical approach. Because all P&G managers worldwide tend to share these values, they are in a sense more similar to each other than they are geographically different. Having such global unanimity makes it easier to develop and implement standardized HR practices worldwide.

Developing a More Effective Global HR System

Similarly, researchers found that these companies engaged in several best practices in developing effective worldwide HR systems:

1. *Form global HR networks.* The firm's HR managers around the world should feel that they're not merely local HR managers, but are part of a greater whole, namely, the firm's global HR network. These six firms did this in various ways. For instance, they formed global HR development teams, and involved them in developing the new HR systems. In fact, the researchers found that in developing global HR systems, the most critical factor for success is "creating an infrastructure of partners around the world that you use for support, for buy-in, for organization of local activities, and to help you better understand their own systems and their own challenges." Treat the local HR managers as equal partners, not just implementers.

2. *Remember that it's more important to standardize ends and competencies than specific methods.* For example, with regard to screening applicants, the researchers concluded, "while companies may strive to standardize tools globally, the critical point is [actually] to standardize what is assessed but to be flexible in how it is assessed." Thus, IBM uses a more or less standardized recruitment and selection process worldwide, but "details such as who conducts the interview (hiring manager versus recruiter) or whether the pre-screen is by phone or in person, differ by country."

Implementing the Global HR System

Finally, in actually implementing the global HR systems, several best practices can help ensure a more effective implementation:

1. *Remember, "You can't communicate enough."* For example, "there's a need for constant contact with the decision makers in each country, as well as the people who will be implementing and using the system."

2. *Dedicate adequate resources for the global HR effort.* For example, do not expect local HR offices to suddenly start implementing the new job analysis procedures unless the head office provides adequate resources for these additional activities. **Table 17.2** summarizes these best practices for instituting global HR systems.

TABLE 17.2 Summary of Best Global HR Practices

Do ...	Don't ...
• Work within existing local systems—integrate global tools into local systems	• Try to do everything the same way everywhere
• Create a strong corporate culture	• Yield to every claim that "we're different"—make them prove it
• Create a global network for system development—global input is critical	• Force a global system on local people
• Treat local people as equal partners in system development	• Use local people for implementation
• Assess common elements across geographies	• Use the same tools globally, unless you can show that they really work and are culturally appropriate
• Focus on what to measure and allow flexibility in how to measure	• Ignore cultural differences
• Allow for local additions beyond core elements	• Let technology drive your system design—you can't assume every location has the same level of technology investment and access
• Differentiate when necessary	• Assume that "if we build it they will come"—you need to market your tools or system and put change management strategies in place
• Train local people to make good decisions about which tools to use and how to do so	
• Communicate, communicate, communicate!	
• Dedicate resources for global HR efforts	
• Know, or have access to someone who knows, the legal requirements in each country	

Source: Ann Marie Ryan et al., "Designing and Implementing Global Staffing Systems: Part 2—Best Practices," *Human Resource Management,* Spring 2003, Vol. 42, No. 1, p. 93. Copyright © 2003 John Wiley & Sons. Reprinted with permission of John Wiley & Sons, Inc.

Chapter Review

Summary

1. Intercountry differences include cultural factors (such as Hofstede's power distance, individualism versus collectivism, and masculinity versus femininity), economic systems, labour cost factors, and industrial relations factors. These affect HRM in a variety of ways.

2. Selecting managers for expatriate assignments means screening them for traits that predict success in adapting to dramatically new environments. Such expatriate traits include adaptability and flexibility, job knowledge and motivation, relational skills, extracultural openness, and family situation. Adaptability screening that focuses on the family's probable success in handling the foreign transfer can be an especially important step in the expatriate selection process.

3. The most common approach to formulating expatriate pay is to equalize purchasing power across countries, a technique known as the balance sheet approach. With this approach, the employer estimates expenses for income taxes, housing, goods and services, and reserve, and pays supplements to the expatriate in such a way as to maintain the same standard of living that he or she would have had at home.

4. Repatriation problems are very common but can be minimized. They include the often-well-founded fear that the expatriate is "out of sight, out of mind," and difficulties in re-assimilating the expatriate's family back into home-country culture. Suggestions for avoiding these problems include using repatriation agreements, assigning a sponsor/mentor, offering career counselling, keeping the expatriate plugged in to home-office business, building in return trips, providing financial support to maintain the expatriate's home-country residence, and offering reorientation programs to the expatriate and his or her family.

5. Employers who successfully implement global HR systems apply various international HR best practices in doing so. These enable them to create global HR systems that are globally *acceptable*, that they can *develop* more effectively, and that their HR staffs can then *implement* more effectively.

Review and Discussion Questions

1. What are some of the specific uniquely international activities that an international HR manager typically engages in?

2. Explain three broad global HR challenges.

3. What special training do overseas candidates need? In what ways is such training similar to and different from traditional diversity training?

4. How does appraising an expatriate's performance differ from appraising that of a home-office manager? How can some of the unique problems of appraising the expatriate's performance be avoided?

5. What accounts for the fact that worker participation has a long and relatively extensive history in Europe? How has this relatively extensive participation affected the labour relations process?

6. Describe five actions that can be taken by expatriate managers in other countries to increase their personal safety.

Critical Thinking Questions

1. You are president of a small business. In what ways do you expect that being involved in international business activity will affect HRM in your business?

2. A firm is about to send its first employees overseas to staff a new subsidiary. The president asks why such assignments fail and what can be done to avoid such failures. Write a memo in response to these questions.

3. What can an organization do to ensure that the skills acquired on an international assignment are utilized when the employee returns to his or her home country?

4. How would you implement a geocentric staffing policy?

Application Exercises

Running Case: LearnInMotion.com

Going Abroad

According to its business plan, and in practice, LearnInMotion.com "acquires content globally but delivers it locally." In other words, all the content and courses and other material that it lists on its site come from content providers all over the world. However, the "hard copy" (book and CD-ROM) courses are delivered, with the help of independent contracting delivery firms, locally, in Ontario and Quebec.

Now the company is considering an expansion. Although the most logical strategic expansion would probably entail adding cities in Canada, one of LearnInMotion.com's major content providers—a big training company in England—believes there is a significant market for LearnInMotion.com services in England, and particularly in London, Oxford, and Manchester (all of which are bustling business centres, and all of which have well-known universities). The training company has offered to finance and co-own a branch of LearnInMotion.com in London.

They want it housed in the training firm's new offices in Mayfair, near Shepherds Market. This is an easily accessible (if somewhat expensive) area, within easy walking distance of Hyde Park and not far from the London Underground Piccadilly line, which runs directly through the city to Heathrow airport.

Everyone concerned wants to make sure the new operation can "hit the ground running." This means either Jennifer or Pierre will have to move to London almost at once and take one salesperson and one of the content management people along. Once there, this small team could hire additional employees locally, and then, once the new operation is running successfully, return to Ottawa, probably within three or four months.

Jennifer and Pierre have decided to go ahead and open the London office, but this is not a decision they've taken lightly, since there are many drawbacks to doing so. The original, Ottawa-based site is not generating anywhere near the sales revenue it was supposed to at this point, and being short three key employees is not going to help. Neither the board of directors nor the representatives of the venture capital fund were enthusiastic about the idea of expanding abroad, either. However, they went along with it, and the deciding factor was probably the cash infusion that the London-based training firm was willing to make. It basically provided enough cash to run not just the London operation but the Ottawa one for an additional six months.

Having made the decision to set up operations abroad, Jennifer and Pierre now need to turn to the multitude of matters involved in the expansion—for instance, obtaining the necessary licences to open the business in England, and arranging for phone lines (all carried out with the assistance of the London-based training firm). However, it's also obvious to Jennifer and Pierre that there are considerable human resource management implications involved in moving LearnInMotion.com employees abroad, and in staffing the operation once they're there. Now, they want you, their management consultant, to help them actually do it. Here's what they want you to do for them.

Questions

1. What are the main HR-related implications and challenges as a result of opening the operation in London?

2. How should the person who will be the permanent manager for the new operation be chosen? Should he or she be hired locally, or should one of the people from the existing operation be used? Why?

3. Based on any sources available to you, including the Internet, research the comparative cost of living of London and Ottawa, including housing and transportation, as well as comparative salaries.

4. Write a short position paper on the subject: "a list of the HR-related things we need to do in sending our three people abroad."

Case Incident

"Boss, I Think We Have a Problem"

Central Steel Door Corporation has been in business for about 20 years, successfully selling a line of steel industrial-grade doors, as well as the hardware and fittings required for them. Focusing mostly in the United States and Canada, the company had gradually increased its presence from the New York City area, first into New England and then down the Atlantic Coast, then through the Midwest and West, and finally into Canada. The company's basic expansion strategy was always the same: Choose an area, open a distribution centre, hire a regional sales manager, then let that regional sales manager help staff the distribution centre and hire local sales reps.

Unfortunately, the company's traditional success in finding sales help has not extended to its overseas operations. With the introduction of the new European currency in 2002, Mel Fisher, president of Central Steel Door, decided to expand his company abroad, into Europe. However, the expansion has not gone smoothly at all. He tried for three weeks to find a sales manager by advertising in the *International Herald Tribune*, which is read by businesspeople in Europe and by American expatriates living and working in Europe. Although the ads placed in the *Tribune* also run for about a month on the *Tribune*'s website, Mr. Fisher so far has received only five applications. One came from a possibly viable candidate, whereas four came from candidates whom Mr. Fisher refers to as "lost souls"—people who seem to have spent most of their time travelling aimlessly from country to country sipping espresso in sidewalk cafés. When asked what he had done for the last three years, one told Mr. Fisher he'd been on a "walkabout."

Other aspects of his international HR activities have been equally problematic. Fisher alienated two of his U.S. sales managers by sending them to Europe to temporarily run the European operations, but neglecting to work out a compensation package that would cover their relatively high living expenses in Germany and Belgium. One ended up staying the better part of the year, and Mr. Fisher was rudely surprised to be informed by the Belgian government that his sales manager owed thousands of dollars in local taxes. The managers had hired about 10 local people to staff each of the two distribution centres. However, without full-time local European sales managers, the level of sales was disappointing, so Fisher decided to

fire about half the distribution centre employees. That's when he got an emergency phone call from his temporary sales manager in Germany: "I've just been told that all these employees should have had written employment agreements and that in any case we can't fire anyone without at least one year's notice, and the local authorities here are really up in arms. Boss, I think we have a problem."

Questions

1. Based on this chapter and the case incident, compile a list of 10 international HR mistakes Mr. Fisher has made so far.

2. How would you have gone about hiring a European sales manager? Why?

3. What would you do now if you were Mr. Fisher?

Experiential Exercises

1. Choose three traits that are useful for selecting international assignees, and create a straightforward test (not one that uses pencil and paper) to screen candidates for these traits.

2. Describe the most common approach to formulating expatriate pay. Use a library source to determine the relative cost of living in five countries as of this year, and explain the implications of such differences for drafting a pay plan for managers being sent to each country.

Handmaster Plus—Made in China

Dr. Terry Zachary is a chiropractor who has developed a product called "Handmaster" to strengthen all the muscles in the hand. It comprises a polyurethane sponge ball and an elastic cord. He has decided to make the product in China because the manufacturing cost will be half of what it would be in Canada. He has also decided to use separate manufacturers for each component in order to avoid counterfeiting.

He has ten days to visit eight manufacturers in five cities in China, and he shoots a video chronicling his trip. Communication is a challenge, but with the help of interpreters, he gets the information he needs. When he is finished, he chooses to have the ball made by the Yuming company in the city of Changzhou, and the cord made by the Lelpro company in the city of Wuxi.

Six weeks later, he returns to view samples and runs into some difficulty with discrepancies between what is said to him and what actually happens. However, in the end, a problem with the cord is resolved, and Zachary's mission is accomplished. His Chinese manufacturing partners are happy and are eager to do more business with other Canadian companies.

Questions

1. Why is the cost of manufacturing half as much in China as in Canada?

2. Are there any additional benefits to manufacturing in China?

3. What are some potential problems associated with manufacturing in China?

4. What could Zachary do to utilize Canadian talent to improve communication with his Chinese manufacturing partners?

Source: Based on "Handmaster Plus—Made in China," *CBC Venture 918* (March 14, 2004).

NOTES

Chapter 1

1. O. Parker, *The Strategic Value of People: Human Resource Trends and Metrics* (Ottawa: The Conference Board of Canada, July 2006); E. Andrew, "Most Canadian Companies Are Still Not Treating Human Resources as a Serious Strategic Issue," *Workspan Focus Canada* (February 2006), pp. 14–16; S. Prashad, "All Aligned: How to Get HR on Board with Business," *HR Professional* (February/March 2005), pp. 19–29.

2. B. Becker and M. Huselid, "The Strategic Impact of High Performance Work Systems," working paper, www.markhuselid.com (January 6, 2007); B. Becker, M. Huselid, P.S. Pickus, and M.F. Spratt, "HR as a Source of Shareholder Value: Research and Recommendations," *Human Resource Management* 36, no. 1 (Spring 1997), pp. 39–47; B. Becker and B. Gerhart, "The Impact of Human Resource Management on Organizational Performance: Progress and Prospects," *Academy of Management Journal* 39, no. 4 (August 1996), pp. 779–801; *Watson Wyatt 2005 Human Capital Index Report* (Watson Wyatt, 2005); *HR Rises to the Challenge: Unlocking the Value of M&A*; Towers Perrin 2004; Ilene Gochman Watson Wyatt & Human Resource Planning Society 2006.

3. O. Parker, *The Strategic Value of People: Human Resource Trends and Metrics* (Ottawa: The Conference Board of Canada, July 2006).

4. Ibid.

5. Watson Wyatt Human Capital Index: Human Capital as a Lead Indicator of Shareholder Value (Watson Wyatt, 2002).

6. R. Kaplan and D. Norton, *The Strategy-Focused Organization: How Balanced Scorecard Companies Thrive in the New Business Environment* (Boston, MA: Harvard Business School Press, 1996); S. Mooraj, D. Oyon, and D. Hostettler, "The Balanced Scorecard: A Necessary Good or an Unnecessary Evil?" *European Management Journal* 17, no. 5 (October 1999), pp. 481–491; B. Becker, M. Huselid, and D. Ulrich, *The HR Scorecard: Linking People, Strategy and Performance* (Boston, MA: Harvard Business School Press, 2001); M. Huselid, B. Becker, and R. Beatty, *The Workforce Scorecard: Managing Human Capital to Execute Strategy* (Boston, MA: Harvard Business School Press, 2006).

7. D. Ulrich and W. Brockbank, *The HR Value Proposition* (Boston, MA: Harvard University Press, 2005); D.M. Cox and C.H. Cox, "At the Table: Transitioning to Strategic Business Partner," *Workspan* (November 2003), pp. 20–23; D. Brown, "HR Pulled in Two Directions at Once," *Canadian HR Reporter* (February 23, 2004), pp. 1, 6; R. Morgan and M. Serino, "Mapping Human Capital DNA," *WorldatWork Journal* (Third Quarter 2002), pp. 42–51.

8. J. Jamieson, "People Skills Required," *National Post* (October 19, 2005); L. Abrahamsen and D. Ruth, "Getting the Job Done, from the Outside In," *Workspan* (October 2003), pp. 22–25; D. Brown, "Lessons form HR Outsourcing Pioneers," *Canadian HR Reporter* (June 16, 2003), pp. 1, 12–13.

9. S. Singh, "Exulted Expectations," *HR Professional* (August/September 2004), pp. 21–24; D. Brown, "Calgary Health Outsources HR," *Canadian HR Reporter* (February 23, 2004), pp. 1, 7; "CIBC Extends HR Outsourcing Deal," *Canadian HR Reporter* (December 15, 2003), p. 2; "Air Canada Plans to Outsource HR," *Canadian HR Reporter* (May 17, 2004), p. 2); D. Brown, "After Experiment with Outsourcing, RBC Brought Recruitment Back In-House," *Canadian HR Reporter* (April 19, 2004), pp. 8–9; J. Melnitzer, "Locating the Ouch Source," *Workplace News* (August 2005), pp. 12–13.

10. T. Belford, "HR Focusing on How It Can Add Value," *Globe & Mail* (March 25, 2002), p. B11.

11. B.E. Becker, M.A. Huselid, and D. Ulrich, *The HR Scorecard: Linking People, Strategy and Performance* (Boston, MA: Harvard Business School Press, 2001); D. Brown, "Measuring the Value of HR," *Canadian HR Reporter* (September 24, 2001), pp. 1, 5. See also E. Beaudan, "The Failure of Strategy: It's All in the Execution, *Ivey Business Journal* (January/February 2001).

12. "CEOs Talk," *Canadian HR Reporter* (March 11, 2002), p. 19.

13. D.S. Cohen, "Behaviour-Based Interviewing," *Human Resources Professional* (April/May 1997), p. 29.

14. R. Wright, *Measuring Human Resources Effectiveness Toolkit* (Ottawa: The Conference Board of Canada, 2004); U. Vu, "The HR Leader's Contribution in an Engaged Organization," *Canadian HR Reporter* (May 22, 2006); D. Brown, "Measuring Human Capital Crucial, ROI Isn't, Says New Think-Tank Paper," *Canadian HR Reporter* (October 25, 2004), pp. 1, 4; J. Douglas and T. Emond, "Time to Pop the Question: Are Your Employees Engaged?" *WorldatWork Canadian News* (Third Quarter 2003), pp. 12–14.

15. R. Baumruk, "The Missing Link: The Role of Employee Engagement in Business Success," *Workspan* (November 2004), pp. 48–52; N. Winter, "Tuned in and Turned On," *Workspan* (April 2003), pp. 48–52.

16. O. Parker, *The Strategic Value of People: Human Resource Trends and Metrics* (Ottawa: The Conference Board of Canada, July 2006).

17. R. Stringer, *Leadership and Organizational Climate* (Upper Saddle River, NJ: Prentice-Hall, 2002).

18. "Highly Skilled Workers Still Hard to Find," *Canadian HR Reporter* (February 3, 1999), p. 6.

19. W.B. Werther, Jr., W.A. Ruch, and L. McClure, *Productivity Through People* (St. Paul, MN: West Publishing, 1986), pp. 3–5.

20. M. Townson, *Women in Non-Standard Jobs: The Public Policy Challenge* (Ottawa: Status of Women Canada, 2003); M. Townson, "The Impact of Precarious Employment," in L.O. Stone (ed.), *New Frontiers of Research on Retirement,* Statistics Canada, Catalogue No. 75-511-XIE, 2006, pp. 355–382; R.P. Chaykowski, *Non-standard Work and Economic Vulnerability*, Canadian Policy Research Network, Vulnerable Workers Series, No. 3 (March 2005); G. Valeé, *Towards Enhancing the Employment Conditions of Vulnerable Workers: A Public Policy Perspective,* Canadian Policy Research Network, Vulnerable Workers Series, No. 2 (March 2005).

21. G. Ferris, D. Frink, and M.C. Galang, "Diversity in the Workplace: The Human Resources Management Challenge," *Human Resource Planning* 16, no. 1 (1993), p. 42.

22. A. Belanger, L. Martel, and E. Caron-Malenfant, *Population Projections for Canada, Provinces and Territories: 2005-2031*, Statistics Canada Catalogue No. 91-520-XIE, (December 2005), pp. 16–17; *Canada's Demographic Revolution: Adjusting to an Aging Population* (Ottawa: The Conference Board of Canada, March 2006).

23. N. Spinks and C. Moore, "Compassionate Care Leave Takes Effect," *WorldatWork Canadian News* (Second Quarter 2004), pp. 1, 21; U. Vu, 'Sandwich Generation' Challenges Big, and Getting Bigger," *Canadian HR Reporter* (October 25, 2004), pp. 1, 8.

24. Based on material cited in "News and Views: Flex Appeal," compiled by M. Griffin, *HR Professional* (February/March 1999), p. 10; research reported by P.L. Nyhof in "Managing Generation X: The Millennial Challenge," *Canadian HR Reporter* (May 22, 2000), pp. 7–8.

25. R. Berry, "Observations on Generational Diversity," *Profiles in Diversity Journal* 4, no. 3 (2002).

26. Jean-Philippe Naud, "Generation Y at Work," *WorldatWork Canadian News* (Second Quarter 2005), pp. 6–8; D. Piktialis, "The Generational Divide in Talent Management," *Workspan* (March 2006), pp. 10–12; G. Kovary and A. Buahene, "Recruiting the Four Generations," *Canadian HR Reporter* (May 23, 2005), p. R6.

27. A. Campbell and N. Gagnon, *Literacy, Life and Employment: An Analysis of Canadian International Adult Literacy Survey (IALS) Microdata* (Ottawa: Conference Board of Canada, January 2006).

28. P. Bleyer, "Let's Make Productivity Work for Canadians," Canadian Council on Social Development, 2005, www.ccsd.ca/pr/2005/ccsd_prebudget.htm (January 6, 2007).

29. "Study: Canada's Visible Minority Population in 2017," *The Daily*, Statistics Canada (March 2005); *Canada's Ethnocultural Portrait: The Changing Mosaic*, Statistics Canada, Catalogue No. 96 F0030 XIE 2001 0082004.

30. G. Rowe and H. Nguyen, *Convergence of Male and Female Patterns of Employment Activity (IV-F)*, Statistics Canada, November 2004.

31. M. Hutchinson, *Aboriginal Workforce Poised to Replace Retiring Baby Boomers*, www.aboriginaltimes.com/science/immigration-baby-boom/view (August 17, 2006).

32. C. Williams, "Disability in the Workplace," *Perspectives on Labour and Income* 18, no. 1 (February 2006), pp. 16–24.

33. K. Williams, "Privacy in a Climate of Electronic Surveillance," *Workplace News* (April 2005), p. 10.

34. "Employment Insurance (EI) Compassionate Care Benefits," www.hrsdc.ca/asp/gateway.asp?hr=/en/ei/types/compassionate_care.shtml (January 6, 2007).

35. C.W. Hill, *International Business* (Burr Ridge, IL: Irwin, 1994), p. 6.

36. "Multinational Corporation," http://en.wikipedia.org/wiki/Multinational_corporation (August 17, 2006).

37. S. Nolen, "Step 1: Keep Workers Alive," *Globe & Mail* (August 5, 2006), pp. B4–B5.

38. F.W. Taylor, "The Principles of Scientific Management," in J.M. Sharfritz and J.S. Ott (eds.), *Classics of Organization Theory*, 2nd ed. (Chicago: The Dorsey Press, 1987), pp. 66–81.

39. D.G. Nickels, J.M. McHugh, S.M. McHugh, and P.D Berman, *Understanding Canadian Business*, 2nd ed. (Toronto: Irwin, 1997), p. 220.

40. This discussion is based on E.E. Lawler III, "Human Resources Management," *Personnel* (January 1988), pp. 24–25.

41. R.J. Cattaneo and A.J. Templer, "Determining the Effectiveness of Human Resources Management," T.H. Stone (ed.), *ASAC: Personnel and Human Resources Division Proceedings* (Halifax: St. Mary's University, June 1988), p. 73.

42. J. Pfeffer, *Competitive Advantage Through People* (Boston, MA: Harvard Business School Press, 1994); E.E. Lawler, *Treat People Right* (San Francisco, CA: Jossey-Bass, 2003); O. Parker, *It's the Journey That Matters: 2005 Strategic HR Transformation Tour* (Ottawa: The Conference Board of Canada, 2005).

43. E. Lawler III, "Becoming a Key Player in Business Strategy," *Workspan* (January 2006), pp. 10–13.

44. *Unfinished Business: Mastering HR Business Design* (Mercer Human Resource Consulting, 2004); S. Klie, "HR Locked in Transactional Mode," *Canadian HR Reporter* (May 8, 2006); E. Andrew, "Most Canadian Companies Are Still Not Treating Human Resources as a Serious Strategic Issue," *Workspan Focus Canada* (February 2006), pp. 14–16; S. Klie, "Business Approach Key for HR Leaders," *Canadian HR Reporter* (September 12, 2005), p. 3; D. Brown, "HR Taking Steps to Prove Strategic Value," *Canadian HR Reporter* (November 17, 2003), pp. 1, 11.

45. *The CHRP Designation: Ensuring Excellence* (Toronto: Canadian Council of Human Resources Associations).

46. M. Belcourt and V. Catano, "HR Morphs from a 'Job' to a Profession," *Canadian HR Reporter* (April 10, 2006).

47. D. McDougall, "Employees Want an Ethical Work Environment," *Canadian HR Reporter* (April 10, 2000), p. 4.

48. "KPMG's Ethics Survey 2000—Managing for Ethical Practice," cited in L. Young, "Companies Not Doing Right," *Canadian HR Reporter* (April 10, 2000), p. 17.

49. Based on Walker Information Canada Inc. study, cited in J. Martin, "Studies Suggest a Link between Employees' Perception of a Firm's Ethics—and Loyalty," *Recruitment & Staffing*, Supplement to *Canadian HR Reporter* (September 20, 1999), p. G7; D. McDougall, "Employees Want an Ethical Work Environment," *Canadian HR Reporter* (April 10, 2000), p. 4.

Chapter 2

1. *Canadian Charter of Rights and Freedoms*, as part of the Constitution Act of 1982.

2. *Canadian Charter of Rights and Freedoms*, Section 15(1).

3. *Annual Report of the Canadian Human Rights Commission* (Ottawa: Government of Canada, 1991), p. 65.

4. Ontario Human Rights Commission, *Human Rights at Work* (Toronto: Government of Ontario, 1999), pp. 63–64.

5. L. Sukerman, "Small Employers, Big Duties," *Canadian HR Reporter* (January 31, 2005), p. R8.

6. A.P. Aggarwal, *Sex Discrimination: Employment Law and Practices* (Toronto: Butterworths Canada, 1994).

7. H.J. Jain, "Human Rights: Issues in Employment," *Human Resources Management in Canada* (Toronto: Prentice-Hall Canada, 1995), p. 50.

8. *Bona Fide Occupational Requirements and Bona Fide Justifications Under the Canadian Human Rights Act: The Implications of Meiorin and Grismer* (Ottawa: Canadian Human Rights Commission, January 2003); see also A. Wahl, "Where There's Fire, There's Smoke," *Canadian Business* (October 8, 1999), pp. 16, 20.

9. *Anti-Discrimination Casebook: Race, Colour, National or Ethnic Origin* (Case Summaries—Discrimination in Employment), 2001, Canadian Human Rights Commission, www.chrc-ccdp.ca/publications/anti_discrimination_case-en.asp#employment (August 13, 2006).

10. "Key Provisions of Ottawa's Same-Sex Legislation," *Canadian HR Reporter* (March 27, 2000), p. 11.

11. Canadian Human Rights Commission, www.chrc-ccdp.ca/adr/settlements/archives2/page5-en.asp (August 13, 2006).

12. Canadian Human Rights Commission, www.chrc-ccdp.ca/discrimination/age-en.asp (August 13, 2006).

13. Ontario Human Rights Commission, www.ohrc.on.ca/english/publicatoins/age-policy_5.shtml (June 2, 2006).

14. S. Klie, "Muslims Face Discrimination in Workplace," *Canadian HR Reporter* (February 27, 2006).

15. Canadian Human Rights Commission, www.chrc-ccdp.ca/adr/settlements/archives2/toc_tdm-en.asp#disability (August 13, 2006).

16. B. Kuretzky, "When Push Comes to Shove," *Workplace News* (November/December 2005), p.22; U. Vu, "Employers Waiting for Courts to Define Bullying," *Canadian HR Reporter* (September 12, 2005), pp. 1, 13.

17. *Anti-Harassment Policies for the Workplace: An Employer's Guide* (Canadian Human Rights Commission, March 2006), p. 3.

18. "Business Owner Found Responsible for Sexual Harassment in the Workplace," *Manitoba Human Rights Commission News Release* (September 22, 2005).

19. B. Orser, *Sexual Harassment Is Still a Management Issue* (Ottawa: Conference Board of Canada).

20. A.P. Aggarwal, *Sexual Harassment in the Workplace*, 2nd ed. (Toronto: Butterworths Canada, 1992), pp. 10–11.

21. "RCMP to pay $950,000 in Harassment Case," *Canadian HR Reporter* (February 13, 2006), p. 2.

22. *Anti-Harassment Policies for the Workplace: An Employer's Guide* (Canadian Human Rights Commission, March 2006), pp. 16–25.

23. This section is based on *Moving Forward 2002: Barriers and Opportunities for Executive Women in Canada* (Toronto: Women's Executive Network).

24. *Women in Canada: Work Chapter Updates*, Statistics Canada, Catalogue No. 89F0133XIE, 2003, Housing, Family and Social Statistics Division.

25. *2002 Annual Report—Employment Equity Act*, Human Resources Development Canada, p. 4.

26. Statistics Canada, www.tbs-sct.gc.ca/report/govrev/04/cp-rc5_e.asp (August 13, 2006).

27. C. Williams, "Disability in the Workplace," *Perspectives on Labour and Income* 7, no. 2 (February 2006), pp.16–23.

28. P. Gorrie, "Discrimination Costly: Study," *Toronto Star* (March 20, 2002), p. A23.

29. R.S. Abella, *Equality in Employment: A Royal Commission Report* (Ottawa: Supply and Services Canada, 1984).

30. A.B. Bakan and A. Kobyashi, *Employment Equity Policy in Canada: An Interprovincial Comparison* (Ottawa: Status of Women Canada, March 2000), pp. 9–10.

31. *Employment Equity: A Guide for Employers* (Ottawa: Employment and Immigration Canada, May 1991), Catalogue No. LM-143.

32. M.B. Currie, "Destined for Equity," *Human Resources Professional* (July/August 1993), pp. 7–8.

33. J. Gandz, "A Business Case for Diversity," *Paths to Equal Opportunity* (Ontario Ministry of Citizenship, 2001), www.equalopportunity.on.ca/userfiles/item/5859/BusCase.pdf (July 23, 2003).

34. This section is based on *2002 Canadian Human Rights Commission Annual Report*.

35. J. Schilder, "The Rainbow Connection," *Human Resources Professional* (April 1994), pp. 13–5.

36. M. Swartz, "Employers Are Learning to Embrace Diversity," *Toronto Star* (January 8, 2004).

37. Ibid.

38. M. Ruby, "In Living Colour," *Workplace News* (May/June 2006), pp. 16–19.

39. B. Siu, "Making Sense of Diversity Assessment Approaches," *Canadian HR Reporter* (November 1, 1999), p. 10.

40. U. Vu, "FedEx Holds Managers Accountable for Diversity," *Canadian HR Reporter* (November 8, 2004), p. 3.

Chapter 3

1. P. Mirza, D. Moss, T. Shea, L. Rubis, and A. Fox, "Ten Changes That Rocked HR," *HR Magazine* (December 2004), p. 39.

2. S. Shrivastava and J.B. Shaw, "Liberating HR Through Technology," *Human Resource Management* (Fall 2003), p. 201.

3. W.J. Jones and R.C. Hoell, "Human Resource Information System Courses: An Examination of Instructional Methods," *Journal of Information Systems Education* (Fall 2005), p. 321.

4. A.S. Targowski and S.P. Deshpande, "The Utility and Selection of an HRIS," *Advances in Competitiveness Research* (Autumn 2001), p. 42.

5. J. Sullivan, "The Six Levels of HRIS Technology," in R.H. Stambaugh (ed.), *21 Tomorrows: HR Systems in the Emerging Workplace of the 21st Century*, pp. 79–86 (Dallas, TX: Rector Duncan & Associates, 2000).

6. "Client Server," www.webopedia.com/term/c/client.html (June 29, 2006).

7. "Client Server," http://en.wikipedia.org/wiki/Client-server (June 29, 2006).

8. "Technology @ Your Fingertips: Glossary," http://nces.ed.gov/pubs98/tech/glossary.asp (June 29, 2006).

9. "Bridgefield Group ERP/Supply Chain Glossary," http://bridgefieldgroup.com/bridgefieldgroup/glos2.htm (June 29, 2006).

10. "Interactive Voice Response," www.hr-software.net/pages/216.htm (June 8, 2006).

11. J. Sullivan, "The Six Levels of HRIS Technology," in R.H. Stambaugh (ed.), *21 Tomorrows: HR Systems in the Emerging Workplace of the 21st Century*, pp. 79–86 (Dallas, TX: Rector Duncan & Associates, 2000).

12. J. Collison, "2005 HR Technology Survey Report," *SHRM Research*, pp. 3–4.

13. R. Henson, "HR 20/20: Clarifying the View of HR in Year 2020," in R.H. Stambaugh (ed.), *21 Tomorrows: HR Systems in the Emerging Workplace of the 21st Century*, pp. 11–16 (Dallas, TX: Rector Duncan & Associates, 2000).

14. Hackett Group, *World-Class HR Metrics: World-Class Spend Less Yet Achieve Higher Effectiveness* (July 25, 2006).

15. S. Shrivastava and J.B. Shaw, "Liberating HR Through Technology," *Human Resource Management* (Fall 2003), p. 201.

16. J. Johnston, "What Does It Take to Put in an HRMS?" *Canadian HR Reporter* (October 22, 2001), p. G3.

17. W.J. Jones and R.C. Hoell, "Human Resource Information System Courses: An Examination of Instructional Methods," *Journal of Information Systems Education* (Fall 2005), pp. 321–329; A.R. Hendrickson, "Human Resource Information Systems: Backbone Technology of Contemporary Human Resources," *Journal of Labor Research* (Summer 2003), p. 381.

18. E.W.T. Ngai and F.K.T. Wat, "Human Resource Information Systems: A Review and Empirical Analysis," *Department of Management and Marketing, The Hong Kong Polytechnic University* (July 7, 2004), p. 297.

19. M. Mayfield, "Human Resource Information Systems: A Review and Model Development," *Advances in Competitiveness Research* (January 1, 2003), pp. 139–152.

20. A.R. Hendrickson, "Human Resource Information Systems: Backbone Technology of Contemporary Human Resources," *Journal of Labor Research* (Summer 2003), p. 381.

21. A.S. Targowski and S.P. Deshpande, "The Utility and Selection of an HRIS," *Advances in Competitiveness Research* 9, no. 1 (2001), pp. 43–47.

22. A.R. Hendrickson, "Human Resource Information Systems: Backbone Technology of Contemporary Human Resources," *Journal of Labor Research* (Summer 2003), pp. 389–392.

23. M. Mayfield, "Human Resource Information Systems: A Review and Model Development," *Advances in Competitiveness Research* (January 1, 2003), pp. 139–152.

24. Human Resources and Social Development Canada, "Employment Equity Computerized Reporting System (EECRS) Software," www.hrsdc.gc.ca/asp/gateway.asp?hr=en/lp/lo/lswe/we/ee_tools/software/eecrs/index-we.shtml&hs=wzp (August 17, 1006).

25. J. Sullivan Ph.D., "The Six Levels of HRIS Technology," in R.H. Stambaugh (ed.), *21 Tomorrows: HR Systems in the Emerging Workplace of the 21st Century*, pp. 79–86 (Dallas, TX: Rector Duncan & Associates, 2000).

26. "The Plain English Geek Glossary," www.pdacortex.com/glossary.htm (January 6, 2007).

27. W.J. Jones and R.C. Hoell, "Human Resource Information System Courses: An Examination of Instructional Methods," *Journal of Information Systems Education* (Fall 2005), p. 326.

28. J.W. Boudreau, "Talentship and HR Measurement and Analysis: From ROI to Strategic Organizational Change," *Human Resource Planning* (2006), p. 30.

29. J. Schramm, "HR Technology Competencies: New Roles for HR Professionals," *2006 SHRM Research Quarterly*, p. 2.

30. Halogen Software, www.halogensoftware.com (June 29, 2006).

31. S. Shrivastava and J.B. Shaw, "Liberating HR Through Technology," *Human Resource Management* (Fall 2003), pp. 201–215.

32. S. Shrivastava and J.B. Shaw, "Liberating HR Through Technology," *Human Resource Management* (Fall 2003), p. 205; "Bridgefield Group ERP/Supply Chain Glossary," http://bridgefieldgroup.com/bridgefieldgroup/glos2.htm (June 29, 2006).

33. J. Johnston, "What Does It Take to Put in an HRMS?" *Canadian HR Reporter* (October 22, 2001), p. G3.

34. S. Shrivastava and J.B. Shaw, "Liberating HR Through Technology," *Human Resource Management* (Fall 2003), p. 203.

35. S. Shrivastava and J.B. Shaw, "Liberating HR through Technology," *Human Resource Management* (Fall 2003), p. 202.

36. J.G. Meade, *The Human Resources Software Handbook* (San Francisco, CA: Jossey-Bass/Pfeiffer, 2003) p. 85.

37. J.C. Hubbard, K.A. Forcht, and D.S. Thomas, "Human Resource Information Systems: An Overview of Current Ethical and Legal Issues," *Journal of Business Ethics* (September 1998), pp. 1320–1321.

38. K.A. Kovach, A.A. Hughes, P. Fagan, and P.G. Maggitti, "Administrative and Strategic Advantages of HRIS," *Employment Relations Today* (Summer 2002), p. 46.

39. J. Caplan, "eHR in Greater China: The Future of HR Takes Flight," *China Staff* (March 2004), p. 3.

40. J. Collison, "2005 HR Technology Survey Report," *SHRM Research*, pp. 3–4.

41. J. Caplan, "eHR in Greater China: The Future of HR Takes Flight," *China Staff* (March 2004), p. 2.

42. B. Jorgensen, "eHR Is Playing a Larger Role in Corporate Communications: But Companies Must Make a Business for Additional Spending," *Electronic Business* (August 2002), p. 36.

43. "Which HRIS Technologies Best Support the Vital Workplace?" *HR Focus* (February 2000), p. 6.

44. "Glossary of Distance Education Terms," www.tamu.edu/ode/glossary.html (January 8, 2007).

45. G. Downey, "Use of Self-Service HR Skyrockets," *Computing Canada* (February 1, 2002), pp. 1–2.

46. H.C. Gueutal and D.L. Stone, *The Brave New World of eHR* (San Francisco, CA: Jossey-Bass, 2005), p. 192.

47. "Do More to Get More from HR Systems," *HR Focus* (Jun 2006), p. 3.

48. P. MacInnis, "Toronto Police Services Ramps Up for Self-Serve HR," *Computing Canada* (October 11, 2002), p. 10.

49. D. Robb, "Unifying Your Enterprise with a Global HR Portal," *HRMagazine* (March 2006), p. 110.

50. "Do More to Get More from HR Systems," *HR Focus* (June 2006), pp. 1–4.

51. Ibid.

52. Industry Canada, "Strategis: Canada's Business and Consumer Site," http://strategis.ic.gc.ca (January 8, 2007).

53. H.C. Gueutal and D.L. Stone, *The Brave New World of eHR* (San Francisco, CA: Jossey-Bass, 2005), p. 200.

54. T.J. Keebler and D.W. Rhodes, "E-HR Becoming the 'Path of Least Resistance'," *Employment Relations Today* (Summer 2002), pp. 57–58.

55. D. Brown, "eHR—Victim of Unrealistic Expectations," *Canadian HR Reporter* (March 11, 2002), p. 2.

56. H.C. Gueutal and D.L. Stone, *The Brave New World of eHR* (San Francisco, CA: Jossey-Bass, 2005), p. 24; S. Greengard, "Putting It All Together," *Workforce Management* (2005), p. 9.

57. H.C. Gueutal and D.L. Stone, *The Brave New World of eHR* (San Francisco, CA: Jossey-Bass, 2005), pp. 22–53.

58. J.G. Meade, *The Human Resources Software Handbook* (San Francisco, CA: Jossey-Bass/Pfeiffer, 2003), pp. 313–332.

59. "Law Firm Moves to Paperless Human resources and Payroll with Ultimate Software's UltiPro," *PR Newswire (U.S.)* (June 7, 2006), pp. 1–2.

60. "SAP AG," www.en.wikipedia.org/wiki/SAP_(company) (June 17, 2006); SAP Canada, www.sap.com (January 8, 2007).

61. "PeopleSoft," http://en.wikipedia.org/ciki/PeopleSoft (June 17, 2006); Oracle, www.oracle.com (June 17, 2006).

62. V. Gerson, "CIBC Taps PeopleSoft HR System," *Bank Systems + Technology* (February 2002), p. 16.

63. A.R. Hendrickson, "Human Resource Information Systems: Backbone Technology of Contemporary Human Resources," *Journal of Labor Research* (Summer 2003), p. 385.

64. J.G. Meade, *The Human Resources Software Handbook* (San Francisco, CA: Jossey-Bass/Pfeiffer, 2003)pp. 353–358.

65. A.R. Hendrickson, "Human Resource Information Systems: Backbone Technology of Contemporary Human Resources," *Journal of Labor Research* (Summer 2003), pp. 381–394.

66. "What's New," *HRMagazine* (January 2005), p. 107.

67. ExecuTRACK Solutions, www.executrack.com (June 29, 2006).

68. Organizational Charts by Human Concepts, www.orgplus.com (June 29, 2006).

69. M. Morales, "Ergowatch Gives Canadian Software a Lift," *Canadian HR Reporter* (April 22, 2002), p. 27.

70. J. Schramm, "HR Technology Competencies: New Roles for HR Professionals," *2006 SHRM Research Quarterly*, p. 2.

71. W. Brockbank, "If HR Were Really Strategically Proactive: Present and Future Directions in HR's Contribution to Competitive Advantage," *Human Resource Management* (Winter 1999), p. 337.

72. J. Collison, "2005 HR Technology Survey Report," *SHRM Research*, p. vii.

73. "HRIS for the HR Professional: What You Need to Know," *HR Focus* (June 2005), pp. 10–11.

74. W. Brockbank, "If HR Were Really Strategically Proactive: Present and Future Directions in HR's Contribution to Competitive Advantage," *Human Resource Management* (Winter 1999), p. 337.

75. "HRIS in 2010 (or Sooner!): Experts Predict Use of Wrist Mounted Devised, Virtual HR Access, and HR Voice Recognition," *Managing HR Information Systems* (February 2002), pp. 1–4.

76. J. Sullivan, "The Six Levels of HRIS Technology," in R.H. Stambaugh (ed.), *21 Tomorrows: HR Systems in the Emerging Workplace of the 21st Century*, pp. 79–86 (Dallas, TX: Rector Duncan & Associates, 2000).

77. L.A. Weatherly, "HR Technology: Leveraging the Shift to Self-Service—It's Time to Go Strategic," *HRMagazine* (March 2005), p. A1.

78. S. Greengard, "Putting It All Together," *Workforce Management* (2005), p. 10.

79. "Human Resource Outsourcing Gains Traction, Says Aberdeen Group; Report Cites Growing Use of Outsourcing," *Business Wire* (January 23, 2006), p. 1.

80. J. Schramm, "HR Technology Competencies: New Roles for HR Professionals," *2006 SHRM Research Quarterly*, p. 6.

Chapter 4

1. C. Babbage, *On the Economy of Machinery and Manufacturers* (London: Charles Knight, 1832), pp. 169–76; reprinted in Joseph Litterer, *Organizations* (New York: John Wiley and Sons, 1969), pp. 73–75.

2. F. Herzberg, "One More Time, How Do You Motivate Employees?" *Harvard Business Review* 46 (January–February 1968), pp. 53–62.

3. J.R. Hackman and G. Oldham, "Motivation through the Design of Work: Test of a Theory," *Organizational Behavior and Human Performance* 16 (August 1976), pp. 250–279.

4. J.R. Hackman and G. Oldham, "Motivation through the Design of Work: Test of a Theory," *Organizational Behavior and Human Performance* 16 (August 1976), pp. 257–258.

5. D.A. Nadler, J.R. Hackman, and E.E. Lawler, *Managing Organizational Behavior* (Boston: Little, Brown, 1979).

6. J.R. Hackman and G. Oldham, "Motivation through the Design of Work: Test of a Theory," *Organizational Behavior and Human Performance* 16 (August 1976), pp. 255–256.

7. G.M. Parker, *Cross-Functional Teams: Working with Allies, Enemies and Other Strangers* (San Francisco, CA: Jossey-Bass, 2003), p. 68.

8. B. Gebor, "Saturn's Grand Experiment," *Training* (June 1992), pp. 27–35.

9. "Collaboration for Virtual Teams," *HR Professional* (December 2002/January 2003), p. 44.

10. J.A. Veitch, K.E. Charles, and G.R. Newsham, "Workstation Design for the Open-Plan Office," *Construction Technology Update*, 61 (October 2004), http://irc.nrc-cnrc.gc.ca/pubs/ctus/61_e.html (August 16, 2006).

11. For a good discussion of job analysis, see J. Clifford, "Job Analysis: Why Do It, and How Should It Be Done?" *Public Personnel Management* 23, no. 2 (Summer 1994), pp. 321–340.

12. R. I. Henderson, *Compensation Management in a Knowledge-Based World* (Upper Saddle River, NJ: Prentice-Hall, 2003), pp. 135–138. See also P.W. Wright and K. Wesley, "How to Choose the Kind of Job Analysis You Really Need," *Personnel* 62 (May 1985), pp. 51–55; C.J. Cranny and M.E. Doherty, "Importance Ratings in Job Analysis: Note on the Misinterpretation of Factor Analyses," *Journal of Applied Psychology* (May 1988), pp. 320–322.

13. Note that the PAQ (and other quantitative techniques) can also be used for job evaluation.

14. E. Cornelius III, F. Schmidt, and T. Carron, "Job Classification Approaches and the Implementation of Validity Generalization Results," *Personnel Psychology* 37 (Summer 1984), pp. 247–260; E. Cornelius III, A. DeNisi,

and A. Blencoe, "Expert and Naïve Raters Using the PAQ: Does It Matter?" *Personnel Psychology* 37 (Autumn 1984), pp. 453–464; L. Friedman and R. Harvey, "Can Raters with Reduced Job Description Information Provide Accurate Position Analysis Questionnaire (PAQ) Ratings?" *Personnel Psychology* 34 (Winter 1986), pp. 779–789; R. J. Harvey et al., "Dimensionality of the Job Element Inventory, A Simplified Worker-oriented Job Analysis Questionnaire," *Journal of Applied Psychology* (November 1988), pp. 639–646; S. Butler and R. Harvey, "A Comparison of Holistic versus Decomposed Rating of Position Analysis Questionnaire Work Dimensions," *Personnel Psychology* (Winter 1988), pp. 761–772.

15. This discussion is based on H. Olson et al., "The Use of Functional Job Analysis in Establishing Performance Standards for Heavy Equipment Operators," *Personnel Psychology* 34 (Summer 1981), pp. 351–364.

16. Human Resources Development Canada, *National Occupation Classification Career Handbook*, 2001.

17. J. Evered, "How to Write a Good Job Description," *Supervisory Management* (April 1981), pp. 14–19; R. J. Plachy, "Writing Job Descriptions That Get Results," *Personnel* (October 1987), pp. 56–58. See also M. Mariani, "Replace with a Database," *Occupational Outlook Quarterly* 43 (Spring 1999), pp. 2–9.

18. J. Evered, "How to Write a Good Job Description," *Supervisory Management* (April 1981), p. 16.

19. J. Evered, "How to Write a Good Job Description," *Supervisory Management* (April 1981), p. 18.

20. P.H. Raymark, M.J. Schmidt, and R.M. Guion, "Identifying Potentially Useful Personality Constructs for Employee Selection," *Personnel Psychology* 50 (1997), pp. 723–726.

21. All Business, "Periodical Titles by Alphabet," www.allbusiness.com/periodicals/article/617401-1.html; "Associate Professor Ram Ganeshan: Digital Technology to Enhance the Efficiency of Supply Chains," *The W&M MBA Monthly Newsletter* 2, no. 1 (January 15, 2004).

22. B. Gomolski, "New E-commerce Food Chain Breaks the Bond between Employee and Employer," *Network World Canada* (November 2000), p. 28.

23. J. Heerwagen, K. Kelly, and K. Kampschroer, "The Changing Nature of Organizations, Work, and Workplace," *Whole Building Design Group (WBDG), National Institute of Building Sciences* (February 2006), www.wbdg.org/design/chnorgwork.php (August 17, 2006).

24. W. Bridges, "The End of the Job," *Fortune* (September 19, 1994), p. 68.

Chapter 5

1. J.W. Walker, "Human Resource Planning, 1990s Style," *Human Resource Planning* 13, no. 4 (1990), pp. 229–240; D. Ulrich, "Strategic and Human Resource Planning: Linking Customers and Employees," *Human Resource Planning* 15, no. 2 (1992), pp. 47–62.

2. L. Young, "Government's Unique Incentive Plan Falls Short of Retention Mark, Nurses Contend," *Canadian HR Reporter* (March 13, 2000), p. 8.

3. U.Vu, "Aging Nurses Spell Trouble," *Canadian HR Reporter* (January 17, 2005), pp. 1–2; U. Vu, "Nursing Needs Mending: Reports," *Canadian HR Reporter* (June 6, 2005), pp. 1, 3.

4. P. Kieran, "Early Retirement Trends," *Perspectives* (Winter 2001), Statistics Canada Catalogue No. 75-001-XPE, pp. 7–13; C. Graham and S. Roy, "Early Retirement on the Bargaining Table," *Canadian HR Reporter* (January 27, 2003), p. 12.

5. J. Langton, "Accountants Offer Two Cents on Aging Workforce," *Canadian HR Reporter* (February 28, 2005).

6. G. Milkovich, A.J. Annoni, and T.A. Mahoney, "The Use of Delphi Procedures in Manpower Forecasting," *Management Science* (1972), pp. 381–388.

7. A.L. Delbecq, A.H. Van DelVen, and D.H. Gustafson, *Group Techniques for Program Planning: A Guide to Nominal and Delphi Processes* (Glenview, IL: Scott Foresman, 1975).

8. S. Klie, "Successors Only Two Years Younger Than Retiring Execs," *Canadian HR Reporter* (July 17, 2006).

9. This is a modification of a definition found in P. Wallum, "A Broader View of Succession Planning," *Personnel Management* (September 1993), pp. 43–44.

10. C. Graham and S. Roy, "Early Retirement on the Bargaining Table," *Canadian HR Reporter* (January 27, 2003), pp. 12–13.

11. J. Langton, "Accountants Offer Two Cents on Aging Workforce," *Canadian HR Reporter* (February 28, 2005).

12. S. Klie, "Business and Labour to Address Aging Workforce," *Canadian HR Reporter* (November 7, 2005).

13. G. Lowe, "Retiring Baby Boomers Open to Options, But Get Them Before They Leave," *Canadian HR Reporter* (March 10, 2003), p. 6.

14. B. Cheadle, "High-Skill Immigrants Drive Labour Force Growth but Job Prospects Still Grim," *Canadian Press Newswire* (February 11, 2003).

15. S. Klie, "Immigration Not a 'Permanent Phenomenon,'" *Canadian HR Reporter* (March 27, 2006); D. Brown, "Ottawa Asks Why Skilled Immigrants Drive Cabs," *Canadian HR Reporter* (January 31, 2005), pp. 1, 5; U. Vu, "Canada Invites Foreign Workers but Neglects Them on Arrival," *Canadian HR Reporter* (May 3, 2004), pp. 1, 3.

16. G. Nixon, "The Immigrant Imperative: Why Canada Can't Afford to Continue to Waste the Skills of Newcomers," *Canadian HR Reporter* (July 18, 2005), p. 19.

17. U. Vu, "Labour Force Growth Depends on Immigrants," *Canadian HR Reporter* (March 10, 2003), pp. 1, 3.

18. A. Coughlin, *Alberta's Labour Shortage Just the Tip of the Iceberg* (Conference Board of Canada Executive Action, 2006); G. Hodgson and G. McGowan, "Taking Sides: Is Alberta's Labour Shortage a Doomsday Scenario?" *Canadian HR Reporter* (July 17, 2006); P. Brethour, "Oil Patch Labour Crisis Seen Spreading to Rest of Country; Husky Head Raises Alarm Over Rising Costs, Saying Projects at Risk," *Globe and Mail* (April 20, 2006).

19. U. Vu, "Trades Tackle Image Problem," *Canadian HR Reporter* (October 11, 2004), pp. 1, 4; "Colleges Warn of Skilled Worker Shortage," *Toronto Star* (February 20, 2006), p. A12.

20. H. Sokoloff, "Legal Exodus," *National Post* (March 17, 2005), p. FP3; "Baby Boomers an HR Problem for Funeral Services," *Canadian HR Reporter* (January 16, 2006), p. 2; "Today's Forecast: Meteorologist Shortage," *Canadian HR Reporter* (December 5, 2005), p. 2; "Engineers in Short Supply," *Canadian HR Reporter* (November 21, 2005), p. 2; S. Klie, "Fewer Accountants Is a Bad Thing—Really," *Canadian HR Reporter* (February 13, 2006), p. 3; "Alberta Labour Shortage Draining Civil Service," *Canadian HR Reporter* (January 30, 2006), p. 2.

21. O. Parker, *Too Few People, Too Little Time: The Employer Challenge of an Aging Workforce* (Conference Board of Canada Executive Action, July 2006).

22. M. MacKillop, "Ballpark Justice," *Human Resources Professional* (September 1994), pp. 10–11.

23. W.F. Cascio and C.E. Young, "Financial Consequences of Employment Change Decisions in Major U.S. Corporations: 1982–2000," in K.P. DeMeuse and M.L. Marks (eds.), *Resizing the Organization*, pp. 131–156 (San Francisco, CA: Jossey-Bass, 2003).

24. O. Parker, *Too Few People, Too Little Time: The Employer Challenge of an Aging Workforce* (Conference Board of Canada Executive Action, July 2006).

25. *Labour Shortages of 1 Million Workers by 2016*, Watson Wyatt, 2006, www.watsonwyatt.com (August 10, 2006).

26. D. Brown, "Training Older Workers Can Offset Shortages Due to Aging: Report," *Canadian HR Reporter* (September 13, 2004), pp. 3, 13; M. Potter, "A Golden Opportunity: Older Workers Step Up to the Plate," *WorldatWork Canadian News* (Third Quarter 2005), pp. 8–11; V. Galt, "Firms See Value in Putting Retirees Back to Work," *Globe & Mail* (September 8, 2004), p. B7; G. Lowe, "Are You Ready to Tap Older Workers' Talents?" *Canadian HR Reporter* (February 27, 2006); S. Klie, "Poor Health Thinning Ranks of Older Workers," *Canadian HR Reporter* (March 27, 2006).

27. S. Klie, "Cities Face Off over Talent," *Canadian HR Reporter* (February 13, 2006), pp. 1, 4; S. Klie, "Nunavut Trade School Will Tackle Labour Shortage," *Canadian HR Reporter* (April 24, 2006); "B.C. Sets Aside $400

Million for Training and Skills," *Canadian HR Reporter* (March 13, 2006), p. 2; K. Howlett, "Ontario Expands College Apprentice Programs," *Globe & Mail* (August 27, 2005), p. A9.

28. G. Lowe, "Are You Ready to Tap Older Workers' Talents?" *Canadian HR Reporter* (February 27, 2006).

29. H. Sokoloff, "Legal Exodus," *National Post* (March 17, 2005), p. FP3; S. Klie, "Work-Life Balance Elusive for Most Lawyers," *Canadian HR Reporter* (January 16, 2006), pp. 1, 3.

30. "Work Pressure Is Top Cause of Stress," *Workplace Today* (January 2001), p. 6.

31. L. Duxbury, *Dealing with Work-Life Issues in the Workplace: Standing Still Is Not an Option*, 2004, Don Wood Lecture in Industrial Relations, Industrial Relations Centre, Queen's University.

32. B. Parus, "Pump Up Your Flexibility Quotient," *Workspan* (August 2004), pp. 47–53; J.T. Bond, E. Galinsky, and E.J. Hill, "Flexibility: A Critical Ingredient in Creating an Effective Workplace," *Workspan* (February 2005), pp. 17–20; F. Giancola, "Flexible Schedules: A Win-Win Reward, *Workspan* (July 2005), pp. 52–54.

33. P. Kulig, "Flextime Increasing in Popularity With Employers," *Canadian HR Reporter* (September 7, 1998), pp. 1, 3.

34. L. Cassiani, "Women Consider Leaving for Better Work-Life Balance," *Canadian HR Reporter* (August 13, 2001), pp. 1, 14.

35. S. Singh, "When the Going Gets Tough, the Tough Hold on to Top Employees," *Canadian HR Reporter* (January 13, 2003), p. 17.

36. M. Madigan, J. Norton, and I. Testa, "The Quest for Work–Life Balance," *Benefits Canada* (November 1999), p. 113.

37. N. Verma, "Making the Most of Virtual Working," *WorldatWork Journal* (Second Quarter 2005), pp. 15–23.

38. D. Brown, "Telework Not Meeting Expectations—But Expectations Were 'Nonsense,'" *Canadian HR Reporter* (February 24, 2003), pp. 3, 11.

39. B. Aldrige, "Innovative Workplace Practices," *Workplace Gazette* (May 15, 2006), www.hrsdc.gc.ca/en/lp/wid/win/2006_1st_quarter.shtml (May 5, 2006).

Chapter 6

1. "Effective Recruiting Tied to Stronger Financial Performance," *WorldatWork Canadian News* (Fourth Quarter 2005), pp. 18–19.

2. "Recruitment Tops HR Areas Expecting 'Enormous Change,'" *Canadian HR Reporter* (December 6, 2004), p. G3; *Hewitt Associates Timely Topic Survey* (February 2004).

3. D. Dahl and P. Pinto, "Job Posting, an Industry Survey," *Personnel Journal* (January 1977), pp. 40–41.

4. J. Daum, "Internal Promotion—Psychological Asset or Debit? A Study of the Effects of Leader Origin," *Organizational Behavior and Human Performance* 13 (1975), pp. 404–413.

5. See, for example, A. Harris, "Hiring Middle Management: External Recruitment or Internal Promotion?" *Canadian HR Reporter* (April 10, 2000), pp. 8–10.

6. "Canadian Web Recruiting Lags behind Americans," *Workplace Today* (June 2001), p. 5.

7. "CareerBuilder.com Launches CareerBuilder.ca, Enters Strategic Alliance with AOL Canada," *Click Weekly*, 80 (May 2006), www.dmn.ca/Click/articles/vol80/vol80_c.htm (August 9, 2006). See also T. Humber, "CanWest Launches New Job Board," *Canadian HR Reporter* (December 6, 2004), p. G7.

8. Y. Lermusiaux, "Recruiting Effectively over the Internet," *Canadian HR Reporter* (April 5, 1999), p. 2.

9. U. Vu, "Security Failures Expose Resumes," *Canadian HR Reporter* (May 24, 2003); P. Lima, "Talent Shortage? That Was Yesterday. Online Recruiters Can Deliver More Candidates for Your Job Openings and Help You Find Keepers," *Profit: The Magazine for Canadian Entrepreneurs* (February/March 2002), pp. 65–66; "Online Job Boards," *Canadian HR Reporter* (February 11, 2002), pp. G11–G15.

10. U. Vu, "Security Failures Expose Resumes," *Canadian HR Reporter* (May 24, 2003).

11. G. Stanton, "Recruiting Portals Take Centre Stage in Play for Talent," *Canadian HR Reporter* (September 25, 2000), pp. G1–G2.

12. A. Altass, "E-Cruiting: A Gen X Trend or Wave of the Future?" *HR Professional* (June–July 2000), p. 29.

13. D. Brown, "Canadian Government Job Boards Lag on Best Practices," *Canadian HR Reporter* (January 13, 2003), p. 2.

14. T. Martell, "Resume Volumes Push Firms to Web," *ComputerWorld Canada* (April 7, 2000), p. 45.

15. A. Altass, "E-Cruiting: A Gen X Trend or Wave of the Future?" *HR Professional* (June–July 2000), p. 33.

16. Ibid., p. 29.

17. "Corporate Spending Millions on Ineffective Web Recruiting Strategies," *Canadian HR Reporter* (September 25, 2000), p. G5.

18. A. Snell, "Best Practices for Web Site Recruiting," *Canadian HR Reporter* (February 26, 2001), pp. G7, G10.

19. D. Brown, "Who's Looking Online? Most Firms Don't Know," *Canadian HR Reporter* (August 13, 2001), pp. 2, 12; "Corporate Spending Millions on Ineffective Web Recruiting Strategies," *Canadian HR Reporter* (September 25, 2000), p. G5; A. Snell, "Best Practices for Web Site Recruiting," *Canadian HR Reporter* (February 26, 2001), pp. G7, G10.

20. D. Lu-Hovasse, "Headhunters: Doomed by the Mouse?" *Financial Post* (February 19, 2001), p. E4.

21. L. Barrington and J. Shelp, "Looking for Employees in *All* the Right Places," *The Conference Board Executive Action Series* (December 2005).

22. A. Pell, *Recruiting and Selecting Personnel* (New York: Regents, 1969), pp. 16–34.

23. Statistics Canada, *The Daily* (April 8, 2005); Association of Canadian Search, Employment and Staffing Services (ACSESS), "Media Kit: Media Fact Sheet," www.acsess.org/NEWS/factsheet.asp (August 9, 2006).

24. J.A. Parr, "7 Reasons Why Executive Searches Fail," *Canadian HR Reporter* (March 12, 2001), pp. 20, 23.

25. Association of Canadian Search, Employment and Staffing Services (ACSESS), www.acsess.org (August 8, 2006).

26. A. Doran, "Technology Brings HR to Those Who Need It," *Canadian HR Reporter* (October 6, 1997), p. 8.

27. U. Vu, "EnCana Builds Talent Pipeline into High School Classrooms," *Canadian HR Reporter* (April 11, 2005), p. 3.

28. Halifax Career Fair, www.halifaxcareerfair.ns.ca (June 23, 2006).

29. Career Edge, www.careeredge.ca (August 9, 2006).

30. N. Laurie and M. Laurie, "No Holds Barred in Fight for Students to Fill Internship Programs," *Canadian HR Reporter* (January 17, 2000), pp. 15–16.

31. Service Canada, Job Bank, http://srv601.hrdc-drhc.gc.ca/JobMatching/common/login.aspx (August 5, 2006).

32. Human Resources Professionals Association of Ontario, www.hrpao.org (June 25, 2003).

33. D. Hurl, "Letting the Armed Forces Train Your Managers," *Canadian HR Reporter* (December 3, 2001), pp. 8–9.

34. L. MacGillivray, "Cashing in on the Canadian Forces," *Workplace Today* (October 2001), pp. 40–41.

35. I.D.D. Livermore, "Award and Recognition Await Supportive Employers and Educational Institutions," *Alliance: Employer Support for the Reserve Force*, 2nd Issue (2004).

36. T. Lende, "Workplaces Looking to Hire Part-Timers," *Canadian HR Reporter* (April 22, 2002), pp. 9, 11.

37. K. LeMessurier, "Temp Staffing Leaves a Permanent Mark," *Canadian HR Reporter* (February 10, 2003), pp. 3, 8.

38. J. Pearce, "Toward an Organizational Behavior of Contract Laborers: Their Psychological Involvement and Effects on Employee Co-Workers," *Academy of Management Journal* 36 (1993), pp. 1082–1096. See also A. Ryckman, "The 5 Keys to Getting Top Value from Contractors," *Canadian HR Reporter*

(December 2, 2002), p. 25; S. Purba, "Contracting Works for Job Hunters," *Globe & Mail* (April 24, 2002).

39. "Flexible Staffing in the Aerospace Industry," *Airfinance Journal I Aircraft Economic Yearbook* (2001), pp. 14–17.

40. "Outsourcing HR," *Industry Week* (May 15, 2000), p. 10.

41. M. Potter, "A Golden Opportunity for Older Workers to Energize Firms," *Canadian HR Reporter* (April 25, 2005), p. 13.

42. E. Miller, "Capitalizing on Older Workers," *Canadian HR Reporter* (June 16, 1997), p. 14. See also L. Cassiani, "Looming Retirement Surge Takes on New Urgency," *Canadian HR Reporter* (May 21, 2001), pp. 1, 10.

43. O. Parker, *Too Few People, Too Little Time: The Employer Challenge of an Aging Workforce* (Ottawa: The Conference Board of Canada Executive Action, July 2006).

44. S.B. Hood, "Generational Diversity in the Workplace," *HR Professional* (June/July 2000), p. 20.

45. G. Kovary and A. Buahene, "Recruiting the Four Generations," *Canadian HR Reporter* (May 23, 2005), p. R6.

46. Inclusion Network, www.inclusionnetwork.ca, and Aboriginal Human Resources Development Council of Canada, www.ahrdcc.com (August 8, 2006).

47. WORKInk, www.workink.com (August 8, 2006).

48. Society for Canadian Women in Science and Technology, www.harbour.sfu.ca/scwist/index_files/Page1897.htm (August 9, 2006); C. Emerson, H. Matsui, and L. Michael, "Progress Slow for Women in Trades, Tech, Science," *Canadian HR Reporter* (February 14, 2005), p. 11.

49. H.N. Chait, S.M. Carraher, and M.R. Buckley, "Measuring Service Orientation with Biodata," *Journal of Management Issues* (Spring 2000), pp. 109–120; V.M. Catano, S.F. Cronshaw, R.D. Hackett, L.L. Methot, and W.H. Weisner, *Recruitment and Selection in Canada*, 2nd ed. (Scarborough, ON: Nelson Thomson Learning, 2001), p. 307; J.E. Harvey-Cook and R.J. Taffler, "Biodata in Professional Entry-Level Selection: Statistical Scoring of Common-Format Applications," *Journal of Occupational and Organizational Psychology* (March 1, 2000), pp. 103–118; Y.Y. Chung, "The Validity of Biographical Inventories for the Selection of Salespeople," *International Journal of Management* (September 2001).

Chapter 7

1. D. Brown, "Waterloo Forced to Fire Top Bureaucrat Weeks after Hiring," *Canadian HR Reporter* (October 11, 2004), p. 3.

2. British Columbia Criminal Records Review Act; www.pssg.gov.bc.ca/criminal-records-review/index.htm (June 27, 2003).

3. C. Kapel, "Giant Steps," *Human Resources Professional* (April 1993), pp. 13–16.

4. S.A. Way and J.W. Thacker, "Selection Practices: Where Are Canadian Organizations?" *HR Professional* (October/November 1999), p. 34.

5. L.J. Katunich, "How to Avoid the Pitfalls of Psych Tests," *Workplace News Online* (July 2005), p. 5; *Testing and Assessment—FAQ/Finding Information About Psychological Tests*, APA Online, www.apa.org/science/faq-findtests.html (August 1, 2006).

6. M. McDaniel et al., "The Validity of Employment Interviews: A Comprehensive Review and Meta-analysis," *Journal of Applied Psychology* 79, no. 4 (1994).

7. Canadian Psychological Association, *Guidelines for Educational and Psychological Testing*, www.cpa.ca/documents/PsyTest.html (August 1, 2006).

8. "Emotional Intelligence Testing," *HR Focus* (October 2001), pp. 8–9.

9. Results of meta-analyses in one recent study indicated that isometric strength tests were valid predictors of both supervisory ratings of physical performance and performance on work simulations. See B.R. Blakley, M. Quinones, M.S. Crawford, and I.A. Jago, "The Validity of Isometric Strength Tests," *Personnel Psychology* 47 (1994), pp. 247–274. See also B. Daniel, "Strength and Endurance Testing," *Personnel Journal* (June 1987), pp. 112–122.

10. C. Colacci, "Testing Helps You Decrease Disability Costs," *Canadian HR Reporter* (June 14, 1999), p. G4.

11. K. Gillin, "Reduce Employee Exposure to Injury with Pre-Employment Screening Tests," *Canadian HR Reporter* (February 28, 2000), p. 10.

12. This approach calls for construct validation, which, as was pointed out, is extremely difficult to demonstrate.

13. Myers-Briggs Type Indicator (MBTI) Assessment, www.cpp.com/products/mbti/index.asp (August 1, 2006).

14. See, for example, D. Cellar et al., "Comparison of Factor Structures and Criterion Related Validity Coefficients for Two Measures of Personality Based on the Five-Factor Model," *Journal of Applied Psychology* 81, no. 6 (1996), pp. 694–704; J. Salgado, "The Five Factor Model of Personality and Job Performance in the European Community," *Journal of Applied Psychology* 82, no. 1 (1997), pp. 30–43.

15. M.R. Barrick and M.K. Mount, "The Big Five Personality Dimensions and Job Performance: A Meta-Analysis," *Personnel Psychology* 44, (Spring 1991), pp. 1–26.

16. T. Judge, J. Martocchio, and C. Thorensen, "Five-Factor Model of Personality and Employee Absence," *Journal of Applied Psychology* 82 (1997), pp. 745–755.

17. E. Silver and C. Bennett, "Modification of the Minnesota Clerical Test to Predict Performance on Video Display Terminals," *Journal of Applied Psychology* 72, no. 1 (February 1987), pp. 153–155.

18. L. Siegel and I. Lane, *Personnel and Organizational Psychology* (Homewood, IL: Irwin, 1982), pp. 182–183.

19. J. Weekley and C. Jones, "Video-Based Situational Testing," *Personnel Psychology* 50 (1997), p. 25.

20. Ibid, pp. 26–30.

21. D. Chan and N. Schmitt, "Situational Judgment and Job Performance," *Human Performance* 15, no. 3 (2002), pp. 233–254.

22. S. Klie, "Screening Gets More Secure," *Canadian HR Reporter* (June 19, 2006).

23. Canadian Human Rights Commission, *Canadian Human Rights Commission Policy on Alcohol and Drug Testing* (June 2002).

24. M. McDaniel et al., "The Validity of Employment Interviews: A Comprehensive Review and Meta-analysis," *Journal of Applied Psychology* 79, no. 4 (1994), p. 599.

25. J.G. Goodale, *The Fine Art of Interviewing* (Englewood Cliffs, NJ: Prentice Hall Inc., 1982), p. 22. See also R.L. Decker, "The Employment Interview," *Personnel Administrator* 26 (November 1981), pp. 71–73.

26. M. Campion, E. Pursell, and B. Brown, "Structured Interviewing: Raising the Psychometric Properties of the Employment Interview," *Personnel Psychology* 41 (1988), pp. 25–42.

27. M. McDaniel et al., "The Validity of Employment Interviews: A Comprehensive Review and Meta-analysis," *Journal of Applied Psychology* 79, no. 4 (1994).

28. D.S. Chapman and P.M. Rowe, "The Impact of Video Conferencing Technology, Interview Structure, and Interviewer Gender on Interviewer Evaluations in the Employment Interview: A Field Experiment," *Journal of Occupational and Organizational Psychology*, 74 (September 2001), pp. 279–298.

29. M. McDaniel et al., "The Validity of Employment Interviews: A Comprehensive Review and Meta-analysis," *Journal of Applied Psychology* 79, no. 4 (1994), p. 601.

30. Ibid.

31. A. Pell, *Recruiting and Selecting Personnel* (New York: Regents, 1969), p. 119.

32. J.G. Goodale, *The Fine Art of Interviewing* (Englewood Cliffs, NJ: Prentice Hall Inc., 1982), p. 26.

33. See R.D. Arvey and J.E. Campion, "The Employment Interview: A Summary and Review of Recent Research," *Personnel Psychology* 35 (1982), pp. 281–322; M. Heilmann and L. Saruwatari, "When Beauty Is Beastly: The Effects of Appearance and Sex on Evaluation of Job Applicants for

Managerial and Nonmanagerial Jobs," *Organizational Behavior and Human Performance* 23 (June 1979), pp. 360–722; C. Marlowe, S. Schneider, and C. Nelson, "Gender and Attractiveness Biases in Hiring Decisions: Are More Experienced Managers Less Biased?" *Journal of Applied Psychology* 81, no. 1 (1996), pp. 11–21; V. Galt, "Beauty Found Not Beastly in the Job Interview," *Globe & Mail* (April 15, 2002).

34. A. Pell, "Nine Interviewing Pitfalls," *Managers* (January 1994), p. 29; T. Dougherty, D. Turban, and J. Callender, "Confirming First Impressions in the Employment Interview: A Field Study of Interviewer Behavior," *Journal of Applied Psychology* 79, no. 5 (1994), p. 663.

35. See A. Pell, "Nine Interviewing Pitfalls," *Managers* (January 1994), p. 29; P. Sarathi, "Making Selection Interviews Effective," *Management and Labor Studies* 18, no. 1 (1993), pp. 5–7; J. Shetcliffe, "Who, and How, to Employ," *Insurance Brokers' Monthly* (December 2002), pp. 14–16.

36. G.J. Sears and P.M. Rowe, "A Personality-Based Similar-to-Me Effect in the Employment Interview: Conscientious, Affect-versus-Competence Mediated Interpretations, and the Role of Job Relevance," *Canadian Journal of Behavioural Sciences* 35 (January 2003), p. 13.

37. This section is based on E.D. Pursell, M.A. Campion, and S.R. Gaylord, "Structured Interviewing: Avoiding Selection Problems," *Personnel Journal* 59 (1980), pp. 907–912; G.P. Latham, L.M. Saari, E.D. Pursell, and M.A. Campion, "The Situational Interview," *Journal of Applied Psychology* 65 (1980), pp. 422–427. See also M. Campion, E. Pursell, and B. Brown, "Structured Interviewing: Raising the Psychometric Properties of the Employment Interview," *Personnel Psychology* 41 (1988), pp. 25–42, and J.A. Weekley and J.A. Gier, "Reliability and Validity of the Situational Interview for a Sales Position," *Journal of Applied Psychology* 72 (1987), pp. 484–487, except as noted.

38. P. Lowry, "The Structured Interview: An Alternative to the Assessment Center?" *Public Personnel Management* 23, no. 2 (Summer 1994), pp. 201–215.

39. Steps two and three are based on the Kepner-Tregoe Decision-Making Model.

40. A. Pell, *Recruiting and Selecting Personnel* (New York: Regents, 1969), pp. 103–115.

41. W.H. Wiesner and R.J. Oppenheimer, "Note-Taking in the Selection Interview: Its Effect upon Predictive Validity and Information Recall," *Proceedings of the Annual Conference Meeting. Administrative Sciences Association of Canada* (Personnel and Human Resources Division, 1991), pp. 97–106.

42. V. Tsang, "No More Excuses," *Canadian HR Reporter* (May 23, 2005); L.T. Cullen, "Getting Wise to Lies," *TIME* (May 1, 2006), p. 27.

43. L. Fischer, "Gatekeeper," *Workplace News* (August 2005), pp. 10–11.

44. Ibid.

45. T. Humber, "Recruitment Isn't Getting Any Easier," *Canadian HR Reporter* (May 23, 2005).

46. M. Stamler, "Employment Gaps, References Should be Scrutinized," *Canadian HR Reporter* (April 8, 1996), pp. 11, 15. See also P. Israel, "Providing References to Employees: Should You or Shouldn't You?" *Canadian HR Reporter* (March 24, 2003), pp. 5–6; T. Humber, "Name, Rank and Serial Number," *Canadian HR Reporter* (May 19, 2003), pp. G1, G7.

47. J.A. Breaugh, "Realistic Job Previews: A Critical Appraisal and Future Research Directions," *Academy of Management Review* 8, no. 4 (1983), pp. 612–619.

48. P. Buhler, "Managing in the '90s: Hiring the Right Person for the Job," *Supervision* (July 1992), pp. 21–23; S. Jackson, "Realistic Job Previews Help Screen Applicants and Reduce Turnover," *Canadian HR Reporter* (August 9, 1999), p. 10.

49. S. Jackson, "Realistic Job Previews Help Screen Applicants and Reduce Turnover," *Canadian HR Reporter* (August 9, 1999), p. 10.

50. B. Kleinmutz, "Why We Still Use Our Heads Instead of Formulas: Toward an Integrative Approach," *Psychological Bulletin* 107 (1990), pp. 296–310.

Chapter 8

1. B.W. Pascal, "The Orientation Wars," *Workplace Today* (October 2001), p. 4.

2. L. Shelat, "First Impressions Matter—A Lot," *Canadian HR Reporter* (May 3, 2004), pp. 11, 13.

3. For a recent discussion of socialization see, for example, G. Chao et al., "Organizational Socialization: Its Content and Consequences," *Journal of Applied Psychology* 79, no. 5 (1994), pp. 730–743.

4. S. Jackson, "After All That Work in Hiring, Don't Let New Employees Dangle," *Canadian HR Reporter* (May 19, 1997), p. 13.

5. B. Pomfret, "Sound Employee Orientation Program Boosts Productivity and Safety," *Canadian HR Reporter* (January 25, 1999), pp. 17–19.

6. A. Macaulay, "The Long and Winding Road," *Canadian HR Reporter* (November 16, 1998), pp. G1–G10.

7. R. Biswas, "Employee Orientation: Your Best Weapon in the Fight for Skilled Talent," *Human Resources Professional* (August/September 1998), pp. 41–42.

8. A. Macaulay, "The Long and Winding Road," *Canadian HR Reporter* (November 16, 1998), p. G1.

9. D. Barnes, "Learning Is Key to Post-merger Success," *Canadian HR Reporter* (July 12, 1999), pp. 16–17.

10. C. Gibson, "Online Orientation: Extending a Welcoming Hand to New Employees," *Canadian HR Reporter* (November 30, 1998), pp. 22–23.

11. D. Brown, "Execs Need Help Learning the Ropes Too," *Canadian HR Reporter* (April 22, 2002), p. 2.

12. Ibid.

13. "The Critical Importance of Executive Integration," *Drake Business Review* (December 2002), pp. 6–8.

14. S. Mingail, "Employers Need a Lesson in Training," *Canadian HR Reporter* (February 11, 2002), pp. 22–23.

15. U. Vu, "Trainers Mature into Business Partners," *Canadian HR Reporter* (July 12, 2004), pp. 1–2.

16. S. Klie, "Training Isn't Always the Answer," *Canadian HR Reporter* (December 5, 2005), pp. 13–14.

17. V. Galt, "Training Falls Short: Study," *Globe & Mail* (July 9, 2001), p. M1.

18. *Knowledge Matters: Skills and Learning for Canadians* (Government of Canada, 2002), p. 3, www11.sdc.gc.ca/sl-ca/doc/summary.shtml (June 7, 2006).

19. A. Tomlinson, "More Training Critical in Manufacturing," *Canadian HR Reporter* (November 4, 2002), p. 2.

20. D. Brown, "PM Calls for Business to Spend More on Training," *Canadian HR Reporter* (December 16, 2002), pp. 1, 11; D. Brown, "Budget Should Include More for Training: Critics," *Canadian HR Reporter* (March 10, 2003), pp. 1–2; D. Brown, "Legislated Training, Questionable Results," *Canadian HR Reporter* (May 6, 2002), pp. 1, 12.

21. N.L. Trainor, "Employee Development the Key to Talent Attraction and Retention," *Canadian HR Reporter* (November 1, 1999), p. 8.

22. Industry Canada, *Canadian Training Solutions*, http://strategis.ic.gc.ca/epic/internet/incts-scf.nsf/en/s100019e.html (June 13, 2006).

23. D. LaMarche-Bisson, "There's More than One Way to Learn," *Canadian HR Reporter* (November 18, 2003), p. 7.

24. M. Belcourt, P.C. Wright, and A.M. Saks, *Managing Performance Through Training and Development*, 2nd ed. (Toronto: Nelson Thomson Learning, 2000). See also A.M. Saks and R.R. Haccoun, "Easing the Transfer of Training," *Human Resources Professional* (July–August 1996), pp. 8–11.

25. J.A. Colquitt, J.A. LePine, and R.A. Noe, "Toward an Integrative Theory of Training Motivation: A Meta-analytic Path Analysis of 20 Years of Research," *Journal of Applied Psychology* 85 (2000), pp. 678–707.

26. K.A. Smith-Jentsch et al., "Can Pre-Training Experiences Explain Individual Differences in Learning?" *Journal of Applied Psychology* 81, no. 1 (1986), pp. 100–116.

27. J.A. Cannon-Bowers et al., "A Framework for Understanding Pre-Practice Conditions and Their Impact on Learning," *Personnel Psychology* 51 (1988), pp. 291–320.

28. This is based on K. Wexley and G. Latham, *Developing and Training Human Resources in Organizations* (Glenview, IL: Scott, Foresman, 1981), pp. 22–27.

29. K. Sovereign, *Personnel Law* (Englewood Cliffs, NJ: Prentice Hall, Inc., 1994), pp. 165–166.

30. B.M. Bass and J.A. Vaughan, "Assessing Training Needs," in C. Schneier and R. Beatty, *Personnel Administration Today,* p. 311 (Reading, MA: Addison-Wesley, 1978). See also R. Ash and E. Leving, "Job Applicant Training and Work Experience Evaluation: An Empirical Comparison of Four Methods," *Journal of Applied Psychology* 70, no. 3 (1985), pp. 572–576; J. Lawrie, "Break the Training Ritual," *Personnel Journal* 67, no. 4 (April 1988), pp. 95–77; T. Lewis and D. Bjorkquist, "Needs Assessment—A Critical Reappraisal," *Performance Improvement Quarterly* 5, no. 4 (1992), pp. 33–54.

31. See, for example, G. Freeman, "Human Resources Planning—Training Needs Analysis," *Human Resources Planning* 39, no. 3 (Fall 1993), pp. 32–34.

32. J.C. Georges, "The Hard Realities of Soft Skills Training," *Personnel Journal* 68, no. 4 (April 1989), pp. 40–45; R.H. Buckham, "Applying Role Analysis in the Workplace," *Personnel* 64, no. 2 (February 1987), pp. 63–55; J.K. Ford and R. Noe, "Self-Assessed Training Needs: The Effects of Attitudes towards Training, Management Level, and Function," *Personnel Psychology* 40, no. 1 (Spring 1987), pp. 39–54.

33. K. Wexley and G. Latham, *Developing and Training Human Resources in Organizations* (Glenview, IL: Scott, Foresman, 1981), p. 107.

34. "German Training Model Imported," *BNA Bulletin to Management* (December 19, 1996), p. 408; L. Burton, "Apprenticeship: The Learn While You Earn Option," *Human Resources Professional* (February/March 1998), p. 25; H. Frazis, D.E. Herz, and M.W. Harrigan, "Employer-Provided Training: Results from a New Survey," *Monthly Labor Review*, 118 (1995), pp. 3–17.

35. "New Funding for Apprenticeships," *Canadian HR Reporter* (May 3, 2004), p. 2; "Ontario Boosts Apprenticeship Program with $37 Million Investment," *Canadian HR Reporter* (April 7, 2000); ThinkTrades (Alberta Aboriginal Apprenticeship Project) www.thinktrades.com/candidates.htm (June 13, 2006).

36. N. Day, "Informal Learning Gets Results," *Workforce* (June 1998), p. 31.

37. M. Emery and M. Schubert, "A Trainer's Guide to Videoconferencing," *Training* (June 1993), p. 60.

38. G.N. Nash, J.P. Muczyk, and F.L. Vettori, "The Role and Practical Effectiveness of Programmed Instruction," *Personnel Psychology* 24 (1971), pp. 397–418.

39. K. Wexley and G. Latham, *Developing and Training Human Resources in Organizations* (Glenview, IL: Scott, Foresman, 1981), p. 141. See also R. Wlozkowski, "Simulation," *Training and Development Journal* 39, no. 6 (June 1985), pp. 38–43.

40. "Pros and Cons of E-learning," *Canadian HR Reporter* (July 16, 2001), pp. 11, 15; D. Murray, *E-learning for the Workplace* (Ottawa: Conference Board of Canada, 2001). See also M. Rueda, "How to Make E-Learning Work for Your Company," *Workspan* (December 2002), pp. 50–53; U. Vu, "Technology-Based Learning Comes of Age," *Canadian HR Reporter* (April 21, 2003), pp. 3, 17.

41. S. Mingail, "Good e-Learning Built on Good Instructional Design," *Canadian HR Reporter* (March 22, 2004), p. 12.

42. S. Carliner, M. Ally, N. Zhao, L. Bairstow, S. Khoury, and L. Johnston, *A Review of the State of the Field of Workplace Learning: What We Need to Know About Competencies, Diversity, E-Learning, and Human Performance Impact* (Canadian Society for Training and Development, 2006).

43. See, for example, T. Falconer, "No More Pencils, No More Books!" *Canadian Banker* (March/April 1994), pp. 21–25.

44. W. Powell, "Like Life?" *Training & Development* (February 2002), pp. 32–38. See also A. Macaulay, "Reality-Based Computer Simulations Allow Staff to Grow through Failure," *Canadian HR Reporter* (October 23, 2000), pp. 11–12.

45. A. Czarnecki, "Interactive Learning Makes Big Dent in Time, Money Requirements for T&D," *Canadian HR Reporter* (November 18, 1996), pp. L30–L31.

46. L. Young "Self-Directed Computer-Based Training That Works," *Canadian HR Reporter* (April 24, 2000), pp. 7–8.

47. F. Manning, "The Misuse of Technology in Workplace Learning," *Canadian HR Reporter* (April 24, 2000), pp. 7, 10; T. Purcell, "Training Anytime, Anywhere," *Canadian HR Reporter* (July 16, 2001), pp. 11, 15; L. Cassini, "Student Participation Thrives in Online Learning Environments," *Canadian HR Reporter* (May 2, 2001), p. 2.

48. O. Diss, "Deploying a New E-Learning Program?" *HR Professional* (October–November 2005), p. 16.

49. P. Weaver, "Preventing E-Learning Failure," *Training & Development* (August 2002), pp. 45–50; K. Oakes, "E-Learning," *Training & Development* (March 2002), pp. 73–75. See also P. Harris, "E-Learning: A Consolidation Update," *Training & Development* (April 2002), pp. 27–33; C.R. Taylor, "The Second Wave," *Training & Development* (October 2002), pp. 24–31; E. Wareham, "The Educated Buyer," *Computing Canada* (February 18, 2000), p. 33; A. Tomlinson, "E-Learning Won't Solve All Problems," *Canadian HR Reporter* (April 8, 2002), pp. 1, 6.

50. P. Weaver, "Preventing E-Learning Failure," *Training & Development* (August 2002), pp. 45–50.

51. M. Belcourt, P.C. Wright, and A.M. Saks, *Managing Performance through Training and Development*, 2nd ed. (Toronto: Nelson Thomson Learning, 2002), pp. 188–202.

52. Ibid, p. 9.

53. D. Kirkpatrick, "Effective Supervisory Training and Development," Part 3, "Outside Programs," *Personnel* 62, no. 2 (February 1985), pp. 39–42. Among the reasons training might not pay off on the job are a mismatching of courses and trainees' needs, supervisory slip-ups (with supervisors signing up trainees and then forgetting to have them attend the sessions when the training session is actually given), and lack of help in applying skills on the job.

54. N.L. Trainor, "Evaluating Training's Four Levels," *Canadian HR Reporter* (January 13, 1997), p. 10.

55. C. Knight, "Awards for Literacy Announced," *Canadian HR Reporter* (December 29, 1997), p. 10.

56. S. Coulombe, J-F Tremblay, and S. Marchand, *International Adult Literacy Study: Literacy Scores, Human Capital and Growth Across 14 OECD Countries*, Statistics Canada, Catalogue No. 89-552-MIE, 2004; S. Mingal, "Tackling Workplace Literacy a No-Brainer," *Canadian HR Reporter* (November 22, 2004), pp. G3, G10; D. Brown, "Poor Reading, Math Skills a Drag on Productivity, Performance," *Canadian HR Reporter* (February 28, 2005), pp. 1, 10.

57. K. Wolfe, "Language Training for the Workplace," *Canadian HR Reporter* (June 6, 2005), pp. 1, 13.

58. B. Siu, "Cross-Cultural Training and Customer Relations: What Every Manager Should Know," *Canadian HR Reporter* (November 15, 1999), pp. G3, G15.

59. D. Roberts and B. Tsang, "Diversity Management Training Helps Firms Hone Competitive Edge," *Canadian HR Reporter* (June 19, 1995), pp. 17–18.

60. Handidactis, www.handidactis.com (July 18, 2006).

61. L. Young, "Retail Sector Seeks to Upgrade Education, Training to Solve Human Resource Woes," *Canadian HR Reporter* (February 8, 1999), p. 11. See also B. Nagle, "Superior Retail Training Blends Customer Service, Product Knowledge," *Canadian HR Reporter* (July 15, 2002), pp. 7–8; D. Brown, "Is Retail Ready to Buy Training?" *Canadian HR Reporter* (July 15, 2002), pp. 7–8.

62. Canadian Retail Institute, www.retaileducation.ca/cms/sitem.cfm/ certification_&_training (July 19, 2006).

63. This is based on J. Laabs, "Team Training Goes Outdoors," *Personnel Journal* (June 1991), pp. 56–63. See also S. Caudron, "Teamwork Takes Work," *Personnel Journal* 73, no. 2 (February 1994), pp. 41–49.

64. A. Tomlinson, "A Dose of Training for Ailing First-Time Managers," *Canadian HR Reporter* (December 3, 2001), pp. 7, 10.

65. L.C. McDermott, "Developing the New Young Managers," *Training & Development* (October 2001), pp. 42–48; A. Tomlinson, "A Dose of Training for Ailing First-Time Managers," *Canadian HR Reporter* (December 3, 2001), pp. 7, 10.

66. S. Odenwald, "A Guide for Global Training," *Training & Development* (July 1993), pp. 22–31.

67. R. Rosen and P. Digh, "Developing Globally Literate Leaders," *Training & Development* (May 2001), pp. 70–81.

Chapter 9

1. Towers Perrin, *Talent Management: The State of the Art* (Toronto: Towers Perrin, 2005).

2. M.B. Arthur and D.M. Rousseau, *The Boundaryless Career: A New Employment Principle for a New Organizational Era* (New York: Oxford University Press, 1996), pp. 1–7. See also B. Moses, "Career Planning Mirrors Social Change," *Canadian HR Reporter* (May 17, 1999), p. G10.

3. S. O'Neal and J. Gebauer, "Talent Management in the 21st Century: Attracting, Retaining and Engaging Employees of Choice," *WorldatWork Journal* (First Quarter 2006), pp. 6–17.

4. These are quoted from F. Otte and P. Hutcheson, *Helping Employees Manage Careers* (Englewood Cliffs, NJ: Prentice Hall, 1992), pp. 5–6.

5. W. Enelow, *100 Ways to Recession-Proof Your Career* (Toronto: McGraw-Hill, 2002), p. 1. See also K. Gay, "Planning Future Path Is Key to a Successful Career," *Financial Post* (July 8, 1995), p. 13.

6. M. Watters and L. O'Connor, *It's Your Move: A Personal and Practical Guide to Career Transition and Job Search for Canadian Managers, Professionals and Executives* (Toronto: Harper Collins, 2001).

7. For example, one survey of "baby boomers" concluded that "allowed to excel" was the most frequently mentioned factor in overall job satisfaction in an extensive attitude survey of Canadian supervisors and middle managers between 30 and 45 years old. J. Rogers, "Baby Boomers and Their Career Expectations," *Canadian Business Review* (Spring 1993), pp. 13–18.

8. E. Schein, *Career Dynamics: Matching Individual and Organizational Needs* (Reading, MA: Addison-Wesley, 1978).

9. J. Holland, *Making Vocational Choices: A Theory of Careers* (Englewood Cliffs, NJ: Prentice-Hall, 1973).

10. E. Schein, *Career Dynamics: Matching Individual and Organizational Needs* (Reading, MA: Addison-Wesley, 1978), pp. 128–129; E.H. Schein, *Career Anchors Revisited: Implications for Career Development in the 21st Century*, Society of Organizational Learning—Working Paper 10.009, 1996.

11. R. Bolles, *What Color Is Your Parachute?* (Berkeley, CA: Ten Speed Press, 1976), p. 86.

12. R. Payne, *How to Get a Better Job Quicker* (New York: New American Library, 1987).

13. J. Ross, *Managing Productivity* (Reston, VA: Reston, 1979).

14. H.G. Kaufman, *Obsolescence and Professional Career Development* (New York: AMACOM, 1974).

15. D. Hall and F. Hall, "What's New in Career Management?" *Organizational Dynamics* 4 (Summer 1976), p. 350.

16. See, for example, T. Scandurg, "Mentorship and Career Mobility: An Empirical Investigation," *Journal of Organizational Behavior* 13, no. 2 (March 1992), pp. 169–174.

17. E. Schein, *Career Dynamics: Matching Individual and Organizational Needs* (Reading, MA: Addison-Wesley, 1978), p. 19. See also R. Jacobs and R. Bolton, "Career Analysis: The Missing Link in Managerial Assessment and Development," *Human Resource Management Journal* 3, no. 2 (1994), pp. 55–62.

18. F. Otte and P. Hutcheson, *Helping Employees Manage Careers* (Englewood Cliffs, NJ: Prentice Hall, 1992), pp. 15–16.

19. Ibid, p. 143.

20. B. Moses, "Implementing an Employee Career Development Program—Part Two: Tools to Support Career Development," *HR Professional* (December 1985), pp. 6–10.

21. T. Newby and A. Heide, "The Value of Mentoring," *Performance Improvement Quarterly* 5, no. 4 (1992), pp. 2–15; A.M. Young and P.L. Perrewé, "What Did You Expect? An Examination of Career-Related Support and Social Support Among Mentors and Protégés," *Journal of Management* 20 (2000), pp. 611–632; "Mentoring Makes Better Employees," *Workplace Today* (June 2001), p. 12; S. Butyn, "Mentoring Your Way to Improved Retention," *Canadian HR Reporter* (January 27, 2003), pp. 13, 15; L. Allan, "Mentoring: The Need to Move to Newer Models," *Canadian HR Reporter* (March 22, 1999), pp. 12–13.

22. L. Young, "Potential of Mentoring Programs Untapped," *Canadian HR Reporter* (April 10, 2000), pp. 1–2; S. Butyn, "Mentoring Your Way to Improved Retention," *Canadian HR Reporter* (January 27, 2003), pp. 13, 15.

23. D. Lewis, "That's Right, Double Click There, Sir," *Globe & Mail* (May 31, 2001), p. B14.

24. D.A. Garvin, "Building a Learning Organization," *Harvard Business Review* (July–August 1993), p. 80.

25. D. Quinn Mills, *Labor–Management Relations* (New York: McGraw-Hill, 1986), pp. 387–396.

26. G. Dessler, *Winning Commitment* (New York: McGraw-Hill, 1993), pp. 144–149.

27. See J. Famularo, *Handbook of Modern Personnel Administration* (New York: McGraw-Hill, 1972), p. 17.

28. For a discussion, see S. Schmidt, "The New Focus for Career Development Programs in Business and Industry," *Journal of Employment Counseling* 31 (March 1994), pp. 22–28.

29. R. Tucker, M. Moravee, and K. Ideus, "Designing a Dual Career-Track System," *Training and Development* 6 (1992), pp. 55–58; S. Schmidt, "The New Focus for Career Development Programs in Business and Industry," *Journal of Employment Counseling* 31 (March 1994), p. 26.

30. See, for example, R. Chanick, "Career Growth for Baby Boomers," *Personnel Journal* 71, no. 1 (January 1992), pp. 40–46.

31. R. Sheppard, "Spousal Programs and Communication Curb Relocation Rejections," *Canadian HR Reporter* (November 1, 1999), p. 17.

32. J. Swain, "Dispelling Myths about Leadership Development," *Canadian HR Reporter* (June 3, 2002), p. 27.

33. J. Cooper, "Succession Planning: It's Not Just for Executives Anymore," *Workspan* (February 2006), pp. 44–47.

34. P. Cantor, "Succession Planning: Often Requested, Rarely Delivered," *Ivey Business Journal* (January/February 2005).

35. R. Cheloha and J. Swain, "Talent Management System Key to Effective Succession Planning," *Canadian HR Reporter* (October 10, 2005), pp. 5, 8.

36. U. Vu, "Beware the Plan That's Led Too Much by HR," *Canadian HR Reporter* (October 10, 2005), pp. 6–7.

37. J. Cooper, "Succession Planning: It's Not Just for Executives Anymore," *Workspan* (February 2006), pp. 44–47.

38. For discussions of the steps in succession planning see, for example, K. Nowack, "The Secrets of Succession," *Training and Development* (November 1994), pp. 49–55, and D. Brookes, "In Management Succession, Who Moves Up?" *Human Resources* (January/February 1995), pp. 11–13.

39. K. Spence, "The Employee's Role in Succession Planning," *Canadian HR Reporter* (February 14, 2000), p. 13.

40. J. Orr, "Job Rotations Give Future Leaders the Depth They Need," *Canadian HR Reporter* (January 30, 2006), pp. 17, 20.

41. "TDBFG Associate," TD Bank Financial Group, www.td.com/hr/CTA.jsp (June 14, 2006).

42. D. Yoder, H.G. Heneman, J. Turnbull, and C.H. Stone, *Handbook of Personnel Management and Labor Relations* (New York: McGraw Hill, 1958). See also Jack Phillips, "Training Supervisors Outside the Classroom," *Training and Development Journal* 40, no. 2 (February 1986), pp. 46–49.

43. K. Wexley and G. Latham, *Developing and Training Human Resources in Organizations* (Glenview, IL: Scott, Foresman, 1981), p. 207.

44. This is based on N. Fox, "Action Learning Comes to Industry," *Harvard Business Review* 56 (September–October, 1977), pp. 158–168; D. Brown, "Action Learning Popular in Europe, Not Yet Caught on in Canada," *Canadian HR Reporter* (April 25, 2005), pp. 1–17.

45. K. Wexley and G. Latham, *Developing and Training Human Resources in Organizations* (Glenview, IL: Scott, Foresman, 1981), p. 193.

46. D. Rogers, *Business Policy and Planning* (Englewood Cliffs, NJ: Prentice Hall, 1977), p. 533. See also J. Kay, "At Harvard on the Case," *National Post Business* (March 2003), pp. 68–78.

47. For a discussion of management games and other noncomputerized training and development simulations, see C.M. Solomon, "Simulation Training Builds Teams through Experience," *Personnel Journal* (June 1993), pp. 100–105; K. Slack, "Training for the Real Thing," *Training and Development* (May 1993), pp. 79–89; B. Lierman, "How to Develop a Training Simulation," *Training and Development* (February 1994), pp. 50–52.

48. Development Dimensions International, www.ddiworld.com (August 16, 2006).

49. IPM Management Training and Development, "Workplace.ca," www.workplace.ca (March 31, 2003).

50. D. McKay-Stokes, "Sleeping in the Snow Together Does Wonders for Morale," *Financial Post* (April 25, 1995), p. 20. See also L. Cassiani, "Taking Team Building to New Heights," *Canadian HR Reporter* (February 26, 2001), pp. 8, 17.

51. J. Famularo, *Handbook of Modern Personnel Administration* (New York: McGraw-Hill, 1972), pp. 21.7–21.8.

52. J. Hinrichs, "Personnel Testing," in M. Dunnette (ed.), *Handbook of Industrial and Organizational Psychology* (Chicago: Rand McNally, 1976), p. 855.

53. D. Swink, "Role-Play Your Way to Learning," *Training and Development* (May 1993), pp. 91–97; A. Test, "Why I Do Not Like to Role Play," *The American Salesman* (August 1994), pp. 7–20.

54. This section based on A. Kraut, "Developing Managerial Skill via Modeling Techniques: Some Positive Research Findings—A Symposium," *Personnel Psychology* 29, no. 3 (Autumn 1976), pp. 325–361.

55. T. Cummings and C. Worley, *Organizational Development and Change* (Minneapolis, MN: West Publishing Company, 1993), p. 3.

56. B. Schneider, S. Ashworth, A.C. Higgs, and L. Carr, "Design Validity, and Use of Strategically Focused Employee Attitude Surveys," *Personnel Psychology* 49 (1996), pp. 695–705.

57. B. Hamilton, "Developing New Leaders to Meet the Talent Shortage," *Canadian HR Reporter* (February 8, 1999), pp. 18–19.

58. D. Brown, "Banking on Leadership Development," *Canadian HR Reporter* (January 17, 2005), pp. 7, 9.

59. Maple Leaf Foods, "Developing Leaders," www.mapleleaf.com/Working/YourDevelopment.aspx (June 13, 2006).

60. Banff Centre, www.banffcentre.ca/departments/leadership/programs/framework.asp#model (July 13, 2006).

Chapter 10

1. J.T. Rich, "The Solutions for Employee Performance Management," *Workspan* (February 2002), pp. 32–37.

2. J.A. Rubino, "Aligning Performance Management and Compensation Rewards Successfully," *WorldatWork Canadian News* (Fourth Quarter 2004), pp. 12–16.

3. D. Brown, "HR Improving at Performance Management," *Canadian HR Reporter* (December 2, 2002), pp. 1, 14.

4. D. Brown, "Re-evaluating Evaluation," *Canadian HR Reporter* (April 8, 2002), p. 2.

5. S. Nador, "A Properly Crafted Performance-Management Program Aids Professional Development," *Canadian HR Reporter* (May 17, 1999), p. 10.

6. J.E. Oliver, "Performance Appraisals That Fit," *Personnel Journal* 64 (June 1985), p. 69.

7. D. Brown, "HR Improving at Performance Management," *Canadian HR Reporter* (December 2, 2002), pp. 1, 14.

8. A. Sung and E. Todd, "Line of Sight: Moving Beyond the Catchphrase," *Workspan* (October 2004), pp. 65–69.

9. R. Greenberg and L. Lucid, "Beyond Performance Management: Four Principles of Performance Leadership," *Workspan* (September 2004), pp. 42–45.

10. For a recent discussion see G. English, "Tuning Up for Performance Management," *Training and Development Journal* (April 1991), pp. 56–60.

11. C.L. Hughes, "The Bell-Shaped Curve That Inspires Guerrilla Warfare," *Personnel Administrator* (May 1987), pp. 40–41.

12. Commerce Clearing House Editorial Staff, "Performance Appraisal: What Three Companies Are Doing" (Chicago, 1985). See also R. Girard, "Are Performance Appraisals Passé?" *Personnel Journal* 67, no. 8 (August 1988), pp. 89–90.

13. J. Ivancevich, "A Longitudinal Study of Behavioral Expectation Scales: Attitudes and Performance," *Journal of Applied Psychology* (April 1980), pp. 139–146.

14. U. Wiersma and G. Latham, "The Practicality of Behavioral Observation Scales, Behavioral Expectations Scales, and Trait Scales," *Personnel Psychology* 30, no. 3 (Autumn 1986), pp. 619–628.

15. J. Goodale and R. Burke, "Behaviorally Based Rating Scales Need Not Be Job Specific," *Journal of Applied Psychology* 60 (June 1975).

16. K.R. Murphy and J. Constans, "Behavioral Anchors as a Source of Bias in Rating," *Journal of Applied Psychology* 72, no. 4 (November 1987), pp. 573–577.

17. See M. Levy, "Almost-Perfect Performance Appraisals," *Personnel Journal* 68, no. 4 (April 1989), pp. 76–83.

18. C. Howard, "Appraise This!" *Canadian Business* (May 23, 1998), p. 96.

19. R.C. Mayer and J.H. Davis, "The Effect of the Performance Appraisal System on Trust for Management: A Field Quasi-Experiment," *Journal of Applied Psychology* 84 (1999), pp. 123–136.

20. J. Kochanski and A. Sorenson, "Managing Performance Management," *Workspan* (September 2005), pp. 20–27.

21. K.S. Teel, "Performance Appraisal: Current Trends, Persistent Progress," *Personnel Journal* 59, no. 4 (April 1980), pp. 296–316.

22. D. Brown, "Performance Management Systems Need Fixing: Survey," *Canadian HR Reporter* (April 11, 2005), pp. 1, 10; M. Waung and S. Highhouse, "Fear of Conflict and Empathic Buffering: Two Explanations for the Inflation of Performance Feedback," *Organizational Behavior and Human Decision Processes* 71 (1997), pp. 37–54.

23. Y. Ganzach, "Negativity (and Positivity) in Performance Evaluation: Three Field Studies," *Journal of Applied Psychology* 80 (1995), pp. 491–499.

24. T.J. Maurer and M.A. Taylor, "Is Sex by Itself Enough? An Exploration of Gender Bias Issues in Performance Appraisal," *Organizational Behavior and Human Decision Processes* 60 (1994), pp. 231–251. See also C.E. Lance, "Test for Latent Structure of Performance Ratings Derived from Wherry's (1952) Theory of Ratings," *Journal of Management* 20 (1994), pp. 757–771.

25. S.E. Scullen, M.K. Mount, and M. Goff, "Understanding the Latent Structure of Job Performance Ratings," *Journal of Applied Psychology* 85 (2001), pp. 956–970.

26. A.M. Saks and D.A. Waldman, "The Relationship Between Age and Job Performance Evaluations for Entry-Level Professionals," *Journal of Organizational Behavior* 19 (1998), pp. 409–419.

27. W.C. Borman, L.A. White, and D.W. Dorsey, "Effects of Ratee Task Performance and Interpersonal Factors in Supervisor and Peer Performance Ratings," *Journal of Applied Psychology* 80 (1995), pp. 168–177.

28. K. Murphy, W. Balzer, M. Lockhart, and E. Eisenman, "Effects of Previous Performance on Evaluations of Present Performance," *Journal of Applied Psychology* 70, no. 1 (1985), pp. 72–84. See also K. Williams, A. DeNisi, B. Meglino, and T. Cafferty, "Initial Decisions and Subsequent Performance Ratings," *Journal of Applied Psychology* 71, no. 2 (May 1986), pp. 189–195.

29. B. Davis and M. Mount, "Effectiveness of Performance Appraisal Training Using Computer Assistance Instruction and Behavior Modeling," *Personnel Psychology* 37 (Fall 1984), pp. 439–452.

30. J. Hedge and M. Cavanagh, "Improving the Accuracy of Performance Evaluations: Comparison of Three Methods of Performance Appraiser Training," *Journal of Applied Psychology* 73, no. 1 (February 1988), pp. 68–73.

31. B. Davis and M. Mount, "Effectiveness of Performance Appraisal Training Using Computer Assistance Instruction and Behavior Modeling," *Personnel Psychology* 37 (Fall 1984), pp. 439–452.

32. T. Athey and R. McIntyre, "Effect of Rater Training on Rater Accuracy: Levels of Processing Theory and Social Facilitation Theory Perspectives," *Journal of Applied Psychology* 72, no. 4 (November 1987), pp. 567–572.

33. M.M. Greller, "Participation in the Performance Appraisal Review: Inflexible Manager Behavior and Variable Worker Needs," *Human Relations* 51 (1998), pp. 1061–1083.

34. L. Axline, "Ethical Considerations of Performance Appraisals," *Management Review* (March 1994), p. 62.

35. M. McDougall and L. Cassiani, "HR Cited in Unfair Performance Review," *Canadian HR Reporter* (September 10, 2001), pp. 1, 6.

36. "Health Worker's Performance Review Unfair," *Workplace Today* (June 2001), p. 23.

37. G. Barrett and M. Kernan, "Performance Appraisal and Terminations: A Review of Court Decisions Since Brito v. Zia with Implications for Personnel Practices," *Personnel Psychology* 40, no. 3 (Autumn 1987), pp. 489–504.

38. M.M. Harris and J. Schaubroeck, "A Meta-Analysis of Self-Supervisor, Self-Peer, and Peer-Supervisor Ratings," *Personnel Psychology*, 41 (1988), pp. 43–62.

39. G.P. Latham and K.N. Wexley, *Increasing Productivity Through Performance Appraisal*, 2nd ed. (Reading, MA: Addison-Wesley, 1994).

40. J. Barclay and L. Harland, "Peer Performance Appraisals: The Impact of Rater Competence, Rater Location, and Rating Correctability on Fairness Perceptions," *Group and Organization Management* 20, no. 1 (March 1995), pp. 39–60.

41. M. Mount, "Psychometric Properties of Subordinate Ratings of Managerial Performance," *Personnel Psychology* 37, no. 4 (Winter 1984), pp. 687–702.

42. V.V. Druskat and S.B. Wolff, "Effects and Timing of Developmental Peer Appraisals in Self-Managing Work Groups," *Journal of Applied Psychology* 84 (1999), pp. 58–74.

43. M.M. Harris and J. Schaubroeck, "A Meta-analysis of Self-Supervisor, Self-Peer, and Peer-Supervisor Ratings," *Personnel Psychology* 41 (1988), pp. 43–62.

44. W.C. Borman, "The Rating of Individuals in Organizations: An Alternate Approach," *Organizational Behavior and Human Performance* 12 (1974), pp. 105–124.

45. B.D. Cawley, L.M. Keeping, and P.E Levy, "Participation in the Performance Appraisal Process and Employee Reactions: A Meta-analytic Review of Field Investigations," *Journal of Applied Psychology* 83 (1998), pp. 615–633.

46. J.W. Lawrie, "Your Performance: Appraise It Yourself!" *Personnel* 66, no. 1 (January 1989), pp. 21–33; includes a good explanation of how self-appraisals can be used at work. See also A. Furnham and P. Stringfield, "Congruence in Job-Performance Ratings: A Study of 360° Feedback Examining Self, Manager, Peers, and Consultant Ratings," *Human Relations* 51 (1998), pp. 517–530.

47. P.A. Mabe III and S.G. West "Validity of Self-Evaluation of Ability: A Review and Meta-Analysis," *Journal of Applied Psychology* 67, no. 3 (1982), pp. 280–296.

48. J. Russell and D. Goode, "An Analysis of Managers' Reactions to Their Own Performance Appraisal Feedback," *Journal of Applied Psychology* 73, no. 1 (February 1988), pp. 63–67; M.M. Harris and J. Schaubroeck, "A Meta-analysis of Self-Supervisor, Self-Peer, and Peer-Supervisor Ratings," *Personnel Psychology* 41 (1988), pp. 43–62.

49. H.J. Bernardin and R.W. Beatty, "Can Subordinate Appraisals Enhance Managerial Productivity?" *Sloan Management Review* (Summer 1987), pp. 63–73.

50. M. London and A. Wohlers, "Agreement between Subordinate and Self-Ratings in Upward Feedback," *Personnel Psychology* 44 (1991), pp. 375–390.

51. Ibid, p. 376.

52. D. Antonioni, "The Effects of Feedback Accountability on Upward Appraisal Ratings," *Personnel Psychology* 47 (1994), pp. 349–355.

53. T.J. Maurer, N.S. Raju, and W.C. Collins, "Peer and Subordinate Performance Appraisal Measurement Equivalence," *Journal of Applied Psychology* 83 (1998), pp. 693–702.

54. R. Reilly, J. Smither, and N. Vasilopoulos, "A Longitudinal Study of Upward Feedback," *Personnel Psychology* 49 (1996), pp. 599–612.

55. K. Nowack, "360-Degree Feedback: The Whole Story," *Training and Development* (January 1993), p. 69. For a description of some of the problems involved in implementing 360-degree feedback, see M. Budman, "The Rating Game," *Across the Board* 31, no. 2 (February 1994), pp. 35–38.

56. C. Romano, "Fear of Feedback," *Management Review* (December 1993), p. 39. See also M.R. Edwards and A.J. Ewen, "How to Manage Performance and Pay With 360-Degree Feedback," *Compensation and Benefits Review*, 28, no. 3 (May/June 1996), pp. 41–46.

57. G.P. Latham, J. Almost, S. Mann, and C. Moore, "New Developments in Performance Management," *Organizational Dynamics* 34, no. 1 (2005), pp. 77–87; R. Brillinger, "The Many Faces of 360-Degree Feedback," *Canadian HR Reporter* (December 16, 1996), p. 21.

58. J.F. Milliman, R.A. Zawacki, C. Norman, L. Powell, and J. Kirksey, "Companies Evaluate Employees from All Perspectives," *Personnel Journal* 73, no. 11 (November 1994), pp. 99–103.

59. R. Brillinger, "The Many Faces of 360-Degree Feedback," *Canadian HR Reporter* (December 16, 1996), p. 20.

60. Ibid.

61. D.A. Waldman, L.A. Atwater, and D. Antonioni, "Has 360-Degree Feedback Gone Amok?" *Academy of Management Executive* 12 (1998), pp. 86–94.

62. P.E. Levy, B.D. Cawley, and R.J. Foti, "Reactions to Appraisal Discrepancies: Performance Ratings and Attributions," *Journal of Business and Psychology* 12 (1998), pp. 437–455.

63. M. Derayeh and S. Brutus, "Learning from Others' 360-Degree Experiences," *Canadian HR Reporter* (February 10, 2003), pp. 18, 23.

64. A.S. DeNisi and A.N. Kluger, "Feedback Effectiveness: Can 360-Degree Appraisal Be Improved?" *Academy of Management Executive* 14 (2000), pp. 129–139.

65. T. Bentley, "Internet Addresses 360-Degree Feedback Concerns," *Canadian HR Reporter* (May 8, 2000), pp. G3, G15.

66. D. Brown, "Performance Management Systems Need Fixing: Survey," *Canadian HR Reporter* (April 1, 2005), pp. 1, 10.

67. See also J. Greenberg, "Using Explanations to Manage Impressions of Performance Appraisal Fairness," *Employee Responsibilities and Rights Journal* 4, no. 1 (March 1991), pp. 51–60.

68. R.G. Johnson, *The Appraisal Interview Guide*, Chapter 9 (New York: AMACOM, 1979).

69. J. Block, *Performance Appraisal on the Job: Making It Work* (New York: Executive Enterprises Publications, 1981), pp. 58–62. See also T. Lowe, "Eight Ways to Ruin a Performance Review," *Personnel Journal* 65, no. 1 (January 1986).

70. J. Block, *Performance Appraisal on the Job: Making It Work* (New York: Executive Enterprises Publications, 1981), pp. 58–62.

71. M. Feinberg, *Effective Psychology for Managers* (New York: Simon & Schuster, 1976).

72. J. Pearce and L. Porter, "Employee Response to Formal Performance Appraisal Feedback," *Journal of Applied Psychology* 71, no. 2 (May 1986), pp. 211–218.

73. D.B. Jarvis and R.E. McGilvery, "Poor Performers," *HR Professional* (June/July 2005), p. 32.

74. J. Kochnarski and A. Sorenson, "Managing Performance Management," *Workspan* (September 2005), pp. 20–37.

75. E.E. Lawler and M. McDermott, "Current Performance Management Practices," *WorldatWork Journal* 12, no. 2, pp. 49–60.

76. D. Bell, J. Blanchet, and N. Gore, "Performance Management: Making It Work Is Worth the Effort," *WorldatWork Canadian News* 12, no. 11 (Fourth Quarter 2004), pp. 1, 27–28.

Chapter 11

1. S. O'Neal, "Total Rewards and the Future of Work," *Workspan* (January 2005), pp. 18–26; S. Watson, "Total Rewards: Building a Better Employment Deal," *Workspan* (December 2003), pp. 48–51.

2. S. O'Neal, "Total Rewards and the Future of Work," *Workspan* (January 2005), pp. 18–26; L. Wright, "Total Rewards Can Mean More HR Work than You Think," *Canadian HR Reporter* (October 6, 2003), pp. 9, 12; K.D. Scott, D. Morajda, and J.W. Bishop, "Increase Company Competitiveness: 'Tune Up' Your Pay System," *WorldatWork Journal* (First Quarter 2002), pp. 35–42.

3. *Towers Perrin 2005 Workforce Study* (Toronto: Towers Perrin, November 2005).

4. S. O'Neal, "Total Rewards and the Future of Work," *Workspan* (January 2005), pp. 18–26

5. J. Dawe, "Compassionate Care Benefit: A New Alterative for Family Caregivers," *Workplace Gazette* (Summer 2004); S. Klie, "Feds Expand Eligibility For Compassionate Care," *Canadian HR Reporter* (July 17, 2006).

6. "GM, Daimler-Chrysler Workers Ratify Agreements," *Workplace Today* (December 1999), p. 11.

7. E. Hay, "The Attitude of the American Federation of Labour on Job Evaluation," *Personnel Journal* 26 (November 1947), pp. 163–169; H. James, "Issues in Job Evaluation: The Union's View," *Personnel Journal* 51 (September 1972), pp. 675–679; Harold Jones, "Union Views on Job Evaluations: 1971 vs. 1978," *Personnel Journal* 58 (February 1979), pp. 80–85.

8. B. Ellig, "Strategic Pay Planning," *Compensation and Benefits Review* 19, no. 4 (July–August 1987), pp. 28–43; T. Robertson, "Fundamental Strategies for Wage and Salary Administration," *Personnel Journal* 65, no. 11 (November 1986), pp. 120–32. One expert cautions against conducting salary surveys based on job title alone. He recommends using job-content salary surveys that examine the content of jobs according to the size of each job so that, for instance, the work of the president of IBM and that of a small clone manufacturer would not be inadvertently compared. See R. Sahl, "Job Content Salary Surveys: Survey Design and Selection Features," *Compensation and Benefits Review* (May–June 1991), pp. 14–21.

9. M.A. Thompson, "Rewards, Performance Two Biggest Words in HR Future," *WorldatWork Canadian News* 10 (2002), pp. 1, 2, 11.

10. Job analysis can be a useful source of information on compensable factors, as well as on job descriptions and job specifications. For example, a quantitative job analysis technique like the position analysis questionnaire generates quantitative information on the degree to which the following five basic factors are present in each job: having decision making/communication/social responsibilities, performing skilled activities, being physically active, operating vehicles or equipment, and processing information. As a result, a job analysis technique like the PAQ is actually as appropriate as a job evaluation technique (or, some say, more), in that jobs can be quantitatively compared with one another on those five dimensions and their relative worth thus ascertained.

11. M.E. Lo Bosco, "Job Analysis, Job Evaluation, and Job Classification," *Personnel* 62, no. 5 (May 1985), pp. 70–5. See also H. Risher, "Job Evaluation: Validity and Reliability," *Compensation and Benefits Review* 21 (January–February 1989), pp. 22–36; D. Hahn and R. Dipboye, "Effects of Training and Information on the Accuracy and Reliability of Job Evaluations," *Journal of Applied Psychology* 73, no. 2 (May 1988), pp. 146–153.

12. See, for example, D. Petri, "Talking Pay Policy Pays Off," *Supervisory Management* (May 1979), pp. 2–13.

13. As explained later, the practice of red circling is used to delay downward adjustments in pay rates that are presently too high given the newly evaluated jobs. See also E.J. Brennan, "Everything You Need to Know about Salary Ranges," *Personnel Journal* 63, no. 3 (March 1984), pp. 10–17.

14. J.B. Cunningham and S. Graham, "Assessing the Reliability of Four Job Evaluation Plans," *Canadian Journal of Administrative Sciences* 10 (1993), pp. 31–47.

15. S. Werner, R. Konopaske, and C. Touhey, "Ten Questions to Ask Yourself about Compensation Surveys," *Compensation and Benefits Review* 31 (May/June 1999), pp. 54–59.

16. P. Cappelli, *The New Deal at Work: Managing the Market-Driven Workforce* (Boston, MA: Harvard Business School Press, 1999).

17. "Compensation Surveys on the Internet," *Canadian HR Reporter* (February 10, 1997), p. 6.

18. F.W. Cook, "Compensation Surveys Are Biased," *Compensation and Benefits Review* (September–October 1994), pp. 19–22.

19. K.R. Cardinal, "The Art and Science of the Match, or Why Job Matching Keeps Me Up at Night," *Workspan* (February 2004), pp. 53–56; S. Werner, R. Konopaske, and C. Touhey, "Ten Questions to Ask Yourself about Compensation Surveys." See also U. Vu, "Know-how Pays in Comp Surveys," *Canadian HR Reporter* (April 7, 2003), p. 13.

20. S. Werner, R. Konopaske, and C. Touhey, "Ten Questions to Ask Yourself about Compensation Surveys," *Compensation and Benefits Review* 31 (May/June 1999), pp. 54–59.

21. D. Hofrichter, "Broadbanding: A 'Second Generation' Approach," *Compensation and Benefits Review* (September–October 1993), pp. 53–58.

22. D. Hofrichter, "Broadbanding: A 'Second Generation' Approach," *Compensation and Benefits Review* (September–October 1993), pp. 53–58. See also G. Bergel, "Choosing the Right Pay Delivery System to Fit Banding," *Compensation and Benefits Review* 26, (July–August 1994), pp. 34–38.

23. C. Bacca and G. Starzmann, "Clarifying Competencies: Powerful Tools for Driving Business Success," *Workspan* (March 2006), pp. 44–46; G. Ledford Jr., "Three Case Studies on Skill-Based Pay: An Overview," *Compensation and Benefits Review* (March–April 1991), pp. 11–23.

24. C. Bacca and G. Starzmann, "Clarifying Competencies: Powerful Tools for Driving Business Success," *Workspan* (March 2006), pp. 44–46.

25. P.K. Zingheim and J.R. Schuster, "Reassessing the Value of Skill-Based Pay," *WorldatWork Journal* (Third Quarter 2002).

26. R. Long, "Paying for Knowledge: Does It Pay?" *Canadian HR Reporter* (March 28, 2005), pp. 12–13.

27. S. St.-Onge," Competency-Based Pay Plans Revisited," *Human Resources Professional* (August/September 1998), pp. 29–34; J. Kochanski and P. Leblanc, "Should Firms Pay for Competencies: Competencies Have to Help the Bottom Line," *Canadian HR Reporter* (February 22, 1999), p. 10.

28. P.K. Zingheim, J.R. Schuster, and M.G. Dertien, "Measuring the Value of Work: The 'People-Based' Pay Solution," *WorldatWork Journal* (Third Quarter 2005), pp. 42–49.

29. D. Yoder, *Personnel Management and Industrial Relations* (Englewood Cliffs, NJ: Prentice Hall, 1970), pp. 643–645.

30. E. Lewis, "New Approaches to Executive Pay," *Directors and Boards* 18 (Spring 1994), pp. 57–58. See also B.R. Ellig, "Executive Pay: A Primer," *Compensation & Benefits Review* (January–February 2003), pp. 44–50.

31. "The Top 1000: Executive Compensation Report 2005," *ROB Magazine*, www.theglobeandmail.com/ceocompensation2005 (August 28, 2006).

32. H.L. Tosi, S. Werner, J.P. Katz, and L.R. Gomez-Mejia, "How Much Does Performance Matter? A Meta-analysis of CEO Pay Studies," *Journal of Management* 26 (2000), pp. 301–339.

33. M.A. Thompson, "Investors Call for Better Disclosure of Executive Compensation in Canada," *Workspan Focus Canada 2006*, pp. 5–6; "CEO Pay More Accountable," *Canadian HR Reporter* (December 19, 2005), p. 2; "Study Probes Executive Compensation," *Workplace News* (April 2005).

34. P. Moran, "Equitable Salary Administration in High-Tech Companies," *Compensation and Benefits Review* 18 (September–October 1986), pp. 31–40.

35. R. Sibson, *Compensation* (New York: AMACOM, 1981), p. 194.

36. B. Bridges, "The Role of Rewards in Motivating Scientific and Technical Personnel: Experience at Egland AFB," *National Productivity Review* (Summer 1993), pp. 337–348.

37. M. Commanducci, "Women Make Gains in Wage Equity as Young Fall Behind," *Canadian HR Reporter* (April 20, 1998), p. 16. See also M. Drolet, "The Male–Female Wage Gap," *Perspectives,* Statistics Canada, Spring 2002, pp. 29–37; E. Carey, "Gender Gap in Earnings Staying Stubbornly High," *Toronto Star* (March 12, 2003), p. A9.

38. "Female Grads Make Less Than Males," *Canadian HR Reporter* (April 19, 2004), p. 2.

39. D. Brown, "StatsCan Unable to Explain Gender Wage Gap," *Canadian HR Reporter* (January 31, 2000), p. 3.

40. "Air Canada Loses Pay Equity Decision, For Now," *Canadian HR Reporter* (February 13, 2006), p. 2.

41. *Canadian Master Labour Guide 2002*, 16th ed. (Toronto: CCH Canadian Limited, 2002), pp. 549–590.

42. *Ontario Pay Equity Commission Newsletter*, "Pay Equity Nets Gains for Women" (October 1995), p. 4; D. Brown, "StatsCan Unable to Explain Gender Wage Gap," *Canadian HR Reporter* (January 31, 2000), p. 3.

43. D. Brown, "New Rules Proposed for Pay Equity," *Canadian HR Reporter* (May 31, 2004), pp. 1, 3; "Pay Equity Nets Gains for Women," *Ontario Pay Equity Commission Newsletter* (October 1995), p. 4.

44. C. Shelton and L. Shelton, "What HR Can Do about the 'Opt-Out' Revolution," *Canadian HR Reporter* (May 8, 2006).

Chapter 12

1. C. Baarda, *Compensation Planning Outlook 2006* (Ottawa: Conference Board of Canada, 2006); "Employers Turn to Pay for Performance Rather Than Salary Increases in 2006 Says Hewitt Survey," *Hewitt Associates Press Release* (September 15, 2005).

2. P.K. Zingheim and J.R. Schuster, *Pay People Right!: Breakthrough Reward Strategies to Create Great Companies* (San Francisco, CA: Jossey-Bass, 2000); D. Brown, "Top Performers Must Get Top Pay," *Canadian HR Reporter* (May 8, 2000), pp. 7, 10; V. Dell'Agnese, "Performance-Based Rewards, Line-of-Sight Foster Ownership Behaviour in Staff," *Canadian HR Reporter* (October 8, 2001), p. 10.

3. S. Klie, "'Employees First' at CPX," *Canadian HR Reporter* (September 26, 2005), pp. 1, 3.

4. This section is based on "Non-Traditional Incentive Pay Programs," *Personnel Policies Forum Survey*, no. 148 (May 1991), The Bureau of National Affairs, Inc., Washington, D.C.

5. R. Henderson, *Compensation Management* (Reston, VA: Reston, 1979), p. 363. For a discussion of the increasing use of incentives for blue-collar employees, see, for example, R. Henderson, "Contract Concessions: Is the Past Prologue?" *Compensation and Benefits Review* 18, no. 5 (September–October 1986), pp. 17–30. See also A.J. Vogl, "Carrots, Sticks and Self-Deception," *Across-the-Board* 3, no. 1 (January 1994), pp. 39–44.

6. D. Belcher, *Compensation Administration* (Englewood Cliffs, NJ: Prentice Hall, 1973), p. 314.

7. For a discussion of these, see T. Wilson, "Is It Time to Eliminate the Piece Rate Incentive System?" *Compensation and Benefits Review* (March–April 1992), pp. 43–49.

8. Measured day work is a third type of individual incentive plan for production workers. See, for example, M. Fein, "Let's Return to MDW for Incentives," *Industrial Engineering* (January 1979), pp. 34–37.

9. R. Henderson, *Compensation Management* (Reston, VA: Reston, 1979), pp. 367–368. See also D. Swinehart, "A Guide for More Productive Team Incentive Programs," *Personnel Journal* 65, no. 7 (July 1986); A. Saunier and E. Hawk, "Realizing the Potential of Teams through Team-Based Rewards," *Compensation and Benefits Review* (July–August 1994), pp. 24–33; S. Caudron, "Tie Individual Pay to Team Success," *Personnel Journal* 73, no. 10 (October 1994), pp. 40–46.

10. Another suggestion is as follows: equal payments to all members on the team; differential payments to team members based on their contributions to the team's performance; differential payments determined by a ratio of each group member's base pay to the total base pay of the group. See K. Bartol and L. Hagmann, "Team-Based Pay Plans: A Key to Effective Teamwork," *Compensation and Benefits Review* (November–December 1992), pp. 24–29.

11. J. Nickel and S. O'Neal, "Small Group Incentives: Gainsharing in the Microcosm," *Compensation and Benefits Review* (March–April 1990), p. 24. See also J. Pickard, "How Incentives Can Drive Teamworking," *Personnel Management* (September 1993), pp. 26–32; S. Caudron, "Tie Individual Pay to Team Success," *Personnel Journal* (October 1994), pp. 40–46; J.P. Alston, "Awarding Bonuses the Japanese Way," *Business Horizons* 25 (September–October 1982), pp. 6–8; P. Daly, "Selecting and Assigning a Group Incentive Plan," *Management Review* (December 1975), pp. 33–45. For an explanation of how to develop a successful group incentive program, see K. Dow Scott and Timothy Cotter, "The Team That Works Together Earns Together," *Personnel Journal* 63 (March 1984), pp. 59–67.

12. L.N. McClurg, "Team Rewards: How Far Have We Come?" *Human Resource Management* 40 (Spring 2001), pp. 73–86. See also A Gostick, "Team Recognition," *Canadian HR Reporter* (May 21, 2001), p. 15.

13. W.E. Reum and S. Reum, "Employee Stock Ownership Plans: Pluses and Minuses," *Harvard Business Review* 55 (July–August 1976), pp. 133–43; R. Bavier, "Managerial Bonuses," *Industrial Management* (March–April 1978), pp. 1–5. See also J. Thompson, L. Murphy Smith, and A. Murray, "Management Performance Incentives: Three Critical Issues," *Compensation and Benefits Review* 18, no. 5 (September–October 1986), pp. 41–47.

14. C. Baarda, *Compensation Planning Outlook 2006* (Ottawa: Conference Board of Canada, 2006).

15. B.R. Ellig, "Incentive Plans: Short-Term Design Issues," *Compensation Review* 16, no. 3 (Third Quarter 1984), pp. 26–36; B. Ellig, *Executive Compensation—A Total Pay Perspective* (New York: McGraw-Hill, 1982), p. 187.

16. B. Ellig, *Executive Compensation—A Total Pay Perspective* (New York: McGraw-Hill, 1982), p. 188–189; R. Bavier, "Managerial Bonuses," *Industrial Management* (March–April 1978), pp. 1–5. See also C. Tharp, "Linking Annual Incentive Awards to Individual Performance," *Compensation and Benefits Review* 17 (November–December 1985), pp. 38–43.

17. F.D. Hildebrand, Jr., "Individual Performance Incentives," *Compensation Review* 10 (Third Quarter 1978), p. 32.

18. Ibid., pp. 28–33.

19. C. Baarda, *Compensation Planning Outlook 2006* (Ottawa: Conference Board of Canada, 2006).

20. P. Brieger, "Shareholders Target CEO Compensation," *Financial Post* (April 7, 2003), p. FP5. See also S.M. Van Putten and E.D. Graskamp, "End of an Era? The Future of Stock Options," *Compensation and Benefits Review* (September–October 2002), pp. 29–35; N. Winter, "The Current Crisis in Executive Compensation," *WorldatWork Canadian News* (Fourth Quarter

2002), pp. 1–3; R.M. Kanungo and M. Mendonca, *Compensation: Effective Reward Management* (1997), p. 237.

21. E. Redling, "The 1981 Tax Act: Boom to Managerial Compensation," *Personnel* 57 (March–April 1982), pp. 26–35.

22. C. Baarda, *Compensation Planning Outlook 2006* (Ottawa: Conference Board of Canada, 2006); R. Murrill, "Stock Options Still the Preferred Incentive," *Canadian HR Reporter* (June 20, 2005), pp. 12–13.

23. R. Murrill, "Executive Share Ownership," *Watson Wyatt Memorandum* 11, no. 1 (March 1997), p. 11.

24. R.J. Long, "Ensuring Your Executive Compensation Plan Is an Asset Rather Than a Liability," *Canadian HR Reporter* (October 19, 1998), pp. 15–16. See also D. Brown, "Bringing Stock Options back to the Surface," *Canadian HR Reporter* (May 7, 2001), p. 2; A. Tomlinson, "Stock Options: Last Year's Darling, This Year's Headache," *Canadian HR Reporter* (October 8, 2001), p. 2; J.M. Bodley, "Incentive Plan Management in Volatile Markets," *Canadian HR Reporter* (May 17, 1999), p. 8.

25. S.J. Chadwick, "Extending Stock Option Plans to All Employees a Growing Trend," *Canadian HR Reporter* (October 5, 1998), pp. 10, 12. See also B. Cline, "Stock Option Plans . . . A New Trend?" *HR Professional* (June/July 1999), pp. 24–26; I. Huss and M. Maclure, "Broad-Based Stock Option Plans Take Hold," *Canadian HR Reporter* (July 17, 2000), p. 18; D. Brown, "Stock Options Grow," *Canadian HR Reporter* (March 26, 2001), pp. 1, 10; D. Brown, "Bringing Stock Options back to the Surface," *Canadian HR Reporter* (May 7, 2001), p. 2; J. Staiman and C. Thompson, "Designing and Implementing a Broad-Based Stock Option Plan," *Compensation and Benefits Review* (July–August 1998), p. 23.

26. *CPP Investment Board Proxy Voting Principles and Guidelines* (February 7, 2006).

27. "No Options at Microsoft," *Canadian HR Reporter* (August 11, 2003), p. 3. See also S.M. Van Putten and E.D. Graskamp, "End of an Era? The Future of Stock Options," *Compensation and Benefits Review* (September–October 2002), pp. 29–35; E. Elliott and C. Kapel, "Market Downturn Puts Stock Options under the Microscope," *Canadian HR Reporter* (June 17, 2002), pp. 17, 19; A. Tomlinson, "Stock Options Still Popular, Firms Picky about Recipients" *Canadian HR Reporter* (June 3, 2002); D. Brown, "Pressure Mounts to Reform Stock Option Accounting," *Canadian HR Reporter* (June 17, 2002), pp. 1, 12; D. Brown, "Stock Options: End of a Trend?" *Canadian HR Reporter* (September 9, 2002), pp. 1, 12; "Accounting Body Calls for Options Expensing," *Canadian HR Reporter* (November 4, 2002), p. 2.

28. Basically, book value per share equals the firm's assets minus its prior (basically debt) liabilities, divided by the number of shares.

29. R. Stata and M. Maidique, "Bonus System for Balanced Strategy," *Harvard Business Review* 59 (November–December 1980), pp. 156–163; Alfred Rappaport, "Executive Incentives versus Corporate Growth," *Harvard Business Review* 57 (July–August 1978), pp. 81–88. See also C. Graef, "Rendering Long-Term Incentives Less Risky for Executives," *Personnel* 65, no. 9 (September 1988), pp. 80–84.

30. J. Kanter and M. Ward, "Long-Term Incentives for Management, Part 4: Performance Plans," *Compensation and Benefits Review* (January–February 1990), p. 36.

31. P. Singh and N.C. Agarwal, "Executive Compensation: Examining an Old Issue from New Perspectives," *Compensation and Benefits Review* (March/April 2003), pp. 48–54.

32. This section is based on M. Meltzer and H. Goldsmith, "Executive Compensation for Growth Companies," *Compensation and Benefits Review* (November–December 1997), pp. 41–50.

33. J. Tallitsch and J. Moynahan, "Fine-Tuning Sales Compensation Programs," *Compensation and Benefits Review* 26, no. 2 (March–April 1994), pp. 34–37.

34. Straight salary by itself is not, of course, an incentive compensation plan as we use the term in this chapter; J. Steinbrink, "How to Pay Your Sales Force," *Harvard Business Review* 57 (July–August 1978), pp. 111–122.

35. T.H. Patten, "Trends in Pay Practices for Salesmen," *Personnel* 43 (January–February 1968), pp. 54–63. See also C. Romano, "Death of a Salesman," *Management Review* 83, no. 9 (September 1994), pp. 10–16.

36. D. Harrison, M. Virick, and S. William, "Working Without a Net: Time, Performance, and Turnover under Maximally Contingent Rewards," *Journal of Applied Psychology* 81 (1996), pp. 331–345.

37. G. Stewart, "Reward Structure as Moderator of the Relationship Between Extroversion and Sales Performance," *Journal of Applied Psychology* 81 (1996), pp. 619–627.

38. In the salary plus bonus plan, salespeople are paid a basic salary and are then paid a bonus for carrying out specified activities. For a discussion of how to develop a customer-focused sales compensation plan, see, for example, M. Blessington, "Designing a Sales Strategy with the Customer in Mind," *Compensation and Benefits Review* (March–April 1992), pp. 30–41; S.S. Sands, "Ineffective Quotas: The Hidden Threat to Sales Compensation Plans," *Compensation and Benefits Review* (March/April 2000), pp. 35–42.

39. E. Maggio, "Compensation Strategies Pulling You in Different Directions?" *Canadian HR Reporter* (October 4, 1999), pp. 11, 19. See also B. Serino, "Non-cash Awards Boost Sales Compensation Plans, " *Workspan* (August 2002), pp. 24–27.

40. B. Weeks, "Setting Sales Force Compensation in the Internet Age," *Compensation and Benefits Review* (March/April 2000), pp. 25–34.

41. See, for example, W. Kearney, "Pay for Performance? Not Always," *MSU Business Topics* (Spring 1979), pp. 5–16. See also H. Doyel and J. Johnson, "Pay Increase Guidelines with Merit," *Personnel Journal* 64 (June 1985), pp. 46–50.

42. N. Winstanley, "Are Merit Increases Really Effective?" *Personnel Administrator* 27 (April 1982), pp. 37–41. See also W. Seithel and J. Emans, "Calculating Merit Increases: A Structured Approach," *Personnel* 60, no. 5 (June 1985), pp. 56–68; D. Gilbert and G. Bassett, "Merit Pay Increases Are a Mistake," *Compensation and Benefits Review* 26, no. 2 (March–April 1994), pp. 20–25; *Merit Pay: Fitting the Pieces Together* (Chicago: Commerce Clearing House, 1982).

43. S. Minken, "Does Lump Sum Pay Merit Attention?" *Personnel Journal* (June 1988), pp. 77–83. Two experts suggest using neither straight merit pay nor lump-sum merit pay but rather tying the merit payment to the duration of the impact of the employee's work so that, for instance, the merit raise might last for two or three years. See J. Newman and D. Fisher, "Strategic Impact Merit Pay," *Compensation and Benefits Review* (July–August 1992), pp. 38–45.

44. This section based primarily on R. Sibson, *Compensation* (New York: AMA-COM, 1981), pp. 189–207; C. Shelton and L. Shelton, "What HR Can Do about the 'Opt-Out' Revolution (Guest Commentary)," *Canadian HR Reporter* (May 8, 2006).

45. C. Baarda, *Compensation Planning Outlook 2006* (Ottawa: Conference Board of Canada, 2006).

46. B. Duke, "Are Profit-Sharing Plans Making the Grade?" *Canadian HR Reporter* (January 11, 1999), pp. 8–9.

47. D.E. Tyson, *Profit-Sharing in Canada: The Complete Guide to Designing and Implementing Plans That Really Work* (Toronto: Wiley, 1996), pp. 200–207.

48. C. Baarda, *Compensation Planning Outlook 2006* (Ottawa: Conference Board of Canada, 2006).

49. R. Murrill, "Executive Share Ownership," *Watson Wyatt Memorandum* 11, no. 1 (March 1997), p. 11.

50. P. Robertson, "Increasing Productivity through an Employee Share Purchase Plan," *Canadian HR Reporter* (September 20, 1999), pp. 7, 9.

51. C. Beatty, "Our Company: Employee Ownership May Sound Drastic, but It Can Work," *HR Professional*, June/July 2004, p. 20.

52. B. Moore and T. Ross, *The Scanlon Way to Improved Productivity: A Practical Guide* (New York: Wiley, 1978), p. 2.

53. These are based in part on S. Markham, K. Dow Scott, and W. Cox, Jr., "The Evolutionary Development of a Scanlon Plan," *Compensation and Benefits Review* (March–April 1992), pp. 50–56; J.K. White, "The Scanlon Plan:

Causes and Correlates of Success," *Academy of Management Journal* 22 (June 1979), pp. 292–312.

54. B. Moore and T. Ross, *The Scanlon Way to Improved Productivity: A Practical Guide* (New York: Wiley, 1978), pp. 1–2.

55. J.K. White, "The Scanlon Plan: Causes and Correlates of Success," *Academy of Management Journal* 22 (June 1979), pp. 292–312. For a discussion of the Improshare plan, see R. Kaufman, "The Effects of Improshare on Productivity," *Industrial and Labor Relations Review* 45, no. 2 (1991), pp. 311–322.

56. B.W. Thomas and M.H. Olson, "Gainsharing: The Design Guarantees Success," *Personnel Journal* (May 1988), pp. 73–79. See also "Aligning Compensation with Quality," *Bulletin to Management, BNA Policy and Practice Series* (April 1, 1993), p. 97.

57. See T.A. Welbourne and L. Gomez Mejia, "Gainsharing Revisited," *Compensation and Benefits Review* (July–August 1988), pp. 19–28.

58. This is paraphrased from W. Imberman, "Boosting Plant Performance with Gainsharing," *Business Horizons* (November–December 1992), p. 77; for other examples, see T. Ross and L. Hatcher, "Gainsharing Drives Quality Improvement," *Personnel Journal* (November 1992), pp. 81–89. See also J. McAdams, "Employee Involvement and Performance Reward Plans: Design, Implementation, and Results," *Compensation and Benefits Review* 27, no. 2 (March 1995), pp. 45–55.

59. P.K. Zingheim and J.R. Schuster, "Value Is the Goal," *Workforce* (February 2000), pp. 56–61.

60. B. Aldridge, "Innovative Workplace Practices," www.hrsdc.gc.ca/en/lp/wid/win/2005_4th_quarter.shtml (February 16, 2006).

61. A. Kohn, "Why Incentive Plans Cannot Work," *Harvard Business Review* (September–October 1993), pp. 54–63.

62. J. Cameron and W.D. Pierce, *Rewards and Intrinsic Motivation: Resolving the Controversy* (Westport, CT: Bergin & Garvey, 2002). See also G. Bouchard, "When Rewards Don't Work," *Globe & Mail* (September 25, 2002), p. C3.

63. P.K. Zingheim and J.R. Schuster, *Pay People Right!: Breakthrough Reward Strategies to Create Great Companies* (San Francisco, CA: Jossey-Bass, 2000).

64. S. Gross and J. Bacher, "The New Variable Pay Programs: How Some Succeed, Why Some Don't," *Compensation and Benefits Review* (January–February 1993), pp. 55–56; see also G. Milkovich and C. Milkovich, "Strengthening the Pay-Performance Relationship: The Research," *Compensation and Benefits Review* (November–December 1992), pp. 53–62; J. Schuster and P. Zingheim, "The New Variable Pay: Key Design Issues," *Compensation and Benefits Review* (March–April 1993), pp. 27–34.

65. D. Belcher, *Compensation Administration* (Englewood Cliffs, NJ: Prentice Hall, 1973), pp. 309–310.

66. C. Kapel and T. Kinsman-Berry, "Seven Key Factors for Effective Incentive Plans," *Canadian HR Reporter* (October 4, 1999), pp. 12–13.

67. D. Brown, "Thanks for a Job Well Done. Can We Clean Your House for You?" *Canadian HR Reporter* (January 13, 2003), pp. 18–19.

68. J. Mills, "A Matter of Pride: Rewarding Team Success," *Canadian HR Reporter* (March 8, 1999), p. 16. See also D. Hutson, "New Incentives on the Rise," *Compensation and Benefits Review* (September/October 2000), pp. 40–46; D. Hutson, "Getting the Feel for Employee Rewards," *Canadian HR Reporter* (January 14, 2002), pp. 22–23; B. Parus, "Recognition: A Strategic Tool for Retaining Talent," *Workspan* (November 2002), pp. 14–18; J. Mills, "A Matter of Pride: Rewarding Team Success"; D. Hutson, "New Incentives on the Rise" and D. Hutson, "Getting the Feel for Employee Rewards." See also L. McKibbin-Brown, "Beyond the Gold Watch: Employee Recognition Today," *Workspan* (April 2003), pp. 44–46.

69. J. Mills, "Gratitude à la carte," *Workplace News* (January 2005), p. 12; L. McKibbon-Brown, "Beyond the Gold Watch: Employee Recognition Today," *Workspan* (April 2003), pp. 44–46.

70. A. Welsh, "The Give and Take of Recognition Programs," *Canadian HR Reporter* (September 22, 1997), pp. 16–17, 22; J.M. Kouzas and B.Z. Posner, *Encouraging the Heart: A Leader's Guide to Rewarding and Recognizing Others* (San Francisco, CA: Wiley, 2003); D. Brown, "Canada Wants Nurses Again, but Will Anyone Answer the Call?" *Canadian HR Reporter* (January 15, 2001), pp. 1, 14, 15.

71. J.M. Kouzas and B.Z. Posner, *Encouraging the Heart: A Leader's Guide to Rewarding and Recognizing Others* (San Francisco, CA: Wiley, 2003). See also B. Nelson, "Why Managers Don't Recognize Employees," *Canadian HR Reporter* (March 11, 2002), p. 9; L. Cassiani, "Lasting Impressions through Recognition," *Canadian HR Reporter* (March 12, 2001), p. 7; J. Mills, "A Matter of Pride: Rewarding Team Success," *Canadian HR Reporter* (March 8, 1999), p. 16; L. Young, "How Can I Ever Thank You?" *Canadian HR Reporter* (January 31, 2000), pp. 7, 9.

72. E. Wright and K. Ryan, "Thanks a Million (More or Less)," *Canadian HR Reporter* (March 9, 1998), pp. 19, 21, 23. See also "How to Sell Recognition to Top Management," *Canadian HR Reporter* (June 1, 1998), p. 21; B. Nelson, "Cheap and Meaningful Better Than Expensive and Forgettable," *Canadian HR Reporter* (August 13, 2001), p. 22.

73. L. Davidson, "The Power of Personal Recognition," *Workforce* (July 1999), pp. 44–49. See also A. Gostick and C. Elton, "Show Me the Rewards," *Canadian HR Reporter* (March 12, 2001), pp. 7, 10; V. Scott and B. Phillips, "Recognition Program Links Achievement to Corporate Goals," *Canadian HR Reporter* (December 14, 1998), pp. 22–23. See also R. Clarke, "Building a Recognition Program: Alternatives and Considerations," *Canadian HR Reporter* (November 2, 1998), pp. 17, 19; E. Wright and K. Ryan, "Thanks a Million (More or Less)," *Canadian HR Reporter* (March 9, 1998), pp. 19, 21, 23; L. Davidson, "The Power of Personal Recognition," *Workforce* (July 1999), pp. 44–49; D. Brown, "Recognition an Integral Part of Total Rewards," *Canadian HR Reporter* (August 12, 2002), pp. 25, 27.

74. J. Jackson, "The Art of Recognition," *Canadian HR Reporter* (January 15, 2001), p. 22. See also B.P. Keegan, "Incentive Programs Boost Employee Morale," *Workspan* (March 2002), pp. 30–33; S. Nador, "Beyond Trinkets and Trash," *Canadian HR Reporter* (May 20, 2002), pp. 15, 19.

75. H. Hilliard, "How to Reward Top Performers When Money Is No Object," *Canadian HR Reporter* (August 13, 2001), pp. 21, 23.

76. A. Welsh, "The Give and Take of Recognition Programs," *Canadian HR Reporter* (September 22, 1997), pp. 16–17, 22; E. Wright and K. Ryan, "Thanks a Million (More or Less)," *Canadian HR Reporter* (March 9, 1998).

77. T. Humber, "Beyond the Gold Watch," *Canadian HR Reporter* (January 30, 2006), pp. 23, 29; S. Singh, "'Tis the Season for Recognition," *Canadian HR Reporter* (December 5, 2005), pp. 19–20; A. Gostick, "Confusion, Envy and Other Tales from the Dark Side of Recognition," *Canadian HR Reporter* (December 6, 2004), p. 13; B. Nelson, "Misunderstanding Rewards Hampers Motivation," *Canadian HR Reporter* (May 17, 2004), p. 14.

Chapter 13

1. Based on F. Hills, T. Bergmann, and V. Scarpello, *Compensation Decision Making* (Fort Worth, TX: The Dryden Press, 1994), p. 424. See also L.K. Beatty, "Pay and Benefits Break Away from Tradition," *HR Magazine* 39 (November 1994), pp. 63–68.

2. R.K. Platt, "A Strategic Approach to Benefits," *Workspan* (July 2002), pp. 23–24.

3. S. Beech and J. Tompkins, "Do Benefits Plans Attract and Retain Talent?" *Benefits Canada* (October 2002), pp. 49–53.

4. F. Holmes, "Talking about an Evolution," *Benefits Canada* (September 2001), pp. 30–32; J. Thomas and M. Chilco, "Coming of Age," *Benefits Canada* (March 2001), pp. 36–38.

5. KPMG, *Employee Benefits Costs in Canada* (1998).

6. J. Dawe, "Compassionate Care Benefit: A New Alterative for Family Caregivers," *Workplace Gazette* (Summer 2004); S. Klie, "Feds Expand Eligibility for Compassionate Care," *Canadian HR Reporter* (July 17, 2006).

7. "EI Top-ups Common—Survey," *Canadian HR Reporter* (February 23, 1998), p. 15.

8. See, for example, Bialk, "Cutting Workers' Compensation Costs," *Personnel Journal* 66 (July 1987), pp. 95–97. See also H. Amolins, "Workers Must Cooperate in Return to Work," *Canadian HR Reporter* (November 3, 1997), p. 8; C. Knight, "Ontario Businesses Ready for New WCB," *Canadian HR Reporter* (November 17, 1997), p. 9.

9. U. Vu, "How Purolator Dealt with Skyrocketing Costs," *Canadian HR Reporter* (March 13, 2006).

10. J. Goodings, "Pressure Mounts to Increase Vacation Time," *Canadian HR Reporter* (March 22, 1999), p. 3.

11. S. Klie, "Feds Expand Eligibility for Compassionate Care," *Canadian HR Reporter* (July 17, 2006).

12. D. Gunch, "The Family Leave Act: A Financial Burden?" *Personnel Journal* (September 1993), p. 49.

13. S. Pellegrini, "Considering Critical," *Benefits Canada* (April 2002), pp. 71–73.

14. "Employee Benefits in Small Firms," *BNA Bulletin to Management* (June 27, 1991), pp. 196–197.

15. R. Jain, "Employer-Sponsored Dental Insurance Eases the Pain," *Monthly Labor Review* (October 1988), p. 18; "Employee Benefits," *Commerce Clearing House Ideas and Trends in Personnel* (January 23, 1991), pp. 9–11.

16. S. Lebrun, "Keeping the Lid on Drug Benefit Costs," *Canadian HR Reporter* (December 16, 1996), p. 12; J. Taggart, "HR's Drug Cost Nightmares," *Canadian HR Reporter* (October 21, 2002), pp. 17, 20; J. Curtis and L. Scott, "Making the Connection," *Benefits Canada* (April 2003), pp. 75–79.

17. C. Kapel, "Unitel Asks Employees to Share Costs," *Canadian HR Reporter* (June 17, 1996), p. 17. See also J. Sloane and J. Taggart, "Runaway Drug Costs," *Canadian HR Reporter* (September 10, 2001), pp. 17–18; "Deductibles Could Be Making a Comeback," *Canadian HR Reporter* (February 26, 2001), pp. 2, 16; K. Press, "Canadian Healthcare Checkup," *Benefits Canada* (June 2000), pp. 75–78. See also L. Young, "Employees Willing to Pay Higher Health Premiums," *Canadian HR Reporter* (June 19, 2000), pp. 1, 19.

18. J. Norton, "The New Drug Invasion," *Benefits Canada* (June 1999), pp. 29–32. See also S. Felix, "The New Drug Dilemma," *Benefits Canada* (March 1998), pp. 35–38.

19. S. Felix, "Healthy Alternative," *Benefits Canada* (February 1997), p. 47; A. Dimon, "Money Well Spent," *Benefits Canada* (April 1997), p. 15.

20. A. Dimon, "Money Well Spent," *Benefits Canada* (April 1997), p. 15.

21. J. Taggart, "Health Spending Accounts: A Prescription for Cost Control," *Canadian HR Reporter* (October 22, 2001), pp. 16, 18. See also "How Spending Accounts Work," *Canadian HR Reporter* (February 24, 2003), p. 16.

22. K. Gay, "Post-Retirement Benefits Costing Firms a Fortune," *Financial Post* (June 2, 1995), p. 18; S. Lebrun, "Turning a Blind Eye to Benefits," *Canadian HR Reporter* (February 24, 1997), p. 2; S. Pellegrini, "Keep Benefits Costs Low by Assessing Retiree Health," *Canadian HR Reporter* (June 14, 1999), pp. 9–10; M. Warren, "Uncovering the Costs," *Benefits Canada* (November 1996), p. 41; G. Dufresne, "Financing Benefits for Tomorrow's Retirees," *Canadian HR Reporter* (April 6, 1998), p. 11.

23. A. Khemani, "Post-Retirement Benefits Liability Grows," *Canadian HR Reporter* (November 4, 1996), p. 17. See also M. Warren, "Retiree Benefits Come of Age," *Benefits Canada* (May 2000), pp. 73–77.

24. W. Pyper, "Aging, Health and Work," *Perspectives on Labour and Income* (Spring 2006, p. 48); S. Klie, "Private Health Coverage Enters Benefits Realm," *Canadian HR Reporter* (September 12, 2005), pp. 1, 22; K. Read, "Integration Key to Managing Lost Time," *Canadian HR Reporter* (May 18, 1998), pp. 10–11.

25. A. Blake, "A New Approach to Disability Management," *Benefits Canada* (March 2000), pp. 58–64; P. Kulig, "Returning the Whole Employee to Work," *Canadian HR Reporter* (March 9, 1998), p. 20. See also A. Gibbs, "Gearing Disability Management to the Realities of Working Life," *Canadian HR Reporter* (December 2, 2002), p. G7.

26. J. Curtis and L. Scott, "Making the Connection," *Benefits Canada* (April 2003), pp. 75–79.

27. N. Rankin, "A Guide to Disability Management," *Canadian HR Reporter* (March 22, 1999), pp. 14–15.

28. H. Bryan, "Island Forestry Firms Get Focused," *WorkSafe Magazine* (August 2004), pp. 8–9.

29. "Mental Health Claims On the Rise in Canada," *WorldatWork Canadian News* (Third Quarter 2005), pp. 15–16; U. Vu, "With Mental Illness, Raising Awareness Is Still the Next Frontier," *Canadian HR Reporter* (December 15, 2003), pp. 1, 6; D. Brown, "Mental Illness a Top Concern but Only Gets Band-Aid Treatment," *Canadian HR Reporter* (May 9, 2005), pp. 1, 3; "Mental Health Biggest Workplace Barrier, Women Say," *Canadian HR Reporter* (January 17, 2005), p. 2; "Depression under Wraps," *Canadian HR Reporter* (November 18, 2002), p. 2.

30. M. Acharya, "Depressed Workers Cost Firms Billions, Business Panel Says," *Toronto Star* (July 21, 2000), p. C3; E. Vernarec, "The High Costs of Hidden Conditions," *Business and Health* 16 (1998), pp. 19–23. See also J. Kline Jr. and L. Sussman, "An Executive Guide to Workplace Depression," *Academy of Management Executive* 14 (August 2000), pp. 103–114.

31. J. Melnitzer, "Down and Out," *Workplace News* (September/October 2005), pp. 20–23; M. Cusipag, "A Healthy Approach to Managing Disability Costs," *Human Resources Professional* (June/July 1997), p. 13. See also M. Burych, "Baby Blues," *Benefits Canada* (October 2000), pp 33–35.

32. B. Hayhoe, "The Case for Employee Retirement Planning," *Canadian HR Reporter* (May 20, 2002), p. 18.

33. G.M. Hall, "Pensions: Death by Regulation?" *Canadian HR Reporter* (October 4, 1999), p. 6. See also S. Smolkin, "Changing Canadian Pension Standards," *Canadian HR Reporter* (November 29, 1999), pp. 24–26; S. Smolkin, "Proposals Add to Hodgepodge of Legislative Inconsistencies," *Canadian HR Reporter* (January 17, 2000), p. 8; T. Singeris and M. Mignault, "Tackling Pension Legislation Compliance," *Canadian HR Reporter* (January 31, 2000), p. 16. See also G.M. Hall, "Pensions: Death by Regulation?" See also J. Nunes, "Defined Benefit or Defined Contribution, It's Always Costly," *Canadian HR Reporter* (November 5, 2001), pp. 7, 9.

34. R.E. Sibson, *Wages and Salaries* (New York: American Management Association, 1967), p. 234. For an explanation of how to minimize employee benefits litigation related to pension and health benefits claims, see T. Piskorski, "Minimizing Employee Benefits Litigation through Effective Claims Administration Procedures," *Employee Relations Law Journal* 20, no. 3 (Winter 1994–95), pp. 421–431.

35. U. Vu, "BD Shortfall Could Hit $190 Billion," *Canadian HR Reporter* (December 5, 2005), pp. 1, 6; J. Hobel, "Defined Benefit Pension Plan Sponsors Worry Risk Becoming Too Great," *Canadian HR Reporter* (November 7, 2005), pp. 5, 10; K. Ambachtsheer, "Monsanto Decision a Wakeup Call for Change," *Canadian HR Reporter* (November 7, 2005), p. 7; S. Bonnar, "Last Nails in the Coffin for Defined Benefit System?" *Canadian HR Reporter* (November 8, 2004), pp. 8, 11.

36. M. Banks and M. Lowry, "Changing Workforce Requires Rethinking of Pension Plan," *Canadian HR Reporter* (March 10, 1997), p. 17; J. Pearce, "Switching from Defined Benefits to a Money Purchase Plan? Think Twice," *Canadian HR Reporter* (October 6, 1997), pp. 20, 23.

37. F. Giancola, "The Truth about Employee Investment Behavior," *Workspan* (April 2005), pp. 42–45; L. Maldonado, "You Decided to Convert . . . Now What?" *Canadian HR Reporter* (May 23, 2005), pp. 15, 17; F. Holden and S. Lewis, "The Rules Are Changing for Capital Accumulation Plans," *Canadian HR Reporter* (January 16, 2004), pp. 15–16; A. Shad, "When the Angry Mob Comes Knocking," *Canadian HR Reporter* (December 2, 2002), p. G6; C. Ripsman and O. Sharma, "More Than Ever, Good Governance, Smart Management Crucial," *Canadian HR Reporter* (November 4, 2002), pp. 7, 9; L. Satov, "Time for Sponsors to Rethink Pension Plans," *Canadian HR Reporter* (October 7, 2002), pp. 22, 23; K. Press, "Top 50 Defined Contribution Pension Funds," *Benefits Canada* (August 1999), pp. 33–42.

38. J. Thompson and P.C. Statler, "Sound Options Make for Sound Choices," *Canadian HR Reporter* (February 9, 1998), p. 10; K. Press, "Top 10 Defined Contribution Pension Funds," *Benefits Canada* (August 1999), pp. 33–42.

39. C. I. Genno, "There's More to Pensions Than Defined Benefit versus Defined Contribution," *Canadian HR Reporter* (February 13, 2006), pp. 14, 17; W. Babcock and C. Pitcher, "Building the Perfect Plan," *Benefits Canada* (May 2000), pp. 33–35.

40. R. Stuart and C. Graham, "Early Retirement on the Bargaining Table," *Canadian HR Reporter* (January 27, 2003), pp. 12, 15; J. Chevreau, "Older Workers Plan to Stay," *National Post* (February 15, 2002).

41. D. Brown, "New Brunswick Nurses Find Phased Retirement Solution," *Canadian HR Reporter* (September 22, 2003), pp. 1, 12; Y. Saint-Cyr, "Phased Retirement Agreements," *Canadian Payroll and Employment Law News*, www.hrpao.org/HRPAO/HRResourceCentre/LegalCentre/ (July 11, 2005).

42. *Towers Perrin 2004 SERP Report: Supplementary Pensions Under Pressure* (Toronto: Towers Perrin, 2004).

43. R. Henderson, *Compensation Management* (Reston, VA: Reston, 1979), pp. 336–339. See also L. Burger, "Group Legal Service Plans: A Benefit Whose Time Has Come," *Compensation and Benefits Review* 18 (July–August 1986), pp. 28–34.

44. A. Davis, "Helping Hands," *Benefits Canada* (November 2000), pp. 117–121; P. Davies, "Problem Gamblers in the Workplace," *Canadian HR Reporter* (November 4, 2002), p. 17; F. Engel, "Lost Profits, Increased Costs: The Aftermath of Workplace Trauma," *Canadian HR Reporter* (September 7, 1998), pp. 21–22; G. Kurzawa, "Cooking Up an EAP," *Canadian HR Reporter* (September 7, 1998), p. 19. See also A. Sharratt, "When a Tragedy Strikes," *Benefits Canada* (November 2002), pp. 101–105; D. Rosolen, "Situation Critical," *Benefits Canada* (November 2001), pp. 29–35; J. Hobel, "EAPs Flounder without Manager Support," *Canadian HR Reporter* (June 2, 2003), p. 7.

45. R. Csiernik, "What to Look for in an External EAP Service," *Canadian HR Reporter* (May 31, 2004), p. 7; D. Sharar, "With HR Chasing Lowest Price, EAPs Can't Improve Quality," *Canadian HR Reporter* (May 31, 2004), pp. 6, 8; A. Davis, "Helping Hands," *Benefits Canada* (November 2000), pp. 117–121.

46. "100 Best Companies to Work For," *Fortune* (January 2000).

47. C. Davenport, "Child-Care Solutions for a Harried Work World," *Canadian HR Reporter* (April 21, 1997), p. 16. See also C. Eichman and B. Reisman, "How Small Employers Are Benefiting from Offering Child-Care Assistance," *Employment Relations Today* (Spring 1992), pp. 51–62; D. Brown, "Bringing the Family to Work," *Canadian HR Reporter* (November 6, 2000), pp. 19–20; Kids and Company, "Back-up Solution," www.kidsandcompany.ca/corporations/our_childcare_solutions.aspx (August 27, 2006).

48. L. Johnson, "Effectiveness of an Employee-Sponsored Child-Care Center," *Applied HRM Research* 2 (Summer 1991), pp. 38–67.

49. D. McCloskey, "Caregiving and Canadian Families," *Transition Magazine* (Summer 2005); B. Parus, "Who's Watching Grandma? Addressing the Eldercare Dilemma," *Workspan* (January 2004), pp. 40–43; N. Spinks, "'We Are Taking Gran to the Hospital': Eldercare Unpredictable, Exhausting," *Canadian HR Reporter* (December 16, 2002), pp. 7, 10; P. Kulig, "Eldercare Issues Loom for Canadian Organizations," *Canadian HR Reporter* (May 4, 1998), pp. 1, 2; A. Vincola, "Eldercare—What Firms Can Do to Help," *Canadian HR Reporter* (June 5, 2000), p. G3.

50. "Elder Care to Eclipse Child Care, Report Says," *Canadian HR Reporter* (August 14, 1995), p. 11; A. Vincola, "Eldercare—What Firms Can Do to Help," *Canadian HR Reporter* (June 5, 2000), p. G3.

51. D. Dyck, "Make Your Workplace Family-Friendly," *Canadian HR Reporter* (December 13, 1999), pp. G5, G10.

52. L. Fraught, "At Eddie Bauer You Can Have Work and Have a Life," *Workforce* (April 1997), p. 84.

53. E.E. Kossek and C. Ozeki, "Work-Family Conflict, Policies, and the Job-Life Satisfaction Relationship: A Review and Direction for Organizational Behavior-Human Resources Research," *Journal of Applied Psychology* 83, (1998), pp. 139–149.

54. B. Ellig, *Executive Compensation—A Total Pay Perspective* (New York: McGraw-Hill, 1982), p. 141.

55. P. Clark, "Relocation Perks Are Tops with Executives," *Canadian HR Reporter* (June 1, 1998), p. G4; "Wellness Perks Highly Valued," *Canadian HR Reporter* (November 15, 1999), p. 10; B. Jaworski, " 'I'll Have My People Call Your People . . . ,'" *Canadian HR Reporter* (March 27, 2006).

56. J.B. Chapman and R. Ottermann, *Employee Preference for Various Compensation and Fringe Benefit Options* (Berea, OH: ASPA Foundation, 1975). See also W. White and J. Becker, "Increasing the Motivational Impact of Employee Benefits," *Personnel* (January–February 1980), pp. 32–37; B. Olmsted and S. Smith, "Flex for Success!" *Personnel* 66, no. 6 (June 1989), pp. 50–55.

57. B. McKay, "The Flexible Evolution," *Workplace News* (January/February 2006), pp. 14–15.

58. R. Dawson and B. McKay, "The Flexibility of Flex," *WorldatWork Canadian News* (Fourth Quarter 2005), pp. 1, 6–13.

59. D. Brown, "Everybody Loves Flex," *Canadian HR Reporter* (November 18, 2002), pp. 1, 11; R. Dawson and B. McKay, "The Flexibility of Flex," *WorldatWork Canadian News* (Fourth Quarter 2005), pp. 1, 6–13

60. J. Tompkins, "Moving Out: A Look at Comprehensive Benefits Outsourcing," *Canadian HR Reporter* (May 5, 1997), p. 9.

61. A. Czarnecki, "Employees Show Increasing Interest in Pension Communication Systems," *Canadian HR Reporter* (July 15, 1996), p. 18. See also J. Kopach, "Today's Flexible Benefits Programs Call for Greater Employee Education," *Canadian HR Reporter* (August 9, 1999), p. G3; N. Chaplick, "Enter at Your Own Risk," *Benefits Canada* (May 2000), pp. 37–39. See also M. Reid, "Legal Aid," *Benefits Canada* (June 2000), pp. 46–48; S. Deller, "Five Hot Survival Tips for Communicating Benefits," *Canadian HR Reporter* (July 13, 1998), pp. 9, 19.

62. C. Davenport, "Employers Twig to Value of Ongoing Pension Communication," *Canadian HR Reporter* (December 16, 1996), p. 33.

Chapter 14

1. D. Brown, "Wellness Programs Bring Healthy Bottom Line," *Canadian HR Reporter* (December 17, 2001), pp. 1, 14.

2. Association of Workers' Compensation Boards of Canada, www.awcbc.ca (June 20, 2006); "Working to Death—Millions Die Each Year Due to Work-Related Accidents and Diseases," *IAPA Press Release* (April 19, 2006), www.iapa.ca/about_iapa/2006_apr19_press.asp (June 20, 2006).

3. H. Bryan, "Attitude Is Everything," *WorkSafe Magazine* (October 2005), p. 18.

4. This section is based on T.A. Opie and L. Bates, *1997 Canadian Master Labour Guide* (CCH Canada Inc.), pp. 1015–1034.

5. C.A. Edwards and C.E. Humphrey, *Due Diligence Under the Occupational Health and Safety Act: A Practical Guide* (Toronto: Carswell/Thomson Canada, 2000).

6. M. Pilger, "Conducting a Hygiene Assessment," *Canadian HR Reporter* (April 10, 2000), pp. G3, G4; J. Montgomery, *Occupational Health and Safety* (Toronto: Nelson Canada, 1996), p. 97; D. Brown, "Joint H&S Committees: An Opportunity, Not a Nuisance," *Canadian HR Reporter* (October 20, 2002), pp. 7, 10.

7. J. Grant and D. Brown, "The Inspector Cometh," *Canadian HR Reporter* (January 31, 2005), pp. 13, 17; "It's Time to Wake Up to Health and Safety: Ministry of Labour Increases Number of Inspectors," *Safety Mosaic* 8 (Spring 2005), pp. 5–6.

8. "MOL Shows Increasing Trend of Fines and Convictions," *Gowlings OHS Law Report* (March 2005), p. 3; N. Keith, "Worker Sentenced to 20 Days Imprisonment for Occupational Health and Safety Violation," *Gowlings OHS Law Report* (June 2005), p. 1; M. Love, "Pea Processor Fined after Workplace Fatality," *Workplace News* (May 2005), p. 2; "Woodbridge Foam Corp Fined $175 000 for Health and Safety Violation," *Ontario Ministry of*

Labour News Release (June 7, 2004); "School Board Fined in Caretaker's Death," *Gowlings OHS Law Report* (March 2005), p. 2.

9. "Employer Jailed for H&S Violation," *Canadian HR Reporter* (April 8, 2002), p. 2. See also T. Humber, "Putting the Boss Behind Bars?" *Canadian HR Reporter* (April 7, 2003), pp. 19, 25.

10. B. McCreadie, "Safety Lessons from One of Bill C-45's First Charges," *Workplace News* (January 2005), pp. 10–11; "Legislative Update: Bill C-45," *Safety Mosaic* (Spring 2005), pp. 2–5; *Report on Labour*, McCarthy Tetrault LLP (February 2004), pp. 2–5.

11. J. Montgomery, *Occupational Health and Safety* (Toronto: Nelson Canada, 1996), p. 34.

12. K. Prisciak, "Health, Safety & Harassment?" *OH&S Canada* (April/May 1997), pp. 20–21.

13. P. Strahlendorf, "What Supervisors Need to Know," *OH&S Canada* (January/February 1996), pp. 38–40; N. Tompkins, "Getting the Best Help from Your Safety Committee," *HR Magazine* 40, no. 4 (April 1995), p. 76.

14. Dupont Canada, www2.dupont.com/DuPont_Home/en_CA/index.html (June 20, 2006).

15. *A Safety Committee Man's Guide*, Aetna Life and Casualty Insurance Company, Catalog 872684.

16. J. Roughton, "Job Hazard Analysis," *OH&S Canada* (January/February 1996), pp. 41–44.

17. A. Fowler, "How to Make the Workplace Safer," *People Management* 1, no. 2 (January, 1995), pp. 38–39.

18. List of unsafe acts from *A Safety Committee Man's Guide*, Aetna Life and Casualty Insurance Company; E. McCormick and J. Tiffin, *Industrial Psychology* (Englewood Cliffs, NJ: Prentice Hall, 1974).

19. E. McCormick and J. Tiffin, *Industrial Psychology* (Englewood Cliffs, NJ: Prentice Hall, 1974), pp. 522–523; Norman Maier, *Psychology and Industrial Organization* (Boston: Houghton-Mifflin, 1965), pp. 458–462; Milton Blum and James Nayler, *Industrial Psychology* (New York: Harper & Row, 1968), pp. 519–531. For example, David DeJoy, "Attributional Processes and Hazard Control Management in Industry," *Journal of Safety Research* 16 (Summer 1985), pp. 61–71.

20. E. McCormick and J. Tiffin, *Industrial Psychology* (Englewood Cliffs, NJ: Prentice Hall, 1974), *Industrial Psychology*, p. 523.

21. P. Finn and B. Bragg, "Perceptions of the Risk of an Accident by Young and Older Drivers," *Accident Analysis and Prevention* 18, no. 4 (August 1986). See also O. Mitchell, "The Relation of Age to Workplace Injuries," *Monthly Labor Review* 111, no. 7 (July 1988), pp. 8–13; M. Philp, "Young Workers Face High Risks," *Globe & Mail* (July 10, 2000), p. A2. See also D. Brown, "Good Intentions—Heartbreaking Results," *Canadian HR Reporter* (November 20, 2000), pp. 1, 7.

22. Young Worker Memorial LifeQuilt, "Jared Diduck," www.youngworkerquilt.ca/jareddiduck.htm (June 20, 2006).

23. M. Blum and J. Nayler, *Industrial Psychology* (New York: Harper & Row, 1968), p. 522.

24. P. Kulig, "Behavior-Based Programs Aim to Limit Mishaps," *Canadian HR Reporter* (May 18, 1998), p. 2.

25. J.B. Miner and J.F. Brewer, "Management of Ineffective Performance," in M. Dunnette (ed.), *Handbook of Industrial and Organizational Psychology*, pp. 1004–1005 (Chicago: Rand McNally, 1976); G. Borofsky, M. Bielema, and J. Hoffman, "Accidents, Turnover, and Use of a Pre-employment Screening Interview," *Psychological Reports* (1993), pp. 1067–1076; L. Ebbs, "The Safety Culture," *Human Resources Professional* (October/November 1998), pp. 22–26.

26. L. Scott, "Measuring Employee Abilities," *Benefits Canada* (September 2002), pp. 41–49.

27. K. Gillin, "Reduce Employee Exposure to Injury with Pre-Employment Screening Tests," *Canadian HR Reporter* (February 28, 2000), p. 10.

28. H.A. Amolins, "Safety Perception: What Do Your Employees Really Think?" *Canadian HR Reporter* (September 21, 1998), p. 8; B. Broadbent, "The Training Alternative," *OH&S Canada* (July–August 1996), pp. 36–41.

29. A group of international experts met in Belgium in 1986 and concluded that a successful safety poster must be simple and specific and reinforce safe behaviour rather than negative behaviour. See "What Makes an Effective Safety Poster," *National Safety and Health News* 134, no. 6 (December 1986), pp. 32–34.

30. M. Shaw, "Rewarding Health and Safety," *Canadian HR Reporter* (December 2, 2002), pp. 19–20.

31. L. Young, "Communicating Heath and Safety Where It Matters," *Canadian HR Reporter* (May 17, 1999), p. 12.

32. D. Hofmann and A. Stetzer, "A Cross-Level Investigation of Factors Influencing Unsafe Behaviors and Accidents," *Personnel Psychology* 49 (1996), p. 329.

33. L. Scott, "Measuring Employee Abilities," *Benefits Canada* (September 2002), pp. 41–49.

34. *Workers' Compensation Manual for Managers and Supervisors* (Chicago: Commerce Clearing House, 1992), pp. 36–39.

35. Ibid, p. 51.

36. A. Dunn, "Back in Business," *Workplace News* (April 2005), pp. 16–17.

37. C. Colacci, "Meet Your Return to Work Obligations with a Functional Abilities Evaluation," *Canadian HR Reporter* (April 10, 2000), p. G5. See also L.J. Blake, T. Cuminskey, and H.J. Brown, *Functional Abilities Evaluations: Hiring and Maintaining a Healthy Workforce* (Toronto: Carswell/Thomson Canada Ltd., 1998).

38. A. Bierbier, "Controlling Sky-High Absenteeism," *OH&S Canada* (January–February 1996), pp. 54–63.

39. M. Morales, "Canada All Talk, No Action in Wellness," *Canadian HR Reporter* (April 22, 2002), pp. 23, 29; D. Dyck, "Wrapping Up the Wellness Package," *Benefits Canada* (January 1999), pp. 16–20. See also T. Wallace, "An Ounce of Prevention," *Canadian HR Reporter* (April 23, 2001), pp. 15, 19.

40. J. Taggart and J. Farrell, "Where Wellness Shows Up on the Bottom Line," *Canadian HR Reporter* (October 20, 2003), pp. 12, 15.

41. "Improved Health of Employees and Financial Bottom Line Demonstrated Through Innovative Pilot Program at DaimlerChrysler Canada Plant," *WorldatWork Newsline* www.worldatwork.org/worldatwork.html (May 11, 2006).

42. S. Pellegrini, "The Next 25 Years: Wellness," *Benefits Canada* (June 2002), pp. 83–85.

43. L. Young, "Managers at B.C. Telus Held Accountable for Wellness," *Canadian HR Reporter* (February 28, 2000), p. 9.

44. A. Tomlinson, "Healthy Living a Remedy for Burgeoning Employee Absentee Rates," *Canadian HR Reporter* (March 25, 2002), pp. 3, 12.

45. Homewood Health Centre, "Career," www.homewood.org/healthcentre/main.php?tID=2&IID=1 (June 20, 2006).

46. This section based largely on J.B. Miner and J.F. Brewer, "Management of Ineffective Performance," in M.D. Dunnette (ed.), *Handbook of Industrial and Organizational Psychology*, pp. 1005–1023 (New York: Wiley & Sons, 1976).

47. "Addiction Problems in Manufacturing," *Canadian HR Reporter* (March 24, 2003), p. 3.

48. J. Rehm, D. Ballunas, S. Brochu, B. Fischer, W. Gnam, J. Patra, S. Popova, A. Sarnocinska-Hart, and B. Taylor, *The Cost of Substance Abuse in Canada 2002* (Canadian Centre on Substance Abuse, March 2006), p. 9.

49. A. Chiu, "The Elements of Workplace Drug, Alcohol Policies," *Canadian HR Reporter* (March 13, 2000), p. 17; M. Johne, "Clean and Sober: Dealing with Drugs and Alcohol in the Workplace," *HR Professional* (October/November 1999), pp. 18–22.

50. G.C. Pati and J.I. Adkins, "Employer's Role in Alcoholism Assistance," *Personnel Journal* 62, no. 7 (July 1983), pp. 568–572. See also Commerce Clearing House, "How Should Employers Respond to Indications an Employee May Have an Alcohol or Drug Problem?" *Ideas and Trends* (April 6, 1989), pp. 53–57.

51. Based on J.B. Miner and J.F. Brewer, "Management of Ineffective Performance," in M. D. Dunnette (ed.), *Handbook of Industrial and Organizational Psychology*, pp. 1005–1023 (New York: Wiley & Sons, 1976). The survey was conducted jointly by the American Society for Personnel Administration and the Bureau of National Affairs.

52. D. O'Meara, "Sober Second Chance," *Alberta Venture* 9, no. 2 (March 2005).

53. C. Hall, "Sobering Advice," *Workplace News* 11, no. 10 (November/December 2005), pp. 11–12.

54. *British Columbia (Public Service Employee Relations Commission) v. B.C.G.S.E.U.*, (1999) 176 D.L.R. (4th) 1 (S.C.C.) [*Meiorin*].

55. *Policy on Drug and Alcohol Testing*, Ontario Human Rights Commission, 2005, www.ohrc.on.ca/english/publicatoins/drug-alcohol-policy.shtml (May 25, 2006).

56. A. Chiu, "The Elements of Workplace Drug, Alcohol Policies," *Canadian HR Reporter* (March 13, 2000), p. 17.

57. *Mental Disorders and Addictions in the Workplace*, BC Partners for Mental Health and Addictions Information, 2003, www.heretohelp.ca/publications/factsheets/workplace.stml (May 18, 2006); *Modernizing Part III of the Canada Labour Code*, Canadian Autoworkers, 2005, www.fls-ntf.gc.ca/en/sub_fb_28.asp (May 18, 2006).

58. J.W. Simpson, "Psychopaths Wear Suits, Too," *National Post* (May 10, 2006), p. WK6; A. Gill, "The Psychopath in the Corner Office," *Globe & Mail* (May 27, 2006), p. F1; "Push for Productivity Taking its Toll," *Canadian HR Reporter* (November 6, 2001), p. 15; D. Brown, "Doing More with Less Hurts Employees and Productivity," *Canadian HR Reporter* (October 7, 2002), pp. 3, 13; A. Sharratt, "Silver Linings," *Benefits Canada* (March 2003), pp. 51–53.

59. J. Santa-Barbara, "Preventing the Stress Epidemic," *Canadian HR Reporter* (March 8, 1999), p. 19. See also A. Chiu, "Beyond Physical Wellness: Mental Health Issues in the Workplace," *Canadian HR Reporter* (February 26, 2001), p. 4; L. Hyatt, "Job Stress: Have We Reached the Breaking Point?" *Workplace Today* (January 2002), pp. 14, 15, 37.

60. L. Duxbury and C. Higgins, *Exploring the Link between Work-Life Conflict and Demands on Canada's Health Care System: Report Three* (Public Health Agency of Canada: March 2004); *Staying at Work 2000/2001—The Dollars and Sense of Effective Disability Management*, Catalogue #W-377 (Vancouver BC: Watson Wyatt Worldwide); T. Stephens and N. Joubert, "The Economic Burden of Mental Health Problems in Canada," *Chronic Diseases in Canada* 22, no. 1 (2001), 18–23.

61. *Mental Health at Work: Booklet 1*. IRSST (Laval University, 2005).

62. P. Crawford-Smith, "Stressed Out," *Benefits Canada* (November 1999), pp. 115–117.

63. *Stress at Work: Taking Control* (Industrial Accident Prevention Association, 2002); J. Newman and T. Beehr, "Personal and Organizational Strategies for Handling Job Stress: A Review of Research and Opinion," *Personnel Psychology* (Spring 1979), pp. 1–43. See also Bureau of National Affairs, "Work Place Stress: How to Curb Claims," *Bulletin to Management* (April 14, 1988), p. 120.

64. J.K. Yardley, "Do Your Managers Roll Their Eyes When Employees Say They Are Overworked?" *Canadian HR Reporter* (April 23, 2001), pp. 18–19.

65. U. Vu, "Lip Service to Wellness Abounds," *Canadian HR Reporter* (April 5, 2004), pp. 1, 9.

66. T. Humber, "Stress Attack," *Canadian HR Reporter* (February 10, 2002), pp. G1, G10; M. Shain, "Stress and Satisfaction," *OH&S Canada* (April/May 1999), pp. 38–47.

67. J. Hampton, "HR Execs Key to Combating Workplace Depression," *Canadian HR Reporter* (August 14, 2000), pp. 1, 3; T. Humber, "Stress Attack," *Canadian HR Reporter* (February 10, 2002).

68. J. Hampton, "HR Executives Key to Combatting Workplace Depression," *Canadian HR Reporter* (August 14, 2000), pp. 1, 3. The 12 steps are drawn from the Business and Economic Roundtable on Mental Health.

69. P. Carayon, "Stressful Jobs and Non-stressful Jobs: A Cluster Analysis of Office Jobs," *Ergonomics* 37, no. 2 (1994), pp. 311–323.

70. A. Pihulyk, "When the Job Overwhelms," *Canadian HR Reporter* (January 14, 2002), p. 11.

71. P. Kishchuk, *Yukon Workers' Compensation Act Subsection 105.1 Research Series: Expansion of the Meaning of Disability* (March 2003).

72. M. Gibb-Clark, "The Case for Compensating Stress Claims," *Globe & Mail* (June 14, 1999), p. M1; L. Young, "Stressed Workers Are Suing Employers," *Canadian HR Reporter* (May 3, 1999), pp. 1, 6; D. Brown, "Liability Could Extend to Mental Damage," *Canadian HR Reporter* (October 9, 2000), pp. 1, 8.

73. OPSEU Online, "International RSI Awareness Day—February 28, 2006," www.opseu.org/hands/rsi2006.htm (May 18, 2006); J. Hampton, "RSIs: The Biggest Strain Is on the Bottom Line," *Canadian HR Reporter* (February 10, 1997), pp. 15, 19. See also G. Harrington, "Pushing Ergonomics into Place," *Canadian HR Reporter* (April 24, 1995), pp. 11–12.

74. "Prevent Workplace Pains and Strains! It's Time to Take Action!" Ontario Ministry of Labour, www.labour.gov.on.ca/english/hs/ergonomics/is_ergonomics.html (May 25, 2006); "Repetitive Strain Injury," Institute for Work and Health, www.iwh.on.ca/media/RSI.php (May 25, 2006).

75. S.B. Hood, "Repetitive Strain Injury," *Human Resources Professional* (June/July 1997), pp. 29–34.

76. "Ergonomic Intervention Improves Worker Health and Productivity," Institute for Work and Health (December 15, 2003), www.iwh.on.ca/media/ergonomic.php (July 8, 2006); "Ergonomic Intervention Improves Worker Health and Productivity," *Workplace News* (February 2004), p. 16.

77. G. Harrington, "Older Workers Need Ergonomic Aid," *Canadian HR Reporter* (November 17, 1997), p. 20; B. Weir, "Technology Transforms Workplace Behaviour," *Workplace Today* (October 2000), pp. 36–37.

78. J.A. Savage, "Are Computer Terminals Zapping Workers' Health?" *Business and Society Review* (1994).

79. "Office Ergonomics and Repetitive Strain Injuries: What You Need to Know," Ottawa Valley Physiotherapy, www.ovphysio.com (May 25, 2006); Occupational Health and Safety Agency for Healthcare in British Columbia, www.ohsah.bc.ca/templates/index.php?section_copy_id=5396 (May 25, 2006); S. Tenby, "Introduction to Ergonomics: How to avoid RSI—Repetitive Strain Injury," Disabled Women's Network Ontario, http://dawn.thot.net/cd/20.html (May 25, 2006).

80. "Unions Stress Cancer Prevention," *Canadian HR Reporter* (February 28, 2005), p. 2.

81. D. Brown, "Killer Toxins in the Workplace," *Canadian HR Reporter* (April 23, 2001), pp. 1, 12.

82. A. Tomlinson, "Manitoba Recognizes Firefighting Cancer Risk," *Canadian HR Reporter* (June 17, 2002), pp. 2, 6. See also W.H. Glenn, "Finding the Right Balance," *OH&S Canada* (June 2002) pp. 38–43; W.H. Glenn, "What's Killing Canadian Workers?" *OH&S Canada* (August 2002), p. 20.

83. "'Waitress Who Never Smoked' Dies of Lung Cancer," CTV.ca (May 23, 2006), www.ctv.ca (May 25, 2006).

84. "EI Granted in Second-Hand Smoke Case," *Canadian HR Reporter* (May 19, 2003), p. 3. See also M.M. Finklestein, "Risky Business," *OH&S Canada* (September/October 1996), pp. 32–34.

85. T. Humber, "Snuffing out Smoking," *Canadian HR Reporter* (April 11, 2005), p. 19, 23; *Towards Healthier Workplaces and Public Places* (Health Canada, 2004).

86. *Violence in the Workplace*, Canadian Association of University Teachers (October 4, 2004); W.H. Glenn, "Workplace Violence: An Employees' Survival Guide," *OH&S Canada* (April/May 2002), pp. 26–31.

87. "Dying for a Job: Health Care Workers Beware," CBC News Online (April 24, 2006), www.cbc.ca/news/background/workplace-safety/sick-workplace.html (May 23, 2006). See also "Physician Abuse of Nurses," *Canadian HR Reporter* (October 22, 2001), p. 2.

88. A. Feliu, "Workplace Violence and the Duty of Care: The Scope of an Employer's Obligation to Protect against the Violent Employee," *Employee Relations Law Journal* 20, no. 3 (Winter 1994/95), pp. 381–406; G. French

and P. Morgan, "The Risks of Workplace Violence," *Canadian HR Reporter* (December 18, 2000), pp. 27–28.

89. K. Burkhardt, "Family of Murdered Nurse Sues for $13.5 Million," *Canadian HR Reporter* (April 10, 2006).

90. S. Klie, "Screening New Hires Won't End Workplace Violence, Study Says," *Canadian HR Reporter* (November 21, 2005), pp. 1, 3.

91. A. Tomlinson, "Re-evaluating Your Workplace: Is It Safe and Secure?" *Canadian HR Reporter* (February 25, 2002), pp. 3, 12; L. Martin and D. Tona, "Before It's Too Late," *OH&S Canada* (April/May 2000), pp. 52–53.

92. P. Viollis and C. Mathers, "Companies Need to Re-engineer Their Cultural Thinking About Workplace Violence," *Canadian HR Reporter* (March 14, 2005), p. 19; D. Anfuso, "Workplace Violence," *Personnel Journal* (October 1994), p. 71. See also L. Martin and D. Tona, "Before It's Too Late," *OH&S Canada* (April/May 2000), pp. 52–53; H. Bloom, "Workplace Violence: The Myth That We're Helpless," *Workplace Today* (January 2002), pp. 36–37; W.H. Glenn, "Workplace Violence: An Employees' Survival Guide," *OH&S Canada* (April/May 2002), pp. 26–31.

93. D. Anfuso, "Workplace Violence," *Personnel Journal* (October 1994), pp. 66–77.

Chapter 15

1. Y. Cohen-Charash and P.E. Spector, "The Role of Justice in Organizations: A Meta-analysis," *Organizational Behavior and Human Decision Processes* 86 (November 2001), pp. 278–321.

2. U. Vu, "Telus E-mails Staff, Union Cries Foul," *Canadian HR Reporter* (May 23, 2005), pp. 1, 10.

3. M. Rowbotham, "Mitigate Corporate Liability through Employee Communication," *Canadian HR Reporter* (December 3, 2001), p. G7.

4. "Big Payoff for Employee Suggestions," *Canadian HR Reporter* (September 25, 1995), p. 7.

5. P. Kulig, "The Importance of Being a Good Listener," *Canadian HR Reporter* (April 20, 1998), pp. 15, 19. See also D. Jones, "What If You Held a Survey and No-One Came?" *Canadian HR Reporter* (July 16, 2001), pp. 19, 22.

6. D. Brown, "Getting the Hard Facts in Employee Attitude and Satisfaction," *Canadian HR Reporter* (November 1, 1999), p. 2.

7. A. Massey, "Blogging Phobia Hits Employers," *Canadian HR Reporter* (September 26, 2005), pp. 15, 17.

8. This section is based on D. McElroy, "High Tech with High Touch: A New Communication Contract," *Canadian HR Reporter* (April 7, 1997), p. G6.

9. B. Orr, "Privacy in the Workplace A Growing Challenge for Employers," *Canadian HR Reporter* (January 25, 1999), pp. 8, 10.

10. P. Israel, "Employee Misconduct . . . Employer Responsibility?" *Canadian HR Reporter* (May 20, 2002), p. 5. See also "Developing Internet Policies for Employees," *Canadian HR Reporter* (November 16, 1998), p. 23.

11. "Yukon: Employees Disciplined for Internet Abuse" *Workplace Today* (October 2003), www.workplace.ca/preview/magsecure/2003m10/news/article3673.html#3675 (July 11, 2006).

12. D. Shields and V. Jepson, "When Internet Use Turns to Abuse," *HR Professional* (April/May 2006), p. 28.

13. J. Conforti, "Privacy in the Workplace: Access to Employee Records and Monitoring of Employees in the Internet Age." Paper presented at the Human Resources Professionals Association of Ontario Employment Law Conference (October 1999), Toronto.

14. E.A. Douthitt and J.R. Aiello, "The Role of Participation and Control in the Effects of Computer Monitoring on Fairness Perceptions, Task Satisfaction, and Performance," *Journal of Applied Psychology*, 86 (2001), pp. 867–874.

15. P. Israel, "Spying on Employees . . . and It's Perfectly Legal," *Canadian HR Reporter* (April 21, 2003), p. 5. See also P. Bonifero, "Workplace Privacy and Surveillance Issues," *HR Professional* (February/March 1999), pp. 49–51.

16. M. MacKillop and L. Jessome, "What You Need to Know About Criminal Charges and Just Cause Terminations," *Workplace News Online* (October 2005),
www.wpnonline.com/index.php?option=com_content&task=view&id=21&Itemid=16 (May 29, 2006).

17. S. Rudner, "The High Cost of Internet, E-mail Abuse," *Canadian HR Reporter* (January 31, 2005), pp. R5–R6; N. MacDonald, "You've Got E-mail Problems," *Canadian HR Reporter* (March 10, 2003), pp. G5, G10; A. Tomlinson, "Heavy-Handed Net Policies Push Privacy Boundaries," *Canadian HR Reporter* (December 2, 2002), pp. 1, 26. See also J. Conforti, "Privacy in the Workplace: Access to Employee Records and Monitoring of Employees in the Internet Age." Paper presented at the Human Resources Professionals Association of Ontario Employment Law Conference (October 1999), Toronto.

18. K. Williams, "Privacy in a Climate of Electronic Surveillance," *Workplace News* (April 2005), p. 10; S. Hood, "What's Private, What's Not?" *HR Professional* (February/March 2006), pp. 20–28.

19. R. Hiscock, "A Perspective on Canada's New Privacy Legislation," *Canadian HR Reporter* (June 18, 2001), pp. G8–G9. See also E. Kuzz, "More Rules for Employee Information Protection," *Canadian HR Reporter* (September 9, 2002), p. 16; D. Brown, "10 Months to Get Ready," *Canadian HR Reporter* (February 24, 2003), pp. 1, 11.

20. P. Israel, "If You're Not Protecting Employee Data, It's Time to Get Started," *Canadian HR Reporter* (May 19, 2003), p. 5; I. Turnbull, "Canada's New Privacy Law—What It Means to You," *Canadian HR Reporter* (December 15, 2003), pp. 20–21.

21. S. Ray and D. Holmes, "How to Discipline without Exposure to Lawsuits," *Canadian HR Reporter* (September 6, 1999), p. 31. See also J. Miller, "Procedural Fairness Toward Disciplined Workers an Issue before the Courts," *Canadian HR Reporter* (November 2, 1998), p. 5. See also P. Israel, "How to Tackle Poor Job Performance—and Bring Down Legal Costs," *Canadian HR Reporter* (February 10, 2003), pp. 5, 12.

22. G.A. Ball, "Outcomes of Punishment Incidents: The Role of Subordinate Perceptions, Individual Differences, and Leader Behavior," Unpublished doctoral dissertation, Pennsylvania State University. See also N. Cole, "Yes, Employees Can React Positively to Discipline," *Canadian HR Reporter* (November 4, 1996), p. 11; N.D. Cole and G.P. Latham, "Effects of Training in Procedural Justice on Perceptions of Disciplinary Fairness by Unionized Employees and Disciplinary Subject Matter Experts," *Journal of Applied Psychology* 82 (October 1997), pp. 699–705.

23. D. Grote, *Discipline without Punishment* (New York: American Management Association, 1995).

24. J. Famularo, *Handbook of Modern Personnel Administration* (New York: McGraw-Hill, 1972), pp. 65.3–65.5.

25. Ibid.

26. A. Britnell, "Stop Employee Theft," *Canadian Business Online*, July 16, 2003, www.canadianbusiness.com (May 29, 2006); J. Towler, "Dealing with Employees Who Steal," *Canadian HR Reporter* (September 23, 2002), p. 4.

27. "Air Canada Searches Employee Rooms," *Canadian HR Reporter* (February 10, 2003), p. 2.

28. J. Famularo, *Handbook of Modern Personnel Administration* (New York: McGraw-Hill, 1972), pp. 65.4–65.5.

29. A. Macaulay, "Dealing with Bad Behaviour at Work," *Canadian HR Reporter* (June 19, 2006).

30. T. Humber, "What Would You Do?" *Canadian HR Reporter* (January 16, 2006), pp. 7–8.

31. E.E. Mole, *Wrongful Dismissal Practice Manual*, Chapter 7 (Toronto: Butterworths Canada, 1993).

32. E.E. Mole, *Wrongful Dismissal Practice Manual*, Chapter 4 (Toronto: Butterworths Canada, 1993). See also L. Cassiani, "Dishonesty Not Always Enough to Terminate," *Canadian HR Reporter* (August 13, 2001), pp. 3, 6; P. Israel, "Firing an Employee for Dishonesty? Put Things in Context First," *Canadian HR Reporter* (August 12, 2002), p. 5.

33. "Proving Cause for Termination Getting Harder," *Workplace Today* (January 2001), p. 17; L. Harris, "High Standards Allow Employer to Fire Threatening Employee," *Canadian HR Reporter* (October 22, 2001), pp. 8, 10.

34. K. Blair, "Sports Editor Scores 28-Month Severance," *Canadian HR Reporter* (April 7, 1997), p. 5.

35. M.J. MacKillop, "The Perils of Dismissal: The Impact of the Wallace Decision on Reasonable Notice." Paper presented at the Human Resources Professionals Association of Ontario Employment Law Conference (October 1999), Toronto. See also M.J. MacKillop, "Bad Faith Discharge Dismissed by S.C.C.," *HR Professional* (April/May 1998), pp. 11–12; K. Blair, "The High Cost of Bad Faith Termination," *Canadian HR Reporter* (December 1, 1997), p. 5. See also J. McAlpine, "Don't Add Bad Faith to Wrongful Dismissal," *Canadian HR Reporter* (May 6, 2002), p. 7; P. Israel, "Cut Down on Lawsuits Just by Being Nice," *Canadian HR Reporter* (November 18, 2002), p. 5.

36. J. Miller, "Lower Courts Raise Employers' Costs with Higher Extended-Notice Damages," *Canadian HR Reporter* (May 31, 1999), p. 5.

37. M.J. MacKillop, "The Perils of Dismissal: The Impact of the Wallace Decision on Reasonable Notice." Paper presented at the Human Resources Professionals Association of Ontario Employment Law Conference (October 1999), Toronto, p. 18.

38. K. Blair, "Pay in Lieu Just the Beginning," *Canadian HR Reporter* (July 14, 1997), p. 5. See also K. Blair, "Dismissal Damages, Thy Name Is Mitigation," *Canadian HR Reporter* (February 9, 1998), p. 5.

39. M. MacKillop and L. Jessome, "Manage Disability Claims with Care," *HR Professional* (August/September 2005), p. 30; J.M. Carvalho, "$500,000 Punitive Damages Award Shocks Honda," *McCarthy Tetrault Report on Canadian Labour and Employment Law* (September 2005).

40. J. Melnitzer, "Peril of Coveting thy Neighbour's Employee," *Workplace News* (May 2005), pp. 1–2.

41. J. McApline, "10 Steps for Reducing Exposure to Wrongful Dismissal," *Canadian HR Reporter* (May 6, 2002), p. 8.

42. E. Caruk, "What to Do If a Wrongful Dismissal Action Hits," *Canadian HR Reporter* (May 6, 2002), p. 10.

43. E.E. Mole, *Wrongful Dismissal Practice Manual*, Chapter 3 (Toronto: Butterworths Canada, 1993).

44. "Employer's Letters Impugning Integrity of Key Employees Constituted Constructive Dismissal, Judge Rules," *Wrongful Dismissal and Employment Law News* (Toronto: Lancaster House, November/December 2005), pp. 11–13.

45. This section was based on M. Rothman, "Employee Termination, I: A Four-Step Procedure," *Personnel* (February 1989), pp. 31–35; S. Jesseph, "Employee Termination, II: Some Do's and Don'ts," *Personnel* (February 1989), pp. 36–38. For a good checklist see A.F. Silbergeld, "Avoiding Wrongful Termination Claims: A Checklist for Employers," *Employment Relations Today* 20, no. 4 (Winter, 1993), pp. 447–454.

46. See J. Coil, III and C. Rice, "Three Steps to Creating Effective Employee Releases," *Employment Relations Today* (Spring 1994), pp. 91–94. Wrongful termination is a problem for managerial employees as well. See, for example, C. Longenecker and F. Post, "The Management Termination Trap," *Business Horizons* 37, no. 3 (May–June, 1994), pp. 71–79.

47. E.A. Lind, J. Greenberg, K.S. Scott, and T.D. Welchans, "The Winding Road from Employee to Complainant: Situational and Psychological Determinants of Wrongful Dismissal Claims," *Administrative Science Quarterly* 45 (2000), pp. 557–590.

48. J. Coil, III and C. Rice, "Three Steps to Creating Effective Employee Releases," *Employment Relations Today* (Spring 1994), p. 92.

49. W.J. Morin and L. York, *Outplacement Techniques* (New York: AMACOM, 1982), pp. 101–131; F.L. Branham, "How to Evaluate Executive Outplacement Services," *Personnel Journal* 62 (April 1983), pp. 323–326; S. Milne, "The Termination Interview," *Canadian Manager* (Spring 1994), pp. 15–16.

50. W.J. Morin and L. York, *Outplacement Techniques* (New York: AMACOM, 1982), p. 117. See also Sonny Weide, "When You Terminate an Employee," *Employment Relations Today* (August 1994), pp. 287–293; Commerce Clearing House, *Ideas and Trends in Personnel* (July 9, 1982), pp. 132–146.

51. D. Patient and D. Skarlicki, "Don't Shoot the Messenger! How to Deliver Bad News," *HR Professional* (June/July 2003), pp. 48–49.

52. J. Zarandona and M. Camuso, "A Study of Exit Interviews: Does the Last Word Count?" *Personnel* 62, no. 3 (March 1985), pp. 47–48.

53. Quoted from Commerce Clearing House, *Ideas and Trends in Personnel* (August 9, 1988), p. 133.

54. Commerce Clearing House, *Personnel Practices/Communications* (Chicago: CCH, 1992), p. 1402.

55. Commerce Clearing House, *Personnel Practices/Communications* (Chicago: CCH, 1992), p. 1410.

56. P. Kulig, "Temporary Employment Changing the Character of Canada's Labour Force," *Canadian HR Reporter* (November 16, 1998), pp. 1, 15.

57. This is based on *Mossop Cornelissen Report* (August 1996).

58. S. Stephens, "When Two Worlds Collide," *HR Professional* (April/May 2000), pp. 27–35.

59. J. Emshoff, "How to Increase Employee Loyalty While You Downsize," *Business Horizons* (March–April 1994), pp. 49–57. See also R. Ford and P. Perrewé, "After the Layoff: Closing the Barn Door before All the Horses Are Gone," *Business Horizons* (July–August 1993), pp. 34–40.

60. S. Stephens, "When Two Worlds Collide," *HR Professional* (April/May 2000), pp. 27–35.

61. *Canada's Demographic Revolution: Adjusting to an Aging Population* (The Conference Board of Canada, 2006).

62. *1995 Canadian Dismissal Practices Survey* (Toronto: Murray Axmith & Associates).

63. G. Golightly, "Preparing Employees for Retirement Transitions," *HR Professional* (December 1999/January 2000), pp. 27–33.

64. Ibid.

65. *New Frontiers of Research on Retirement*, Statistics Canada, Catalogue No. 75-511-XPE, 2006, www.statcan.ca/bsolc/english/bsolc?catno=75-511-XIE (July 11, 2006).

Chapter 16

1. T.T. Delaney, "Unions and Human Resource Policies," in K. Rowland and G. Ferris (eds.), *Research in Personnel and Human Resources Management* (Greenwich, CT: JAI Press, 1991).

2. R. Morissette, G. Shellenberg, and A. Johnson, "Diverging Trends in Unionization," *Perspectives on Labour and Income* 17, no. 2, Statistics Canada (Summer 2005); U. Vu, "Low Membership Keeps Unions on the Defensive," *Canadian HR Reporter* (February 13, 2006), pp. 4, 9.

3. C. Hallamore, "Globalization Shifts the Ground in Labour Relations," *Inside Edge* (Spring 2006), p. 14. See also C. Hallamore, *Industrial Relations Outlook 2006: Shifting Ground, Shifting Attitudes* (Ottawa: Conference Board of Canada).

4. D. Chamot, "Unions Need to Confront the Results of New Technology," *Monthly Labor Review* (August 1987), p. 45.

5. S. Levitan and F. Gallo, "Collective Bargaining and Private Sector Employment," *Monthly Labor Review* (September 1989), pp. 24–33; B. Ettorre, "Will Unions Survive?" *Management Review* (August 1993) pp. 9–15; "Union Blasts Privatization," *The Peterborough Examiner* (February 8, 2000).

6. W.C. Hamner and F. Schmidt, "Work Attitude as Predictor of Unionization Activity," *Journal of Applied Psychology* 63, no. 4 (1978), pp. 415–521; A. Okafor, "White Collar Unionization: Why and What to Do," *Personnel* 62, no. 8 (August 1985), pp. 17–20; M.E. Gordon and A. DiNisi, "A Re-examination of the Relationship between Union Membership and Job Satisfaction," *Industrial and Labor Relations Review* 48, no. 2 (January 1995), pp. 222–236.

7. "Union, Non-union Wage Gap Closing," *Canadian HR Reporter* (October 21, 2002), p. 2.

8. Statistics Canada Internet site, "Unionization—An Update" (August 30, 2000).

9. C. Fullager and J. Barling, "A Longitudinal Test of a Model of the Antecedents and Consequences of Union Loyalty," *Journal of Applied*

Psychology 74, no. 2 (April 1989), pp. 213–227; A. Eaton, M. Gordon, and J. Keefe, "The Impact of Quality of Work-Life Programs and Grievance Systems Effectiveness on Union Commitment," *Industrial and Labor Relations Review* 45, no. 3 (April 1992), pp. 592–604.

10. L. Young, "Union Drives: Initiated Within, Prevented Within," *Canadian HR Reporter* (November 29, 1999), pp. 2, 14.

11. Based in part on L. Field, "Early Signs," *Canadian HR Reporter* (November 29, 1999), p. 14.

12. *Canadian Master Labour Guide*, 16th ed. (Toronto: CCH Canadian, 2002).

13. A.W.J. Craig and N.A. Solomon, *The System of Industrial Relations in Canada*, 5th ed. (Scarborough, ON: Prentice Hall Canada, 1996), p. 217.

14. Ibid, p. 218.

15. Ibid, p. 216.

16. D. Yoder, *Personnel Management* (Englewood Cliffs, NJ: Prentice Hall, 1972), p. 486. See also M. Ballot, *Labor–Management Relations in a Changing Environment* (New York: John Wiley and Sons, 1992), pp. 169–425.

17. J. Peirce, *Canadian Industrial Relations* (Scarborough, ON: Prentice Hall Canada, 2000), p. 431.

18. R. Stagner and H. Rosen, *Psychology of Union–Management Relations* (Belmont, CA: Wadsworth, 1965), pp. 95–97.

19. The section on distributive bargaining is based on R.E. Walton and R.B. McKersie, *A Behavioral Theory of Labor Negotiations* (New York: McGraw-Hill, 1965), pp. 4–6.

20. The section on integrative bargaining is based on R.E. Walton and R.B. McKersie, *A Behavioral Theory of Labor Negotiations* (New York: McGraw-Hill, 1965), pp. 4–6.

21. Based on C. Kapel, "The Feeling's Mutual," *Human Resources Professional* (April 1995), pp. 9–13. See also S.D. Smith, "Taking the Confrontation out of Collective Bargaining," *Canadian HR Reporter* (September 10, 2001), pp. 11, 13.

22. Based on D. Cameron, "The Interest-Based Approach to Union–Management Negotiation," *HR Professional* (February/March 1999), pp. 37–39.

23. U. Vu, "Interest Wanes on Interest-Based?" *Canadian HR Reporter* (February 28, 2006), pp. 6, 9.

24. J. Peirce, *Canadian Industrial Relations* (Scarborough, ON: Prentice Hall Canada, 2000), p. 431.

25. Cited in B. Tieleman, "Still Good Reason to Join a Union: Studies Show Union Workers Reap Better Wages and Benefits," *Financial Post* (July 5, 1999), p. C6.

26. D. Hasselback, "Inco Strike to Cost Firm US$20M a Month," *Financial Post* (June 5, 2003), p. FP4.

27. C. Spurr, "A 'Perfect Storm': Stora Enso Lockout in Nova Scotia," *Shunpiking Online* 3, no. 4 (May 3, 2006), www.shunpiking.com/ol0304/0304-AC-CS-perfectstrom.htm (June 1, 2006); "Keep Stora off Campaign Agenda: Mayor," *CBC News* (May 26, 2006), www.cbc.ca/ns/story/nsv-stora20060526.html (June 1, 2006); "Stora Enso Lockout in Canada Ends with Ratification Vote," ICEM InBrief, www.icem.org/?id=19&doc=1861&la=EN (July 6, 2006).

28. V. Lu, "Wildcat Strike Possible Today, TTC Says," *Toronto Star* (May 29, 2006), p. A2; N. Van Rijn, "Blindsided," *Toronto Star* (May 30, 2006), pp. A1, A6; K. McGran and D. Vincent, "Day after Wildcat Strike, Union Leader Is Defiant," *Toronto Star* (May 31, 2006), pp. A1, A18.

29. See J.E. Grenig, "Stare Decisis, Re Judicata and Collecteral Estoppel and Labour Arbitration," *Labour Law Journal* 38 (April 1987), pp. 195–205.

30. Based on M. Gunderson and D.G. Taras, *Union–Management Relations in Canada* (Toronto: Pearson Education Canada, 2001), p. 429; J. Peirce, *Canadian Industrial Relations* (Scarborough, ON: Prentice Hall Canada, 2000), p. 431.

31. This section is based on M. Gunderson and D.G. Taras, *Union–Management Relations in Canada* (Toronto: Pearson Education Canada, 2001), pp. 282–283.

32. *Canadian Master Labour Guide*, 16th ed. (Toronto: CCH Canadian Ltd., 2002).

33. M. Hebert, "Length of Collective Agreements," *Workplace Gazette* 7, no. 4 (Winter 2004), p. 27.

34. G. Sova, "How Long a Contract Should You Sign?" *Canadian HR Reporter* (February 28, 2005), p. 9.

Chapter 17

1. G. Reinhart, "Preparing for Global Expansion: A Primer," *Canadian HR Reporter* (March 14, 2005), pp. 14, 17.

2. D. Brown, "HR Issues Top of Mind for Execs Worldwide: Study," *Canadian HR Reporter* (May 5, 2003), pp. 1, 9. See also A.K. Paul and R.N. Anantharaman, "Impact of People Management Practices on Organizational Performance: Analysis of a Causal Model," *International Journal of Human Resource Management* 14, no. 7 (2003), pp. 1246–1266.

3. S. Cryne, "The Changing World of the Relocation Specialist," *Canadian HR Reporter* (March 8, 2004), pp. 13, 15.

4. "Short-Term Global Assignments Rising," *Canadian HR Reporter* (May 7, 2001), p. 2; S. Cryne, "The Changing World of the Relocation Specialist," *Canadian HR Reporter* (March 8, 2004), pp. 13, 15; G. Reinhart, "Preparing for Global Expansion: A Primer," *Canadian HR Reporter* (March 14, 2005), pp. 14, 17.

5. K. Roberts, E. Kossek, and C. Ozeki, "Managing the Global Workforce: Challenges and Strategies," *Academy of Management Executive* 12, no. 4 (1998), pp. 93–106.

6. J. Head, "How Paper Can Protect International Relocations," *Canadian HR Reporter* (March 13, 2006).

7. *2005 Employee Relocation Survey: Domestic, Cross-Border & International Relocations* (Toronto: Canadian Employee Relocation Council, 2005); D. Bergles, "Let Them Choose," *Canadian HR Reporter* (May 6, 2002), pp. 15, 19.

8. *2005 Employee Relocation Survey: Domestic, Cross-Border & International Relocations* (Toronto: Canadian Employee Relocation Council, 2005); D. Bergles and L. Da Rocha, "Putting Work–life Balance into Relocation Planning," *Canadian HR Reporter* (September 23, 2002), pp. 9–10.

9. S. Cryne, "The Changing World of the Relocation Specialist," *Canadian HR Reporter* (March 8, 2004), pp. 13, 15.

10. R. Melles, "Lost in Translation," *Canadian HR Reporter* (March 8, 2004), p. 14.

11. L. Grobovsky, "Protecting Your Workers Abroad with a Global Diversity Strategy," *Canadian HR Reporter* (November 1, 1999), pp. 15–16.

12. "Expect Corruption Overseas," *Canadian HR Reporter* (September 23, 2002), p. 9; "Oil and Water," *Canadian Business* (November 8–21, 2004), pp. 14, 16.

13. These are based on E. Gaugler, "HR Management: An International Comparison," *Personnel* (August 1988), pp. 24–30. See also Y. Kuwahara, "New Developments in Human Resource Management in Japan," *Asia Pacific Journal of Human Resources* 31, no. 2 (1993), pp. 3–11; C.M. Solomon, "How Does Your Global Talent Measure Up," *Personnel Journal* (October 1994), pp. 96–108.

14. For a discussion of this, see E. Gaugler, "HR Management: An International Comparison," *Personnel* (August 1988), p. 26; see also George Palmer, "Transferred to Tokyo—A Guide to Etiquette in the Land of the Rising Sun," *Multinational Business* no. 4 (1990/1991), pp. 36–44.

15. G. Hofstede, "Cultural Dimensions in People Management," in Vladimir Pucik, Noel Tishy, and Carole Barnett (eds.), *Globalizing Management*, p. 143 (New York: John Wiley & Sons, 1992).

16. G. Hofstede, "Cultural Dimensions in People Management," in Vladimir Pucik, Noel Tishy, and Carole Barnett (eds.), *Globalizing Management* (New York: John Wiley & Sons, 1992).

17. E. Gaugler, "HR Management: An International Comparison," *Personnel* (August 1988), p. 27. See also Simcha Ronen and Oded Shenkar, "Using Employee Attitudes to Establish MNC Regional Divisions," *Personnel* (August 1988), pp. 32–39.

18. "Comparing Employment Practices," *BNA Bulletin to Management* (April 22, 1993), p. 1.

19. M. Higginson, "Hungary's Low Labor Costs Still Lure Big Investors," *Budapest Business Journal* (April 10, 2006).

20. This is discussed in E. Gaugler, "HR Management: An International Comparison," *Personnel* (August 1988), p. 28.

21. This is based on R. Sedel, "Europe 1992: HR Implications of the European Unification," *Personnel* (October 1989), pp. 19–24. See also C. Brewster and A. Hegewish, "A Continent of Diversity," *Personnel Management* (January 1993), pp. 36–39; G. Lowc, "The Quality of Work Features Prominently in Europe's Plan for Competitiveness," *Canadian HR Reporter* (May 19, 2003), pp. 6, 8; *European Union Member States,* http://europa.eu/abc/governments/index_en.htm (August 21, 2006).

22. J.D. Daniels and L.H. Radebaugh, *International Business* (Reading, MA: Addison-Wesley, 1994), p. 764.

23. Based on B.J. Punnett, "International Human Resources Management," in A.M. Rugman (ed.), *International Business in Canada: Strategies for Management,* pp. 330–346 (Scarborough, ON: Prentice Hall Canada, 1989); L.G. Klaff, "Thinning the Ranks of the 'Career Expats,'" *Workforce Management* (October 2004), pp. 84–87.

24. L. Hyatt, "It Takes Two: Relocating Dual Career Couples," *Workplace Today* (January 2002), p. 13.

25. M. Schell, quoted in C.M. Solomon, "Success Abroad Depends on More Than Job Skills," *Personnel Journal* (April 1994), p. 52. See also J. Keogh, "A Win-Win, From Start to Finish," *Workspan* (February 2003), pp. 36–39.

26. B.J. Punnett, "International Human Resources Management," in A.M. Rugman, ed., *International Business in Canada: Strategies for Management* (Scarborough, ON: Prentice Hall Canada, 1989), pp. 334–335; V. Galt, "World Loves to Milk Canada's Executive Pool," *Globe & Mail* (September 5, 2005), p. B10.

27. L. Young, "Let's Make a Deal—When to Offer Relocation Alternatives," *Canadian HR Reporter* (June 14, 1999), pp. 18, 19. See also L. Young, "Family Relocations on the Decline," *Canadian HR Reporter* (June 14, 1999), pp. 1, 19; A.M. Yeargan and R. Herod, "Managing Short-Term International Assignments," *WorldatWork Canadian News* 10 (2002), pp. 1, 3, 8, 17; D. Bergles and R. Peterman, "Selling Relocation Used to Be Easier Than This," *Canadian HR Reporter* (September 27, 2004), p. 8; S. Cryne, "Are Short-Term Gigs Better Than Permanent Moves?" *Canadian HR Reporter* (December 6, 2004), pp. 1–2.

28. Z. Fedder, "Short-Sighted Thinking Shortchanges Short-Term International Assignments," *Canadian HR Reporter* (September 25, 2000), p. 20.

29. J.D. Daniels and L.H. Radebaugh, *International Business* (Reading, MA: Addison-Wesley, 1994), p. 767; Arvind Phatak, *International Dimensions of Management* (Boston: PWS-Kent, 1989), pp. 106–107.

30. J.D. Daniels and L.H. Radebaugh, *International Business* (Reading, MA: Addison-Wesley, 1994); Arvind Phatak, *International Dimensions of Management* (Boston: PWS-Kent, 1989), pp. 106–107.

31. J.D. Daniels and L.H. Radebaugh, *International Business* (Reading, MA: Addison-Wesley, 1994), p. 769; Arvind Phatak, *International Dimensions of Management* (Boston: PWS-Kent, 1989), p. 106.

32. Howard Perlmutter, "The Torturous Evolution of the Multinational Corporation," *Columbia Journal of World Business* 3, no. 1 (January–February 1969), pp. 11–14; Arvind Phatak, *International Dimensions of Management* (Boston: PWS-Kent, 1989).

33. G.W.L. Hill, *International Business* (Burr Ridge, IL: McGraw Hill, 1994).

34. Ibid, p. 509.

35. Ibid.

36. Arvind Phatak, *International Dimensions of Management* (Boston: PWS-Kent, 1989), p. 113; Charlene Marmer Solomon, "Staff Selection Impacts Global Success," *Personnel Journal* (January 1994), pp. 88–101. For another view, see Anne Harzing, "The Persistent Myth of High Expatriate Failure Rates," *International Journal of Human Resource Management* 6, no. 2 (May 1995), pp. 457–574.

37. M.A. Shaffer, D.A. Harrison, K.M. Gilley, and D.M. Luk, "Struggling for Balance Amid Turbulence on International Assignments: Work-Family Conflict, Support and Commitment," *Journal of Management* 27 (2001), pp. 99–121; R. Garonzik, J. Brockner, and P.A. Siegel, "Identifying International Assignees at Risk for Premature Departure: The Interactive Effects of Outcome Favorability and Procedural Fairness," *Journal of Applied Psychology* 85 (2000), pp. 13–20; M.A. Shaffer and D.A. Harrison, "Forgotten Partners of International Assignments: Development and Test of a Model of Spouse Adjustment," *Journal of Applied Psychology,* 86 (2001), pp. 238–54.

38. W. Arthur, Jr. and W. Bennett, Jr., "The International Assignee: The Relative Importance of Factors Perceived to Contribute to Success," *Personnel Psychology* 48 (1995), pp. 99–114; table on pp. 106–107. See also E. Davison and B. Punnett, "International Assignments: Is There a Role for Gender and Race in Decisions?" *International Journal of Human Resource Management* 6, no. 2 (May 1995), pp. 411–441.

39. W. Arthur, Jr. and W. Bennett, Jr., "The International Assignee: The Relative Importance of Factors Perceived to Contribute to Success," *Personnel Psychology* 48 (1995), p. 110.

40. G. Spreitzer, M. McCall Jr., and J. Mahoney, "Early Identification of International Executive Potential," *Journal of Applied Psychology* 82 (1997), pp. 6–29.

41. Arvind Phatak, *International Dimensions of Management* (Boston: PWS-Kent, 1989), p. 119.

42. L. Laroche, "Removing the Unexpected with Pre-Assignment Visits," *Canadian HR Reporter* (May 8, 2000), pp. 17, 20. See also P.M. Caligiuri and J.M. Phillips, "An Application of Self-Assessment Realistic Job Previews to Expatriate Assignments," *International Journal of Human Resource Management* 14, no. 7 (2003), pp. 1102–1116; P. Blocklyn, "Developing the International Executive," *Personnel* (1989), p. 45.

43. Discussed in M. Callahan, "Preparing the New Global Manager," *Training and Development Journal* (March 1989), p. 30. The publisher of the inventory is the New York consulting firm Moran, Stahl, and Boyer; see also Jennifer Laabs, "The Global Talent Search," *Personnel Journal* (August 1991), pp. 38–44, for a discussion of how firms, such as Coca-Cola, recruit and develop international managers, and T.S. Chan, "Developing International Managers: A Partnership Approach," *Journal of Management Development* 13, no. 3 (1994), pp. 38–46.

44. M. Larson, "Background Checking Goes Global," *Workforce Management* (April 2006).

45. M. Callahan, "Preparing the New Global Manager," *Training and Development Journal* (March 1989), pp. 29–30. See also C.M. Solomon, "Global Operations Demand That HR Rethink Diversity," *Personnel Journal* (July 1994), pp. 40–50; A. Bross, A. Churchill, and J. Zifkin, "Cross-Cultural Training: Issues to Consider during Implementation," *Canadian HR Reporter* (June 5, 2000), pp. 10, 12.

46. M. Callahan, "Preparing the New Global Manager," *Training and Development Journal* (March 1989), p. 30. See also D. Feldman, "Repatriate Moves as Career Transitions," *Human Resource Management Review* 1, no. 3 (Fall 1991), pp. 163–178; J. Yanouzas and S. Boukis, "Transporting Management Training into Poland: Some Surprises and Disappointments," *Journal of Management Development* 12, no. 1 (1993), pp. 64–71; J.S. Biteen, "Worldly Relocation Advice," *Canadian HR Reporter* (February 23, 1998), pp. 21, 22; A. Bross, A. Churchill, and J. Zifkin, "Cross-Cultural Training: Issues to Consider During Implementation," *Canadian HR Reporter* (June 5, 2000); C. Shick, "It Wasn't What You Said, It Was How You Said It," *Canadian HR Reporter* (February 28, 2000), p. 18.

47. G. Reinhart, "Going Global," *Canadian HR Reporter* (September 25, 2000), pp. 19, 23.

48. C. Reynolds, "Global Compensation and Benefits in Transition," *Compensation and Benefits Review* (January/February 2000), pp. 28–28; J.E. Richard, "Global Executive Compensation: A Look at the Future," *Compensation and Benefits Review* (May/June 2000), pp. 35–38.

49. L. Laroche, "Negotiating Expatriate Packages," *Canadian HR Reporter* (November 20, 2000), pp. 15, 19.

50. J. Stoner and R.E. Freeman, *Management*, 4th ed. (Englewood Cliffs, NJ: Prentice Hall, 1989), p. 783. See also J. Cartland, "Reward Policies in a Global Corporation," *Business Quarterly* (Autumn 1993), pp. 93–96; L. Mazur, "Europay," *Across-the-Board* (January 1995), pp. 40–43.

51. Hewitt Associates, "On Compensation," (May 1989), p. 1 (Hewitt Associates, 86–87 East Via De Ventura, Scottsdale, Arizona 85258); C. Reynolds, "Global Compensation and Benefits in Transition," *Compensation and Benefits Review* (January/February 2000), p. 37; K. Bensky, "Developing a Workable Global Rewards System," *Workspan* (October 2002), pp. 44–48.

52. C.W. Hill, *International Business* (Burr Ridge, IL: Irwin, 1994), pp. 519–520; L. Molnar, "How Canadian Companies are Paying Expatriates," *WorldatWork Canadian News* (Second Quarter 2005), pp. 1, 22–24; "Tax Equalization Still Ranks First for Canadian, U.S. and U.K. Expatriates" *Workspan Focus Canada 2006*, p. 18.

53. Arvind Phatak, *International Dimensions of Management* (Boston: PWS-Kent, 1989), p. 134. See also L. Laroche, "Negotiating Expatriate Packages," *Canadian HR Reporter* (November 20, 2000), pp. 15, 19.

54. B. Brooks, "Long-Term Incentives: International Executives Need Them, Too," *Personnel* (August 1988), pp. 40–42.

55. V. Frazee, "Keeping Your Expats Healthy," *Global Workforce* (November 1998), pp. 18–23. See also B. Barker and D. Schulde, "Special EAP Helps Expatriates Face International 'Culture Shock,'" *Canadian HR Reporter* (November 29, 1999), p. 20; L. O'Grady, "Using Technology to De-stress on International Assignment," *Canadian HR Reporter* (September 24, 2001), pp. 8, 12; R. Melles, "Lost in Translation," *Canadian HR Reporter* (March 8, 2004), p. 14; E.C. Heher, "Anticipating the Psychological Effects of Expatriate Life," *Workspan* (May 2006), pp. 54–56.

56. A. Bross and G. Wise, "Sustaining the Relocated Employee with an International EAP," *Canadian HR Reporter* (November 29, 1999), pp. 18, 19, 21.

57. Except as noted, this is based on G. Addou and M. Mendenhall, "Expatriate Performance Appraisal: Problems and Solutions," in M. Mendenhall and G. Addou, *International Human Resource Management* (Boston: PWS-Kent Publishing, 1991), pp. 364–374. See also J. Milliman, S. Taylor, and A.J. Czaplewski, "Cross-Cultural Performance Feedback in Multinational Enterprises: Opportunity for Organizational Learning," *Human Resource Planning* 25 (2002), pp. 29–43.

58. M. Mendenhall and G. Addou, *International Human Resource Management* (Boston: PWS-Kent Publishing, 1991), p. 366. See also Maddy Janssens, "Evaluating International Managers' Performance: Parent Company Standards as Control Mechanism," *The International Journal of Human Resource Management* 5, no. 4, (December 1994), pp. 853–873.

59. R. Sauer and K. Voelker, *Labor Relations: Structure and Process* (New York: Macmillan, 1993), pp. 510–525.

60. R. Sauer and K. Voelker, *Labor Relations: Structure and Process* (New York: Macmillan, 1993), p. 516. See also Marino Regini, "Human Resource Management and Industrial Relations in European Companies," *The International Journal of Human Resource Management* 4, no. 3 (September 1993), pp. 555–568.

61. Quoted from R. Sauer and K. Voelker, *Labor Relations: Structure and Process* (New York: Macmillan, 1993), p. 519.

62. M. Higginson, "Hungary's Low Labor Costs Still Lure Big Investors," *Budapest Business Journal* (April 10, 2006).

63. G. Pitts, "Kidnap Consultants Always Have Room for Negotiation," *Globe & Mail* (October 25, 2003), p. B3.

64. S. Merkling and E. Davis, "Kidnap and Ransom Insurance: A Rapidly Growing Benefit," *Compensation and Benefits Review* (November/December 2001), pp. 40–45; T. Appleby, "Kidnap Insurers Stay Shrouded in Secrecy," *Globe & Mail* (September 27, 2004), p. A9.

65. These are based on or quoted from S. Greengard, "Mission Possible: Protecting Employees Abroad," *Workforce* (August 1997), p. 32. See also B. Belisle and W. Cuthbertson, "Anticipate Expat Crises Instead of Responding," *Canadian HR Reporter* (March 10, 2003).

66. Definition based on Dennis Briscoe, *International Human Resource Management* (Englewood Cliffs, NJ: Prentice Hall, 1995), p. 65. See also Linda Stroh, "Predicting Turnover among Repatriates: Can Organizations Affect Retention Rates?" *International Journal of Human Resource Management* 6, no. 2, (May 1995), pp. 443–456; "Views of Employees and Companies Differ on International Assignments," *Workspan Focus Canada 2006*, pp. 22–24.

67. Arvind Phatak, *International Dimensions of Management* (Boston: PWS-Kent, 1989), p. 124. See also Reyer Swaak, "Today's Expatriate Families: Dual Careers and Other Obstacles," *Compensation and Benefits Review* 27, no. 3 (May 1995), pp. 21–26; D. Brown, "Companies Undervaluing Skills Learned during Relocation," *Canadian HR Reporter* (February 28, 2000), pp. 15, 21; G. Reinhart, "Going Global," *Canadian HR Reporter* (September 25, 2000), pp. 19, 23. See also J. Hobel, "The Expatriate Employee Homecoming," *Canadian HR Reporter* (June 1, 1998), pp. G5, G11. See also J. Keogh, "A Win-Win, from Start to Finish," *Workspan* (February 2003), pp. 36–39.

68. These are based on Dennis Briscoe, *International Human Resource Management* (Englewood Cliffs, NJ: Prentice Hall, 1995), p. 66; Arvind Phatak, *International Dimensions of Management* (Boston: PWS-Kent, 1989), pp. 124, 126; J.D. Daniels and L.H. Radebaugh, *International Business* (Reading, MA: Addison-Wesley, 1994), p. 772. See also P. Stanoch and G. Reynolds, "Relocating Career Development," *Canadian HR Reporter* (May 5, 2003), pp. 13, 15; "Global Talk," *HR Professional* (June/July 2006), p. 12.

69. This section is based on Ann Marie Ryan et al., "Designing and Implementing Global Staffing Systems: Part 2—Best Practices," *Human Resource Management* 42, no. 1 (Spring 2003), pp. 85–94.

A

accommodation measures Strategies to assist designated group members.

achievement tests Tests used to measure knowledge and/or proficiency acquired through education, training, or experience.

action learning A training technique by which management trainees are allowed to work full-time, analyzing and solving problems in other departments.

alternation ranking method Ranking employees from best to worst on a particular trait.

annual bonus Plans that are designed to motivate the short-term performance of managers and are tied to company profitability.

appraisal bias The tendency to allow individual differences, such as age, race, and sex, to affect the appraisal ratings that these employees receive.

appraisal interview An interview in which the supervisor and employee review the appraisal and make plans to remedy deficiencies and reinforce strengths.

aptitude tests Tests that measure an individual's aptitude or potential to perform a job, provided he or she is given proper training.

arbitration The use of an outside third party to investigate a dispute between an employer and union and impose a settlement.

attrition The normal separation of employees from an organization because of resignation, retirement, or death.

authorization card A card signed by an employee that indicates his or her willingness to have the union act as his or her representative for purposes of collective bargaining.

B

baby boomers Individuals born between 1946 and 1965.

balanced scorecard A measurement system that translates an organization's strategy into a comprehensive set of performance measures.

bargaining unit The group of employees in a firm, a plant, or an industry that has been recognized by an employer or certified by a Labour Relations Board (LRB) as appropriate for collective bargaining purposes.

bargaining zone The area defined by the bargaining limits (resistance points) of each side, in which compromise is possible, as is the attainment of a settlement satisfactory to both parties.

behaviour modelling A training technique in which trainees are first shown good management techniques, then asked to play roles in a simulated situation, and finally given feedback regarding their performance.

behavioural or behaviour description interview (BDI) A series of job-related questions that focus on relevant past job-related behaviours.

behaviourally anchored rating scale (BARS) An appraisal method that aims to combine the benefits of narratives, critical incidents, and quantified ratings by anchoring a quantified scale with specific narrative examples of good and poor performance.

benchmark job A job that is critical to the firm's operations or commonly found in other organizations that is used to anchor the employer's pay scale and that acts as a reference point around which other jobs are arranged in order of relative worth.

biographical information blank (BIB) A detailed job application form requesting biographical data found to be predictive of success on the job, pertaining to background, experiences, and preferences. As with a WAB, responses are scored.

blind ad A recruitment ad in which the identity and address of the employer are omitted.

bona fide occupational requirement (BFOR) A justifiable reason for discrimination based on business necessity (that is, required for the safe and efficient operation of the organization) or a requirement that can be clearly defended as intrinsically required by the tasks an employee is expected to perform.

boundaryless career A career that spans several organizations and/or industries.

boundaryless organization structure A structure in which relationships (typically joint ventures) are formed with customers, suppliers, and/or competitors, to pool resources for mutual benefit or encourage cooperation in an uncertain environment.

boycott An organized refusal of bargaining unit members and supporters to buy the products or use the services of the organization whose employees are on strike, in an effort to exert economic pressure on the employer.

broadbanding Reducing the number of salary grades and ranges into just a few wide levels or "bands," each of which then contains a relatively wide range of jobs and salary levels.

burnout The total depletion of physical and mental resources caused by excessive striving to reach an unrealistic work-related goal.

business unionism The activities of labour unions focusing on economic and welfare issues, including pay and benefits, job security, and working conditions.

C

Canada/Quebec Pension Plan (C/QPP) Programs that provide three types of benefits: retirement income; survivor or death benefits payable to the employee's dependants regardless of age at time of death; and disability benefits payable to employees with disabilities and their dependants. Benefits are payable only to those individuals who make contributions to the plans and/or available to their family members.

capital accumulation programs Long-term incentives most often reserved for senior executives. Six popular plans include stock options, book value plans, stock appreciation rights, performance achievement plans, restricted stock plans, and phantom stock plans.

career anchor A concern or value that you will not give up if a choice has to be made.

career cycle The stages through which a person's career evolves.

career planning and development The deliberate process through which a person becomes aware of personal career-related attributes, and the lifelong series of activities that contribute to his or her career fulfillment.

career-planning workshop A planned learning event in which participants are expected to be actively involved in career-planning exercises and career-skills practice sessions.

case study method A development method in which a trainee is presented with a written description of an organizational problem to diagnose and solve.

caucus session A session in which only the members of one's own bargaining team are present.

central tendency A tendency to rate all employees in the middle of the scale.

certification Recognition for having met certain professional standards.

certification The procedure whereby a labour union obtains a certificate from the relevant LRB declaring that the union is the exclusive bargaining agent for a defined group of employees in a bargaining unit that the LRB considers appropriate for collective bargaining purposes.

Charter of Rights and Freedoms Federal law enacted in 1982 that guarantees fundamental freedoms to all Canadians.

classes Groups of jobs based on a set of rules for each class, such as amount of independent judgment, skill, physical effort, and so forth. Classes usually contain similar jobs—such as all secretaries.

classification (or grading) method A method for categorizing jobs into groups.

client server A network architecture in which each computer on the network is either a client or a server.

coinsurance The percentage of expenses (in excess of the deductible) that are paid for by the insurance plan.

collective agreement (union contract) A formal agreement between an employer and the union representing a group of its employees regarding terms and conditions of employment.

collective bargaining Negotiations between a union and an employer to arrive at a mutually acceptable collective agreement.

common law The accumulation of judicial precedents that do not derive from specific pieces of legislation.

compensable factor A fundamental, compensable element of a job, such as skill, effort, responsibility, and working conditions.

competencies Individual knowledge, skills, and behaviours that are critical to successful individual or corporate performance.

compressed workweek An arrangement that most commonly allows employees to work four ten-hour days instead of the more usual five eight-hour days.

conciliation The use of a neutral third party to help an organization and the union representing a group of its employees to come to a mutually satisfactory collective agreement.

construct validity The extent to which a selection tool measures a theoretical construct or trait deemed necessary to perform the job successfully.

constructive dismissal The employer makes unilateral changes in the employment contract that are unacceptable to the employee, even though the employee has not been formally terminated.

content validity The extent to which a selection instrument, such as a test, adequately samples the knowledge and skills needed to perform the job.

contingent employees Workers who do not have regular full-time or regular part-time employment status.

contract law Legislation that governs collective agreements and individual employment contracts.

contract workers Employees who develop work relationships directly with the employer for a specific type of work or period of time.

contrast or candidate-order error An error of judgment on the part of the interviewer because of interviewing one or more very good or very bad candidates just before the interview in question.

controlled experimentation Formal methods for testing the effectiveness of a training program, preferably with a control group and with tests before and after training.

craft union Traditionally, a labour organization representing workers practising the same craft or trade, such as carpentry or plumbing.

criterion-related validity The extent to which a selection tool predicts or significantly correlates with important elements of work behaviour.

critical incident method Keeping a record of uncommonly good or undesirable examples of an employee's work-related behaviour and reviewing the list with the employee at predetermined times.

D

data warehouse Primary data storage repository for all data collected by an organization's business systems.

decertification The process whereby a union is legally deprived of its official recognition as the exclusive bargaining agent for a group of employees.

decline stage The period during which many people are faced with the prospect of having to accept reduced levels of power and responsibility.

deductible The annual amount of health/dental expenses that an employee must pay before insurance benefits will be paid.

deferred profit-sharing plan A plan in which a certain amount of company profits is credited to each employee's account, payable at retirement, termination, or death.

defined benefit pension plan A plan that contains a formula for determining retirement benefits.

defined contribution pension plan A plan in which the employer's contribution to the employees' retirement fund is specified.

Delphi technique A judgmental forecasting method used to arrive at a group decision, typically involving outside experts as well as organizational employees. Ideas are exchanged without face-to-face interaction and feedback is provided and used to fine-tune independent judgments until a consensus is reached.

demographics The characteristics of the workforce, which include age, sex, marital status, and education level.

developmental job rotation A management-training technique that involves moving a trainee from department to department to broaden his or her experience and identify strong and weak points.

diary/log Daily listings made by employees of every activity in which they engage, along with the time each activity takes.

differential validity Confirmation that the selection tool accurately predicts the performance of all possible employee subgroups, including white males, women, visible minorities, persons with disabilities, and Aboriginal people.

disability management A proactive, employer-centred process that coordinates the activities of the employer, the insurance company, and health-care providers in an effort to minimize the impact of injury, disability, or disease in a worker's capacity to successfully perform his or her job.

discipline A procedure intended to correct an employee's behaviour because a rule or procedure has been violated.

discrimination As used in the context of human rights in employment, a distinction, exclusion, or preference, based on one of the prohibited grounds, that has the effect of nullifying or impairing the right of a person to full and equal recognition and exercise of his or her human rights and freedoms.

dismissal Involuntary termination of an employee's employment.

distributive bargaining A win–lose negotiating strategy, such that one party gains at the expense of the other.

distributive justice Fairness of a decision outcome.

diversity Any attribute that humans are likely to use to tell themselves, "that person is different from me," and thus includes such factors as race, gender, age, values, and cultural norms.

diversity management Activities designed to integrate all members of an organization's multicultural workforce and use their diversity to enhance the firm's effectiveness.

downsizing Refers to the process of reducing, usually dramatically, the number of people employed by the firm.

E

early retirement buyout programs Strategies used to accelerate attrition, which involve offering attractive buyout packages or the opportunity to retire on full pension, with an attractive benefits package.

e-learning Delivery and administration of learning opportunities and support via computer, networked, and Web-based technology, to enhance employee performance and development.

electronic HR (e-HR) A form of technology that enables HR professionals to integrate an organization's HR strategies, processes, and human capital to improve overall HR service delivery.

electronic performance support systems (EPSS) Computer-based job aids, or sets of computerized tools and displays that automate training, documentation, and phone support.

emotional intelligence (EI) tests Tests that measure ability to monitor one's own emotions and the emotions of others and use that knowledge to guide thoughts and actions.

employee assistance plan (EAP) A company-sponsored program to help employees cope with personal problems that are interfering with or have the potential to interfere with their job performance, as well as issues affecting their well-being and/or that of their families.

employee benefits Indirect financial payments given to employees. They may include supplementary health and life insurance, vacation, pension, education plans, and discounts on company products, for instance.

employee engagement The emotional and intellectual involvement of employees in their work.

employee leasing An arrangement that typically involves a company transferring specific employees to the payroll of an employee leasing firm/professional employer organization (PEO) in an explicit joint-employment relationship.

employee opinion surveys Communication devices that use questionnaires to ask for employees' opinions about the company, management, and work life.

employee orientation A procedure for providing new employees with basic background information about the firm and the job.

employee retention The extent to which employees are retained by the organization over a relatively long time.

employee share purchase/stock ownership plans (ESOPs) A trust is established to hold shares of company stock purchased for or issued to employees. The trust distributes the stock to employees on retirement, separation from service, or as otherwise prescribed by the plan.

employee wellness program   A program that takes a proactive approach to employee health and well-being.

employment (labour) standards legislation   Laws present in every Canadian jurisdiction that establish minimum employee entitlements and set a limit on the maximum number of hours of work permitted per day or week.

employment equity program   A detailed plan designed to identify and correct existing discrimination, redress past discrimination, and achieve a balanced representation of designated group members in the organization.

employment insurance   A federal program that provides income benefits if a person is unable to work through no fault of his or her own.

employment systems review   A thorough examination of corporate policies and procedures, collective agreements, and informal practices, to determine their impact on designated group members so that existing intentional or systemic barriers can be eliminated.

empowerment   Providing workers with the skills and authority to make decisions that would traditionally be made by managers.

enterprise-wide system   A system that supports enterprise-wide or cross-functional requirements, rather than a single department or group within the organization.

environmental scanning   Identifying and analyzing external opportunities and threats that may be crucial to the organization's success.

equality rights   Section 15 of the Charter of Rights and Freedoms, which guarantees the right to equal protection and equal benefit of the law without discrimination.

ergonomics   The art of fitting the workstation and work tools to the individual.

establishment stage   The period, roughly from age 24 to 44, that is the heart of most people's work lives.

exploration stage   The period from around age 15 to 24, during which a person seriously explores various occupational alternatives, attempting to match these alternatives with his or her interests and abilities.

F

factor comparison method   A method of ranking jobs according to a variety of skill and difficulty factors, adding these rankings to arrive at an overall numerical rating for each given job, and then incorporating wage rates.

fair treatment programs   Employer programs aimed at ensuring that all employees are treated fairly, generally by providing formalized, well-documented, and highly publicized vehicles through which employees can appeal any eligible issues.

flexible benefits program   Individualized benefit plans to accommodate employee needs and preferences.

flextime   A plan whereby employees build their workday around a core of midday hours.

flexyear   A work arrangement under which employees can choose (at six-month intervals) the number of hours that they want to work each month over the next year.

flow data   Data tracking designated group members by employment transactions and outcomes.

forced distribution method   Predetermined percentages of ratees are placed in various performance categories.

functional job analysis (FJA)   A quantitative method for classifying jobs based on types and amounts of responsibility for data, people, and things. Performance standards and training requirements are also identified.

G

gainsharing plan   An incentive plan that engages employees in a common effort to achieve productivity objectives and share the gains.

Generation X   Individuals born between 1966 and 1980.

Generation Y   Individuals born since 1980.

glass ceiling   An invisible barrier, caused by attitudinal or organizational bias, which limits the advancement opportunities of qualified designated group members.

globalization   The tendency of firms to extend their sales or manufacturing to new markets abroad.

grade/group description   A written description of the level of compensable factors required by jobs in each grade. Used to combine similar jobs into grades or classes.

grades   Groups of jobs based on a set of rules for each grade, where jobs are similar in difficulty but otherwise different. Grades often contain dissimilar jobs, such as secretaries, mechanics, and firefighters.

graphic rating scale   A scale that lists a number of traits and a range of performance for each. The employee is then rated by identifying the score that best describes his or her level of performance for each trait.

grievance   A written allegation of a contract violation, filed by an individual bargaining unit member, the union, or management.

group life insurance   Insurance provided at lower rates for all employees, including new employees, regardless of health or physical condition.

group termination laws   Laws that require an employer to notify employees in the event that an employer decides to terminate a group of employees.

growth stage   The period from birth to age 14, during which the person develops a self-concept by identifying with and interacting with other people, such as family, friends, and teachers.

guaranteed piecework plan   The minimum hourly wage plus an incentive for each piece produced above a set number of pieces per hour.

H

halo effect   A positive initial impression that distorts an interviewer's rating of a candidate, because subsequent information is judged with a positive bias.

halo effect In performance appraisal, the problem that occurs when a supervisor's rating of an employee on one trait biases the rating of that person on other traits.

harassment Unwelcome behaviour that demeans, humiliates, or embarrasses a person, and that a reasonable person should have known would be unwelcome.

hiring freeze A common initial response to an employee surplus. Openings are filled by reassigning current employees, and no outsiders are hired.

HR technology Any technology that is used to attract, hire, retain, and maintain human resources, support HR administration, and optimize human resource management.

human capital The knowledge, education, training, skills, and expertise of an organization's workforce.

human engineering (ergonomics) An interdisciplinary approach that seeks to integrate and accommodate the physical needs of workers into the design of jobs. It aims to adapt the entire job system—the work, environment, machines, equipment, and processes—to match human characteristics.

human relations movement A management philosophy based on the belief that the attitudes and feelings of workers are important and deserve more attention.

human resources information system (HRIS) Integrated systems used to gather, store, and analyze information regarding an organization's human resources.

human resources management (HRM) The management of people in organizations through formulating and implementing human resources management systems that are aligned with organizational strategy in order to produce the workforce competencies and behaviours required to achieve the organization's strategic goals.

human resources movement A management philosophy focusing on concern for people and productivity.

human resources planning (HRP) The process of reviewing human resources requirements to ensure that the organization has the required number of employees, with the necessary skills, to meet its goals.

I

industrial engineering A field of study concerned with analyzing work methods; making work cycles more efficient by modifying, combining, rearranging, or eliminating tasks; and establishing time standards.

industrial union A labour organization representing all workers eligible for union membership in a particular company or industry, including skilled tradespersons.

in-house development centre A company-based method for exposing prospective managers to realistic exercises to develop improved management skills.

insubordination Willful disregard or disobedience of the boss's authority or legitimate orders; criticizing the boss in public.

integrative bargaining A negotiating strategy in which the possibility of win–win, lose–win, win–lose, and lose–lose outcomes is recognized, and there is acknowledgement that achieving a win–win outcome will depend on mutual trust and problem solving.

intelligence (IQ) tests Tests that measure general intellectual abilities, such as verbal comprehension, inductive reasoning, memory, numerical ability, speed of perception, spatial visualization, and word fluency.

interactional justice Fairness in interpersonal interactions by treating others with dignity and respect.

interactive voice response (IVR) A telephone technology in which a touch-tone phone is used to interact with a database to acquire information from it or enter data into it.

interest arbitration The imposition of the final terms of a collective agreement.

interest dispute A dispute between an organization and the union representing its employees over the terms of a collective agreement.

interest inventories Tests that compare a candidate's interests with those of people in various occupations.

intranet A network that is interconnected within one organization, using Web technologies for sharing information internally.

J

job A group of related activities and duties, held by a single employee or a number of incumbents.

job analysis The procedure for determining the tasks, duties, and responsibilities of each job, and the human attributes (in terms of knowledge, skills, and abilities) required to perform it.

job description A list of the duties, responsibilities, reporting relationships, and working conditions of a job—one product of a job analysis.

job design The process of systematically organizing work into tasks that are required to perform a specific job.

job enlargement (horizontal loading) A technique to relieve monotony and boredom that involves assigning workers additional tasks at the same level of responsibility to increase the number of tasks they have to perform.

job enrichment (vertical loading) Any effort that makes an employee's job more rewarding or satisfying by adding more meaningful tasks and duties.

job evaluation A systematic comparison to determine the relative worth of jobs within a firm.

job instruction training (JIT) The listing of each job's basic tasks, along with key points, in order to provide step-by-step training for employees.

job pathing Selecting carefully sequenced job assignments to enable employees to test their aptitudes and preferences.

job posting The process of notifying current employees about vacant positions.

job rotation Another technique to relieve monotony and employee boredom that involves systematically moving employees from one job to another.

job sharing A strategy that involves dividing the duties of a single position between two or more employees.

job specification A list of the "human requirements," that is, the requisite knowledge, skills, and abilities, needed to perform the job—another product of a job analysis.

K

KSAs Knowledge, skills, and abilities.

L

labour union (union) An officially recognized association of employees practising a similar trade or employed in the same company or industry, who have joined together to present a united front and collective voice in dealing with management.

labour–management relations The ongoing interactions between labour unions and management in organizations.

layoff The temporary withdrawal of employment to workers for economic or business reasons.

learning organization An organization focused on creating, acquiring, and transferring knowledge, and at modifying its behaviour to reflect new knowledge and insights.

lifelong learning Providing extensive continuing training throughout employees' careers.

local A group of unionized employees in a particular location.

lockout Temporary refusal of a company to continue providing work for bargaining unit employees involved in a labour dispute, which may result in closure of the establishment for a time.

M

maintenance stage The period from about age 45 to 65, during which the person secures his or her place in the world of work.

management assessment centre A strategy used to assess candidates' management potential that uses a combination of realistic exercises, management games, objective testing, presentations, and interviews.

management by objectives (MBO) Involves setting specific measurable goals with each employee and then periodically reviewing the progress made.

management development Any attempt to improve current or future management performance by imparting knowledge, changing attitudes, or increasing skills.

management game A computerized development technique in which teams of managers compete with one another by making decisions regarding realistic but simulated companies.

management inventories Records summarizing the qualifications, interests, and skills of management employees, along with the number and types of employees supervised, duties of such employees, total budget managed, previous managerial duties and responsibilities, and managerial training received.

Markov analysis A method of forecasting internal labour supply that involves tracking the pattern of employee movements through various jobs and developing a transitional probability matrix.

mediation The use (usually voluntary) of a neutral third party to help an organization and the union representing its employees to reach a mutually satisfactory collective agreement.

memorandum of settlement A summary of the terms and conditions agreed to by the parties that is submitted to the constituent groups for final approval.

mentoring An experienced individual (the mentor) teaching and training another person (the protégé) who has less knowledge in an area.

merit pay (merit raise) Any salary increase awarded to an employee based on his or her individual performance.

micro-assessment A series of verbal, paper-based, or computer-based questions and exercises that a candidate is required to complete, covering the range of activities required on the job for which he or she is applying.

mixed (semi-structured) interview An interview format that combines the structured and unstructured techniques.

multiple-hurdle strategy An approach to selection involving a series of successive steps or hurdles. Only candidates clearing the hurdle are permitted to move on to the next step.

must criteria Requirements that are absolutely essential for the job, include a measurable standard of acceptability or are absolute, and can be screened initially on paper.

mutual gains (interest-based) bargaining A win–win approach based on training in the fundamentals of effective problem solving and conflict resolution, in which the interests of all stakeholders are taken into account.

N

National Occupational Classification (NOC) A reference tool for writing job descriptions and job specifications. Compiled by the federal government, it contains comprehensive, standardized descriptions of about 30000 occupations and the requirements for each.

nepotism A preference for hiring relatives of current employees.

nominal group technique A decision-making technique that involves a group of experts meeting face to face. Steps include independent idea generation, clarification and open discussion, and private assessment.

O

occupation A collection of jobs that share some or all of a set of main duties.

occupational health and safety legislation Laws intended to protect the health and safety of workers by minimizing work-related accidents and illnesses.

occupational orientation The theory, developed by John Holland, that there are six basic personal orientations that determine the sorts of careers to which people are drawn.

occupational segregation The existence of certain occupations that have traditionally been male dominated and others that have been female dominated.

online recruitment The use of the Internet to aid in recruiting.

organization chart A "snapshot" of the firm, depicting the organization's structure in chart form at a particular point in time.

organization development (OD) A method aimed at changing the attitudes, values, and beliefs of employees so that employees can improve the organization.

organizational climate The prevailing atmosphere that exists in an organization and its impact on employees.

organizational culture The core values, beliefs, and assumptions that are widely shared by members of an organization.

organizational structure The formal relationships among jobs in an organization.

outplacement counselling A systematic process by which a terminated person is trained and counselled in the techniques of self-appraisal and securing a new position.

outsourcing The practice of contracting with outside vendors to handle specified functions on a permanent basis.

outsourcing The subcontracting of work that is not considered part of a company's core business.

P

paired comparison method Ranking employees by making a chart of all possible pairs of employees for each trait and indicating whom the better employee of the pair is.

panel interview An interview in which a group of interviewers questions the applicant.

pay equity Providing equal pay to male-dominated job classes and female-dominated job classes of equal value to the employer.

pay grade A pay grade comprises jobs of approximately equal value.

pension plans Plans that provide income when employees reach a predetermined retirement age.

performance analysis Verifying that there is a performance deficiency and determining whether that deficiency should be rectified through training or through some other means (such as transferring the employee).

performance management The process encompassing all activities related to improving employee performance, productivity, and effectiveness.

personality tests Instruments used to measure basic aspects of personality, such as introversion, stability, motivation, neurotic tendency, self-confidence, self- sufficiency, and sociability.

phased retirement An arrangement whereby employees gradually ease into retirement by using reduced workdays and/or shortened workweeks.

physical demands analysis Identification of the senses used and the type, frequency, and amount of physical effort involved in the job.

picket Stationing groups of striking employees, usually carrying signs, at the entrances and exits of the struck operation to publicize the issues in dispute and discourage people from entering or leaving the premises.

piecework A system of pay based on the number of items processed by each individual worker in a unit of time, such as items per hour or items per day.

point method The job evaluation method in which a number of compensable factors are identified, the degree to which each of these factors is present in the job is determined, and an overall point value is calculated.

portability A provision that employees who change jobs can transfer the lump-sum value of the pension they have earned to a locked-in RRSP or their new employer's pension plan.

portal A single site that can be accessed within an existing Internet site.

position The collection of tasks and responsibilities performed by one person.

position analysis questionnaire (PAQ) A questionnaire used to collect quantifiable data concerning the duties and responsibilities of various jobs.

positive measures Initiatives designed to accelerate the entry, development, and promotion of designated group members, aimed at overcoming the residual effects of past discrimination.

pre-hearing vote An alternative mechanism for certification, used in situations in which there is evidence of violations of fair labour practices early in the organizing campaign.

pre-retirement counselling Counselling provided to employees some months (or even years) before retirement, which covers such matters as benefits advice, second careers, and so on.

primary sector Agriculture, fishing and trapping, forestry, and mining.

procedural justice Fairness of the process used to make a decision.

process chart A diagram showing the flow of inputs to and outputs from the job under study.

productivity The ratio of an organization's outputs (goods and services) to its inputs (people, capital, energy, and materials).

profit-sharing plan A plan whereby most or all employees share in the company's profits.

programmed learning A systematic method for teaching job skills that involves presenting questions or facts, allowing the person to respond, and giving the learner immediate feedback on the accuracy of his or her answers.

promotion Movement of an employee from one job to another that is higher in pay, responsibility, and/or organizational level, usually based on merit, seniority, or a combination of both.

R

ranking method The simplest method of job evaluation, which involves ranking each job relative to all other jobs, usually based on overall difficulty.

rate ranges A series of steps or levels within a pay grade, usually based on years of service.

ratification Formal approval by secret-ballot vote of the bargaining unit members of the agreement negotiated between union and management.

ratio analysis A forecasting technique for determining future staff needs by using ratios between some causal factor (such as sales volume) and the number of employees needed.

realistic job preview (RJP) A strategy used to provide applicants with realistic information—both positive and negative—about the job demands, the organization's expectations, and the work environment.

reality shock The state that results from the discrepancy between what the new employee expects from his or her new job, and the realities of it.

reasonable accommodation The adjustment of employment policies and practices that an employer may be expected to make so that no individual is denied benefits, disadvantaged in employment, or prevented from carrying out the essential components of a job because of grounds prohibited in human rights legislation.

recency effect The rating error that occurs when ratings are based on the employee's most recent performance rather than on performance throughout the appraisal period.

recruiter A specialist in recruitment, whose job it is to find and attract capable candidates.

recruitment The process of searching out and attracting qualified job applicants, which begins with the identification of a position that requires staffing and is completed when résumés and/or completed application forms are received from an adequate number of applicants.

red circle pay rate A rate of pay that is above the pay range maximum.

reduced workweek Employees work fewer hours and receive less pay.

regression analysis A statistical technique involving the use of a mathematical formula to project future demands based on an established relationship between an organization's employment level (dependent variable) and some measurable factor of output (independent variable).

regulations Legally binding rules established by the special regulatory bodies created to enforce compliance with the law and aid in its interpretation.

relational database Database in which data can be stored in more than one file, each one containing different types of data. The different files can be linked so that information from the separate files can be used together.

reliability The degree to which interviews, tests, and other selection procedures yield comparable data over time; in other words, the degree of dependability, consistency, or stability of the measures used.

repetitive strain injuries (RSIs) Activity-related soft-tissue injuries of the neck, shoulders, arms, wrist, hands, back, and legs.

replacement charts Visual representations of who will replace whom in the event of a job opening. Likely internal candidates are listed, along with their age, present performance rating, and promotability status.

replacement summaries Lists of likely replacements for each position and their relative strengths and weaknesses, as well as information about current position, performance, promotability, age, and experience.

representation vote A vote conducted by the LRB in which employees in the bargaining unit indicate, by secret ballot, whether or not they want to be represented, or continue to be represented, by a labour union.

request for proposal (RFP) Request to vendors to schedule demonstrations of the various systems and ultimately choose one that most closely aligns with their needs analysis, budgets, and management requirements.

reverse discrimination Giving preference to designated group members to the extent that nonmembers believe they are being discriminated against.

rights arbitration The process involved in the settlement of a rights dispute.

rights dispute A disagreement between an organization and the union representing its employees regarding the interpretation or application of one or more clauses in the current collective agreement.

role-playing A training technique in which trainees act the parts of people in a realistic management situation.

S

Sandwich Generation Individuals with responsibility for rearing young dependants as well as for assisting elderly relatives who are no longer capable of functioning totally independently.

Scanlon plan An incentive plan developed in 1937 by Joseph Scanlon and designed to encourage cooperation, involvement, and sharing of benefits.

scatter plot A graphical method used to help identify the relationship between two variables.

scientific management The process of "scientifically" analyzing manufacturing processes, reducing production costs, and compensating employees based on their performance levels.

secondary sector Manufacturing and construction.

selection The process of choosing among individuals who have been recruited to fill existing or projected job openings.

selection interview A procedure designed to predict future job performance on the basis of applicants' oral responses to oral inquiries.

selection ratio The ratio of the number of applicants hired to the total number of applicants.

seniority Length of service in the bargaining unit.

severance package A lump-sum payment, continuation of benefits for a specified period of time, and other benefits that are provided to employees who are being terminated.

sexual annoyance Sexually related conduct that is hostile, intimidating, or offensive to the employee but has no direct link to tangible job benefits or loss thereof.

sexual coercion Harassment of a sexual nature that results in some direct consequence to the worker's employment status or some gain in or loss of tangible job benefits.

sexual harassment Offensive or humiliating behaviour that is related to a person's sex, as well as behaviour of a sexual nature that creates an intimidating, unwelcome, hostile, or offensive work environment, or that could reasonably be thought to put sexual conditions on a person's job or employment opportunities.

short-term disability and sick leave Plans that provide pay to an employee when he or she is unable to work because of a non-work-related illness or injury.

similar-to-me bias The tendency to give higher performance ratings to employees who are perceived to be similar to the rater in some way.

situational interview A series of job-related questions that focus on how the candidate would behave in a given situation.

situational tests Tests in which candidates are presented with hypothetical situations representative of the job for which they are applying and are evaluated on their responses.

skills inventories Manual or computerized records summarizing employees' education, experience, interests, skills, and so on, which are used to identify internal candidates eligible for transfer and/or promotion.

social (reform) unionism Activities of unions directed at furthering the interests of their members by influencing the social and economic policies of governments at all levels, such as speaking out on proposed legislative reforms.

social responsibility The implied, enforced, or felt obligation of managers, acting in their official capacities, to serve or protect the interests of groups other than themselves.

socialization The ongoing process of instilling in all employees the prevailing attitudes, standards, values, and patterns of behaviour that are expected by the organization.

spot bonus A spontaneous incentive awarded to individuals for accomplishments not readily measured by a standard.

staffing table A pictorial representation of all jobs within the organization, along with the number of current incumbents and future employment requirements (monthly or yearly) for each.

standard hour plan A plan by which a worker is paid a basic hourly rate plus an extra percentage of his or her base rate for production exceeding the standard per hour or per day. It is similar to piecework payment but is based on a percentage premium.

statistical strategy A more objective technique used to determine to whom the job should be offered that involves identifying the most valid predictors and weighting them through statistical methods, such as multiple regression.

stock data Data that provide a snapshot of the organization at a particular point in time, in terms of how many designated group members are employed, in what occupations, and at what salaries.

stock option The right to purchase a stated number of shares of a company stock at today's price at some time in the future.

straight piecework plan A set payment for each piece produced or processed in a factory or shop.

strategy The company's plan for how it will balance its internal strengths and weaknesses with external opportunities and threats in order to maintain a competitive advantage.

strictness/leniency The problem that occurs when a supervisor has a tendency to rate all employees either high or low.

strike The temporary refusal by bargaining unit members to continue working for the employer.

strike vote Legally required in some jurisdictions, it is a vote seeking authorization from bargaining unit members to strike if necessary. A favourable vote does not mean that a strike is inevitable.

structured interview An interview following a set sequence of questions.

succession planning The process of ensuring a suitable supply of successors for current and future senior or key jobs, so that the careers of individuals can be effectively planned and managed.

succession planning A process through which senior-level openings are planned for and eventually filled.

supplemental employee retirement plans Plans that provide the additional pension benefit required for employees to receive their full pension benefit in cases where their full pension benefit exceeds the maximum allowable benefit under the Income Tax Act.

supplemental unemployment benefits (SUBs) A top-up of EI benefits to bring income levels closer to what an employee would receive if on the job.

supportive measures Strategies that enable all employees to achieve better balance between work and other responsibilities.

survey feedback A method that involves surveying employees' attitudes and providing feedback so that problems can be solved by the managers and employees.

survivor sickness A range of negative emotions experienced by employees remaining after a major restructuring initiative, which can include feelings of betrayal or violation, guilt, and detachment, and can result in stress symptoms, including depression, proneness to errors, and reduced productivity.

T

task analysis A detailed study of a job to identify the skills and competencies it requires so that an appropriate training program can be instituted.

team A small group of people, with complementary skills, who work toward common goals for which they hold joint responsibility and accountability.

team building Improving the effectiveness of teams through the use of consultants, interviews, and team-building meetings.

team or group incentive plan A plan in which a production standard is set for a specific work group, and its members are paid incentives if the group exceeds the production standard.

team-based job designs Job designs that focus on giving a team, rather than an individual, a whole and meaningful piece of work to do and empowering team members to decide among themselves how to accomplish the work.

termination Permanent separation from the organization for any reason.

termination interview The interview in which an employee is informed of the fact that he or she has been dismissed.

tertiary or service sector Public administration, personal and business services, finance, trade, public utilities, and transportation/communications.

360-degree appraisal A performance appraisal technique that uses multiple raters including peers, employees reporting to the appraisee, supervisors, and customers.

tombstone data List of basic employee information.

top-down communication programs Communication activities, including in-house television centres, electronic bulletin boards, and newsletters, that provide continuing opportunities for the firm to update employees on important matters.

total rewards An integrated package of all rewards (monetary and nonmonetary, extrinsic and intrinsic) gained by employees arising from their employment.

training The process of teaching employees the basic skills/competencies that they need to perform their jobs.

transfer Movement of an employee from one job to another that is relatively equal in pay, responsibility, and/or organizational level.

transfer of training Application of the skills acquired during the training program into the work environment, and the maintenance of these skills over time.

trend analysis The study of a firm's past employment levels over a period of years to predict future needs.

U

unclear performance standards An appraisal scale that is too open to interpretation of traits and standards.

underemployment Being employed in a job that does not fully utilize one's knowledge, skills, and abilities (KSAs).

undue hardship The point to which employers are expected to accommodate under human rights legislative requirements.

unintentional/constructive/systemic discrimination Discrimination that is embedded in policies and practices that appear neutral on the surface, and are implemented impartially, but have an adverse impact on specific groups of people for reasons that are not job related or required for the safe and efficient operation of the business.

union security clause The contract provisions protecting the interests of the labour union, dealing with the issue of membership requirements and, often, the payment of union dues.

union steward A union member elected by workers in a particular department or area of a firm to act as their union representative.

unstructured interview An unstructured, conversational-style interview. The interviewer pursues points of interest as they come up in response to questions.

utilization analysis The comparison of the internal workforce profile with external workforce availability.

V

validity The accuracy with which a predictor measures what it is intended to measure.

variable pay Any plan that ties pay to productivity or profitability.

vestibule or simulated training Training employees on special off-the-job equipment, as in airplane pilot training, whereby training costs and hazards can be reduced.

vesting Provision that employer money placed in a pension fund cannot be forfeited for any reason.

videoconferencing Connecting two or more distant groups by using audiovisual equipment.

W

wage curve A graphic description of the relationship between the value of the job and the average wage paid for this job.

wage/salary survey A survey aimed at determining prevailing wage rates. A good salary survey provides specific wage rates for comparable jobs. Formal written questionnaire surveys are the most comprehensive.

want ad A recruitment ad describing the job and its specifications, the compensation package, and the hiring employer. The address to which applications and/or résumés should be submitted is also provided.

want criteria Those criteria that have been culled from the must list. They represent qualifications that cannot be screened on paper or are not readily measurable, as well as those that are highly desirable but not critical.

Web-based applications Applications that use a Web browser as a user interface (i.e., the "front-end"). Users can access the applications from any computer connected to the Internet via a secure, password-protected login page and from that point forward all the data are encrypted.

weighted application blank (WAB) A job application form on which applicant responses have been weighted based on their statistical relationship to measures of job success.

wildcat strike A spontaneous walkout, not officially sanctioned by the union leadership, which may be legal or illegal, depending on its timing.

work sharing Employees work three or four days a week and receive EI benefits on their non-workday(s).

work simplification An approach to job design that involves assigning most of the administrative aspects of work (such as planning and organizing) to supervisors and managers, while giving lower-level employees narrowly defined tasks to perform according to methods established and specified by management.

workers' compensation Workers' compensation provides income and medical benefits to victims of work-related accidents or illnesses and/or their dependants, regardless of fault.

workforce analytics The use of HRIS data to assess the performance of an organization's workforce by using statistics and research design techniques.

Workplace Hazardous Materials Information System (WHMIS) A Canada-wide legally mandated system designed to protect workers by providing information about hazardous materials in the workplace.

wrongful dismissal An employee dismissal that does not comply with the law or does not comply with a written or implied contractual arrangement.

Y

yield ratio The percentage of applicants that proceed to the next stage of the selection process.

NAME AND ORGANIZATION INDEX

SUBJECT INDEX

Note: Key terms and the pages on which they are defined are indicated in bold.